RELIGIONS OF THE UNITED STATES IN PRACTICE

RELIGIONS OF THE

UNITED STATES

IN PRACTICE · *Volume Two*

Colleen McDannell, Editor

PRINCETON READINGS IN RELIGIONS

PRINCETON UNIVERSITY PRESS

PRINCETON AND OXFORD

Library of Congress Cataloging-in-Publication Data
Religions of the United States in practice / Colleen McDannell, editor.
p.cm. — (Princeton readings in religions)
Includes bibliographical references and index.
ISBN 0-691-00998-8 (vol. 1) — ISBN 0-691-00999-6 (vol. 1 : pbk.) — ISBN
0-691-01000-5 (vol. 2) — ISBN 0-691-01001-3 (vol. 2 : pbk.)
1. United States--Religious life and customs. I. McDannell, Colleen. II. Series.
BL2525 .R4688 2002
200.973—dc21
2001036269
British Library Cataloging-in-Publication Data is available

This book has been composed in Berkeley.

Printed on acid-free paper. ∞
www.pup.princeton.edu
Printed in the United States of America
1 3 5 7 9 10 8 6 4 2
1 3 5 7 9 10 8 6 4 2
(Pbk.)

PRINCETON READINGS

IN RELIGIONS

Princeton Readings in Religions is a new series of anthologies on the religions of the world, representing the significant advances that have been made in the study of religions over the last thirty years. The sourcebooks used by previous generations of students, whether for Judaism and Christianity or for the religions of Asia and the Middle East, placed a heavy emphasis on "canonical works." Princeton Readings in Religions provides a different configuration of texts in an attempt to better represent the range of religious practices, placing particular emphasis on the ways in which texts have been used in diverse contexts. The volumes in the series therefore include ritual manuals, hagiographical and autobiographical works, popular commentaries, and folktales, as well as some ethnographic material. Many works are drawn from vernacular sources. The readings in the series are new in two senses. First, very few of the works contained in the volumes have ever been made available in an anthology before; in the case of the volumes on Asia, few have even been translated into a Western language. Second, the readings are new in the sense that each volume provides new ways to read and understand the religions of the world, breaking down the sometimes misleading stereotypes inherited from the past in an effort to provide both more expansive and more focused perspectives on the richness and diversity of religious expressions. The series is designed for use by a wide range of readers, with key terms translated and technical notes omitted. Each volume also contains a substantial introduction by a distinguished scholar in which the histories of the traditions are outlined and the significance of each of the works is explored.

Religions of the United States in Practice is the tenth title in the series. The forty-two contributors include many of the leading scholars of American religions. Each scholar has provided one or more selections of key works, some of which are published here for the first time. These works include prayers and songs from Christian, Jewish, and Native American traditions, accounts of visions and trances, instructions on healing and health, and rites of passage. Each chapter begins with a substantial introduction that discusses the history and influence of the work, identifying points of particular difficulty or interest. Colleen McDannell, the editor of these groundbreaking volumes, opens the book with a masterful introduction to the multiple worlds of the religions of United States.

Donald S. Lopez, Jr.
Series Editor

CONTENTS

————

Healing: Health, Happiness, and the Miraculous

Imagining: The Unseen World

Persuading: Witnessing, Controversies, and Polemics

CONTRIBUTORS

Dianne Ashton teaches in the Department of Philosophy and Religion at Rowan University.

Wallace Best teaches in the Department of Religious Studies at the University of Virginia.

Betty DeBerg teaches in the Department of Philosophy and Religion at the University of Northern Iowa.

Gastón Espinosa is director of the Hispanic Churches in American Public Life project and teaches at the University of California, Santa Barbara.

Peter Gardella teaches in the Department of World Religions at Manhattanville College.

Philip Goff is the Director of the Center for the Study of Religion and American Culture and teaches at Indiana University — Purdue University.

Paul Harvey teaches in the Department of History at the University of Colorado.

Julie Ingersoll teaches in the Department of Philosophy and Religion at the University of North Florida.

Tazim R. Kassam teaches in the Department of Religion at Syracuse University.

Patricia O'Connell Killen teaches in the Department of Religion at Pacific Lutheran University.

Gary Laderman teaches in the Department of Religion at Emory University.

Bernhard Lang teaches in the Department of Theology and Religion at the University of Paderborn in Germany.

Iain S. Maclean teaches in the Department of Philosophy and Religion at James Madison University.

Elizabeth McAlister teaches in the Department of Religion at Wesleyan University.

Michael McClymond teaches in the Department of Theological Studies at St. Louis University.

Michael D. McNally teaches in the Department of Religion at Carleton College.

Timothy J. Meagher is the Director of Archives, Manuscripts, and Museum Collections and teaches at the Catholic University of America.

Pamela S. Nadell teaches in the Jewish Studies Program at American University.

Vanessa L. Ochs teaches in the Department of Religious Studies at the University of Virginia.

Mark Oppenheimer is an independent scholar in New Haven, Connecticut.

Amanda Porterfield teaches in the Religious Studies Program at the University of Wyoming.

Craig R. Prentiss teaches in the Department of Theology and Religious Studies at Rockhurst University.

Stephen Prothero teaches in the Department of Religion at Boston University.

Jana Kathryn Riess is Religion Book Review Editor for *Publishers Weekly*.

Richard Hughes Seager teaches in the Department of Religious Studies at Hamilton College.

Manuel A. Vásquez teaches in the Religion Department at the University of Florida.

Judith Weisenfeld teaches in the Department of Religion Vassar College.

RELIGIONS OF THE UNITED STATES IN PRACTICE

INTRODUCTION

———

Colleen McDannell

This anthology presents the contours of religious practices in the United States by examining a selection of primary documents. There are many virtues to this varied collection. It offers readers a series of texts, in the broadest sense of that term, that impart a sense of the remarkable diversity and range of practices that have existed throughout American religious history. Each text is preceded by an essay that sets the document in context. The primary documents and essays bring readers into contact with people of the past by introducing voices that have recently caught the attention of scholars. These voices urge us to broaden the range of what we consider religious and to consider the many significant ways that religious practice shapes American life. The documents also provide examples of the kinds of source materials scholars use when trying to understand religious impulses at specific moments in American history.

By constructing an anthology based on primary documents, the contributors to this volume introduce a fresh perspective into the discussion of American religious history. The two volumes present religion as a dynamic process of borrowing, conflict, and interaction between and within religious traditions. The volumes focus on religious *behaviors* rather than on historical movements, church-state issues, or theological developments. Religious thought and ethics are approached from the perspective of the lived experiences of average people. An introductory essay accompanying each primary text clarifies the practice described in the document. The essay sets the historical scene and explains difficult ideas contained in the primary text. Rather than assemble the documents chronologically or by faith communities, I have thematically grouped the texts around the common activities of religious people: praying, singing, healing, teaching, imagining, and persuading. These aspects of religious life are shared by many people. I have deliberately juxtaposed materials from different religious traditions, time periods, geographical areas, and modes of expression in order to encourage readers to reflect on the relationship between religious practices often regarded as separate and distinct. Too often we take traditional periodization as a type of natural ordering of the messiness of human affairs. Fortunately, religious people behave in ways that scholars cannot predict. Religious events happen at times when we least expect them. Rather than present a neatly ordered system of thought and action, the volumes offer a multiplicity of religious expressions. Like the overarching themes and categories, the documents and their introductions should be considered starting points for discussion and reflection. If the anthology accomplishes its purpose, it will encourage readers to challenge my way of dividing the "American pie" and to discover other ways of handling the complexity of religion in the United States.

The documents and essays should also raise—but not unequivocally answer—the question of whether or not an "American religion" is apparent in these diverse practices. What, if any, are the common elements in praying from a homemade Passover Haggadah, singing at a Catholic folk mass, or visualizing with a Tibetan community? Most of the texts included in this volume come from recognizable religious communities, while a few, such as the lecture by Martin Luther King, Jr., are of a more general character. These documents, especially those from Native American communities, illustrate the difficulty of separating "religion" from culture and society. I hope that the anthology will challenge readers to find evidence within these texts of what might be called the religion of American nationalism (Robert Bellah's "civil religion") or the religion of pop culture (Catherine Albanese's "cultural religion") and then to evaluate these concepts.

The anthology is indebted to the recent movement in the study of American religions that places religious practice at the center of religious life. Religious practice and behavior range from formal, communal rituals with long histories to spontaneous actions that an individual may understand as religious. Regardless of their history, all religious practices convey knowledge through action. In a very obvious way, information is contained in the words of a ritual, the lyrics of a hymn, or the instructions of a vision. When contemporary Christians sing, "I love you Lord, / And I lift my voice / To worship you," the meaning is clear. Every text in this anthology is made up of words, and those words have meanings. Meanings, of course, are multiple, and words are notoriously slippery. Sometimes people say and sing things they wish were the case rather than articulating what is the case. Meanings are created by religious practices, but they can also be challenged and remade. The introductory essays are designed to make sense of the information contained in the words and practices. Knowledge and meaning, however, is conveyed in many ways: the movements of liturgical gestures, the design of vestments, the poetics of place, the emotion of music, and so on. Religious practices are visceral and sensual. They involve the body in action. We must be prepared not only to analyze religious practices but to feel their poetic expression. If we are to understand how religious individuals, as well as religious communities, create, re-create, and sustain themselves through their practices, we must be sensitive to the many different ways practices can be interpreted.

Recent scholarship not only stresses the importance of religious practice in the United States but also recognizes a wide range of religious actors. This volume extends the trend by presenting texts that reveal the everyday thinking and doing of laypersons. The essays and documents illustrate how people become engaged with their religious traditions. This engagement can occur in a variety of places:

in churches and synagogues, of course, but also in former storefronts, in front of national monuments, in living rooms, and in the streets. Women and children engage in religion perhaps even more than adult men. The texts produced by average people, even people who have had extraordinary religious experiences, may be more straightforward, basic, or even aggressive than texts produced by an educated elite. These documents reveal the ways that religion may contribute to pain and suffering, social chaos, domestic discord, uncertainty, and intolerance. Consequently, we need to acknowledge that religion as it is lived out has rough edges and may not always be as subtle—or as virtuous—as we would like.

The texts in this volume, though, do not merely describe *lived* religion. Religious practice certainly is lived out in the family circle, in religious communities, and in the marketplace. People pray, sing, dance, shout, and sit quietly. They struggle to raise their children, fend off bad influences, and adapt to changing social environments, all using guidelines set by their religious communities. And, being an inventive people, Americans creatively adapt and improvise. They create living, as well as lived, religion. Religious practice, however, is more than merely lived. Religious practice is also imagined. In dreams, visions, and fictional accounts, people participate in worlds that are not a part of everyday life. These special worlds can eventually become as real as everyday life, or they can remain speculative fantasies. Just as through rituals people learn and construct religious worldviews, so they build religious environments through vision and imagination. In both lived and imagined religion, people use the cultural forms of their society. They may stretch and modify those forms, but they cannot entirely escape the givens of their culture.

In the introductions to the texts the "givens of culture" are laid out for the reader. At times the primary documents read as if religious practices are free from historical contingency. Religious people often assert that their beliefs and behaviors are absolutely natural and have rarely changed. As a historian, however, I cannot understand a text apart from the society that produced it, uses it, and modifies it. Even though a ritual may have a set of words and movements that everyone performs in the same way, people bring to the ritual the world in which they live. After the establishment of the state of Israel, for instance, Hanukkah songs carried different messages for American Jews. People participate in religion at a particular time and in a particular place. Religious practices are not stable but are constantly in process. Consequently, the authors of the introductory essays place religious practices in their historical and social contexts. At times the authors reach far back into history to show the development of a particular practice. At other times they connect religious behavior with the economic, sociological, scientific, or artistic forces of a given time period.

When we see how religious practices are intimately connected to society and culture, we notice that people "use" religion in many different ways. Religious practices can reflect social harmony and consensus just as they can inspire dissent and subversion. People can feel empowered or restricted, unified or divided by the religions they live and imagine. There are no simple formulas, and thus one goal of the student of religious practices is to make sense of what people *do* with their texts, visions, rituals, sermons, tracts, songs, or letters. To accomplish this, we must read critically. Who wrote (or dreamed or sang or danced) the text? Was the text addressed to a small coterie of fellow believers or to an entire nation? Was the text intended to slander, uplift, inform, or transform, and which participants intended what ends? When was a particular practice recorded, by whom, and for what purpose? In reading an anthology of religious texts we need to do the impossible—to be sympathetic to practices while at the same time being aware of their limits.

Religious practices are "multimedia events," where speech, vision, gesture, touch, and sound combine. Unfortunately, in an anthology we can never do justice to the ways the senses converge in religious practices. Book form sets severe limits on understanding. It forces us to rely on the descriptive power of scholars and then on our own imaginations to conjure what it might have been like to see an Apache girl dancing on buckskin, hear weary marchers sing "We Shall Overcome," or watch a Muslim draw his palms over his face in prayer. The anthology's limits, however, should motivate readers to find supplemental texts that more directly engage our ears and eyes, our senses of touch, smell, and taste. Readers can bring into the discussion various forms of material culture that cannot be collapsed into a book. The documents have been chosen because they are rich, stimulating, or controversial. They should provoke conversation and reflection, as well as further research. This anthology is a starting point for raising questions, pointing out continuities, examining juxtapositions, and contemplating what it means to be religious.

Like the other volumes in The Princeton Readings in Religions series, this anthology presents its documents in thematic sections. The section categories seek to illustrate some of the common ways that people participate in their religions. Putting the documents and essays in categories helps us see how religious beliefs and values are created and maintained. Within the categories are long-established, formal rites and ceremonies as well as more spontaneous practices. Some of the categories are familiar—most of us understand prayer to be a religious practice—but others ask us to expand our notion of what constitutes a religious practice. The religious practices of "imagining" or "persuading" are equally important in the makeup of religious life in the United States. These categories ask us to consider such activities as watching a movie or passing out a leaflet as religous practices. All of the categories are elastic and texts that appear in one category might easily fit into another. When a baby boy is baptized in a Vodou ceremony, not only is he introduced to the spirits and angels but his family learns valuable information about the child and how he should be brought up. Jehovah's Witnesses know that door-to-door preaching is not merely a form of persuasion but also an act of worship. While the introductory essays stress a particular theme, the clever reader will be able to construct his or her own essays based on other themes embedded within the primary documents.

Within each category the texts and introductory essays are arranged in approximate chronological order. Some texts, however, do not have precise dates of composition. No one knows when, for example, the Navaho Indians first performed the Male Shooting Chant Evil. Other practices have existed for centuries, but the essays pin the practices to a specific time. Benediction of the Blessed Sacrament, for instance, is still conducted in churches across the country, but here we describe its meaning prior to the Second Vatican Council. The essays in this volume focus on the twentieth century, although some texts—like the Jehovah's Witness chart—span the year 1900. Religious practices do not easily fall into chronological boxes. One of their distinctive features is the practitioners' effort to transcend time boundaries, to claim that, within a ritual or while singing a hymn, time is no longer important. Rituals can transport the individual to another time and place. How do we date, for instance, the memories of Adolfo C. Valdez, who, after a lifetime as a Pentecostal preacher, remembered the Azusa Street Revival of the early twentieth century in his 1980 autobiography? Religious practices collapse time in addition to being bound by it.

The problem of establishing the dates of religious practices is similar to the problem of fixing the borders of the United States. Most of the documents included here were produced within the current U.S. national boundaries. The religious practices of Canada and Mexico have their own stories. On the other hand, national borders are continuously crossed in the anthology. Buddhists fled persecution in Vietnam and became United States citizens. Hymns written in Spanish in El Salvador were sung in Long Island churches as well as charismatic Catholic communities throughout North and South America. Evangelical novels, such as *This Present Darkness,* are translated and sold throughout the world. Americans invent a "Hinduism" that says more about their own society than that of India. Religious communities facilitate transnationalism. So, while the United States is the locus of the volume, the borders of both the nation and the anthology are porous.

The anthology begins with the part *Praying: Individual and Communal Worship.* The texts in this section include formal liturgies as well as more spontaneous expressions of praise. The Christian, Muslim, and Jewish texts recount God's deeds and virtues, express wonder and awe, and celebrate the human/divine relationship. At times the texts call for repentance after recognition of sin. In testimonials such as those from Latter-day fast and testimony meetings, individuals praise God in story form. Autobiographical accounts articulate personal relationships with God, which may include episodes of trouble, distress, and deliverance. Although there is an informal quality to the testimonials, the narratives reflect specific theological and cultural frameworks. Worship may be designed for adults or for children. In all the texts we see the creation and re-creation of the transcendental as a permanent reality.

For many people, the most positive memories they have of religion are connected with music. In the part *Singing: Songs of Devotion, Praise, and Protest,* sound and text combine to praise, teach, and express the human situation. The spaces of singing are varied—churches, synagogues, community halls, homes, buses, and even prisons. New styles of music reflect cultural, theological, and geographical change. Songs may be tightly connected to traditional scriptures, as with the

Soka Gakkai chanting, or reworked for specific purposes, as with the transformation of black spirituals into civil rights movement songs. Like all communal rituals, singing connects people with each other and links the living with those who have sung the same songs in the past. People adapt music, as they do all behaviors, to their own needs. The text of the songs might stay the same, but where the songs are sung, how they are sung, and who sings them, changes.

The part *Teaching: Learning How to Live Correctly* explores the practices that socialize people into a particular religious culture. Through religious practices we learn appropriate behavior. We learn right and wrong. We gain information about our gender roles and sexuality. And, of course, we are partial learners, not passive learners. Religious and social ethics are created and sustained in relationship to wider social realities. People respond in many different ways to how they are told to act. In the *na ih es,* a girl grows in her knowledge of Apache culture, its sacred narratives and core values, while learning how to behave properly as an Apache woman. Not all religious practices, however, are embedded within specific rituals or ceremonies. Religions also have "intellectual rituals" that center on the reading and study of texts. People learn about what they should do in life by reading novels, letters, and polemical pamphlets. The creation, distribution, and consumption of written materials is an important part of religious practice in the United States. In the twentieth century, religious communities used every medium of modern communication to teach their values, beliefs, and rituals. Harry Emerson Fosdick did not hesitate to preach both from the pulpit of Riverside Church and from the pages of the *Ladies' Home Journal.* African American churches and segregated movie houses showed movies carrying distinct moral messages. Religious practices come in many forms. Teaching as a religious practice inculcates morality, passes on knowledge, provokes emotional responses, and shapes notions of ethnicity, sexuality, gender, class, place, and time.

A major function of religion is transformation. In the section *Healing: Health, Happiness, and the Miraculous,* we examine practices that move people from states of ill health (broadly defined) to health. For many religious people, physical health is a sign of blessing, a part of the empowerment that comes through close contact with what is sacred. Some people see close contact—sometimes even a shared nature—between the physical and spiritual worlds. Healing may come from an outside, supernatural power, as reported by those who experienced the Azusa Street revivals. In these accounts, God's help is not confined to a past age but reaches down to our own generation and will continue into the future. For other religious people, healing power is within everyone. The writings of Norman Vincent Peale and Michael Harner suggest how people make themselves whole by using their faith, spirit, and creativity. Healing practices form a central part of the religious lives of many Americans.

In the part *Imagining: The Unseen World,* we explore realms of experience considered "unnatural" or "abnormal." I use *unseen* to mean *typically* unseen, *usually* unseen. This is the uncanny world, the ideal world, the hoped-for world. The texts included here explore the supernatural. They discuss places outside of the natural world, and they describe people who are intimately in contact with these other worlds. An important task of religious practice is to define this "seen unseen" world and to set the boundaries between the commonplace and the extraordinary. Through religious practices one can cross these boundaries and bring together various ways of experiencing reality. For some people, these boundaries are crossed in dreams and visions. For others, they are crossed via literary fiction. The unseen world can be experienced through imagining. *Imagining* means forming a mental image of something not typically present to the senses. The documents in this part illustrate how people form ideas and pictures of things that are not typically part of the everyday world but may become intimately connected to people's lives. These mental images help construct an ongoing relationship with supernatural characters, beings that range from saviors to devils. By imagining, people visualize the Buddha or momentarily live in a world of old-fashioned simplicity. The dreams, visions, possessions, and miracles reported in these texts do not merely provide evidence of the supernatural. The practice of imagining prompts changes in other religious practices. Martin Luther King, Jr.'s vision of a renewed earth inspired civil rights workers and average Americans to fight for social justice. The battling angels and demons in Frank Peretti's novels remind conservative Protestants of their responsibility to maintain social order. Experiencing the unseen world is intense and dramatic. Imagining stimulates the senses and motivates action.

In the final part, *Persuading: Witnessing, Controversies, and Polemics,* texts illustrate the exchange, often tense and unpredictable, between different religious communities in the United States. To a certain extent, these documents illustrate the competitive spirit that religious communities developed in the pluralistic religious marketplace of the United States. Through their sermons, jokes, pamphlets, lectures, and writings, people try to overturn old ways and establish new viewpoints. Or, they try to restate the old ways in hopes of fending off competing ideas. Protestants, who promoted tales of a sex-obsessed India, thought they were preserving the virtue of susceptible American women. At the same time, the very popularity of their writings leads us to suspect there was something enviable (as well as despicable) in Indian sensuality and religious intensity. In other texts, pleas are addressed to people who may already be sympathetic "fellow travelers." To appreciate the humor in *The Wittenburg Door,* a reader would have to know something about evangelical Protestant culture. The magazine writers assume that readers want to make fun of the excesses in their own faith communities. In persuading, people convince themselves as well as others. It is in this part in particular that we find examples of the dark side of religion. The language of persuading, in contrast to that of teaching, is often polemical, inflammatory, and even macabre. Lies may be spread and careful reasoning rejected in favor of rhetorical flare. The practices of persuasion are often fueled by hatred.

Taken together, the contents of this volume and the first volume should dispel the old views of American religion that stressed institutional development and disembodied theology or focused on religion in a narrowly construed public context.

This collection, among other things, asks us to rethink the division between public and private in religious experience and practice. By offering a sampling of perspectives rather than an authoritative canon, the anthology more closely approximates the living texture of religious thought and practice in the United States. Readers should place the texts and practices in conversation with one another, and listen in on their discussion of mutual concerns and fears.

Further Reading

Sydney E. Ahlstrom, *A Religious History of the American People* (New Haven and London: Yale University Press, 1972); Catherine L. Albanese, *America: Religions and Religion* (Belmont, Calif.: Wadsworth, 1999); David Hall, ed., *Lived Religion in America: Toward a History of Practice* (Princeton: Princeton University Press, 1997); Bernhard Lang, *Sacred Games: A History of Christian Worship* (New Haven and London: Yale University Press, 1997); Colleen McDannell, *Material Christianity: Religion and Popular Culture in America* (New Haven and London: Yale University Press, 1995); Robert A. Orsi, *Thank You, St. Jude: Women's Devotion to the Saint of Hopeless Causes* (New Haven and London: Yale University Press, 1996); Thomas A. Tweed, ed., *Retelling U.S. Religious History* (Berkeley and Los Angeles: University of California Press, 1997).

Praying: Individual and
Communal Worship

— 1 —

Lucy Smith and Pentecostal Worship in Chicago

Wallace Best

Lucy Smith arrived in Chicago from Atlanta, Georgia, by train on the first day of May 1910. She had never been to the great northern city, nor did she know anyone there. Her material belongings were few, but she did have possesion of her nine children, her superior skill as a seamstress, and her hope for a better life. Within a few years after migrating to Chicago, Smith, sensing a divine call to do so, organized a roving Pentecostal congregation and then a permanent church with the help of one of her daughters. Having purchased land in the African American section of Chicago known as the "Black Belt," Smith laid the cornerstone of the Langley Avenue All Nations Pentecostal Church in 1926, adopting the name from Isaiah 56:17, "My house shall be called a house of prayer for all nations." Tall in stature and weighing over three hundred pounds, Smith considered herself primarily a "faith healer," one endowed with the power to be a conduit of divine healing through physical touch, and would claim to have healed two hundred thousand people in her lifetime. For nearly forty years, her ministry and the church she founded were highly acclaimed on Chicago's south side and beyond. By the time of her death in 1952, All Nations Pentecostal Church had become highly influential, racially integrated, and five thousand members strong. The *Chicago Defender* declared Smith's funeral one of the largest in Chicago's history. Sixty thousand people made their way to view her body, as a reported fifty thousand lined the streets to watch the seventy-five-car processional travel to Lincoln cemetery.

Elder Lucy Smith, as she came to be called, left her native Georgia as one among millions of African Americans who in the early twentieth century were forsaking the rural South for life in the urban Northeast and Midwest. As a child she had faced the deprivations common to most black families in the postemancipation South. The one-room log cabin where she lived with her mother and siblings contained a few furnishings, a fireplace made of two stones, and an open-roof loft where the children slept. Their food was meager, usually syrup and gravy, with meat eaten only a few times a week, from a tin pan. Though Smith never knew her father, she remembered her mother to be affectionate and kind. Because she was allowed only to attend school a few times a year, her formal education was negligible. In later years, however, Smith not only learned to read but also conducted numerous business transactions for the church.

Soon after she arrived in Chicago, Smith proclaimed a call to preach the gospel and to heal the sick. Pursuing this call led her to organize a small group of women, who met with her for prayer, into what eventually became All Nations Pentecostal. Although the building on Langley Avenue looked prosperous on the exterior, the congregation was drawn primarily from the area surrounding it—a blighted, deteriorating neighborhood of desperately poor blacks. Most of the homes were virtually uninhabitable despite exorbitant rents charged by absentee property owners. By the late 1930s, the Federal Slum Clearance Committee determined that the entire area needed demolition. Many of the area residents who attended All Nations Pentecostal Church for spiritual succor also relied on the church for material help. Throughout the Depression era, therefore, Smith established a systematic program of social outreach that clothed and fed thousands of people from her own congregation, as well as those from other parts of the city. The "Saints," a small coterie of women recognized for their spiritual gifts and extreme piety, constituted the core of the congregation and assisted Smith in her work. These women, primarily poor and from the South, also rendered crucial help to Smith in the church's large faith-healing ministry. Although the "Saints" remained the central spiritual and administrative component of All Nations Pentecostal, second only to Smith, by the late 1930s and early 1940s the church had reached such renown in Chicago that a wide spectrum of people— men and women, white and black, rich and poor—attended services at the church.

The periodical reprinted here, the *Pentecostal Ensign,* gives a summary of the activities of All Nations Pentecostal Church during February of 1936. Eight pages long in the original, the periodical is an intimate glimpse into the daily life of the church and reveals much about the beliefs and practices of Lucy Smith and her followers. Producing and distributing periodical literature (often in the form of newsletters) is a common activity for most religious organizations. This literature often provides information regarding the schedule of services, the various organizations that operate from the church, and the names of church administrators. The church's mission statement, a statement of doctrinal beliefs, a message from the pastor, and testimonials from members of the congregation are also common features of church periodical literature. All these features appear in this edition of the *Pentecostal Ensign,* along with information regarding some of the church's most important rituals. We also get a sense of the general content of Smith's sermons.

The production of church periodicals is often a type of religious practice in itself. The effort to write and routinely distribute church literature can reveal strong religious commitments, particularly when those producing it have little or no education. Many of those responsible for the *Pentecostal Ensign* fit this description. In view of the high quality of the church paper and the low level of education of Smith and much of her congregation, the production of the paper was unquestionably an enormous undertaking, as well as an act of faith. But the production of the *Pentecostal Ensign* was a type of religious practice in another way. Used as a healing tool, it was an important element in the practice of faith healing at All Nations Pentecostal Church. For the price of ten cents, those convinced of its healing power bought the paper and, as with anointed handkerchiefs and other objects of divine unction, laid it on the body of the sick person, believing it to bring the recovery of health in body and mind.

At the top of the periodical, a biblical quotation states the fundamental eschatological conviction of the church: "Behold, He Cometh with Clouds; and every eye shall see Him" (Rev. 1:7). Lucy Smith and the members of All Nations Pentecostal espoused a premillennial eschatology and regarded Christ not as a distant God but rather as a powerful savior, who promised a return to earth soon. As a "full Gospel" church, the members of All Nations took the words of the Bible seriously and literally. Every service contained numerous Bible quotations and biblical allusions. Each statement in the "Our Belief" section of the *Pentecostal Ensign* includes supportive, evidential biblical texts. Elder Smith understood Mussolini's invasion of Ethiopia, for example, through the lens of the Old Testament prophet Daniel and the New Testament Gospel of Matthew.

The "Our Belief" section also clearly shows that Lucy Smith founded All Nations as a sanctified and spirit-filled church. She followed in the tradition of holiness women preachers such as Phoebe Palmer (1807–1874), whose interpretation of the teachings of John Wesley led her to preach that sanctification—a postconversion experience of spiritual growth and devoutness—could be complete and permanent. Having obtained sanctification, Palmer believed, Christians need no longer sin. Lucy Smith taught, as did Phoebe Palmer and others in the nineteenth century, that all Christians could receive this dramatic "second blessing," which would assure them that they were cleansed from sin—the selfish intent of the heart—and free to act in conformity to the will of God. Aligned with Pentecostal doctrine (as distinct from "Holiness" doctrine), however, Smith and her congregation also believed in a "third blessing" after conversion, the baptism of the Holy Spirit. Spirit baptism was not for purification, as in the case of water baptism and sanctification. This baptism was meant for spiritual empowerment. Once the Holy Spirit descended on an individual, they believed, that person was graced with special divine gifts. The most important of these was the gift of speaking in tongues in accordance with Acts 2 and 1 Corinthians 12.

The list of religious activities offered at All Nations Pentecostal Church indicates that the congregation met frequently and for a variety of services. In addition to Sunday worship, which was held both morning and evening, midweek services rounded out the church's busy activities calendar. There were meetings of the missionaries, choir and orchestra rehearsals, Sunday school classes, and discussions of the ushers boards. For the members of All Nations Pentecostal, church was much more than an hour or two on Sunday morning. Church activities took up much of a member's leisure time and infused his or her life with an intense spiritual dimension. Wednesdays were devoted to healing, with a service in the afternoon and a radio broadcast in the late night. Thursdays were devoted to fasting and prayer. The church sponsored Friday meetings primarily to provide diversion and entertainment for the large number of young people in the congregation. Periodic special services included a monthly observance of the Lord's Supper, a simple albeit lively ceremony complete with bread and grape juice blessed by church leaders and distributed among the congregation. A footwashing ritual was a crucial component to the observance of the

Lord's Supper. The ritual, common among most Pentecostal and Holiness churches, was based on John 13:14—"Now that I, your Lord and Teacher, have washed your feet, you also should wash one another's feet"—and the practices of the early church as described in 1 Timothy 5:10. Additionally, All Nations practiced the sacraments of baptism by immersion and infant consecration. The "consecration services," as they were called, were held each second Sunday afternoon.

Although Elder Smith staged at least one revival meeting every year, she deemed it necessary that her congregation seek spiritual renewal and empowerment at closer intervals. She established weekly "refilling services" to meet this need. Like annual revivals, "refilling services" were designed to bring believers to a point of contrition, cleansing, and renewed spiritual energy. They also provided regular opportunities for those who had not received the baptism of the Holy Spirit to do so. At All Nations Pentecostal, "refilling services" were second only to healing services in terms of importance.

The Sunday morning services, as with all meetings held at All Nations, were opened with loud and enthusiastic music. Music was an essential component of all activities held at All Nations—whether spiritual or administrative in orientation—because it expressed the members' devotion and stimulated an environment of praise. All Nations Pentecostal Church became noted for its music, presented by adult and children's choirs, ensembles, and numerous soloists. The choirs were frequently accompanied by what the *Pentecostal Ensign* calls the "church orchestra," made up of an organist, a pianist, a drummer, and a guitarist. Lucy Smith's granddaughter, "Little Lucy," served as the church's music director for many years and later became a gospel music recording artist who wrote and produced for the Lucy Smith Singers, as well as the Roberta Martin Singers. Due mainly to the high quality of the gospel music emanating from All Nations, the church's radio broadcast, which began in 1933, became a huge success and increased Elder Smith's stature within the city. The broadcast, called "The Glorious Church of the Air," became a proving ground for the early careers of some of gospel music's legendary artists. Mahalia Jackson, Robert Anderson, "Singing" Sammy Lewis, the Norfleet Brothers, the Roberta Martin Singers, and, of course, the Lucy Smith Singers all made frequent appearances on the program. This edition of the *Pentecostal Ensign* mentions that Thomas A. Dorsey, "the father of the gospel music," was present at the Wednesday broadcast.

Following the opening hymn, in a typical worship service the members of the church stood and raised their hands in adoration and praise. All worship services at All Nations Pentecostal consisted of members praising and thanking Jesus for their salvation and for his support. This ritual very often led to even more frenzied expressions of praise, as some worshipers would become "filled" with the Holy Spirit. The *Pentecostal Ensign* describes how "the power fell while Sister Holmes sang 'Jesus is Mine.' The Holy Ghost had his way for 20 minutes the young and the old danced under the mighty power of God." When the Holy Spirit "had his way," members became overcome with religious emotion and enthusiasm, clapped their hands, threw their hands over their heads, and shouted "thank you, Jesus." Some would dance to the point of frenzy. "Truly," explained the church paper, "the Glory of the Lord was in the building and many wonderful praises went up to God and the power fell and many rejoiced in the God of their Salvation."

The ecstatic praise, exuberant music, and "holy dancing"—evidence that the Holy Spirit was present—were integral parts of All Nations Pentecostal Church. Enthusiastic praise, however, did not deter Smith and her congregation from concerns of a more earthly nature. Throughout the church paper, we read how the pastor sought to inform her congregation of national and international events. This impulse often informed what biblical texts Smith chose for her sermons. In October 1935, Italian troops under the direction of Benito Mussolini invaded Ethiopia. By February 1936, the Italian offensive included air power and poison gas to destroy the Ethiopian armies, inflicting severe civilian casualties. African Americans around the world watched helplessly as one of the few independent nations in Africa fell to Italian colonial aggression. In the "Signs of the Times" section of this edition of the paper, Smith describes the effort by Emperor Haile Selassie to halt the Italian invasion, and other events occurring in Ethiopia and Egypt, as evidence of the "last days" spoken of in the book of Revelation. Elder Smith presented the events of the 1930s, particularly those meaningful to the African Americans in her congregation, as signs that "redemption draweth nigh." Worship services at All Nations Pentecostal, therefore, were not always exclusively devoted to music, praise, and religious enthusiasm. Smith also attempted to show her congregation how the tribulations of the world, at home and abroad, fulfilled the predictions of the prophets. Her constant admonition to her followers was that they "be ready when the Master comes."

Although Elder Smith believed that divine healing could take place at any time, she held special healing services on Wednesday afternoons and evenings. Like Sunday worship, healing services began with the choir singing, accompanied by piano and drum. After a brief message by Smith, those who had come especially for healing were called forward. Then Smith and her coworkers, robed all in white, attended to them, rubbing ailing spots with olive oil and praying audibly. The emotional tone of the healing services was very high, most often escalating to the point of frenzy. Although most of the church's membership and those who sought Smith's healing touch were African American, a few immigrants and poor whites living in the neighborhood also joined the church, and they, too, often sought her healing. As a testimony of those who claimed physical recovery after coming to All Nations, Smith converted the church's basement into what she called the "trophy room," where crutches and canes abandoned by their former owners were stored. The *Pentecostal Ensign* also contained personal testimonies of healing. Smith and her staff included in each issue short letters from people who had been healed by God through Smith's prayers and those of her coworkers. The letters detailed the problems suffered, the duration of the illness, and the "miraculous healing."

The religious worship at All Nations Pentecostal Church often occurred throughout the entire week, taking various forms and involving a variety of different activities. From praise services, to talks by visiting missionaries, to letter writing, the activities at All Nations were designed to spread a specific Christian message in many different ways. At times the congregation was caught up in the Holy Spirit, praying loudly and incessantly. At other times they sat and listened to Lucy Smith describe the biblical implications of certain world events. The breadth and depth of the activities and services offered at All Nations explains, in part, the church's broad appeal. A wide range of Chicagoans, black, white, and immigrant, were attracted to Lucy Smith's church, making it the only decidedly interracial congregation on Chicago's predominately black South Side during the migration era. Also, although the lively worship style and unschooled speech of Lucy Smith appealed to the thousands of poor southern migrants filtering into Chicago during these years, middle-class and elite blacks also became friends and supporters of the church. Two decades of religious broadcasting, and an even longer time ministering to those who came to her church, allowed Lucy Smith to enter the lives of thousands of Chicagoans. It also permitted many people to experience a type of religious worship new to the urban north and to recognize the spiritual leadership of one of Chicago's first and most innovative African American Pentecostal woman preachers. The text below reprints All Nations Pentecostal Church, *Pentecostal Ensign*, no. 16 (February 1936).

Further Reading

Wallace Best, "'Passionately Human, but No Less Divine': Racial Ideology and Religious Culture in the Black Churches of Chicago, 1915–1963," Ph.D. dissertation, Northwestern University, 2000; Eric Lincoln and Lawrence H. Mamiya, *The Black Church in the African American Experience* (Durham, N.C.: Duke University Press, 1990); Melvin D. Williams, *Community in a Black Pentecostal Church: An Anthropological Study* (Pittsburgh, Pa.: University of Pittsburgh Press, 1974); Cheryl J. Sanders, *Saints in Exile: The Holiness-Pentecostal Experience in African-American Religion and Culture* (New York: Oxford University Press, 1999); Milton C. Sernett, *Bound for the Promised Land: African American Religion and the Great Migration* (Durham, N.C.: Duke University Press, 1997).

The Pentecostal Ensign

Report of the Langley Avenue All Nations Pentecostal Church Issue No. 16, February 1936

Behold, He Cometh With Clouds
And Every Eye Shall See Him. Rev. 1:7

Come and Hear
Elder Lucy Smith . . .

She preaches a Full Gospel. Teaches how to be saved, sanctified and filled with the Holy Ghost. Sick prayed for at every service except Sunday morning. We get letters from all over the United States asking us to pray for people. If you want anointed handkerchief send it to us with an addressed envelope. We anoint it free.

Divine healing service every Wednesday afternoon 1:30 P.M. Thursday is a day of fasting and prayer, meet at 11 A.M. Friday night, young people's meeting at 8 P.M. Foot washing every Thursday night before the 1st Sunday. Lord's supper every 1st Sunday night. Refilling service once a month. Consecration service for the babies every 2nd Sunday at 3 P.M. Missionary offering every 1st Sunday night. . . . I am the Lord that healeth thee. Exodus 15:26.

SERVICE REPORT
Watch Service Anniversary

Dec. 31, 1936 [1935?]

The meeting was open[ed] by the choir singing, "Saved by the Blood." Regular song service followed, after song service, all stood with lifted hands in praise to God. Announcements made as usual. Remarks by the Pastor, telling how glad she was to be here and kept almost another year, she warned all the saints to leave all their failures in the old year. Then she spoke from Peter fifth chapter. She spoke of how she had fed the flock with a willing mind and not for filthy lucre, we want to submit our selves and be subject one to the other. Cast all our cares upon him for he careth for you. God picked me up in 1916 and sent me and tonight I thank God for he has given me many souls, now the God of all grace is going to be with you this year and we must be obedient to him. The praise service was led by Sis[ter] Porter. Truly the Glory of the Lord was in the building and many wonderful praises went up to God and the power fell and many rejoice in the God of their Salvation.

January 1—1936,
New Years

The meeting opened by singing "Hide You in the Blood." All stood and praised God. Announcement by the pastor. We were so glad to have Sis[ter] Mattie Neeley with us from Africa. The sick was prayed [for] and many were healed. Sister Neely gave a short talk. "If you can't say down in your heart, 'even so Lord Jesus come quickly,' you are not ready." She told us how wonderfully the Lord saved a native and right away he wanted his house cleaned out and burned up his jujues. These jujues are very expensive costing from $5.00 to $40.00 dollars. She related how 30 educated natives were killed and their heads cut off. Sister Neely said that she hated to leave the native babies for when they learn to trust God for their healing they never fail to trust him when sick. She told us also how a native got saved at his relative's funeral. His father wanted him to serve the devil and he later was converted, then he gave his son permission to serve God.

Jan. 1st 1936

The meeting was open[ed] by singing "When I See the Blood." A lovely song service was rendered. All stood and praise[d] the Lord with uplifted hands. Request for prayer taken up by Elder R. J. Porter. Announcement made. Praise service led by Bro[ther] Jesse Edwards. Offering taken up for the broadcast. The pastor told how this work began and how the Lord called her and gave her the gift of healing. While she and other sisters prayed, the Lord showed Sister Morris a candle stick in the middle of [the] floor on Jan. 1st 1919 the Mission was crowded but no one said to have a church or a tent, but the Lord showed me a huge tent in a vision and brought it to pass in 1921, this work came out from one room. Then the Lord told me to build him a Church. This church was buil[t] by faith.

Thanksgiving Service

The meeting was open[ed] by prayer and a lovely song service, then all stood with uplisted [uplifted] hands praising God Announcements made. The Pastor talked from I Chronicles 16th Chapter 10th verse. She talked under the anointing of the Holy Ghost. Offering lifted for thanksgiving. Praise service led by Sister Evans. The saints and visitors gave praises and thanks to the Almighty God. The power fell while Sister Holmes sang "Jesus is Mine." The Holy Ghost had his way for 20 minutes the young and the old danced under the mighty power of God, praise his holy name. Thank God for the rain. The pastor said that the Lord proved that he was well pleased of us being here on this thanksgiving day. Amen Praise God!

CHURCH HAPPENINGS

Celebrated

Our Pastor Elder Lucy Smith was highly celebrated Tuesday, January 14th on her 62nd birthday with a splendid program. Many distinguished visitors help[ed] in a great way to make the program a real success. Many beautiful birthday cards was [were] received from her radio listeners. A paper from Elder J. E. Greenfield of Omaha, Nebr. Also one from Mrs. Rose Wilton and her sister Mrs. Ethel Hooper of Wisconsin was read.

Sick List

Those around the church who is ill at present are: Sister Felicia Evans at 466 E. 41st Street, Sister Daisy Johnson, at 3730 Cottage Grove Ave. Mother Copeland address unknown. Sister Lula Langford 3726 Vincennes Ave.

Convalescing

Mother Ella Harvey who has been down for quite awhile but is now up and waiting on the weather that she may mingle her voice once more with the saints of the most high. Praises be to God. We are happy to see Sister Wilson up and about. Our radio announcer has been ill but we [are] glad that she is back on the job again. . . .

BROADCAST RALLY

The Broadcast rally was a real success last Wednesday night when many in spite of the cold wave packed the auditorium to enjoy the Musical program. A lovely offering was taken up that the program might remain on the air. Those who took part on the program were: The Morning Star Baptist Church Gospel Choir. Miss Salle Martin. Mr. Thomas A. Dorsey, The Four Morning Glorys, Mrs. Emma Jackson, Mrs. Jessie Matthews. The Jr. Gospel Chorus. Everyone retired having enjoyed a glorious evening. . . .

HEALING SERVICE

January 1st 1936

I thank God for healing me of a growth that I had in my nose and the Doctors said that I would have to be operated on; but thank God after that Elder Smith and her co-workers prayed for me the Lord wonderfully healed me and saved and baptized my soul with the Holy Ghost and fire, praise God. I suffered with this growth for two months.

Mary Rounds, 4528 Prairie Ave. Chicago Ill.

I have suffered with spells for about 4 years. When I eat I have to take medicine. Whenever I have these spells I would fall out unconscious; but praise God after Elder Smith prayed for me God healed me. I gave him all the glory.

Robert Walker 4635 St. Lawrence Ave. Chicago Ill.

I am thankful to the Lord, to Elder Smith and co-workers for praying for me and the Lord healed me of heart trouble that I had for years. Praise his great name.

Agnes Hammons 5617 Indiana Ave.

I have suffered about 7 or 8 years with neuritis, after Elder Lucy Smith prayed for me I was healed. Praise God.

Emma Balthrop 4549 Indiana Ave. Chicago, Ill.

I praise God for healing me of a backache I suffered with for 4 years. It was what they called a nervous backache. Elder Smith prayed for me and the Lord healed me.

Mrs. Lizzie Norwood Market St. Waukegan Ill.

I praise God for healing me of stomach trouble that I suffered with since 1915. He also baptized me also with the Holy Ghost, praise his name.

Daisy Swan, 4137 Calumet Ave. Chicago Ill. . . .

Jan. 15, 1936

I have suffered with my eyes about two years. I had a growth on my left eye also suffered with my stomach. Elder Smith and her workers prayed for me and praise God I'm healed.

Ida Wright 4923 Calumet [Chicago, Ill.]

I had a Rupture for four or five years. Anytime I would get sick or feel anyways bad it would cause a terrible hurting in my side. It was so severe I couldn't sleep at night. I was prayed for and the Lord healed me.

Sadie Collins 3730 Cottage Grove [Chicago, Ill.]

Jan. 23, 1936

I have had rheumatism four weeks. My hands were so stiff I could hardly use them. Elder Smith prayed for me and I was healed. Now I am able to use my hands and praise God for it.

Jane Tompkins 3938 State St. [Chicago, Ill.]

I thank God for healing me of a pain that I had in my stomach also a soreness under my arm. I was prayed for and was healed.

Ruby Davis 4332 Michigan [Chicago, Ill.]

OUR BELIEF ACCORDING TO GOD'S HOLY WORD

The Father

We believe in God the Father Almighty the author and creator of all things. Gen. 1:1 In the beginning God created heaven and earth. Psalms 90:2 Before the mountains were brought forth even thou hadst formed the earth and the world even from everlasting to everlasting thou art God.

The Son

We believe that Jesus was and is the Son of God co-equal in wisdom, power and holiness with the Father and that through his atonement the world is saved from sin and reconciled to God. Matt. 3:17. And lo a voice from heaven saying "This is my beloved Son in whom I am well pleased hear ye him."

The Holy Ghost

We believe in the personality of the Holy Spirit. That he proceedeth from the Father and the Son, and that he is the operator of the trinity through which the plan of salvation is carried on in earth. John 14. Even the spirit of truth whom the world cannot receive because it seeth it not neither knoweth him;

but we know him because he dwelleth in us. But the comforter which is the Holy Ghost whom the Father will send in my name, shall teach you all things and bring all things to your rememberance whatsoever I have said unto you. Acts 1:5–8. For John truly baptized with water but ye shall be baptized with the Holy Ghost not many days hence. Ye shall receive power after that the Holy Ghost shall come upon you; and ye shall be a witness unto me unto the uttermost parts of the earth.

The Blood of Christ

We believe that without the blood of Christ there is no remission for sin and no cleansing of sin. Hebrews 9:22. Without the shedding of blood there is no remission for sin.

Justification

We belief that when a person repents of his sins with godly sorrow, and accepts Jesus as personal Savior he is justified before God and righteousness is imputed to him. Romans 4:7,8,24.

Sanctification

We believe that Jesus was sanctified according to Hebrews 12:14 also Ephesians 5:18. We must be like him. The Holy Spirit sanctifies and imparts true righteousness to us.

Heaven and Hell

Heaven is the final abode of the saints, the place of eternal rest and joy. Hell is the final abode of the wicked and sinners. Romans 6:26 and Revelation 20:13–15.

SIGNS OF THE TIMES

Ethiopia

The activities of the Ethiopians extend far back, as some believe, to the very beginning of history. They evidently were a powerful people in the days of David and Solomon. Though many of the jungle of Abyssinia are only partly civilized, yet many of her people are numbered among the best educated of any nation. The emperor, Haile Selassie, voluntarily gave to his country a representative parliament similar to that of Great Britain. Selasie says: We do not want territorial expansion, but to live in peace, and more fully contribute our part toward human progress. He has done seeming[ly] everything in his power to bring about a peaceful settlement with Mussolini, and in doing so has won the sympathy of the nations of the world.

Mussolini and the Bible.

As an of set [?] to many paragraphs being published at the present time against Mussolini and especially in his attitude toward Abyssinia. All teachers and school-masters should read the New Testament and should explain this divine book to the children and see that they learn its divine passages by heart. The Bible should not be missing from one school library for it is ever new through the centuries. It is the greatest of all books—the most necessary book because it is divine.

Egypt Fears

In Egypt we constantly see airplanes roaring overhead, and are reminded that war, ruthless and cruel is near. Just now Italy has 80,000 and 350 bombing planes on the west coast of Egypt ready to come any moment bringing death and awful destruction. We are only safe in God's keeping.

Signs of the End

MATT. 24

When ye therefore shall see the abomination of desolation spoken of by Daniel the prophet, stand in the holy place. Let him which is on the house top not come down to take anything out of house. For then shall be great tribulation such as was not since the beginning of the world until now. And except those days shall be shortened, there shall no flesh be saved.

If anyone shall say unto you, Lo, here is Christ, or there; believe it not.

For there shall rise false Christs, and false prophets, and shall show great signs and wonders; in so-much that if it were possible, they shall deceive the very elect.

When you see these things coming to pass, look up for your redemption draweth nigh. Watch ye therefore and be sober for the moment that ye think not the son of man cometh. Therefore, in order to be ready when our Master comes let us lay aside every weight and sin and run this race with patience. . . .

The newsletter concludes with lists of names of church members and the roles they play within the community: ordained ministers, coworkers, ordained missionaries, church orchestra members, choir directrices, Christian workers, church mothers, ushers, board members, presidents (of various organizations), Sunday school teachers, and staff.

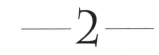

2

Lutheran Family Devotions

Betty DeBerg

The Protestant Reformers of the sixteenth century put new emphasis on the religious education of children by their parents within the home. Some of the premises of Reformation theology, such as *sola scriptura* ("the Bible alone") and *sola fide* ("faith alone"), called all Christians, male or female, lay or clergy, adult or child, to an individual encounter with the Bible through regular reading and study of the Scriptures. Creation of an individual saving relationship with Christ was cultivated through interaction with the text of the Bible. Both Martin Luther and John Calvin demanded that all Christians be taught to read the Bible and the various Protestant catechisms that were developing to explain Protestant doctrines. Mothers and fathers were, according to Luther, to be "apostles and bishops" to their children. Calvin assigned mothers a significant role in both instructing their children and influencing them toward Christian piety. Mothers were to listen to their children read the Bible and were to give catechism lessons to them. Frequently, the mother was the parent more available to conduct family worship.

In the United States, Puritan and other Protestant families generally conformed to classical Reformation teaching about the importance of family literacy and religious education. The father was always described as the head of the household, with the wife owing him obedience. Nevertheless, the role of women in both congregations and family religious life expanded gradually over the eighteenth and early nineteenth centuries. Within mainstream white Protestant culture, women were identified as the passive and naturally more religious gender, whose natural God-given spheres of activity and influence were supposed to be the home and the church. Victorian women were to provide for the Christian nurture of their families, especially of their children. While men were seen as the head of the home, just as Christ was the head of the Church, in reality women often took over the religious leadership of their families. Historians have documented how this exaltation of motherhood and womanly Christian piety led, ironically, to women assuming more and more active roles in individual congregations and in Protestant denominational structures. Especially after the Civil War, women formed all kinds of organizations with a variety of religious and social reform missions. In the late nineteenth century, the "Home Worship" movement became an important aspect of Protestant foreign and domestic women's missionary societies. Middle-class women believed that their virtuous, patient, self-sacrificing methods of child rearing could be passed on to other women who were not familiar with them. "Educated motherhood" became the focus of many women's organizations and activities such as Mother's Clubs, which sprang up all over the nation. Both denominational organizations and interdenominational ones encouraged the Christian nurture of children–those of their own members and the needy children of others. The Lutheran church was only one among many Protestant denominations that supported federated women's work for and with children.

The first Lutherans to come to North America came from Sweden and established a short-lived colony on the Delaware River in 1638. Soon other Lutherans—from Germany and the Netherlands—established farming settlements, primarily in the Middle Colonies. On the eve of the American Revolution in 1771, there were eighty-one German congregations in Pennsylvania and surrounding states. Although there was some movement in the early nineteenth century to create an English-language-based "American" Lutheranism, the large influx of immigrants during the remainder of the century made this difficult. Swedes, Danes, and Norwegians—in addition to Germans—all wanted to speak their own languages at church and practice their own traditional religious customs. Many of them settled in isolated regions of the old Northwest and later farmed on the upper Midwestern plains. In 1870 there were less than half a million Lutherans in the country, but immigration quintupled their numbers by 1910. Although they all followed a similar liturgy and claimed a common belief system, ethnicity and theological orientation divided the communities of Lutherans. The twentieth century, however, was marked by a series of mergers of various independent Lutheran groups. As more and more members spoke English and embraced an "American" identity, they found that their rituals and beliefs brought them together in a common faith. After a merger in 1988, the majority of American Lutherans belonged to the Evangelical Lutheran Church in America, with much smaller numbers belonging to the Lutheran Church–Missouri Synod and the Wisconsin Evangelical Lutheran Synod.

One of the common beliefs that Lutherans possessed in the early twentieth century was the religious importance of the mother in the family. Emma Miller Bolenius, writing for the General Council women's Lutheran Mission Worker in 1914, declared that "every woman is a mother in the making. Whether she has married and borne children matters little. The instinct for motherhood is so strongly inherent in the sex that it seeks expression from childhood to old age." At the very center of the idea of educated motherhood was the understanding of the importance of early childhood and the role that adults had in shaping children's moral and religious character. Bolenius compared the power of the parents to shape their child to that of the Creator God to give the child life in the first place. The mother had a particularly distinctive role in training the body and mind, the personality and soul. "By constant repetition, she must create in the child habits of health and personal hygiene," Bolenius wrote. "She must foster correct standards of thinking and conduct. She must develop his will along proper lines. She must equip him with all that is needed to bring him into right relationship with people and conditions." According to Bolenius, the first seven years of the child's life were the most important because during this period the foundations of later thinking, speaking, and acting then were laid. The responsibility of mothers, who oversaw their children in their early years, could not be overestimated. "No people can rise higher than the status of its young," Bolenius could then conclude.

Each woman was encouraged to view her day-to-day parenting activities as a special arena for reflection on, and practice of, her spirituality. This spirituality of child nurture, of women's sacred trust, was not merely a particular motherly attitude toward education. Christian nurture also was a spiritual discipline of habits and rituals both individual and corporate. Family devotions or home worship were promoted by women's missionary societies as an integral part of child nurture. The Women's Missionary Federation of the Norwegian Lutheran Church of America, for example, published extensively on home worship between 1923 and 1933. Lutheran women were not alone in their appeal for "the family altar." This was also a theme in the rhetoric of male leaders of many of the newly emerging Protestant fundamentalist organizations and networks.

The structure of Lutheran family devotions in the twenties and thirties was summarized in a didactic and inspirational essay called "Christian Nurture" by Mrs. H. Hanson. For Hanson, home worship is the first and primary way in which Christian devotion manifests itself. Family devotions are to be held daily— "the hour is of minor importance"—and are to consist of common "prayer, praise and thanksgiving." This family worship occasion was to be supplemented daily by "grace at meals" and "religious training in the home" for preschool children, consisting of "Bible stories and Christian hymns." It was considered especially important that children hear the Bible read to them and that they begin to read it themselves as soon as they are able. Hanson cautioned that families not overlook Luther's *Small Catechism* as a resource for family devotion and religious formation. "Sunday school and church papers" might help "develop an intelligent interest in church work" and may be a valuable resource, too.

Lutheran women's missionary societies encouraged parents to plan together with their children for some special time of prayer and reflection. Breakfast time, the evening meal, or before retiring at night might be a good time for Bible stories, prayers, and songs. Older children were encouraged to read the Bible aloud or perhaps responsively, so that all the family could participate in worship. Reciting sentence-length prayers, memorizing hymns, reading chapters from a devotional book, and studying the lives of Christian heroes and famous missionaries were all appropriate activities for family worship. Lutheran organizations for women, such as the Women's Missionary Federation, promised to make materials available for facilitating the construction of a home altar. Throughout the twenties and thirties they published prayer books for children, devotional pamphlets, inspirational articles, and reading lists of useful religious books for mothers. Lutheran women realized the difficulty of consistently conducting family worship, but they insisted that the nurturing character of the devotions was essential to Christian living. As Mrs. M. A. Kjeseth explained, "Home worship is like meals. Some meals are joyous, some are tiresome, some are dry. But—well planned, regular meals give us food. Some home devotions are joyous, some are tiresome, some are dry. But—well planned, regular home devotions give us food. Food for our bodies gives us strength, vigor and a soul's desire to go heavenward." For Mrs. Kjeseth, the Bible was the most nutritious spiritual food, but families could also benefit from reading children's books about the Bible such as Jesse Hurlbut's *Story of the Bible* (1904), Elsie Egermeier's *Bible Story Book* (1922), and Catherine Vos's *The Child Story Bible* (1935).

Many Lutherans kept family devotions going after World War II. Religious activities became a part of suburban family living, which, with the G.I. Bill, became a reality for many middle-class white Americans. Men who had fought overseas wanted to return to a secure family life, where sex roles were traditional and familiar. Women, many of whom had worked in the domestic war industry, were being told by the media and their own families to resume their focus on home activities. Churchgoing reached a high level in the Eisenhower years, and this, combined with postwar domestic ideology, encouraged families to bring religion into the home. Protestant and Catholic presses produced new, updated materials to help families create Christian homes through family worship and the celebration of Christian holidays. Ministers, priests, and educators taught adults and children how to make a strong bond between worship in church and worship in home.

In the late 1950s and into the 1960s, one children's book designed to be used in family worship became a religious bestseller. *Little Visits with God* was published in 1957 by the Lutheran Church–Missouri Synod through its Concordia Publishing House. *Little Visits with God* perhaps best represents the survival of the practice of Lutheran family devotions into the second half of the twentieth century. In 1959 the Missouri Synod reported to its convention delegates that by the end of the convention over 105,000 copies of *Little Visits with God* would be in print. The excellent sale of the volume encouraged them to develop another children's devotional booklet, *My Devotions*. Within a few months the circulation of this new periodical grew to more than 100,000 copies. The sale of *Little Visits with God* encouraged Concordia Publishing House to issue a sequel, *More Little Visits with God*, in 1961. (A revised edition of *Little Visits with God* was published in 1997. For this new edition, the original text was revised by Mary Manz Simon and Allan Hart Jahsmann, and illustrated by Hal Lund.) The authors of the original edition of short devotional pieces were Allan Hart Jahsmann, editor of the *Christian Parent* magazine, and Martin P. Simon, a specialist in Sunday school materials designed for small children. They specifically composed the devotions in a language that would make sense to young children. Consequently, they used incorrect grammar and simplified some of the Bible verses at times. The authors included short life-experience stories in order to make the devotional reading more interesting and meaningful. Along with Lutheran women from the nineteenth and early twentieth centuries, the authors of such primers believed that parents needed regularly to take time as a family to visit with God. Family worship could occur either at the breakfast table or supper table or in a family circle at the children's bedtime hour. Older children should be encouraged to read *Little Visits with God* on their own. The authors included discussion questions to help with informal conversation about spiritual matters, and they suggested that families sing a hymn preceding or following the reading of the text.

Little Visits with God contains two hundred short devotional readings, each prefaced by a Bible verse, and each concluding with a "Bible reading for older children and grownups" and a prayer. Most of the devotional pieces teach Christian doctrine—especially the doctrine of God and Christology—and morality. Some of the doctrinal or theological essays include "Where God Is," "God Can Do Anything," "How Strong God Is!" "God Can See Who Believes," "Jesus Obeyed for Us," "Jesus Never Changes," "What Jesus Can Do for Us," "Why Jesus Died," and "How God Forgives Sins." Some of the titles of the pieces devoted to teaching morality include "How Others Get to Know You," "The Fun of Being Kind," "God Wants Us to Be Thankful," "How to Treat Mean People," "Are You a Liar?" "Our Lord Is Never Proud," "Smile before Sundown," and "How to Keep from Sinning." There are several devotionals on death and heaven, several about the importance of church attendance, and several that admonish children to respect and obey their parents. Over half of these short narratives feature boys as the primary actor, one-quarter feature girls, and nearly one-quarter feature at least one boy and one girl. The color illustration on the cloth book cover depicts a young blond mother reading to two small brown-haired boys and a small blond girl, an indication of the on-going role of mothers in mid-century middle-class Protestant homes.

The selection below is from Allan Hart Jahsmann and Martin P. Simon, *Little Visits with God: Devotions for Families with Small Children* (St. Louis: Concordia Publishing House, 1957), pp. 1–2, 5–6, 11–12, 18–19. Used with permission.

Further Reading

Barbara J. MacHaffie, *Her Story: Women in Christian Tradition* (Philadelphia: Fortress, 1986); Colleen McDannell, *The Christian Home in Victorian America, 1840–1900* (Bloomington: Indiana University Press, 1985); Patricia R. Hill, *The World Their Household: The American Woman's Foreign Mission Movement and Cultural Transformation, 1870–1920* (Ann Arbor: University of Michigan Press, 1985), p. 71; Lani L. Johnson, *Led by the Spirit: A History of Lutheran Church Women* (Philadelphia: Lutheran Church Women, 1980); Barbara Welter, "The Cult of True Womanhood, 1820–1860," in her *Dimity Convictions: The American Woman in the Nineteenth Century* (Athens, Ohio: Ohio University Press, 1976), pp. 21–41; Betty A. DeBerg, *Ungodly Women: Gender and the First Wave of American Fundamentalism* (Minneapolis: Fortress, 1990), pp. 59–74; Emma Miller Bolenius, "Motherhood and Everywoman," *Lutheran*

Mission Worker 18, no. 1 (December 1914), p. 43; Mrs. H. Hanson, "Christian Nurture," in *Program Helps: Christian Nurture* (n.p., n.d.); Mrs. M. A. Kjeseth, *Home Worship* (Minneapolis: Women's Missionary Federation, NLCA, n.d.).

Little Visits with God

WHY WE CAN ALWAYS BE HAPPY

> *Blessed is he whose sin is forgiven. Psalm 32:1*

Jerry wasn't happy. When his father came home from work, Jerry hurried upstairs. Mother had to call him four times before he came down to supper.

At the table his father asked, "Who broke the window in the garage?" Jerry said nothing, but he felt his face get hot. "You played ball over there, didn't you?" said his father. "And we told you not to."

Jerry looked at his plate and still said nothing. He could hardly swallow the bread he was chewing. Then he began to cry.

"I'm sorry," he said. "I'll pay for it from my allowance. And I promise I won't play ball there again."

His parents were glad to hear Jerry talk that way. He was sorry he had done wrong. And he promised to do better. "All right, Jerry," said his father softly, "we'll forget it. God forgives you when you are sorry, and we will, too. But please don't disobey us again."

Next morning Jerry whistled as he went along to school. He was happy. God had put joy into his heart. "I wonder why it feels so good to be forgiven," he thought. "Thank You, God," he said, "for always being willing to forgive us."

Let's talk about this: Why didn't Jerry want to meet his father? What wrong had Jerry done? Was it easy for Jerry to say, "I'm sorry"? Why did Jerry feel so good the next day? The Bible says, "Be glad in the Lord. . . and shout for joy," because God forgives us our sins every day for Jesus' sake.

Older children and grownups may now read: Psalm 32:8–11.

Let us pray together: Dear Lord, we are glad that we can come to You at any time and can always receive forgiveness. Keep us from doing wrong, make us sorry for our sins, and help us to believe in Jesus, our Savior. Then we shall always be happy children of God. We ask this in Jesus' name. Amen.

SERVICE WITH A SMILE

> *Without having seen Jesus, you love Him. 1 Peter 1:8*

"What's Ella doing?" asked Mr. James.
    "She's helping Mother," said Fred.

Mr. James went to the kitchen to see how Ella was helping. She wasn't helping very much. She had a face a mile long, and it was sour enough to can pickles.

"Well, well," said her daddy, "something must be wrong. My little girl isn't happy helping her Mother, is she?

"No," said Ella.

"O.K.," said her daddy, "I'll finish drying the dishes for you if you'll learn a little Bible verse for me."

That was fine with Ella. "Which Bible verse?" asked Ella when her daddy was finished with the dishes.

"It's in Psalm 100," said Mr. James. "That makes it easy to find in the Bible. Hunt for verse 2."

Ella found it and read, "Serve the Lord with gladness."

"How are we to serve the Lord?" asked her father, as though he didn't know.

"With gladness," said Ella. "Do I serve the Lord when I help Mother?"

"You can," said Mr. James. "But I'm afraid you didn't do it with gladness this time."

"I'm sorry," said Ella; "next time I'll try to smile. I want to please Jesus in what I do," she said. This made her father happy.

Let's talk about this: What was Ella doing? How did she show that she wasn't glad to do it? Who did it for her? Which Bible verse did he ask her to learn? Why did Ella want to serve the Lord Jesus with gladness?

Older children and grownups may now read: Psalm 100.

Let us pray together: Dear Lord Jesus, we are glad that You are our God and Savior and that we are Your children. Please help us to remember that we can serve You in whatever we do. Then even our work will become pleasant, and we will do it gladly. Amen.

HOW TO GET CLEAN INSIDE

Wash me, and I shall be whiter than snow. Psalm 51:7.

"Did you wash your hands, Dick?" his mother asked. "Yes, I did," said Dick. But when he showed his hands to his mother, she said, "You didn't use soap, did you? And you didn't wash here and here and here." So Dick had to go and wash again. This time he tried to wash clean with soap.

There is a way in which boys and girls can get real clean the first time. When they let their mothers wash them, they usually get clean, at least on the outside.

But even mothers can't wash away the bad things that their children think and say and do. They can't wash their sins away. Only God can do that. When He forgives a person's sins, He washes them all away. That is why King David said in a psalm, "Wash me, and I shall be whiter than snow."

Mothers like to have their wash real white when it hangs on a line. White clothes with black marks on them are not clean and beautiful. Black marks on white clothes make most mothers unhappy.

When we are naughty, we sin. Sin is like a black spot on a clean white sheet. God wants His children to be clean on the inside. And we want to be clean and white for God inside. We want to be clean from sin even when our hands and clothes get dirty. Only a clean and decent person can be a child of God.

David said, "If God will wash me, then I will be perfectly clean from sin, whiter than snow." Sometimes snow is dirty, but when God washes us, we are whiter than snow. Not one speck of sin is left when God forgives us. Isn't that wonderful?

Let's talk about this: Who could have washed Dick cleaner than he washed himself? What could Dick's mother not wash away? Who alone can wash us on the inside? When God washes away sins, how many are left? How does God wash away our sins?

Bible reading for older children and grownups: Psalm 51:1–7.

Let us pray: Forgive us all our sins, dear God, so that we may be whiter than snow and holy in Your eyes. In Jesus' name we ask this. Amen.

HOW JESUS OBEYED FOR US

> *Children obey your parents in all things. Col. 3:20.*

Guess who was the only perfect boy who ever lived. It was Jesus. When his mother Mary asked Him to get some water for her, He gladly did it. Joseph was a carpenter. When he needed somebody to hold a board, Jesus did it. Jesus didn't grumble; He didn't disobey. He even noticed things He could do without being asked.

The Bible says, "Jesus was subject to them." That means He willingly obeyed His parents.

But didn't He ever play at all? Oh, yes. His parents gave Him time to play, and they had fun together with Him. It was a happy little home, down there in Nazareth. His parents were happy because Jesus obeyed them in all things.

Jesus is God. God doesn't have to obey people. But He had a special reason for obeying Mary and Joseph. He did so that we could be saved. He also showed us that God's children are to obey their parents in all things. If we love Jesus, we will want to obey our parents.

Let's talk about this: Can you say the Bible verse? Who was the best boy that ever lived? How well did He obey His parents? Why did He want to obey them? How well does He want us to obey our parents? Will children obey their parents when they try to be like Jesus?

Older children and grownups may now read: Colossians 3:20–25.

Let us ask Jesus to help us obey our parents: Dear Jesus, please forgive us for not always obeying our parents the way You did. Help us to become more like You by gladly doing whatever our parents want us to do. Amen.

—— 3 ——

The Daily Prayer (*Du'a*) of Shi'a Isma'ili Muslims

Tazim R. Kassam

Establish worship at the going down of the sun until the

dark of the night, and [the recital of] the Qur'an at dawn.

Lo! [the recital of] the Qur'an at dawn is ever witnessed.

And some part of the night awake for it, a largess

for thee. It may be that thy Lord will raise thee

to a praised estate (17:78–79).

Every day before sunrise and around sunset a familiar scene occurs in many cities across Canada and the United States: Shi'a Isma'ili Muslims assemble in their *jamatkhanas* (places of assembly) to pray in fellowship (diacritical marks have been omitted for readability). Following the Qur'anic injunction to be in a state of ritual purity (*ghusl* or *wudu*) during prayer, they bathe and dress in fresh and formal attire before they set out to "establish worship at the two ends of the day" (11:114). They enter the jamatkhana, remove their coats and shoes in an ante-room while greeting each other *ya ali madad* (Ali help us!), and walk into a modest prayer hall for a worship service that takes about half an hour. The focal point of this service is called the *du'a*, a ritual supplication that is recited in Arabic. Isma'ilis are required to recite the du'a thrice daily in the jamatkhana. Those unable to attend a jamatkhana to pray in congregation must recite the obligatory du'a in a timely fashion at dawn and dusk wherever they find themselves.

The du'a embodies, expresses, and confirms the religious life and identity of the Isma'ili Muslims. The Isma'ilis are part of the growing Muslim *ummah* (community) living in North America that consists of Muslim immigrants from around the world, as well as African-American converts. Current estimates put the North American Muslim population at six million people, about 2 percent of the population of Canada and the United States combined. The majority of Muslims are in diasporic communities that constitute a multicultural mosaic from countries in the Middle East, Central Asia, South and Southeast Asia, Africa, and Europe. By and large, Muslims migrated to North America for economic betterment and education. Some Muslims, including the Palestinians and Bosnians, however, came to North America as refugees to escape political turmoil and persecution in their homelands. The largest ethnic groups among North American Muslims are South Asians and African-Americans (29 percent each), followed by Arab Americans (20 percent). The Muslim community in North America is unique because it mirrors the global diversity of the Islamic world and is marked by a diversity of race, language, practice, and interpretation.

The Isma'ili Muslim community similarly reflects the diversity of peoples and cultures to be found in the global Muslim community. Although the largest proportion of Isma'ilis in Canada and the United States who immigrated from East Africa and South Asia are of South Asian descent, a small proportion also come from Central Asia and the Middle East and possess a Perso-Arabic cultural identity. Prior to the 1970s, there were very few Isma'ilis in North America, but their numbers multiplied after former dictator Idi Amin evicted all Asians living in Uganda in 1972. Since then, Isma'ilis have steadily migrated to North America from different parts of the world. Although no official statistics are available, their present population is estimated at one hundred thousand people. They tend to be well-educated professionals and entrepreneurs, and they constitute one of the most organized of Muslim communities in North America. They have readily assimilated to the lifestyle of North American society and are known for their annual Partnership Walks that encourage philanthropy and raise consciousness about sustainable development.

Muslims consist of a variety of subgroups. The two main streams of interpretation and practice in Islam are the Sunni and the Shi'a. About 90 percent of Muslims are Sunni. Regardless of their affiliation, all Muslims believe in the absolute Oneness of God (tawhid), the Prophet Muhammad as the Seal of Prophets (khatm al-anbiya'), the Qur'an as God's conclusive revelation (kitab), and the final reckoning or Day of Judgment (qiyamah). The Sunni and Shi'a differ, however, on the question of whether or not Prophet Muhammad appointed a successor to assume his functions as leader of the Muslim community. The Sunni believe that the Prophet did not appoint a successor and that his religious office and authority came to an end at his death in 632 C.E.; It was, therefore, up to the faithful to interpret the Qur'an and the Prophet's example to determine how to obey God's message.

The Shi'a believe, however, that although divine revelation ceased, the need for divinely inspired leadership continued. They assert that the Prophet explicitly designated 'Ali—his companion, cousin, and son-in-law—as "Commander of the Believers" (amir al-mu'minin) and "Leader of the Devout" (imam al-muslimin) for this purpose. As the Prophet's trustee (wasi), 'Ali (d. 661) was vested the spiritual authority and wisdom to provide religious guidance and secular leadership by interpreting God's divine revelations in the Qur'an and the Prophet's example (*sunnah*). This divine guidance would continue without interruption till the Last Day (*qiyamah*) through the descendants of 'Ali and his wife Fatima, the Prophet's daughter (d. 632). The Shi'a refer to the holders of this hereditary office, which is passed on by explicit designation (*nass*), as Imam.

The Isma'ili du'a is best understood within the context of the highly cultivated inner devotional life in Islam. God says in the Qur'an: "Remember Me and I shall remember thee" (2:152). With respect to prayer and worship, Prophet Muhammad said: "For everything there is a polish to clear away rust and the polish of the heart is remembrance of God." In response to the commandment to worship and in the personal quest for God, Muslim societies over the centuries have evolved a rich, expressive tradition of prayers and devotions.

In Islam, prayer is associated with several Arabic terms, including *salah, du'a, dhikr,* and *ibadah*. These four terms are mentioned often in the Qur'an. *Salah* refers to the obligatory, canonical prayer performed five times daily by Sunni Muslims. The salah is a set prayer rite consisting of a series of bodily movements, such as bowing and prostrating, done in conjunction with a fixed recitation in Arabic that includes verses from the Qur'an. The form and content of this ritual prayer was established centuries ago on the basis of the Prophet's example (*sunnah*) and consensus (*ijma'*) of Sunni schools of law. Salah (pl. *salawat*) also refers to the formulaic prayer of calling down blessings on the Prophet and his descendants enjoined in the Qur'an on all Muslims: "May God bestow peace and blessings upon (Prophet) Muhammad and upon the family of Muhammad!"

Du'a (call, plea) is generally regarded by Muslims to be a spontaneous, individual prayer consisting of personal supplications and petitions to God. Du'a (pl. *ad'iyah*) both incorporates and imitates the plentiful invocations and prayers present in the Qur'an, which is itself the matrix of Muslim devotions. Unlike the ritual salah, which is an established communal liturgy offered at specific times, du'a is offered individually at any time and is usually voiced silently, inwardly, with hands upraised and palms held open to receive blessings. It is customary for Muslims to remain seated in the *masjid* (place of prostration, mosque) after performing the salah to invoke God's name (*dhikr*) thirty-three times and then to offer a du'a. Completing the supplication with words of gratitude (*al-hamdulillah*), the palms are drawn over the face and down, crossing the shoulders, as if one were anointing oneself with divine blessings (*barakah*).

Although spontaneous and informal in origin, many individual prayers have been composed for special needs and compiled into prayer handbooks. Du'a is a distinctive feature of the Shi'a tradition that lovingly rehearses and transmits from one generation to the next the supplications of its imams. The first imam, Hazrat 'Ali, was much given to du'a and urged his followers to recite them. Because the imams were oppressed by those who rejected their divine right to leadership, they adopted du'a as a medium for teaching the meaning of the Qur'an, the principles of Islam, and the message of the Prophet's household. Through their own example, they taught du'a as a means to instill piety, devotion, and righteous conduct. Hundreds of prayer books have been preserved by the Shi'a containing these supplications, the most famous of which are drawn from Imam 'Ali's *Nahj al-Balaghah* and Imam Zayn al-'Abidin's (d. 714) *al-Sahifah al-Sajjadiyyah,* also known as *Zabur 'ahl-i Muhammad* (Psalms of the Prophet's Household).

Regardless of the type of prayer, the primary aim of all Muslim devotions is to seek spiritual and worldly peace (*salam*) through surrender and submission (*islam*) to God's will; hence, the word *muslim* literally means one who submits or surrenders oneself to God. This sentiment is echoed in numerous ways in the ordinary conduct of Muslim life including the customary Muslim greeting "May peace be upon you and God's mercy and blessings!" (*as salamu alaykum wa rahmatulahi wa barakatahu*). The most comprehensive term for worship in Islam is *ibadah.* Derived from the verb "to serve," it emphasizes that the ideal response of humanity toward God is veneration and obedience, adoration, and servitude. God's servant (*abd*) follows God's will out of a profound love and awe of God as Creator, Sustainer, and Lord of all worlds (*rabb al-'alamin*). The simple acts of lifting up the hands with palms open, bowing (*ruku*), and prostrating the body (*sujud*) manifest these feelings of penitence, reverence, humility, and adoration.

The term *du'a* is used in a special way by present-day Isma'ili Muslims to denote a prescribed obligatory ritual prayer in Arabic that is recited thrice daily in a congregational service held in the jamatkhana. The services held in the jamatkhana at the two ends of the day also include other devotional activities such as singing hymns, reading sermons, and making food offerings. However, the recitation of the fixed Arabic du'a is the key ritual prayer without which the service remains incomplete. An Isma'ili who arrives at a service after the du'a has been recited must quietly recite it alone to fulfil this obligation. Thus, the du'a occupies a functional status similar to that of the obligatory ritual salah observed by Muslims generally.

The Isma'ili du'a is in Arabic, the universal language of Islam, and is composed of six cycles or parts. Parallel structures within the du'a create an internal rhythm and balance. Each of the six parts opens with the Qur'anic formula *basmala* (In the Name of God, the Compassionate, the Merciful) and closes with *sujud* or prostration (O God, to Thee is my prostration and prayer). The first half of each part contains select verses from the Qur'an that convey fundamental Islamic and Isma'ili principles. The second half of each part consists of a supplication followed by a salah or *tasliyah,* namely, calling down blessings upon the Prophet and his household. In parts II, IV, V, and VI the hands are raised up with open palms before making supplications for forgiveness, sustenance, and divine aid. During the fifth part, a few moments of silence are observed for repetition (*dhikr*) of *ya ali, ya muhammad.* The whole du'a itself is tied together elegantly with the formula of gratitude, *al-hamdullilah* or "Praise be to God!" which is the first phrase after the basmala at the start of the du'a and the last phrase before the final sujud at the end of the du'a. This structure is shown in the table.

Part I	Part II	Part III	Part IV	Part V	Part VI
Basmala	Basmala	Basmala	Basmala	Basmala	Basmala
Qur'an Ayat Al-Hamd	Qur'an Ayat	Qur'an Ayat	Qur'an Ayat	Qur'an Ayat	Qur'an Ayat
Du'a	Du'a (raisehands)	Shahadah Du'a	Du'a (raise hands)	Silent dhikr Du'a (raise hands)	Salah on Ahl al-Bayt and 48 Imams
Salah	Salah	Salah	Salah	Salah	Du'a (raise hands) Al-Hamd
Living Imam	Living Imam	Living Imam	Living Imam	Living Imam	Shah jo didar (handshake)
Sujud	Sujud	Sujud	Sujud	Sujud	Sujud

The repetition of *bismillah al-rahman al-rahim* to mark the beginning of the du'a as a whole and its six discrete parts is noteworthy. The basmala phrase begins all but Surah 9 of the 114 surahs or chapters in the Qur'an. One of the most frequently repeated pious utterances in Islam, Muslims utter the basmala formula before eating a meal, undertaking a journey, reciting a prayer, and commencing virtually any important task. The basmala phrase attests that all power belongs to God and nothing occurs outside God's will and grace. The Shi'a understanding of the basmala is derived from one of Imam 'Ali's sermons in the *Nahj al-Balaghah* in which he explains that Divine Revelation, Prophets, and Imams are a mercy to humankind, for they are beacons of light that reveal the path of return to God. 'Ali explains that all the treasure that is in the Qur'an is in the first opening chapter called al-Fatiha; all that is in the Fatiha is in the basmala; all that is in the basmala is in its first letter 'b' (which has a dot under it in Arabic script); all that is in the b is in the dot; and 'Ali, who was the wasi or trustee of the Prophet, is that dot. The first imam is thus the *bab* or gate who opens up the treasures of Divine Revelation. For the Shi'a, the Prophet, 'Ali, and the Imams are divinely inspired paradigms for the rest of humanity. Possessors of higher knowledge (*'ilm*), they manifest God's mercy and divine attributes, and they have been sent as a bounty to lead God's creatures to spiritual enlightenment (*ma'rifah*).

God in Islam is Absolute, Unique, and Incomparable. This concept is expressed in Surah al-Ikhlas (112:1–4), which appears in Part VI of the du'a. God is Transcendent, which means it is impossible for the human mind to grasp or comprehend God. Thus, it is only through God's revealed divine attributes (*sifat*) that humans can relate to him and draw near to him. The Qur'an mentions ninety-nine beautiful names of God (*al-asma al-husna*) that Muslims invoke in remembrance (*dhikr*) of God. In the basmala phrase are found two most frequently recited of God's attributes, *rahman* and *rahim*, which come from a single Arabic root *r-h-m*. Literally, *al-rahman al-rahim* means the Compassionate, the Merciful. The attribute *rahman* or Mercy is considered to be the very essence of God.

In Surah al-Fatiha, the first Qur'anic verse in Part I of the Isma'ili du'a, in addition to the divine attributes of Compassion and Mercy, God is described as "Lord of all worlds" (*rabb al-'alamin*) and "Master of the Day of Judgment" (*malik yaum al-din*). God in the Qur'an is not a distant and remote Creator who creates and then leaves His creation alone. Creation is not a single act in time but a perpetual event sustained by God's will. The Qur'an says: "God! There is no God save Him, the Alive, the Eternal. Neither slumber nor sleep overtakes Him. Unto Him belongs whatsoever is in the Heavens and whatsoever is in the Earth" (2:255). All things are thus dependent on God for their existence. God alone is self-sufficient; "All things perish save the Face of God" (55:27). This relationship of utter dependence on God both elicits and demands from creation a response of gratitude and wonderment. Hence, the very first verse of the Qur'an in Surah al-Fatiha is an exclamation of gratitude: "Praise be to God, Sustainer of all beings!" Daily Muslim conversation is punctuated with *al-hamdullilah* (Praise be to God!) to thank God for virtually any circumstance, be it success or misfortune.

The importance of expressing gratitude and singing God's praise is indicated in the Isma'ili du'a by its occurrences at the beginning and end of the six parts. Except for human beings, who possess free will, all creation instinctively bears witness to and praises God: "The seven heavens and the earth and all that is therein praise Him, and there is not a thing but hymns His praise; but ye understand not their praise!" (17:44). Gratitude goes hand-in-hand with submission to God's will since God is also "Master of Judgment Day" (*malik yaum al-din*). Creation is not a frivolous diversion but a momentous and purposeful act of God. Like Jews and Christians, Muslims believe that at the end of time (*qiyamah*) all creatures will be weighed for their deeds and misdeeds. Death does not mean extinction. The body may perish but the soul, which is eternal, must face the consequence of its deeds in the hereafter. Hence, life in this material world (*al-dunya*) is believed to be a preparation for divine felicity in the next world (*al-akhirah*). The Qur'an states that an abode of peace (*dar al salam*) awaits the righteous in the hereafter: "For them will be an abode of peace in the presence of their Lord. He will be their protective friend because they acted (righteously)" (6:128). Part II of the du'a contains the prayer, "Give us, O Sustainer, a life of peace and usher us into the abode of peace." Peace is a state of integrity and harmony that may apply to many dimensions of everyday life, but the ultimate destiny of the soul is to attain everlasting peace.

How, then, is one to discern right from wrong, the path of sanctity from the path of ruin? Is it possible for humankind to discover God's truth without divine aid? It is interesting to note that the first prayer in the Surah that opens the Qur'an is not a plea for forgiveness or for sustenance but for guidance: "Guide us to the straight path, the path of those whom Thou hast bestowed favors, not of those who earned Thine anger nor of those who have gone astray" (1:5–7). The foundation of Islam is the belief that over the centuries God has sent His guidance through prophets and messengers to every society. Illumined by divine grace, Noah, Abraham, Moses, Jesus, the prophets of Israel, and still others disclosed to their people the way of truth and holiness. According to the Qur'an, the human soul has thus never been left without a specially inspired messenger from the Lord, who is Creator and Sustainer of all beings. However, each time God has sent his revelation, humans, by their capricious natures, have distorted its teachings to suit themselves. Muhammad, the Seal of the Prophets, was sent again as a warner and messenger to restore the purity of God's guidance to his previous prophets and to reveal once and for all God's complete revelation. Islam is thus the Straight Path—*sirat al-mustaqim*. Human nature is such, however, that, even when Prophet Muhammad is called upon to be witness to his people on the Last Day, he will declare, "O my Lord! My own people have cast aside this Qur'an" (25:30).

All six parts of the Isma'ili du'a end with salah, or calling down blessings on the Prophet, 'Ali and the Prophet's family, and the Imam of the time. No Muslim prayer is complete without the salah or tasliyah in keeping with the command; "Verily, God and his Angels send blessings upon the Prophet. O ye who believe! Call down blessings upon him and peace" (33:56). Most blessings on the Prophet are variations on a single sentence, "May God call down blessings on our lord Muhammad and on the family of our lord Muhammad and greet them with peace." This prayer extends to all prophets; whenever the name of Muhammad or a biblical prophet such as Abraham is mentioned, Muslims utter *sallalahu alayhi wa al-salam*: "May God bless him and give him peace!"

This brings us to the core of the Isma'ili du'a, which is the recognition of the authority and leadership of 'Ali and the Isma'ili Nizari line of imams. Before the sujud, every part of du'a ends with the testimony, "Our lord Shah Karim al-Husayni is the present living Imam." Several Qur'anic verses in the du'a pertain to the Shi'a understanding of 'Ali and the imams as trustees of the Prophet's teachings and God's revelation. In Part II, verse 4:59 commands the believers to obey God, the Messenger, and *ulu al-amr*, the "Holders of Authority." According to the Shi'a, the ulu al-amr are 'Ali and the divinely appointed imams. Their authority refers to their office as interpreters par excellence of the Qur'an. Isma'ilis, a subsect of the Shi'a, believe that Revelation has two aspects: the formal, literal, external text of the Qur'an (*tanzil*) and its spiritual, symbolic, hidden meanings (*ta'wil*). God entrusted the Prophet with both the exoteric and esoteric aspects of the Qur'an. Following God's command, the Prophet, in turn, entrusted the ta'wil or esoteric wisdom of the Qur'an to 'Ali. This divine inheritance is passed on from one imam to the next through explicit designation (*nass*). After the Prophet, the imams alone were endowed with the capacity to mine the Qur'an for its divine secrets because God had bestowed upon them knowledge (*'ilm*) of all things.

Without the divinely sanctioned appointment of 'Ali, the Prophet's mission would have remained incomplete because, although the exoteric aspect of divine revelation and law ceased with the Prophet's death, the esoteric aspect of divine guidance continues through symbolic and contextual interpretation. For the Shi'a, the

Qur'anic verse "O Messenger! Proclaim what has been sent down to thee from thy Lord, for if thou did not do so, thou hast not delivered His Message" (5:67) indicates that the Prophet was divinely commanded to proclaim 'Ali as his vicegerent and as the *amir al-mu'minin*, Commander of the Believers. God thus ensured that the message of the Qur'an and the teachings of Islam would remain alive and relevant for all time through 'Ali and successive imams. In gratitude and recognition of their imams' timely guidance, in Part VI of the du'a, the Isma'ilis recite the names of forty-nine imams including that of the present, living imam, Shah Karim al-Husayni (b. 1936).

During Muhammad's lifetime, those who embraced Islam would go up to him and testify one by one, "There is no god but God and Muhammad is his messenger" (*shahadah*). Then they would extend their right hand and the Prophet would place his hand on their hand and swear they were to be loyal and faithful to the message of God. Thus, the first Muslims declared their fealty to God by performing this act of allegiance (*bay'ah*) to the Prophet. Part IV of the du'a contains a Qur'anic verse that bears witness to this practice(48:10). After Muhammad died, the Shi'a made this oath to the imams to declare their faith and affirm the imams' authority. A bay'ah ceremony is performed for every Isma'ili child at birth to establish its permanent spiritual bond with the imam, a bond that extends beyond this life. This relationship of love and obedience to the imam is manifest in the everyday practical and devotional life of Isma'ili Muslims. The various supplications to the imam in the du'a for help and support gives expression to this trust and anticipation of material and spiritual aid.

Weber's idea of charisma may help us to understand the authority of the Isma'ili imam. Not to be confused with the idea of a charming personality, charisma as defined by Weber is a certain quality possessed by individuals by virtue of which they are set apart from ordinary people and treated in a way that marks them out as possessing exceptional qualities and powers. These qualities and powers are not accessible to ordinary people but are believed to be of divine origin and exemplary. On this basis, the charismatic figures such as prophets and imams are treated as ideal leaders whose authority is thus voluntarily acknowledged by their followers. Isma'ilis express the charismatic nature of the imam in terms of the metaphor of Light upon Light (*nur 'ala nur*) a divine grace that is the special prerogative of each successive imam. The concept of imam as the possessor of Light (*nur*) is related to one of the most enigmatic and striking verses in the Qur'an, called the verse of Light:

> God is the Light of the Heavens and the Earth. His Light is as a niche in which is a lamp. The lamp is in a glass. The glass is as though it were a shining star. (This lamp) is lit from a blessed tree, an Olive neither of the East nor of the West, the oil of which would well-nigh give Light though no fire touched it. Light upon Light; God guides to His Light whom He wills. And God strikes out parables for men and God doth know all things. (24:35)

God's Light cannot be contemplated directly by the human mind, which is too imperfect an organ of knowledge. As long as it is confined by the limits of the material world, God can speak to human kind only through symbols and parables. According to Imam Ja'far as-Sadiq, "The light descends upon the most noble men; it shone through our Imams, so that we are the lights of the heavens and the earth. To us is heaven committed and from us are the secrets of science derived, for we are the destination that all strive to reach . . . we are the Proofs of the Lord of the Worlds." For the Shi'a the imams are thus illuminated and irradiated with divine light (nur).

At the end of reciting the du'a, each member of the Isma'ili Muslim congregation turns to the person on the right and on the left to shake hands while saying shah jo didar, which means: "May you glimpse His divine countenance!" While it may not be possible to see God with physical eyes, God may be witnessed spiritually through single-minded devotion and prayer. This is the ultimate goal of the Isma'ili devotee (murid)—to be blessed with a glimpse of the divine countenance. The Qur'an describes the shining faces of those who have had that beatific vision as follows: "Some faces on that day will be bright, looking upon their Lord" (75:22).

In conclusion, the ritual prayer of the Isma'ilis is at once a daily act of devotion and submission as well as a clear affirmation of their Shi'a Muslim identity. As an obligatory prayer for all Isma'ilis, the recitation of the du'a unites this diverse and scattered community in a frontierless faith of fellowship. By testifying to the Oneness of God, the authority of God's divine revelation in the Qur'an and the example and teachings of the Prophet Muhammad as God's last Messenger, the Isma'ilis affirm their participation in the Muslim ummah. Their recognition of 'Ali and the imams as Commander of the Believers who are divinely appointed and inspired to interpret the Qur'an identify them as Shi'a. And finally, their declaration of allegiance to the forty-ninth Imam Shah Karim al-Husayni, His Highness Prince Aga Khan IV, as the present living imam anchors their historical lineage as Nizari Isma'ilis.

The Arabic text of the Isma'li du'a, together with an official Urdu translation, is published in Du'a (Karachi: Shia Imami Isma'ili Tariqah and Religious Education Board for Pakistan, 1993). An English transliteration with official Gujarati and English translation is published in Holy Du'a (Nairobi: Shia Imami Isma'ilia Association for Africa, 1970). The following is an adaptation of the official translation of the Arabic text.

Further Readings

Sultan Muhammad Shah, Aga Khan III, The Memoirs of the Aga Khan (New York: Simon and Schuster, 1954); Henry Corbin, Cyclical Time and Isma'ili Gnosis (New York: Kegan Paul International, 1983); Farhad Daftary, A Short History of the Isma'ilis: Traditions of a Muslim Community (Edinburgh: Edinburgh University Press, 1998); Shihabu'd-Din Shah al-Husayni's True Meaning of Religion or Risala dar

Haqiqat-i Din, translated by Wladimir Ivanow (Bombay: Ismailia Research Association Series, 1933); *Islamic Spirituality: Foundations,* edited by Seyyed Hossein Nasr (New York: Crossroad, 1987); Constance E. Padwick, *Muslim Devotions: A Study of Prayer-Manuals in Common Use* (Oxford: 1961, Oneworld reprint, 1996); *The Meaning of the Glorious Koran,* trans., M. Marmaduke Picthall (New York: NAL/Dutton, 1953); Jane I. Smith *Islam in America* (New York: Columbia University Press, 1999); Yvonne Yazbeck Haddad and Jane Idleman Smith, eds. *Muslim Communities in North America* (Albany, N.Y.: State University of New York Press, 1994).

Isma'ili Du'a

PART I

In the name of God, the Compassionate, the Merciful.

All praise is due to God, the Sustainer of all beings, the Compassionate, the Merciful, the Lord of the Day of Judgment. Thee alone we worship and Thee alone we seek for help. Guide us to the straight path, the path of those whom Thou hast blessed, not of those who earned Thine anger nor of those who have gone astray. (Surah al-Fatiha 1:1–7)

I prostrate before Thee and I rely upon Thee; from Thee is my strength and Thou art my protection, O Sustainer of all beings!

O God! Let Thy peace be upon Muhammad—the chosen, and upon 'Ali—the favorite, and upon the Imams—the pure, and upon the evidence of Thy authority—the lord of the age and the time, the present living Imam, our lord Shah Karim al-Husayni.

O God! To Thee is my prostration and prayer.

PART II

In the name of God, the Compassionate, the Merciful.

O ye who believe! Obey God and obey the Messenger and (obey) the holders of authority from amongst you. (Surah an-Nisah 4:59)

And We have vested (the knowledge of) everything in the manifest Imam. (Surah Ya-Sin 36:12)

(Raise hands) O God! O our Lord! Thou art the peace, from Thee is the peace, and to Thee returneth the peace. Give us, O our Sustainer, a life of peace, and usher us into the abode of peace. Blessed art Thou, our Lord, the most High, O the Lord of Majesty and Reverence.

O God! O our Lord! From Thee is my support and upon Thee is my reliance. Thee alone we worship and from Thee alone we seek for help. O 'Ali! Help me with thy kindness.

There is no god except God. Muhammad is the Messenger of God. 'Ali—the master of believers—is from God.

Our lord Shah Karim al-Husayni is the present living Imam.

O God! To Thee is my prostration and prayer.

PART III

In the name of God, the Compassionate, the Merciful.

O Messenger! Proclaim what has been sent down to thee from thy Lord, for if thou did not do so, than thou hast not delivered His Message; and God will protect thee from the people. (Surah al-Ma'ida 5:67)

There is no god except God, the Ever-Living, the Eternal. There is no god except God, the Sovereign, the Truth, the Evident. There is no god except God, the Sovereign, the Truth, the Certainty. There is no god except God, the Lord of the Day of Judgment.

There is no hero except 'Ali, there is no sword except (his sword) Dhu'lfiqar. Seek in times of difficulty the help of your lord, the present living (Imam) Shah Karim al-Husayni.

O God! To Thee is my prostration and prayer.

PART IV

In the name of God, the Compassionate, the Merciful.

Lo! Those who swear allegiance unto thee (Muhammad), in truth they swear allegiance unto God; God's hand is upon their hands. Then he who breaks his oath breaks it hurting his own soul. And he who fulfils what he has pledged with God, God will grant him a mighty reward. (Surah al-Fatah 48:10)

(Raise hands) O God! Forgive us our sins, give us our bread, have mercy upon us in the name of Thy closest Messengers and Thy pure Imams, and in the name of our lord and our Imam, Shah Karim al-Husayni.

O God! To Thee is my prostration and prayer.

PART V

In the name of God, the Compassionate, the Merciful.

O ye who believe! Betray not God nor the Messenger, and betray not your trusts while you know. (Surah al-Anfal 8:27)

O our Lord! Forgive us our sins, make our tasks easy, give us our bread, and have mercy upon us. Verily, Thou art powerful over all things.

(Repeat silently) O 'Ali, O Muhammad! O Muhammad, O 'Ali!

(Raise hand) O Imam of the time! O our lord! Thou art my strength and thou art my support and upon thee I rely. O present living Imam Shah Karim al-Husayni, thou art the true manifest Imam.

O God! To Thee is my prostration and prayer.

PART VI

In the name of God, the Compassionate, the Merciful.

Say: He is God, One! God is Absolute, Everlasting. He did not beget nor was He begotten and there is none like unto Him. (Surah al-Ikhlas 112:1–4)

O God! In the name of Muhammad–the chosen, and 'Ali–the favorite, and Fatima–the radiant, and Hasan and Husayn.

O God! In the name of our lord 'Ali; our lord Husayn; our lord Zayn al-'Abidin; our lord Muhammad al-Baqir; our lord Ja'far al-Sadiq; our lord Isma'il; our lord Muhammad bin Isma'il; our lord Wafi Ahmed; our lord Taqi Muhammad; our lord Razi al-Din Abd Allah; our lord Muhammad al-Mahdi; our lord al-Qa'im; our lord al Mansur; our lord al-Mu'izz; our lord al-'Aziz; our lord Hakim al-Amr Allah; our lord al-Zahir; our lord al-Mustansir bi'llah; our lord al-Nizar; our lord al-Hadi; our lord al-Muhtadi; our lord al-Qahir; our lord 'Ala Dhikri al-Salam; our lord 'Ala al-Din Muhammad; our lord Jalal al-Din Hasan; our lord 'Ala al-Din Muhammad; our lord Rukn al-Din Khurshah; our lord Sham al-Din Muhammad; our lord Qasim Shah: our lord Islam Shah; our lord Muhammad bin Islam Shah; our lord Mustansir bi'llah; our lord Abd al-Salam; our lord Gharib Mirza; our lord Abu Dharr 'Ali; our lord Murad Mirza; our lord Dhu'l Fiqar 'Ali; our lord Nur al-Din 'Ali; our lord Khalil Allah 'Ali: our lord Nizar; our lord Sayyid 'Ali: our lord Hasan 'Ali; our lord Qasim 'Ali; our lord Abu al-Hasan 'Ali: our lord Khalil Allah 'Ali; our lord Shah Hasan 'Ali; our lord Shah 'Ali Shah; our lord Sultan Muhammad Shah.

(Raise hands) And in the name of our lord and our present living Imam Shah Karim al-Husayni, have mercy upon us and forgive us.

Verily Thou art powerful over all things. And all praise is due to God, the Sustainer of all beings.

May you glimpse the Lord's divine countenance! (handshake)

O God! To Thee is my prostration and prayer.

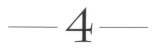

4

Benediction of the Blessed Sacrament

Patricia O'Connell Killen

Perhaps more powerfully than any other ritual act in American Catholicism between 1800 and 1965, Benediction of the Blessed Sacrament made divine power and presence available to ordinary people. Benediction comes from the Latin word for "bless." In the ritual of Benediction, people experienced being blessed by the host, or consecrated communion bread. This blessing was the highlight or climactic event in many rituals of devotional Catholicism: novenas (a series of prayers performed over a period of time, often nine days), missions (a series of devotional practices and sermons over a set number of days designed to increase the fervor and practice of Catholic Christians), Forty Hours' Devotion (a period of exposition of the consecrated host involving private prayer and community prayer), and even the mass. For ordinary people, Benediction was an event of particular intimacy between themselves and God, especially Jesus Christ. In Benediction people saw the divine presence with their own eyes, they gazed on God. They also felt the power of divine grace bestowed on them directly through blessing from a God whom they could see.

In the nineteenth and first half of the twentieth centuries, the Catholic sense of intimacy with divine power was reinforced by attaching Benediction to other kinds of liturgical services designed to increase devotion and commitment to the sacramental and canonical life of the Roman Catholic Church. Benediction fits within the rich and elaborate array of devotional practices that made the supernatural palpable and real for Catholics. Rituals that made the supernatural real, visible, and perceptible through all the senses reinforced the truth and credibility of Catholicism for generations of immigrants and their children in the United States, many of whom were confronted for the first time with other religious options. A majestic, yet intimate, devotional Catholicism made Catholics proud of their faith in a country that looked down on them. It provided immigrants the psychological and imaginative resources necessary to negotiate the challenges of life in a new country. By 1950, the elaborate system of devotional Catholicism, including Benediction, had become the ritual counterpart to the grand neo-Thomistic intellectual synthesis that the Roman Catholic Church in the

United States used to articulate its self-understanding as a supernatural body in history. This intellectual synthesis and its ritual counterpart helped the church to overcome divisions among ethnic groups, and to demonstrate to those outside the church the power of Catholic sacramental life.

In addition to conveying the grandeur of Catholic sacramental life and providing intimacy with the divine, Benediction also subtly undercut the hierarchical structures of Catholicism. The structure of Benediction, unlike any other ritual except the ordination of a priest (which few lay people saw), showed the lowliness of the clergy in relation to God. In the ritual of Benediction, at the point where the actual blessing with the Eucharist took place, the priest's hands did not directly touch the monstrance, the container in which the host was visible. His hands were covered The priest as servant of a God who blesses the ordinary people was expressed more directly in Benediction than in any other ritual. For ordinary people, Benediction was a direct, intimate encounter with God unencumbered by the close contact with a priest that the formal seven sacraments entailed.

Benediction involves the exposition or display of the sacred host, the consecrated communion wafer, on the altar. The host is placed in a pyx, a magnified glass case that is in the center of the monstrance, an elaborate cruciform container used only for exposition of the sacred host. The monstrance sits on the highest part, or throne, of the altar. Bathed in candle light in a church often otherwise darkened, the priest and assembly honor Jesus Christ present in the Eucharistic bread. This honoring involves incensing the monstrance, reciting prayers, sitting in silence while gazing on God, and singing hymns. Benediction's most sublime moment comes when the priest blesses the assembly by making the sign of the cross over them with the monstrance. This is the ritual point where the power of Christ, the one who died on the cross for our sins and continues to atone for the sins of all, flows out directly to the believer. For those participating, Benediction is a powerfully sensuous, intimate experience of the divine that carries participants out of profane space and time into sacred space and time. Benediction is a preview of the beatific vision, eternity in the intimate companionship and presence of God.

The ritual of Benediction of the Blessed Sacrament falls into the category of a Eucharistic devotion—a practice focused on Jesus the Christ present in the bread of the Eucharist or communion. Such devotions in Christianity go back at least to the second century. Christians took bread from the Eucharistic celebration to members of the community who could not attend the service. During periods of persecution in the third and fourth centuries, Christian communities could not gather regularly for the Eucharistic celebration. After a service, members would take consecrated bread to their homes, place it in a location where they could reverence it, and eat the bread in intervals between times when participation in the celebration of Eucharist was possible.

Historically, Benediction emerged in the 1220s in western Europe as a particular form of Eucharistic devotion. The ritual probably grew out of the practice of exposing or showing the host at various locations on the route of the Corpus Christi (Body of Christ) processions. These processions, somewhat like a religious parade, became part of Catholic practice during the late medieval period. The earliest record describing the ritual of Benediction dates from the 1400s and came from the monastery of Hildesheim in present-day Germany.

The origins of the ritual of Benediction rest in a profound cultural realignment that occurred during the 1200s in western Europe. Notions of truth shifted from hearing and receiving wisdom or truth passed on from past generations, to observation and seeing on the part of individuals. Advances in optics, such as refinements in grinding magnifying glasses and the use of spectacles, contributed to this change. At the same time that this epistemological shift was occurring, theological controversy over the Eucharist increased. Theologians engaged in heated debates over two main issues. The first was how to explain the presence of Jesus in the Eucharistic bread. The second was determining at what moment in the mass (central Eucharistic celebration of the community) the bread became the body of Jesus. In addition, the liturgical practice and theology of the period steadily increased the sense of the gulf between God and the ordinary believer, to the point that people rarely received communion at mass, often doing so only yearly. Mass was said in Latin with the priest's back to the people. Unable to understand what was said or to see what was happening, for laity the moment that the bread was raised high during the consecration became their point of contact with God. The theological controversy and the structure of liturgical practice converged to increase the desire of the faithful to "see" Jesus. Merely seeing the body of Christ during Corpus Christi processions and the moments at mass when a priest held the Eucharistic bread aloft both at the consecration and before distributing it to communicants did not suffice. Benediction of the Blessed Sacrament provided the occasion for the faithful to view Jesus directly for a longer period of time, to gaze on God in a relatively unencumbered manner. Widely popular by 1400, Benediction generally was performed at the conclusion of evening prayers or vespers in a local parish or monastery church, a service that laity, Christians who were not ordained or vowed religious, were encouraged to attend. Benediction, then, helped to reinforce the reality of God for people in a world where sight was rapidly becoming the privileged sense and where the language of religion was unintelligible.

Eucharistic devotion, and Benediction in particular, became more significant for Catholics after the Reformation. The Council of Trent (1545–63), a meeting of the leadership of the Roman Catholic Church, deliberately defined Catholicism over and against Protestant forms of Christianity. This council reaffirmed Catholic belief in the real presence of Christ in the Eucharist. Eucharistic devotions were encouraged and churches were built to provide sight lines that focused the eye on the tabernacle, the place where consecrated Eucharistic bread was kept. Paying homage to the Eucharistic bread and seeing it with one's own eyes already separated Catholics from Protestants at this early point in history.

In the United States of the nineteenth century, mass still was said in Latin, which few people other than priests understood. Communion still was infrequent, for most Catholics a yearly occurrence during the Easter season. Physical sight continued to carry epistemological privilege, so viewing the consecrated bread still reinforced Catholic belief about Jesus' real presence in the Eucharist. Hence, it is not surprising that by 1800 in the United States Benediction had become the culmination to novenas, missions, and Forty Hours' Devotion. From late in that century until 1965, Benediction frequently was performed at the conclusion of one of the Sunday masses each week, at Sunday evening vespers, and, in some parishes with sufficiently large staffs, even daily, usually in the early evening. Until the renewal of the liturgy in the Roman Catholic Church in the United States occasioned by Vatican Council II, Benediction was one of the few services where the congregation participated by singing and reciting prayers. It provided more opportunity for participation by the faithful than weekly Sunday mass. Not only could the faithful "see" Jesus in the host, they did so in a paticipatory ritual congruent with the democratic impulses that Catholics had absorbed in the United States. This state of affairs reinforced Benediction's significance and meaningfulness for the people.

Benediction of the Blessed Sacrament continues today in the Roman Catholic Church, and to a lesser extent in the Episcopal Church in the United States. It was practiced more frequently in the Roman Catholic Church in the United States from the 1830s until the liturgical and devotional revisions instituted by Vatican Council II (1962–65). Benediction was not mentioned in the "Constitution on the Liturgy" promulgated by Vatican Council II. In the wake of the Council, the devotion was discontinued or minimized in many parishes. This was because Benediction was associated with an understanding of mass and Eucharist as a replication or reenactment of the salvific sacrifice of Jesus through his death on Calvary, something emphasized by the Council of Trent. After Vatican Council II, many bishops and priests wanted the emphasis in the understanding of the mass and Eucharist to be on the Eucharistic assembly of the faithful enacting the eschatological (fullness of time) banquet of God's kingdom or reign. The former view of Eucharist, to the minds of the Vatican II bishops, objectified and focused the entire celebration of the mass on Christ present in the host. The latter made the gathered assembly and Jesus Christ's presence in the midst of the assembly more central. The Eucharistic theology arising from Vatican Council II, then, left most theologians of liturgy and many pastors ambivalent toward Benediction as a practice. Despite the concerns of experts, however, Benediction remained and remains popular with large numbers of laity.

Theologically, Benediction and all other Eucharistic practices are rooted in the incarnational character of Catholic Christianity—God's becoming enfleshed in Jesus. This gives Catholic Christianity a strong appreciation for the material world. In Catholic understanding, God becoming human shows that all of creation, everything, is shot through with the divine. To put it differently, every aspect of creation is transparent. For those with eyes to see, it reveals God, the source of all.

In print, the ritual for Benediction of the Blessed Sacrament does not convey the power that this rite held for Catholics prior to Vatican Council II. Of the many devotions in which the Catholic faithful participated, Benediction stands out for its contemplative quality and its utterly gratuitous, intimate, embodied contact between God and the devotee. Unlike other Eucharistic practices, such as eating the consecrated bread as part of the celebration of the mass, no elaborate preparation through fasting, prayer, or other practices, such as confessing one's sins to a priest in the sacrament of penance, was required for Benediction of the Blessed Sacrament. Simply by attending, the devotee was free to gaze on Jesus Christ—God present in the Eucharistic bread—and to be blessed by Jesus. Benediction was the most direct, unmediated, unconstrained contact a devotee had with Jesus Christ present in matter—the bread of the Eucharist. Once the practice of communion became more frequent in American Catholicism around 1910, the gazing on God during Benediction complemented the eating of God by receiving the Eucharistic bread at mass.

The ritual of Benediction was simple, solemn, yet grand. It created an air of awesome presence, of closeness to divine power for the devotee. Silence, darkness, light, incense, song, seeing—all the senses were stimulated in a practice that, for many Catholics, was as close as they would get on earth to the beatific vision—intimacy with God promised in heaven.

The ritual of Benediction contains four main parts. The first part is focused on gazing on God, contemplative presence with the divine. The environment supports this. Traditionally, the faithful gathered in silence. The church often was dark, with what light there was focused on the altar. Once the host was exposed for adoration, the lights were raised slightly, with the greatest light around the host on the altar.

The second part is adoration. Often a time of silence, readings, psalms, songs, even a homily might be included, depending on the setting in which Benediction took place. The period of silent adoration for many was deeply personal and intimate. Most often kneeling, but sometimes sitting in the presence of God embodied in the consecrated host, the faithful poured out their hearts in petitions, in sorrow, in gratitude. This was a time of unmediated contact with the divine, a time of contemplative presence, not a time during which they had to do anything.

The third and climactic part of Benediction in terms of evident ritual action is the blessing of all present with the Blessed Sacrament or Eucharistic bread. The bread is visible to the congregation in a pyx, a magnified glass container into which the consecrated Eucharistic bread has been placed. The pyx itself is in the center of a monstrance, an elaborate cruciform container made of precious metal. The monstrance has only one function, to display the consecrated host. After a prayer, the priest, having donned the humeral veil—a long cape that extends beyond the priest's hands—takes up the monstrance with the humeral veil between his hands and the actual monstrance, and blesses the people with the consecrated host by making the sign of the cross over them with the monstrance. The faithful respond to the blessing with praise, traditionally the "Divine Praises."

The fourth part of Benediction is the reposition or replacing of the sacred host into the tabernacle, a container for housing the consecrated bread. This was a point of physical distancing or separation from the divine. Though the devotees believed that Jesus was present in the bread reserved in the tabernacle, that believing was not the same as seeing Christ in the bread displayed in the monstrance. The service closed with a prayer led by the priest and then a hymn, often "Holy God, We Praise Thy Name."

The translation of the prayers and hymns from the Latin is from *Saint John's Sunday Missal and Every Day Prayer Book with a Forward by Rev. Henry J. Gebhard of the Archdiocese of New York* (Dublin: Eason and Son, 1952), pp. 550–53. The instructions on how the ritual should be conducted are summarized from John Baptist Mueller, S.J., *Handbook of Ceremonies for Priests and Seminarians*, seventeenth English edition entirely revised and reedited by Adam C. Ellis, S.J. (St. Louis: B. Herder, 1956), pp. 241–56. The rubric is in conformity with the most recent decrees of the Sacred Congregation of Rites of 1955 and 1936.

Further Reading

Rev. Joseph A. Jungmann, S.J., *The Mass of the Roman Rite: Its Origins and Development* (New York: Benzinger Brothers, 1961); James J. Mcgivern, *Concomitance and Communion: A Study in Eucharistic Doctrine and Practice*, Studia Friburgensia, New Series no. 33 (New York: Herder, 1963); Nathan Mitchell, *Cult and Controversy: The Worship of the Eucharist Outside Mass* (New York: Pueblo, 1982).

Benediction of the Blessed Sacrament (1952)

The priest, vested in surplice, stole, and cope, approaches the altar, genuflects, and then kneels for a short time in adoration of the Blessed Sacrament. Then, without genuflecting or bowing, he ascends to the altar, spreads (unfolds) the corporal, a square linen cloth, and unveils the monstrance, and places it upon the corporal. He then opens the tabernacle, genuflects, and takes the custodia, a container holding the consecrated bread, from the tabernacle. He then opens the monstrance, opens the custodia, and places the lunula, the large Eucharistic wafer, in the monstrance, closes it and then the custodia. He then returns the custodia to the tabernacle which he closes. Then he places the monstrance in the middle of the altar, makes a simple genuflection, ascends the steps, takes the monstrance and puts it on the throne, descends, genuflects again, and, turning to his right (and stepping a bit towards the gospel side so as not to turn his back to the Blessed Sacrament), descends to the foot of the altar.

Kneeling at the foot of the altar, he bows (medium bow of the body), rises, steps back a little to the gospel side, and, without turning his back to the Blessed Sacrament, puts incense into the censer. He kneels again, receives the censer from the assistant, and, bowing before and after (medium bow of the body), incenses the Blessed Sacrament with three double swings of the censer. He then returns the censer to the assistant.

When the priest opens the Tabernacle and incenses the Blessed Sacrament, is usually sung the hymn O Salutaris Hostia:

> O saving Victim, opening wide
> The gate of heav'n to man below.
> Our foes press on from every side;
> Thine aid supply, thy strength bestow.
> To Thy great name be endless praise,
> Immortal godhead, one in three!
> O grant us endless length of days.
> In our true native land with Thee. Amen.

After which follows some Psalm, or Antiphon, or Hymn in honor of the Most Holy Sacrament. Then is sung the hymn Tantum ergo Sacramentum, *all present making a profound inclination while the words* Veneremur cernui *are being said. (The priest incenses the monstrance again during this hymn at the words, "To the everlasting Father.")*

> Down in adoration falling,
> Lo! The sacred host we hail;
> Lo! O'er ancient forms departing
> Newer rites of grace prevail;
> Faith for all defects supplying
> Where the feeble senses fail.
> To the everlasting Father,
> And the Son who reigns on high,
> With the Holy Ghost proceeding
> Forth from each eternally,
> Be salvation, honor, blessing,
> Might, and endless majesty! Amen.

Verse (said by the priest). Thou didst give them bread from heaven. (Alleluia).

Response (said by the people). Containing in itself all sweetness. (Alleluia).

Priest: Let us pray.

All: O God, who, under a wonderful Sacrament, hast left us a memorial of Thy passion; grant us, we beseech Thee, so to venerate the sacred mysteries of thy body and blood that we may ever feel within us the fruit of Thy redemption. Who livest and reignest, One God for ever and ever. Amen.

After the oration, having received the humeral veil, without bowing he ascends to the platform, genuflects there on one knee, takes the monstrance from the throne (with or without a bow, as the custom may be), and places it on the altar with the ornamented side toward himself. Then he kneels on both knees and receives the humeral veil (or, if he has already received it, he genuflects), rises, and (again without genuflecting) takes hold of the monstrance with the extremities of the veil, the right hand at the knob, the left hand below the knob.

He turns the ornamented side of the monstrance away from himself and, turning to his right, gives the blessing.

Here the Benediction is given with the Blessed Sacrament, all bowing down in profound adoration, and beseeching this blessing on themselves, and on the whole Church, and upon the world.

The priest raises the monstrance from the level of his breast to his eyes, then lowers it below his breast, raises it again to the level of his breast, and turns with the monstrance first to the left, then to the right, then back again to the middle; and from that position he completes the circle by turning again to his right and facing the altar.

The priest then places the monstrance on the altar (the ornamented side turned toward himself), genuflects, and facing right about, kneels at the edge of the platform, and returns the veil. He again (without bowing: Decr. 4179 ad 3) advances to the altar, genuflects, (takes the custodia from the tabernacle unless it is already on the altar), opens the custodia and then the monstrance, places the lunula in the custodia, closes it (as well as the monstrance, which he moves to one side), opens the tabernacle (without genuflecting), returns the custodia, genuflects, and closes the tabernacle. Then he folds the corporal and places it in the burse, which he leans against the altar, and veils the monstrance. Without further genuflection or bow he turns to his right and descends to the foot of the altar.

At this point the priest leads the people in concluding prayers.

DIVINE PRAISES

> Blessed be God.
> Blessed be His Holy Name.
> Blessed be Jesus Christ, true God and true man.
> Blessed be the name of Jesus.
> Blessed be His most Sacred Heart.
> Blessed be Jesus in the most holy Sacrament of the Altar.
> Blessed be the great Mother of God, Mary most holy.
> Blessed be her holy and Immaculate Conception.
> Blessed be her glorious Assumption.
> Blessed be the name of Mary, virgin and mother.
> Blessed be St. Joseph, her most chaste spouse.
> Blessed be God in His Angels and in His Saints.

Indulgence three years every time they are said; five years after Benediction. (Where approved by the Ordinary:)

May the Heart of Jesus in the Most Blessed Sacrament be praised, adored and loved with grateful affection at every moment.

Ant. May we forever adore the Most Holy Sacrament.

PSALM 116

Oh! praise the Lord, all ye nations: praise Him, all ye people.
For His Mercy is confirmed upon us; and the truth of the Lord remaineth
for ever.
Glory be to the Father, and to the Son, and to the Holy Ghost. As it was
in the beginning, is now and ever shall be, world without end. Amen.

Ant. May we for ever adore the Most Holy Sacrament.

The priest genuflects and returns to the sacristy. The people may participate in a
closing hymn or a period of silent prayer and then depart the church.

—5—

The Homemade Passover Haggadah

Vanessa L. Ochs

The Haggadah is the text used at the seder, the festive ritual holiday meal of Passover. This popular observance is held on the first, or both the first and second, nights of Passover (Israeli Jews hold one seder; outside of Israel, Reform Jews hold one seder, and other observant Jews hold two). Usually the seder is held in the homes of one's extended family and friends, although community-oriented seders are also held in synagogues, college campuses, hotels, and restaurants.

The Haggadah (literally, the *telling*) provides instructions for the rituals performed by each family at its own seder (ordered meal). A text that has grown larger over the centuries, the Haggadah is sometimes lavishly illustrated; over the centuries and continuing into the present, wealthy families might commission an artist to write and illuminate a Haggadah for their own use.

The Haggadah tells the story of the Exodus from Egypt as drawn from the Torah and from ancient, modern, and even contemporary rabbinic commentaries and legends, and includes blessings for ritual hand washing, for wine, matzah, and other symbolic foods, as well as prayers, psalms of praise, and folk songs. The intention of the Passover observance is not just to remember the history of the Jews' slavery in Egypt and subsequent salvation by God, delivery to freedom, and eventual passage to a promised land. Rather, Jews are obliged to reenact the story of the Exodus from Egypt with their children in such a way that all who are present experience the Exodus, as if it had been they themselves who had once been slaves but now are free women and men. Thus, appealing to intellectual curiosity and the evocative, sensual symbols of various texts, foods, and activities, the seder is a pedagogic experience par excellence; it is engaging, evocative, compelling, and memorable, and it offers points of entry for those whose learning styles are intellectual, sensual, or physical.

This night is "different from all other nights" in many ways. On all other nights, one does not recline at the table on a pillow (reflecting the way a free person, and not a slave, might have dined in antiquity). On all other nights, one does not drink multiple cups of wine (symbolizing liberty) throughout the meal, thus fulfilling God's commandment to mark this holy day. On all other nights, one does not celebrate spring in a Jewish way, being attentive to the eternal blessing of renewal and the possibility of celebrating and creating "second chances" in one's own life. On Passover, the story of Jewish oppression is told not as an end in and of itself but as a lesson. This story obliges every Jew who has been blessed with freedom to notice wherever people in the world are troubled by slavery, oppression, hunger, poverty, and unhealthful living conditions, and to work actively and aggressively on their behalf. Thus, the seder is an exercise in responsibility that extends to one's family and beyond, to the local and even worldwide community of Jews. The story expands to include all the people of the world who have needs that can be addressed, just as God of the Passover story hears and answers the cries of the Hebrew people.

Most Jewish American families now acquire a set of illustrated mass-produced Haggadahs. In fact, when many American Jews picture Moses or the crossing of the Red Sea, it is the images of their childhood Haggadahs, seen year after year at family seders, that come to mind. For instance, over the years, many families have collected complementary Haggadahs produced by the makers of Maxwell House Coffee. Ironically, the "Maxwell House Haggadah," originally an advertising gimmick, is considered by many to be the "traditional" Haggadah, the "real thing" against which "new-fangled" (feminist or liberation) Haggadahs are measured.

American Haggadahs include the Hebrew with some transliteration and translation into English, and sometimes they provide commentary and music for popular Passover songs. Until the 1960s, it was not uncommon for a grandfather or father sitting at the head of the table to chant the text of the Haggadah in Hebrew all by himself, as women scurried back and forth from kitchen to dining room and as children and petulant grownups whined "When do we eat?" throughout the long pre-meal part of the ceremony.

With the passing of the generation that raced through the Haggadah in Hebrew, a new generation took over the seders, one that preferred an egalitarian and participatory model and, except for the major blessings, used much more English. Liberal Jews, feeling freer to add, alter, and innovate liturgies and rituals, began to type, cut and paste, and photocopy texts to distribute at their ceremonies, thus demonstrating their "ownership" of traditions, which they were recasting for greater personal relevance. Given that the goal of a Passover seder is to tell the Exodus story in such a way that it is meaningful (for children in particular) and provocative, it is no surprise that Haggadah creators felt free to compose, elaborate, and abridge for the sake of creating a memorable and often child-centered learning experience. The homemade Haggadahs or brief Haggadah addenda of a page or more reflected such contemporary concerns as feminism, egalitarianism, liberation, Jewish pluralism, Holocaust memorialization, ecumenicism, racial relations, sexual tolerance, ecological awareness, and a wide range of expressions of political concern for Jews endangered in far-off places such as the Soviet Union or Ethiopia. Some families or communities used these alternative Haggadahs for their Passover seders, whereas others used them as supplementary material that seder guests could turn to on their own for selected readings or for private perusal. Jewish organizations, for fundraising, sent out their own Haggadah addenda, reflecting their particular mission.

Homemade Haggadahs began to appear in the 1970s. They reflected the countercultural, homespun, do it yourself aesthetic of the *Whole Earth Catalog* that would be captured in the best-selling *The First Jewish Catalog* (edited by Richard

Siegel, Sharon Strassfeld, and Michael Strassfeld in 1973) as well as in the second and third catalogs. Jewish couples, too, were making wedding booklets, which they gave out to their guests, explaining the service, explaining deviations from tradition made in the name of modernity, and making the ceremony more contemporary and intimate with personally chosen readings. If Jewish couples eventually gave birth to daughters, it was likely that they would produce their own booklet for the baby-naming ceremony for their newborn. Such rituals had come about in the last few decades as a response to the male baby circumcision ceremony in order that daughters might also formally enter the covenantal community of the Jewish people.

In 1977, *Ms.* magazine published an edited version of *The Women's Haggadah*, composed in 1975 by Jewish feminist author Esther Broner with Nomi Nimrod, for use in what would become an annual seder of leading Jewish feminists. The creators of this Haggadah experienced the responsibility of their project, to create a feminist text out of an age-old patriarchal sacred text. In their text, Miriam, rather than Moses, became the central figure, a choice that perhaps empowered the authors and certainly empowered Jewish women who would use this new text. *Ms.* magazine was deluged by requests for photocopies of *The Women's Haggadah*.

In the 1990s, despite the availability of many attractive, artistic, and intellectually and spiritually compelling commercially published Haggadahs, it became common for individuals, families, or communities to create their own Haggadahs, particularly if they were for "model seders" held before Passover and were pedagogic or political in theme. In America, the ecumenical "model seder" became popular, and even more popular was the feminist seder, one that emphasized the theme of the liberation of women from all forms of oppression. As a model seder held in a communal setting was less bound by the traditions that acquire weight in the family setting, there was more freedom to innovate.

The spirit of innovation caught on, and people either brought their newly acquired "model seder" Haggadahs to their real seders, or they clipped parts of the model seders and introduced them to their families. Thus, new readings were "imported" into the regular family seders, as were new rituals, such as drinking a cup of spring water to honor the prophetess Miriam.

Hundreds of privately created, cut-and-paste, photocopied Haggadahs became available and were passed freely around. Their number increased as personal computers made desktop publishing possible and as the Internet provided templates of Haggadahs on which people could improvise. Creating one's own Haggadah was seen by many as a part of one's spiritual preparation for the holiday. The creation process became an intellectual and creative supplement to the overwhelming physical tasks of scouring one's house for crumbs and replacing all of one's dishes, utensils, pots, and pans with kitchen equipment set aside for Passover only. At root, it was a way to make the Jewish tradition one's own.

The text included here is "The Rosenblum-Adler Family Hagaddah," created by Susan Adler of Randolph, New Jersey, in 1998. Adler explains that after the death of her father, who had lead the family seder for years, the family was committed to still have a meaningful seder, but it had to be one that was appropriate for the family, something they could realistically and comfortably perform. Using a copying machine, she reproduced passages from other Haggadahs she had collected, and cut and pasted a text that honored her father but also helped the family, with its adjustments and deviations, to move forward. The cover of the eleven-page, stapled, photocopied document called "The Rosenblum-Adler Family Hagaddah" is a work of computer-generated clip art featuring a multigenerational family in a circle dance (see Figure 5.1). At the center is a happy family toasting with cups of Passover wine, humorously extending from their mouths read: "L'Chaim! Yummy! Welcome! Passover Rocks!" (referring to the matzah balls). In the "Rosenblum-Adler Family Hagaddah," the entire second half of the seder, that which follows the festive meal, is omitted, reflecting a common practice in many Jewish American homes. Still, it does present the basic "signposts" of a Jewish American seder: Included are blessings over wine, but only two of the four traditional cups are drunk: one to start the ceremony and one just before the holiday meal is served, meant as a toast to freedom and to the blessings of family. A green vegetable, matzah, horseradish, and charoset are served. The Haggadah also retains the hiding of the matzah, called the *afikomen,* the telling of the Passover story, the four questions asked by the youngest person present, the answers given to four different kinds of children, and the recitation of the ten plagues (with a drop of wine spilled as each plague is mentioned, suggesting that the pain of the Egyptians whose lives were lost diminishes the joy of the Israelite's freedom). The family also retains the singing of "Dayenu" in ancient and contemporary versions. Adler's Haggadah is essentially an abridgement of *A Different Night: The Family Participation Haggadah* by Noam Zion and David Dishon, a project of the Shalom Hartman Institute of Jerusalem. Adler's version, however, is about one-third as long and it contains questions and reflections Adler poses to her seder guests, which are intended to spark thoughtful, and even heated, discussion at the table, a Passover seder hallmark.

Susan Adler, "The Rosenbaum-Adler Family Hagaddah" (Randolph, N.J.: privately printed, 1998).

Further Reading

E. M. Broner, *The Women's Haggadah* (San Francisco: Harper San Francisco, 1994); Arnold M. Eisen, *Rethinking Modern Judaism* (Chicago: University of Chicago Press, 1998), pp. 242–63; Elie Wiesel, *A Passover Haggadah, as commented upon by Elie Wiesel* (New York: Touchstone, 1993); Noam Zion and David Dishon, *A Different Night: The Family Participation Haggadah* (Jerusalem: Shalom Hartman Institute, 1997).

Our Seder

(Based on the hot-off-the-printer ROSENBLUM-ADLER FAMILY HAGADDAH*)*

Welcome to our Seder. The word "Seder" means "order"—and there is a particular order, or road map, for conducting this special family celebration. Just as we sometimes deviate from the exact route on a printed map when we travel, we can

Figure 5.1. The Rosenblum-Adler Family Hagaddah.

make adjustments and deviations in this Seder (order), too. But the basic signposts are here for us, and for all Jews around the world. THE CELEBRATION OF PASSOVER, AND ATTENDANCE AT SEDER, IS THE MOST OBSERVED RITUAL IN THE JEWISH WORLD.

One of the central questions asked at every Seder, which we will hear later, is "Why is this night different?" To each of us, this year, last year, in fact, every year, is different. We celebrate with some of the same family members and friends, but not all; we hold our Seder in different homes; we share many common characteristics, but there are differences among us; we share many holiday memories, but some of those vary, too. So this night is "different," and that is what makes it interesting.

KIDDUSH

Remember, it is ok, even correct, to sit on a pillow, or recline at the Seder. WHY?

> BLESSED ARE YOU, Lord
> Our God, King of the Universe
> who creates the fruit of the vine.

> BLESSED ARE YOU, Lord, our God, King of the
> Universe, who has chosen us from among the nations
> and the languages, sanctifying us by your mitzvot.
> Lovingly You have given us Shabbat for rest and
> festivals for happiness, including today—
> the Shabbat and the Holiday of the
> Matzot, the season of our liberation,
> a sacred day to gather together and to
> commemorate the Exodus from
> Egypt. For you have chosen us and
> sanctified us among the nations.
> You have granted us lovingly the
> Shabbat and joyfully the
> Holidays. Blessed are You,
> Lord, who sanctifies The
> Shabbat and the people of
> Israel and the festivals

FYI—A NOTE ON THE IMPORTANCE OF WOMEN ON PESACH—

According to the Sages, women must be involved with honor in the celebration of Pesach because they had a huge role in the survival and redemption of the Jews. It was the women who continued to have babies and hide them in Egypt even in the face of slavery and the decree of Pharoah that all Jewish male babies be killed.

CAN YOU IDENTIFY OTHER SPECIFIC WOMEN WHO HAD SPECIAL ROLES IN THE PASSOVER STORY?

KARPAS

We dip a green vegetable in salt water or charoset and say the following blessing. WHAT IS THE SIGNIFICANCE OF THE GREEN VEGETABLE? OF THE CHAROSET?

For vegetables (like celery, parsley, or potatoes):

BLESSED ARE You, Lord, our God, King of the Universe, who creates the fruit of the earth.

Spring traditionally reminds us of new beginnings. Think of this as "prime time." Can you draw a connection between the word "prime" and the word for "spring" in other languages? What does the word "spring" itself call to mind?"

YACHATZ—BREAKING THE MATZAH

The middle matzah is broken in two, and one part is hidden for the AFIKO-MEN. An old custom in Tunisia was to compare the breaking of the middle matzah with the way God parted the Red Sea. (This is an example of the way the Seder offers us visual aids in the telling of the Passover story.)

Remember, the Seder will not be complete until the AFIKOMEN is retrieved, and eaten as part of dessert.

WHAT DOES THE SEDER HAVE IN COMMON WITH THE CELEBRATION OF THANKSGIVING?

MAGGID—THE TELLING OF THE STORY

We are all familiar with the Hagaddah, the book we are accustomed to using at our Seders. There are almost an infinite variety of Hagaddahs, from the simple ones given out at the supermarket, to extremely artistic and original ones. Some Hagaddahs have particular agendas, such as a Women's Hagaddah, a Hagaddah of Liberation, a Reform or Conservative Hagaddah, etc.

The important thing to know, however, is that the Hagaddah is only a guide. There is no hard and fast rule about which Hagaddah to use or how closely to follow it. The word Ha'Agadan means "The Telling," and it is "The Telling" that is the most important ingredient of any Seder.

HA LACHMA ANYA

We lift up the matzah and show it to everyone. We are told, "This is the bread of poverty and affliction that our ancestors ate in the land of Egypt." Does this agree with the widely accepted story that matzah was invented at the time the Jews fled Egypt because there was no time for their bread to rise?

> THIS IS THE BREAD of poverty and persecution
> that our ancestors ate in the land of Egypt. As it
> says in the Torah "seven days shall you eat . . . mazot"
> the bread of poverty and persecution (Deut. 16.3) so that
> you may "remember that you were a slave in Egypt"
> (Deut. 16.12)
>
> LET ALL who are hungry, come and eat
> LET ALL who are hungry, come and share
> the Pesach meal.

THIS YEAR we are still here—
Next year, in the land of Israel.

THIS YEAR we are still slave—
Next year, free people.

We recite, "Let all who are hungry, come and eat; let all who are in need, come and share the Pesach meal." WHAT DOES THIS SAY ABOUT OUR VALUES?

We also say, "This year we are still here—next year, may we be in Israel. This year we are still slaves; next year, may we be free."

MUST WE TAKE THIS PRAYER LITERALLY? WHAT OTHER MEANING CAN WE FIND IN THESE SENTENCES? THINK ABOUT WHAT ELSE CAN ENSLAVE US OTHER THAN THE ANCIENT EGYPTIANS. WHAT ARE SOME OF THE THINGS IN OUR OWN LIVES THAT OPPRESS US? HOW DO WE BECOME FREE?

A CONTEMPORARY MEDITIATION ON SLAVERY AND FREEDOM

By Leonard Fein, founder of MOMENT Magazine (1975) and MAZON: A Jewish Response to Hunger (1985)

"This year we are slaves"
    WHAT CAN these words mean?
    We are slaves because yesterday our people were in slavery, and memory makes yesterday real for us.
    We are slaves because today there are still people in chains around the world and no one can be truly free while others are in chains.
    We are slaves because freedom means more than broken chains. Where there is poverty and hunger and homelessness, there is no freedom; where there is prejudice and bigotry and discrimination, there is no freedom; where there is violence and torture and war, there is no freedom.
    And where each of us is less than he or she might be, we are not free, not yet.
    And who, this year, can be deaf to the continuing oppression of the down-trodden, who can be blind to the burdens and the rigors that are now to be added to the most vulnerable in our midst?
    If these things be so, who among can say that he or she is free?

THE FOUR QUESTIONS

ARE THERE REALLY FOUR?

Some people ask them this way—Pourquoi cette nuit se distingue-t-elle de toutes les autres nuits? or Por que es diferente esta noche de las demas noches?

A few quotes from our Sages show the importance that has always been given to asking questions:

"Whoever is not ashamed to ask, will the in the end be exalted."—Talmud
"Whoever is ashamed to ask, he will diminish in wisdom among
men."—Moses ibn Ezra (11th c.)
"Unless you call out, who will answer the door?"—Ethiopian proverb

It is traditional for the youngest at the Seder to ask the Four Questions.

MA NISHTANA

HOW IS THIS NIGHT different from all other nights?

> ON ALL other nights
> we eat
> either leavened bread or matza,
> but on this night we eat only matza.

> ON ALL other nights
> we eat other kinds of vegetables,
> but on this night we eat maror (bitter herbs).

> ON ALL other nights,
> we need not dip
> our vegetables even once,
> but on this night we dip twice.

> ON ALL other nights,
> we eat
> either sitting
> upright or reclining,
> but on this night
> we all recline.

WHAT ARE SOME WAYS IN WHICH THE JEWISH PEOPLE WERE ABLE TO MAINTAIN
THEIR IDENTITY AS A PEOPLE AND AS A COMMUNITY DURING ALL THE YEARS OF
SLAVERY?

ARE THERE DIFFERENCES IN THE WAY PHAROAH TREATED THE JEWS AND THE WAY
THE NAZIS TREATED THEM?

SOME ANSWERS TO THE FOUR QUESTIONS

As often happens after the youngest child recites the four questions, the family
and guests applaud but do not bother to answer the questions. Since a young
child's questions should not go unanswered, we shall present one answer to
each of the four questions.

ON THE ONE HAND, the matza and the maror belong to the menus of the slaves
and the oppressed:

1. Why eat plain matza which is hard to digest?
Poor laborers and slaves are fed matza not only because it is cheap but because
it is filling and requires a long digestion period. The diet was designed by the
oppressor to exploit the people efficiently.

2. Why eat raw, bitter vegetables ?
Maror is eaten plain only by the most oppressed workers who are given little
time to prepare their meals. With more time they would have made these
herbs into a tasty salad.

ON THE OTHER HAND dipping and reclining typify the manners of the leisure
class in Roman times.

3. Why dip twice before eating?
On seder night we are obligated to dip twice—karpas in salt water and maror in
charoset—before the meal begins. Even today, finger foods dipped in tangy sauces
are typical hors d'oeuvres with cocktails (the first cup of wine) at banquets.

4. Why recline on pillows while drinking wine?
The body language of the free reflects their ease and comfort. Reclining on
sofas or pillows, everyone—big and small alike—experiences the freedom of
the upper classes. On seder night these foods and these table manners are
props and stage directions in the script acted out by all.
(Based on Don Isaa Abrabanel, Zebach Pesach)

WE WERE SLAVES—AVADIM HAYINU

When, in time to come, your children ask you: "What is the meaning of the
decrees, laws, and rules that the Lord our God has enjoined upon you?" You shall
say to your children: "We were slaves to Pharaoh in Egypt and the Lord freed us
from Egypt with a mighty hand and an outstretched arm. The Lord produced
before our eyes great and awful signs and wonders in Egypt, against Pharaoh and
all his household; and God freed us from there, so that God could take us and give
us the land that had been promised on oath to our ancestors." (Deut. 6:20–23).

THE FOUR CHILDREN

The Torah alludes to 4 children—wise, wicked, simple, and one who does not
know how to ask. WHY DO WE MAKE THESE FOUR CHILDREN PART OF THE SEDER?
WHAT DOES IT TEACH US? WHAT KIND OF PROBLEMS DO WE HAVE AS PARENTS, AS
TEACHERS, AND AS A SOCIETY WHEN WE PUT LABELS ON CHILDREN?

THE TEN PLAGUES

"God took us out of Egypt with a strong hand, and an outstretched arm, with awesome power, signs, and wonders." These signs, wonders, and awesome power

refer to the Ten Plagues. We recite them, dripping a little bit of wine as we say each plague.

1. Blood
2. Frogs
3. Lice
4. Wild beasts (or insects)
5. Cattle plague
6. Boils
7. Hail
8. Locust
9. Darkness
10. Death of the Firstborn

AN AFRICAN-AMERICAN SPIRITUAL

Sing:
When Israel was in Egypt's land,
"Let My people go" (Ex. 5:1)
Oppressed so hard they could not stand,
"Let My people go."

Go down, Moses, way down in Egypt's land
Tell old Pharaoh: "Let My people go."

Thus said the Lord, bold Moses said,
"Let My people go."
If not, I'll smite your first-born dead,
"Let My people go."

Go down, Moses, way down in Egypt's land
Tell old Pharaoh: "Let My people go."

No more shall they in bondage toil,
"Let My people go."
Let them come out with Egypt's spoil,
"Let My people go."

Go down, Moses, way down in Egypt's land
Tell old Pharaoh: "Let my people go."

HARRIET TUBMAN escaped in 1849 from her plantation in Maryland with the help of the "Underground Railroad." Soon she became a major "conductor" bringing more than 300 slaves to freedom. Despite the high price on her head, her faith in God gave her the courage to persist and earn the nickname "Moses of her people."

Something to ponder on this holiday which marks our deliverance from slavery into freedom. We as Jews know the importance of remembering not only our deliverance, but the times throughout history when we have been oppressed, forced into ghettos, attacked, and in recent history, the Holocaust, when we were targeted for annihilation.

However, when we dwell on being victims, those memories may either corrupt us, or they may help us grow in empathy for others. Consider the negative effects of suffering—self-pity, dreams of vengeance, self-righteousness, self-blame. Often, one loses the ability to feel anything for others, thinking only, "But I suffered much worse."

ARE THERE ANY OTHER, PERHAPS OPPOSITE REACTIONS THAT CAN BE BROUGHT ON BY PAIN AND SUFFERING?

DAYEINU

We sing this song, which liberally translated means, "Thank you God, for overdoing it." Literally, dayeinu means, "It would have been enough."

> Had God taken us out of Egypt but had not divided the sea for us . . . Dayeinu!
> (It would have been enough for us)!
> Had God given us the Sabbath but not brought us to Mount Sinai . . . Dayeinu!
> Had God brought us to Mount Sinai but not brought us into the land of Israel . . .Dayeinu!

A Contemporary Dayeinu
By Rabbi Steven Greenberg and Rabbi David Nelson
"It Would Have Been Enough . . ."

> Had God upheld us throughout 2,000 years of Dispersion,
> But not preserved our hope for return   Dayeinu!
>
> Had God preserved our hope for return,
> But not sent us leaders to make the dream a reality   Dayeinu!
>
> Had God sent us leaders to make the dream a reality,
> But not given us success in the U.N. vote in 1947   Dayeinu!
>
> Had God given us success in the U.N. vote,
> But not defeated our attackers in 1948   Dayeinu!
>
> Had God defeated our attackers in 1948,
> But not unified Jerusalem   Dayeinu!
>
> Had God unified Jerusalem,
> But not led us towards peace with Egypt and Jordan   Dayeinu!

Had God returned us to the land of our ancestors,
But not filled it with our children   Dayeinu!

Had God filled it with our children,
But not caused the desert to bloom   Dayeinu!

Had God caused the desert to bloom,
But not built for us cities and towns   Dayeinu!

Had God rescued our remnants from the Holocaust,
But not brought our brothers from Arab lands   Dayeinu!

Had God brought our brothers from Arab lands,
But not opened the gate for Russia's Jews   Dayeinu!

Had God opened the gate for Russia's Jews,
But not redeemed our people from Ethiopia   Dayeinu!

Had God redeemed our people from Ethiopia,
But not strengthened the State of Israel   Dayeinu!

Had God strengthened the State of Israel,
But not planted in our hearts a covenant of one people   Dayeinu!

Had God planted in our hearts a covenant of one people,
But not sustained in our souls a vision of a perfected world   Dayeinu!

MATZAH, MAROR, AND CHAROSET

The Rabbis, in their infinite wisdom, made a time in the Seder for Hors d'oeuvres. At this time, we make a sandwich of matzah, maror, and charoset, and discuss how good it is, and the symbolism it represents.

The modern Hagaddah, *A Different Night,* on which most of our Hagaddah is based, recounts an ironic tale of Matzah, maror, and charoset. It seems that during the American Civil War, when a group of Jewish Union soldiers made a Seder for themselves in the wilderness of West Virginia, they had none of the ingredients for traditional charoset. Instead of eliminating this important ingredient from their Seder plate, they put a real brick in its place! [Source: Ira Steingroot, *Keeping Passover,* 1995]

This is a good time to reflect on the various Charoset recipes, and which you prefer.

A TOAST TO FREEDOM

With this reading, we conclude the storytelling portion of the Seder and drink the second cup of wine.

Each cup we raise this night is an act of memory and of reverence. The story we tell, this year as every year, is not yet done. It begins with them, then; it continues with us, now. We remember not out of curiosity or nostalgia, but because it is our turn to add to the story.

> Our challenge this year, as every year, is to feel the Exodus,
> To open the gates of time and become one with those
> Who crossed the Red Sea from slavery to freedom.
>
> Our challenge this year, as every year, is to know the Exodus,
> To behold all those in every land who have yet to make the crossing.
>
> Our challenge this day, as every day, is to reach out
> Our hands to them and help them cross to freedomland.

We know some things that others do not always know—how arduous is the struggle, how very deep the waters to be crossed and how treacherous their tides, how filled with irony and contradiction and suffering at the crossing and then the wandering.

We know such things because we ourselves wandered in the desert for forty years. Have not those forty years been followed by thirty-two centuries of struggle and of quest? Heirs to those who struggled and quested, we are old-timers at disappointment, veterans at sorrow, but always, always, prisoners of hope. The hope is the anthem of our people (Hatikvah), and the way of our people.

For all the reversals and all the stumbling-blocks, for all the blood and all the hurt, hope still dances within us. That is who we are, and that is what this seder is about. For the slaves do become free, and the tyrants are destroyed. Once, it was by miracles; today, it is by defiance and devotion.
(Leonard Fein, American social activist)

BLESSED ARE YOU, OUR GOD, KING OF THE UNIVERSE, CREATOR OF THE FRUIT OF THE VINE. BLESSED ARE YOU, OUR GOD, KING OF THE UNIVERSE, WHO HAS REDEEMED US AND BROUGHT US TO THIS NIGHT. MAY YOU BRING US IN PEACE AND GOOD HEALTH TO FUTURE HOLIDAYS AND CELEBRATIONS WITH OUR FAMILY AND FRIENDS. AMEN.

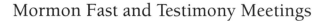

—6—

Mormon Fast and Testimony Meetings

Jana Kathryn Riess

Fast and testimony meetings occur in every local Latter-day Saint (Mormon) ward on the first Sunday of each month, although meetings may be rescheduled so as to avoid conflicts with General Conferences on the first Sundays of April and October. Although regular Sundays will feature two or three prepared talks by members of the ward, testimony Sunday is an "open mike" tradition in which area members take approximately forty minutes of the church meeting to share their extemporaneous thoughts.

Mormons believe that the Holy Ghost is present at such meetings and will prompt some members to bear their testimonies. Every member who feels moved to do so may testify. Even small children, aided by parental prompting, lisp their testimonies into the microphone. Testimonies usually expound on Mormons' core beliefs about the restoration of the gospel through Joseph Smith, the sacred nature of the Book of Mormon, and the role of the current Latter-day Saint prophet, Gordon B. Hinckley. Members express gratitude for blessings such as family, health, and spiritual abundance. Often, they share "faith-promoting" personal stories to underscore gospel principles such as tithing, keeping the Word of Wisdom, reading the Scriptures, doing missionary work, or attending the temple. As they testify, contemporary Mormons discuss how their beliefs affect their work, family relationships, and life goals.

The tradition of fast and testimony meetings arises from a verse in the Book of Mormon, which speaks of church members coming "together oft, to fast and to pray, and to speak with one another concerning the welfare of their souls" (Moroni 6:5). In 1836, when the first LDS temple was dedicated in Kirtland, Ohio, many Mormons reported seeing visions and experiencing a general outpouring of the Spirit. Testifying to such experiences eventually became a regular feature of Mormon life. Until the 1980s, when Mormon church meetings were consolidated into a single three-hour block schedule on Sundays, fast and testimony meetings were held on Thursdays.

Today, Mormon testimonies are more formulaic than in the past. One sociologist who tracked a year's worth of one ward's testimonies found that the overwhelming majority "were preoccupied with expressions of gratitude" rather than reflections on doctrine. Most testimonies follow a fairly predictable pattern as compared to the more spontaneous testimony bearing in the nineteenth-century church. It is less common today to hear mention of miraculous healings, whereas early church meetings regularly featured healings and other charismatic gifts, including glossolalia (speaking in tongues). Testimony meetings are marked by a distinctive language with recurrent phrases; Mormons speak of "knowing" that the Church is true, that Joseph Smith was a true prophet, and that the Book of Mormon is the word of God. Each testimony ends with the phrase "in the name of Jesus Christ," as do all Mormon prayers.

The testimony meeting is an important community ritual for Mormons. Many meetings feature new members who introduce themselves, or others who offer a tearful farewell to ward members, who have become like family. For active Mormons, social life revolves around the local ward, and testimony meetings often reflect the intimate trust of a small, tight-knit community. Members mention one another by name and describe how other members have bolstered their testimonies or helped them in some way. Often, these public expressions of friendship hinge on quotidian, tangible signs of community exchange; a young mother might use testimony time to thank the ward women who fed her family and cleaned her house while she nursed her new baby, or a college student might acknowledge the ward for issuing multiple invitations for a first Thanksgiving away from home.

Mormon testimony meetings are accompanied by a two-meal fast (ideally over a twenty-four-hour period), in which adult members abstain from all food and drink. Many Mormons begin fasting after dinner on Saturday evening and continue fasting until dinner on Sunday evening, but individual practices vary. Adult members who are pregnant, nursing, or in delicate health are not expected to fast, nor are small children.

Fasting is designed to foster spiritual growth and to remind Mormons of their dependence upon their Heavenly Father. Often, members fast with a particular purpose in mind, such as divine guidance for a challenge they are facing. Many Mormons say that the discipline of fasting helps them to focus their prayers. Occasionally, an entire ward will fast and pray together for the same purpose, such as an ill or injured community member. Sometimes the local bishop will suggest that the members fast and pray for missionary work or other churchwide issues. Individual Mormons fast at other times, such as when they attend the temple, and very occasionally the entire worldwide church will be asked to fast for a particular purpose on a special day apart from Fast Sunday. Month in, month out, however, Fast Sunday is the only regularly scheduled time in which the worldwide Mormon community fasts together.

Mormons are asked to donate the money they would have spent on their own food to the Church Welfare Program, to feed others. The Latter-day Saint Welfare Program is the largest private (nongovernmental) welfare organization in the world. Begun during the Great Depression, it now operates hundreds of storehouses and canneries, sixty-one social service centers, ninety-nine employment offices, and numerous agricultural enterprises. Fast offerings constitute the bulk of the program's funding and are used to feed and educate impoverished church members. Such aid is seen as a temporary measure, until members can become self-reliant. To maintain the strong and far-reaching welfare program, members are encouraged to give as generous a fast offering as they can afford.

Fast and testimony meetings adhere to the same basic sequence as all Mormon sacrament meetings. Opening hymns, prayers, and announcements are followed by the blessing and distribution of the sacrament, the bread and water that Mormons share to remember the body and blood of Jesus Christ. One of the three members of the ward bishopric (the bishop and his two counselors) will conduct the meeting, opening the testimony time with his own thoughts.

The following three testimonies were recorded at a fast and testimony meeting on August 1, 1999. (Information on location/ward is considered confidential.)

Further Reading

David Knowlton, "Belief, Metaphor, and Rhetoric: The Mormon Practice of Testimony Bearing," *Sunstone* 15, no. 1 (April 1991): 20–27; Garth L. Mangum and Bruce D. Blumell, *The Mormons' War on Poverty: A History of LDS Welfare, 1830–1990* (Salt Lake City: University of Utah Press, 1993); Armand L. Mauss, *The Angel and the Beehive: The Mormon Struggle with Assimilation* (Urbana: University of Illinois Press, 1994); Susan Buhler Taber, *Mormon Lives: A Year in the Elkton Ward* (Urbana: University of Illinois Press, 1993).

Fast and Testimony Meeting

The ward bishop, who is conducting the meeting, begins the testimony time by describing a talk by President Gordon B. Hinckley that he had watched on videotape earlier in the morning.

[President Hinckley] does such a wonderful job when he bears his testimony, to tell us that he knows that Jesus Christ lives. And that he died on the cross for us. And he just brings it all together in such a great manner that you know that what he is saying is true, and you can feel it in your heart and soul. . . .

I know that in the Hill Cumorah, that there is still a stone box there. Nobody knows where it is. And someday, that box will be opened up again, and the world will know that this church is true, and at the Sacred Grove Joseph Smith did see Heavenly Father and Jesus Christ standing before him in a pillar of light. That he did wrestle with the devil at that time. . . . When we were baptized in this church, we took upon ourselves the name of Christ, and should use him as the example in our lives. I'm thankful for Him that died for my sins. I sometimes feel

that I'd done more than my share of sins to make him have pain, before I became
a member of this church, and I'm thankful for [Christ], my elder brother.

You know, [Heavenly Father] tells us in the Scriptures that he knew us
before he formed us in the belly. And that tells me there's a pre-existence, and I
knew that before I joined this church. It's hard to change your life, when you
become baptized. I'm thankful for my wife, who stayed with me for . . .[those]
first few years, when I wasn't a member of the church. And she showed me by
example. And all of you, all the selfless acts and deeds that you do for each
other, I'm thankful for that. I feel the love growing in this ward, the concern
that each and every one of us has for the other. I can feel that, sometimes, if
I'm looking for the good. I think that's a key in our lives, that we need to look
for the good in each and every one of us. . . .

I know that President Hinckley is a prophet of God. Being able to watch him on
the tape this morning, that helped me out a lot. . . . He's a wonderful man. And I
get to listen to him on the tapes, and when we have General Conference we get to
listen to a Prophet of our Heavenly Father. And I'm thankful for that, to be able to
even see him. . . . Things are advancing more every year. The devil's at work against
us; we need to keep ourselves strong. Pray every day. Read your scriptures. . . .

I'm thankful for the youth that we have. We have a great bunch of youth
here. I probably don't understand all the things that they have to go through in
school, and all the pressures that they have, but it's a wonderful thing to know
that they have seminary in the mornings . . . and they have a little bit of Christ
in their hearts when they get to school. And I think that sets their school day
off in a good manner. I'm thankful for each and every one of you, and I say
these things in the name of Jesus Christ. Amen.

The bishop then announces, "Brothers and sisters, the time is now yours,"
encouraging members to observe the meeting's time limits. In some wards, members of the Aaronic priesthood (generally boys ages twelve to eighteen) pass the
microphone around the room, with testifying members standing at their seats. In
other wards, members walk to the front podium to testify.

SMALL GIRL, AGE 6:

I want to bear my testimony that I'm thankful for the church, and for my family,
and for my Primary [early religious school] teachers. I'm thankful for Heavenly
Father, that blesses me daily, and I say this in the name of Jesus Christ. Amen.

RETIRED MAN, AN ADULT SUNDAY SCHOOL TEACHER :

There's never a time that I sit in a fast and testimony meeting . . . that I don't
think about how grateful I am for a young boy who wanted to know which
church to join. It's this time of the year that the pageant in Palmyra is going
on, the Hill Cumorah. . . . I'm grateful for him and the many struggles he had

in his short life, and what he accomplished. Surely the Prophet Joseph Smith was a prophet of God. And I'm grateful for President Hinckley, and the message he leaves and the kind of life he lives. You can't go wrong if you follow the prophet. I'm grateful for my wife and our children and grandchildren for their commitment to serve the Lord, and their desire to do so. I know that Jesus is the Christ, the Son of God, that he is the only person whereby we can receive exaltation in our lives, that this is his church, that the Bible and the Book of Mormon are true. [The Book of Mormon] is a powerful book and can be a great solace to us, which solves our problems, answers our questions, and is a guidance to us throughout our lives. The scriptures are a great blessing to us, but they are only a blessing when we search and ponder and pray about them. Again I testify that this is the Lord's work, and that Jesus is the Christ, and that we have a prophet. And I leave these things with you in the name of Jesus Christ. Amen.

Singing: Songs of Devotion, Praise, and Protest

Hanukkah Songs of the 1950s

Dianne Ashton

The delightful winter holiday of Hanukkah, now a favorite among American Jews, achieved its current popularity in the 1950s. Although Hanukkah has been part of the Jewish holiday calendar for over two thousand years, it is considered a minor festival. Before the twentieth century it was one among many American Jewish customs that sometimes fell by the wayside. In the late nineteenth century, a Philadelphia group attempted to rescue Hanukkah from near oblivion with a pageant. Today, it is one of the holidays most likely to be celebrated by American Jews.

Hanukkah was easy to overlook because it is a simple holiday. Its ritual requires neither the elaborate meal and liturgy of Passover, which celebrates the Exodus from Egypt, nor the strict discipline of Yom Kippur, the day of fasting and prayer to atone for sins. Hanukkah demands only lighting evening candles and reciting three brief blessings and a hymn at home and adding certain psalms to the synagogue morning service, including a distinctive paragraph inserted into the Amidah. In America after World War II, however, Hanukkah's customs of gift-giving, songs, games, and the eating of symbolic foods grew more complex as the festival increased in popularity.

The Hebrew word "Hanukkah" means "dedication," and the holiday commemorates the rededication of the Temple in Jerusalem by Jews in 165 B.C.E. Hanukkah's history begins with Alexander The Great, who conquered the land on which the Jews lived, along with most of the Near East, although he did not interfere directly with Jewish worship. After Alexander's death, control of the Hellenic empire fell to different families, and in the early second century B.C.E. Antiochus IV Epiphanes took control of Syrian and Jewish land. By then, broad and deep cultural differences had emerged between urban Jews who tended to embrace Hellenic culture and those in the coutryside who did not. To stem an internal rebellion arising from that conflict, Antiochus IV issued decrees forbidding many Jewish practices and commanding observance of his own Hellenized Syrian customs and rites. Toward that goal, he transformed the Jerusalem Temple, then the most holy site of Judaism, into a shrine to his own gods and himself.

The Jews' battle against Antiochus was led by the family of the High Priest, Mattathias, and his five sons. Tradition holds that one of the sons, Judah, earned the nickname "the Hammer" (*maccabee* in Hebrew), and ever since then the brothers have been called "the Maccabees" in Jewish holiday lore. After three years of fighting, their small army won a significant battle for Jerusalem and immediately cleansed and rededicated the Temple. They removed altars to foreign gods and cleaned out residue left from their Syrian sacrifices. After cleaning, they began rededicating the Temple to the God of the Hebrew Bible. They lit the oil lamps that symbolized the spirit of God, which were to remain constantly lit. Legend has it that although only enough oil was found to burn for one day, the flame lasted eight days until sufficient oil could be found and brought to renew the flame.

The story of these events is told in four books of the Maccabees that were written between the latter part of the second century B.C.E. and about 100 C.E. Although these are not included in biblical texts, they were considered important enough to include in the semicanonical collection called the Apocrypha. Written by different authors, the books offer different viewpoints on the Maccabees and the rededication commemorated by Hanukkah. The first book is the oldest and is largely an historical account of the revolt. The second book stresses divine deliverance of the Jews. The third book, although inspired by the Maccabean revolt, does not mention it directly. Instead, it describes a parallel event that occurred later, when Ptolemy Philopater, a Roman governor, was thwarted in his plan to convert the Jerusalem Temple into a shrine to his gods. Finally, the fourth book of Maccabees is a philosophical work that simply uses examples from the Maccabean revolt to illustrate its points.

According to the second book of Maccabees, the first Hanukkah celebration was patterned after the autumnal Jewish holiday of Sukkot, an eight-day event commemorating the time early Jews spent traveling in the wilderness from Egypt to Canaan. Thus Hanukkah, like Sukkot, lasts eight days. On both holidays, Psalms 113–118 are recited in the synagogue, where the dedication of the tabernacle in the wilderness, described in the biblical book of Numbers, is also read. Both holidays are joyous occasions.

Hanukkah has also been understood to commemorate a miracle. For children, the miracle is the oil that lasted eight days. For adults, the ancient rabbis who established the ritual insisted that it was God's miraculous aid that enabled the Maccabees to defeat Antiochus's larger army. To underscore that point, the rabbis decreed that a verse from the prophet Zechariah, "Not by might, nor by power, but by my spirit, saith the Lord of hosts," be read in the synagogue on the Sabbath that occurs during Hanukkah. Despite its historical import, the early rabbis strived to dim the militaristic tone of the holiday. Perhaps they did so because they worked under the suspicious watch of Roman rule, or perhaps because they opposed the influential descendants of the Maccabees, who collaborated with Roman governors. Whatever their reasoning, Hanukkah became a holiday whose motto is "A great miracle happened there."

The lighting of the Hanukkah lamp underscores the importance of God's spirit in Jewish lives. The menorah's light, which grows brighter with each evening's additional candle, symbolizes gradual spiritual enlightenment as well as the slow but steady victory over those who have tried to destroy Judaism. Because it represents a miracle, the lighted menorah is often placed in a window to proclaim divine action. No work can be done while the slender candles burn, and Jews use that time to sing songs, play games, offer gifts to children, and eat foods fried in oil, such as potato pancakes (the European tradition) or doughnuts (the Mediterranean tradition), which symbolize the oil found in the Jerusalem Temple. A traditional game is played with a spinning top called a *dreidl*, whose four sides are inscribed with the initials of the Hebrew words for "A great miracle happened there." (In Israel the dreidl's letters stand for "A Great Miracle Happened Here.") Thus, the sheer fun of Hanukkah takes place amid reminders of God's power. These cultural icons are memorialized in the popular songs, "Chanukah, O Chanukah" and "My Dreidl."

Living as minorities for much of their history, Jews often felt that their survival depended on God's miracles. Hanukkah's story sparked the imaginations of many Jewish writers and artists. In countries as distant as Italy and Yemen, Jews shared the custom of reading an elaboration of the story of Hanukkah in their synagogues from a scroll which was probably written in the seventh century. By the sixteenth century, among Jews living in Germanic lands it had become customary to sing a hymn called "Maoz Tsur," or "O Fortress, Rock of My Salvation," immediately after lighting the Hanukkah candles. Sung to the tune of an old German folk tune, "Maoz Tsur" was probably composed in the thirteenth century. Its five verses praise God and offer thanks for saving Jews (Ze-er-iu-ba-bel, referred to in the third stanza, was the leader of Jewish exiles returning from Babylon c. 520 B.C.E., who supervised rebuilding of the Jerusalem Temple.) The song's first and last verses beg God to speed the day when Jews will be restored to their former land on the eastern shore of the Mediterranean Sea, when they will be free to practice their religion. "Maoz Tsur"'s stirring melody was commonly heard in homes and synagogues throughout northern Europe. Jewish artists frequently used the image of the oil lamp in Jewish folk and ritual art. It appeared in illuminated manuscripts, on jewelry, in architectural carvings, and on ritual objects. In recent centuries, however, the Hanukkah lamp has been modeled on the seven-branched candelabrum which was used in the Jerusalem Temple.

Although Hanukkah spoke to the hopes of oppressed Jews that God would continue to save them from destruction, among American Jews, Hanukkah found haphazard celebration. In the colonial period, the dominant Protestant culture frowned on the sort of jubilant display we today associate with Christmas, and the winter holidays passed calmly. In part because the few Jews living in colonial America were not confronted with a vivid Christian holiday at the same time of the year, some among them found it easy to let Hanukkah observances lapse. By the mid-nineteenth century, however, Hanukkah faced new challenges as the synagogues' power to enforce religious discipline were thwarted by three new circumstances. First, American laws guaranteeing freedom of religion made it more difficult for synagogues to control their members' religious observances. Second, between 1820 and 1870 almost 150,000 Jews from central and western Europe came to the United States, bringing the total number of American Jews to 250,000 by 1880. As the number of synagogues increased, the power of any one synagogue to control its members diminished. Third, some Jews from central and western Europe embarked on a program of reforming Judaism to accommodate Enlightenment ideals, focusing on Judaism's central beliefs and ethics while trimming away many rituals and translating many Hebrew prayers into German or English. For these people working to reshape Judaism to fit their modern, integrated experience, the minor holiday of Hanukkah could easily be overlooked or discarded.

Not all reformers agreed that Hanukkah's meaning was best left to the past. American Reform's most vocal and influential leader, Isaac Mayer Wise, a rabbi in Cincinnati, Ohio, viewed much of post–biblical Jewish history as heroic and inspiring. His novel based on Hanukkah, called *The First Maccabees,* was serialized in 1860 in forty installments in his weekly national newspaper. On the eve of the Civil War, his tale of Jewish courage in battle may have inspired some enlistments among Wise's readership. A more likely goal was to inspire American Jews to celebrate Hanukkah. Wise would have agreed with those more traditional Jews who staged Philadelphia's Hanukkah pageant nineteen years later.

Other Reform rabbis also took steps to urge their congregants to celebrate Hanukkah. Near the close of the nineteenth century, a New York rabbi who led the Reform movement on the east coast, Gustav Gottheil, tried to revive interest in Hanukkah by rewriting the hymn "Maoz Tsur." Although his new hymn fit the traditional melody, his lyrics reshaped the holiday's meaning to conform to the Reform perspective on Judaism. First, he shortened it from five stanzas to three. His opening did not hope to rededicate the Temple in Jerusalem, as did "Maoz Tsur," but instead praised God for saving Jews in the past. Gottheil's second stanza emphasized the cheer of Hanukkah, which has included lighting lamps and singing songs since its first celebration. This stanza encouraged American Jews to view Hanukkah as a thoroughly joyous occasion. Gottheil's conclusion reinterpreted Judaism's historic hope for a messiah who would signal the Jews' return to their homeland. Instead of an actual messiah, reformers like Gottheil called instead for a Messianic Age in which all people would be free to practice their religions in peace. As a Reform teacher, Gottheil wrote his last stanza to instruct American Jews that Judaism's message is one of expanding freedom: a Messianic Age that all Americans could embrace. Thus, he gave Judaism's historic hope a universal meaning and gave American Jews a message for all people.

Gottheil's hymn shows us something of the American Jewish intellectual world at the end of the last century. Using the nineteenth-century idea that each nation was a distinct race, Gottheil referred to Jews as "children of the martyr race." His phrase reminded Jews that their coreligionists in eastern Europe still experienced persecution. Efforts to help those Jews would soon compel the aid of many

American Jews. Gottheil's hymn illustrates American Jews' familiarity with the Protestant Christian culture that dominated America. Calling his work "Rock of Ages," Gottheil used a popular Christian hymn title to refer to the God of Israel, emphasizing the similarities between Protestant Christianity and Judaism. By trimming the tune's five stanzas to three, he made it more likely that American Jews, who spent less time on religious practice than did Jews in other parts of the world, might take the time to sing the song. When Gottheil eliminated requests for returning to the ancient homeland and for rebuilding the Jerusalem Temple, he not only pulled the hymn into line with a basic principle of Reform Judaism in the last century, he echoed the sentiments of American Jews who were happy in the United States.

However, it was the immigration of more than one million Jews from eastern Europe at the turn of the twentieth century that made the glow of Hanukkah candles a common sight in American Jewish homes. Between 1881 and 1924, Jewish families came to the industrial cities of the United States to escape violent anti-Jewish riots in Russia and Poland. These immigrants had left behind one of the world's preeminent Jewish communities, noted for fine rabbinical schools, prestigious rabbis, and strong mystical traditions. By and large, these immigrants maintained most of Judaism's religious practices. Largely because of these immigrants and their children, by 1950 almost five million Jews lived in the United States and Jews comprised almost 4 percent of its population.

The immigrants' piety was soon reshaped by American life. The private prayers of some female immigrants expressed faith in God's understanding that long working hours forced them to abandon some religious practices. Before the 1940s, more than half of the Jewish children living in New York City, then the largest Jewish community in the country, received no formal Jewish education. Only eighteen Jewish day schools could be found in New York in 1935. These trends might soon have led American Jewry to the same condition that Gottheil and others decried in the mid nineteenth century: a steady decline in Jewish observance, leaving Hanukkah and other practices by the wayside.

But while Jewish piety faced obstacles, Jewish culture thrived and music played a key role in American Jewish culture. The National Jewish Music Council held its festival each year, and twenty-five different record companies published a growing body of Jewish music. New efforts were made to musically educate Jewish folk musicians. The annual Cantor's conference that year noted new research into the history of Jewish prayer chants, and steps were taken to establish a cantorial school. In New York City, the Festival of Jewish Arts held at Carnegie Hall and public choral programs elsewhere proved so popular that exhibitions of Jewish music were staged in major department stores.

Hanukkah's place in that vibrant Jewish musical culture can best be traced through songbooks. Published by local Jewish school boards, Jewish book publishers, synagogues, clubs, and various Jewish denominations, these small volumes were inexpensive to produce and easy to distribute. Teachers, rabbis, and cantors who worked with religious schools often compiled songbooks. As early as 1918, *The Jewish Songster,* a simple compilation for voice and piano, proved so popular that it went through three printings its first year and was reissued and expanded into two volumes eleven years later. Its earliest version contained seven Hanukkah songs, including the blessings for the candle-lighting ceremony, "Maoz Tsur," Gottheil's "Rock of Ages," a Yiddish song about Hanukkah fun, and an English ditty called "Hear the Voice of Israel's Elders," which asks the question "Who will continue the work they began?" The volume focused its Hanukkah collection on transmitting traditional values and religious knowledge. In addition, movement toward a Jewish homeland had begun, and with it emerged a new interest in Jewish culture of all kinds. Thus, the 1929 *Jewish Songster* offered eighteen Hanukkah songs, most in Hebrew. Clearly, American Hanukkah celebrations had grown more important, and some Jewish schools had already felt the need for diverse Hanukkah songs that would appeal to children of various ages, even before World War II.

Enthusiasm for Jewish music in the mid twentieth century was fired by three different interests shared by American Jews. Jewish educators frequently turned to Jewish music to aid in meeting educational goals. Musical activities engaged children in a lively way while helping them learn Hebrew vocabulary and pronunciation, understand Jewish culture, build communal bonds, and absorb concepts of Jewish religious life and history. Local Boards of Jewish Education helped to produce albums of holiday music that could be used in religious schools. As the 1950s began, the Los Angeles board brought out four albums featuring choral performances of traditional chants. Second, professional musicians and composers such as Leonard Bernstein saw their arrangements and original compositions produced, serving the audience of sophisticated music lovers who appreciated both fine music and Jewish folk traditions. By 1950, however, the single greatest influence in American Jewish music was Israel. Of three albums of Jewish music produced that year, two included or were devoted to dances and songs from the new state. On one, Bernstein and other Jewish composers arranged traditional horas (circle dances) for orchestra and voices. Israel itself helped to bring out new music by supporting research and documentation of both the folk tunes sung by its pioneers and the European melodies remembered by Jewish refugees in Israel. Thus, through music, American Jews expressed their religious commitments, their aesthetic sense, their desire to learn about the life of once-vibrant, destroyed communities, and their joy in Israel's new spirit.

Three mid-twentieth-century events reshaped Hanukkah into a vibrant occasion widely celebrated. The establishment of the state of Israel in 1948 gave new meaning to Hanukkah's celebration of a fight for Jewish independence. Suddenly a tale over two thousand years old seemed like a modern story. The sharp rise in the birth rate after World War II, sustained for almost fifteen years, made home festivities and occasions for gift-giving to children, both part of Hanukkah customs, especially popular among American Jews. This same baby boom among American Christians enhanced the popularity of Christmas celebrations, and Jews found that Hanukkah suited their need for a timely Jewish occasion to provide their own children with parties, gifts, and celebrations. Finally, by the 1950s, Jews throughout America began to understand the depth of the disaster wrought by the Holocaust. Between 1933 and 1945, most Jewish communities in Europe had been destroyed. Postwar American Jews realized that they constituted the world's largest Jewish community and thus carried a new duty to keep Judaism alive and to aid Jews in need around the world. Just as the United States emerged as a global leader after the war, so its Jews took on a new responsibility for Jewish life. Even minor holidays such as Hanukkah became important.

In America's Jewish religious schools and educational venues of the 1950s, Hanukkah became well understood, meaningful, and popular. Many of the children in these schools lived in new suburbs along the eastern seaboard, or in Chicago, Los Angeles, or in industrial towns. Most Jewish children attended local public schools but many in addition enrolled either in Jewish schools that met after school on weekday afternoons or in Sunday schools. Although slightly more girls than boys received only a Sunday school education, over the course of the 1950s religious training for most Jewish boys and girls increasingly equalized.

In 1951, when Jewish educators met for the first time as a national body, they concluded that their goal was to make American Jewish life creative, culturally vibrant, and spiritual. Hebrew language instruction grew increasingly important as Israel, soon to hold the largest concentration of Jews from around the world, became Judaism's religious and cultural center. American Jewish educators hoped to cultivate a sense of closeness with Jews worldwide while, at the same time, stressing common elements in both Jewish and American culture. American Jewish education was largely elementary education, and educators agreed that it must address the character development and emotional needs of Jewish children. With these changes enrollment in Jewish schools increased faster than the growth in Jewish population. By 1961 almost 80 percent of American Jewish children attended some kind of Jewish school, thus ensuring their socialization into Jewish customs.

American Jews embraced Israel's music because it provided an emblem of Jewish survival. After the Holocaust, Jews everywhere felt less secure. In the United States, although the 1950s is generally remembered as a period when anti-Semitism sharply declined, hundreds of hate crimes against American Jewish institutions during the early 1950s culminated in synagogue bombings in several states during the 1960s. Yet, perhaps because Israel offered the promise of Jewish survival, despite threats of violence, Jewish educators noted that a new feeling of optimism characterized Jewish schools. Emphasizing the spiritual and cultural relationship between the United States and Israel, schools taught Israeli pronunciation of Hebrew (unfamiliar to most American Jews), sent their faculty to seminars on education offered by the Hebrew University in Jerusalem, published more educational material in Hebrew, and reinforced all these new skills and values with Israeli music.

Hanukkah songs of this period expressed these changing values and attitudes. Because Jewish educators needed a broad selection of songs, appropriate to students of many ages and abilities, which would enrich a varied curriculum, new songs were written and new compilations of songs were published. Since the 1930s, new songs for young children had been written by Jewish educators to engage young children in Hanukkah play and teach about the holiday. Songs became a focus for school group activities, by asking children to act out parts as candles shining in a menorah, spinning tops, or potato pancakes frying in a pan. Record albums with these songs often were given as Hanukkah gifts to children. Thus from very young ages, American Jewish children learned to eagerly anticipate Hanukkah. These songs helped postwar families tending the "baby boom" turn American Hanukkah into a child-centered holiday.

At the same time, new collections of Hanukkah songs expressing a wider range of meanings were provided for young adults. One 1939 collection of 225 Jewish songs included only six Hanukkah melodies, but among them was a ditty that became prominent in postwar Hanukkah celebrations. Originally offered in Hebrew, "Who Can Retell?" never mentions God. Instead it claims that *human* effort has aided Jews in every age. Indeed, its final line asserts that, although heroes saved Jews in the past, all Jews must now "arise" and save themselves, suggesting that only collective effort will be effective in the modern world.

These new songs helped to inculcate an activist attitude. Record albums and songbooks, whose tunes helped children to act out a pancake sizzling in a pan of oil, also asked them to march like a Maccabee, be brave and strong, and to beat a drum. As these children grew older, they might be ready to answer the call to action of "Who Can Retell?" With this new song, the literal meaning of Hanukkah, dedication, expanded. Formerly, Hanukkah celebrated the rededication of the Jerusalem Temple and God's aid to ancient Jews defending Judaism. After the Holocaust, Hanukkah inspired contemporary Jews to dedicate themselves to defending Jews everywhere.

"Who Can Retell?" stresses human responsibility and appeared in American songbooks as part of a collection compiled by the Society for the Advancement of Judaism, the forerunner of Reconstructionist Judaism, a denomination that embraces a humanist approach to religion. Its spritely melody, sung in a round, creates an impression of the richness and power of the human voice. That humanist perspective linked Hanukkah with American Jewish postwar efforts to ensure Jewish survival in the United States and in Israel. Another songbook compiler, who described Hanukkah as commemorating the first battle for religious freedom, found "Who Can Retell?" so important that he placed the song immediately after the candle blessings and "Maoz Tsur," whose praise of God's miracles is directly contradicted, rather than including it with a selection of party tunes at the back of the volume. Widely sung in both Hebrew and English, "Who Can Retell?" remained a favorite among American Jews throughout the rest of the century.

By 1950, other American Jewish religious denominations were also publishing songbooks for classroom use that reflected their own religious commitments. The Conservative movement, which grew to be the largest denomination, published the largest collections. Noting the "upsurge of religious feeling . . . during the war years" along with a recent "renaissance of Jewish music," Conservative educators hoped not only to inculcate faith in God but to "spiritually bind Jews together" through song. Although these compilations usually included "Who Can Retell?" it was only one among many songs in Hebrew, Yiddish, and English suitable for children as well as teens and adults. Within five years the Reform movement, whose children spent less time than Conservative children in religious schools, published a smaller songster that included an entire Hanukkah worship service modified for American children. It contained only twelve songs, all in English, including both Gottheil's "Rock of Ages" and "Who Can Retell?"

As Jews moved to the suburbs after World War II, Hanukkah became an occasion for synagogue parties and pageants sponsored by men's clubs or other groups. At these occasions, children would be called on to light candles, lead in singing Hanukkah songs, and perform original dramatic works on the holiday's theme. These events made Hanukkah into an important social and communal occasion that brought together Jewish children, families, and religious communities.

Not all American Jews embraced this humanistic and activist trend. When Orthodox educators brought out an album of holiday songs for Jewish children in 1962, after "Who Can Retell?" had won a wide audience, the song was omitted. These teachers taught the "joy of religion, love of torah, and delight in the wondrous world that G-d has made." For these Brooklynites, the best way to defend Judaism was through faith in God. A mother and daughter team wrote or arranged many of the tunes. Their photos, along with those of the children in their classes who performed on the album, were prominently displayed on the cover. To assure Orthodox purchasers that the album upheld traditional values, brief biographies proving both the piety and the musical accomplishment of every adult who worked on the project filled the back cover.

Although Hanukkah was propelled to prominence during the 1950s largely on the strength of its appeal to the many children in postwar families, recordings of Jewish music for adults that included Hanukkah songs also found a wide audience. Soon after World War II, American Jews embraced Hanukkah as a celebration of religious liberty whose meaning, they felt, embraced America's defeat of Nazism. For them, Hanukkah was an American holiday. One of the first albums of Jewish holiday music to appear in the early 1950s appealed to its audience's patriotism as well as its piety. Marketed to the American Jewish family, the cover art blended images from both Jewish tradition and contemporary postwar America. Above a depiction of a Torah opened for reading, red-lettered text assured listeners that its songs and stories were authoritative and rabbinically approved by all major American Jewish denominations. A black-and-white photo of a family—dad, mom, and daughter, all boasting blond hair and hats—looked up toward the Torah from the cover's bottom right corner. The Hammond Organ Company's advertising office, who provided the photo, also used it in their brochures for church groups. A booklet inserted in the album explained that "the lights of Chanukah stand for the achievement of religious liberty."

Although the trend began in earlier materials, by the mid 1950s Hanukkah took root in American culture, as recordings of Jewish holiday music marketed to adults boasted their artistic quality rather than their religious or patriotic appeal. Album covers listed vocalists' credits, musicians' accomplishments, and composers' successes. Many vocalists either had performed on the professional stage or were cantors who had achieved fame in television or radio. Composers and musicians performed at Carnegie Hall, served as musical directors for television stations, or wrote for the Broadway theater. Because New York was home to television, radio, opera, theater, concert halls, and the record industry, as well as the country's largest Jewish community, Jewish music albums produced there often featured highly talented individuals. When Jews around the country purchased recordings made in New York, they were promised "New York quality."

American Jews of the 1950s found meaning for their own time and experiences in Hanukkah, and Hanukkah maintained its malleable quality as the century progressed. As Hanukkah was shaped into a central holiday marking Jewish identity amid ever more elaborate Christmas celebrations, it became an occasion for activities that brought Jews together as families, synagogue members, club members, and neighbors. Hanukkah songs became a centerpiece for both specialized activities designed for specific age groups and for intergenerational gatherings. These melodies reflect the cultural roots and interests that American Jews have found meaningful. Israel's emergence on the heels of the Holocaust and America's victory in World War II transformed Hanukkah from a historic commemoration into an occasion for hope. Melodies from a now-lost European culture (to which most American Jews traced their family origins) slowly were replaced by Israeli songs that inspired American Jews and assuaged their grief. Slowly but inevitably, American Jews replaced their familiar pronunciation of Hebrew, the northern European dialect they heard their parents use, with the Israeli pronunciation they learned in religious school, sang in Hanukkah and other sorts of songs, and used on visits to Israel. As Hebrew became a living language again, so Hanukkah songs were enlivened to reflect contemporary tastes, values, and rhythms.

The sources of the songs printed here are as follows: "Chanukah, O Chanukah" and "My Dreidl," in Harry Coopersmith, *The Songs We Sing* (New York: United Synagogue of America, 1950) reprinted with permission of the United Synagogue of Conservative Judaism; "Maoz Tsur," or "Rock of My Salvation," translated by Emily Solis-Cohen, in *When Love Passed By and Other Poems* (1929) and in Emily Solis-Cohen, *Hanukkah* (Philadelphia: Jewish Publication Society, 1937); "Rock of Ages," in *Union Songster/Shiru Ladonay* (New York: Central Conference of American Rabbis, 1955); "Hear the Voice of Israel's Elders," in *Neighborhood Center Club Leader Guide* (Philadelphia, 1946) Philadelphia Jewish Archives, Neighborhood Center Collection, box 7, folder 12; "Maccabee March," words and music by Shirley R. Cohen, "Chanukah Music Box" (Kinor Records, 1951); "Mi Yimalel:

Who Can Retell?" in Harry Coopersmith, *The Songs We Sing* (New York: United Synagogue of America, 1950) reprinted with permission of the United Synagogue of Conservative Judaism.

Further Reading

Theodore Gaster, *Festivals of the Jewish Year* (New York: William Morrow, 1953); Yael Zerubavel, *Recovered Roots: Collective Memory and the Making of Israeli National Tradition* (Chicago: University of Chicago Press, 1995); Shlomo Deshen, Charles S. Liebman, and Moshe Shokeid, *Israeli Judaism: The Sociology of Religion in Israel* (New Brunswick, N.J.: Transaction, 1995), Theodor H. Gaster, *Purim and Hanukkah in Custom and Tradition* (New York: Schuman, 1950); Ruth Eis, *Hanukkah Lamps of the Judah L. Magnes Museum* (Berkeley, Calif.: Judah L. Magnes Museum, 1977); David Roskies, *The Jewish Search for a Useable Jewish Past* (Bloomington: Indiana University Press, 1999); Jack Wertheimer, *A People Divided* (New York: Basic Books, 1990); Jack Wertheimer, ed., *The Uses of Tradition: Jewish Continuity in the Modern Era* (New York: Jewish Theological Seminary, 1992).

Chanukah, O Chanukah

Chanukah, O Chanukah,
Come light the menorah.
Let's have a party,
We'll all dance the *hora*.

Gather round the table,
I'll give you a treat.
Dreidls to play with and *latke* to eat.

And while we are dancing
The candles are burning low.
One for each night
They shed a sweet light
To remind us of days long ago.
One for each night
They shed a sweet light
To remind us of days long ago.

My Dreidl

I have a little dreidl
I made it out of clay

And when it's dry and ready
then dreidl I shall play.

Oh! Dreidl, dreidl, dreidl
I made it out of clay
And when it's dry and ready
Then dreidl I shall play.

Maoz Tsur (Rock of My Salvation)

Mighty, praised beyond compare,
    Rock of my salvation
Build again my house of prayer,
    For Thy habitation!
Offering and libation, shall a ransomed nation
    Joyful bring
    There, and sing
Psalms of dedication!

Woe was mine in Egypt-land,
    (Tyrant kings enslaved me);
Till Thy mighty, out-stretched Hand
    From oppression saved me.
Pharoah, rash pursuing, vowed my swift undoing—
    Soon, his host
    That proud boast
'Neath the waves was rueing!

To Thy Holy Hill, the way
    Madest Thou clear before me;
With false gods I went astray—
    Foes to exile bore me.
Torn from all I cherished, almost had I perished—
    Babylon fell,
    Ze-er-ru-ba-bel
Badest Thou to restore me!

The vengeful Haman wrought
    Subtly, to betray me;
In his snare himself he caught—
    He that plann'd to slay me.
(Hailed from Esther's palace; hanged on his own gallows!)
    Seal and ring
    Persia's king
Gave Thy servant zealous.

When the brave Asmoneans [Hasmoneans = Maccabees] broke
   Javan's chain in sunder
Through the holy oil, Thy folk
   Didst Thou show a wonder—
Ever full remained the vessel unprofaned;
   These eight days
   Lights and praise,
Therefore were ordained.

Lord, Thy Holy Arm make bare,
   Speed my restoration;
To my martyr's blood Thy care—
   Judge each guilty nation.
Long is my probation; sore my tribulation—
   Bid, from Heaven,
   Thy shepherds seven
Haste to my salvation!

Rock of Ages
Gustav Gottheil

Rock of Ages, let our song
Praise Thy saving power;
Thou, amidst the raging foes,
Wast our shelt'ring tower.
Furious they assailed us,
But thine arm availed us.
And thy word
Broke their sword
When our own strength failed us.

Kindling new the holy lamps,
Priests approved in suffering,
Purified the nation's shrine,
Brought to God their offering.
And His courts surrounding
Hear, in joy abounding,
Happy throngs
Singing songs
With a mighty sounding.

Children of the martyr race,
Whether free or fettered,
Wake the echoes of the songs
Where ye may be scattered.

Yours the message cheering,
That the time is nearing
which shall see
All men free,
Tyrants disappearing.

Hear the Voice of Israel's Elders

Hear the voice of Israel's elders
Calling on Judea's sons
Who will be the future leaders
When the older men are gone?
Who will do what we have started,
Bring the Jew to ancient station?
Who will urge the weary hearted,
Fight for right to live a nation?

Maccabee March

One, two, three, four,
One, two, three, four,
Take your drum and march and sing along with me.
One, two, three, four,
Step, two, three,
Everyone can be a Maccabee.

Brave and strong,
Come march along.
We've lots to do before the day is done.
Chanukah time is here again.
Happy holiday to everyone!

Mi Yimalel: Who Can Retell?

(Round—group 2 begins the song when group 1 has reached the asterisk.)

Who can retell
The things that befell us?
Who can count them?*

In every age
A hero or sage,
Came to our aid!

Hark! In days of yore, in Israel's ancient land,
Brave Maccabeus led the faithful band.
But now all Israel must as one arise,
Redeem itself thru deed and sacrifice.

—8—

Freedom Songs and

the Civil Rights Movement

Paul Harvey

"You sing the songs which symbolize transformation, which make that revolution of courage inside you," an activist said of the singing that was an integral part of the civil rights movement, the great black freedom struggle of the 1950s and 1960s. The ordinary citizens who made up the rank-and-file of the black freedom struggle empowered themselves through song to a degree exceeding that of any protest movement in American history. During the civil rights movement, singing sustained black protestors through years of turmoil. As Martin Luther King, Jr., suggested, freedom songs played "a strong and vital role in our struggle. . . . I think they keep alive a faith, a radiant hope in the future."

The civil rights movement had legislative aims, and to that extent it was a political movement. It was more than that, however; it was also a religious movement sustained by the deeply Protestant religious imagery and fervor of southern black churches. As one female sharecropper and civil rights activist in Mississippi explained her conversion to the movement, "Something hit me like a new religion." Many activists, both white and black, experienced conversions, moments when the grim reality of southern racism hit them like the blinding light that felled the apostle Paul on the road to Damascus. The civil rights movement was also religious in its rituals of mass meetings, revivalistic preaching to inspire activism, and, most especially, in its singing. The thoughts of Pat Watters, a white journalist, kept returning to "the powerful pounding of the music of the mass meetings as a counterpoint to my words of discovery and analysis." He wrote of the "mystical, inspired and excited, ecstatic—and reverent mood of those meetings," an experience that helped him overcome his own fears derived from a conventionally racist childhood. It was only in these churches that he "experienced real religious feeling, in a lifetime within the South's church-oriented society."

Freedom songs arose in a variety of ritual contexts. Most familiarly, they came at the beginning and end of mass meetings, as civil rights organizers allowed the large crowds to energize themselves with song. Traditional Protestant hymns, familiar especially to older black folk raised in church, often began the services. Newer freedom songs increasingly took their place as the movement progressed. Sometimes the music was accompanied with piano or organ, sounding much like Protestant hymn-singing on Sunday mornings. Often, especially in places dominated by students and younger participants, the music was a cappella, with spirited hand clapping and foot stomping providing the rhythmic force that propelled the music forward. Freedom songs transmitted movement culture itself, as mass meetings became in effect mass singing and praying conventions.

Freedom songs were accompanied by swaying, singing, shouting, foot stomping, and other bodily movement and rhythmic accompaniment, a legacy of the rituals of black religious song dating from the antebellum spirituals and ring shouts. Historically, the spirituals exalted Old Testament heroes such as Moses as well as more obscure figures, and often turned New Testament figures such as Jesus into Old Testament avenging heroes. These biblical heroes were available in the present day because the slaves' sacred world invoked a kind of "eternal now." Sacred time merged with real time. In this sense, the freedom songs recaptured and revitalized the black folk religious song tradition, updating lyrics and settings while also importing the resolve and spirit to persevere and triumph over the hosts of Pharaoh—now understood to be Ross Barnett, George Wallace, and the other functionaries of the Jim Crow regime. The freedom songs grew from the roots of the black church. The very fact that the lyrics were easily adaptable was fully in accord with the black folk song tradition, in which communal call-and-responses encouraged individual creativity in lining out new verses to familiar tunes and themes. The popular theology contained in the traditional songs, moreover, held out the promise of freedom—a theme easily captured, updated, and made more urgent in the civil rights movement era.

Jailhouses also served as a prime center and motivating force for freedom songs. As civil rights protestors filled southern jail cells, they sang to each other, consciously modeling themselves on Paul and Silas in the New Testament. Activists sang to each other and to the sheriffs arresting them as they filed into police vehicles for transport to jail. To no avail, prison guards threatened protestors with physical harm if they did not stop singing and praying. Jail cells themselves became creative centers from which dozens of new verses to freedom songs spontaneously arose. Picket and boycott lines became another ritual center, as did mass marches down city streets in Birmingham, Selma, and dozens of other locations.

In 1954 the Supreme Court issued its epochal *Brown v. Board of Education* decision mandating an end to the facade of "separate but equal" education. Separate educational facilities, the justices unanimously ruled, were inherently unequal. During the same year, black residents of Montgomery, Alabama, organized to protest separate and unequal rules that governed bus transportation in their city. They initially sought not an end to segregation on the bus lines but simply more fair and equal treatment for black citizens riding segregated bus lines. The city resisted. In short order, the black community mobilized. A seamstress named Rosa Parks refused to give up her seat to a white passenger and was arrested. Civil rights organizers deliberately portrayed Parks as a humble working woman who simply was tired. In fact, Parks had been trained in civil rights activism through her work with the NAACP and her visits to the Highlander Folk School, an institute in Tennessee run by a white radical organizer named Myles Horton. At Highlander, Parks was introduced to a hymn used by the labor movement earlier in the century, one that would soon emerge as the anthem of the civil rights movement: "We Shall Overcome." And at a mass meeting held to protest Parks's arrest, Martin Luther King and his ministerial associate Ralph Abernathy led parishioners in the refrain from "Leaning on the Everlasting Arms," a gospel hymn from the nineteenth century.

Singing freedom songs made up a critical aspect of the civil rights movement from its very inception in the 1950s. Mass meetings held to organize civil rights protests began with songs and then proceeded to the business of the meeting. Freedom songs often ended these meetings, providing that last bit of spiritual fortitude needed to face the hostile racism outside. Freedom songs soothed congregants surrounded by rampaging whites, National Guardsmen, and tear gas. Songs fortified marchers as they tramped down streets. Freedom songs accompanied the ordinary black working men and women who stayed off the buses in Montgomery, Alabama, for over one year in 1955 and 1956. Freedom songs sustained the thousands of ordinary black citizens who faced jail time for the audacious act of trying to exercise their constitutionally protected rights.

Freedom songs came to full fruition in the 1960s, especially with the formation of the Student Non-Violent Coordinating Committee (SNCC). Movement activists in SNCC were masters at taking traditional church anthems and spirituals and converting them into sung versions of civil rights manifestos. This was first evidenced in the Freedom Rides of the spring of 1961. An interracial group of thirteen freedom riders from the Congress of Racial Equality and SNCC set out on a fateful Greyhound bus trip from Washington, D.C., intending to ride down to North Carolina and then westward through the Deep South—Georgia, Alabama, Mississippi—before heading south again to end up in New Orleans. The riders met only limited resistance until they hit Alabama, where mobs firebombed one bus in Anniston and attacked a group of riders in Birmingham (while local police conspicuously absented themselves). Several riders, including two whites, took severe beatings. Despite the Kennedy administration's advice to stage a "cooling-off period," the riders insisted on continuing, wanting to make their way from Birmingham to Jackson, Mississippi. As they traveled the road to Mississippi, they took up a renewed version of a song used in black protest movements since at least the 1940s, "Hallelujah, I'm A-Traveling." They sang

I'm paying my fare on the Greyhound bus lines.
I'm riding the front seat to Jackson this time.
Hallelujah, I'm a-traveling,
Hallelujah, ain't it fine,
Hallelujah, I'm a traveling,
Down freedom's main line.

The concluding verse told a bit of civil rights history:

> In Nineteen Fifty-four, the Supreme Court has said,
> Looka here, Mr. Jim Crow, it's time you were dead.
> Hallelujah, I'm a-traveling, . . .

Upon the riders' arrival in Jackson, state authorities (who had made a deal with the Kennedy administration) escorted the riders to jail. In Mississippi, "jail" sometimes meant the city penitentiary and sometimes places such as Parchman Farm, a gigantic and brutal convict labor farm in the Mississippi Delta, controlled by the state's notoriously racist senator, James O. Eastland. As the riders sat in jail, however, they followed the example of Paul and Silas in the New Testament, singing through the evenings. True to form, jail authorities tried to stop the singing, in some cases taking away mattresses as punishment. But the riders kept on, singing verses such as

> Freedom, freedom, freedom's coming, and it won't be long
> Freedom, freedom, freedom's coming, and it won't be long

Freedom riders took up an old gospel song, "I Woke Up This Morning with My Mind Stayed on Jesus," and converted the tune to their own uses: "Woke up this morning with my mind (My mind it was) stayed on freedom." While in jail, Bob Zellner, an SNCC activist and son of a white Methodist minister from Alabama invented new verses such as "Ain't no harm in keep'n' your mind, / In keepin' it stayed on freedom," and "Singin' and prayin' with my mind, / My mind it was stayed on freedom."

The Albany, Georgia, movement in 1961 and 1962 was best known for its singing. Indeed, Albany was the mother lode of freedom song (and home to Bernice Johnson Reagon, founder of the a cappella group Sweet Honey in the Rock, which in recent years has kept alive traditional forms of black singing that ranged from spirituals to freedom songs). For months in 1961 and 1962, blacks in Albany, a small town in southwest Georgia, protested Jim Crow. For much of this time, the well-known national movement leaders—Martin Luther King, Andrew Young, and others—were absent. The movement was sustained instead by the actions of thousands of ordinary black citizens. The black churches of Albany provided the organizing base and the spiritual inspiration for the movement. Thus, the movement in Albany provides an excellent case study in the nature of freedom songs themselves.

Derived from hymns and folk music, freedom songs were adaptable to a variety of movement purposes. Black churches for years had sung "Don't You Let Nobody Turn You 'Roun'":

> Don't you let nobody turn you 'roun',
> Turn you 'roun'
> Don't you let nobody turn you 'roun',
> Keep the straight an' the narrow way.

In the Albany movement, civil rights protestors faced a dilemma. Historically, movement leaders baited local authorities by breaking local segregation laws, anticipating that the federal government would intervene and trump segregationist local law by applying federal civil rights statutes or the Fourteenth Amendment. In Albany, however, the judicial system proved to be a hindrance rather than an ally. The local sheriff of Albany, Laurie Pritchett, understood that civil rights activists planned to break local laws and fill the jails with the intent of creating a crisis. He also understood that the movement wanted confrontation with local authorities. Pritchett refused to provide it. Instead, he allowed strictly regulated street protests for a limited period of time and then secured a federal court injunction against further protests. This was a turning point for the movement, for now civil rights activists had to break the federal court order. They continued protesting and filling up jails, and freedom songs, especially "Ain't Gonna Let Nobody Turn Me 'Roun'," became anthems of empowerment. "Ain't gonna let nobody turn me 'roun'," they sang. "I'm gonna keep on a-walkin', / "Keep on a-talkin', / Marching up to freedom land." As they walked the streets, and as police officers led them into paddy wagons, protestors sang endless variations on the verses. "Ain't gonna let Chief Pritchett, / Turn me 'roun', turn me 'roun', turn me 'roun'," a group of young women sang as officers escorted them into police vehicles for transport to jail. "Ain't gonna let no injunction, / Turn me 'roun', turn me 'roun', turn me 'roun'," they sang upon hearing of the federal court order against their demonstrations.

In the jail of Doughery County, civil rights protestors took up a traditional spiritual entitled "Rocking Jerusalem":

> O Mary O Martha O Mary ring dem bells
> I hear arch angels a-rockin' Jerusalem
> I hear arch angels a-ringin' dem bells,
> Church gettin' higher!
> Rockin' Jerusalem!
> Church gettin' higher!
> Ring-a dem bells.

Sitting in Chief Pritchett's jails, young activists sang "O, Pritchett, O, Kelley, O, Pritchett, open them cells" and endless variations on the theme, such as "I hear God's children cryin' for mercy, I hear God's children, prayin' in jail" and "I hear God's children you know they're suff'rin', I hear God's children, prayin' in jail."

Following the Albany campaign, which ended inconclusively, civil rights organizers turned their attention to Birmingham, Alabama, a city known for its brutality and racism. Birmingham's de facto ruler was the city police chief, Theophilus "Bull" Connor, who had made his career refining tactics of racial repression and police terrorism. A black minister in the town named Fred Shuttlesworth, who had endured years of bombings and racial harassment from Klansmen and policemen, encouraged Martin Luther King and his organization (the Southern Christian Leadership Conference) to attack segregated institutions in Birmingham. During the campaign, in the spring of 1963, the movement reached an impasse when boycotts failed to open city stores, and support from the adult community grew tepid. Civil rights organizers responded with a new tactic, referred to as the "children's crusade." Soon, hundreds of black schoolchildren were marching, being arrested, and filling up the city's jails, creating a renewed crisis that forced the city to the negotiating table. Again, freedom songs empowered protestors. "I'm on my way, to freedom land, / Oh yes, oh Lord, I'm on my way," the children sang while lining up to be carted off in police wagons.

> If my mother don't go, I'll go anyhow,
> If my mother don't go, I'll go anyhow.
> If my mother don't go, I'll go anyhow,
> Oh yes, oh Lord, I'm on my way.
> I'm on my way, to freedom land. . . .

A final example of the role of freedom songs came during the Mississippi Freedom Summer in 1964. Freedom Summer arose from SNCC's efforts to dramatize the difficulties of voter registration for tens of thousands of black Mississippians, residents of a state so deeply entrenched in racism that other civil rights groups had been fearful of attacking segregation there. The white Mississippi establishment lived up to its reputation of brutality. The state formed a "Sovereignty Commission" to provide a state-sanctioned way to conduct harassment and terrorism against civil rights organizers, dubbed "outside agitators" by hostile whites. Shortly after the beginning of Freedom Summer, as hundreds of college student volunteers from across the country descended on the state, three civil rights workers (two out-of-state whites and one black Mississippian) turned up dead. While driving to investigate the burning of a black church, they had been kidnapped by Klansmen (who had recieved the activists' license plate number from state authorities), murdered, and buried deep in an earthen dam just outside the local town of Philadelphia.

But Mississippi also had a coterie of ordinary black citizens who were extraordinarily courageous in the face of the most intense racial terrorism experienced by the movement. One particularly legendary figure was a sharecropper from Ruleville, Mississippi, named Fannie Lou Hamer. Mrs. Hamer endured beatings and torture in county jails after attempting to register to vote in the early 1960s. In 1964, Hamer became a nationally known spokeswoman for the Mississippi Freedom Democratic Party, an interracial group of Mississippians who traveled to the Democratic National Convention to challenge the credentials of the "regular" (and all-white) Democratic party delegation. At the convention, Freedom Party personnel refused to accept a compromise proffered by Democratic party authorities, insisting that they represented the true Democratic party. Queried by reporters on her feelings, Hamer responded with an impromptu speech that captured the sentiment of rank-and-file participants in the movement, pointing out that black Mississippians still risked their lives simply trying to vote. "I question America," she concluded. Hamer led the participants in her favorite freedom song, "This Little Light of Mine," a tune belted out by Sunday schoolers everywhere. In Hamer's version, and in the verses added by movement activists depending on the needs of various situations, the sweet song became a manifesto of freedom:

> This-a little light of mine,
> I'm gonna let it shine, let it shine,
> Let it shine, let it shine.
> We've got the light of freedom,
> We're gonna let it shine. . . .
> Tell Chief Pritchett,
> I'm gonna let it shine. . . .
> All over the state of Georgia,
> We're gonna let it shine. . . .
> Voting for my freedom,
> I'm gonna let it shine. . . .

Hamer was known for her inspirational singing, which she, like so many others, drew directly from the music of the black church.

More than any other tune, "We Shall Overcome" became associated with the black freedom struggle, and it symbolized as well the movement's religious, interracial, and nonviolent emphasis up to 1965. The song dates back to the antebellum era, when South Carolina slaves sang a tune entitled "I'll Be Alright," which quickly entered the black sacred music repertoire. Another version of the song, with the words "We Shall Overcome," came out of the labor movement when striking tobacco workers used it in their southern campaigns in the 1940s. From there, folksinger Pete Seeger carried the song through the country, introducing it to civil rights activists at the Highlander Folk School in Tennessee in the 1940s and 1950s. Indeed, it was at Highlander that the tune became identified with civil rights.

> We shall overcome, we shall overcome,
> We shall overcome, someday.
> Oh, deep in my heart, I do believe, that
> We shall overcome, someday.

Later in the 1960s, movement activists replaced "someday" with the more insistent "today." As with the other songs, a seemingly infinite number of verses were added, many spontaneously. Birmingham residents in 1963 sang

> We shall go to jail,
> We shall go to jail,
> We shall go to jail,
> Today. . . .

The turmoil in Birmingham ended in triumph for the Southern Christian Leadership Conference and especially for Martin Luther King. On August 28, 1963, over a quarter million Americans of all races and religions gathered in Washington, D.C. They marched to the Lincoln Memorial and heard King deliver his greatest speech, "I Have a Dream." The march was alive with freedom song, including a concluding benediction of "We Shall Overcome." Two years later, President Lyndon Johnson stood before Congress, urging passage of what became the Voting Rights Act of 1965. He told a national television audience, "And we shall overcome," giving his own imprimatur to the struggles of the movement. In this way, freedom songs symbolized the entire epochal struggle of the civil rights era.

Later in the 1960s, freedom songs gave way to the cries of anguish heard in the urban riots in Watts, Detroit, Newark, and other cities. The themes of Christian nonviolence ceded to music and speeches of a more black nationalist orientation. The religious ritual of the freedom song could not ensure continued unity for a movement that had achieved many of its aims only to find an even more intractable gulf of economic inequality facing it. But the meaning of the freedom songs as rituals of sustenance, encouragement, and healing live on in the memory of the participants. The freedom songs remain some of the most powerful and politically potent ritual music in American history.

Song lyrics are taken from Kerran L. Sanger, "When the Spirit Says Sing": The Role of Freedom Songs in the Civil Rights Movement (New York: Garland, 1995); and Crossing the Danger Water: Four Hundred Years of African-American Writing, edited by Deirdre Mullane (New York: Anchor Books, 1993), pp. 651–56.

Further Reading

Kerran L. Sanger, "When the Spirit Says Sing": The Role of Freedom Songs in the Civil Rights Movement (New York: Garland, 1995); Guy Carawan and Candie Carawan, comps. and eds., Sing for Freedom: The Story of the Civil Rights Movement through Its Songs (Bethlehem, Pa.: Sing Out, 1990); Charles Payne, I've Got the Light of Freedom: The Organizing Tradition and the Mississippi Freedom Struggle (Berkeley and Los Angeles: University of California Press, 1995); Eyes on the Prize (Blackside Production, 1987), film series; Pat Watters, Down to Now: Reflections on the Civil Rights Movement (New York: Pantheon Books, 1971); Voices of Freedom: Songs of the Civil Rights Movement (Folkways Recordings, 1997).

We Shall Overcome

We shall overcome, We shall overcome,
We shall overcome, Someday.
Oh, deep in my heart, I do believe, that
We shall overcome, Someday.

We'll walk hand in hand, We'll walk hand in hand,
We'll walk hand in hand, Someday.
Oh, deep in my heart, I do believe, that
We shall overcome, Someday.

We are not afraid, We are not afraid,
We are not afraid, Oh, no, no, no,
'Cause deep in my heart, I do believe, that
We shall overcome, Someday.

O Freedom

O Freedom!
O Freedom!
O Freedom over me!
And before I'd be a slave,
I'd be buried in my grave,
And go home to my Lord and be free!

No more mournin'
No more weepin'
No more misery over me.
And before I'd be a slave,
I'd be buried in my grave,
And go home to my Lord and be free.

Keep Your Eyes on the Prize

Paul and Silas bound in jail,
Had no money for to go their bail.
Keep your eyes on the prize,
Hold on, hold on.
Hold on, hold on.
Keep your eyes on the prize,
Hold on, hold on.

Paul and Silas begin to shout,
The jail door open and they walked out.
Keep your eyes on the prize,
Hold on, hold on.

Freedom's name is mighty sweet,
Soon one day we're gonna meet.
Keep your eyes on the prize,
Hold on, hold on.

Got my hand on the Gospel plow,
I wouldn't take nothing for my journey now.
Keep your eyes on the prize,
Hold on, hold on.

The only chain that a man can stand,
Is that chain of hand in hand.
Keep your eyes on the prize,
Hold on, hold on.

The only thing that we did wrong,
Stayed in the wilderness a day too long.
Keep your eyes on the prize,
Hold on, hold on.

But the one thing we did right,
Was the day we started to fight.
Keep your eyes on the prize,
Hold on, hold on.

We're gonna board that big Greyhound,
Carryin' love from town to town.
Keep your eyes on the prize,
Hold on, hold on.

We're gonna ride for civil rights,
We're gonna ride both black and white.
Keep your eyes on the prize,
Hold on, hold on.

We've met jail and violence too,
But God's love has seen us through.
Keep your eyes on the prize,
Hold on, hold on.

Haven't been to Heaven but I've been told,
Streets up there are paved with gold.
Keep your eyes on the prize,
Hold on, hold on.

Ain't Gonna Let Nobody Turn Me 'Round

Ain't gonna let nobody, Lordy, turn me 'round,
    Turn me 'round, turn me 'round,
Ain't gonna let nobody turn me 'round,
    I'm gonna keep on a-walkin',
Keep on a-talkin',
Marching up to freedom land.

Ain't gonna let no jail house turn me 'round,
    Turn me 'round, turn me 'round,
Ain't gonna let no jail house turn me 'round,
    I'm gonna keep on a-walkin',

Keep on a-talkin',
Marching up to freedom land.

Ain't gonna let no sheriff turn me 'round,
   Turn me 'round, turn me 'round,
Ain't gonna let no sheriff turn me 'round,
   Turn me 'round, turn me 'round,
Keep on a-talkin',
Marching up to freedom land.

Ain't gonna let Chief Pritchett,
   Turn me 'round, turn me 'round. . . .

I'm on My Way to Freedom Land

I'm on my way, to freedom land,
I'm on my way, to freedom land.
I'm on my way, to freedom land,
Oh yes, oh Lord, I'm on my way.

If my mother don't go, I'll go anyhow,
If my mother don't go, I'll go anyhow.
If my mother don't go, I'll go anyhow,
Oh yes, oh Lord, I'm on my way.

Hallelujah, I'm A-Traveling
Civil Rights Version

Stand up and rejoice, a great day is here.
We're fighting Jim Crow and the vic'try is near.

Chorus:
Hallelujah, I'm a-traveling,
Hallelujah, ain't it fine,
Hallelujah, I'm a-traveling,
Down freedom's main line.

I'm paying my fare on the Greyhound bus line.
I'm riding the front seat to Jackson this time.
Chorus

In Nashville, Tennessee, I can order a coke.
The waitress at Woolworth's knows it's no joke.
Chorus

I walked in Montgomery, I sat in Tennessee,
And now I'm riding for equality
Chorus

I'm traveling to Mississippi on the Greyhound bus lines.
Hallelujah, I'm a-riding the front seat this time.
In old Fayette County, set off and remote,
The polls are now open for Negroes to vote.

In Nineteen Fifty-four, the Supreme Court has said,
Looka here, Mr. Jim Crow, it's time you were dead.

(Everybody Says) Freedom
Civil Rights Version

(Everybody says) Freedom
(Everybody says) Freedom
(Everybody says) Freedom, freedom, freedom.

(In the cottonfield) Freedom,
(In the schoolroom) Freedom,
(In the jailhouse) Freedom, freedom, freedom.

(Everybody says) Civil rights. . . .
(All across the South) Freedom. . . .
(In Mississippi) Freedom. . . .

Woke Up This Morning with My Mind on Freedom

Woke up this morning with my mind
(My mind it was) Stayed on freedom,
(Oh yes I) Woke up this morning with my mind
Stayed on freedom,
(Well I) Woke up this morning with my mind
(My mind it was) Stayed on freedom,
Hallelu, hallelu, hallelu, hallelu,
Hallelujah!

Ain't no harm in keep'n' your mind,
In keepin' it stayed on freedom. . . .

Walkin' and talkin' with my mind
My mind it was stayed on freedom. . . .

Interlude:
You got to walk walk,

You got to walk walk,
You got to walk with your mind on freedom,
You got to talk talk,
You got to talk talk,
You got to talk with your mind on freedom,
Oh oh oh you got to walk walk, talk talk.

Singin' and prayin' with my mind,
My mind it was stayed on freedom. . . .

This Little Light of Mine

This-a little light of mine,
I'm gonna let it shine (oh)
This little light of mine,
I'm gonna let it shine, let it shine,
Let it shine, let it shine.

We've got the light of freedom,
We're gonna let it shine. . . .

Deep down in the South
We're gonna let it shine. . . .

Down in Birmingham (Mississippi, Alabama, etc.),
We're gonna let it shine. . . .

Everywhere I go,
I'm gonna let it shine. . . .

Tell Chief Pritchett,
I'm gonna let it shine. . . .

All in the jail house,
I'm gonna let it shine. . . .

All over the state of Georgia. . . .

All over the southland. . . .
All over America. . . .

—— 9 ——

Folk Music in the Catholic Mass

Mark Oppenheimer

By the 1960s, American Catholics realized that they were no longer on the margins of American ethnic or religious life. Although the "Catholic question" was asked of Senator John F. Kennedy as he sought to occupy the Oval Office—could someone loyal to a pope in Rome be entrusted with the federal government?—he answered it to most Americans' satisfaction. In 1960 Kennedy was elected our thirty-fifth, and first Catholic, president. The work of sociologists such as Andrew Greeley was demonstrating that young Catholics had achieved income and education parity with Protestants. Most important, the Second Vatican Council revolutionized the style of Catholic worship, unmooring it from some hallowed traditions but also lowering the walls separating Roman Catholicism from mainline Protestantism. Although many Protestants and Jews hardly noticed the changes, Catholics themselves began to think of their faith and rituals in a new light.

The Second Vatican Council, or Vatican II as it is popularly known, was called in 1959 by Pope John XXIII and met from 1962 to 1965 (by which time Pope Paul VI had succeeded the late John). The bishops who attended its sessions hoped to fulfill John's charge to usher the church into modernity. In that spirit of *aggiornamento,* or "updating," the Council promulgated sixteen documents generally meant to foster an ecumenical spirit and to urge Catholics to see the world as a partner in dialogue rather than a threat to an insular church. Most noticeable, though, were the changes in the liturgy. The Latin Mass was now replaced by the vernacular tongue of the congregants. No longer would the priest officiate with his back to the parishioners; instead he would face them in a spirit of familiarity. And no longer would the laity see themselves as servants of an irreproachable hierarchy; they were now encouraged to speak and be heard.

President Kennedy, Pope John XXIII, and the message of Vatican II ensured that American Catholics would be bolder both within their church and without. That spirit was enhanced by turns in American culture. The Civil Rights movement, the free speech activism of college students, and the effect of youth culture—rock and roll music, sexual libertinism, and drug experimentation—affected Catholics, too.

These cultural changes pushed the freedom allowed by Vatican II to its limits. The Vatican II bishops had hardly set foot in their home dioceses before they had to cope with "folk masses." Folk masses could take many forms, but they often included, in addition to folk music, priests in casual clothing; communal, circular seating; worship in people's houses, rather than in churches; and popular instruments like the guitar, fiddle, or flute, rather than just an organ and choir.

These masses still included the traditional elements: prayers, including the Apostles' Creed; readings from the Old and New Testaments; and the ingestion of the Eucharist, the wafer and wine that represent the body and blood of Christ. Historically, church music, interspersed throughout the other elements of the mass, had included Gregorian chants or psalms set to classical music. In the folk masses, however, guitar music became especially commonplace, bringing the feel of the protest rally to the church nave. "I can remember attending those first parish 'folk masses' back in the 1960s," the musicologist Thomas Day writes. "At the entrance they sang *Michael, Row Your Boat Ashore*. At the Offertory [the giving of the Eucharist] there was *Kumbaya*. A somewhat nervous clergy, not quite sure of what it should do with the folk believers, often put them 'downstairs' in the basement church. . . . Back in those days (the 1960s), all signs indicated that nothing would stop the 'downstairs' revolution."

In exceptional cases, the masses got more colorful still: Thomas Day describes a "basketball mass," during which the local hoops team dribbled balls; Catholic music publisher Dan Onley calls the decade an era "when swinging young priests in turtlenecks used beer and pretzels for Eucharist and said for us to read 'anything meaningful' for the Word, including the sayings of Chairman Mao." But surely this was unusual; what united folk masses were an informality and popular mood that were reflected in the music, much of which was original. Catholic folk singer/songwriters, such as Joe Wise, Sister Miriam Therese Winter and the Medical Mission Sisters, Skip Sanders, and Carey Landry, wrote hymnody that was closer to Bob Dylan than to the Gregorian chants of European cathedrals.

Today, with thirty years' hindsight, we can see that there was no revolution in the mass; Latin gave way to people's native tongues, informality became acceptable. Nevertheless, the replacement of old chants and classical arrangements was of profound psychological importance. The old ways were old indeed, and more important, they were revered. Symbolic gestures as part of worship played a part in the religious formation of most Catholics. Catholics made the sign of the cross, they bowed and genuflected, they struck their breasts with their closed fists. However, from the reformers' perspective, reverence and obligation were stressed by such movements while beauty and emotion were ignored or hardly mentioned. Reformers rejected such empty gestures as "old church."

The new music, then, made the experience of the mass seem exciting and strange by introducing new gestures. Instead of sitting, standing, and kneeling, there might be swaying in a circle. The music might, on occasion, be accompanied by interpretive dance or drumming. Such new innovations had to be democratic; even interpretive dance, a specialized art form, should not be restricted to the artist any more than singing would be limited to a professional musician. In other words, *anybody* should feel free to jump in and perform.

To a people reared on a mass conducted entirely by the male priest, aided by male altar boys, *anybody* meant, most remarkably, women. Only priests could give communion or perform other sacramental rites—Vatican II had not changed that. But many of the new traditions being inaugurated, especially folk music, had no sexual preferences. Women could play guitar and lead songs, just as men could. In the late 1960s and early 1970s, there was also a strong push by some female Catholics to allow the ordination of women priests. Even the Vatican's own biblical commission examined the subject and found no prohibition in the Bible against women priests. While women still were kept from ordination, they did have more than the convent to which to turn. After the Second Vatican Council women could exercise actual ceremonial duties by leading parts of experimental Catholic liturgies. By aligning themselves even in some small way with the surging feminist movement, new styles of mass could seem (to their supporters) like radical political statements or (to their opponents) "a thing . . . of youth culture fads instead of ancient rites," as Garry Wills writes.

Nobody had a greater role in spreading these "fads" than the songwriters. Initially, their songs were distributed on the inky blue mimeographs that powered radicals and innovators before the advent of the Xerox machine. Eventually, the songwriters discovered copyrights and publishing, sometimes by accident. "Clarence Rivers was a black priest from the a cappella tradition," Joe Wise (b. 1939), an early Catholic folk composer who now lives in Arizona, remembers about his early benefactor of circa 1966. "He was in Memphis, and he heard my music, and he gave me three thousand dollars of his own money. He said, 'If you don't sell enough to pay me back, fine. If you do earn the money, pay me back without interest.' It was an awesome gift." Wise made a monaural demo tape, later found a publisher, quit his job running a coffee shop, and toured with his music and records. Eventually, publishers like G.I.A., Pastoral Arts Associates, and Oregon Catholic Press came to specialize in Catholic folk music.

Some Catholics disapproved of the new music, believing that it demeaned the mass, shifted the liturgical focus away from God, severed important links with tradition, or simply failed as art. In 1967, when the conservative political writer William F. Buckley's sister Aloise died, the family requested and received a Latin mass. Both Buckley and Thomas Day note that, in the nearly forty years since Vatican II, Catholics have never taken to singing aloud with anything like the Protestant fervor. Still, in certain sizable precincts, the folk music endures.

Reprinted here are songs by Joe Wise and Sister Miriam Therese Winter (b. 1938), who in the 1960s led the singing Medical Mission Sisters and who is now a professor at Hartford Seminary. Wise and Winter remain two of the most appreciated, and best-selling, Catholic folk singers. Winter's "Joy Is Like the Rain" (which alludes to Luke 8:22–27) was written in 1965. Wise's "Take Our Bread" came a year later and his "Lord, Teach Us to Pray" four years after that. Also included are two songs by Ed Gutfreund (b. 1946) that became popular somewhat later, in the 1970s. Gutfreund wrote in Cincinnati, which had an extremely active Catholic counterculture, including a parish, the Community of Hope, specially created for Catholics in the archdiocese who wanted nontraditional masses.

Accompanied by the guitar, all three writers' songs draw heavily on the folk tradition, in both melodies and lyrical tropes. All the songs feature, for example, the symbolism of nature, weather, and the earth's bounty. When Winter sang "I saw raindrops on my window" or Wise sang "Spirit filled yet hungry we await your food," they were simultaneously alluding to the religious dimensions of nature, such as rain coming from heaven or food growing in the earth created by God, and playing on the environmentalism and naturalism so powerful in our culture from the 1960s onward. These themes are even more explicit in Ed Gutfreund's "Encircle Us": "feast on the bread of life again. . . . God comes to nourish and feed ev'ryone." Bread, of course, has an especially immediate meaning for Christians, who imbibe bread wafers that symbolize—or, for Catholics, become—the body of Christ. Gutfreund even titled one of his songs "Your Bread Is for the World."

Catholic folk songs emphasized the primacy of interpersonal relations, often those with God. Historically, Christians have treated prayer as a form of supplication, making requests of a distant, almighty God. However, the God of these songs is kinder and gentler. He is a benevolent father rather than a judgmental overlord. Joe Wise makes this point by treating man's and woman's relationship with God as a partnership: "Yours as we stand at the table you set," he sings, "We are the sign of your life with us yet." For Miriam Therese Winter, God is a facilitator of human amity, one who "ask[s] us to care for each other."

Finally, Catholic folk songs encourage, in addition to naturalism and familiarity, a noncreedal universalism. Religion is not about doctrine or catechism but about the spirit. Whereas traditional Catholic liturgical music, whether chanting or classical, reminds people of the complexity and fanciness of specifically Catholic ritual, the folk songs could be sung just as easily in a Methodist, Lutheran, or Presbyterian church. Ed Gutfreund's "Alleluia, Praise to the Lord," does not even mention Jesus, resurrection, atonement, or any other religious doctrine. It could conceivably appeal to Muslims or Jews. "I will bring you all together" seems to be its only message.

That inclusive spirit may be the key to understanding how these songs functioned in the actual mass. After the Second Vatican Council removed Latin from the mass, invited the priest to face his congregation, and invited lay people to exert more sway in directing the church, there was among young and liberal Catholics a pervasive feeling that they all had something to contribute. To reinforce that spirit, they brought folk melodies and lyrics inside the church walls. These were songs that required no knowledge of a foreign language, no extensive training in theology, and no instrument except maybe a guitar. Most important, the lyrics seemed to speak to concerns of the day: the environment, peace, and racial harmony.

Especially around 1970, when the shooting of antiwar protestors at Kent State University was just the most famous example of intergenerational conflict, these songs represented a new, more up-to-date spirit in the Roman Catholic Church. (Recall that *aggiornamento,* the task of Vatican II, translates loosely as "updating.")

The baby boomers who felt that the church's traditions were old and tired welcomed this new spirit. Many other Catholics felt that too much had changed too fast, and they resented the new music. Even though the most radical folk masses were rare, and many churches stuck to the old church music, the new songs were common enough to cause both excitement and hard feelings.

While the songwriters have moved on to other careers—Winter teaches liturgy and feminist studies, Wise is an artist, and Gutfreund is a clinical counselor and massage therapist—their songs remain easily recognizable to legions of Catholics, at once children of the Church and of the tumultuous era through which it has lived.

"Joy Is Like the Rain," Medical Mission Sisters (Hartford Ct., 1965); "Take Our Bread," (Cincinnati, Ohio, G.I.A. Publications, 1966); "Lord, Teach Us to Pray," (Cincinnati, Ohio, G.I.A. Publications, 1970); "Encircle Us," Edward J. Gutfreund, Jr., and North American Liturgy Resources. (Phoenix, Ariz., 1978); "Alleluia, Praise the Lord," Ed Gutfreund and North American Liturgy Resources. (Phoenix, Ariz., 1975).

Further Reading

William F. Buckley, Jr., *Nearer My God: An Autobiography of Faith* (New York: Doubleday, 1997); Thomas Day, *Why Catholics Can't Sing: The Culture of Catholicism and the Triumph of Bad Taste* (New York: Crossroad, 1990); Jay P. Dolan, *The American Catholic Experience: A History from Colonial Times to the Present* (Garden City, N.Y.: Doubleday, 1985); Michael Harrington, "The New Radicalism," *Commonweal* 82, no. 20 (September 3, 1965): 623–27; Mark S. Massa, *Catholics and American Culture: Fulton Sheen, Dorothy Day, and the Notre Dame Football Team* (New York: Crossroad, 1999); Garry Wills, *Bare Ruined Choirs: Doubt, Prophecy and Radical Religion* (Garden City, N.Y.: Doubleday, 1972).

Joy Is Like the Rain

I saw raindrops on my window,
Joy is like the rain.
Laughter runs across my pain,
slips away and comes again.
Joy is like the rain.

I saw clouds up on a mountain,
Joy is like a cloud.
Sometimes silver, sometimes gray,
always sun not far away.
Joy is like a cloud.

I saw Christ in wind and thunder,
Joy is tried by storm.

Christ asleep within my boat,
whipped by wind, yet still afloat.
Joy is tried by storm.

I saw raindrops on the river,
Joy is like the rain.
Bit by bit the river grows,
till all at once it overflows.
Joy is like the rain.

Take Our Bread

Take our bread, we ask you;
take our hearts, we love you.
Take our lives, O Father;
we are yours, we are yours.

Yours as we stand at the table you set;
Yours as we eat the bread our hearts can't forget.
We are the sign of your life with us yet;
we are yours, we are yours.

Take our bread, we ask you;
take our hearts, we love you.
Take our lives, O Father;
we are yours, we are yours.

Your holy people standing washed in your blood.
Spirit filled yet hungry we await your food.
We are poor, but we've brought ourselves the best we could;
we are yours, we are yours.

Take our bread, we ask you;
take our hearts, we love you.
Take our lives, O Father;
we are yours, we are yours.

Lord, Teach Us to Pray

Chorus:
Lord, teach us to pray.
It's been a long and cold December kind of day.
With our hearts and hands all busy in our private little wars,
we stand and watch each other now from sep'rate shores;
we lose the way.
Lord, teach us to pray.

We still believe that we can find a better way.
Teach us to pray.
We lose the way.
Teach us to pray.

I need to know today
The way things should be in my head;
I need to know for once now
The things that should be said.
I've got to learn to walk around
As if I were not dead;
I've got to find a way to learn to live.

Chorus:
Lord, teach us to pray.
It's been a long and cold December kind of day. . . .

I still get so distracted
By the color of my skin;
I still get so upset now
When I find that I don't win.
I meet so many strangers;
I'm so slow to take them in.
I've got to find a way to really live.

Chorus:
Lord, teach us to pray.
It's been a long and cold December kind of day. . . .

I stand so safe and sterile
As I watch a man all flat;
I'm silent with a man
Who'd like to know just where I'm at.
With the aged and the lonely
I can barely tip my hat;
I need to see the sin of "I don't care."

Chorus:
Lord, teach us to pray.
It's been a long and cold December kind of day. . . .

I stand so smug and sure
Before the people I've outguessed;
To let a man be who he is
I still see as a test.
And when it all comes down to must,
I'm sure my way is best.
I've got to find what "room" means in my heart.

Chorus:
Lord, teach us to pray.
It's been a long and cold December kind of day. . . .

I walk and fall, myself alone,
Can't tolerate a guide.
And when the camps split up
I'm sure to put you on my side
And dare someone to challenge me
And swear I will not hide.
I've got to find a better way to live.

Chorus:
Lord, teach us to pray.
It's been a long and cold December kind of day. . . .

I mouth so many things,
Take so little time to weigh;
I've let it all slip by
In the sweep of yesterday.
I can't believe you mean it all
To grace me on my way;
I've got to find a way to really live.

Chorus:
Lord, teach us to pray.
It's been a long and cold December kind of day.

With our hearts and hands all busy in our private little wars,
we stand and watch each other now from sep'rate shores;
we lose the way.
Lord, teach us to pray.
We still believe that we can find a better way.
Teach us to pray.
We lose the way.
Teach us to pray.

Encircle Us

Sisters and brothers welcome here;
feast on the bread of life again.
You have come in Jesus' name;
remember his word for us all.

Chorus:
Circle around the table now.
Circle and dance in his love.

You ask us to care for each other, Lord;
encircle us now in your love.
You ask us to care for each other, Lord,
encircle us now in your love.

God comes to nourish and feed ev'ry one;
his word among us spoken strong.
Born again in his holy name;
we never go hungry for love.

Chorus:
Circle around the table now.
Circle and dance in his love. . . .

Risen and living, passing through death,
he will return to take us home.
Fire your lamp and set it high;
your gift can now brighten the world.

Chorus:
Circle around the table now.
Circle and dance in his love.

Alleluia, Praise to the Lord

Alleluia, alleluia, alleluia,
praise to the Lord!

I will bring you all together;
a new heart will be the bond.

Alleluia, alleluia, alleluia,
praise to the Lord!

New clean water, a new spirit;
these will help you love my Word.

Alleluia, alleluia, alleluia,
praise to the Lord!

Then the darkness will be clearing;
a new light will guide our lives.

— 10 —

Buddhist Chanting in Soka Gakkai International

Richard Hughes Seager

Buddhism began to differentiate into two great traditions around 100 C.E. An older form represented today by Theravada became dominant in South and Southeast Asia, while a second, Mahayana Buddhism, flourished in Central and East Asia. Within the Mahayana traditions, new scriptures or sutras were written that recast the Buddha's teaching. A pantheon of cosmic Buddhas and bodhisattvas, enlightened beings thought to have realized the essence of the Path, emerged as great exemplars and teachers of new forms of philosophy and practice. Mahayana became further transformed as it took on national and regional forms in China, Japan, and Korea, where many reformers arose over the course of centuries to further develop the Buddha's teachings. One such leader was Nichiren, a thirteenth-century Japanese monk, whose name was given to a powerful current of Buddhism in Japan. Some Buddhists consider Nichiren an incarnation of a bodhisattva, others a new Buddha who restored the religion for a new era. There are today some thirty-six Nichiren sects in Japan, at least three of which have taken root in the United States.

One group is the Nichiren Buddhist Church of America, which has a largely Asian-American constituency primarily in the western states. A second is Nichiren Shoshu Temple which has six temples nationwide, staffed by Japanese priests and a lay membership of both Asians and non-Asians. The third is Soka Gakkai International–USA, the American wing of an international lay movement, whose membership is composed of Euro-, Afro-, Asian-, and Hispanic-Americans. Until 1991, Nichiren Shoshu and Soka Gakkai International formed a single group. But at that time, the two underwent a schism, the result of long-standing tensions between the Nichiren Shoshu priesthood and the laity in Soka Gakkai. Since that time, Soka Gakkai has emerged as the largest, most visible, and most studied Nichiren movement in the West.

All three groups, however, teach similar philosophies and practices that can be traced to the reforms inaugurated by Nichiren. Like some other reformers of his day, Nichiren grew dissatisfied with a perceived elitism and corruption in Japanese monasteries. He and others viewed Buddhism as having arrived in a degenerate, latter-day age, an idea derived from one of the greatest scriptures of the Mahayana tradition, the *Lotus Sutra*. Nichiren set out both to purify Buddhism and to simplify its practice to make it more accessible to common people. To do this, he rejected other Buddhist scriptures to focus exclusively on the importance of the *Lotus Sutra*. The powerful populist and reformist elements in Nichiren's life and thought have led many observers to liken him to Martin Luther. His view that other forms of Buddhism were not simply partial and incomplete but false and deluded contributed to a tendency for Nichiren movements to break into sects and to remain aloof from other forms of Buddhism. This remains largely the case in the United States today, where 1960s-era converts to Nichiren Buddhism travel in different circles from those of converts in Zen, Tibetan, and other Buddhist groups.

Nichiren Buddhists, moreover, have a way of practicing Buddhism that is very different from sitting meditation, the primary practice in those other groups. The primary practice in Nichiren groups is to chant *daimoku,* which in the Soka Gakkai movement normally consists of the single phrase *Nam-Myoho-Renge-Kyo*. Even an elementary understanding of its meaning, which is the subject of a great deal of philosophical commentary, underscores the importance of the *Lotus Sutra* to all Nichiren groups. *Myoho-Renge-Kyo* is a Japanese phonetic pronunciation of the Chinese title of the sutra. In English, the phrase literally means "*Lotus Sutra* of the True Law." The introductory *Nam* (or *Namu*) means homage or devotion. Hence, the daimoku is roughly translated in as "Hail to the mystic law of the *Lotus Sutra*." In Nichiren's view, to chant the title of the sutra was to express the spiritual essence of the entire text. With this simple practice, he saw himself freeing the wisdom of the Buddha from arcane monastic practice and making it available to all people. Daimoku is not a song of praise, hymn of edification, or prayer of supplication but a means by which Nichiren Buddhists become infused with, and empowered by, the wisdom of the Buddha, which is understood to be a dynamic force inherent in the universe.

Soka Gakkai Buddhists usually chant daimoku at least twice a day, either in group practice or at home. In group meetings, *Nam-Myoho-Renge-Kyo* is repeated for about ten minutes before proceeding with an extended liturgy. At home in private, it is often chanted for much longer, depending on the disposition of the practitioner. The frequency and duration of chanting is likely to increase when a Buddhist is under duress, seeking solace, or in need of emotional and spiritual clarification. Both group and private chanting is done before a *gohonzon,* a scroll or plaque that is a replica of mandala-like representations of the *Lotus Sutra* said to be originally inscribed by Nichiren himself.

The extended Nichiren liturgy is referred to as *gongyo*. It consists of morning and evening sessions in which sections of the *Lotus Sutra* identified by Nichiren as containing the essence of Buddhism are chanted in conjunction with daimoku. These are a portion of chapter two, called the Hoben chapter, and chapter sixteen, the Juryo, which is divided into prose and verse sections. Like daimoku, gongyo is also chanted in Japanese phonemes based on the Chinese text. Nichiren taught the importance of faith, practice, and study, so after chanting gongyo, a group leader, usually the host, leads a study session on an aspect of Nichiren philosophy. The floor is then opened for those assembled to share their experiences as to how chanting has transformed their lives. Such experiences, which range from the cure of life-threatening diseases to the overcoming of everyday obstacles, are circulated in the movement's publications and play a significant role in popular Nichiren Buddhism.

One cannot overestimate the degree to which Nichiren Buddhists consider chanting to be efficacious. Regularly undertaken, practice is thought to be a way to secure benefits, be these material or spiritual. Soka Gakkai Buddhists often make the distinction between conspicuous and inconspicuous benefits. The former are tangible improvements in the life of a practitioner, be these an increase in financial resources, having better health, or enhancing one's personal relationships. Inconspicuous benefits are more subtle, such as attaining greater wisdom, deeper faith, or a stronger sense of personal self-worth. People in Soka-Gakkai International–USA are remarkably tolerant about the different needs and aspirations members bring to their practice. But long-time Buddhists tend to emphasize the efficacy of chanting in terms of inconspicuous benefits. Many extol them in terms of characteristically American values such as personal empowerment, the ability to take charge of one's life, and becoming more self-reliant.

The first text below is the instructions for gongyo taken from the liturgical manual published by Soka Gakkai. Guides to the correct pronunciation and rhythm of the phonetic chants have been omitted. "Prolonged daimoku" refers to a portion of the practice in which each syllable, including the "u" in *namu,* is chanted slowly and deliberately to foster contemplation and to create a resonance between the practitioner and the perfect wisdom of the Buddha. The five silent prayers have been omitted, but these express appreciation for the mystic law, Nichiren Daishonin, early leaders of the Nichiren tradition, the gohonzon, and Tsunesaburo Makiguchi, the liberal educator who founded the Soka Gakkai movement in the 1930s. One prayer is devoted to expressing the hope that Nichiren Buddhism will be disseminated worldwide in these latter-days of the law, a very important missionary dimension of the tradition referred to as *kosen-rufu.*

The precise structure of gongyo as indicated in the instructions conveys the importance of the chanting ritual but also obscures the familiar and informal nature of most Soka Gakkai gatherings. The host of a home meeting usually leads the chant, and those who have gathered in a living room or family room often know each other on a first-name basis. They sit in chairs or on the floor, facing a small altar displaying the gohonzon. Some practitioners hold rosary-like strings of beads in their hands, rubbing them together from time to time to enhance their concentration. The chant proceeds in an even tone, but no effort is made to have those assembled chant at a uniform pitch. The pace is steady, may be very rapid, and extends for about half an hour. The entire effect of the liturgy is to create an intimate, upbeat, and highly charged atmosphere.

The second text is the portion of the Hoben chapter of the *Lotus Sutra* chanted during gongyo. Only the English translation has been reproduced because the phonetic chant itself is not intelligible to the uninitiated. New practitioners usually find mastering gongyo to be a formidable task, but seasoned Buddhists assist them and audiocassette practice tapes are readily available. The chapter opens as the World Honored One (a title of the Buddha) emerges from samadhi, a deep meditative trance. He explains to his disciple Shariptura that some people (voice-hearers or *pratyekabuddhas*) have not understood his teachings, which over the course of many lifetimes he has preached in many different ways to myriad beings. This capacity to teach perfect wisdom in a wide variety of ways is conveyed in the phrase "expedient means," a key idea in Mahayana Buddhism that has enabled it to be inclusive of many different forms of practices. But the Buddha (also referred to as the Thus Come One) says he is expounding a new teaching never known before, which is that all phenomena in the universe (appearance, nature, entity, and so on) are wholly pervaded by the "true entity," the perfect wisdom of the Buddha. The gist of this is that the Buddha is found in all people and that they can cultivate his perfect wisdom together. This universalistic perspective is developed throughout the sutra in parables and discourses and is expanded on in Mahayana philosophical systems.

Nichiren traditions, however, give portions of the sutra distinctive interpretations that vary from sect to sect. The World Honored One is sometimes identified with Nichiren himself, who is considered a buddha or bodhisattva for a new, latter-day age. Shariputra is often said to represent the common people, who his new teachings will liberate. The practice the Buddha refers to as "the Law that is profound and never known before" and "rarest and most difficult-to-understand Law" is chanting daimoku. The latter-day aspects implied in much of this has given an apocalyptic cast to some Nichiren groups in Japan and underlies the idea of kosen-rufu noted above. Among Soka Gakkai Buddhists in America, however, apocalyptic thinking plays little or no role, although the importance of preaching and teaching the practice of daimoku gave a marked evangelical tone to the movement into the mid 1970s. At about that time, the movement took on a more introspective character and began to interpret the idea of kosen-rufu in more liberal ways. Since the schism in 1991, this evangelical impulse has been further moderated.

The third and fourth texts are portions of experiences published in the *World Tribune,* a weekly Soka Gakkai newspaper published in the United States. The first is from a new practitioner in California that exemplifies the way in which chanting can be understood to have secured conspicuous benefits. The second is from a Wisconsin practitioner of twenty years. It explores a more complex situation in which a potentially severe medical condition, testing positive for hepatitis C, and a difficult personal relationship were resolved together as a result of intense chanting. The language the two use reflects the view that obstacles are opportunities for strong practice and that chanting can effect a human revolution, ideas commonly expressed in Soka Gakkai. As is the case in many situations that involve faith, the precise way in which religious practice actually created the change described can remain somewhat elusive to an outside observer.

In the last several decades, Soka Gakkai International—USA has emerged as a dynamic element in America's complex Buddhist landscape. It claims, moreover, the distinction of having the largest African American and Latino membership of any convert Buddhist organization. This characteristic of the movement has been attributed to a number of things—an early interest in recruitment in the inner city, the tendency for Soka Gakkai to grow through networks of family and friends, and, perhaps most importantly, its philosophy that teaches that the practice of chanting is personally empowering and enables one to change one's karma or life condition.

Under the leadership of Daisaku Ikeda, its current international president, it has become involved in many liberal social issues from environmentalism to feminism and world peace. Its American headquarters are in Santa Monica, California, and it has a strong national organization with many centers across the country, but family and group meetings in homes remain the movement's institutional foundation. Since the schism, the lay character of the movement has been enhanced. Sacramental roles once played by Nichiren Shoshu priests, which were limited to initiation ceremonies and, at times, rites of passage such as weddings, have been taken up by laity on a nonpaying, voluntary, and rotating basis.

The texts below are from: *The Liturgy of the Buddhism of Nichiren Daishonin* (Santa Monica, Calif.: Soka Gakkai International, 1992); *Lectures of the Sutra: The Hoben and Juryo Chapters* (Tokyo: Nichiren Shoshu International Centre, 1978); "I'm Not Turning Back Now!" *World Tribune,* May 21, 1999; "The Key is Inner Revolution," *World Tribune,* July 16, 1999.

Further Reading

Richard Causton, *The Buddha in Daily Life: An Introduction to the Buddhism of Nichiren Daishonin* (London: Rider, 1995); Phillip Hammond and David Machacek, *Soka Gakkai in America: Accommodation and Conversion* (New York: Oxford University Press, 1999); Jane D. Hurst, *Nichiren Shoshu Buddhism and the Soka Gakkai in America: the Ethos of a New Religious Movement* (New York: Garland, 1992); Daniel A. Meraux, *The Lotus and the Maple Leaf: The Soka Gakkai Buddhist Movement in Canada* (Lanham, Md.: University Press of America, 1996); Richard Hughes Seager, "Soka Gakkai and Its Nichiren Humanism," in *Buddhism in America,* edited by Richard Seager (New York: Columbia University Press, 1999); Thomas A. Tweed and Stephen Prothero eds., *Asian Religions in America: A Documentary History* (New York: Oxford University Press, 1999); Bryan Wilson and Karel Dobbelaere, *A Time to Chant: The Soka Gakkai Buddhists in Britain* (Oxford: Clarendon Press, 1994).

Instructions for Gongyo

HOW TO DO GONGYO

Gongyo, a series of prayers that include the recitation of excerpts from the Lotus Sutra along with chanting Nam-Myoho-Renge-Kyo, is conducted twice daily. All five prayers are offered in the morning, and the second, third, and fifth prayers in the evening. . . .

TONE

Along with correct pronunciation and steady rhythm, it is also important to maintain a stable tone, neither raising nor lowering one's pitch unnecessarily.

ORDER OF RECITATION

The sutra in this book is divided into three sections:
Pages 1–5   Excerpt from the "Hoben" chapter
Pages 6–27   *Chogyo*, or prose section of the "Juryo" chapter
Pages 27–38   Jigage, or verse section of the "Juryo" chapter

FIRST PRAYER

Face the Gohonzon and chant daimoku (Nam-Myoho-Renge-Kyo) three times. Then, face eastward, chant daimoku three times and recite the "Hoben" chapter and the jigage (verse portion) of the "Juryo" chapter. After finishing the jigage, chant prolonged daimoku (Namu-Myoho-Renge-Kyo) three times. Chant daimoku three times and offer the [first] silent prayer. Afterward, chant daimoku three times. (The bell is not rung during the first prayer.)

SECOND PRAYER

Face the Gohonzon, sound the bell and recite the "Hoben" chapter. After reciting the "Hoben" chapter, sound the bell and recite both the chogyo (long prose portion) and the jigage of the "Juryo" chapter. Chant prolonged daimoku three times, sound the bell, chant daimoku three times and offer the [second] silent prayer. Chant daimoku three times.

THIRD PRAYER

Sound the bell, recite the "Hoben" chapter and sound the bell. Recite the jigage, chant prolonged daimoku three times and sound the bell. Chant daimoku three times and offer the silent prayer. After each section of this silent prayer, chant daimoku three times.

FOURTH PRAYER

Sound the bell, recite the "Hoben" chapter and sound the bell. Recite the jigage, chant prolonged daimoku three times and sound the bell. Chant daimoku three times and offer the silent prayer. After each section of the [fourth] silent prayer, chant daimoku three times.

FIFTH PRAYER

Sound the bell, recite the "Hoben" chapter, sound the bell, and recite the jigage. Sound the bell and then chant daimoku continuously for as long as you wish. Sound the bell, chant daimoku three times and offer the [fifth] silent prayer. After the first section of this silent prayer, chant daimoku three times. Offer the second section of the silent prayer while sounding the bell continuously, and then chant daimoku three times. After the last silent prayer, sound the bell and chant daimoku three times to conclude gongyo.

Hoben Chapter of the Lotus Sutra

1. At that time the World-Honored One calmly arose from his samadhi and addressed Shariputra, saying: "The wisdom of the Buddhas is infinitely profound and immeasurable. The door to this wisdom is difficult to understand and difficult to enter. Not one of the voice-hearers or pratyekabuddhas is able to comprehend it.

2. "What is the reason for this? A Buddha has personally attended a hundred, a thousand, ten thousand, a million, a countless number of Buddhas and has fully carried out an immeasurable number of religious practices. He has exerted himself bravely and vigorously, and his name is universally known. He has realized the Law that is profound and never known before, and preaches it in accordance with what is appropriate, yet his intention is difficult to understand.

3. "Shariputra, ever since I attained Buddhahood I have through various causes and various similes widely expounded my teachings and have used countless expedient means to guide living beings and cause them to renounce their attachments.

4. "Why is this? Because the Thus Come One is fully possessed of both expedient means and the perfection of wisdom.

5. "Shariputra, the wisdom of the Thus Come One is expansive and profound. He has immeasurable mercy, unlimited eloquence, power, fearlessness, concentration, emancipation and meditations, and has deeply entered the boundless and awakened to the Law never before attained.

6. "Shariputra, the Thus Come One knows how to make various kinds of distinctions and to expound the teachings skillfully. His words are soft and gentle and can delight the hearts of the assembly.

"Shariputra, to sum it up: the Buddha has fully realized the Law that is limitless, boundless, never attained before.

7. "But stop, Shariputra, I will say no more. Why? Because what the Buddha has achieved is the rarest and most difficult-to-understand Law.

8. "The true entity of all phenomena can only be understood and shared between Buddhas. This reality consists of the appearance, nature, entity, power, influence, internal cause, relation, latent effect, manifest effect and their consistency from beginning to end."

I'm Not Turning Back Now!

Two months after I started chanting, my apartment was broken into and all of my saxophones and jewelry were stolen. Nothing was insured and I suffered a loss of over $13,000 as well as the sentimental value, which was worth more than money. I felt violated, and couldn't understand why this had happened to me. My Buddhist friends said, "Congratulations! You have many obstacles!" I did not see why this was a reason to rejoice, but continued chanting with all my heart. One month later, I received a settlement from a prior lawsuit that had been ensuing for five years. The money I received was just enough to pay the lawyers and buy new saxophones.

In the meantime, I called every musician I knew to tell them to keep an eye out for my stolen instruments. One of the people I called was an old friend named Julie whom I hadn't spoken to in many months. She and her husband, Steve, were happy to hear from me and invited me over to see them. They had been composing the music for Warner Brothers cartoons and put me to work reorganizing their home offices.

At our district meeting, I was told to be specific while chanting in front of the Gohonzon. I chanted for lots of high-paying work as a musician that did not involve much driving. Four days later, Steve asked me if I wanted to start orchestrating for him on the cartoons for "lots of money." He would fax me his musical sketches, and I could work from my home. Of course I accepted.

I love my work and am making more money than I have ever made before. It turned out that on the other side of what I thought was the worst thing in the world was an enormous benefit.

The Key to Inner Revolution

For several years I have struggled on and off with a relationship at work that has progressively worsened. I determined to face the situation head on. I began to notice that when I was feeling really stressed out and upset about the situation I would experience pain in my right side by the liver. I realized that my low life-condition was contributing to the Hepatitis C.

This was an incredible awakening. I began to chant about my work relationship and the Hepatitis virus as if they were definitely connected. I saw overcoming my ill feelings as the direct link to clearing out the virus. Besides doing my usual morning and evening prayers, I began chanting inside all the time, in the car, whenever I could.

It was extremely difficult for me to remember that this situation was entirely my responsibility. Every fiber of my being wanted to rebel against that thought. One minute I would tell myself, "She's so arrogant, I have every right to be upset," or "she's so mean to me, why should I be nice to her?" Then I would remind myself that everything in my environment was a reflection of my life and that I needed to change myself from within.

Every bone in my body resisted, but eventually I started seeing her suffering and was able to feel some compassion for her life. I felt like I was cleaning dirt out of my life. I think I've gone deeper into my life than ever and I'm beginning to understand what courage really is. In "The Strategy of the Lotus Sutra" it says, "A coward cannot have any of his prayers answered." President Ikeda also says about courage, "whether or not you have courage will determine your happiness or unhappiness in life." I realized it takes much more courage to face the demons within than the demons outside us. I've also come to the conclusion that doing human revolution can sometimes be a painful process, but it surely leads to absolute happiness.

In the process of all this, my doctor wanted to do a liver biopsy. I was tested every two months for a particular liver enzyme that could indicate liver damage. In the past, I had two slightly elevated readings. I was very reluctant to have a biopsy and was chanting that I would not have to have one. In the mean time, he decided to retest my P.C.R., which indicates how much virus is in the blood.

Much to my doctor's amazement and my own, my P.C.R. test came back negative, which means I've completely cleared the virus from my blood. I feel such incredible appreciation for my Buddhist practice and to the SGI for the encouragement I received. Apparently, the virus can still be harboring in my liver, so this ordeal may not be over yet. The doctor said I have to test negative for three consecutive years in a row before he will say I am completely cured. I am determined to continue to do human revolution, work for world peace and be 100 percent clear of the virus by the year 2001.

— 11 —

Contemporary Christian Worship Music

Julie Ingersoll

It is Sunday morning and across America people make their way to church. Many
end up in warehouse spaces that are home to a growing number of conservative
Christian congregations. Some people belong to Pentecostal, evangelical, or fundamentalist Protestant communities. Some call themselves "born-again Christians"
or just plain "Christians." As people trickle into these churches, those who arrived
earlier mill about. Some pray as others dance and shout, singing along to rock and
roll music that ranges from a soft "easy-listening" or "pop-rock" style, to a reggae
beat, and to harder "classical" rock music.

Absent from these warehouse-church spaces are the traditional markings of
church buildings. They have no stained-glass windows. Instead of hymnals
there is an overhead projector to project the words to the songs onto a big screen
in the front of the room. Instead of traditional church pews, the rows are lined
with cushioned stacking chairs. There are no formal religious artifacts, no classical organ music. Many of these evangelical churches have either a single "worship leader" or a "worship team" consisting of a dozen or so members. In
addition to acoustic and electric guitars, the worship bands, often professional
in quality, may use flutes, drums, trumpets, pianos, electric keyboards, and tam-
bourines. The worship bands lead the congregations in singing praise songs
composed by contemporary Christian artists—many of the same praise songs the
congregations' members listened to in their cars on the way to church. Worship
services also typically include contemporary arrangements of classic Christian
hymns as well.

As nontraditional as these church services seem, it is also true that they are in
many ways quite "traditional." Teachings from these pulpits represent conservative
evangelical interpretations of the Bible and align closely with historic Christian
orthodoxy. The social organization of these congregations is also conservative.
Church leadership is centralized and typically held tightly by appropriately
credentialed males. Most churchgoers are solidly middle class and the children tend
to live in two-parent families.

For many years, scholars of American religion sought to define evangelical Christianity according to distinct theological positions evangelicals were thought to hold. One problem with this approach was that evangelicalism arose from the melding of various strands of conservative American Protestantism that often disagreed with each other on points of theology. What those traditions shared was not theology but a particular religious culture and an opposition to modernism.

But although evangelicals opposed many of the trappings and mores of modern culture, they also readily used modern cultural forms and developments to promote their own culture and worldview. They were innovators in using radio and television to spread their message across America. By the late twentieth century, they had adopted the satellite television technology necessary to reach across the globe. By combining computer technology and the postal service to facilitate mass mailings, they could quickly mobilize political supporters. Pastors experimented with innovative business and management strategies that helped make strides in church growth and organization. So, even as they criticize secular American society, they easily embrace modern technology as a worthy medium of evangelization.

There is significant demographic and sociological diversity to be found among those who attend evangelical churches. Some are filled with professionals who are well dressed and who drive expensive cars. Many others attract middle- to working-class people who wear jeans and T-shirts and drive older cars. Some of these churches have several thousand members and fill multiple Sunday morning services, whereas others are tight-knit groups consisting of fewer than fifty or so people. Some exhibit a loose, free-flowing character, with people moving about as they wish, some sitting, others standing. Others are much more structured; ushers meet people at the doors and take them to seemingly assigned seats. These contemporary evangelical churches typically exhibit a greater degree of racial and ethnic diversity than more traditional churches (in which de facto segregation persists), but they still rarely match the demographics of their surrounding communities.

The most striking demographic similarity found among those who attend the churches is their ages. There are very few senior citizens; the oldest members are aging baby boomers and the youngest members are the children of Generation Xers. With few exceptions, those attending the churches where contemporary Christian worship music—also called praise music—is a central focus are those who grew up in the 1960s (or later), when popular music had become an almost constant presence in American culture.

In the first half of this century, people might have listened to radio programming in the evenings, and some people undoubtedly owned phonographs. But the presence of mass-produced music in the lives of common folk in the first fifty years of the twentieth century pales in significance with the increasing presence of music in the second half of the century. Personal-sized, portable transistor radios became widely available in the 1960s and have now been replaced by high-quality personal music devices ("Walkmans"). People began spending an increasing amount of time in their cars with their radios, 8-track tape decks, cassette tape decks or, now, compact-disc players. Baby boomers were the first Americans to grow up with popular music as a continual backdrop to their lives.

In the 1970s the Jesus Movement was the youthful, baby boomer expression of American evangelicalism, and from it came contemporary Christian rock. "Jesus Freaks," as they were called, embraced many of the central convictions of evangelicalism: the necessity of being "born again," the emphasis on Jesus as a personal savior, the conviction that real salvation leads to a transformed life. At the same time, they were determined to "make the Gospel relevant" and did so, centrally, through the development of Christian music geared to their primary target audience: hippies.

It should not surprise us then that churches designed to appeal to the heirs of the Jesus Movement—baby boomers and their children—would make Christian rock music a centrally important cultural form. Indeed, such music is increasingly characteristic of evangelical churches, as well as churches in denominations like the Assemblies of God and the International Church of the Foursquare Gospel. Contemporary Christian worship music typically is the only type of music heard in "nondenominational fellowships" such as the Vineyard Christian Fellowship, Calvary Chapel, and Hope Chapel. In general, the more strongly a church can trace its roots to the Jesus Movement, the more important contemporary Christian worship music is as a cultural and religious expression in the faith community.

It would be hard to overestimate the importance of Christian pop and rock music in the church communities of which it is a part. These churches tend to have services that last two hours or more, with at least a full hour devoted to music. Many emphasize music as a key descriptive characteristic in advertising their churches; at least one lists its focus on inspirational music as one of seven points in its "Statement of Faith" printed in its church bulletin. Most important, contemporary Christian music serves to bind the members of the religious community together emotionally. Church members are connected to each other, in part, because they share a musical language. Members of similar churches are also connected to each other across geographical distances. Believers see this as an embodiment of the universal Church. The power of music to create these connections is recognized by the worshipers themselves as they adapt centuries-old hymns and create new "worship songs" in an effort to connect the members of the Church across generations and through time.

Insofar as contemporary Christian music is a religious expression of popular culture, it is characterized by the drive to seek the new, most often by creatively blending existing forms in new ways. Most everyone agrees that American religious communities are still the most racially segregated institutions in our culture. Yet the widespread adoption of contemporary Christian praise music by conservative evangelicals has brought about the importation of aspects of African-American culture into predominantly white Protestant Christianity. The influence of traditional African-American musical styles (specifically reggae and rap) is apparent in many of the worship songs. At times, white Protestant churches even adopt an African-American singing style. The church choir members may wear colorful robes, sway to the rhythm of their songs, and raise their hands in the manner of African-American gospel singers, which is distinctively different from the raised hands of charismatic or Pentecostal worshipers.

The centrality of contemporary Christian music also represents a broader trend in evangelicalism: a move away from an emphasis on doctrine and beliefs and a return to experiential religion reminiscent of earlier forms of evangelicalism born out of the revivals of the nineteenth century. Lengthy and emotional worship sessions lend themselves to an experiential, even mystical, faith. Such faith is freed from tedious doctrinal questions about how old someone should be when baptized, when Jesus will return, or even whether the Bible is inerrant. Interestingly, many of the churches that trace their roots to the Jesus Movement and make use of contemporary Christian music are also loosely tied to the charismatic movement. Unlike earlier Pentecostals, they do not place overt emphasis on the "gifts of the Spirit" (speaking in tongues, miraculous healings, and so forth). That is, earlier Pentecostals made these "gifts of the Spirit" badges of orthodoxy; "true Christians" were expected to speak in tongues. Churches that use contemporary Christian music endorse moderate expression of the gifts, but the gifts are not seen as indicators of the strength of one's faith. During a meditative worship song, for example, the worship band may continue playing while the worship leaders stop singing and begin praying to themselves. The members of the congregation will follow suit, some praying informally and extemporaneously, while others pray softly "in tongues." If you were a visitor in the congregation and unaware of what they were doing you might think that people were just quietly praying and humming along to the music. Using contemporary music in an experiential worship service is another avenue for expressing the emotional, expressive, mystical dimension of charismatic evangelicalism. The emphasis is on experiencing a relationship with God (or Jesus) rather than on giving assent to a creed.

Many of the artists who write contemporary Christian songs and produce sheet music for worship teams also market their work to Christian consumers for personal use. As an integral part of evangelical culture, and within the context of American consumer culture, the use of this music in church services, not surprisingly, helps to create consumer demand for mass-produced Christian music for use by individuals, and vice versa. The result is a specialized music industry (which scholars have estimated at $300 to $500 million annually). Worship songs that are familiar to evangelical churchgoers across the nation are readily available on cassettes and compact discs to Christian consumers in the many Christian bookstores around the country. A few Christian artists have developed followings among secular audiences; Amy Grant is the best known of these musicians. Evangelical Christians listen to Christian recording artists in their homes and in their cars—just as other people listen to their pop music of choice.

The songs reprinted here are representative of the range of worship/praise music from the 1980s and 1990s. Each of these songs has been used widely in church services and has been popular on cassettes and compact discs for personal enjoyment as well as in songbooks with "transparency masters" to be used in church worship. The first three songs represent the earliest of the widely popular praise music targeted to, and produced by, baby boomers. "El Shaddai," sung by crossover artist Amy Grant, uses several Hebrew names for God. Like the other two songs, it has a light rock rhythm and is softly devotional. The second three songs represent more recent examples characteristic of Generation Xers and their musical tastes. The group Deliriou5 (pronounced "delirious") is one of the more popular current Christian rock groups. Their song "I Could Sing of Your Love Forever" is sung in a worshipful, meditative style. "Freedom" is the title cut to Darryl Evans's new album and is sung with laughter and enthusiasm. All of the songs have straightforward, personal lyrics that proclaim the glory of God and emphasize the transformative character of faith.

The songs printed here are as follows: Laurie Klein, "I Love You Lord," © 1978 House of Mercy Music (administered by MARANTHA! Music c/o the copyright company, Nashville, TN). All rights reserved. International copyright secured. Used by permission; Jack Hayford, "Majesty," © 1981 Rocksmith Music c/o Trust Music Management, Inc., P.O. Box 22274, Carmel, Calif. 93922. Used by permission. All rights reserved; Amy Grant, "El Shaddai," words and music by Michael Card and John Thompson (Mole End Music/Word Music, Inc., 1981); Sonic Flood, "I Want to Know You" (also known as "In the Secret," by Andy Park, © 1995 Mercy/Vineyard Publishing (ASCAP). All rights reserved. Used by permission); Deliriou5, "I Could Sing of Your Love Forever," from the album *Cutting Edge* (Sparrow Records, 1997); Darryl Evans, "Freedom," (© 1998 Integrity's Hosanna! Music/ASCAP. All rights reserved. International copyright secured. Used by permission. c/o Integrity Music, Inc., 1000 Cody Rd., Mobile, Ala. 36695).

Further Reading

Ray R. Howard and John Streck, *Apostles of Rock: The Splintered World of Contemporary Christian Music* (Lexington: University Press of Kentucky, 1999); Carol Flake, *Redemptorama: Culture Politics and the New Evangelicalism* (New York: Viking Penguin, 1984); Quentin Schultze, *American Evangelicals and the Mass Media* (Grand Rapids, Mich.: Zondervan, Academie Press, 1990); Donald E. Miller, *Reinventing American Protestantism: Christianity in the New Millennium* (Berkeley: University of California Press, 1997); Kimon Howland Sargeant, *Seeker Churches: Promoting Traditional Religion in a Nontraditional Way* (Brunswick, N.J.: Rutgers University Press, 2000). William D. Romanowski, "Roll Over Beethoven, Tell Martin Luther the News: American Evangelicals and Rock Music," *Journal of American Culture* 15, no. 3 (Fall 1992): 79–88, and "Evangelicals and Popular Music," in *Religion and Popular Culture in America,* edited by Bruce David Forbes and Jeffrey H. Mahan (Berkeley and Los Angeles: University of California Press, 2000).

I Love You Lord
Laurie Klein

I love you Lord,
And I lift my voice

To worship you
Oh my soul rejoice

Take joy, my King
In what you hear
Let it be a sweet sweet song
In your ear

Majesty
Jack Hayford

Majesty, worship His majesty
Unto Jesus be all glory, power, and praise
Majesty, kingdom authority
Flows from His throne unto His own
His anthem raise

So exalt, lift up on high, the name of Jesus
Magnify, come glorify, Christ Jesus the king
Majesty, worship His majesty
Jesus who died, now glorified
King of all kings

El Shaddai
Michael Card and John Thompson

Chorus:
El Shaddai, El Shaddai
El El Yonna Adonai
Age to Age you're still the same
By the power of the name
El Shaddai, El Shaddai
En Kamkanna Adonai
We will praise and lift you high, El Shaddai

Through your love and through the ram
You saved the son of Abraham
Through the power of your hand
You turned the sea into dry land
To the outcast on his knees
You were the God who really sees
And by your might you set your children free, El Shaddai
Chorus [ending:] I will praise you 'til I die, El Shaddai

Through the years you made it clear
That the time of Christ was near

Though the people couldn't see
What Messiah ought to be
Though your Word contained your plan
They just couldn't understand
Your most awesome work was done
By the frailty of your son, El Shaddai

I Want to Know You
Sonic Flood

In the secret, in the quiet place
In the stillness you are there
In the secret, in the quiet place
I wait only for you
'Cause I want to know you more

I want to know you
I want to hear your voice
I want to know you more
I want to touch you
I want to see your face
I want to know you more

I am reaching for the highest goal
That I might receive the prize
Pressing onward, pushing every
Hindrance aside
Out of my way
'Cause I want to know you more

I Could Sing of Your Love Forever
Deliriou5

Over the mountains and the sea
Your river runs with love for me
And I will open up my heart
And let the healer set me free

I'm happy to be in the truth
And I will daily lift my hands
For I will always sing

I could sing of your love forever [sing four times]

Oh I feel like dancing
It's foolishness I know

But when the world has seen the light
They will dance with joy
Like we're dancing now

Freedom
Darryl Evans

Where the spirit of the Lord is
There is Freedom
Where the Spirit of the Lord is
There is Freedom
Where the Spirit of the Lord is
There is Peace
There is Love
There is Joy

It is for freedom you've set us free
It is for freedom you've set us free

I'm free
I'm free

So we will walk in your freedom
Walk in your liberty

So we will walk in your freedom
Walk in your liberty

So we will dance in your freedom
Dance in your liberty

So we will dance in your freedom
Dance in your liberty

Teaching: Learning How to Live Correctly

—12—

Teaching Morality in Race Movies

Judith Weisenfeld

From the early 1910s through the late 1940s, African-Americans had available a vibrant cinema that was largely separate from the world of Hollywood. The black and white directors, producers, and actors who made these films (known as "race movies") understood and capitalized on the desire of black audiences to experience their own stories at the center of at least some of the films they paid to see. Filmmakers sought to provide a broader range of characterization than the hackneyed stereotypes of the black maid and butler permitted. In many ways, race movies set themselves up as a counter to the overtly racist displays of African-Americans in mainstream American popular culture. D. W. Griffith's *Birth of a Nation* (1915) stands as the most significant and influential example of film's ability to promote Christian white supremacy. Film historians generally cite *The Railroad Porter* (Bill Foster, 1912) as the first race movie and *Souls of Sin* (William Greaves, 1948) as the last, and estimate that during this period filmmakers produced more than 350 race movies. Historians have also surmised that some twelve hundred theaters across the country exhibited these films. In addition, black audiences had access to race movies in venues such as churches and schools. With regard to viewing practices, Diane MacIntyre has counted 429 theaters for exclusively black audiences in the year 1929. Although most of these were in the South, a significant number were found in the north.

Race movies devoted particular attention to religious experience, expression, and institutional structures in an attempt to counter the distinctive uses of black religiosity in mainstream American culture. A number of Hollywood's "all-black cast" films used religious contexts to frame their stories and, in these films, black religion is always simple, instinctive, emotional, and extraordinarily embodied. These films include Paul Sloane's *Hearts in Dixie* (Fox, 1929), King Vidor's *Hallelujah!* (MGM, 1929), Marc Connelly's *The Green Pastures* (Warner Brothers, 1936), the final segment of Julien Duvivier's *Tales of Manhattan* (20th Century Fox, 1942), and Vincente Minnelli's *Cabin in the Sky* (MGM, 1943). Fantasies in American popular culture about the nature of African-American religiosity understand it to function in a compensatory manner, diverting attention from the political, economic, and social needs of the here and now. At the same time, such images typically make African-Americans grotesque in an excessive display of what inevitably appears to be mere mimicry of the Christianity of whites. King Vidor's 1929 film, *Hallelujah!*, which he produced as a meditation on what he believed was a connection between the sexual drives of African-Americans and their religious expressions, exemplifies this type of film.

Although the makers of most race movies did not seek to cultivate religious commitment in their viewers, many of the films often devoted considerable attention to religious themes. No doubt, filmmakers sought both to mark the significance of religion in African-American life and to counter racist depictions of black religion. Films such as *Body and Soul* (Oscar Micheaux, 1924), *The Black King* (Bud Pollard, 1932), *Sunday Sinners* (Arthur Dreifuss, 1940), and *Dirty Gertie from Harlem, U.S.A.* (Spencer Williams, 1946), as well as others, feature ministers as central characters and use churches and other religious settings as important parts of the story. Many race movies from the 1930s and 1940s that deal with religious themes give evidence of concern among African-Americans about the place of churches and their leaders in an increasingly urbanized and modernized community, in which institutions other than the church (including the press, secular political organizations, entertainment venues) were now prominent. These films also frequently explored the relationship between Christian commitment and participation in entertainments such as card playing, dancing, and listening to jazz music. Although none of the films names movies as a threat to faith, one can conjecture that the medium's popularity also raised concerns among church members and leaders.

Among the race film directors of the 1940s, Spencer Williams stands out for producing two religious melodramas that assume and promote a Christian perspective. *The Blood of Jesus* (1941) and *Go Down, Death* (1944) are self-consciously religious films in which the audience is meant to identify with the two female protagonists in their struggles to overcome the forces of evil that seek their downfall. Williams's work is unusual when set against other race movies because of his use of special effects—most often through the superimposition of one image over another—to represent divine interventions in the lives of believers and to underscore his belief in the literal existence of heaven and hell. In *The Blood of Jesus* Williams also insists upon the reality of angels and of the devil and includes them as characters in the film, clothing angels in white-winged costumes and the devil in a shiny suit complete with horns and a tail. There is a precedent for Williams's approach to sacred drama in black church theater productions. In 1930, for example, two female members of Atlanta's Big Bethel African Methodist Episcopal Church wrote and produced *Heaven Bound*. The play presents twenty-four pilgrims and their journeys toward heaven or hell, with saints, angels, and the devil also appearing as major characters. Williams's costuming choices in *The Blood of Jesus* are quite similar to those in this play.

Most of the race movies extant today are narrative films that were produced for theatrical distribution. Although they often dealt with religious themes or engaged in debates concerning religious life and leadership, their primary audience was meant to be broad and general within African-American communities.

A number of other surviving films that fall within the category of race movies targeted a more narrow audience, however, and have much clearer religious intent than did *Sunday Sinners* or *The Black King*. Rev. L. O. Taylor of Memphis, Tennessee, for example, made short films of his trips to National Baptist Convention meetings during the 1930s and 1940s, in addition to filming his congregation on various occasions. Taylor traveled to other churches, exhibiting the films in the evening and preaching the following day. Little is known about Eloyce King Gist and James Gist and the context for the production of *The Hell-Bound Train*, but it is probable that it was made in the early 1930s. Eloyce was born in the last years of the nineteenth century in a small town near Galveston, Texas, and James about the same time in Indianapolis. James, a lifelong Baptist, and Eloyce, a convert to Baha'i, met and married in Washington, D.C., in the 1930s. By this time, James had already begun producing films and Eloyce joined him in these projects. They rewrote the script to produce a second version of James's *The Hell-Bound Train* and then the two made *Verdict, Not Guilty* together.

The Gist films have none of the polish of most race movies or of Hollywood films, nor do they make use of conventional narrative structures so central to the classical Hollywood cinema of the 1930s. In general, these silent films are underexposed and often out of focus, but nevertheless they sometimes provide compelling viewing. In contrast to Spencer Williams's narrative and often humorous approach to projecting his faith, *Verdict, Not Guilty* and *The Hell-Bound Train* are straightforwardly dogmatic and derive their drama largely from promoting fear in viewers. *The Hell-Bound Train* uses the structure of a sermonic form popular in African-American Christianity in which the preacher likens the spiritual journey to a journey by train. In this case, each car carries those who have committed a particular type of sin, and the film provides extended descriptions of the activities that will inevitably lead the viewers to hell if they do not repent.

In the opening scene of *The Hell-Bound Train*, we see the devil—a black actor dressed in a shiny suit, with horned hood, pointed tail, and cape—standing behind a ticket window, above which a sign reads: "No Roundtrip Ticket; One Way Only; Free Admission to All; Just Give Your Life and Soul." The words projected in the first title of this silent film warn us: "The Hell-bound train is always on duty and the devil is the engineer." A man and woman stand before the window considering their options, and the next title reads: "Well, we'll take a chance." The film goes on to warn viewers against jazz music, dancing, intemperance, sex, disobedience in children, theft, murder, gambling, Sabbath-breaking, dishonesty in business, and backsliding. And in the final dramatic sequence the train speeds toward hell as the title implores, "Get off this train by repenting, believing and being baptized, before it's too late." Death stands at the entrance to a tunnel, dancing before a sign that reads, "Entrance to Hell, Welcome to All." The titles warn, "The fast, sinful life of the hell-bound train moves on until it's too late," and "Our bible reads, 'The wicked shall be turned into hell; and all nations that forget God.' Psalms 9:17." The train finally enters hell and we see its passengers burning in agony.

Many of the activities that the film insists will trap viewers on the hell-bound train are aspects of general popular culture and hallmarks of black popular culture in particular. In its critique of these activities, the film warns against certain kinds of display as excessive and un-Christian. For the Gists, chief among these are dancing and listening to jazz. They warn viewers that "the indecent dance of the day" leads to drunken fighting and other kinds of sin, and they point to a more general lesson about how things may provide pleasure for us during this lifetime but doom us in the next life. Dancing and jazz are accorded their own cars on the train and receive particular attention in the film, whereas murderers and gamblers share a car, as do "thieves, boot-leggers and law-breakers."

Not surprisingly, the way in which the film attempts to proscribe behavior is deeply gendered. The majority of sins that men commit in the film involve failures to devote themselves first and foremost to their families. Thus, the film contains a variety of scenes of men squandering their paychecks through drinking and gambling. Women also receive particular attention in the film, and almost every activity denoted as sinful also leads to sex and pregnancy. One scene illustrates the consequences of a married woman's attempt to abort her child, showing her dying while her husband looks on. The title reads, "She has taken medicine to avoid becoming a mother. She'd better get right with God, for it's murder in cold blood." In another scene we are treated to the consequences of "women who don't care what happens before children." Here a mother entertains a man in her living room and the two kiss, drink liquor, dance, and smoke in front of her small daughter. When the two leave, the little girl imitates them, taking a sip of the drink left on the table, pretending to smoke the cigarette butt, and dancing with and kissing her doll. "Children practice just what they see," the film concludes. The majority of women's sinful activities in the film have a direct, negative impact on children's behavior, whereas men's sins create a general misery for all who come into contact with them.

A good deal more work needs to be done on how black Protestants used film as an evangelizing tool and as a way of delineating and reinforcing standards of religious belief and comportment in the wider world outside the church. African-Americans were certainly not alone in recognizing the potential of the movies as a tool for teaching morality, as some white evangelicals also used film in proselytizing and in religious education. In The Hell-Bound Train, the Gists are particularly concerned with conduct but, unlike producers of the commercially released narrative race films that also considered behavior standards, the Gists do not envision the consequences of "bad" behavior according to its effect on relations with white Americans. Although in most of the narrative race films the world of whites is strikingly absent, it is clear to what degree a concern for what whites will think is included in the depiction of black religious leadership and the relationship between church and world.

It is difficult to gauge the efficacy of such films for moral education, and audience responses are not preserved in the historical record. Certainly one can imagine that the explicit presentation of criminal activities and other behavior marked as sinful might have intrigued and facinated a viewer in ways contrary to the filmmakers' goals. This notion that such representations would motivate young people to engage in similar behavior undergirded the movement in the late 1920s and early 1930s to censor the content of Hollywood movies, an effort that resulted in the adoption of the Production Code in 1930. The general principle behind the Code was an insistence that a film not "lower the moral standards of those who see it" and required that when filmmakers felt it necessary to include characters who engage in "immoral" behavior, those characters be chastised or punished in keeping with the "rule of compensating moral values." The question of the relationship between exposure to popular culture and the behavior of young people remains controversial, and neither studies from the 1930s nor more recent studies on the subject convincingly resolve the issue. It is notoworthy that, for the Gists, movies do not receive the same critical attention as a threat to the moral well-being of black Christians as do other aspects of popular culture.

It is also quite possible that the Christian viewers who attended exhibitions of the Gists' films and others like them found a safe arena in which they could imagine what it might be like to engage in taboo behavior. The actors, Gist family and friends, certainly seem to be enjoying themselves in pretending to be criminals, gamblers, and adulterers and in their demonstrations of lascivious jazz dancing. And given that many, if not most, of the showings of the film took place in churches and were, in effect, "preaching to the converted," it seems important to consider the vicarious thrill that viewing these films made possible for committed Christians. *The Hell-Bound Train* is an extremely rich and complex example of an attempt by black Protestants to harness the popular medium of film to promote a particular religious sensibility and to teach Christian morality in church and beyond.

The Library of Congress has preserved a video copy of the film; however, the segments are out of sequence. Because it is a silent film that uses titles—frames with words that provide the viewer with dialogue, narration, or descriptions of the action—and does not present a narrative of events in a causal sequence, it is particularly difficult to know in what order the filmmakers presented the scenes. My discussion relies on notes in the library's files that record the likely sequence of the original reels, as well as my own sense of the possible order of scenes. The transcription of the film's titles and description of the action in the scenes are my own.

The Hell-Bound Train, by James Gist and Eloyce King Gist, c. 1930, is in the Motion Picture, Broadcast, and Sound Division of the Library of Congress, Washington, D.C.

Further Reading

Gregory D. Coleman, *We're Heaven Bound! Portrait of a Black Sacred Drama* (Athens: University of Georgia Press, 1992); Thomas Cripps, *Slow Fade to Black: The Negro in American Film, 1900–1942* (New York: Oxford University Press, 1977), and

Black Film as Genre (Bloomington: Indiana University Press, 1978); G. William Jones, *Black Cinema Treasures Lost and Found* (Denton: University of North Texas Press, 1991); Lynne Sacks, *Sermons and Sacred Pictures: The Life and Work of Rev. L. O. Taylor* (29 min. 1989); Judith Weisenfeld, "For Rent: 'Cabin in the Sky': Race, Religion, and Representational Quagmires in American Film," *Semeia* 74 (1996): 147–65; Diane MacIntyre, "Movie Houses in Segregated America of 1929," *The Silents Majority,* http://www.mdle.com/ClassicFilms/SpecialFeature/theaters.htm, July 1, 1998; Francis G. Couvares, ed., *Movie Censorship and American Culture* (Washington, D.C.: Smithsonian Institution Press, 1996).

The Hell-Bound Train

In the film's opening sequence we see the devil standing behind a ticket window as a group of people crowd around to purchase tickets. A sign next to the window reads: "No Roundtrip Ticket; One Way Only, Free Admission to All; Just Give Your Life and Soul."

Title: THE HELL-BOUND TRAIN IS ALWAYS ON DUTY AND THE DEVIL IS THE ENGINEER.

A man and woman stand before the window.

Title: WELL, WE'LL TAKE A CHANCE.

Shot of the exterior of the train. Shot of the devil taking the engineer's seat. Shot of people on the train.

Title: DANCING IS THE FIRST COACH. BECAUSE THE DANCE OF TODAY IS INDECENT. THE DANCE DISMISSES WITH DRUNKENNESS, JEALOUSY, AND EVIL.

Scene of a party as people begin to get angry and shove each other.

Title: THE DEVIL REJOICES.

Title: THIS HAPPENS AT THE DANCE.

Scene of fighting at the party.

Title: MANY A GIRL FOLLOWED THE DANCE UNTIL . . .

Shot of a woman in bed with an infant.

Title: SECOND COACH DRUNKENNESS. WIFE AND CHILDREN OF A DRUNKEN MAN MUST SUFFER.

Shot of a family gathered at a table. The father sits with his head down on the table.

Title: PAPA, PLEASE WAKE UP. MAMA'S CRYING ABOUT SOMETHING.

The children try to wake their father. Shot of a letter from the landlord indicating that money is owed.

Title: DRUNKARDS ARE ROBBED BY THEIR BEST FRIENDS.

We see an obviously drunk man staggering while walking along a snow-covered street. Two men walk up to him and take his money. Shot of the family at the table and the father sitting with his head down on the table.

Title : WOMEN AND GIRLS ARE MISTREATED WHILE DRUNK.

Scene in which a man leads a drunken young woman to an empty house (the sign on it says that it is for rent). They go inside and, in the next shot, exit the house after he has presumably "mistreated" her.

Title: THE THIRD COACH IS JAZZ MUSIC. IT STARTED TO FAME IN CABARETTE LIFE
Shot of a train in motion.

Title: THEN AS ENJOYMENT TO SPORTING WOMEN.

Title: AND NOW IT HAS WEAVED ITS WAY INTO CHRISTIAN HOMES.

Shot of a woman and man sitting in their living room reading Bibles and their young daughter sitting on the floor listening to a phonograph. We see a picture of Jesus on the wall.

Title: IT MAY BRING HAPPINESS TO YOU THROUGH LIFE.

Shot of a woman dancing in a living room.

Title: BUT AT THE POINT OF DEATH.

Suddenly the woman falls into a chair and clutches her chest as two other women rush toward her.

Title: MARY, EMMA, COME QUICK, STOP THOSE BLUES, BRING HYMN BOOK.

Shot of the pages of a hymn book.

Title: TOO LATE THEN.

The woman is dead and we see her distraught children. Later in the film we read the following title.

Title: DISOBEDIENT CHILDREN ARE ON THE ROAD TO DOWNFALL.

Scene of children playing in the street until their mother comes out and signals for them to come inside.

Title: I'VE TOLD YOU NOT TO PLAY IN THE STREET.

Shot of the children running out of the house and beginning to play in the street again.

Title: A FEW DAYS LATER.

Once again the children play ball on a busy street. Shot of a man jumping out of car. He picks up one of the children from the street as the mother comes outside. The man and the child's mother carry the child inside the house.

Title: BOY WHO MISTREATS DUMB ANIMALS.

Shot of a boy playing with a dog. A group of other boys tie a can to the dog's tail and run off. Shot of the train in motion.

Title: THOU SHALT NOT STEAL.

Scene with two teenage boys walking along a commercial street. Suddenly they grab apples from a market and run away, toppling the basket in which the pile of apples is displayed. The owner comes outside and sees them as they run off. He flags down a policeman walking by and shows the policeman the basket and apples on the ground.

Title: YES, THEY RAN THAT WAY.

The policeman goes after the boys and finds them around the corner eating apples. He drags them back to the market.

Title: THAT'S THEM. THEY ARE ALWAYS STEALING.

Shot of the policeman taking the boys away.

Title: I'LL PUT THEM WHERE THEY CAN'T STEAL.

Another shot of the policeman and the boys.

Title: GIRLS SHOULDN'T BE IMPUDENT TO MOTHER.

Scene of a girl putting on makeup and then heading for the front door of the house. Her mother, who has been sitting in a chair near the door, gets up to stop her from going out.

Title: I'M OLD ENOUGH TO KNOW AND I'M GOING WHERE I PLEASE.

The girl leaves and heads out with a young man. Shot of the couple entering a café, sitting down, ordering drinks, and then getting up to dance.

Title: FOR AS MONTHS PASS YOU MAY BE BROUGHT TO SORROW.

The girl has a young baby now and sits in the living room crying. Her mother comes over to comfort her. Shot of the train in motion. Later in the film we read the following.

Title: COACH NUMBER SEVEN IS OVERCROWDED WITH LIARS.

Shot of the inside of one of the cars of the train. The passengers are stepping on Bibles.

Title: WHILE SOME SERVE GOD ON THE SABBATH, OTHERS WORSHIP AUTOMOBILES.

A car pulls up and stops before a house. A group of men and women run out of the house and get in the car, which then drives away. Shot of a train in motion.

Title: SABBATH BREAKERS TO CHURCH IN MORNING, WITH THE DEVIL THE REST OF THE DAY.

The devil watches people exit a church and then begins walking down the street with them. Shot of a train in motion. Three men walk down the street. Cut to a man standing in front of a door, reading. The camera pulls back to a long view to show that the man is standing outside a church.

Title: IF WE GET RID OF HIM WE'LL BE ALL RIGHT.

Three men stand in front of the church door talking. Shot of people entering the church, then of the congregation seated, and then of the minister preaching.

Title: FALSE PREACHERS WILL GET WITH THE OFFICERS AND STEAL THE CHURCH'S MONEY.

Title: FALSE PREACHERS JOIN IN PLOTS AGAINST ONE ANOTHER.

Title: OFTEN THEY WALK HAND IN HAND WITH THE DEVIL.

Title: SOME WILL BEAT THEIR ROOM AND BOARD BILL.

Title: WHILE RIGHTEOUS PREACHER STRIVES TO CARRY THE PROGRAM OF JESUS CHRIST.

Shot of a minister preaching. Shot of people playing craps and others dancing. Shot of the train in motion.

Title: THE LAST COACH IS RESERVED FOR BACKSLIDERS, HYPOCRITES AND USED TO BE CHURCH MEMBERS, AND THE GOOD-HEARTED SINNERS WHO TREAT FRIENDS RIGHT BUT MISTREAT GOD ABOVE.

Two men walking down the street meet. One, an older man, holds a Bible, opens it, and talks to the young man, who answers,

Title: I DON'T DRINK, GAMBLE OR STEAL, I TREAT EVERYBODY RIGHT, I PAY MY DEBTS, EVEN IF I HAVEN'T REPENTED, BEEN BAPTIZED, OR JOINED CHURCH.

Title: I'M AS GOOD AS SOME OF THOSE IN CHURCH.

The young man walks away.

Title: POOR BOY, YOU'LL REGRET IT SOME DAY.

Shot of the young man in bed, clutching his heart. Shot of the man staggering around a house and finally to the living room. He sits in a chair, picks up a Bible from the table, and drops dead. The devil comes in and does a dance around the body.

Shot of people riding inside the train.

Title: GET OFF THIS TRAIN BY REPENTING, BELIEVING AND BEING BAPTIZED, BEFORE IT'S TOO LATE.

Title: THE FAST, SINFUL LIFE OF THE HELL-BOUND TRAIN MOVES ON UNTIL IT'S TOO LATE.

Title: OUR BIBLE READS 'THE WICKED SHALL BE TURNED INTO HELL; AND ALL NATIONS THAT FORGET GOD.' PSALMS 9:17

Title: FLAG DOWN THE TRAIN AT . . .

Shot of a train going into a tunnel as Death dances near the entrance. The sign at the entrance reads: "Entrance to Hell, Welcome to All."

Title: DEATH RECEIVES MESSAGE THAT SIN IS RUSHING TOO FAST.

The devil leans out the train window and waves. Flames burn the train. Shots of people in the flames of hell.

Title: THUS I'VE DEMONSTRATED TO YOU THIS PICTURE WHICH I PAINTED AS A VISION FROM HEARING A SERMON IN A REVIVAL MEETING.

Shot of a minister in front of a large poster with a map that reads: "Midnight excursion with no headlights. It's a hell-bound train."

Title: WHICH COACH DO YOU RIDE?

——13——

Harry Emerson Fosdick
and Liberal Protestant Teaching

Bernhard Lang

Between 1922 and his retirement in 1946, Harry Emerson Fosdick (1878–1969) ranked as one of America's most famous Protestant preachers. A best-selling author and pastor of Riverside Church in New York, he was known for his radio ministry, his long-term association with millionaire John D. Rockefeller, and his program of pastoral counseling.

Fosdick stands in the tradition of liberal Protestantism that began in nineteenth-century Germany and eventually become a major movement in American Christianity. From its founding father, Friedrich Schleiermacher (1768–1834), American Protestant liberalism inherited an emphasis on religion as a disposition present in every human being. If that religious orientation could be adequately developed, it would lead to a clear consciousness of being connected to, and in harmony with, the divine and transcendent reality of God. When properly stimulated in worship, especially through the sermon, religious sentiment would lead to peace and composure of mind. Schleiermacher called the sermon the "medicine" that helps restore the inner balance of those who have lost it, and will lose it again, in the many worries and troubles of life. Schleiermacher, and all liberal theologians in both Europe and America, were interested not so much in Christianity as a body of doctrine but in a practical spirituality that helps one to cope with life.

It was while he was studying at Colgate Seminary in Hamilton, New York, and Union Theological Seminary in New York City that Fosdick adopted Schleiermacher's belief in the joyful experience of the divine presence in the human heart. He became a Baptist minister, and in 1915 he exchanged his pastorate for a chair in practical theology at Union Theological Seminary. An experienced preacher and author of best-selling devotional books, he was also invited to serve at the First Presbyterian Church in New York. It was there in the 1920s that he exercised his extraordinary gifts, attracting large crowds every Sunday.

As a pastor and preacher, Fosdick promoted the liberal orientation to faith. From his student days, he had embraced biblical criticism, intellectual honesty in matters of belief, the idea of biological evolution, and the nondogmatic, experiential nature of Christian teaching. One of Fosdick's early sermons, preached in 1922, received national attention and made him a famous man. Entitled "Shall the Fundamentalists Win?" it commented on and contributed to the debate between "modernists" (like Fosdick himself) and conservatives ("fundamentalists"). In the sermon, Fosdick rejected belief in the Bible's literal inspiration and pleaded for a church that would be intellectually hospitable, tolerant, and liberty loving. Calling fundamentalism an "immeasurable folly," he ridiculed those who believed that Darwinism should not be taught in American schools. The widely read sermon established Fosdick as an intellectual force within the American Protestant community. The first text reprinted here, "First Things First," dates from this period and was a commissioned article for the *Ladies' Home Journal*.

Fosdick knew that liberalism had its perils, and he named ethical disloyalty to Jesus as one of its greatest weaknesses. Accordingly, he saw his task as a preacher to show how Christians could apply Jesus' ethical teaching to their personal and social lives, economic systems, racial relations, and international affairs. Fosdick took his task seriously and preached hundreds of sermons on all of these issues. After its inauguration in 1930, Riverside Church became the place where many of these sermons (including the one here anthologized) were given. Funded with money from the Rockefeller family, Riverside Church was a huge and beautiful Gothic Revival structure positioned on the Hudson River in New York City. Fosdick wanted a combination of a glorious cathedral and an efficient lecture hall. In the new, dignified environment, regular Sunday worship assumed a splendor that sometimes bordered on liturgical vanity. The stained-glass windows, the huge Gothic nave, the altar, the pulpit, the well-dressed ushers, the robed choir, and of course the solemn organ music all conspired to create a sacred atmosphere—much to the liking of the chief minister, Dr. Fosdick. Although sacred architecture might not be able to replace the saving word, it could at least support it.

Fosdick's sermons, including "Six Ways to Tell Right from Wrong," were not merely preached within the grandeur of Riverside Church. Although the attendance at any given Sunday service included many more visitors than members, the vast church could only hold twenty-five hundred people. In order to spread his message across the country, Fosdick began broadcasting his sermons over the radio. Before coming to Riverside, he had established "National Vespers," a Sunday evening program eventually carried by the National Broadcasting Company (NBC) that ran for twenty years. In this time, Fosdick sent 480 sermons over the national airwaves, reaching millions of Americans. By 1941, National Vespers was carried by 125 stations and his radio audience comprised an estimated twenty million people. Over the years, more than 740,000 people wrote for copies of his sermons, which were sent by Fosdick's secretaries. His listeners also sent him thousands of letters telling him of their sorrows and triumphs. Many of the tourists who attended services at Riverside Church did so because they had heard Fosdick preach over the radio. Since NBC donated radio time, no fundraising was conducted on the air. Appreciative listeners, however, sent money that was used to support the program. Through his radio presence and publishing efforts, Fosdick accomplished his goal of bringing to modern, affluent, middle-class Americans his message of Christian virtue, behavior, and personal religion.

Fosdick's sermons reflect his desire to be a spiritual counselor to the American people. Teaching was not merely instructing people in proper forms of behavior or explicating Christian doctrine. Teaching was a way to help people understand their own existential situation and educate them in possible ways of rearranging their lives. For him, a sermon was meant to serve people, and he referred to it as personal counseling on a group scale. Therefore, he started a sermon not by ana lyzing and commenting on a biblical lesson but by presenting a real problem experienced by real people, which he then discussed in light of the Bible. In the pulpit, Scripture served as an amazing compendium of every kind of situation in human experience, accompanied by the wisdom of the ages to help in meeting problems. Fosdick knew his audience, and he met many of them in his office for personal counseling. The key to being a good preacher for him was to make himself available as a counselor to his parishioners, his audience, and whoever approached him. Although his plans to establish a professional counseling center or clinic at Riverside Church never materialized, he did establish regular counseling hours, kept reading in the current psychological literature, and discussed problems and cases with a professional psychologist. Teaching, preaching, and healing were all closely aligned in Fosdick's ministry.

Fosdick insisted that individuals and their stories mattered to Jesus. Like the Master, the Christian minister must touch lives and must deal directly with individual needs if he (or now she) hoped to teach anything important. Only contact with individuals could prevent a minister from living isolated and aloof from life's real problems. Since Fosdick did not take Christianity as a fixed set of theoretical teachings and practical commandments, he relied on what he considered the essential biblical experience. For him, common sense and psychological insight counted as much as what a person might learn from specific biblical stories.

Consequently, it is not surprising that Fosdick would begin his series of articles for the Ladies' Home Journal with, "A recent ride upon a Fifth Avenue bus threatened to waste time. The talk of two women, however, whose conversation was too plainly audible to be escaped, made it well worth while." Fosdick had been asked by the editor of the magazine to prepare a monthly essay on the topic of modern morals to appear in the 1923 edition of the journal. The first article, "First Things First," appeared among ads for Cream of Wheat cereal and Ivory soap, a short story by Zane Grey, and illustrations of Paris frocks. In keeping with Fosdick's desire to reach a wide audience with a broad, nonsectarian message, there are no evidential biblical texts to support his ideas. Indeed, the one time the Bible is mentioned it is used to point out how one of its proverbial characters, Methuselah, is recorded to have lived over nine centuries, but "he never did anything or thought anything to make such longevity worthwhile." Even Jesus is vaguely referred to as "The Master," who tells stories about missed opportunities.

Fosdick eventually published his year's worth of articles in a small book called *Twelve Tests of Character,* but the original venue more aptly captures Fosdick's desire to help the modern, consumer-oriented men and women of the twenties find a spiritual center.

And yet, Fosdick's message in "First Things First" reflected concerns of long-standing interest to Protestant clergy. Addressing the predominant female, white, and affluent readers of the *Ladies' Home Journal,* he criticizes the frivolous lives that many modern Americans lead. Gambling while playing bridge, attending musical comedies, reading light novels, traveling to Europe but not appreciating the history and culture of the Ages—all of these activities distracted men and women from more serious and valued pursuits. Fosdick echoed preachers from the Puritans onward who had warned their listeners not to fritter away their lives by cultivating pastimes that had no moral, cultural, intellectual, or spiritual purpose. Life is short, Fosdick warns, and the energy of life is limited—don't make a fool of yourself with trivial preoccupations. Although women have historically been accused of wasting their time on fashions and fads, Fosdick attacked male preoccupations, as well. Men play bridge, too, but more problematic is their attachment to the business world. Overinvolvement with the material ends of business, a frequent complaint of nineteenth-century ministers, not only ruins one's appreciation for things of the spirit but also attacks the very foundation of society—the family. In the article's only positive reference to the Bible, Fosdick makes a witty paraphrase of Psalm 27:10 ("When my father and my mother forsake me, then the Lord will take me up."): "When my father and my mother forsake me, then the Boy Scouts will take me up." Fosdick sets out for the modern readers of the *Ladies' Home Journal* a traditional teaching: take care of your families, live up to your responsibilities, read serious literature, appreciate the finer arts, and study the hand of God in the natural world. It is not skepticism that undermines faith and is at the root of irreligion, he argues—taking a dig at the fundamentalists—it is preoccupation with the scraps and the leftovers of life.

"Six Ways to Tell Right from Wrong" was originally a sermon given at Riverside Church in New York City on October 30, 1932, and then given again for the National Vespers radio program on January 3, 1933. Typical of many of Fosdick's sermons, it was reprinted with other sermons by a secular press in 1933 as *The Hope of the World* and again within a different collection of sermons in 1958 as *Riverside Sermons*—twelve years after he had left the pulpit at Riverside Church.

In this sermon, Fosdick more directly addressed a churchgoing, Protestant audience. He referred to his listeners not only as fellow Christians but as people who had the Pilgrims as their forefathers. These Protestants, however, were modern men and women who no longer could rely on old customs, simple codes of behavior, or traditional family relationships for knowing how to lead their lives. They are Christians who are "trying to be intelligent" and have given up their belief in hell. How do such modern people sort out a basic code of ethics that will help them choose right from wrong? The question of how to cope with moral and theological relativism had to be answered by liberal thinkers if they were to counter biblical fundamentalists. Obviously, this question was not limited to liberal Protestants trying to understand how to live in a world filled with many faiths and many value systems. Most Americans of the 1930s experienced some form of the "cosmopolitanism" that Fosdick observed. Christian or not, many would find the question to be a fair one and the answers Fosdick gave to be meaningful.

Fosdick's "six ways" of determining how to act are pragmatic and detached from theological systems or religious imagery. They assume that all of us desire the good and that our problem is that we are confused and weak. If we would merely follow our own common sense, cultivate the character of a good sportsman, and seek to cultivate our most noble values and tastes, then we would be on the right track. Fosdick's insights into ethical behavior assumes that people are basically good; they are just lazy at times or do not look far enough into the future to see what type of community their actions would build. As with all of Fosdick's sermons, he moves easily between personal anecdotes, general biblical references, and cultural allusions. He assumes his audience to be of a sufficient educational and social class to understand his references to Shakespeare, Cervantes, and Pasteur while not rejecting as hopelessly old-fashioned his condemnation of cheap jazz and Coney Island amusements.

The sermon's optimism reflects the progressive spirit of liberal Protestantism that had survived the attacks of biblical fundamentalism but would have a more difficult time arguing for the basic goodness of humanity in the following years. In the United States, social and economic upheavals of the Great Depression were taking their toll on millions of Americans. The stock market crash of October 1929 shook first the American economy and then the world. By 1932, wages had dropped 60 percent and as many as seventeen million Americans were unemployed. An estimated one million were moving around the country trying to find jobs while others were begging on street corners. In 1933, Adolf Hitler would be appointed chancellor of Germany and the Nazi terror would begin.

In more than one sermon, Fosdick did try to address the hellish reality confronting the country. Preaching on Christianity and unemployment, he drove home the magnitude of the suffering with statistics and quotations of letters he had received from those desperately unemployed. He called for increased government aid and the establishment of unemployment insurance. Moreover, he asked the businessmen in the congregation to abandon the spirit of competition and opt for cooperative planning under wise social control. He even castigated the cruelties of the capitalistic system and promoted some form of socialism.

Nevertheless, despite his social and political awareness, many of Fosdick's sermons simply ignored the pressing problems caused by unemployment in New York and around the country. Almost two years after the stock market crash, "Six Ways to Tell Right From Wrong" uses anecdotes that focus on the wealthy members of Riverside Church—those whose problem was not finding a job but "trying to be aimlessly happy, [yet] not going anywhere." Fosdick chides people who gamble on stocks but only offers honest "sportsmanship" as the alternative. Dishonest businessmen get their comeuppance, but nothing is said of the workers who are fired as American industry crumbles. Although "Six Ways to Tell Right

from Wrong" presents its truth as applicable to the average American, its oblivi-
ousness to the dramatic times of the early 1930s weakens its effect. The sermon
reflects the heady times of the Roaring Twenties rather than the serious worries of
a nation facing economic depression and rising worldwide fascism.

The sermons reprinted here are from Harry Emerson Fosdick, "Twelve Tests of
Character: First Things First," *Ladies' Home Journal,* January 1923, pp. 15, 42;
and "Six Ways to Tell Right from Wrong," in *Riverside Sermons* (1932; reprint,
New York: Harper & Brothers, 1958), pp. 203–11. Copyright © 1958 by Harry
Emerson Fosdick, renewed © 1986 by Elinor Fosdick Downs and Dorothy Fos-
dick. Reprinted by permission of HarperCollins Publishers, Inc.

Further Reading

Bernhard Lang, *Sacred Games: A History of Christian Worship* (New Haven: Yale
University Press, 1997); Robert Miller, *Harry Emerson Fosdick—Preacher, Pastor,
Prophet* (New York: Oxford University Press, 1985); William B. Lawrence, *Sundays in New York: Pulpit Theology at the Crest of the Protestant Mainstream* (Lanham,
Md.: American Theological Library Association and Scarecrow Press, 1996); Hal-
ford R. Ryan, *Harry Emerson Fosdick: Persuasive Preacher* (New York: Greenwood,
1989).

First Things First

A recent ride upon a Fifth Avenue bus threatened to waste time. The talk of
two women, however, whose conversation was too plainly audible to be
escaped, made it well worth while. They were bosom friends, and in an hour's
tête-à-tête they gave a comprehensive résumé of their characters.

They loved to play bridge, and they played it, apparently, a good deal of the
time. They were gambling at it. To be sure, one of them had had some trouble
with her husband, who, having been brought up a Presbyterian, had scruples
about gambling. "But," she had said to him, "you see that we must give up
the game if we do not gamble." So he had come over just recently. They were
all gambling now and were happy. They loved the theater, especially musical
comedies. They loved to dance and evidently, when they were not playing
bridge, dancing was their chief diversion. They loved their automobile trips,
and as for dress how shall a mere man report their conversation about that?
One listened to see if any other interest in life would be revealed, but this was
all. Their talk had struck bottom.

These women live in one of the most needy and critical generations in history, when a shaken civilization is striving desperately to get on its feet again,
when there are great enterprises to serve, great books to read, great thoughts to
think; and yet their lives, like a child's doll, are stuffed with sawdust. They rep-

resent in an extreme form one of the commonest failures in character—the crowding out of things that really matter by things that do not matter much. They are absorbingly busy with trivialities. They have missed the primary duty and privilege of life—putting first things first.

The basic facts about us which make such promiscuous preoccupation ruinous is that our life's time and our life's energy are limited. We are like street cars: we can hold our quota and no more; when all seats are taken, the standing room absorbed, and the "Car Full" sign put up in front, whoever hails us next, though he be the most prominent citizen in the community, must be passed by.

It never was so easy to fail in this particular way as it is today. There may have been times when life was sluggish and folk could drift listlessly through apathetic years. The Bible tells the story of Methuselah's living over nine centuries, but, so far as the record shows, he never did anything or thought anything to make such longevity worthwhile. If ever life could be dragged out through such dull continuance, that time has gone. Today the currents of life are swift and stimulating, the demands of life absorbing. There are more things to do than we ever shall get done; there are more books to read than we ever can look at; there are more avenues to enjoyment than we ever shall find time to travel. Life appeals to us from innumerable directions, crying, "Attend to me here!" In consequence, we are continually tempted to dabble. We litter up our lives with indiscriminate preoccupation. We let first come be first served, forgetting that the finest things do not crowd. We let the loudest voices fill our ears, forgetting that asses bray, but gentlemen speak low. Multitudes of people are living not bad but frittered lives—split, scattered, uncoordinated. They are like pictures into which a would-be artist has put, in messy disarray, everything that he has chanced to see; like music into which has been hurled, helter-skelter, every vagrant melody that strayed into the composer's mind.

Preoccupation is the most common form of failure.

Consider, for example, the effect of preoccupation on our reading. Some time ago an airship collapsed above Chicago and dumped itself ruinously down upon a public building. People woke up at that, to see that new inventions like airplanes require special regulation. Now, the printing press is a comparatively new invention. Five hundred years ago there was no such thing. And while it is important that aircraft should not be allowed to empty themselves into our households, it is just as important to consider what the printing press is emptying into our heads.

An entirely new set of problems has arisen since the printing press arrived and reading became one of the dominant influences of human life. When one considers how reading seeps in through all the cracks and crannies of our days, what power there is in books to determine our views of life, and how cheaply these possibilities lie at every man's hand, it is plain that the quality of a man's reading is one of his foremost responsibilities.

It is plain, too, that while a few people deliberately read perversive [improper] books, most of us miss the best books, not because we choose the bad but because we litter up our minds with casual trash. We stop to pass the time of day with any printed vagabond who plucks at our sleeve. We have forgotten Ruskin's exclamation: "Do you know, if you read this, that you cannot read that?"

It is no longer necessary that anybody should plead with us to read. We read enough. "What do you read, my lord?" says Polonius, and Hamlet answers, "Words, words, words." That is a fair description of a great deal of reading in a world which someone has described as "a blur of printed paper."

But how many put first books first? How many would think of saying with Mrs. Browning, "No man can be called friendless when he has God and the companionship of good books"?

To be sure, there are minor kinds of reading of which we all must do more or less. We read for efficiency in daily work. Modern business in every realm, from domestic science to international commerce, has been broken up into an indefinite number of specialties, and books convey to us the results of other men's labors. Any man, to be an adept, must read the specialists. But if a man uses books only so, as Pharaoh might use his slaves to build the pyramid of his success and renown, he does not know what real reading means.

Moreover, we read to keep up with the times—an endless stream of papers, magazines, and books, resecting every changing situation in this fluid world, until we are fairly dizzy with the flood of them. And we read the books that are talked about just because they are talked about. Of all social compulsions what is more urgent than the oft-repeated question: "Have you read?" That club flogs us to our reading "What!" says our friend, "you have not read so and so?" Whereupon we fly to the nearest bookstore and against the necessity of conversation at the next dinner we buy a best seller.

Yet, so continuously reading, we read everything except the books that we should read first of all. The great books habitually are crowded out. The little books that are menially useful to us, our slaves, running errands for us to further our convenience or success, or to dress us in the tinsel of a ready conversation— we read those. But the books that are not slaves, but masters, at whose feet the wise sit to be taught and illumined and inspired—they are crowded out. We should hardly think of saying, as Charles Lamb did, that we should like to say grace over our books; or with Charles Kingsley, "Except a living man, there is nothing more wonderful than a book."

Nevertheless, the great books are waiting for us all. If the world's poets and seers, prophets and apostles were alive, we could hardly meet them one by one, much less talk with them. But in a book they will come to each of us as though there were no one else in all the world for them to call upon. Though we are so poor that we must have them in paper covers, they will be all there. Though we are so dull that we cannot understand at first, they will repeat the message to us again and again. Though we are so foolish as to forget, they will be there on the morrow to tell it to us once more with tireless patience. Great books are the perfect democrat. The shame of many of us is that, with such books waiting to be read, we stop to barter gossip with every corner loafer on our way. Any vagrant straggler down the literary street can waste our attention and our time. And because time and attention are limited, having read this, we cannot read that.

Reading is but one illustration of the way in which habitually the best in life is lost to us by being crowded out. Dean Briggs, of Harvard, describes a company of American young people whom he saw in Rome. They were on their first visit to the Eternal City. Morning after morning they arose with the opportunity of a lifetime awaiting them. The Forum, the Coliseum, Saint Peter's, the whole city, fabulously rich in historical association, was at their disposal. And every day they settled down in the hotel for a long morning at bridge. Cries Dean Briggs: "What business had such people in Rome? What business had they anywhere?"

So far as our amusements are concerned, this loss of the best, through the preposterous cramming of our lives with wastage, is the more common because the old Puritanical attitude against popular recreations has gone to pieces. Fortunately we can only with difficulty imagine ourselves back in the time when drama had to be presented, if it was to be presented at all, under the guise of a free extra, interspersed between the musical numbers of a concert. . . .

That day happily has gone. Concerning popular recreations which were once under a rigid interdict, most of us have come to the conclusion voiced by the late President Hyde of Bowdoin, that they are altogether too good to be monopolized by the devil. Plenty of folk, however, having decided concerning popular amusements that they are right, forget that there is still a further question to be faced: how much time and attention do they deserve?

"Mr. Jones," said an effusive youth, "is the most wonderful man I ever knew. He remembered every card that I held at bridge last week!" To which a girl with a level head answered: "Has it ever occurred to you that Mr. Jones is forty-five years old, and that he doesn't know anything else?" The trouble with Mr. Jones is one of our commonest maladies. . . .

The seriousness of this problem involved in putting first things first is not, however, adequately represented by folk like Mr. Jones or the young people in Rome or the chatterers on the Fifth Avenue bus. A young lad in Brooklyn was almost given up in despair by his mother because he seemed addicted to trash, enjoying nothing so much as cheap cigarettes to smoke and cheap tales to read. Then a librarian got hold of him. "What do you like to read?" he asked.

"Detective stories."

"Have you ever read Thomas Bailey Aldrich's 'The Story of a Bad Boy'? It is one of the best detective stories ever written," said the librarian.

So the boy took the book home and, retaining it a week longer than he usually kept books, returned it, saying: "That is the best book I ever read. Got any more?"

The librarian was also a field lecturer in geology, and along with feeding the boy better and better books, he persuaded him to go on a field trip with his class. At the foot of the Palisades he began telling about the leisureliness of God laying the foundation of the earth, when he saw the boy, legs apart, arms akimbo, eyes protruding with amazed interest.

Going home the lad sidled up to him. "I never heard anything like that in all my life. Are there any books about it?"

So he began reading geology and, to make a long story short, that lad, once absorbed in trash, is now professor of geology in a great university.

The tragedy of preoccupation, however, is often caused, not by flippant triviality, but by life's ordinary and necessary business. The cause of alarm about Niagara Falls has been simply that business has been drawing off a little stream here and another little stream there until through many small dispersions the cataract which the Indians called "Thundering Water" may in the end leave only bare and ugly rock.

Business is doing that to people as well as to Niagara. The problem may be intensified in modern times, but it is not new. The Greeks had a proverb, "Zeus frowns upon the overbusy." The Master himself told a story about men who, being absorbed in a farm, in a newly purchased team of oxen or in a freshly established home, missed the greatest opportunity of their lives.

The consequences of this sort of preoccupation are often pathetic. An American once stormed through one of the great European galleries of art. He sniffed at this picture an instant; he sniffed an instant at that; and then he stormed out. But before he went he turned on the venerable attendant at the door and said; "Not a thing here worth seeing—not a thing!" To which the attendant replied, "If you please, sir, these pictures are no longer on trial—the spectators are." That dull-eyed visitor doubtless was a very busy man. He had started with normal capacities to appreciate the finest gifts of life, but, preoccupied with many tasks, he had lost through atrophy the power to love the highest when he saw it.

One result of this absorbing material business, which so crowds out attention to the things of the spirit, is the appalling vulgarity of our personal and public life. We forget that, while we may not be able to create those forms of beauty which will last forever, we have another ability which is almost as wonderful: we can love them when they are created; we can rejoice in them and grow rich because of them.

We do not deliberately decide to lose all this beauty from our lives—the best books, the best music, the best art; we are simply busy. There are so many other things which press upon us with urgent clamor to be done that we let the best things go. In the end, for all the money that we make, we are like the Mohammedan beggars on the steps of St. Sophia in Constantinople, standing with their backs to the great mosque, careless of its history, its symbolism, its beauty, crying "Baksheesh! Baksheesh!"

The climax of this test's application concerns a deeper matter than the lost esthetic values in which excessive busyness results. It concerns some of our lost moral and religious values. The problem of the family, for example, would be in a fair way toward solution if fathers and mothers would once more put first things first in their relationships with their children.

One of the troubles with this much-berated younger generation is not primarily with this younger generation at all, but with the older generation. The younger generation does not so much need critics as it needs examples. "When my father and my mother forsake me, then the Boy Scouts will take me up"—such is the rendering given to an ancient Psalm by an observant watcher of our family life. For fathers and mothers, preoccupied with many tasks, have farmed their children out to any agency, from school and scout troop to a summer camp, where they can be rid of their responsibility. They use these helps, not as helps, but as substitutes for the family life.

A father, whose son had been dropped from several schools and colleges and who confessed that he knew nothing whatever about the boy, recently took him to another college and demanded that, as a *quid pro quo* for money given, that institution should assume the problem of his son. "I am a very busy man," he said, "and I have no time to attend to him."

The trouble with that father is not lack of time. He has time to do those things which he considers essential. His difficulty is that he thinks some things are more important than caring about his son, that some entrustments are more sacred than that. Once, in the gray of a winter dawn, an early riser watched a stooped and aged woman groping about a building in process of construction, picking up bits of lath and sawed-off ends of lumber. It was a pathetic sight to see a woman reduced to the off-scourings of the wood for fire to warm her household. But even more pathetic is it to see the finest relationships of human life, our friends, our families, and at last our God, seeking around the main business of our days for the scraps and leftovers of our attention. We give the logwood of our life to secondary matters; to the highest we give the chips.

More than anything else one suspects that this is at the root of irreligion. It is not skepticism, but preoccupation, which generally makes the inner-most relationships of a man's soul with God of no account. The highest is in us all. At times it flames up and we know that we are not dust but spirit, and that in fellowship with the Spiritual Life, from whom we came, is our power and our peace. But many a man who has known the meaning and the might of this relationship has largely lost it, not because theoretically he has disbelieved, but because practically he has crowded it out.

"Sometime," the man says, "I will attend to these deepest and finest relationships."

Meanwhile he picks up his life as a football runner does the ball and speeds across the field. He does not notice the ground across which he runs; his eyes are set upon the goal. He has no present; he has only a future. The most enriching relationships of life, from family love and friendship to religious faith, offer their best to him, but he runs by. "Sometime," he says.

That time never comes; it never will come. What he needs most to learn is that the days are not a football field to be run over, but gardens to be tilled, and that, if tilled well, they can grow now the things of which heaven is made. "*Carpe diem*," said the Latins—"Seize the day." Some people who for many years have been doing the opposite, crowding out the best by preoccupation and postponement, might well begin a new year with the single resolution to put first things first.

For the ultimate trouble with preoccupation is that it takes no account of the flight of time. Someone has figured human life as covering the span of a single day's waking hours from six in the morning until ten at night. Then if a man is twenty years old, it is ten o'clock in the morning with him; if he is thirty, it is high noon; if he is forty, it is two in the afternoon; if he is sixty, it is six in the evening. So the day passes and the enriching experiences which fellowship with the Highest offers us are lost, not because we deliberately discard them, but because our time and attention are pre-engaged.

The famous Bargello portrait of Dante was lost for years. Glen knew there was such a portrait, but they did not know where it was. Then an artist, resolved on finding it, started his search with the room where tradition had located it. The room was a storehouse for wastage; straw and lumber littered the floor and whitewash covered the walls. But when the rubbish had been carted out and the whitewash was being removed, old lines long obscured began to appear and colors long hidden became visible, until at last the grave, lofty, noble face of the great poet was recovered for the world. Nobody had destroyed the Bargello portrait, but somebody had littered it up. Straw and lumber and whitewash had seemed to somebody more important than the face.

Six Ways to Tell Right from Wrong

Our thought starts with the plain fact that it is not always easy to tell the difference between right and wrong. Any pulpit, therefore, which keeps up the traditional exhortation, Do right! Do right! as though, with a consensus of popular opinion as to what right is, all that the world needs is to be urged to do it, is indulging in a futile kind of preaching. Behind a great deal of our modern immoralism is not so much downright badness as sincere confusion as to what is right. In many a dubious situation how we wish that someone would tell us that!

The factors that enter into this condition must be obvious to anybody.

For one thing, change of circumstances. Old customs and old codes of behavior in family life or in the relationships between men and women, let us say, undertake to tell us how to act, but the circumstances in which those codes and customs are supposed here to function are radically different from the circumstances in which they first emerged, so that although their basic principles may be valid, their applications are endlessly perplexing. In consequence, old patterns of behavior smash up and old prescriptions for right and wrong do not seem pertinent, and every day human beings, who always like to have their roadways plainly marked, go astray, not because they deliberately want to but because they are honestly confused about which the right road is.

Again, our cosmopolitanism, pouring all the cultures of the earth into one melting pot, has, among other consequences, resulted in ethical confusion. Our Pilgrim forefathers, with a wilderness on one side and a sea on the other, in their comparatively isolated community and with their comparatively homogeneous population, could reach a popular consensus of moral judgment or even a dogmatic certainty as to how men ought to act. But in a city like this most of the ways of behaving known on earth are poured together, so that the issue is not a single clear right against a single clear wrong, but such diverse and competing ideas of right as to befuddle the minds even of the elect.

The upshot of all this is that conscience is not enough. Of course conscience never has been enough. Many of the most terrific deeds in history, from the crucifixion of our Lord down, were conscientiously done. Listen even to Paul in his first letter to Timothy: "I was before a blasphemer, and a persecutor, and injurious: howbeit I obtained mercy, because I did it ignorantly in unbelief." Paul throughout his life had been conscientious. Toward the end of it he could say to his Jewish brethren, "I have lived before God in all good conscience until this day." That did not mean, however, that as he looked back over his life all the things he had conscientiously done seemed to him to have been right. Upon the contrary, he confessed: a blasphemer, a persecutor, an injurious person, such was I, conscientiously but ignorantly.

Today I propose talking about this matter with homely practicality to my own soul and to yours. We may take it for granted that we would not be here in a Christian church if in general we did not desire to do right. We may even take it for granted that if, as in Shakespeare's "As You Like It," some one should ask us Touchstone's question, "Hast thou any philosophy in thee, shepherd?" we would say, Yes indeed, we have; we believe the basic ideas of Christianity about life's meaning—that is our philosophy. But we had better take it for granted also that this general desire to do right and this general acceptance of the Christian philosophy of life do not solve our problem. So as automobilists our problem is not solved when we desire to take the right road or when we hold a true cosmology about the solar relationships of the earth on which the right road runs. Oh, for a homely signpost now and then, some practical, directive help: amid the confusion of competing ways to tell us where to turn! So this morning I invite you to no airplane trip into the lofty blue but to a practical land journey as we set up six homely guideposts to the good life.

In the first place, if a man is sincerely perplexed about a question of right and wrong, he might well submit it to the test of common sense. Suppose that some one should challenge you to a duel. What would you say? I would advise you to say, Don't be silly! As a matter of historic fact, dueling, which was once a serious point of conscientious honor, was not so much argued out of existence as laughed out. The common sense of mankind rose up against it, saying, Don't be silly! So Cervantes in *Don Quixote* finished off the ridiculous leftovers of the old knighthood, saying, Don't be silly! So Jesus, in his parable of the rich man who accumulated outward things but cared nothing for the inward wealth of the spiritual life, did not say, Sinner! but Fool!—"Thou fool, this night thy soul shall be required of thee: then whose shall those things be, which thou hast provided?"

So, too, more intimately, here is a youth whom you may know whose behavior burdens with anxiety his family, his teachers, and his friends. They argue with him; they exhort him; they penalize him to no effect. But some day a fine girl for whom he cares says to him, it may be no more than three words, Don't be silly! and lo, something happens in that boy that home and school and church together could not achieve.

What we are saying now is that this is a healthy thing for a man to say to his own soul before somebody else has to say it to him. One wonders how many here would be affected by it. You do not really care anything about drink, and left to yourself you would not drink at all, but it is so commonly offered to one nowadays and is so generally taken as a matter of course, that you are drinking too much. Don't be silly! Or you may have in your hands today a choice between promiscuous sexual liaisons and a real home where two people love each other so much that they do not care to love anybody else in the same way at all; where romance deepens into friendship and overflows into children; where, as the sun grows westerly, the family life becomes every year more beautiful. And with that choice in your hands you are playing with promiscuity. Don't be silly!

Or it may be that you have a good set of brains and real ability that if you wanted to you could prepare yourself for some worthwhile work in the world, and just because you are financially able you are trying to be aimlessly happy, not going anywhere,—just meandering,—endeavoring to pick up all the sensations that you can accumulate. I should not think it worth while to call you first of all bad, but I am sure it would be true to call you silly.

That is the first test and, alas! twenty years from now somebody here this morning, listening to this and paying no heed to it, will be looking back on life and saying that bitter thing, "God be merciful to me, a fool!"

In the second place, if a man is sincerely perplexed about a question of right and wrong, he may well submit it to the test of sportsmanship. Now the essence of sportsmanship is that in a game we do not take for ourselves special favors which we deny to other players but, making the rules equal for all, abide by them. In daily life that means that a man should always question concerning his conduct whether, if everybody acted on the same principle, it would be well for all. There is no doubt, then, why it is wrong to crowd in ahead of your turn in a line at a ticket office. Play the game! There is no doubt why it is wrong to cheat the government with petty smuggling or to join whispering campaigns about people when you do not know the facts, or to treat contemptuously a person of another race or color. Play the game! In all such cases we know well that we would not wish to be treated ourselves as we are treating others and that if everybody acted on that principle it would not be well for all. Sometimes one thinks that half the evil in the world is simply cheating. People do not play the game.

Do not, I beg of you, restrict the application of this test within the limits of individual behavior. There are ways of making money in our economic system, not simply illegal but legal, speculative gambling with the securities of the people, using public utilities as a football to be kicked all over the financial field in hope of making a goal of private profit with it, or betting day after day on stocks that represent genuine values which honest business once created but which now can be used merely for a gambler's chance without creating anything. If everybody acted like that there would be no values even to gamble with and no welfare for any one. Be sure of this, that this rising tide of public indignation against the economic wrongs has this much justification: we have a right at least to ordinary sportsmanship and in wide areas we have not been getting it. The Golden Rule, my friends, is a grand test. Husband and wife, parents and children, employers and employees, black and white, prosperous and poor, Occident and Orient—what if we did not cheat! what if we did as we would be done by! what if we played the game!

In the third place, if a man is sincerely perplexed about a question of right and wrong, he may well submit it to the test of his best self. Notice, I do not say to his conscience, for the conscience merely urges us to do right without telling us what the right is, but deeper than conscience and more comprehensive is this other matter, a man's best self. For, of course, no one of us is a single self. How much simpler life would be if we only were! There is a passionate self, reaching out hungrily for importunate sensations, good, bad, and indifferent. There is the careless self taking anything that comes along, excellent and vulgar, fine and cheap. There is the greedy self in whose eyes an egoistic want blots out all the wide horizons of humanity beside. But deeper than all these is that inner self where dwells the light that, as the Fourth Gospel says, lighteth every man coming into the world.

Let us illustrate it from biography. You know the story of Pasteur, great scientist, devout Christian, builder of modern medicine. In 1870, when the Germans invaded France, he already had had a paralytic stroke and was a cripple. He could not help repel the invaders. His friends urged him out of Paris that he might not be "a useless mouth" to be fed through the siege. His biographer tells us that sometimes when he was sitting quietly with his wife and daughter, in the little village of Arbois, the crier's trumpet would sound, and forgetting all else, he would go out of doors, mix with the groups standing on the bridge, listen to the latest news of disaster, and creep like a dumb, hurt animal back to his room. What could he do? What ought he to do? "Unhappy France," he wrote to a friend, "dear country, if I could only assist in raising thee from thy disasters!" Then something happened inside Pasteur that has changed the world. He, half paralyzed, a man already warned of his end, determined that he would raise France again to glory by a work of pure beneficence, that he would erect a monument to his country's honor that would make the military monuments of the conquerors seem puerile. In his biography you can read it all, how by years of inspired and sacrificial labor he at last fulfilled his purpose.

So Pasteur, wondering what he ought to do, what he could do in a perplexing situation, carried the decision up to that finest self.

Sometimes when I preach here, I wonder if there may not be in this congregation a youth who, so choosing his vocation, so testing his ambition, so dedicating his intelligence, will not help to raise America again. She needs it, unhappy country!

Be sure of this, that if, in large ways or small, any one of us does help to ennoble our society and build a better nation for our children and their children to be born into, it will be because we have taken our secret ambitions up to the tribunal of our finest self. There *is* something in us like a musician's taste, which discriminates harmony from discord. There *is* something in us like a bank teller's fingers, which distinguish true money from counterfeit: "To thine own self be true, / And it must follow, as the night the day, / Thou canst not then be false to any man."

In the fourth place, if a man is sincerely perplexed over a matter of right and wrong he may well submit the question to the test of publicity. What if everybody knew what we are proposing to do? Strip it of secrecy and furtiveness. Carry it out into the open air, this conduct we are unsure about. Suppose our family and friends knew about it. Imagine it publicly talked of whenever our name is mentioned. Picture it written in the story of our life for our children afterwards to read. Submit it to the test of publicity. Anybody who knows human life with its clandestine behavior understands what a searching and healthy test this is. . . .

I know one business firm in this city which in a few weeks will crash into a receivership under the tremendous blow of a righteous court decision. Ten years ago that firm did a secret thing which would not stand the test of open knowledge. For ten years those men have lived in deadly fear that it might be known. And now the light has fallen. Yes, and just the other day in personal conference I talked with an individual on the ragged edge of nervous prostration because in the secret furtiveness of private life something was afoot which it would be disastrous to have known.

Things that cannot stand sunlight are not healthful. There is a test for a perplexed conscience. How many here do you suppose would be affected by it? Imagine your behavior public.

In the fifth place, if a man is perplexed about a question of right and wrong he may well submit it to the test of his most admired personality. Carry it up into the light of the life which you esteem most and test it there. Why is it that some of us do not like cheap jazz? It is because we have known and loved another kind of music. Why is it that some of us do not think that Coney Island is a beautiful place? It is because on autumn days when the artistry of heaven has been poured out in lavish loveliness upon the trees we have walked in the spacious woods alone with our own souls and God. Why is it that some of us regard with a deep distaste all this promiscuous sexuality? It is because we have lived in homes where love was deep and lasting and dependable.

My friends, it is the beauties and the personalities that we positively have loved that set for us the tests and standards of our lives. Why is it, then, that conduct which seems to some people right seems to some of us cheap and vulgar, selfish and wrong? It is because for years we have known and adored the Christ. There is a test for a perplexed conscience. Carry your behavior up into the presence of the Galilean and judge it there.

If some one protests that he does not propose to subjugate his independence of moral judgment to any authority, not even Christ's, I answer, What do you mean by authority? There are all kinds of authorities—ecclesiastical, creedal, external, artificial—against the imposition of whose control on mind and conscience I would as vigorously fight as you. But there is one kind of authority for which I hunger, the insight of the seers. In science, in philosophy, in literature, in art, in music, not simply in morals and religion, I would, if I might, enrich my soul with the insights of the seers. A modern essayist says of Wordsworth, the poet, that he "saw things that other people do not see, and that he saw with quite unique clearness and frequency things which they see at most rarely and dimly." Aye! More than once some of us have carried our perplexed consciences up into the presence of the Christ and have made a saving use of his eyes.

In the sixth place, if a man is perplexed about a question of right and wrong, he may well submit it to the test of foresight. Where is this course of behavior coming out? All good life, my friends, depends upon the disciplining of clamorous and importunate desires in the light of a long look. We Christians who are trying to be intelligent long since gave up our belief in hell, but one suspects that many of us, throwing over the incredible and picturesque impossibilities of that belief, have dropped also a basic truth which our forefathers carried along in it. Every man who picks up one end of a stick picks up the other. Aye! Every man who chooses one end of a road is choosing the other. Aye! Every course of behavior has not only a place where it begins but a place where it comes out.

Life is like a game of chess. Some youth is here this morning with all his pieces on the board and freedom to commence. They tell me, however, that when a man has once played his opening, he is not so free thereafter. His moves must conform to the plan he has adopted. He has to follow the lead with which he has begun. The consequence of his opening closes in on him until at last, when checkmate is called. See! says the expert, when you chose those first moves you decided the end. Well, with what gambit are we opening our game?

We really do not need to be so perplexed about right and wrong as we sometimes are. To be sure, there is nothing infallible about all this. Goodness is an adventure and "Time makes ancient good uncouth." Nevertheless, the test of common sense, of sportsmanship, of the best self, the test of publicity, of our most admired personality, of foresight,—these are sensible, practical, high-minded ways to tell right from wrong. I call you to witness that in all this I have not been imposing on you a code of conduct; I have been appealing to your own best moral judgment. Alas for a man who neglects that! For though, as in Paul's case, one may come out at last to a good life, it is a bitter thing to have to look back and say, A blasphemer, and a persecutor, and injurious—such was I ignorantly.

— 14 —

Reconciling Patriotism and Catholic Devotion:
Catholic Children's Literature in Postwar America

Timothy J. Meagher

The effort to reconcile the Catholic Church and American culture is a persistent theme in American Catholic history. America, after all, was founded as a Protestant country. Most colonies proscribed the practice of the Catholic religion, and Catholics were thus scarcely visible in any of the colonies outside Maryland and Pennsylvania. As important, Catholicism seemed an integral part of the Old World's corruption, hierarchies, and ignorance, which American republicans had explicitly rejected in setting up the new nation. Catholics, therefore, had to prove their worth as citizens to a nation of skeptics who saw them as, at best, aliens and, at worst, potential fifth columnists for Old World monarchism.

The effort to Americanize the Catholic Church, however, did not proceed, only nor perhaps even principally, out of a need to convince non-Catholics that Catholics could be good Americans. It proceeded as much from internal as from external reasons. English-speaking leaders of the church, largely Irish American in origin, sought to make the church American in order to weld together an ethnically diverse and potentially fragmented Catholic people under their own leadership.

Ethnic conflicts troubled the church in America throughout the nineteenth and early twentieth centuries. Clashes between French Canadian priests and laymen and their Irish American bishops wreaked havoc in Catholic dioceses from Maine to Connecticut, and German- or Polish-Americans battled largely Irish-American English-speaking bishops from Pennsylvania through the Midwest. English-speaking Catholic leaders believed that in making the church American they would not only eventually eliminate such conflicts but also make the church enormously powerful and influential as Catholics of all ethnic ancestries shared a single culture and began to conceive of a single political and economic interest. Making the church American, they concluded, was not just essential to its survival in the United States, but could someday help it to dominate the new republic.

Catholics developed a number of rhetorical strategies of Americanism that served both to unite their diverse communities and to make their case for Catholic patriotism to outsiders. One rhetorical strategy was to search for early American ancestors, Catholics in the colonial, Revolutionary, or Early Republican eras who offered proof that Catholics had been integral parts of the American experiment from the beginning. Catholic heroes of the Revolution such as Charles Carroll, who signed the Declaration of Independence, or Commodore John Barry, who commanded ships in the Revolutionary navy, or even earlier explorers of America—Fr. Jacques Marquette, Hernando De Soto, or Christopher Columbus himself—helped American Catholics make a "genealogical" claim to America. They also served as universal ancestors for Catholics of all ethnic backgrounds, ancestors that could stand beside or even replace the heroes of their homelands. Catholics also ritually invoked the sacrifices that their coreligionists had made defending America in wartime. War heroes, especially fallen ones, suggested the Catholic commitment to American ideals and offered even the newest immigrant object lessons in patriotic piety. A final rhetorical strategy that Catholics used was to suggest that Catholics were the fiercest opponents in America of radical ideas and movements that might be dubbed "un-American." The very ferocity of Catholic opposition to socialism and radicalism, Catholic spokesmen asserted, offered proof of Catholics' American loyalties. Such opposition also helped to suggest the fundamental similarities between Catholic and American values by implying differences between them were insignificant in the face of the alien and dangerous radical other. Such positions, again, also gave the American church a rallying point of political action to unite all Catholic ethnics.

Though efforts to reconcile Catholicism with American culture were constant from the emergence of Catholicism after the Revolution through the nineteenth century, the first great controversy over Catholicism and Americanism did not come until the 1880s and 1890s. At that time a group of Catholic liberals led by Archbishop John Ireland and Bishop John J. Keane argued strongly that if sufficiently Americanized the Catholic Church could become a powerful force in America. That Americanized Catholic Church could then capitalize on America's rising economic and political power to project reformed Catholicism's power throughout the world. These liberals attacked German-Americans' and other groups' attempts to preserve their cultures and demanded that immigrants assimilate quickly. Liberals were also confident about Catholic participation in the American social and cultural mainstream and worried that walling off Catholics in their own schools and societies would alienate non-Catholics and limit Catholic power. The liberals encountered stiff opposition both in the United States and in the Vatican. At home, German- and French Canadian-Americans resented the largely Irish-American liberals' insistence on forced Americanization of their people. Yet even some bishops, who were more sympathetic to the Americanization of immigrants, bridled at the liberals' eagerness to accommodate non-Catholics. Pope Leo XIII seemed to agree. The Vatican eventually insisted on separate societies and schools for Catholics in America, and in 1899 the pope condemned a heresy vaguely defined as "Americanism."

Liberal defeat did not put an end to Catholic efforts to reconcile American and Catholic culture. In the first half of the twentieth century, a definition of American Catholicism as patriotically American but militantly Catholic began to dominate the church in the United States. Bishops like Cardinal O'Connell of Boston and later Cardinal Spellman of New York helped define this new militant American Catholicism, but upwardly mobile American-born lay men and women eagerly participated in its promotion through associations like the Knights of Columbus or the Catholic Daughters of America. One of the Knights' ceremonials or rituals proclaimed, for example, "Proud in the olden days was the boast: 'I am a Roman Catholic'; prouder yet today is the boast, 'I am an American citizen'; but the proudest boast of all times is ours to make, 'I am an American Catholic citizen.'"

In 1938, alarmed by the recent rise of "dangerous theories" and "public subversion" of morality, Pope Pius XI asked American bishops to encourage study of the "science of civics" and to create a "program of social action" that would address the "disorientation" of the times. Heeding the pope's "injunction," the bishops decreed that "our people from childhood to mature age be instructed in the true nature of Christian democracy. . . . They must be held to the conviction that love of country is a virtue and that disloyalty is a sin." The bishops thus created a Commission on American Citizenship at Catholic University in Washington, D.C., and directed it to develop a citizenship curriculum for Catholic school teachers, and a series of readers, the *Faith and Freedom* series, for students in Catholic elementary schools around the United States. In addition to these projects, the commission published a number of other books, pamphlets, youth magazines, and even a series of comic books, called *Treasure Chest*. Finally, the commission promoted the formation of civics clubs in every Catholic elementary school, under guidelines that it issued.

In 1884 the bishops of the United States had met in Baltimore and decreed that every Catholic parish in the nation should build its own school within two years and that Catholic parents should make every effort to send their children to such schools. Despite the mandate, the growth of Catholic schools varied significantly by region. The Massachusetts dioceses of Boston and Springfield were slow to build their own schools, while in the Chicago archdiocese school construction followed almost immediately upon completion of the parish church—and sometimes even preceded it. If there was no consistency among dioceses in building schools, there was also little uniformity in their curricula and management practices through most of the nineteenth century. Most parish schools ran more or less independently, since dioceses had no central supervisory administrations until the turn of the century (the first diocesan school superintendent was appointed in New York in 1888).

In the twentieth century, the development of Catholic education became more consistent, Catholic school administration more systematic, and curricula increasingly standardized. In the new atmosphere of militant Catholicism, dioceses such as Boston or Springfield, which had once lagged in school construction, now picked up the pace. In 1940 over seventy-five hundred Catholic parishes in the United States had their own schools, and those schools enrolled over two million students. It was a vast system supported entirely by

Catholics and dwarfed the private schooling efforts of any other religious group in the country. All the dioceses also eventually appointed school superintendents and expanded diocesan school bureaucracies. As early as 1902, this emerging class of Catholic school administrators and parochial school teachers and principals formed a national organization, the Parish School Conference, to encourage professionalization and to provide a forum for discussing common problems. The conference merged two years later with other associations to create the Catholic Education Association.

The size and breadth of the Catholic school system, the evolution of centralized diocesan school systems, and the emergence of national forums for Catholic educators undoubtedly facilitated the Commission on American Citizenship's success in quickly spreading its message of "Christian citizenship" among Catholic children. By 1964, sales of the *Faith and Freedom* readers had risen to over three million volumes, and three-fifths of the eleven thousand Catholic elementary schools in the United States were using the books as their basic readers. Commission-sponsored civics clubs became just as popular. In 1947, 657 Catholic schools had such civics clubs; by 1965, 5,000 schools—192 in Chicago alone—had clubs.

The selections enclosed here include two readings from the *Faith and Freedom* reader for the seventh grade, *These Are Our Freedoms*. The book was compiled (and partially written) by Sister Mary Charlotte of the Sisters of Mercy and Dr. Mary Synon, who was a longtime member of the Commission's staff, and was published by Ginn and Company in 1944. These two selections reflect some of the rhetorical strategies Catholics used to prove the harmony between Catholic and American loyalties and to provide a common American Catholic culture for an ethnically diverse people. The first selection, "The Spirit of the Navy," for example, stresses Catholics' sacrifice in war on behalf of their country; in this case, World War II, still raging when *These Are Our Freedoms* was published. Catholics played a critical role in the war, making up an estimated 25 to 35 percent of the nation's armed forces. Yet they probably assumed an even larger role in public consciousness of the conflict as Hollywood lionized Catholics as the embodiment of American fighting men in movies such as the *Fighting Sullivans*. "The Spirit of the Navy" emerges naturally from such a context as well as from the celebrated exploits of actual heroes such as the pilot Colin Kelly. More important, it explicitly hammers home a consistent point of Catholic Americanist rhetoric: the virtual identification or unity between Catholic and American values. "Be a good Catholic," the flight commander John J. Shea tells his son Jackie, "and you can't help being a good American."

The second selection, "The Judge and Young Sebastian," is somewhat different. It is set in the early years of the nation's history and thus helps establish Catholicism's legitimacy by pointing to its presence at the very birth of the American nation. More interesting, however, is the fact that it raises the existence of discrimination against Catholics in early America. The text does this not to challenge American ideals but to make a point about the ultimate power of American ideals. "In a free country like ours, men will, in time, correct such injustice," the story predicts. The tale teaches and underlines proper, patient, nonviolent participation in the American political system. "The only way we could win justice was by proving that we were good citizens, loyal citizens, honest citizens."

We should note that William Gaston was not the strong democrat portrayed in the story. He was a Federalist and later a Whig, and a staunch opponent of Thomas Jefferson, James Madison, and Andrew Jackson. He hated the French Revolution and believed that "property" as well as people deserved representation in state and national legislatures. He also owned slaves. He did, however, believe that slavery, "more than any other cause, keeps us back in the career of improvement." He helped North Carolina's Quakers manumit their slaves and, in a celebrated decision during his career as a judge, freed a slave accused of slaying his overseer by claiming that the slave had a right to self-defense. As described in "The Judge and Young Sebastian," Gaston also fought hard in the Constitutional Convention of 1835 to retain suffrage for free African Americans, a fight he lost in a close vote. As also described in the story, he was a devoted Catholic, who fought for and won the deletion of anti-Catholic discriminatory clauses from the Constitution.

What is perhaps most intriguing about this story, however, is its focus on the issue of African-American struggles for civil rights at such an early period. The counsel the story offers African-Americans is conservative, advising them to wait and work hard but peacefully for change; that the story addresses such an issue at all is somewhat surprising. Though the Civil Rights movement was picking up momentum after World War II, Catholics were somewhat slow to enlist in that crusade. The inclusion of this and several other stories on race relations and African-Americans may reflect the influence of Monsignor Francis Haas, who was both chairman of the Executive Committee of the Commission on American Citizenship and President Roosevelt's second chairman of the federal government's Fair Employment Practices Commission.

The stories printed here are from Sister M. Charlotte, R.S.M., and Dr. Mary Synon, *These Are Our Freedoms* (Washington, D.C.: Ginn for the Catholic University of America, 1944): "The Spirit of the Navy" in *The Continental Navy* pp. 71–74, and "The Judge and Young Sebastian," pp. 209–20.

Further Reading

Christopher Kauffman, *Faith and Fraternalism: The History of the Knights of Columbus, 1882–1982* (New York:Harper and Row, 1982); Jay P. Dolan, *The American Catholic Experience: A History from Colonial Times to the Present* (Garden City, N.Y.: Doubleday, 1985); Timothy J. Walch, *Parish School: American Parochial Education from Colonial Times to the Present* (New York: Crossroads, 1996); John T. McGreevy, *Parish Boundaries: The Catholic Encounter with Race in the Twentieth-Century Urban North* (Chicago: University of Chicago Press, 1996); Donald F. Crosby, *God, Church and Flag: Senator Joseph McCarthy and the Catholic Church, 1950–1957* (Chapel Hill: University of North Carolina Press, 1978).

The Continental Navy

How did the men of the Continental Navy feel as they went into battle under John Barry, John Paul Jones, Joshua Barney, and the other brave captains of that time?

Nearly every man above decks or below decks was a plain man, come from a plain home. It was not a time of easy writing or much writing. No one of them left a record of his thoughts as he prepared to go into action; but we know that they established a tradition of service which has come down through the years.

This tradition has been expressed by a man who lived, not in that time, but just a little while ago. He was John J. Shea of Boston, the flight-deck commander of the aircraft carrier *Wasp*. Out in the South Pacific in the dark times of the Second World War, he set down that spirit of love of God, of home, and of country which the first sailors of the American Navy had known.

On the feast day of Saint Peter and Saint Paul, as the carrier sailed bravely and perilously, under the Southern Cross, this man wrote a letter. He had not thought that anyone but a member of his own family would ever see it; and in it he set down the thoughts of his soul. It was a letter to his five-year-old son. It read:

June 29, 1942

Dear Jackie:

This is the first letter I have ever written directly to my little son, and I am thrilled to know that you can read it all by yourself. If you miss some of the words, I am sure it will be because I do not write very plainly. Mother will help you in that case, I am sure.

I was certainly glad to hear your voice over the long-distance telephone. It sounded as though I were right in the living room with you. You sounded as though you missed your Daddy very much. I miss you too, more than anyone will ever know. It is too bad that this war could not have been delayed a few more years so that I could grow up again with you and do with you all the things I planned to do when you were old enough to go to school.

I thought how nice it would be for me to come home early in the afternoon and play ball with you, and go mountain climbing and see the trees and brooks, and learn all about woodcraft, hunting, fishing, swimming and things like that. I suppose we must be brave and put things off for a little while.

When you are a little bigger you will know why your Daddy is not home so much any more. You know we have a big country and we have ideals as to how people should live and enjoy the riches of it, and how each is born with equal rights to life, freedom, and the pursuit of happiness. Unfortunately, there are some countries in the world where they don't have these ideals, where a boy cannot grow up to be what he wants to be with no limit on his opportunities to be a great man, such as a great priest, statesman, doctor, soldier, businessman, etc.

Because there are people and countries who want to change our nation, its ideals, form of government, and way of life, we must leave our homes and families to fight. Fighting for the defense of our country, ideals, homes and honor is an honor and a duty which your Daddy has to do before he can come home to be with you and mother. When it is done he is coming home to be with you always and forever. So wait just a little while longer. I am afraid it will be more than the two weeks you told me on the phone.

In the meantime take good care of Mother. Be a good boy and grow up to be a good young man. Study hard when you go to school. Be a leader in everything good in life. Be a good Catholic and you can't help being a good American. Play fair always. Strive to win, but if you must lose, lose like a gentleman and a good sportsman. Don't ever be a quitter either in sports or in your business or profession when you grow up. Get all the education you can. Stay close to Mother and follow her advice. Obey her in everything, no matter how you may at times disagree. She knows what is best and will never let you down or lead you away from the right and honorable things in life. If I don't get back, you will have to be Mother's protector because you will be the only one she has. You must grow up to take my place as well as your own in her life and heart.

Love your Grandmother and Granddad as long as they live. They too will never let you down. Love your aunts and see them as often as you can. Last of all, don't ever forget your Daddy. Pray for him to come back, and if it is God's will that he does not, be the kind of boy and man your Daddy wants you to be.

Write me very often and tell me everything. Kiss mother for me every night. Good-bye for now, with all my love and devotion for Mother and you.

Your Daddy

A little while afterward, in the battle for the Solomon Islands, the *Wasp* was sunk. The flight-deck commander, John J. Shea, United States Navy, was reported "missing in action." He was dead long before his son was able to read what his father had written to him; but that letter, the "Letter to Jackie," has become one of the famous human documents of American history because it speaks so truly and so well the spirit of the men of our nation who go down to the sea in ships for God, country, and home.

DISCUSSION

You will probably want to discuss the "Letter to Jackie" in class. It is interesting and helpful to exchange ideas with your fellow pupils. To make your opinion worthwhile, you must explain to your classmates why you think as you do.

These questions are suggested for discussion. If you were impressed by any other point, you may bring it to the attention of the class.

1. What kind of mood do you think Commander Shea was in when he wrote this letter?
2. Why do you suppose he wrote this sort of letter to Jackie?
3. Do you think he expected a small boy to understand everything he said?
4. Contrast the first three paragraphs with paragraphs six and seven. What are the two chief differences?
5. Judging him from his own statements in this letter, what idea have you formed of Commander Shea as a father? a citizen? a Catholic? a naval officer?

6. Which sentence in the letter impressed you most?
7. Is there any one sentence that you think the commander might have
   meant more earnestly than all the others?
8. Do you think Commander Shea's letter will have any effect on the life of his son?

The Judge and Young Sebastian

The Judge and Young Sebastian were riding to Raleigh. The judge was nearly
sixty. Young Sebastian was twenty-one. The judge was white. Young Sebastian
was black. The judge was a great and famous statesman, William Gaston, who
had been a member of Congress from his North Carolina district, and, until a
little while earlier, chief justice of the supreme court of his native state. Young
Sebastian was a servant, the grandson of a slave, Old Sebastian, who had been
set free by the Gastons, with all their other slaves.

The judge and Young Sebastian were friends. They rode in quiet comradeship on that June day through the North Carolina pine woods. Young Sebastian's sorrel horse followed the judge's chestnut mare over narrow trails; but as
they came to open country, they rode side by side.

Sometimes the old man and the young man smiled at each other as a wild
turkey ran across the road or they heard the drumming of a partridge. "Mighty
good dinner for someone," Young Sebastian said. But since he knew why Judge
Gaston was silent, he too stayed silent.

"You're like your grandfather, Young Sebastian," the judge said at last. They
were passing through a little settlement where a few men stood before the general store. The men bowed to Judge Gaston, but stared angrily at his companion. There was an excitement about them which Young Sebastian understood.
Did not every man in North Carolina, who knew anything at all, know that
delegates were about to meet in a convention which would change the voting
laws of the state? And that votes for Catholics, and votes for free Negroes, and
votes for men without any property were to be considered by that convention?

That was why Judge Gaston was going to Raleigh. He had resigned from his
place on the supreme court of the state so that he would be free to fight against
the law which prevented Catholics from holding office in North Carolina. The
judge was a Catholic. He had always been a Catholic, a good Catholic. His fellow citizens knew that, and they had put him into one office after another, in
spite of the law. He was, they said, always the best man for the place. "Let the
law be a dead letter!" they cried. But Judge Gaston said that no law was dead
while it stayed on the books, and he had set out to have it taken from the
books.

Young Sebastian thought of all this before he spoke to the judge. He
thought, too, of many qualities that the judge had: honesty, fairness, devotion
to his family, his friends, his servants, particularly to Old Sebastian. "I'm not as
good a man as Old Sebastian, Sir," he said.

"Who said you were?" the judge demanded. "I said you were like him. Perhaps, if you live long enough, you may be as good a man as he is."

"That would take a long, long time, Judge."

"Old Sebastian started a long time ago," Judge Gaston said. "He was working for us when the British soldiers killed my father, although my father was a doctor, not a soldier. Sebastian could have left us then. They were only my mother and my sister Jane and I—and I was three years old. My mother did not like slavery. She was an English Catholic who wanted freedom of all kinds for all men, just as her people had always wanted freedom of worship for themselves. She offered to set Sebastian free. He said he would not take his freedom until I was of legal age and gave it to him "

"Old Sebastian always says your mother was a fine woman, Judge," the young man said.

"There never was a better woman." The judge looked ahead as if he were watching the road; but Young Sebastian knew that he was not looking forward at all. "I was baptized an American in the blood of my father. I was baptized a Catholic in the faith of my mother. I have always thanked God for that."

"We don't get much chance down here to be good Catholics," Young Sebastian said. "Once a year, maybe, the bishop can come to baptize, and confirm and marry folks, and hear their confessions, and say Mass, and give Communion."

"You could be a good Catholic if you were wrapped up in a bale of cotton," the judge said sharply. "Remember this, Young Sebastian. After I die, even if there's a long time when no priest can come as far as our settlement, you must keep your faith. Promise me that!"

"Oh, I promise, Judge," said Young Sebastian.

"My mother was a long way from any Catholic settlement," the judge went on. "After my father's death some people wanted her to take Jane and me to her people in England. Other people told her to take us to a Catholic country, France or Spain or Italy. We Catholics should be more welcome there, they said, than we were in North Carolina. My mother said no. This was our home, our country. My father had died for it. Here we would stay, and stay Catholics."

"We could not have stayed, I sometimes think, if it had not been for your grandfather. He was young, but he was strong, the only strong man on the place. He cut down trees. He plowed fields. He sowed crops. He reaped harvests. He built houses. And until I had the legal right to give him his freedom, he would not take it. Somehow, I never thought of him as a slave. Sebastian was my helper, my friend."

"Did he ever tell you," the judge went on, "how he saved my life? He was about your age, and I was not quite nine years old. I had followed him into the woods. A wildcat attacked me. Sebastian killed it with his bare hands. He never let me tell my mother for fear it would worry her when I was away from the house; but he made me promise not to go into the woods without him."

"We got so much in the way of being together that he asked my mother to let him ride north with me when I started to college. I was the first student at

Georgetown. I did not believe I could have made the journey to Maryland without Sebastian. He cared for everything, food and shelter for us on the way, my room in the college. He almost studied for me through the first weeks while he stayed. Afterward he rode back and forth, between Georgetown and North Carolina, with messages for me, and clothes, and even cakes. Once he brought me a watermelon."

"All the time," the judge continued, "he kept up the work of the plantation. I was of age when I came home, a graduate of Georgetown and of the College of New Jersey. I was a lawyer then; and my first use of the law was to give freedom to Sebastian and all his family and to every other Negro on the place. I have always been glad that I did that. God has made all men free. The least that we, His creatures, can do is to follow His law."

"We're all certainly glad you feel like that, Judge," Young Sebastian said. "There are plenty of men hereabout who don't think so. People tell that this convention where you are going will take away the right to vote which free Negroes have in North Carolina."

"Yes I know." All the kindliness went out of Judge Gaston's face. "I know what some of the men in that convention plan to do, and I am going to fight them to the last ditch. They are the same men who want to keep in the institution the law which is an insult to us Catholics, even though they say it is nothing now but a dead letter."

"It is a dead letter, Judge," the young man said. "The voters of the state of North Carolina have elected you to office, time and again, although the law says that Catholics can't hold office. Everyone knows that you are a good Catholic, and everyone keeps on voting for you."

"But that law is wrong," the judge shouted. "What if the voters elect me? Someday they'll keep a better man out of office because of it. I will not rest until it is out of the lawbooks." He frowned deeply as they came within sight of Raleigh, a community big for its time and place, but still only a little city. "What do you know about voting, Young Sebastian?" he asked.

"I know what you have taught me, sir."

"Then let me tell you something more. The right of freemen to vote is the safeguard of this republic, as it is of any democracy. Unless all good, decent responsible adult citizens may use this right to vote, the republic is in danger."

"Not very many men can use that right now, Judge," the Negro said.

"No," said the judge. "It's a right, but all men don't realize that, Young Sebastian."

"I'll be able to vote next election," Young Sebastian said, "unless they take my vote away from me. If they do—"

"If they do, there's nothing you can do about it," said the judge.

"Oh yes, there is," Young Sebastian cried; but the judge was paying him no heed. A party of riders was waiting for them at a crossroads. Shouts of welcome greeted Judge Gaston as men surrounded him. Young Sebastian fell in with the riders, and they jogged on into town.

Around the tavern where Judge Gaston found lodging Young Sebastian heard the talk of stableman and slaves, of newspaper writers and politicians. The Convention called to revise the constitution of North Carolina was of more than usual importance. The questions of removing the handicaps under which Catholics suffered, of taking out the rule which required that a man own property before he could vote, and of taking away the vote of free Negroes had aroused men to fever heat. Every group around the tavern argued for or against the law as it stood. There was discontent among the poor men who could not vote because they had not enough property and among the free Negroes, whose right to vote was threatened. Everywhere Young Sebastian heard words of hate, of threat

The words fanned in him a determination which had been growing ever since he had heard that his right to vote might be taken from him. From the time he had been a little boy on the Gaston plantation, he had looked forward to the day when he would cast his ballot. It was true that many free Negroes in North Carolina did not, for one reason or another, use their voting right; but Old Sebastian's children and grandchildren had always cherished and exercised that right. They had voted proudly, election after election, for those candidates who they had come to believe were the best men for the offices. Young Sebastian had planned already how he would write his ballot. Now, if the vote were taken away, he had another plan.

If he could not vote in the land where he had been born, the land where his grandfather had won freedom by honesty and loyalty and courage, then he would go to another land. He would go to Liberia, the place in Africa which had been founded some ten years earlier as a colony for Free Negroes. There he would have not only freedom but the rewards of freedom. "If they pass that law against my people," he told himself sullenly, "I'll just throw this North Carolina dust off my feet so fast that not even the judge can hold me."

For a little while he could not tell the frame of mind of the men who were meeting for the convention. They might believe, as Judge Gaston believed, that men, regardless of color or property ownership or form of worship, should be given the vote when they were of proper age. They might, on the other hand, believe that the vote should be taken from freemen who were Negroes or had not sufficient property to qualify, and they might also believe that Catholics should be kept from holding office. No one knew yet which way the tide would run.

There were several free Negroes in the town, most of them servants to men who, like Gaston, had freed their slaves. Young Sebastian had little to say to them, however, for his work for the judge kept him busy. Dimly he knew that he was fighting his way through his own problem, just as the judge was striving to find a solution for the questions which the convention would decide. Always, however, he went back to his promise to himself: "If they don't let me vote at the next election, I'll go to Liberia." That, he told himself, was the answer for him.

Young Sebastian knew that the convention was in session in the big hall, but he knew that he had no chance of hearing anything of its meetings. The best he could learn came to him in scraps of talk from men who had come from the sessions. From them he could not tell what the convention would do. Some said it would uphold all Judge Gaston asked. Others said that the judge would be defeated on every one of the three issues for which he was fighting.

At the end of the first day the judge came wearily back to the tavern. Young Sebastian rushed to serve him, but so many men crowded into the room that the young man had no chance to ask any question of the elder. In the morning men came early to take Judge Gaston off to the convention hall, and again Young Sebastian lived through hours of doubt.

The days which followed were little better. Hour after hour, the delegates to the convention talked in the hot rooms of the hall. For a time it seemed as if the meeting would never end. Then, suddenly, came the news that the voting on the questions had begun. People rushed toward the hall and stood outside in crowds, watching the windows and the doors. Finally, through the big door, delegates began to come out into the hot afternoon sunshine.

Judge Gaston was one of the last to come. Young Sebastian saw instantly how old and weary he looked. He rushed to his side. "What can I do for you, Judge?" he asked before he put the question which burned in his brain.

"Nothing, nothing," the judge said. He leaned heavily upon the Negro's arm. "It was not a good day for us, Young Sebastian. We gained one point—but we lost two."

"Which one did you win?" Young Sebastian asked huskily.

"Catholics may now be elected to office in the state of North Carolina," the judge said. "The convention passed that amendment unanimously. It voted, though, that men must have some property to vote for state senators. That was a compromise. And it voted that free Negroes can no longer vote in our state. I am sorry, Young Sebastian. I did my best to prevent that."

"Yes, sir," Young Sebastian said. He walked silently with the judge through the crowd; but when they came near the tavern, he spoke, "Judge," he said, "would you mind, if I didn't go back home with you now?"

"Where do you want to go?" the judge asked.

"I'm going to Liberia," Young Sebastian said. "I can be really free there. I can vote there. I shall be with my own people there—and with no other people. I can't stay here any more. I'm going, Judge. I'm going fast."

"Listen to me Young Sebastian." The judge's voice was weary, but it was also firm. You may say you want to be with your own people. What of your father and mother? They won't go to Liberia. What of your brothers? Do they want to go away from here?"

"They can decide for themselves," the Negro said sullenly.

"No, they can't," said the judge. "Your father and mother are too old to leave this place, which has long been home to them. They feel about this country as my mother felt after my father was killed. She was an American then. Her children were Americans. Your people here are Americans, Young Sebastian. It is true that you have been treated unjustly; but in a free country like ours men will, in time, correct such injustice. This is your country too, and it is cowardly of you to run away."

"What good will it do me or anyone else if I stay?" the young man protested.

"I'll tell you what good it will do," the judge shouted. "Look what has happened today. For years and years we Catholics have suffered under an unjust law. What if we had all run away from our home place because of that law? Would it be changed today if we'd done that? No, sir! I tell you the only way we could win justice was by proving that we were good citizens, loyal citizens, honest citizens. We did not like that law, but we lived under it until we could change it by our conduct. And it'll be that way with you, with your people. You free Negroes should have the vote that has just been taken from you, but you won't win it back by going to Liberia. You'll win it back, Young Sebastian, by doing what your grandfather did through his long lifetime. Be good, be honest, be loyal. Stay on your jobs. Stay at your posts. Do your work better than anyone else can do it. Believe in God, and have faith in your fellow men!"

He turned on his heel and went into the tavern. For a moment Young Sebastian could not follow him. The bitterness of defeat, of humiliation, the blasting of his hopes, and his human pride held him back. He was standing, staring at the tavern door, when the crowd from the convention hall came behind him.

"Gaston," men were shouting, "Judge Gaston! Hurrah for Gaston!" Then, in their shouts, Young Sebastian realized the truth of what the judge had said. Nothing but a lifetime of goodness, of justice, could have won any man not only this praise but the vote on Catholics which the convention had given. It was a triumph, a personal triumph, for William Gaston, and, through him a triumph for all Catholics of the state of North Carolina. Through his leadership his state had given expression in its constitution to ideals of true democracy.

Staring at the old man as he came through the tavern door to face the crowd, Young Sebastian made a promise to himself; but it was also a promise to the judge. "I'll stay," he said. "I won't go to Liberia. I'll stay right here in North Carolina; and maybe someday I'll do for my people what Judge Gaston has done for his people."

He was still staring at the judge as the crowd lifted the old man on their shoulders and bore him joyously through the streets of Raleigh.

READING TO UNDERSTAND PEOPLE

Become acquainted with the characters in the stories that you read. Picture to yourself what people looked like. Try to get their tone of voice and their manner of acting. Feel what is in their minds. Use these helps to understanding "The Judge and Young Sebastian":

1. Do you see the two men coming along the road on horseback? Contrast them in as many ways as you can.
2. What idea do you get of both of them from this statement: "They rode in quiet comradeship"?

3. Read aloud Young Sebastian's first remark as you think he must have made it. Answer him in the tone in which you think the judge answered.
4. At the end of paragraph 6 Young Sebastian made a statement. What do you think of the judge's reply to it and to Sebastian's next remark?
5. Read silently the paragraph that contains this statement: "But Young Sebastian knew that he was not looking forward at all." What do you learn from the characters of the two men?
6. How did the judge feel toward Old Sebastian? What do you think of the judge's attitude toward his servant?
7. What do you learn about Young Sebastian from the speech which he made to himself about going to Liberia?
8. Did the judge seem to feel that he had any obligation toward Young Sebastian?
9. With one pupil impersonating the judge, and another taking the part of Young Sebastian, read aloud the dialogue which begins with the servant's request not to return home.

— 15 —

Sex and Submission in the Spirit

Peter Gardella

In *The Total Woman* (1973), Marabel Morgan became the first evangelical Christian to tell women that they should have orgasms. She also taught women how to manage their households, their husbands, and their spiritual lives. Morgan addressed the "problem that has no name," the misery of married women that Betty Friedan revealed in *The Feminine Mystique* (1963). Though Morgan never challenged patriarchy, her influence earned her a chapter in what some historians have called "the feminization of sex."

The Total Woman was the best-selling book of 1974; in that year of President Nixon's resignation, it outsold *All the President's Men* by one hundred thousand copies. Even after sales reached one and one-half million in 1975, Americans were still buying between ten and twenty thousand copies *per week*. Because many of these sales occurred at Total Woman class sessions and in small, family-owned Christian bookstores, the compilers of best-seller lists did not notice the phenomenon at first.

The book grew out of Morgan's experience running Total Woman workshops, which in the early 1970s had become a small Christian industry. Morgan had trained a network of Total Woman teachers, who offered eight hours of instruction in four classes for fifteen dollars. Seventy-seven of these teachers, each trained by Morgan herself, were traveling the country in 1975. Because the fourth class always included a call to accept Christ, the Total Woman program was a form of evangelism, but it was a parachurch evangelism that bridged a gap between churches and the secular world. Usually, a local Baptist or Methodist church sponsored the course, and the sessions took place in church basements. At the classes, not only *The Total Woman* but other books of advice on marriage and Christian life were displayed and sold. Teachers sent students from class to clothing stores in search of new nightgowns and material for costumes.

Morgan often provoked ridicule, particularly for her recommendation that wives greet their husbands in provocative costumes (black net stockings, high heels, and an apron) and seduce them every night for a week. Even at the height of the Total Woman movement, accounts by the mainstream press tended toward mockery, while some experts condemned Morgan in startlingly vivid terms. A psychiatrist went so far as to call *The Total Woman* "hogwash and bullshit" in an interview for *Time* magazine, while Masters and Johnson said that Morgan taught "a patchwork quilt of impressions, intuitions, and out-of-style dogma." In a review for *Christian Century,* church historian Martin Marty grumbled about Morgan's combination of "total submission, total materialism, total sex and total Bible reading" and hoped he would be around to see evangelicals raptured in costume to meet their Lord. Though Marty pronounced it "fine" for evangelical couples to overcome their hang-ups, he also concluded, "I am not sure this obsessiveness is what the Bible had in mind."

To judge by Morgan's testimony, she was not so much obsessed as responding to an acute need. "In class one wife heard for the first time that she, too, should experience a climax. She went home and told her young executive husband, who replied, 'I didn't think women were supposed to!'" Such ignorance conflicted with the postwar explosion of sexual knowledge, technology, and activity with which married women had to cope. In 1960 the first birth control pills became available, and in 1966 William Masters and Virginia Johnson documented the female capacity for as many as fifty orgasms an hour. In 1973, the *Roe v. Wade* decision struck down all state laws against abortion. A sexual revolution on college campuses and in high schools missed most of Marabel Morgan's audience, but expectations for sexual pleasure in marriage increased, while the constraints that fear of pregnancy imposed on frequency of intercourse and infidelity decreased in force. Looking back from our own day, when young women record songs filled with praise for masturbation and sexual instructions for men, it can be easy to forget that the 1970s provided a large market for Dr. David Reuben's *Any Woman Can!* (1971), which Morgan cited as a guide for the nonorgasmic woman, and that *The Hite Report* (1976) found only 30 percent of women reporting orgasm during intercourse. Morgan took part in a process of education that extended an ethic of mandatory orgasm, which began to prevail among advanced thinkers in the 1920s, to the whole population of the United States.

Orgasm for women moved into evangelical advice literature as the world of evangelical Christians grew dramatically in absolute numbers, cultural expressions, and doctrinal flexibility. Between 1973 and 1983, the Southern Baptist Convention grew by 15 percent, the Assemblies of God by 71 percent, the Church of the Nazarene by 22 percent, and independent churches sprung up across the nation. Christian books and Christian popular music, sold at Christian bookstores, reached a wider audience. Meanwhile, the "Jesus people" revival of the 1960s and 1970s transcended traditional Reformed theologies and denominations to emphasize faith and the power of the Holy Spirit. The scene was set for Morgan to become the first practicing evangelical to write a popular book insisting on the innocence of sex.

"Sex was not the first sin," Morgan taught, agreeing with all theologians. Then she went beyond what biblical scholars had found in Genesis by declaring, "Sex was going strong before sin ever entered the world." Picturing Adam and Eve, she called God a "great romantic" for designing people as "He" did. "With no marriage manuals or doctors to consult," she coyly asked, "can't you imagine their fun and games experimenting with their newfangled parts?" Nor did sin make a difference in sex after Eden. Mining the New Testament, Morgan found Hebrews 13:4 ("Marriage is honorable in all and the bed undefiled") and came to the striking conclusion that "sex is as clean and pure as eating cottage cheese."

Having freed sex from sin, Morgan declared it good and therefore obligatory. Morgan found both physical and spiritual obligations to mutual orgasm. "A Total Woman knows that sex is vital to her marriage," she wrote. "Unless both she and he are satisfied while making love, her marriage rates only a C+ at best." Only through mutual orgasm could sex fulfill its purpose of enabling husband and wife to "know each other in the depths of their being." Biology demanded orgasm, Morgan insisted; "Physically, the climax during intercourse is the greatest pleasure on earth. Medical research reveals that a climax renews and restores the body. Better physical health also results. What marvelous therapy!" Morgan also connected orgasm with spiritual rebirth. "For sexual intercourse to be the ultimate satisfaction, both partners need a personal relationship with God," she wrote. If they have such a bond, "their union is sacred and beautiful. . . . Intercourse becomes the place where man and woman discover each other in a new dimension." But unless sexual experience reached these sacred heights, "Sex becomes frustrating to the wife, and even destructive."

By claiming that sex was free from guilt, physically healthy, and spiritually meaningful, Morgan gave evangelical Christians an obligation to sexual pleasure that resembled the standards imposed by Alex Comfort in *The Joy of Sex* (1974) and by sex researchers who counted and measured orgasms. *The Total Woman* introduced Christian women to an ethic of innocent ecstasy that pervaded American culture in the years before AIDS. Carrying this process forward, the Reverend Tim LaHaye and Beverly LaHaye wrote *The Act of Marriage* in 1976, and another evangelical couple, Dr. Ed and Gaye Wheat, wrote *Intended for Pleasure* in 1977. While both books gave much more technical guidance regarding sexual positions, Kegel exercises, clitoral stimulation, and common sexual problems than Morgan offered, they merely inherited and continued her high expectations for sexual pleasure and her association of orgasm and spiritual fulfillment. Morgan provided a few specifics in the sequel to *The Total Woman*, called *Total Joy* (1976). Citing a letter from a woman "married twenty-five years with five kids," who had never had an orgasm because her husband "doesn't know where the clitoris is," she advised: "If your husband is also in the dark on this matter, tell him where your clitoris is, and anything else that you particularly like to have caressed. You will probably reach a beautiful orgasm when he gently and patiently applies a rhythmic pressure to your clitoris. But knowing its location is essential! Don't give up. It may take time, but it's worth the wait."

Unlike Christian sex manuals and most secular advice literature, Marabel Morgan imposed the duty of taking sexual initiative on wives. Although Morgan's counsel that "a woman's hands should never be still when she is making love" was rather vague, and her advice to spray the sheets with cologne and to drape a red nightgown over the bedside lamp might seem dangerous, Morgan did make women the active agents in their marriages. She wrote for women who needed to make their marriages work.

Her sense of that need grew out of personal history. Born in 1937 in Mansfield, Ohio, a rustbelt city of less than forty thousand near Akron, Morgan suffered the loss of her father to divorce when she was three years old and the loss of her step-father, a policeman who had adopted her, to a heart attack when she was four-teen. "I never saw a happy marriage when I was young," she told *Time* magazine; instead, she saw "a lot of fighting." Her family had no automobile and took no vacations. Morgan claimed never to have tasted steak until a boyfriend took her to dinner when she was eighteen.

Despite hardships, the girl who was then named Marabel Hawk did well at school, won the titles of Miss Mansfield and Miss Congeniality in the Ohio Miss America pageant, and became a beautician who "made good money" and "had freedom." By the time she was twenty-two, she had enough money to go to Ohio State University, where she was named May Queen. Her money and interest ran out after a year of college, and she went back to the beauty shop in Mansfield, where, "with the water running," she experienced rebirth in Jesus. While on a vacation in Miami, she found a new job with the Campus Crusade for Christ and met a law student, Charles Morgan, whom she married in 1964.

The Total Woman rejected equality in marriage because Morgan claimed to have tried it and failed. Morgan's vision of domestic bliss dawned after seven years of marriage, which had produced three daughters (including one who died after being born one month premature) and a growing alienation from her husband. Shocked when her husband called her "uptight," she found herself screaming at him for dumping his briefcase and packages on the table she had just polished. She noticed that he told her less and less about what happened during his day and seemed less and less romantic. Urging him to do what she wanted could not make him take out the garbage, buy a new refrigerator, or give her the money to redecorate the family room. Then came the moment of rebirth.

One night at dinner, Charles Morgan told his wife that he had accepted an invitation to go out with another couple on the next evening. She protested that she had made other plans. He responded with a new policy: from now on he would tell her twenty minutes before they were going out. Bursting into tears, Marabel Morgan left the table and went to her room. When her husband did not come up to console her, she had the epiphany that became *The Total Woman*. She could never change him, but she could change herself. If she recognized what he needed in a wife, she could get what she wanted from him. She would walk him to the door and wave until his car was out of sight; she would make the salad and set the table for the evening meal at nine in the morning, so that she could take a bubble bath at five; she would put on heels and pearls (or perhaps a baby-doll nightgown and boots, her first costume) and greet him in the evening. She would practice "the four A's" in relation to her husband: accept, admire, appreciate, and adapt. In sex, she would "be the seducer, rather than the seducee." Within a week, according to *The Total Woman,* Charles Morgan was leading his daughters in applauding their mother at breakfast. He sent a new refrigerator to their home without being asked; one night he told her to go ahead and redecorate the family room. He even began to talk with her again.

According to the Total Woman legend, friends noticed how happy the Morgans were, and wives began to ask Marabel for advice. She held luncheons and organized outings to the lingerie store. Several wives of Miami Dolphins football players, whom Charles Morgan represented as a sports attorney, gave Marabel good publicity and the numbers grew until "women would call every half-hour until midnight." Morgan knew she had to write a book. Like many self-help writers, she consulted experts to support what she already had discovered for herself, and she admitted to trying for a fifth-grade reading level in her use of written language. Yet she succeeded in writing about household management (and husband management) with humor and about sex with modesty.

A feminist might observe that Morgan had discovered the wisdom that Jean Baker Miller ascribed to all subordinate groups in *Toward a New Psychology of Women* (1976). As Miller explained, all social systems in which inequality is regarded as permanent result in dominant and subordinate groups with very different sets of knowledge. Permanent subordinates—whether peasants or slaves or women—become highly aware of the opinions of the dominants, become able to predict their reactions of pleasure and displeasure, and so learn how to get what they want. Though critics complained that Morgan was teaching women to manipulate their husbands, indirect action may be an inevitable tactic for a permanent subordinate. And most of the aims of a Total Woman—a happy husband, orgasmic sex, and a beautiful, or at least well-equipped, home—could be attained within a system of subordination.

Accepting subordination constituted more than practical wisdom to Morgan, however. She also believed from her Bible that "God ordained man to be the head of the family" and that "when this order is turned around, the family is upside down." Subordination appeared to Morgan as a religious duty. Becoming a Total Woman involved a pattern of spiritual experience resembling the process of becoming a born-again Christian. In the chapter of *The Total Woman* Morgan called "Power Source," she told a story of effort and exhaustion, conviction of sin, realization of grace, rebirth, and life in the Spirit, with regard to her acceptance of Jesus, that paralleled her story of accepting her husband. Just as she had worked to be a good wife and to get what she wanted from marriage, so as a child and young woman she had tried to be a good person. She studied philosophy in college, won "academic honors and campus and state beauty contest awards," traveled to Europe, and left school to make money, but she found life to be empty. Though she never doubted her "love for God" and "believed in Him with all [her] heart," she could not make contact with God's love; her "prayers seemed to bounce off the ceiling." A feeling of unreality pursued her as she looked at her hands and wondered who she was. Then a friend pointed out Isaiah 59, where the prophet says that Israel's iniquities have separated its people from God. Morgan suddenly saw her "garden variety" bad habits—worry, unbelief, gossiping, pride—as real sins. She could then accept her need for a savior and ask Jesus to take away her sins. Instead of trying to make life meaningful for herself, she found that Jesus became her purpose and the source of her power.

Morgan said she was reborn in Christ at twenty-three, which dates that event to 1960. She married on her twenty-seventh birthday, in 1964, and the epiphany that led to The Total Woman could not have happened before 1971; but the problem and the pattern of solution were the same. When she worked to control herself, her marriage, and her husband, her efforts bred resentment. Only after she saw herself as the source of tension—the moment analogous to conviction of sin—and accepted her husband as he was did Charles Morgan begin to share his power. Though "a Total Woman is not a slave," Marabel Morgan now knew that God ordained marriage as an unequal relationship on the analogy of His relations with humanity. Women who found this unacceptable should stay single. As Simone de Beauvoir wrote in The Second Sex that no one is born a woman, so Morgan could have written that no one is born a Total Woman; to attain that spiritual state, you must be born again.

Morgan feared that when she quoted Ephesians 5:22, "wives must submit to your husbands' leadership in the same way you submit to the Lord," women would "scream and throw this book away"; yet millions continued to read the book and go to Total Woman classes. Perhaps they found the message acceptable because the submission Morgan counseled followed an individualistic, Protestant pattern suitable for American women. During the 1970s, other kinds of patriarchal marriage, such as the Catholic model reasserted by Pope Paul VI in the encyclical against birth control, Humanae vitae (1968), or the traditions of orthodox Jews, came under direct attack from feminists and liberals. Catholic and Jewish ideals demanded that women subordinate their desires not so much to their husbands as to their religions, which entailed restraints on sexuality and other behavior. Morgan's evangelical model, on the other hand, urged a woman to seek pleasure in sex, to seek power from God, and to put her husband in the mood to "spoil her with goodies" in the material world. All of these goals reinforced each other, and only the most abstract self-denial was required.

The dream of marriage as a round of sex and goodies may have been appealing as wish fulfillment for the many women who experienced marriage as grinding work inside and outside the home—in addition to coping with the demands of husbands at night. Very few of the examples in The Total Woman or its sequel, Total Joy, even mentioned women with paying jobs, except to say that the schedule of bubble baths could be adjusted. Some women must have read the books to help them imagine what they might do if they could stay at home during the day. For others, Morgan may have provided a way to cope with the new sexual expectations of American men. In Worlds of Pain (1976), a study of working-class marriages, sociologist Lillian Rubin described women with husbands who had recently begun to expect their wives to have orgasms, multiple orgasms, and oral sex, yet who became frightened if their women did become orgasmic or begin to take the sexual initiative. Wives dealing with such husbands could have used *The Total Woman* (which never mentioned oral sex) both as a fantasy and as a guide to unthreatening behavior.

Morgan's advice that wives should submit reflected a cultural consensus about healthy development and gender roles. According to that consensus, when women tried for equality or leadership in marriage, disaster ensued not only for the couple but also for their children. To drive this point home, Morgan told the story of a woman who decided to ignore her husband and concentrate on the children. Gradually, her son lost respect for his father and identified with his mother. "Physically, he can appear quite masculine. Emotionally, however, because of his strong attachment to his mother, the door is open to homosexuality." Marabel Morgan here echoed a warning that Betty Friedan had issued a decade before in *The Feminine Mystique*. Both women feared that a matriarchal society of dominant mothers and passive fathers would encourage what Friedan called "parasitical mother-love," which the feminist held responsible for "the homosexuality that is spreading like a murky smog over the American scene" (Friedan, p. 276).

Morgan and Friedan saw some startlingly similar problems but differed in their prescriptions. Friedan recommended "a new life plan for women" that included meaningful work outside the family. The heart of Morgan's advice appears in the following selections, which include a few pages about costumes and the chapters on "Super Sex" and "Power Source" from *The Total Woman*. Although these passages led Martin Marty to call his review of Morgan "Fundies and Their Fetishes," and although Barbara Ehrenreich referred to "Fundamentalist S/M" and the "slave mentality" of evangelical women, Morgan could also be seen as a woman taking control.

The selections are from Marabel Morgan, *The Total Woman* (Old Tappan, N.J.: Fleming H. Revell, 1973), pp. 94–99, 114–28, 171–81.

Further Reading

Barbara Ehrenreich, Elizabeth Hess, and Gloria Jacobs, *Re-Making Love: The Feminization of Sex* (New York: Doubleday, 1986) has a good chapter on "Fundamentalist Sex." Other sources are Betty Friedan, *The Feminine Mystique* (1963; rev. ed., New York: W. W. Norton, 1997); Peter Gardella, *Innocent Ecstasy: How Christianity Gave America an Ethic of Sexual Pleasure* (New York: Oxford University Press, 1985); Shere Hite, *The Hite Report: A Nationwide Study of Female Sexuality* (New York: Dell, 1976); Tim and Beverly LaHaye, *The Act of Marriage: The Beauty of Sexual Love* (Grand Rapids, Mich.: Zondervan, 1976); Jean Baker Miller, *Toward a New Psychology of Women* (Boston: Beacon, 1976); Mark Oppenheimer, "In the

Biblical Sense: A Guide to the Booming Christian Sex-Service Industry," found at: http://Slate.msn.com/Features/Sex/Sex.asp (November 15, 2000). Slate has links to websites on sex advice for evangelicals.

The Total Woman

COSTUME PARTY

One morning, Charlie remarked about the pressures of the day that lay ahead of him. All day I remembered his grim face as he drove away. Knowing he would feel weary and defeated, I wondered how I could revive him when he came home.

For an experiment I put on pink baby-doll pajamas and white boots after my bubble bath. I must admit that I looked foolish and felt even more so. When I opened the door that night to greet Charlie, I was unprepared for his reaction. My quiet, reserved, nonexcitable husband took one look, dropped his briefcase on the doorstep, and chased me around the dining-room table. We were in stitches by the time he caught me, and breathless with that old feeling of romance. Our little girls stood flat against the wall watching our escapade, giggling with delight. We all had a marvelous evening together, and Charlie forgot to mention the problems of the day.

Have you ever met your husband at the front door in some outrageously sexy outfit? I can hear you howl, "She's got to be kidding. My husband's not the type, and besides, we've been married twenty-one years!"

Nope, I'm not kidding, *especially* if you've been married twenty-one years. Most women dress to please other women rather than their own husbands. Your husband needs you to fulfill his daydreams.

I have heard women complain, "My husband isn't satisfied with just me. He wants lots of women. What can I do?" You can be lots of different women to him. Costumes provide variety without him ever leaving home. I believe that every man needs excitement and high adventure at home. Never let him know what to expect when he opens the front door; make it like opening a surprise package. You may be a smoldering sexpot, or an all-American fresh beauty. Be a pixie or a pirate—a cowgirl or a show girl. Keep him off guard.

You don't think you're the type? I didn't either. It took me seven years of marriage to try costumes on him. I only tried them because my marriage needed some sizzle. But my silly costumes got such fabulous results that now I'm hooked. And so is Charlie. My first costume, the pink baby-dolls and boots, was among my more conservative outfits. For a corn-fed gal from a small Ohio town, I must admit I've branched out quite a bit since then!

You may not want a costume party every night, but you can work toward it. Keep a step ahead of your husband. Keep him guessing. If you have older children, naturally use discretion when they are around. You may not wish to parade around in nylon net at half-past five with your fifteen-year-old son all eyes. But the children will love your costumes. It makes life exciting. Can't you just imagine Junior on the sandlot telling his friends, "I've got to go now, guys. Got to see Mom's outfit for tonight."

One son came home from college while his mother was taking the course. He told her, "Mom, you look so cute lately. I hope I can find a woman like you for a wife." . . .

Still another gal took the course being held in her Southern Baptist Church. She welcomed her husband home in black mesh stockings, high heels, and an apron. That's all. He took one look and shouted, "Praise the Lord!" He was flabbergasted, but extremely pleased. He could hardly eat his dinner!

One middle aged woman who had been married for many years found this part of the assignment rather difficult. She ruled out the baby-doll route, but put on a new dress for dinner and said demurely, "Dear, I'm wearing my new dress with the no-bra look." Her husband couldn't quite believe it, but said, "This is one of the happiest moments of my life; I just don't want it to end."

These stories may sound unbelievably naive, but I can assure you that costumes bring a surefire response. Two last words of caution are suggested as you start:

First of all, don't use costumes as a gimmick to manipulate your husband. He will sense it if you are not sincerely trying to please him out of love. Be sure your attitude matches your costume. . . .

Secondly, make sure you recognize your husband's car door or knock at the door when he arrives. Zealous to surprise her husband, a Fort Lauderdale housewife, dressed a la gypsy with beads, bangles, and bare skin, greeted the equally surprised water meter reader!

Recently, I said to Charlie, "I wish I could be gorgeous and ravishing in the mornings when you leave but between breakfast and getting the girls off to school, I just can't." "That's okay," he grinned, "as long as you're gorgeous and ravishing when I come home."

Your husband will love it too. And he will love you for wanting to please him. When his need for an attractive and available wife is met, he'll be so grateful that he will begin to meet your needs. Try it tonight!

SUPER SEX

Sex is an hour in bed at ten o'clock; super sex is the climax of an atmosphere that has been carefully set all day. Your attitude during your husband's first four waking minutes in the morning sets the tone for his entire day. The atmosphere for love in the evening can be set by you even before breakfast. Give him a kiss first thing tomorrow morning. Rub his back as he's waking up. Whisper in his ear. Slip into the bathroom to clear a few cobwebs before he wakes.

Remember, he can stand almost anything but boredom. The same nightgown month after month is not too exciting to any man. Treat him and yourself to some snazzy new ones. Have you ever looked so sexy in the morning that your husband called in late to the office? At least you can make him wish he could stay home.

One wife changes the sheets every few days while her husband is dressing for work. As she sprays the sheets with cologne, she purrs, "Honey, hurry home tonight." It gives him incentive for the whole day. If you expect great sex tonight, it should definitely start in the morning, with words. That's basic. Sex 201.

Edna St. Vincent Millay wrote, "'Tis not love's going hurts my days, but that it went in little ways." Marriage is but a basketful of those little things.

Tomorrow morning as your husband leaves for work, stand at the door and wave until he's out of sight. That's his last memory of you, in the open doorway. Make him want to hurry home.

In class recently, one cute girl I'll call Janet told how she had anxiously anticipated her husband's coming home one day. At four o'clock she called his office somewhat nervously and said, "Honey, I'm eagerly waiting for you to come home. I just crave your body."

Jack said, with great consternation, "Ummmmmmph."

"Is there someone there with you, darling?" she asked.

"Ummhum," came the same reply.

"Well, I'll see you soon, darling," she said.

"Ummhum," was his final utterance.

And they both hung up.

Five minutes later the phone rang. It was Jack. In unbelief he said, "Would you please repeat slowly what you said five minutes ago?"

The sequel to the story was almost as amusing. Janet called her girl friend, Barbara, to tell what had happened. Barbara couldn't wait to try it on her husband, Pete. She called his office number and when the male voice answered, she said, "Darling, I wanted to call to say that I just crave your body. Hurry home!"

The voice on the other end demanded, "Who is this?" Realizing that another man, not her husband, had answered the phone, Barbara quickly hung up, absolutely mortified.

That night when her husband came in the door, he said, "Wait until I tell you about Ron's phone call today. You'll never believe it!" (She never told him, by the way, who the anonymous caller had been.)

So when you call your husband's office, first be sure you've got the right man! Then keep it short, just long enough to let him know that you're ready and willing. It may be the greatest news he has heard all day.

Luncheon Special

If you pack your husband's lunch in the morning, try tucking in a surprise love note. Mail a beautiful card to his office (marked PERSONAL) that would brighten up his day. Or appear in person. I know of one woman who arrived at her husband's office at lunch hour with a picnic basket. Behind locked doors they spent the longest lunch hour the boss had taken in months. The secretaries are still talking about that one!

Arrange your day's activities so that you'll be totally and eagerly prepared as he walks in the door. A psychiatrist told me, "Lots of men would be less preoccupied with work—or other women—if their wives made coming home the most exciting part of the day."

I find that after a hard day at the office, most husbands don't usually arrange flowers and light the candles in the bedroom. At least mine doesn't, but he appreciates my efforts. And it's my privilege to do it.

Set an atmosphere of romance tonight. Set your table with cloth, flowers, and silver. Prepare his favorite dinner for him. Eat by candlelight; you'll light his candle!

Make up your mind to be available for him. Schedule your day so you won't start projects at nine o'clock. The number-one killer of love is fatigue, but you won't be exhausted if you're using your $25,000 plan. You'll have the energy to be a passionate lover.

Next, be sure the outside of your "house" is prepared. Bubble your troubles away at five o'clock. Of course, you'll be shaven, perfumed, and seductive in an utterly lovely outfit. Perhaps you're thinking, "Since I'm forty pounds overweight, I don't feel very seductive in my baby-doll pajamas." That's all right, he chose you because he loves you. Concentrate on your good points and he will, too. He won't be able to take his eyes off you. Best of all, he'll know how much you care.

Prepare now for making love tonight. This is part of our class assignment. In fact by the second week, the women are to be prepared for sexual intercourse every night for a week. When I gave the homework in one class, a woman muttered audibly, "What's she think I am, a sex maniac?"

Another gal told a Total Woman teacher, "I tried to follow the assignment this past week, but I just couldn't keep up—I was only ready for sex six nights; Monday night I was just too I tired." The teacher gave her a B—, but her husband gave her an A!

One Fort Lauderdale housewife told how she diligently prepared for love for seven straight nights, "whatever, whenever, and wherever," and it was her husband who couldn't take it. "I don't know what's happened to you, honey," he said with a weak grin, "but I love it!"

Secrets of a Mistress

In the book *How to be a Happily Married Mistress*, the author, Lois Bird, asks, "Would he pick you for his mistress? A mistress seduces. A housefrau submits. We all know who gets the most goodies."

I don't approve of a mistress in any way, but maybe we ought to check out the competition occasionally and see why she is competition. Nell Kimball, a madame from a bygone era, published her memoirs. She told about the call girl, who is always bathed, perfumed, curled, and adorned. She is never seen in bright lights, only dimly lit rooms and candlelight. She never refuses her body or talks about her headache. She never criticizes or belittles. He is always the boss. She builds up his ego. She makes sex exciting.

What about it, girls? Are you in a marriage rut? Would your husband pick you for his mistress?

What made Marilyn Monroe the angel of sex? Why was she so desirable and delectable to tens of millions of American males? Norman Mailer, in his book *Marilyn*, writes: "She looked then like a new love ready and waiting between the sheets in the unexpected clean breath of a rare sexy morning, looking like she'd stepped fully clothed out of a chocolate box for Valentine's Day, so desirable as to fulfill each of the letters in the word of the publicity flack, *curvaceous*, so curvaceous and yet without menace as to turn one's fingertips into ten happy prowlers. Sex was, yes, ice cream to her. 'Take me,' said her smile, 'I'm easy. I'm happy. I'm an angel of sex, you bet.'"

A secretary interviewed by the Miami Herald about extracurricular activities between the girls in the office and their bosses was asked, "Do men at the office ever talk much about their wives?"

"Hardly ever," she said. "In all the time I've worked in an office I've never heard a man say, 'I'm married to the best woman in the whole world.' I'm always surprised when a wife comes into the office. She never looks as good as her husband. I think men get better looking with age. But, unfortunately, women don't.

"That's why a woman, it seems to me, has to work extra hard—make a real effort—to be an exceptional wife. To be considerate, attentive, as attractive as she possibly can be, especially when her husband is 35 or 40. She wouldn't get up in the morning and serve him breakfast looking like a witch if she knew how the girls in the office look. She'd be a lot nicer to him in everything she did. She'd try to live in his world."

Remember that the tone for the evening is set during the first four minutes after your husband comes home tonight. His senses will be anticipating food and sex. If he wants to make love tonight, love him extravagantly and wastefully. If you pour out your love on him unconditionally, he'll want to love you in return.

If you are suddenly overprepared for sex after months of denial, don't take it as a personal rebuff if he reacts with apparent disinterest, preoccupation, or suspicion. Perhaps he needs to trust you. Be prepared and patient, it won't be long.

PERFECT WAVE OF LIBIDO

Has it ever dawned on you that making love in bed, with the lights out, week after week and month after month might have become dull to your husband? To prepare your face for love, but not the time and place for love, rates only B −. If the bedroom is your only solution, at least make it romantic. An ancient book on love says fresh flowers are a must. So is music. Spray your sheets with sweet cologne. Immerse him in love.

For a change tonight, after the children are in bed, place a lighted candle on the floor, and seduce him under the dining-room table. Or lead him to the sofa. How about the hammock? Or in the garden? Even if you can't actually follow through, at least the suggestion is exciting. He may say, "We don't have a hammock." You can reply, "Oh, darling, I forgot!" If you are creative and imaginative, he'll love you for it.

For you boating enthusiasts, one smart wife packed a picnic supper and she and her husband shoved off for a late-night cruise. She said it was one of their most exciting evenings of married life. "Just searching for that perfect wave—of libido!" she said.

A Houston doctor gave this advice to a young wife: "I see that you're following the same pattern many of my older patients have followed. Most of them are wealthy, social, and very talented. All of them feel unfulfilled and all of them are neurotic. They are past the point of taking any advice, but you are young and can change the path you are on. My advice is this: Love your husband first and foremost. And, most important of all, don't ever love him at night!" What a startling prescription! This doctor knew that boredom sets in when sex becomes routine. He told her to make love in the morning or afternoon, not in the 10:30 rut.

Mrs. Mackey Brown analyzed why her marriage ended in divorce and told what she could have done to prevent it in an article titled "Keeping Marriage Alive through Middle Age," in *McCalls* magazine. "He found my love-making unimaginative . . . surely it would be better to use one's imagination to seek alternatives, solutions to live afresh before it is too late," she advised. "We never sneaked small vacations away from the children; sex became a bedroom ritual, almost meaningless except as a tension reliever. We never even went out for a quiet dinner alone, to say, 'Who are you and how are you?' When our grown-up children left home, we were left to stare astonished across the breakfast table, strangers in a stranger land."

Dr. David Reuben agrees.

The woman who would never think of serving her husband the same frozen television dinner every evening sometimes serves him the same frozen sexual response every night. Sex, like supper, loses much of its flavor when it becomes predictable. That, of course, is the lure of the other woman; she offers the illusion that sex with her will be different. But if a wife is on the same emotional wave as her husband it will be hard for anyone else to provide greater satisfaction.

Dr. George W. Crane, syndicated columnist, wrote, "Successful wives are superb boudoir actresses for they realize it is vital to serve as a one-wife harem to their mates! Boudoir cheesecake involves a lot of romantic histrionics!"

Just Undersupplied

For super sex tonight, respond eagerly to your husband's advances. Don't just endure. Indifference hurts him more than anything. He may enjoy making love even when you're a limp dishrag, but if you're eager, and love to make love, watch out! If you seduce him, there will be no words to describe his joy. Loving you will become sheer ecstasy.

The proverbs in the Bible speak much of married love. In modern paraphrase, one portion reads, "Man is to be intoxicated continually with the delight and ecstasy of his wife's sexual love" [Prov. 5:19]. I know of one instance where a psychiatrist advised a husband to be "continually intoxicated," literally. He was advised to have intercourse fourteen times a day! And you think you have problems! His wife said he was oversexed; he said he was just undersupplied. That was one man who was willing to follow his doctor's orders to the letter, even if it killed him. He said at least he'd die with a smile on his face.

Sexual intercourse is an act of love. Express your love by giving him all you can give. A woman's hands should never be still when she is making love. By caressing tenderly, you assure him that he's touchable. Tell him "I love you" with your hands.

Psychological test results reveal that infants who are not touched lovingly suffer emotional deprivation as adults. This basic need to be loved, touched, and comforted continues throughout life, in your life and his. He depends on you to reassure him that he's desirable to you. He needs confidence in this area where he may be vulnerable.

Your husband wants you to want him sexually. He wants you to enjoy lovemaking as much as he does. If you fail in this area, he is devastated. Down inside, he feels he is an utter failure. Believe in him and tell him so. Let him know he's your special project in life.

The Speed Demon

Tonight, as you make love, remember that your brain is your control center. Keep it tuned to the subject at hand. Think about his body, not Sunday's dinner menu. One of the secrets of life is to concentrate on the moment. Enjoy the present—not yesterday, or tomorrow, but right now! It's a secret to super sex, too.

In the same way you need words for atmosphere, so does he. Don't clam up. The silent-movie days are gone. He'll respond to your sounds of love. He does not automatically know what pleases you and what you don't like. The only way he'll know is for you to tell him. His enjoyment will be increased when he knows what is pleasing you. Tell him you want him. Treat him as if he is a great lover, and he'll become a great lover.

If your husband is a speed demon in sex and spends only a few minutes with you, your change in attitude will help slow him down. He will want to spend more time loving you. By seeing how you care, he will also want to see that your needs are met.

One important note—don't douse his flame of love once the romance begins. Any little negative word from you, even indirectly, may turn him off completely. If he senses you're not with him in the moment, he will be less than satisfied. He'll read it as a smoke screen or a cop-out.

Don't break the mood. Tell him tomorrow about that dented fender. Don't ask if he locked the back door. Hold back any sentences that start, "By the way." Watch your negative responses and diversions. Sometimes they're subtle and sometimes they're not. Any husband can pick up the vibrations of the more obvious ones like, "Oh, not again," or "Must we?" Others are more difficult to interpret, like, "Not tonight, my head hurts!" A headache on Monday night may be serious or subtle. A headache all week, however, may be very serious, but not very subtle.

Sometimes your passion is not as great as his, but you can still be warm and responsive. Love him whenever he wants to, if you possibly can. If you must refuse, be very gentle. Let him know you are not rejecting him, but you are willing to meet his needs in other ways.

Companion, not Competition

Sex can restore a bad mood or disagreement. One wife felt she had been wronged by her husband. Her pride took over and she refused to give in until he changed. The Bible advises, ". . . let not the sun go down upon your wrath" (Ephesians 4:26). Watch that no bitterness or resentment takes root in you for it causes deep trouble.

Nip it in the bud. Don't let your grudge carry over to the next day. There is no place for resentment in a good marriage. Part of his problem may be his need for your sexual love. Talk it out and change your attitude. Often that's all it takes.

Love never makes demands. Love is unconditional acceptance of him and his feelings. He does not need competition at home; he's had that all day at work. He needs your companionship and compliments instead.

A mature couple does not demand perfection. They do not chase false goals, which can only end in disillusionment. They are willing to work together for each other's good, which produces a happy sexual adjustment.

Don't deprive your husband of intercourse when he acts like a bear. He may be tired when he comes home tonight. He needs to be pampered, loved, and restored. Fill up his tummy with food; soothe away his frustrations with sex. Lovemaking comforts a man. It can comfort you too.

In speaking to a men's service club recently, I told them some of the class assignments for super sex. The reason for the homework, I explained, was that sex comforts a man. The reaction of the men was completely unexpected. These sophisticated businessmen spontaneously shouted, pounded the tables, picked up their spoons, and clanged their water glasses!

Lovemaking is an art you can develop to any degree, according to *How to be a Happily Married Mistress*. You can become a Rembrandt in your sexual art. Or, you can stay at the paint-by-numbers stage. One husband, by the way, felt his wife was more like Grandma Moses because she always wore a flannel granny gown. The benefits in your becoming a Rembrandt just cannot be overemphasized. You can begin now to be a budding artist. Tonight is your night for super sex. Prepare, anticipate, relax, and enjoy!

Assignment

SEX 201

1. Be an atmosphere adjuster in the morning. Set the tone for love. Be pleasant to look at, be with, and talk to. Walk your husband to the car each morning and wave until he's out of sight.

2. Once this week call him at work an hour before quitting time, to say, "I wanted you to know that I just crave your body!" or some other appropriate tender term. Then take your bubble bath shortly before he comes home.

3. Thrill him at the front door in your costume. A frilly new nighty and heels will probably do the trick as a starter. Variety is the spice of sex.

4. Be prepared mentally and physically for intercourse every night this week. Be sure your attitude matches your costume. Be the seducer, rather than the seducee.

5. If you feel your situation involves a deeper problem, either psychological or physiological, seek professional help.

POWER SOURCE

One day recently, Laura came home from school loaded with three books, a doll, and her lunch box. Anxious to play, she dropped them all on the kitchen floor. I heard the crunch of the lunch box and took out the Thermos bottle. It looked fine on the outside, but inside the glass was shattered in a million little pieces. Looking at that lining, I thought, "Little Thermos bottle, I identify with you. How many times I've felt just like you look—shattered!"

When you feel like Humpty Dumpty, who had a great fall, who puts you back together again? When your husband cuts you down, who gives you the power to keep on loving? When you want to pop him one for spoiling your plans, who gives you self-control? Is it possible to maintain a relaxed mental attitude when pressures seem overwhelming? Where are you going, anyway? And why?

So far in this book, we've taken your old house, the fragmented you, and painted the outside. We've planted some new shrubs and repaired a few loose shutters. Inside, we've dusted under the sofa and done some redecorating. All we need now is the power. Without a power source for heat, for light, for life, your shell is nothing more than a glorified outhouse.

Ten years ago I "plugged in" to the world's greatest power source. I established contact with my Creator, the Source and Essence of love—perfect love. He gave me life, with a capital L. He turned on all the lights, brighter than I had ever seen. And He put all my pieces together again.

MY SEARCH

From my earliest recollection of my childhood, I recall my love for God. I believed in Him with all my heart, but somehow I couldn't seem to make contact. I never doubted He existed, but my prayers seemed to bounce off the ceiling. I was frustrated over my one-way love affair. I pleaded with Him, but He never seemed to respond.

My father's death when I was fourteen completely broke my heart. After the funeral, I remember taking a long walk through a cornfield behind my house. I sobbed and prayed. No answer. Dad was gone and God wouldn't answer. "God, if you're out there," I shouted, "why don't you let me know it?" But there was still no answer. My prayers bounced again.

In the years that followed, I began to search for Him in stained-glass windows. I called ministers and priests at random and asked for an appointment to discuss my search. Some were too busy, they said. Others never bothered to return my call. One minister said he, too, was looking, and to call if I ever found it. Religion left me cold.

I had always tried to be a "good little girl." On Saturdays I baked cookies and delivered them to sick people's doorsteps anonymously. I took presents on holidays to the less fortunate across town. I wanted to make the world a better place. My search continued.

At Ohio State University, I studied philosophy. I read the various philosophers until I collapsed each night. I found myself confused, however, as I tried to take the best from each. So many claimed to be "truth," yet they contradicted each other. Some of these were real humdingers. They seemed good enough to live by, but not good enough to die by.

My involvement with people was the most fun, and brought me the most happiness. College life was active with academic honors and campus and state beauty contest awards. Even a trip to Europe didn't satisfy. Under it all, there was that one problem. My song was the pop song, "Laughing on the Outside, Crying on the Inside." And I didn't even know why I was crying!

I felt empty inside. I felt guilty. I longed for something more. I was afraid to be alone with my thoughts. Turning the radio on full blast helped drown out my searching questions. Why am I here? Where am I going? What's it all about, Marabel? As I walked to class each morning I sang to keep up my courage. My favorite was, "Let a Smile Be Your Umbrella." No one ever suspected otherwise. I played the role well.

When I first realized the importance of money, I was sure I had found the real secret to life. Dollars could buy happiness. The more dollars, the greater the options, the greater the joy. In the tenth grade, I remember shopping for a sweater and then I saw it—the most luscious, furry, beige sweater I'd ever seen. That sweater had to be mine. I wanted it more than anything in the world. I stood at the department store window every day on my way home and pictured it on me.

Money was hard to come by then, but I finally saved enough to buy it. I still remember how anxious I was during classes that day and how I rushed downtown after school. Oh, it was such a big deal. I remember every detail, even the closet-like fitting room with pins on the floor, where I slipped it on and the miracle took place. That sweater made me look ethereal.

That night, however, when I tried it on again at home, that terrible lonely feeling swept over me. "So! I've got the sweater," I thought, "but I still feel empty inside." It left a permanent impression. Things didn't satisfy. That sweater was my goal of the moment. "If only it was mine," I had thought, "I'd be satisfied." But I wasn't. To have it turn to ashes in my mouth was so unexpected. It really rocked me.

What *was* the answer? I asked myself that question repeatedly while walking to work on clear summer mornings. I watched the yellow butterflies darting over the waving wheat fields and knew that the God who created all this must have something more for me. I said aloud, "If only I could really see; if I could just pull the blinders off my eyes and see life as it really is." I looked at my hands and thought about the blood coursing through those veins. I was awed by the magnitude of the human body. I thought, "*I'm* in this body. The real me lives in here. But, who am I actually? Who am I?"

I felt there must be something more, a dimension of life that I just could not perceive, but I knew by this time that it had to come from a greater source than myself.

Transformed, not Reformed

My search finally led me to truth—ageless truth, satisfying and relevant. A friend told me that God loved me and had a wonderful plan for my life. I knew that God is love and I could quote John 3:16 even as a child. "For God so loved the world, that he gave his only begotten Son, that whosoever believeth in him should not perish, but have everlasting life."

God's love, for me! And Jesus said He came to give us abundant life [John 10:10] That sounded good to me. But how did I plug into this God of the universe?

Thousands of years ago, the Jewish prophet Isaiah said, "Your iniquities have separated between you and your God . . ." [Isa. 59:2]. Thousands of years ago, or yesterday, or today? Were my iniquities, my sins, keeping me from God and His power? I wasn't a bad kid and I wanted to see what qualified as "sin." I came across a list in the Bible that astounded me. They weren't gross sins, but the garden variety—worry, unbelief, gossiping, pride.

Wow, I hit the jackpot. That was me. I was separated and unplugged. I had spent twenty-three lonely years separated from God. At times it was nearly unbearable to experience that devastating loneliness, that emptiness.

And there was more bad news. "The penalty for sin," my friend said, "is death—spiritual death—according to Romans 6:23."

"Oh, no, I'm a goner," I remember thinking. "I'm a sinner for sure, and the sentence has been pronounced." I looked at my dear friend and she must have seen my total despair.

"But there's good news, too," she said, "right there in the same verse '. . . but the gift of God is eternal life through Jesus Christ our Lord'" [Rom. 6:23]. I saw that Marabel couldn't bridge the chasm back to God, so God reached down to Marabel. That was good news. That was great news! My friend then showed me a verse in the Bible which seemed to contradict all my attempts to reach God. It read, "For by grace are ye saved through faith; and that not of yourselves: it is a gift of God. Not of works . . ." [Eph. 2:8,9].

I saw how, long ago, God stepped out of eternity and stepped into time. He came so that man could come out from wherever he was hiding and be free. The world had been expecting Him ever since the prophets had described the coming Messiah.

I eagerly read His writings. His life was one of total unselfishness. He seemed to spend so much of His life healing broken bodies and broken hearts. His personal claims were unique. He claimed, for example, to be the sole way any man could reach God the Father. He even spoke of His impending death, explaining that He came to be our Passover Lamb, my Passover Lamb.

Because He died, I could live. He promised me life. My friend showed me Revelation 3:20, where Jesus stood knocking at a symbolic door of my heart: "Behold, I stand at the door, and knock: if any man hear my voice, and open the door, I will come to him, and will sup with him, and he with me."

I could hardly wait to ask Him into my life, once I realized the importance of this step. I had always believed in God and in Jesus, His Son. I believed He had died some years ago as the Saviour of man. But now He became my Saviour.

I prayed to God silently. "Dear God, I've been looking for You for so long. Thank you for finding me. I believe that Jesus died—for me, as my Saviour. I invite Him into my life right now. Thank you very much. Amen."

I looked up at my friend and began to weep with joy. I realized that my search was over; my lifelong, agonizing search. I felt so clean, so complete. I was plugged in, at last! Not reformed, but transformed—hooked up to the true power source—the Light of the world. The lights came on and they've never gone out.

FOREVER FAMILY

Since that all-important day, I've experienced the most wonderful benefits of the abundant life, which He promised to give.

First of all, I have peace—inner peace from God Himself, the Prince of Peace. Jesus said, ". . . my peace I give unto you . . ." [John 14:27]. I am His very own child, spiritually born into the forever family!

Secondly, I have pardon. Jesus paid the penalty for my sins, all I ever did or ever will do wrong. Jesus promised, "Ye shall know the truth, and the truth shall make you free" [John 8:32]. By receiving Him, I was acquitted, set free, made a liberated woman.

Thirdly, I have a purpose in life. For so many years, I wondered, "Who am I? Where am I going?" My Jesus is the Way—the Way out—the Way through. He is my reason for living.

Lastly, I have power. His power. He is not dead. He arose from the dead. He's alive. He said that His same resurrection power can be mine. I have the power to live the abundant life—power to love—power to transform my natural love for my husband and children into a super love, a divine love, flowing out of me.

You, too, can plug into this power Source. Your life can have peace, pardon, purpose, and power. Because God is love, contact with Him means abundant life for you, and a super love for others. The Bible promises that you will become a new person inside and a new life will begin.

To invite Him into your life, simply open the door. Talk to Him. The following is a suggested prayer which many in the classes have used successfully:

Dear Jesus, I need You. I open the door of my life and receive You as my Saviour. Thank You for forgiving my sins. Make me the kind of person You want me to be. Thank You for coming in as You promised you would.

Please, don't be satisfied with a new paint job and some redecoration. Plug yourself into the One, the only One, who can give you life. Pascal said, "There is a god-shaped vacuum in the heart of every man, which cannot be satisfied by any created thing, but only by God, the Creator . . ." God is waiting and wanting to fill your vacuum, to make you complete. Total. Right now you can become a Total Woman.

ASSIGNMENT

Building Bridges

To Your Husband

1. When you have good rapport with your husband this week, ask him to write out your three main strengths and weaknesses. Thank him for his helpful list. Don't be defensive as you read it.
2. Celebrate something special tonight. Make dinner time a time of fun and sharing. Plan to have a serendipity time for him and the children.

To Your Children

1. Put into practice today with each child the blueprint for blessings:
   a. Accept him
   b. Love and touch him
   c. Play with him
   d. Encourage him

  e. Talk with him
  f. Discipline him in love
  g. Encourage spiritual growth
2. List the characteristics that you would like to develop in your children.

Begin to compliment these traits as you see them appear.

To Your God

1. Read the third chapter of Saint John in a modern translation of the Bible. Buy a copy if you don't have one.
2. Jesus has bridged the gap between you and God. This free gift of life is now yours for the asking.

— 16 —

An Apache Girl's Initiation Feast

Michael D. McNally

Among Apache peoples in the American Southwest, the ceremony that honors a girl's passage to womanhood and that teaches her how to live properly as an Apache woman is a ceremony central to the religious traditions of the entire people. The *na ih es,* as the ceremony is known in the language of the San Carlos Apache of eastern Arizona, marks an individual girl's rite of passage. In addition, because the girl is ritually "sung into" her identity as Changing Woman, a primary deity for the Apache, the ceremony is also understood to bring renewal to the entire community and to the entire world.

The Apache-language story of Changing Woman is so detailed that it requires many hours to tell fully. She is regarded by Apaches as one of the deities present at creation and is the key agent in the transformation of the world. She brings to the people knowledge of how to use sacred power from the earth to bring healing, renewal, and the restoration of balance. The "sing," as it is called in Apache, was inaugurated by Changing Woman at the time of her own first menses. The songs, dance steps, organization of sacred space, and sequence of events that give structure to the ceremony are understood as gifts granted the people by Changing Woman. Consequently, the ritual is adhered to with great care so that the community can tap into the sacred power that effectively makes present Changing Woman's power to heal and renew. According to Inés Talamantez, an Apache scholar, a properly performed ceremony accomplishes an exchange of the girl's youth for Changing Woman's womanhood, making the girl a woman while ensuring that Changing Woman, a personification of earth, continues to live through the next year's cycle.

The ceremony transpires over four to eight days, depending on which of the several contemporary Apache communities is practicing it. At the Mescalero Reservation in New Mexico, an annual gathering marks the ceremonial passage to womanhood for a larger number of girls at the same time, although additional ceremonies are sponsored for individual girls. In either case, age-old traditions mingle with modern life in a most extraordinary way in these ceremonial complexes.

Although the feasts center on the ceremony involving girls becoming women, they are also busy intersections of community life—part family reunion, part social dance, part county fair.

The ritual practices of the ceremony proper are understood as the culmination of a year of reflection and preparation on the part of the girl, her family, the male "singer" who is asked to preside at the ceremony with his knowledge of the elaborate cycle of songs, and the elder woman "sponsor," or *na ihl esn,* who takes the girl under her care and educates her in the meaning of the ceremony and in the traditions of Apache womanhood. The family saves up the considerable resources to provide gifts and to feed the guests. They make shawls for guests and put up food sufficient to feed as many as hundreds over several days. They also help the principals prepare the sacred paraphernalia necessary for an effective ceremony: a fringed buckskin dress made from a deer killed ceremonially, a cane, a scratching stick, a drinking tube, sacred minerals, and large amounts of cattail pollen to symbolize the sacred power, fertility, and blessing that Changing Woman will confer on the people as she did in the moment of creation.

The transformation of a girl into an Apache woman involves a great deal of teaching and learning. Instruction is offered by the many women who surround the girl and support her before and during the ceremony. It is the female elder sponsor, however, who plays the crucial role in the girl's education. Although she must be from another clan than the girl, the two and their families form a lifelong kinship bond. The girl grows in knowledge of Apache culture, its sacred narratives and core values, and she learns how to behave properly as an Apache woman does. Inés Talamantez describes the transformation into womanhood as a process of ceremonially "awakening the initiate to the world around her." "For some girls," Talamantez explains, "the ceremony is said to calm their adolescent imbalances. The Mescalero [Apaches] conceive of 'fixing' the young initiate, ridding her of her baby ways and helping her though the door of adolescence. At this young age the girls are said to be soft and moldable, capable of being conditioned and influenced by their female kin and others around them." Likewise, "timid girls may need to be awakened to their powerful female identities; others may need to be taught to settle down and be more sensible and feminine" (Talamantez, 1989, 250). Keith Basso writes that the ceremony's function "is largely an educative one," concerning the four "life objectives" to which the girl becoming woman should aspire: "physical strength, a good disposition, prosperity . . . and a sound, healthy, uncrippled old age" (160–61). For Apaches to live well and beautifully to a ripe old age is an important goal of the religious tradition. Living well on this earth requires the appropriate knowledge of, and relations with, the sacred.

In the Apache worldview, the ritual is far more than a mere dramatization or communication of cultural information. It effectively transforms the girl into the deity Changing Woman. If properly performed in accord with Changing Woman's original instructions, the ceremony generates the sacred power originally gifted by Changing Woman to the people. The real presence of Changing Woman in the figure of the ritualized girl is considered a blessing for all within her broad reach. As one girl was told, "When you become Changing Woman, in the ceremony, you will have her power to heal because it is Changing Woman who handed this knowledge to us. There is a sacred story about this. Since you will be Changing Woman, you will be asked to heal and bless people who come to see you" (Talamantez, 1989, 252–53). A singer charged the same girl to "think in images about the tribe—to visualize troubles and illness and to send them over the mountain and away from the tribe."

In its faithful attention to proper performance in accord with Changing Woman's instruction, the Apache ceremony seems to collapse all time. But there is a peculiar timeliness to the felt timelessness of na ih es. Feasts for Apache girls minister afresh to novel historical situations in which Apache women find themselves. The intersection of ritual and history make this ceremonial practice an especially powerful one at the brink of the twenty-first century. Although the Apaches say that the songs and dances go back to first times, the performance of the ceremony today can be read as a ritual act of resistance, a bold performance of the Apache language, of Apache music, and of Apache traditions in a world that would try to fix that language and those songs in books and museum dioramas. Na ih es is a ritual recreation of the world according to Apache understandings of the sacred, an annual reminder of the urgency of human respect and responsibility for the continuation of the earth and for each other. It is a ritual blessing on a beleaguered community, a healing assertion of sacred power and centrality to a people marginalized from positions of economic, political, and social power.

The na ih es is perhaps most remarkable for its bold performance of a profoundly countercultural way of imagining womanhood in America. The na ih es celebrates womanhood among Apaches and brings the resources of ritual and tradition to honor teenage girls becoming women. It proclaims publicly that becoming a woman is a powerful thing, and it does so at a critical juncture in the development and socialization of wider American gender norms. As a consequence, while Apache people live in multiple worlds, and while Apache women face all the challenges that other American women face, they are instructed to remember always what it felt like to be Changing Woman. In the words of one sponsor to a girl: "You must always remember how you felt during your ceremony, when you were the living Changing Woman, then later in life, you can call on her for help whenever you face problems; you will remember how you felt when you were her, when you became her" (Talamantez, 1989, 253).

As with other oral traditions among native peoples, it is difficult if not impossible to find a written document that serves as an authoritative guide to the ceremony; consequently, we must rely on disciplined observations of particular ceremonies. The text that follows is based on observation of four such ceremonies during the summers of 1960 and 1961, and fifty-seven interviews about the ceremony with sixteen different Apaches. These observations and interviews were conducted by Keith Basso, an anthropologist who has distinguished himself over the years for his knowledge, creativity, and continued commitment to the San Carlos community of Apaches. The following selection begins on the first day of the actual ceremony, although this in itself means beginning in medias res, because much of Basso's larger purpose is to document the preceremony arrangements of ceremonial relationships, sacred space, and ritual paraphernalia. For readability's sake, the Apache-language terms for the ceremony are omitted in favor of Basso's exegetical translations, indicated in the text by quotation marks.

Keith H. Basso, *The Gift. of Changing Woman*, Smithsonian Institution Bureau of American Ethnology Bulletin 196, Anthropological Papers no. 76 (1966), pp. 153–59.

Further Reading

Keith Basso, *The Gift of Changing Woman;* Ernestine Cody Begay with Robert Preucel, *Is Dzan Naadleeshe' Bi Chaghashe: The Children of Changing Woman* (Cambridge, Mass.: Peabody Museum Publications, 1995); Pliny E. Goddard, *Myths and Tales from the White Mountain Apache*, American Museum of Natural History Anthropological Papers no. 24 (1920), pp. 371–527; Inés Talamantez, "In the Space Between Earth and Sky: Contemporary Mescalero Apache Ceremonialism," in *Native Religious and Cultures of North America*, Lawrence E. Sullivan, ed. (New York: Continuum, 2000), pp. 142–59; Anne Dhu Shapiro and Inés Talamantez, "The Mescalero Apache Girls' Puberty Ceremony: The Role of Music in Structuring Ritual Time"; *Yearbook of the International Council for Traditional Music* 18 (1986), pp. 17–90.; Inés Talamantez, "The Presence of Isanaklesh: A Native American Goddess and the Path of Pollen," in *Unspoken Worlds: Women's Religious Lives,* Nancy Auer Falk and Rita Gross, eds., 2nd ed. (Belmont, Calif.: Wadsworth, 1989), pp. 246–55.

Na Ih Es

As performed in Cibecue [Arizona] today, *na ih es* is made up of eight distinct parts or phases. Each phase has a unique meaning, name and set of ritual actions; each is initiated, perpetuated, and terminated by a group of songs, or "song set." The Apaches do not conceive of *na ih es* as an unbroken continuum, but rather tend to emphasize and stress its different parts.

Each medicine man arranges the thirty-two or more "Changing Woman's power songs" which comprise *na ih es* to fit his own stylistic scheme. This produces great variation as to the number of songs in a given phase. But the sequence of phases is a stable pattern from which there is rarely any deviation. For example, one medicine man may sing twelve songs in phase I, while another may sing eight or sixteen. Nevertheless, phase I always proceeds phase II. In short, regardless of the number of songs in a phase, the order of the phases never changes.

PHASE I. "ALL ALONE, SHE DANCES"

During the first phase of *na ih es,* which may consist of eight, twelve, or sixteen songs, the pubescent girl dances on the buckskin with her [maternal rela-
tive] companion. In all respects, the method of dancing is identical to that at
"she is dressed up ceremony" [held the previous night]. The dancers bounce
lightly, first on one foot, then on the other, always in time to the drums. With
each beat, the girl strikes the bottom of her cane on the buckskin, causing the
bells attached to the cross thong to jingle loudly. Her face is expressionless, her
eyes fixed on the buckskin. At the end of each song, the medicine man and his
drummers pause briefly, while the older woman wipes the girl's face with a
handkerchief or smooths her hair.

The songs sung in phase I deal primarily with the Western Apache creation
or, as the people say, "when the earth was set up." Changing Woman is mentioned frequently. With his songs, the medicine man asks for Changing
Woman's power on behalf of the pubescent girl. Apparently, there is no given
point (or song) at which this force enters her. It is understood however, that
she receives it before the end of phase I. At the beginning of the fifth, sixth, or
seventh song, the medicine man tells the girl to pray to Changing Woman.
One informant said: "She couldn't make that prayer if she didn't have power."
The girl's prayer is a short one—"Long life, no trouble, Changing Woman."

PHASE II. "SITTING"

At the end of phase I, which may have lasted as long as forty-five minutes if
sixteen songs were sung, the singing and dancing cease. Five or ten minutes
elapse before the start of phase II. During this recess, the medicine man and
his drummers take a drink of *tulipay* [fermented pulp of mashed corn shoots]
from a can or a pot provided by the girl's camp or smoke a cigarette. They do
not move from their positions behind the girl. Welcoming this chance to rest,
she remains on the buckskin.

Shortly before the first song in phase II, "the Sponsor" makes her first formal appearance of the day. She comes out of her shade and walks unescorted
toward the center of the dance area. She is dressed in a spotless new camp
dress. Her loose unbraided hair has been freshly washed. As she approaches
the buckskin, the woman with whom the girl has been dancing in phase I
departs. For the remainder of *na ih es,* "the Sponsor" will be the girl's partner.

Unlike the pubescent girl, "the Sponsor" does not personify a mythological
character. Her function is to instruct the girl throughout *na ih es,* nothing
more. She does not receive power and consequently is never considered holy.
As was explained to me:

> "The Sponsor" tells the girl what to do, and not to be scared or bashful.
> The girl does not know what to do next, and someone must tell her.

That's what she does. She doesn't have any power at all, and the reason that she does that (instruct the girl) is because she helped put on the dance, and because they are not relatives.

For the two or four songs that make up the structure of phase II, the pubescent girl recreates the impregnation of Changing Woman by the Sun. In 1920, P. E. Goddard was given the following version of this incident.

This maiden (Changing Woman when she was young) running as you say the sun began it they say. Then in this fashion sun toward this way she sat they say. Then sun from it shone in rays it was they say. Then in here it shone it became they say. (Goddard 426–7)

Goodwin's account, taken from a man named Bane Tithla of the Eastern White Mountain Apache, relates:

Then as the Sun came up she pulled up her dress toward Sun and spread her legs apart, so that Sun shone between her legs. When Sun came up one of his beams went right into her, a red one. Then she got her menstrual period and the blood started to come. After that she became pregnant. (Goodwin, 17)

A somewhat fuller description of this episode was told to me by a Cibecue Apache named Teddy Peaches, who is nearly sixty years old.

This way I heard it from my grandfather. He was from Carrizo, but they tell it always the same way over here (at Cibecue). She was living all by herself and went out one day for berries to get. It was before the Sun came up that she went out. Then when the Sun came up, she felt tired and sat down. She looked at the Sun and kneeled down like the girl does in *na ih es* in front of it. When she did that one of the Sun's red rays came and went in there. After that she noticed that she was bleeding from there and she didn't know what it meant because it was her first time. When it stopped she found out she was pregnant. That's all I know about that part of the story. I don't think there is any more to it.

Before the first song in phase II, "the Sponsor" takes the girl's cane and places it upright between the two baskets or boxes farthest from the buckskin. Then the girl takes a kneeling position, with her knees some twenty to twenty five inches apart. As the song begins, she raises her hands to the level of her shoulder, and then, looking into the rising sun, begins to sway from side to side not necessarily following the beat of the drums. "The Sponsor" dances beside her.

The emphasis on phase II is on Changing Woman's first menstruation, and not on the conception of [Changing Woman's firstborn,] "Monster-Slayer." The all important fact that the pubescent girl has recently had her first period is given a vivid symbolic portrayal by her assumption of the posture in which Changing Woman is generally believed to have experienced her initial menstruation. Pubescent girl and mythological figure "share" this in common during phase II, and never is their identification with each other more thorough.

Despite the unmistakable sexual nature of phase II, it is not intended to promote the girl's fertility. Apaches assume that any girl who menstruates is fertile and, moreover, that this quality cannot be heightened effectively by supernatural means.

PHASE III. "LYING"

Phase III of *na ih es* is based on the belief that certain parts of the girl's body are made strong by ritualistic massage. The reasoning behind this belief is explained in the following quotation.

> Changing Woman's power is in the girl and makes her soft, like a lump of wet clay. Like clay she can be put into different shapes. "The Sponsor" puts her in the right shape and Changing Woman's power in the girl makes her grow up that way, in that same shape. When "the Sponsor" rubs her the right way, she will grow up strong and hard and never get tired.

Shortly after the end of phase II, the medicine man instructs the girl to lie prone on the buckskin, with her arms at her sides and her legs together. (She may also be told to raise her head and stare into the sun.) During phase III, which consists of one or two songs, the girl remains in this position while "the Sponsor" kneads the muscles in her legs, back, and shoulders.

> "The Sponsor" rubs her legs so she will never have any trouble walking long ways. Also, so she can stand up for long time and never get tired. She rubs her back so that when she gets to be really old age she won't bend over and not straighten up. Her shoulders . . . so she can carry heavy things for her camp and never get tired doing that either; carry wood and water and groceries long ways. "The Sponsor" rubs her back and legs so she can always work hard for a long time and never get tired out. "The Sponsor" does that for her so she will grow up strong and in good shape and always be able to help out at her camp and whenever her relatives need help.

PHASE IV. "CANE SET OUT FOR HER, SHE RUNS AROUND IT"

During the pause (eight to twelve minutes) between phase III and phase IV, the pubescent girl remains on the buckskin and the medicine man and his drummers relax. The cane, which has been lodged between two baskets or cardboard cartons in phases II and III, is retrieved by "the Sponsor." Directly east of the buckskin, and approximately twenty-five feet from it, one of the medicine man's assistants makes a shallow cylindrical hole in the earth with a crowbar. Here, "the Sponsor" inserts the cane, standing it upright.

When the opening song of phase IV begins, the girl runs to the cane, circles it once, and runs back again. She is closely followed by "the Sponsor" who, after going around the cane, takes it from the hole and returns with it to the buckskin. There, she hands it to the girl, and the remainder of the song is danced in place.

This procedure is repeated during each of the three additional songs that comprise phase IV. At the start of each, the cane is placed farther away from the buckskin, thereby increasing the distance the girl has to run. In song two, the cane is about thirty-five feet from the buckskin; in song three, about fifty feet; and in song four, sixty feet.

Each of the four "runs" in phase IV symbolizes a stage of life through which the pubescent girl has passed, or hopes to pass in the future. The first and shortest is childhood. The second represents young womanhood. The third run symbolizes adulthood and the fourth, which is the longest, is old age. Apaches believe that as soon as the girl circles the cane, she "owns" the stage of life it stands for. Thus, after completing the final run, the girl has symbolically passed through all the stages of life and is assured of living until she is very old. This is the gift of Changing Woman, and the essence of *na ih es*. If the girl trips and falls while making one of the four "runs" she is required to return to the buckskin and repeat the entire sequence. Such a mishap is not viewed with alarm, nor is it interpreted as symbolic of early death.

> For the girl, that is the most important part. That is where she prays for long life. She has the power to make herself very old when she runs around the cane that way. Each time she runs around the cane that way she will live to be that age. That way, after she makes the last time—when it is far away—she will live until a very old lady. She goes through her life running around that cane. Changing Woman did that one time and it made her very old. The girl has her power to grow up to a long age.

PHASE V

The structure of phase V does not differ greatly from that of phase IV, and its alleged function is similar to phase III. Before the first four songs, the cane is placed in a hole about twenty feet east of the buckskin. When the singing begins the pubescent girl and "the Sponsor" run to the cane and circle it, just as they did in phase IV. For the second song, the cane is placed south of the buckskin. Again, the girl runs around it, followed by "the Sponsor." During song III, they run to the west, and in song IV, to the north.

Whereas phase III is thought to strengthen the pubescent girl's body, phase V supposedly enables her to run fast without feeling fatigue.

> After she runs around the cane in the four ways, she will never get tired and will always be able to run fast. Changing Woman gives her power to the girl and that is why it happens this way. She runs in the four ways so she will never get tired. Changing Woman ran fast long time ago, they say. That is why the girl runs so fast around (the cane). She wants to be like Changing Woman and run good.

PHASE VI. "CANDY IT IS POURED"

In phases I–V, only the pubescent girl profits from Changing Woman's power. However, in phases VI and VII it is used to the advantage of everyone at the dance
ground. Phase VI begins when the medicine man blesses the girl by sprinkling a
small amount of holy powder over her head and shoulders, and on the crook of her
cane. He may be followed in this by one or two of his assistants, or by some of the
girl's old male relatives. Next, the medicine man picks up a small basket filled with
candy, corn kernels, and coins of low denomination. Standing on the buckskin,
directly in front of the girl, he pours these contents over her head. As the candy and
corn fall to the ground, spectators nearby scramble wildly to pick it up.

> After he pours it over her head, everything in all the baskets gets holy. Not
> just the stuff from the basket he pours over her. All the baskets, even the
> big ones near the buckskin. Because it is holy, all those things, everybody
> wants it. If you get a piece of candy, you will have plenty food all the time.
> If you take one of those corns home and plant it, you have plenty corn to
> bring in later on. You get some money, that means you get rich and never
> be poor. The girl's power makes all those things holy and good to have.

Following the "pouring of the basket," the other cartons and baskets containing candy, fruit, etc. are carried through the crowd by several of the girl's male
relatives who encourage everyone to reach in and take as much as they can.
When all the baskets are empty, they are placed in front of the girl on the
buckskin. This concludes phase VI. There has been no singing.

PHASE VII. "BLESSING HER"

Phase VII begins when the medicine man blesses the pubescent girl and "the
Sponsor" with holy powder. At this point, all the adults at the dance ground
take a small pinch of powder from a basket held by one of the medicine man's
assistants, and line up to repeat the blessing for themselves. Singing continues
until everyone has done so. I have witnessed one *na ih es*, attended by an
unusually large number of people, at which phase VII lasted for twenty-three
songs and approximately fifty minutes.

The significance of phase VII for the community is enormous, for Apaches
believe that whatever wish is made while blessing the girl is certain to come
true. "She has power to do that." In phase VII, the girl's power—Changing
Woman's power—becomes a means by which anyone may attain his own personal ends. It functions in as many ways as there are individual wishes. A few
of these are recorded below.

> To have a good crop of corn and beans; to make my sick wife get better;
> my cattle, to get fat for sale time; to cure up my daughter's face (in refer-
> ence to a severe case of acne); rain; my son in Dallas learning to be a bar-
> ber, not get into any trouble.

PHASE VIII. "BLANKETS, SHE THROWS THEM OFF"

Phase VIII begins shortly after the end of phase VII. It usually is made up of four songs (sometimes six, three of which are danced in place by "the Sponsor" and the pubescent girl). During the final song, the girl steps off the buckskin, picks it up with both hands, shakes it, and then throws it three or four feet towards the east. Following this, she throws a blanket in each of the three other cardinal directions, to the south, then to the west, and finally to the north.

> She does this for two reasons. She throws the blanket so she can always have blankets, plenty of them, in her camp when she gets old. She shakes them out, like if they had dust in them, so her blankets and camp will always be clean. The buckskin she throws so there will always be deer meat in her camp, and good hunting for everyone.

Phase VIII concludes *na ih es*. Immediately after the last song, the girl and "the Sponsor" retire to their wickiups [or tipis]. The medicine man and his drummers leave the dance area in search of shade and a drink. When most of the crowd has dispersed two or three men from the girl's camp gather up the buckskin, blankets, baskets, and tarpaulin and carry them away. Presently, the girl's relatives will complete "food exchange" by bringing food to "the Sponsor's" camp.

FOUR HOLY DAYS

Throughout most of *na ih es,* the girl's power is used to benefit herself. However, immediately after the ceremony, it becomes available to anyone. It is not incorrect, though perhaps an oversimplification, to say that during the four days which follow *na ih es* the girl's power is public property.

At this time she is considered holy and continues to live at the dance ground with her family. She is not obliged to stay there all the time, however, and is free to return to Cibecue during the day or to accompany her parents on trips to other parts of the reservation. Throughout the four days, the girl must observe certain taboos. She may not wash herself, for it is thought that by doing so she would sacrifice her power. She may drink only through her drinking tube. If she were to drink from a container, whiskers would grow around her mouth. A third restriction, and the one I am told is most difficult to maintain, dictates that the girl not touch her skin with her fingernails. She may scratch herself only with a scratching stick. Apaches say that if she did otherwise, ugly sores (and subsequent scars) would appear where she touched herself.

Wherever she goes, the girl wears her drinking tube and scratching stick around her neck. The four colored ribbons and the eagle feather and the abalone shell are still in her hair, but she has discarded the buckskin serape and has left her cane in the wickiup at the dance ground.

During the four holy days, the girl's power is believed to be strong enough to cure the sick. To be healed, a sick person stands facing the girl, who extends her arms in front of her (palms up) and then raises them quickly to shoulder level. She repeats this gesture four times. At no point does she touch the patient. If, after such a blessing, the sick person feels relieved, then the girl's power is considered exceptional in its strength and she is henceforth called "She Can Perform Miracles."

In addition to healing, the girl's power may be used to bring rain. I have never witnessed the rainmaking ritual, but received the following description of it from a trustworthy informant.

> Inside her wickiup, they stand her cane in the ground. Then she takes water and sprinkles it over the cane. They say rain will come that way. There is a medicine man in there and he sings songs when they do it. Four songs, I think.

Around noon on the fourth day after *na ih es,* "the Sponsor" unties the ribbons and the feather in the girl's hair and takes the drinking tube and scratching stick from around her neck. Upon the removal of this paraphernalia, the girl no longer has the ability to cure the sick or bring rain, and her taboos are ended.

— 17 —

Taking or Receiving the Buddhist Precepts

Richard Hughes Seager

The Buddhist eightfold path is a highly succinct statement, said to be delivered by the Buddha in his first sermon, of the way to attain liberation from suffering. According to it, one needs to cultivate: 1) right view, and 2) right resolve to foster wisdom; 3) right speech, 4) right action, and 5) right livelihood to address matters of moral or ethical behavior; and 6) right effort, 7) right mindfulness, and 8) right concentration, which bear most directly on the practice of meditation. Buddhists cultivate wisdom, morality, and meditation as a seamless whole on the path, but each is a distinct arena of thought and practice. Moral and ethical concerns are outlined in what are called the precepts. Ritual expressions of commitment and recommitment to them are generally referred to in the United States as taking or receiving the precepts.

The precepts took on a variety of expressions as Buddhism spread from India across southern, central, and eastern Asia and as numerous sectarian and regional traditions flourished over the centuries. Thus, one can speak of the five, eight, ten, sixteen, and other numbers of precepts and a wide range of ritual contexts in which Buddhists take or receive them. Generally speaking, the precepts are cast as prescriptions not unlike the Ten Commandments. They are not understood to be divinely ordained prohibitions, however, but vows made to oneself to follow the Buddhist path. As in the case of the commandments, these prohibitions also enjoin positive moral action and are the subject of a great many sermons and much religious commentary. The precepts also reflect widely held social norms in Buddhist countries.

The prescriptive nature of the precepts is also reflected in what is called *vinaya*, extensive disciplinary codes for orders of fully ordained monks and nuns that became established throughout Buddhist Asia and are now found in the West. The rules contained within vinaya, which deal with questions about sexuality, matters of dressing, eating, and sleeping, and so on, as well as more abstract ethical concerns, were codified into a list known as the *pratimoksha*. Although the precise number of rules varies somewhat in Buddhist texts and among different sects, one authoritative list contains 227 rules for fully ordained males and 311 for fully ordained women. According to some monastic traditions, the pratimoksa is chanted every two weeks by the assembled community to keep the commitment to their vows vital.

The precepts figure in the practice of American Buddhism in a wide variety of ways, depending on the Asian tradition in question, its nation or region of origin, and the status of the practitioner. Additional variety is being introduced as a result of Americanization, as both immigrant and convert Buddhists create North American interpretations of the teachings and practice of Buddhism in a wide range of social settings. The texts below have been selected to suggest the range of ways in which lay American Buddhists now understand and take the precepts. Two texts illustrate the traditional method of taking precepts in immigrant temples in the Theravada tradition of South and Southeast Asia. By one estimate, there are over 150 organizations in the United States functioning as Theravada temples, called *wats* (Thai) or *viharas* (Sri Lankan), serving around three-quarters of a million immigrants in over thirty states. A third text represents a more innovative form of precept-taking as it is done among students, most of them European American converts, who study under Thich Nhat Hanh, a Mahayana monk in the Thien or Zen tradition of East Asia. Nhat Hanh is a poet, teacher, and leading exponent of "engaged Buddhism," a broad current of contemporary Buddhist practice grounded in social action. Nhat Hanh is the head of the Order of Interbeing, an organization embracing male and female laity and ordained monks and nuns. He is also the inspiration behind a movement called Communities of Mindful Living, of which there are two hundred worldwide, most of them in the United States.

The two Theravada rituals are usually performed in a shrine room in a temple. They are chanted or recited in Pali, the ancient scriptural language of the Theravada tradition, which remains authoritative in this country. Due to the variety of Asian ethnic groups within the American Theravada community, however, some temples use one or another of the vernacular languages of Southeast Asia. With the growth of Anglicized and Americanized second and third generations, moreover, some leaders have begun to encourage the use of English, the form in which they are reproduced here. By and large, lay Theravada Buddhists do not engage in extended sitting meditation. Their religious practices are primarily devotional in kind, some of which take the form of providing support for monastics orders, an activity seen as a source of merit making.

The first text is "Taking the Five Precepts," the most basic expression of the precepts in the Buddhist tradition. These are to abstain from: 1) harming living beings, 2) taking what is not given, 3) sexual misconduct, 4) false speech, and 5) unmindful states due to alcohol or drugs. The ritual begins with a formal request by lay Buddhists of a monastic preceptor, asking him for instruction in the essentials of the path. Immediately thereafter comes a very brief hymn, "Homage to the Blessed One." The monk then instructs the laity in "taking refuge" in what are called the Three Jewels—the Buddha, the *dhamma* (or dharma) or his teaching, and the *sangha* or Buddhist community. The core of the ritual is the taking of the five precepts. The closing consists of the monastic teacher extolling the precepts and their benefits to all beings. The three main parts of this ritual—the hymn, taking refuge, and the precepts—are extremely familiar elements in Theravada temple worship. They are as well known to those raised in a South or Southeast Asian Buddhist culture as the sign of the cross, Our Father, and Hail Mary are to most Catholic Christians. The three are chanted together by monks and lay people in virtually every ritual in an immigrant Theravada temple, from daily morning and evening chanting sessions to special celebrations on Vesak and Kathin, two particularly important Buddhist holidays. They also figure prominently in worship at home, hence they play an important role in the private religious life of lay people.

The second Theravada chant is a portion of a ritual called "Taking the Eight Precepts." On selected occasions, be these retreats, important holidays, or a special season of one's life, Theravada lay people may temporarily take on the lifestyle of a fully ordained monastic for a day, weekend, week, month, or longer period. To do this, they take the eight precepts. These chants occur within the same ritual framework as five precepts—the request, the hymn, and taking refuge—so only the actual taking of the eight precepts is printed below. Compare the five and the eight precepts to note how the more austere standards of the monastic vinaya regarding sexuality, dress, and personal comportment are enjoined on lay Buddhists for the duration of their retreat.

The Thich Nhat Hanh text, "Reciting the Five Wonderful Precepts," provides an interesting counterpoint to the Theravada texts for a number of reasons. First, they are the same five precepts as those discussed above, but stated in a more affirmative way. The ethical content of them is also made far more explicit, at times very strikingly so, in order to bring out how they are to be applied to contemporary society for a constituency that is largely, but not exclusively, comprised of western converts. In many respects, they are the precepts plus contemporary social commentary. Note how issues prominent in the last three decades, from break-down of community, to exploitation of the environment, child abuse, dysfunctional families, the use of preservatives in food, and the effect of violence seen on television, are reflected in the choice of language. At the same time, however, these concerns are set within a transcendental frame of reference that owes a great deal to the expansive philosophical worldview that is one hallmark of Mahayana Buddhism and to Nhat Hanh's poetic nature.

The "Five Wonderful Precepts," which are also referred to as the "Five Mindfulness Trainings," are recited in English. In the text here, the recitation is in the context of a biweekly or monthly recommitment ceremony which is held in a dharma hall, retreat center, or any location where Nhat Hanh's followers assemble to meditate. But anyone seeking to take the precepts for the first time can submit their name at a retreat led by Nhat Hanh himself, which often attract from five hundred to a thousand students, or by one of his authorized teachers. Students receive a Buddhist name, "a dharma name," at that time to mark their entrance onto the Buddhist path and an ordination certificate that signifies they are a lay student in Nhat Hanh's lineage. They are admonished to recite the precepts alone or within a group at least once a month, with a sense that their ordination will automatically lapse should they neglect to do so over the course of a year. "The Five Wonderful

Precepts" play an important role in the Order of Interbeing, but Order members are also expected to live in accord with fourteen precepts, the larger number of vows reflecting a higher degree of spiritual and institutional commitment.

The text of the ritual is more or less self-explanatory. It begins with a leader calling the community together and proceeds to the recitation of the precepts. Those in attendance will either repeat them out loud or listen while mindfully attending to their meaning. A bell, a standard element in Buddhist temples rituals and meditation sessions, punctuates the ceremony. In Nhat Hanh's communities it is referred to as the mindfulness bell, the ringing of which is used to draw assemblies together in silent attention to the import of the proceedings.

The precepts figure prominently in other convert communities, where the form in which they are taken varies significantly. For example, John Daido Loori, the abbott of Zen Mountain Monastery in New York state, transmits the precepts as a rite of initiation for students only once they have achieved a significant level of maturity in their practice. Following the Soto Zen tradition of Japan, Loori's students take sixteen precepts in the course of a ceremony called *jukai*, a term that means to receive the precepts but connotes as well that they are to be realized within oneself. The sixteen include the Three Jewels noted above, the three pure precepts (to do no evil, to do good, and to do good for others), and the ten grave precepts: 1) do not kill, 2) do not steal, 3) do not engage in sexual misconduct, 4) do not lie, 5) do not become intoxicated, 6) do not speak of others' faults, 7) do not elevate yourself while demeaning others, 8) be generous to others, 9) do not be angry, and 10) do not slander the Buddha, Dharma, or Sangha. Loori, while emphasizing much that is traditional in the precepts, also reinterprets elements of them to apply to American men and women who practice together, are often married householders with children, and are concerned about a range of contemporary social concerns such as ecological issues and feminism.

"Taking the Five Precepts" and "Taking the Eight Precepts" are in *A Chanting Guide: Pali Passages with English Translation* (Ontario, Canada: The Dhammayut Order in the United States of America, 1994), Reprinted by permission of the publisher, the Dhammayut Order of the United States of America ©1994; Thich Nhat Hanh, "Reciting the Five Wonderful Precepts," is in *Interbeing: Fourteen Guidelines for Engaged Buddhism*, third edition (1998) by Thich Nhat Hanh with permission of Parallax Press, Berkeley, Calif., edited by Fred Eppsteiner (Berkeley, Calif.: Parallax, 1993).

Further Reading

Peter Harvey, "Buddhist Practice: Ethics," in *An Introduction to Buddhism: Teachings, History, Practices* (Cambridge: Cambridge University Press, 1990); John Daido Loori, *The Heart of Being: Moral and Ethical Teachings of Zen Buddhism* (Boston: Charles E. Tuttle, 1996); Paul David Numrich, *Old Wisdom in the New World: Americanization in Two Immigrant Theravada Buddhist Temples* (Knoxville: University of

Tennessee Press, 1996); Thich Nhat Hanh, *For a Future to Be Possible: Commentaries on the Five Mindfulness Trainings*, rev. ed. (Berkeley, Calif.: Parallax, 1998).

Taking the Five Precepts

Lay people request:

> Venerable Sir, we request the Three Refuges and the Five Precepts.
> Venerable Sir, a second time we request the Three Refuges and the Five Precepts.
> Venerable Sir, a third time we request the Three Refuges and the Five Precepts.

The monk then recites the following passage three times, after which the lay people repeat it three times:

> Homage to the Blessed One, the Worthy One,
> The Rightly Self-awakened One.

The monk then recites the following passages line by line, with the lay people reciting line by line after him.

> I go to the Buddha for refuge.
> I go to the Dhamma for refuge.
> I go to the Sangha for refuge.
> A second time, I go to the Buddha for refuge.
> A second time, I go to the Dhamma for refuge.
> A second time, I go to the Sangha for refuge.
> A third time, I go to the Buddha for refuge.
> A third time, I go to the Dhamma for refuge.
> A third time, I go to the Sangha for refuge.

The monk then says:

> This ends the going for refuge.

The lay people respond:

> Yes, Venerable Sir.

The monk then recites the precepts line by line, with the lay people reciting them line by line after him.

> I undertake the training rule to refrain from taking life.
> I undertake the training rule to refrain from stealing.
> I undertake the training rule to refrain from sexual misconduct.
> I undertake the training rule to refrain from telling lies.
> I undertake the training rule to refrain from intoxicating liquors and drugs that lead to carelessness.

The monk then concludes with the following:

> These are the five training rules.
> Through virtue they go to a good birth.
> Through virtue is wealth attained.
> Through virtue they go to Liberation.
> Therefore we should purify our virtue.

Bow three times

Taking the Eight Precepts

The monk then recites the precepts line by line, with the lay people reciting them line by line after him.

> I undertake the training rule to refrain from taking life.
> I undertake the training rule to refrain from stealing.
> I undertake the training rule to refrain from sexual intercourse.
> I undertake the training rule to refrain from telling lies.
> I undertake the training rule to refrain from intoxicating liquors and drugs that lead to carelessness.
> I undertake the training rule to refrain from eating after noon and before dawn.
> I undertake the training rule to refrain from dancing, singing, music, watching shows, wearing garlands, beautifying myself with perfumes and cosmetics.
> I undertake the training rule to refrain from high and luxurious seats and beds.
> I undertake these eight precepts.
> I undertake these eight precepts.
> I undertake these eight precepts.

Bow three times

Reciting The Five Wonderful Precepts

Head of Ceremony: Has the entire community assembled?

Reply: The entire community has assembled.

Head of Ceremony: Is there harmony in the community?

Reply: Yes, there is harmony.

Head of Ceremony: Is there anyone not able to be present who has asked to be represented and have they declared themselves to have done their best to study and practice the precepts?

Reply: No, there is not.

or

Reply: Yes, _____, for health reasons, cannot be at the recitation today. She has asked _____ to represent her and she declares that she has done her best to study and practice the precepts.

Head of Ceremony: What is the reason for the community gathering today?

Reply: The community has gathered to practice the recitation of the Five Wonderful Precepts. Noble community, please listen. Today, (date), has been declared to be the precept recitation day. We have gathered at the appointed time. The noble community is ready to hear and recite the precepts in an atmosphere of harmony, and the recitation can proceed. Is that correct?

Everyone: That is correct.

Head of Ceremony: Brothers and Sisters, it is now time to recite the Five Wonderful Precepts. Please, those who have been ordained as Upasaka [lay man] and Upasika [lay woman] kneel with joined palms in the direction of the Buddha, our teacher.

Brothers and Sisters, please listen. The Five Precepts are the basis for a happy life. They have the capacity to protect life and to make it beautiful and worth living. They are also the door that opens to enlightenment and liberation. Please listen to each precept, and answer yes, silently every time you see that you have made the effort to study, practice, and observe it.

The First Precept

Aware of the suffering caused by the destruction of life, I vow to cultivate compassion and learn ways to protect the lives of people, animals, plants, and minerals. I am determined not to kill, not to let others kill, and not to condone any act of killing in the world, in my thinking, and in my way of life.

(silence)

This is the first of the Five Precepts. Have you made an effort to study and practice it during the past two weeks?

(bell)

The Second Precept

Aware of the suffering caused by exploitation, social injustice, stealing, and oppression, I vow to cultivate loving kindness and learn ways to work for the well-being of people, animals, plants, and minerals. I vow to practice generosity by sharing my time, energy, and material resources with those who are in need. I am determined not to steal and not to possess anything that should belong to others. I will respect the property of others, but I will prevent others from profiting from human suffering or the suffering of other species on Earth.

(silence)

This is the second of the Five Precepts. Have you made an effort to study and practice it during the past two weeks?

(bell)

The Third Precept

Aware of the suffering caused by sexual misconduct, I vow to cultivate responsibility and learn ways to protect the safety and integrity of individuals, couples, families, and society. I am determined not to engage in sexual relations without love and a long-term commitment. To preserve the happiness of myself and others, I am determined to respect my commitments and the commitments of others. I will do everything in my power to protect children from sexual abuse and to prevent couples and families from being broken by sexual misconduct.

(silence)

This is the third of the Five Precepts. Have you made an effort to study and practice it during the past two weeks?

(bell)

The Fourth Precept

Aware of the suffering caused by unmindful speech and the inability to listen to others, I vow to cultivate loving speech and deep listening in order to bring joy and happiness to others and relieve others of their suffering. Knowing that words can create happiness or suffering, I vow to learn to speak truthfully, with words that inspire self-confidence, joy, and hope. I am determined not to spread news that I do not know to be certain and not to criticize or condemn things of which I am not sure. I will refrain from uttering words that can cause division or discord, or that can cause the family or the community to break. I will make all efforts to reconcile and resolve all conflicts, however small.

(silence)

This is the fourth of the Five Precepts. Have you made an effort to study and practice it during the past two weeks?

(bell)

The Fifth Precept

Aware of the suffering caused by unmindful consumption, I vow to cultivate good health, both physical and mental, for myself, my family, and my society, by practicing mindful eating, drinking, and consuming. I vow to ingest only items that preserve peace, well-being, and joy in my body, in my consciousness, and in the collective body and consciousness of my family and society. I am determined not to use alcohol or any other intoxicant or to ingest foods or other items that contain toxins, such as certain TV programs, magazines, books, films, and conversations. I am aware that to damage my body or my consciousness with these poisons is to betray my ancestors, my parents, my society, and future generations. I will work to transform violence, fear, anger, and confusion in myself and in society by practicing a diet for myself and for society. I understand that a proper diet is crucial for self-transformation and for the transformation of society.

(silence)

This is the fifth of the Five Precepts. Have you made an effort to study and practice it during the past two weeks?

(bell)

Brothers and Sisters, we have recited the Five Wonderful Precepts, the foundation of happiness for the individual, the family, and society. We should recite them regularly so that our study and practice of the precepts can deepen day by day.

Hearing the bell, please bow three times to the Buddha, the Dharma, and the Sangha to show your gratitude.

(three sounds of the bell)

Healing: Health, Happiness,

and The Miraculous

— 18 —

Tongues and Healing at the
Azusa Street Revival

Gastón Espinosa

The following autobiographical excerpt includes a description of the Azusa Street Revival by Adolfo C. Valdez (1896–1988). A fifth-generation Mexican-American who traced his ancestry back to the time of the founding of California by Junipero Serra, Valdez was born and raised in Los Angeles. At the age of ten, his mother, Susie Villa Valdez, began attending the Azusa Street Revival in Los Angeles. After she converted to Pentecostalism, she brought her Catholic husband and family to the Apostolic Faith Mission on 312 Azusa Street, where they, too, converted and joined the Pentecostal movement. She was one of the first Latina Pentecostal evangelists in North America and one of the first to work with the poor and the prostitutes in the red-light district of Los Angeles. As a traveling evangelist, she conducted evangelistic services in migrant farm labor camps in Los Angeles, San Bernardino, and Riverside, California. Although he was less active in the lay ministry than his wife, José Valdez was healed at the Azusa Street Revival.

After his ordination in 1916, A. C. Valdez went on to become one of the most important, if overlooked, Mexican American Pentecostal evangelists of the twentieth century. He preached all over the United States to Anglo-American, Mexican, and Native American audiences, especially in the Southwest. Surprisingly, he also went on evangelistic tours to Australia and New Zealand, countries in which he claimed to be one of the founders of the Pentecostal movement. As is evident in his autobiography, *Fire on Azusa Street,* the revival had a profound impact on his future ministry.

The Azusa Street Revival took place in the black section of Los Angeles from 1906 to 1909. It was led by an African-American holiness minister named William J. Seymour (1870–1922). Born in Louisiana to the son of former slaves, Seymour traveled along the former underground railroad to the Midwest before moving to Houston, Texas, in search of his relatives, with whom he had lost contact. There he met a Midwestern holiness minister named Charles Fox Parham (1873–1929) and embraced his teaching that the baptism with the Holy Spirit was evidenced by speaking in tongues, an unknown language that sounds like ecstatic speech or gibberish. As proof of his claims, Parham asserted that all of Jesus' disciples spoke in tongues on the day of Pentecost as described in the New Testament book of Acts. He further claimed that the Apostle Paul and the New Testament churches practiced speaking in tongues (1 Cor. 12 and 14). In addition to speaking in tongues, they also practiced prophecy, words of knowledge, miracles, and divine healing. Their commitment to the infallibility of the Bible led them to affirm high moral standards that forbade lying, stealing, premarital sex, drunkenness, cheating, smoking, and gambling. In their place, they promoted lively worship services, small-group home Bible studies, annual camp meetings, and Christian books and periodicals. Like other conservative Protestants of their day, Pentecostals stressed the importance of missions and the imminent return of Jesus Christ to earth to set up his thousand-year kingdom.

Needless to say, Parham's views on spiritual gifts and tongues were considered unorthodox by many Protestant and Catholic Christians of his day. They held that the spiritual gifts described in the New Testament ceased to be valid for the church after the death of the apostles. Still, persuaded by Parham's interpretation of the Bible, Seymour took his message to Los Angeles. There he began a prayer meeting that erupted into the now famous Azusa Street Revival in April 1906. This revival, which ran daily from 1906 to 1909, was one of the longest in American history.

What was unique about the revival was not its duration but rather its multiracial composition. More than twenty nationalities reportedly participated in the revival, including large numbers of blacks, whites, and Mexicans. Furthermore, unlike most mainline Protestant and Catholic churches in that day, the Azusa Street Revival allowed women to preach and teach the Bible. They also allowed women to serve as evangelists and on the ordination committee, which was made up of both blacks and whites. In an age dominated by the shadow of Jim Crow segregation, the revival permitted women, ethnic minorities, and the working class to transgress some, though clearly not all, of the social borders and boundaries of their day. Blacks, whites, Mexicans, and other immigrants, for instance, freely intermingled and were healed through the laying-on of hands. Although the multiracial composition of the revival attracted much attention, it was the claims of healing at the mission that attracted the masses. The Azusa Street newspaper, *The Apostolic Faith,* is chock full of testimonies of divine healing.

Valdez's autobiography captures the energy and enthusiasm of the Azusa Street Revival and spirit of the first generation of Pentecostal Christians. Valdez was ten years old when his mother told him about her Azusa Street experience. In the selection excerpted here, he describes his mother's visit to the revival and the biblical basis for speaking in tongues. Valdez then recalls the setting and cadence of the revival, but he confuses Charles Fox Parham with William J. Seymour. What is important about the service, however, is not who is leading it but rather the supernatural activity that is taking place. He refers to a woman who claimed she was healed of blindness, and then he gives a description of the canes, braces, and crutches that leaned against the Azusa Street mission walls as a testimony by those who no longer needed them.

Contrary to the stereotype of Pentecostalism as unrestrained emotionalism, Valdez notes that the revival also had long and profound moments of what he called a "holy quietness." This quietness was often followed by a period of speaking in tongues. During this time of speaking in tongues and singing, people would faint and experience what Pentecostals call being "slain in the Spirit." Valdez remembers the "invisible force" that permeated the revival. Although Pentecostals would claim that this force is the Holy Spirit, their opponents argued that it was demonic activity. Indeed, some claimed that Spiritualists, Theosophists, and other metaphysical practitioners tried to infiltrate the revival, leading to conflict between Seymour and some church participants.

The tremendous emphasis that the Azusa Street Revival placed on the spiritual gifts and speaking in tongues made it an easy target for ridicule in newspapers and among Protestant and Catholic leaders. Valdez recalled how the decision to become a Pentecostal meant almost certain expulsion from traditional Protestant and Catholic churches. It was this expulsion from traditional churches, he argues, that gave birth to the Pentecostal movement. Although this excerpt ends with the miraculous healing of Valdez's father, the autobiography continues with a discussion of how Valdez was ordained to the Pentecostal ministry in 1916. He became an important member of the movement, preaching in South America, India, China, Hawaii, and the South Sea Islands. Throughout his life, he had a profound sense that he was never alone—that God was always watching over him.

Valdez's story illustrates the problems, power, and attraction of Pentecostalism. The power of Pentecostalism lies in its ability to allow people to reimagine their historical identities by using revelation as a divine pretext to cross certain social, racial, gender, and ecclesiastical boundaries. After all, if God is telling you to do something, who is going to argue with God? In this respect, Pentecostalism is a religion of self-empowerment and self-authentication. The role of priest as the mediator between God and humanity is no longer necessary, thus making the Pentecostal movement potentially dangerous to the religious establishment. Since the movement has been made up of largely working-class people and poorly schooled whites, blacks, and Latinos, Pentecostal beliefs and practices were theologically suspect to educated mainline and evangelical Protestants.

The self-authenticating nature of Pentecostalism has contributed to a built-in tendency to fragment. This has been both the Achilles heal of the movement and the secret to its growth. At precisely the time it begins to institutionalize, some charismatic leader claims God told him or her to start a new church based on the New Testament. Although on the one hand this fragmentation weakens the denomination, on the other hand it generates new, indigenous leadership and forces the parent denomination either to adjust to the cultural change or to be left behind. This fragmentation thesis may help explain why the movement now numbers more than twenty million people in the United States and four hundred million people around the world.

The text below is excerpted from A. C. Valdez, Sr., with James F. Scheer, *Fire on Azusa Street* (Costa Mesa, Calif.: Gift Publications, 1980), pp. 3–10, 39–40.

Further Reading

Robert Mapes Anderson, *Vision of the Disinherited: The Making of American Pentecostalism* (Peabody, Mass.: Hendrickson, 1992); Stanley M. Burgess and Gary B. McGee, eds., *Dictionary of Pentecostal and Charismatic Movements* (Grand Rapids, Mich.: Zondervan, 1988); Gastón Espinosa, "*El Azteca* Francisco Olazábal and Latino Pentecostal Charisma, Power, and Faith Healing in the Borderlands," *Journal of the American Academy of Religion* 67 (1999), 597–616.

Fire on the Street

Late one night when I was fast asleep, my mother came into my dark bedroom after a service at the Azusa Street Mission. She bent over and touched my shoulder. As I brushed the sand out of my eyes to wake up, she began talking fast in some language I had never heard before.

I was frightened. Why wasn't she talking English? What had come over her? Then, suddenly, she began crying, but I knew right away she was crying from joy, not sadness. I kept wondering if she would ever use English again. Then the other language stopped, and she said: "Son, I have had a most glorious experience! I have just been baptized in the Holy Ghost and have been given the gift of tongues!" I was puzzled and tried to understand her. "These are blessed times, son," she continues. "The Holy Ghost is here on earth—like at Pentecost. Thank God we are alive to see fulfillment of promises of the Bible!"

I knew that the Holy Ghost was the third member of the Holy Trinity, but not much more. She went on: "Actually, the prophecy of the Holy Ghost's coming was given more than 800 years before Jesus was born. The Bible in Joel 2:28 tells us: 'And it shall come to pass afterward, that I will pour out my Spirit upon all flesh; and your sons and your daughters shall prophesy, your old men shall dream dreams, your young men shall see visions . . .'" She flipped the well-worn pages of her black leather-covered Holy Bible to Matthew 3:11 where it told about John the Baptist in the wilderness and how he announced to the world: "I indeed baptize you with water unto repentance; but he that cometh after me (Jesus) is mightier than I, whose shoes I am not worthy to bear: he shall baptize you with the Holy Ghost and with fire." Quickly she turned to Acts 1 and told me how Jesus, forty days after He was resurrected, commanded His apostles to stay in Jerusalem and wait for the promise of God: "For John truly baptized with water; but ye shall be baptized with the Holy Ghost. . . ." She skipped on to Acts 1:8: "But ye shall receive power, after that the Holy Ghost is come upon you: and ye shall be witnesses unto me both in

Jerusalem, and in all Judea, and in Samaria, and unto the uttermost parts of the earth." And a page farther on, in Acts 2, she read: "And when the day of Pentecost was fully come, they were all with one accord in one place. And suddenly there came a sound from heaven as of a rushing mighty wind, and it filled the house where they were sitting. And there appeared unto them cloven tongues like as of fire, and it sat upon each of them. And they were all filled with the Holy Ghost, and began to speak with other tongues, as the Spirit gave them utterance."

Now I was eager to see what was happening on Azusa Street! On the next night she invited me along. As we came within a block of a two-story white-painted wooden building, I felt a pulling sensation. I couldn't have turned away if I wanted to. Inside, the place looked like a big, plain barn. Most of the seats—rough planks on wooden nail kegs—were taken. There were as many black people as white. I couldn't understand why metal mailboxes were nailed to walls.

As we moved toward an open spot on a rear bench, I suddenly felt a chill. How could that be? It wasn't cold at all. Then the hair on my arms, legs, and head began to stand on end. It felt as if I were surrounded by God. I was trembling. So was mother and everybody else.

On the platform, a black man—mother said it was Pastor W. J. Seymour—sat behind two wooden boxes, one on top of the other. They were his pulpit. Now and then he would raise his head and sit erectly, his large lips moving in silent prayer. He was a plain man with a short beard and a glass eye. He didn't seem like a leader to me, but when I saw what was going on, I knew he didn't have to be.

Something unusual was happening. In most churches, kids would be running up and down aisles or turning seats. Here the children, seated between their parents—even babies in their mothers' arms—were quiet. But it was not their parents who kept them still. Nobody even whispered. All the adults were praying with eyes closed. I knew the Spirit of God was there.

Suddenly, people rose to their feet. Everywhere hands shot toward heaven. Mine went up, and I hadn't tried to raise them. So did the hands of smaller children and even those of babies in the arms of black mothers. Big, strong men began to cry out loud, then women. I felt like crying too. I didn't know why. I just felt, "Thank you, God, for letting me be here with You."

As I looked out over the congregation, another chill ran down my spine. It was as if ocean waves were moving from one end of the congregation to the other—the most thrilling sight I had ever seen.

Wave after wave of the Spirit went through the hall, like a breeze over a corn field. Again the crowd settled back into the seats. And prayers began to buzz through the hall. Then *tongues of fire* suddenly appeared over the heads of so many people, and a black man with a shining face leaped to his feet. Out of his mouth poured words in some language I had never heard before. I began to tremble harder than before.

When he finished, another black man rose and told us in English what the other man had said. It was a prayer to Jesus! Occasionally, as Pastor Seymour prayed, his head would bow so low that it disappeared behind the top wooden box.

Just when quiet settled over the hall, a white woman came off the bench like a jack-in-the-box. "Oh, my blessed Jesus," she cried out in excitement, "I can see. I can *see.*" She placed her hands over her eyes. "Oh, Jesus, thank you. Thank you for this miracle." And she plunged out into the aisle and began to dance, her open palms reaching toward heaven. "Thank you, Father. I can see. I can see!"

Before the night was over, another blind person could see, the deaf could hear and the crippled could walk. It was so exciting! That was my first night of many in over three years at. . . . Azusa Street. . . .

Everything about the Azusa Street Mission fascinated me—especially the prayer or "tarrying room" on the second floor. Usually one hundred or more black, brown, and white people prayerfully waited there for the Holy Spirit to come upon them. Dozens of canes, braces, crutches and blackened smoking pipes leaned against the barnlike walls. Many times waves of glory would come over the tarrying room or meeting room, and people would cry out prayers of thanks or praise as they received the baptism in the Holy Spirit.

Meetings used to go past midnight and into the early hours of the morning. Hours there seemed like minutes. Sometimes after a wave of glory, a lot of people would speak in tongues. Then a holy quietness would come over the place, followed by a chorus of prayer in languages we had never before heard.

Many were slain in the Spirit, buckling to the floor, unconscious, in a beautiful Holy Spirit cloud, and the Lord gave them visions. How I enjoyed shouting and praising God. During the tarrying, we used to break out in songs about Jesus and the Holy Spirit: "Fill Me Now," "Joy Unspeakable," and "Love Lifted Me" about the cleansing and precious blood of Jesus would just spring from our mouths. In between choruses, heavenly music would fill the hall, and we would break into tears. Suddenly the crowd seemed to forget how to sing in English. Out of their mouths would come new languages and lovely harmony that no human beings could have learned.

On the ground floor, where services seemed never to end, the metal mailboxes, the Azusa Street Mission's "collection plates," were always filled with coins and paper money. Never did Seymour or any other preacher behind the shoe-box pulpit ask for money. They had faith. All preachers had to do was preach. Anybody who had been blessed by the service gave generously. Hardly ever did the Azusa Street Mission advertise in newspapers about its services. People heard about them through word of mouth. In the same way that my mother and I felt a strong pull toward the mission, so did others.

Many who came said that they knew nothing about Azusa Street and the Holy Spirit meetings until they had visions of the mission and were instructed to go there. Others were moved by an invisible force to attend. Some who attended Azusa Street at the start had little understanding of what was happening, and feared the unknown.

They had not even been taught by their pastors about being born again. Many had read in their Bibles in John 3:3 what Jesus had told Nicodemus: ". . . except a man be born again, he cannot see the kingdom of God." But they had not given it much thought. Most had not learned about being baptized in the Holy Ghost and the gift or gifts that come with this experience. Old-line churches frowned on the Azusa Street Mission's Bible teachings, "so-called miracles," and "noisy meetings." Their members who came just once to Azusa Street services and were found out, were often asked to leave their congregations. . . .

A sure way to get kicked out of an established church in the early twentieth century was to admit having been baptized in the Holy Spirit. I learned this from experience, as did thousands of others. Some of us were given another chance. We could renounce "this heresy," and then be permitted back in the flock, but no one who has ever been baptized in the Holy Spirit could return to a church that is without the Holy Ghost, without spirit and life. There were no sectarian churches in the charismatic movement, so we had to go it without the establishment. This is why many Pentecostal churches got started. . . .

For some years, my father had had a steadily enlarging malignant growth on his back, which, doctors feared, would spread to every critical part of his body and take his life. After he had been born again and baptized in the Holy Spirit, his condition improved steadily. One day the growth dissolved completely and disappeared from his body.

What a great day for us all! Our family was relieved of anxiety, and father recovered his health enough to take on light work that supported mother and himself. . . .

— 19 —

Navajo Healing Ceremonies

Amanda Porterfield

In small round buildings, or hogans, Navajo singers invoke the powers of the Holy People, the immortal beings with whom the human people, the Diné, share the sacred space of Navajoland. Located in northeastern Arizona and adjacent parts of New Mexico, Utah, and Colorado, Navajoland is a place of changing winds and subtly colored canyons, escarpments, and buttes. The Diné (Navajo) see the physical geography of Navajoland as the outward manifestation of the activities of the Holy People and they conceptualize the Holy People as the inner forms of the mountains, winds, rains, animals, and other natural phenomena. The Diné attempt to influence the personified forces working within their environment with the help of singers trained to draw strength and goodness from the Holy People and to subdue or dissipate their malevolent power. Holy People fall into different classes with regard to their relationship to human beings. Some are persuadable, others are not. Some are helpers and intermediaries between human beings and other Holy People, others are undependable or persistently dangerous.

By means of ceremonies, also known in English as sings or chants, singers attempt to control the Holy People in ways that are therapeutic for human beings. Navajo ceremonies are extremely complex both philosophically and technically, and scholars who have spent years studying them often admit that much eludes them. But some general observations can be made. Particular situations, including potentially propitious events such as weddings and house blessings, as well as unfortunate events such as injuries and disease, prompt the need for ceremonies. Ceremonies are elaborate events that often last several days and require accurate execution. But no organized priesthood exists to prescribe them. Rather, the families of individuals suffering some misfortune, or undergoing an important transition, identify the kind of chant appropriate to the problem at hand, often in consultation with individuals known for their abilities to make such diagnoses. They then contract with a singer who specializes in the performance of the particular chant that is required. Of the numerous chants that exist among the Navajo, there are three main types: *Blessingway* chants, which prevent disease and other misfortune by drawing in the blessings, or good will, of Holy People; *Holyway* chants, which neutralize the potential malevolence of Holy People and transform it into beneficial power; and *Evilway* chants, which exorcise Holy People in situations where their malevolence has erupted.

Evilway chants rarely include sandpaintings, since sandpaintings are used to attract the energies of Holy People, and Evilway chants concentrate on dispelling their malevolence. Some Blessingway chants include sandpaintings, although they resemble Pueblo paintings in their small size and utilization of brightly colored vegetable matter. All Holyway chants include sandpaintings that are distinctively Navajo in their design and utilization of dry pulverized materials from charcoal, flower petals, corn meal, pollens, and various kinds of stone.

Holyway chants are actually collections of individual ceremonies divided into two main parts. Each Holyway chant begins with ceremonies aimed at dissipating the malevolent potential of the Holy People. These preliminary cleansing ceremonies are followed by ceremonies aimed at attracting the Holy People's goodness and strength, and sandpaintings—such as the one reprinted here—are part of these ceremonies of attraction. To receive the sun's blessing, Holyway paintings are made during the day, whereas the chant itself is performed at night. During a two-night Holyway sing, chants focused on sandpainting occur the second night; during a five- or nine-night sing, these chants occur the last four nights, each time over a different painting. Constructed on the floor of a ceremonial hogan covered smoothly with river sand, Holyway sandpaintings depict one or more Holy People, and range in size from one to twelve square feet and average about six square feet. Although a big, elaborate painting can require as much as four hundred hours of work, the average-sized painting takes four or five men about four hours to complete. Beginning at the center and working outward, and using strings held taut to make straight lines, men sift the dried materials between thumb and forefinger to reproduce one of the designs known to the singer, who supervises the work. Although hundreds of different designs are known, each singer specializes only in a few. The execution of these designs must be perfect; errors are dangerous and invite malevolence. If a worker makes a mistake, he covers the spot with river sand and starts again.

During a sandpainting ceremony, the individual for whom the chant is held may sit in the middle of the painting. As the singer calls forth the powers of the Holy People represented in the painting, he applies parts of the painting to various parts of the body of the one sung over, with the intention of facilitating a transfer of power between the Holy People and the patient. Anthropologist Gladys A. Reichard described sandpaintings as "ceremonial membranes" through which a kind of "spiritual osmosis" occurs. The Holy People draw evil out of the one-sung-over through the painting and then infuse him or her with strength and goodness.

The singer's chant guides and controls these activities. In sandpainting, as in all Navajo ceremonies, chanting is the chief means by which human beings compel Holy People to serve human well-being. In one of the stories explaining the origin and significance of chanting, First Man and First Woman learned chanting from Wind at the beginning of creation. This ceremonial language became a source of leadership for First Man and First Woman. It enabled them and other Holy People, some of whom were progenitors of human clans, to become increasingly self-controlled and work their way through foul underworlds into this present fifth world.

In addition to his association with language, Wind made breathing possible and also created the material world through his multicolored components, which are the same winds that blow today in Navajoland. At the beginning of creation, a white wind or mist arose from the east and then a blue wind mist arose from the south. Yellow came from the west at the end of the day, followed by black from the north. These wind mists lay beautifully on top of each other, and from them life was created. But this productive harmony has been disturbed by rituals that give the dark wind a different place. After the birth of First Man and First Woman's two children, who were creatures of incest and hence personifications of inharmonious activity, witches have disturbed the beauty of life. Witches often perform their evil by means of reversing the elements of ceremonial speech.

In the multileveled world of the Navajo, elements at different levels of reality can represent and interact with each other; thus, wind nurtures the development of language, while language can invert the natural harmonies of wind. Moreover, events that took place at the beginning of creation coalesce with present events. Thus, ceremonies performed today recapitulate the work of creation and work to restore the original harmonies of the environment established at the time of creation. This artful coalescence is exemplified by two recurrent elements in many chants—Sa 'ah Naaghaii and Bik 'eh Hozko—which together mean "long life according to beauty." Sa 'ah Naaghaii (long life) and Bik 'eh Hozho (along the path of hozho, or harmony and beauty) represent the ideal each Navajo aspires to achieve, the balanced interplay of forces in the environment, the creative efforts of First Man and First Woman at the time of creation, and the paired forces of thought and speech, which control both individual lives and environmental forces.

Healing is the main purpose of much that goes on in Navajo religious life, and the ceremonies that invoke the creative powers of the environment have real therapeutic effect. As is the case with many systems of religious belief, the ideas involved in Navajo ceremonies offer intellectual explanations that combat feelings of helplessness, anxiety, and fear. But although rituals in many religions impart strength to people by defining relationships between them and powerful forces, the religious practices of Native American and other indigenous groups often identify these forces with aspects of the natural environment. Like many Native religions, Navajo ceremonies facilitate well-being and cause people to feel infused with strength and goodness by fostering a sense of attunement with powerful natural forces.

Although healing is an important component of many Native religions, its all-encompassing role in Navajo ceremonial life distinguishes Navajo religion from other Native religions in which individual healing and efforts to guide environmental forces are both important, but are not so closely linked to each other as they are in Navajo religion. Invocation of the spirits working within environmental forces is an essential part of healing ceremonies in virtually all Native religions, including the Navajo religion, but the latter is unusual in its focus on individual healing as the principal means of regulating the environment and reinstating its original harmony.

Like practitioners of other Native religions, the Navajo visualize the spirits working with their environment, and call on those spirits to effect well-being. This process of visualizing and interacting with the spirits occurs through prayers, songs, and other forms of religious ceremony that give participants a sense of involvement in the inner workings of the world and of contributing to their positive outcome. As a result of this sense of effective engagement in the world, these religious practices have an energizing, even transformative, effect on people's lives.

Although the process of engagement with spirits working within the environment is characteristic of virtually all indigenous religions, the Navajo conceptualization of how the spirit forces in the environment work together is as distinctive as the Navajo focus on the cosmic importance of individual healing. In their outlook on reality, the Navajo conceptualize every aspect of the world as being constantly in motion. Thus, the harmony of the world is not a static thing but a matter of continuous interaction and dynamic balance. This ongoing cosmic balance involves the participation of human beings and requires their constant attention. To maintain the beauty and harmony of the world, every human act, including every sentence spoken, should involve some recognition of surrounding forces and attention to their proper relationships and interactions.

Recognition of this interdependence between human beings and surrounding forces is built into the grammatical structure of the Navajo language. The verb "to go" is as central to the construction of Navajo language as the verb "to be" is in English, and open to even more differentiation; anthropologist Gary Witherspoon counted hundreds of different forms of "to go" in Navajo. Literally everything that can be spoken of involves some kind of action and interaction with other things, however slow of pace; nothing is inert or without involvement with other things. Since accurate information and communication involve some awareness of these interactions, the grammatical construction of Navajo language carries information about which things initiate or dominate motion. Thus nouns representing objects with relatively great force of activity must precede nouns representing objects of lesser activity. As Witherspoon shows, it is customary to say the Navajo equivalent of "the girl drank the water." But it would provoke laughter to say "the water was drunk by the girl," since that way of putting the matter focuses the listener on the activity of the water as it is being drunk by the girl, and conjures up an image of a body of water that is more active and powerful than she is going into the girl's mouth.

Navajo ceremonies raise this underlying attentiveness to interaction to the level of deliberate and formalized religious expression. Their concentration on the natural processes of life, and their effort to establish control over these processes through thought and speech, is important for understanding the history of the

Navajo people and for understanding the crucial role that ceremonies have played in enabling them to survive, and even flourish, during centuries of domination by other cultures. By fostering commitment to the coalescing processes of change and renewal, and by visualizing these processes as patterns deliberately guided by thought and speech, Navajo ceremonies have figured importantly in the ability of the Navajo people to rebound from a state of defeat and utter poverty in the 1860s to become the largest Indian tribe in the United States and one whose religious traditions are among the most securely intact.

In 1863, as part of plans to subdue the Navajo and fund the Civil War by obtaining the gold and other precious metals erroneously believed to exist in Navajoland, the U.S. Army destroyed the hogans and sheep of Navajoland and captured eight thousand Navajo men, women, and children. The soldiers marched the Navajo across New Mexico on rations of rancid bacon and weevily flour and imprisoned them for four years without buildings or tents. During these years of forced removal from their beloved homeland, the Navajo lived without their gods. When they were finally allowed to return to Navajoland, the survivors reestablished their culture through the traditional ceremonies aimed at recreating therapeutic relationships with the Holy People. These ceremonies not only enabled the Navajo to identify with the strength and beauty of their homeland but also to associate the processes of change forced on them by immigrants and U.S. agents with their own traditional respect for movement and hence with their own healing and empowerment. Whereas religious traditions in other Native groups have sometimes become wedded to images of the past, the Navajo investment in process has facilitated an embrace of social change that is a hallmark of Navajo history. Although on the surface it might seem paradoxical, the acceptance of change, along with a deeply entrenched and constant concern for healing and renewal, has enabled Navajo culture to emerge in the twentieth century as one of the most well ensconced Native American cultures.

This willingness to accommodate novelty and change as part of the processes that renew and revitalize the original harmonies of the world has deep roots in Navajo history. Long before the arrival of the Europeans, Navajo culture took shape. Nomadic clans of Navajo ancestors appropriated sandpainting and many other elements of belief and lifestyle from the more highly developed, self-controlled, and sedentary Pueblo cultures of the Southwest. With the arrival of the Spanish in the sixteenth century, the Navajo again altered their lifestyle dramatically by becoming shepherds who developed weaving as a characteristic cultural expression, and horseback riders who developed trading skills and retained mobility even as sheepherding tied them to particular locales. Although elements of both Navajo weaving and sandpainting reflect borrowings from other cultures, these arts have become central to Navajo culture, and scholars agree that the Navajo have developed both of them in highly distinctive ways. In the twentieth century, the Navajo have displayed considerable success in surviving as a religious subculture amid the dominating cash economy and consumerist mentality of American culture. They continue to conduct their ceremonies, tell their stories, and promote their traditions in the Southwest.

Included here are three examples of ways that Navajo heal. Although they each come from different ceremonies, they all are a type of prayer for well-being. The first example (Figure 19.1) is a black-and-white rendition of a sandpainting. The original sandpainting was destroyed after healing, since according to Navajo tradition its purpose for existence had been accomplished. However, at times paintings and sketches of the original sandpaintings were made by non-Navajos. Such is the case with this one, a painting made in 1942 by Maud Oakes after attending a Navajo ceremony. In this drawing of that sandpainting, the first Snake person is made with white pigment, the second with blue pigment, the third with yellow pigment, and the fourth with black pigment. The first and third figures are male and hold rattles made out of hides and turkey-feather bundle prayer sticks. The second and the fourth figures are female and hold ears of corn. From their arms hang attachments made of otter skin. Around the figures is a rainbow-garland guardian with feathers from four birds: eagle, blue hawk, red-wing hawk, and the blackbird.

In the second text, Leland Wyman (b. 1897) recorded the ritual directions for what he called a "minor Navaho ceremony," the Female Shooting Life Chant. Wyman recorded it in August of 1935 when he himself was the patient being treated for a sore knee. At the time, Wyman was an anthropologist working for the Boston University School of Medicine, who was studying Navajo forms of

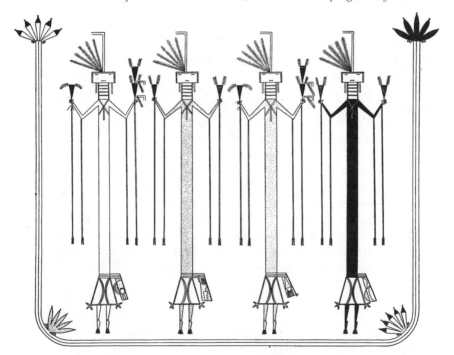

Figure 19.1. "Snake People Who Make Medicine," line drawing based on sand painting.

healing. This chant is performed during the summer and is more a part of the everyday life of the Navajo than the more complicated (and expensive) Night Chant or Mountain Chant. This ceremony in particular took place in the southeastern part of Navajoland, near Pinedale, New Mexico. The chanter is briefly described by Wyman as "an English-speaking man of middle age." As in all Navajo ceremonies, even "minor" ones, great care must be taken to arrange the proper sacred objects in the proper order. Whether accompanied by words or not, the ritual acts described in the text are prayers for well-being. Actions, like sandpaintings, are powerful.

The third text was recorded in the early 1930s, although the exact date is not known. The prayer comes from the Male Shooting Chant Evil Chasing ceremony. It was recorded on a phonographic disc and transcribed by Adolph Bitanny, a Navajo trained to write and transcribe Navajo. The translation was made by Gladys Reichard (1893–1955), a professor from Barnard College who spent more than twenty-five years researching Navajo society and culture. The prayer is one small part of a long ceremony that has many ritual gestures and songs that must be performed correctly before healing may take place. Although both a song and a prayer may be chanted, a typical ceremony will have many songs but only a few short, general prayers. Most of the prayers are decided on between the chanter and the person-chanted-over because each prayer has its own price. Prayers are expensive because they are difficult to learn. The chanter does not learn the prayer line by line, as one might memorize a poem. The chanter must learn the prayer as a whole. He must listen carefully to the whole thing, and then repeat it in its entirety. No word can be repeated out of its correct order. If said incorrectly, the prayer is void and the mistake could bring down wrath, rather than blessing. For a song, some words may be left out and the ritual may still be complete. But with a prayer, nothing must be altered.

This particular prayer comes in the first night of the Male Shooting Chant Evil. This chant belongs to the category of Evilway chants and so is concerned with expelling evil. Evil may come from ghosts (contamination by the dead), sorcery, strangers, or unknown mistakes. In the prayer we see that the sick person is stuck in a circle of confusion and needs protection. This can only come by driving off or deflecting evil. Only after the evil is exorcised can positive power be evoked to keep the negative power away. The prayer is rich in the language of motion; evil is told in many ways to "move on." Once this has happened, the person can call on the good and become healthy. For the Navajo to be healthy means to be in balance, to have happiness and peace, prosperity and safety. To become, as the prayer says, "beautiful again."

"Snake People Who Make Medicine," is Figure 5 from Leland C. Wyman, *Beautyway: A Navajo Ceremonial* (New York: Bollingen Foundation, 1957); Leland C. Wyman, "The Female Shooting Life Chant: A Minor Navaho Ceremony," is in *American Anthropologist* 38 (1936): 634–53. Wyman's transcriptions of Navajo terms and his footnotes have been eliminated for easier reading. Gladys A. Reichard's text appears in her *Prayer: The Compulsive Word* monograph 7 from the American Ethnological Society (New York: J. J. Augustin, 1944), pp. 59–93. The original text includes a Navajo transcription and numbered lines of text.

Further Reading

Sam Gill, "Whirling Logs and Colored Sands," in *Native American Traditions: Sources and Interpretations* edited by Sam D. Gill (1979; reprint, Belmont; Calif.: Wadsworth, 1983); Raymond Friday Lock, *The Book of the Navajo* (1976; reprint, Los Angeles: Mankind, 1992); James Kale McNeley, *Holy Wind in Navajo Philosophy* (Tucson: University of Arizona Press, 1981); Nancy J. Parezo, *Navajo Sandpainting: From Religious Act to Commercial Art* (1983; reprint, Albuquerque: University of New Mexico Press, 1991); Gladys A. Reichard, *Navajo Religion: A Study of Symbolism* (1950; reprint, Princeton: Princeton University Press, 1974); Gary Witherspoon, *Language and Art in the Navajo Universe* (Ann Arbor: University of Michigan Press, 1977); Paul G. Zolbrod, *Diné Bahane: The Navajo Creation Story* (1984; reprint, Albuquerque: University of New Mexico Press, 1989).

The Female Shooting Life

CHANT PRELIMINARIES

The chant took place in the house [hogan] of the medicine man, the patient's own "modernized" [hogan] being unsuitable because of the lack of a smoke hole and central fireplace. The patient, having arrived on the scene during late afternoon, first gave the basket, the calico, and the fee for the medicine man to an intermediary (anyone present) to be delivered to the singer in private, and made arrangements for feeding the guests. About six P.M. he entered the [hogan] and sat at the west side, while an assistant (any participant), seeing that he was dressed properly, brought in and laid out upon one calico spread the fetishes for the altars on the west side of the ho yen at the right of the patient.

The only requirements of costume other than ordinary clothes were a head-band, a turquoise and shell bead necklace, and moccasins. The head-band is worn so that the diyin diné'é [Holy People] will recognize the wearer as the patient. It shows that "he belongs to this chant," but if he wore a hat he would be a stranger to the spirits and the medicine and prayers would not be effective. The medicine man always wears a head-band during a chant for the same reason (recognition). Shell and turquoise beads and moccasins are worn because they were made for the Navaho in the beginning; they are "their own" and must not be lost. In the ceremony they mark the wearer as of "the people." . . .

The patient was instructed to observe certain restrictions for the duration of the ceremony: he was not to break bones or sticks, not to put his fingers in blood, and when turning or walking around anything he was always to turn or go from left to right, i.e. sunwise. . . . Sexual continence is also required during a ceremony. . . .

THE ALTAR

The fetishes which were laid upon the spread of calico constituting the altar will be described in order from north to south (butts pointing eastward).

1. Bull roarer (wood that makes a noise). It is laid with the point towards the east. It is made of lightning-struck oak, covered with burned [charcoal?] and pitch. The face (eyes and mouth) of turquoise show that it is alive. It was given to the people by the lightning spirit. Its sound represents thunder. It is used to chase away evil spirits. . . . It is not whirled in the [ceremony] but its presence on the altar shows that there is danger in the vicinity for evil spirits.

2. Arrow. A length of reed . . . about eight inches long, filled with dirt from a buffalo track, dirt mixed with buffalo blood (from where a buffalo has been killed), and male and female bluebird and yellow-bird live pollen. This is corn pollen shaken from the feathers of these living birds. The top end is decorated with feathers and beads. There are two of these, male and female. The male is distinguished by having a turquoise bead or a stone arrowpoint tied to it (usually both), and the female by white shell beads. One reed must come from the east and the other from the west. . . . In the early days the [Holy People] used these as arrows. Spirit man used the male arrow and spirit woman the female. There were four arrows, but the [Holy People] gave two of them to the Navaho and kept the other two.

3. Digging stick. An oak stick, about eight inches long, shaped like a spatula at one end and decorated like the arrows at the other. Male and female, marked as stated above. The [Holy People] used to dig out the roots of medicinal plants with these. There were also four of these, the Navahos receiving two.

4. Medicine stick. Eagle feathers, wound from butt tip with buckskin and then with colored wool yarns, and decorated with beads. Male and female, marked as above. The colored yarn is for decoration only, not being used before acculturation. It is used to protect the medicine in the medicine cup. There were four of these also, as before.

5. The arrow, digging stick, and medicine stick of the opposite sex from those occupying positions 2, 3, and 4. When the patient is a male, the male fetishes come first; if a female, the female fetishes precede. . . .

6. Live feathers. Fluffy eagle feathers, from living birds, with the butts wound with buckskin containing live pollen. Two male and two female, designated by turquoise beads and white shell beads. Formerly tied in the hair of patients by the [Holy People] and so used today by the Navaho, to designate the patient. The male fetishes are for male, the female ones for female patients. . . .

7. Whistle. Made of eagle bone, and decorated as are the other fetishes. The [Holy People] used to blow this whistle. . . .

8. Some live eagle feathers. Two only are essential. These are used to sprinkle medicine on the patient in order to cool a fever.

9. Fine shaped arrow points (chipped flint). All the prehistoric stone knives or spear-points that the medicine man can obtain or can conveniently carry in his pouch. The [Holy People] used to use them as weapons. Their presence on the altar serves to scare away evil spirits.

All of the fetishes with wrappings also contain ground medicines, thus adding to their curative properties.

In practice the sacks of medicines and pollens are usually placed at the southwest corner of the altar, the grease paints at the south side, and the medicine cup at the southeast corner.

FIRST NIGHT CEREMONY

About nine P.M., all [chanter, patient, families, and guests] having gathered in the [hogan], the house was consecrated. An assistant rubbed some corn meal on the four lower roof beams: first the east beam, then south, west, and north; and sprinkled a handful sunwise around [hogan]. This is so that the [Holy People] will know that this [hogan] is to be the scene of a ceremony. They say to one another: "Let us all come together and go to this place, to see what is going on and to see if things are being done correctly." White corn meal is used if the patient is male, yellow if female; if neither is available corn pollen may be used.

The seating arrangement was the customary one for any Navaho occasion. Since the altar lies near the wall at the west side of the [hogan], the medicine man sits to its right, the patient to its left. Visiting medicine men or others who wish to help with the ceremony sit at the right of the [chanter]. The male onlookers occupy the rest of the south side of the [hogan] and the women and younger children the north side. The number of visitors is entirely a matter of circumstance. [At this ceremony there were approximately 100.]. . .

After the [hogan] was consecrated the medicine man made sure that the fetishes on the calico spread were in the proper order and turned the spread so that the butts of the fetishes were towards the patient. This was so that the [Holy People] would know that the man toward whom they pointed was the patient. Medicine was next prepared.

An abalone shell was made steady on a little heap of earth before the altar, with its lip to the east. It was filled with water, and dry powdered herbs from two small sacks were sprinkled on the water. This was stirred sunwise with the butt of the male medicine stick and tasted twice from the tip of the stick by the medicine man. Then the stick was laid across the shell with its butt pointing east. An abalone shell or a turtle shell is used as a medicine cup in most chants. In ancient times on this earth these animals were like people; they were [Holy People]. They used to chant, and when they went away they said: "As long as the Navaho live on this earth they shall use my shell for taking medicine." . . .

Either shell is placed with the head end to the east, because the earth and sky face the east.

The medicine was life medicine, which consists of several plants, dried and ground together. This medicine is a common one, regarded as a general tonic and painkiller. . . .

Both sacks contained the same kind of medicine, "one sack for the medicine man and one for the patient." Two are kept in readiness, because the medicine man is singing over one patient, and if he improves, the singer may be obliged to start another chant over another patient elsewhere; in which case he leaves one sack of medicine with the first patient and takes the other to the second patient.

The medicine is stirred with the [medicine stick] (the male one for a male patient), so that the power of the fetish may be transferred to the medicine. The medicine is tasted by the medicine-man because the [Holy People] are watching to see what kind of medicine is given. If the medicine-man is willing to taste his own medicine the spirits will know that it is the right kind. The [medicine stick] is laid over the medicine cup until it is used, to protect it, so that bad influences will not get into the medicine ("so bad spirits will not spit in it, or drop something into it").

While the medicine is soaking the chanting is begun. Anyone sings who knows how; the greater the number of singers the more effective the cure. The singing is accompanied by shaking buffalo-hide rattles. These are oblong, contain pieces of the five precious stones, have a fluffy eagle feather attached to each upper corner, are decorated on each side with two parallel zig-zag lines representing lightning and several arrangements of holes representing certain constellations, and are fitted with a handle of oak or cedar wood which is decorated at the proximal end with either buffalo hair or beaver fur and porcupine quills and at the distal end with buffalo tail hair. Such rattles must be made during a chant. As many rattles may be used as are available. [Four were used at this ceremony.] The medicine man shakes one and the others are usually shaken by visiting medicine men, although they may hand them over to any male visitor when they are tired. Sometimes they give one to a small boy who shows interest in learning how to sing.

The first arrow chant was sung. There are three arrow chants, and if the medicine man conducts several of these ceremonies in succession he uses the first, second, and third in rotation on separate first nights.

During the thirteenth song of the chant the medicine man gave the medicine to the patient, holding the abalone shell in his right hand over the [medicine stick] which was held in his left hand with its butt pointing to his right. The brew was administered four times, the last drink exhausting it.

The medicine is given over the medicine stick in order to apply power of the fetish along with the herbs; "it [the fetish] will give you a lift; it will heal sickness." The stick is held just so because the [Holy People] are watching to see if anything is done incorrectly. They say: "Let us see if it is the right stick; if not, he will not hold it properly."

The four drinks of medicine are given to the patient by the [Holy People]. [Holy young man] gives the first one. [Holy young woman] gives the second. [Holy boy] gives the third, and [Holy Girl] gives the fourth. After this thirteenth song was finished there was a short interval while the patient, taking the sunwise course around the [hogan], went outside for a brief rest. . . .

After the patient had reentered the [hogan] and taken his seat, eight more songs were sung; and this completed the first night's ceremony, which had lasted about two hours. The women and children then retired to the shade house while most of the men prepared to sleep in the [hogan]. The principal purpose of the first-night ceremony is to bring back the medicine which was given some time ago and make it new.

BATHING

About eight A.M. the following morning the bath was prepared. Meanwhile the patient sat on the north side of the [hogan], to be out of the way, and removed his clothes except for a gee string (in this and in other ceremonies which require undressing, men strip to a gee string while women retain a skirt). An assistant was given a prehistoric stone knife from the pouch of the medicine man and a sack of pollen, and was sent for a piece of soap-weed root.

He goes toward any one of the cardinal points and finds a perfect, full-grown yucca plant. Upon an adjacent plant he places corn pollen, on the east, south, west, and north, and in the center; and sprinkling some upwards, he prays: "Plant, I want your living medicine. I need your help to cure the sickness; I need your good health. You shall bring back good health to him (or to her)."

Digging around the perfect plant he exposes the roots and with the stone knife cuts a piece about four inches long and an inch in diameter, being careful to remember the bottom and top ends. . . . He then places pollen on the cut ends of the remaining roots, so they "will join again." Taking the piece of root to a shady place, he pounds it carefully with two stones to remove the bark and then brings it to the [hogan].

In the meantime a pile of fresh earth from the cornfield had been placed at the west side of the [hogan] and spread out to form a smooth platform. In front of this a medicine basket, which had been soaked in water to make it tight, was placed with the opening in the design towards the east. The spirits coming from the east enter through this opening. The medicine man poured water into the basket from the east, south, west, and north, into the middle, and then all around, and finally laid the piece of yucca root in the water with the top end towards the east. Then while the soap-weed root song was being sung the assistant rubbed the root in the water and beat up a stiff suds.

On the surface of the suds the medicine man sprinkled material from six small sacks, applying each kind in the following order: twice across the basket from east to west and from west to east, twice across from south to north and back again, sunwise around the circumference, and in the center. The material, in the order used, was: fog flakes or white cornmeal ground by a girl before marriage, mixed with frost crystals gathered from vegetation in the winter and dried in the sun; dry, powdered life medicine from two sacks; blue pollen or powdered [flower]; [and] cattail; corn pollen. The fog flakes, blue pollen, and cattail pollen are used because the [Holy People] formerly used them. . . .

A similar design was made on the earth platform with white corn meal, only the circle was about three feet in diameter, an opening was left at the east, and small crosses (†) of meal were made in the southwest, northwest, southeast, and north-east quadrants. The basket was then set in the eastward opening of this design.

The order in which water is poured into the basket and the designs on the suds and on the platform signify the universe—the four sacred mountains at the cardinal points or quadrants, the sun in the middle, small mountains all around, with the earth and the sky inside.

The bath being ready, the patient walked in the sunwise route around the fireplace and stood behind (west of) the basket. The medicine man picked up some suds from the east, south, west, and north sides of the basket and applied them to the patient's body in the ceremonial order: bottom of right foot, bottom of left foot, right knee, left knee, chest, back, right palm, left palm, right shoulder, left shoulder; and finally suds from the center of the basket to the top of the head.

This ceremonial order is upwards because when you are prostrated by illness you wish to rise. Life proceeds upwards, for "you grow up from a baby; you must not go down. A baby lies, then sits, then stands, and then walks." Just so a sick man must rise and walk.

In all chants, procedures which involve both sides of the body are begun with the right side. Formerly a dead person's moccasins were reversed on his feet before he was buried, and clothing ties were tied crosswise. For the living, therefore, (and especially in a life ceremony) the right side comes first and ties are made straight. This applies to putting on moccasins, trousers, tying shoestrings, etc.

The patient then knelt on the platform of earth, right knee on the southwest cross of corn meal, left knee on the northwest cross, right hand on the south-east cross, and left hand on the northeast cross. Then he washed, first his hair and then the rest of his body, downwards, with the help of the assistant who rinsed away the suds with fresh water.

In the bath bad spirits and disease in the body are washed downwards and away. The hair is washed first because the sun looks on one's head first. Soap-weed root is used because the [Holy People] were wont to use it as soap.

The patient's necklace and other jewelry, which had been placed near the basket at the north, were also washed in the yucca suds. This is because he wishes to keep the jewelry and to get more; so it too must be purified.

The remainder of the bath water in the basket was emptied on the earth platform and the patient was dried with corn meal, first applied in ceremonial order by the medicine man and then rubbed all over the body by the assistant.

The corn meal represents daylight, for the patient is going to "meet the daylight" later in the ceremony. White corn meal is used for a male patient and yellow for a female.

The patient's jewelry was then placed upon him, after which he dressed and sat facing the east while the medicine man placed corn pollen on his tongue and sprinkled some to form a trail from the patient, by the north of the fire-place, to the door of the [hogan]. Pollen is eaten and sprinkled on the trail outwards to make the trail perfect; to make perfect the way before, behind, below, above, all around.

A dose of medicine, prepared in the abalone shell as before, was adminis-tered in four drinks as previously described. After this the patient was sent outside and told to wear a blanket and to wait in the shade-house until called.

The patient goes out to walk around so that the [Holy People] who happen to be outside the [hogan] may see him. Some of these spirits may be outside the house and others inside, just as are the people who are attending the ceremony.

The bath being over, the earth platform was scraped up and carried outside in a blanket, to be deposited in a shady place.

DAY CEREMONY

In a few minutes the patient was recalled to the [hogan] for the day ceremony. This consisted entirely of singing, accompanied by the rattles.

Any one of several groups of songs may be chosen for this portion of the cere-mony; thunder songs, spider songs, etc. Thunder songs were used on this occasion.

After the [day ceremony], which lasted less than an hour, the patient was advised to get some sleep during the afternoon in preparation for the next event, the all-night ceremony.

NIGHT CEREMONY

As the time for the all-night ceremony approached, about nine P.M., the patient was asked to wait in the shade-house until called. Meanwhile the fol-lowing preparations were made: the altar was placed before the patient's seat at the west of the [hogan], between it and the fireplace, with the butts of the fetishes towards the east; and beneath it were placed the pieces of calico and

the money fee for the medicine man. The [Holy People] used to put buck-
skins, arrow points, shell beads, turquoise, and pollen beneath the altar when
they had a ceremony. Various of the [Holy People] wanted to sing their songs,
abalone wanted to sing his song, and in return for singing each received a
present of buckskin or of other things. So it is today: some of the visiting
Navaho wish to help the ceremony by singing, and since the medicine man,
the patient, and the watching [Holy People] appreciate their aid, the visitors
receive presents of calico from beneath the altar.

The grease for painting the patient was prepared—a large ball of red grease
about two inches in diameter and a smaller ball of black about an inch in
diameter. The ingredients and the reasons for their use will be given later. The
medicine man streaked each of his checks with the red grease.

The patient was called to the [hogan], where everyone had assembled, and
after taking his seat at the west he removed first his moccasins and necklace,
placing them at the north of the altar, and then all his clothes except a gee
string. The "first chant" was then begun, and during it the patient was painted.
As an assistant appointed to do the painting rose, the patient also stood. Black
grease was applied, first with small dabs in ceremonial order and then plenti-
fully across the chin from ear to ear. Red grease was rubbed all over the body
including the face, the patient helping to paint his upper portions. Finally
"bright sand" was applied to the face in five places from right to left, two spots
on each cheek, and one on the nose.

As the assistant finished painting with each material he put some of it on his
face and handed the remnants to the women at the north. Here they were
passed along and any one who had pains rubbed some of the grease on the
affected part and put some "bright sand" on the face. (The remnants were
exhausted before they came to the men's side of the [hogan].)

A lock of hair at the top of the patient's head was greased with black paint to
make it stick together, and to this lock one of the male live feathers was
securely tied and made to hang toward the right. The patient then resumed his
seat until the first chant was finished. . . .

When the first chant was over the medicine man gave pollen to the patient and
made a trail of pollen for him to follow outside, as was done in the morning. . . .

After the patient had reentered the [hogan] and taken his seat the first arrow
chant was begun and during it he was given the four drizzles of liquid medicine from the abalone shell, prepared and administered as before.

Then followed the second arrow chant, and during this the assistant gave
the patient the first dose of dry powdered life medicine from the two sacks.
The male and female digging sticks were used as spoons or spatulas, first the
male and then the female for each of the two sacks, making four generous
mouthfuls of the bitter, astringent mixture at each dose. This treatment was
repeated nine times during the night, at about the middle of each of nine
groups of songs which followed in succession. The patient was told that after
the first treatment with dry medicine he could put on his clothes or a blanket

and could smoke if he wished. He was required, however, to sit up straight throughout the ceremony, and of course he must not doze.

The digging stick fetishes are used to remove the dry medicine from the sacks in order to simulate digging roots from the ground, thus showing the [Holy People] that the stuff is medicine dug from the earth.

The patient must sit erect with his feet and hands apart while taking the medicine, because the [Holy People] always held their body erect while taking medicines so that the body would become straight, not twisted with disease. . . . The groups of songs, during which dry medicine was given, follow in the proper sequence.

Second arrow chant.

Third arrow chant.

The slayer of enemies song.

Killing-fear songs. "Nayé·nesɣá·ni and his brother killed fear, so there was no more fear, and then they sang these songs."

Arrow-point. Child-birth. "When a woman is in labor this song is sung and the child comes." . . .

Bear songs. Buffalo songs.

These are the most important songs of this chant.

Attention to other details prevented an accurate count of the number of songs in each group. The medicine man later stated that in this ceremony over two hundred songs are used. Since it took about six hours to complete the nine groups listed above, and since each song lasted about three minutes, there may have been perhaps one hundred and twenty songs in all; that is, about a dozen in each group. This leaves, according to the medicine man's estimate, about eighty songs for the other parts of the ceremony. . . .

At about quarter of four in the morning, when dawn was imminent, the medicine man smeared a handful of white corn meal across the chin of the patient, then put some on his own chin. The principal singers also applied corn meal to their chins.

The patient is going to "meet the daylight," the meal representing daylight. Those who take part in the ceremony are likewise going to meet the daylight, and so are the [Holy People].

The patient then sat cross-legged, close to the altar, while the medicine man picked up all the fetishes on the altar and gave them to the patient in a bundle with their butts pointing eastward, telling him to be very careful not to drop one. The dawn songs (often called the "bluebird songs") were commenced, while the patient beat time to the singing with the bundle of fetishes held in both hands.

Every chant closes with these dawn songs. The patient moves the fetishes up and down in time to the singing because the yellow-birds and bluebirds move like that when they sing to the approaching daylight. They are full of health and move their bodies when daylight comes. Yellowbird and bluebird live pollen are within some of the fetishes, and the patient, now that the ceremony is nearly over, should also be full of health and so should move like the birds.

The butts of the fetishes are pointed to the east, towards the daylight, because the patient wishes to "win the daylight" and thus win back his health.

The dawn songs lasted until about four-thirty. At their completion the assistant filled the medicine basket with water, and followed by the patient who was in turn followed by another man, he walked sunwise around the fireplace four times, sprinkling water on the ground as he walked. After the last trip around, the assistant emptied the basket of water outside of the [hogan], and the patient walked out through the door and a little way to the east. There, facing the dawn which was just breaking, he extended his arms to the sides and four times brought his hands to his mouth as if gathering in the daylight and swallowing it. Then he walked back towards the [hogan] and was met half way by the assistant, who untied the live feather from his hair and rubbed away the grease from the lock of hair with pollen. The assistant took the feather back to the medicine man and the patient retired to the shade-house.

The water is sprinkled on the pathway of the patient so that he will be walking "cool" (without fever) from now on. The remainder is put outside the house in order to make the way cool outside as well as inside. Another man, following the patient, acts as a guard so that no bad spirits can pursue.

In the morning the [Holy People] are ready to go to their homes in the east. After the daylight has arrived they will be gone. The patient is going to "swallow the daylight" in order to get back his health. He must do this while the [Holy People] are still present; for they are watching, and if he does it correctly they will take him away from the bad spirits, from disease. If he does it incorrectly he will still belong to the sickness.

After the patient had left, the altar was dismantled and the fetishes were packed away in the medicine man's bundle, while a "song for packing up" was sung. Then songs of the four sacred mountains were sung to close the ceremony.

After breakfast, when most of the guests were preparing to return to their homes, the medicine man gave a piece of the calico to each of the more important personages who had assisted with the ceremony and had stayed in the [hogan] all night. One woman received a piece because she had helped with the singing throughout the night. The man who had assisted with the bath received the medicine basket as his gift.

The patient was not allowed to sleep until past noon. The ceremony is not officially over until afternoon, and if the patient should sleep before this time he might have bad dreams inimical to health, and so the bad spirits would "win back the chant." Furthermore, although most of the [Holy People] go home before daylight, a few might stay around until noon, as do some of the Navaho who attend the ceremony. It would be improper to sleep in their presence.

POSTCEREMONIAL PROCEDURES

The patient must not wash until the next day, in order to give the medicine in the grease paint time to penetrate the flesh and cure the sickness. Otherwise no special behavior was required of the patient.

On the following morning the patient bathed and put on clean clothes. He first washed his entire body with a lotion which the Franciscan Fathers have termed "ceremonial liniment," although the sense of the term is untranslatable. Every chant has . . . a mixture of plants which are placed in the cold or luke-warm water that is to be used as a surface application. Sometimes it serves as an actual liniment, the medicine being supposed to penetrate the skin, but often it is merely a ceremonial wash. . . . In the bath it is not the intention to wash away the medicine, but to wash the color off and leave the medicine. . . .

After the bath . . . the patient was allowed to scrub away the grease-paint in hot soap and water. He was also enjoined to be careful to wash all the paint from his clothing and blanket before he exposed these articles in public again. In other words all of the sacred paint must be disposed of, now that the ceremony was over. This ended the patient's part in the procedure, and he could now resume his usual activities.

Prayer of the First Night Male Shooting Chant Evil

At Rumbling Mountain,
Holy Man who with the eagle tail-feathered arrow glides out,
    This day I have come to be trustful
    This day I look to you (for help)
With your strong feet rise up to protect me,
With your sturdy legs rise up to protect me,
With your strong body rise up to protect me,
With your healthy mind rise up to protect me,
With your powerful sound rise up to protect me,
Carrying the dark bow and the eagle tail feathered arrow with which you
    transform evil,
    By these means you will protect me,
    These you will hold protecting me,
So that I being at a place behind you, evils will pass me.
Evil ghost power of all kinds will go past me.
    This day from the tips of my toes it will swell out from where it does
        not belong,
    From the tips of my body it will move out (in swelling fashion),
    From the tips of my fingers it will move out,
    From the tips of my speech it will move out,
No weapon of evil sorcery can harm me as I go about.
    This day I shall recover,
    Safely may I go about.
    Your child I have become,
    Your grandchild I have become,
    I have recovered my energy, I say.

That is the reason that this day you are the one who is recovering,
    May I by the same means recover.
You are the one who repeatedly rises up by these means,
    May I repeatedly rise up by these means.
The very one who darts about with you,
    May it dart about with me.
As you are the one who stands suspended above,
    May I be suspended above it,
    May I be the one who goes about by means of these things.
Just as you are the one who is holy because of these things,
    So may I be holy because of them.
There is just one way by which we become holy.
Sorcery of every kind this day has gone far away,
This day evil sorcery previously described
    To a point above it has gone
    Opposite it has gone
    To a place in the interior it has gone.
This day the weapon of sorcery
    Has returned to normal.
    Has returned to normal.
Behind you I survive
    I being behind you evil passes me by,
    I being in your shelter all kinds of evil miss me.
Just as weakness passes away from you,
    So may weakness pass away from me.
Just as you are the one whom weakness merely grazes,
    So may weakness merely graze me.
Just as you are the one who transforms evil,
    So may I transform evil.
Just as you are the one dread by evil because of these things,
    So may I be dreaded by evil because of these things.
Just as you are the one who has become evil because of these things,
    So may I become evil because of them.
Evil sorcery weapons of every kind
    Upward have gone
    Opposite have gone
    Things have returned to normal.
    My mind safe survives.
    My mind safe survives.
    My mind safe survives.
    We all survive.
    We all survive.
    My mind in safety repeatedly survives.
    My mind in safety repeatedly survives.

My mind in safety repeatedly survives.
My mind is safe.
My mind is safe.
Restoration-to-youth According to beauty I have become again.
Restoration-to-youth According to beauty,
Natural Boy I have become again.
It has become beautiful again.
It has become beautiful again.

At Rumbling Mountain,
Holy Woman who with the feathered wand glides out,
　　This day I have come to be trustful
　　This day I look to you.
Rise up to protect me,
Go about protecting me,
With your strong feet rise up to protect me,
With your sturdy legs rise up to protect me,
With your strong body rise up to protect me,
With your healthy mind rise up to protect me,
With your powerful sound rise up to protect me,
With your fine head rise up to protect me.
Carrying the yellow bow and the feathered wand,
　　These you will carry before me.
　　With these you move about protecting me,
　　Thus in their shelter evils miss me,
　　Thus they pass by,
　　Thus in their shelter evil sorcery of every kind will repeatedly go past me,
　　Thus in their shelter evil sorcery of every kind will repeatedly go past me.
Ghost power of every kind with which I may be bothered,
　　From the tips of my toes where it does not belong will move out (in
　　　　swelling fashion),
　　From the tips of my body where it does not belong will move out,
　　From the tips of my fingers where it does not belong will move out,
　　From the tips of my speech where it does not belong will move out,
The weapon of evil sorcery,
　　To a point above it will go
　　To a point above it has gone
　　Opposite it has gone
　　To a place inside it has gone.
Invisible to evil power of every kind I shall go about,
　　So this day I shall be well again,
　　Safely I shall go out,
　　So this day your grandchild I have become, I say.
　　Your child I have become, I say.

Just as you are the one who recovers by these means,
    So may I recover because of them.
Just as you are the one who repeatedly recovers by these means,
    So may I repeatedly recover because of them.
Just as you are the one made holy by them,
    So may I become holy because of them.
Just as you are the one who stands suspended above them,
    So may I stand suspended above.
Just as you are the one who goes about because of them,
    So may I go about because of them.
Just as you are the one avoided by weakness on account of them,
    So may weakness avoid me,
Just as you are the one whom weakness merely grazes,
    So may weakness merely graze me on account of it.
Just as you are the one who warned off evil,
    So may evil be warned off from me for the same reason.
Just as you are the one who transforms evil,
    So may I transform evil with the same power.
Invisible to the weapon of evil sorcery may I go about.
    Surely this day happily I shall be well again.
    In beauty I shall go out.
    This day evil has passed by,
    This day evil will be removed from me,
    Healthy may I be,
    May my feet be strong,
    May my legs be sturdy,
    May my body be healthy,
    May my mind be dependable,
    May my sound power be great,
    May my head be clear,
    May my gait be strengthened,
By means of the one who has become evil,
    May I also become evil.
Evil sorcery of every kind,
    To a point up above has gone
    Opposite has gone
    It has returned to normal.
    It has returned to normal.
    Surely this day I shall go out well.
    Restoration-to-youth According to beauty I have become, I say.
    Restoration-to-youth According to beauty,
    The one who is natural I have become again
    These I have become again,
    It has become beautiful again.
    It has become beautiful again.

At Rumbling Mountain,
Holy Boy with the yellow tail-feathered arrow,
   This day I have come to be trustful
   This day I look to you
Rise up to protect me,
Go about again protecting me,
With your strong feet rise up to protect me,
With your sturdy legs rise up to protect me,
With your strong body rise up to protect me,
With your healthy mind rise up to protect me,
With your powerful sound rise up to protect me,
With your fine head rise up to protect me,
You are the one who carries the dark bow with the yellow-feathered arrow,
   These carry before me to protect me,
   These hold before me.
I being in their shelter evil will pass me by,
I being in their shelter evil has passed me by,
Thus evil will not get hold of me.
Every kind of ghost power fails to grasp me,
   So this day they have missed me.
   This day they have missed me.
Evil power of all kinds,
   To a point above has gone
   Opposite it has gone.
With every kind of ghost power, of evil power of sorcery you have trans-
   formed me with it.
From the tips of my toes where it does not belong it moves out (in swell-
   ing fashion),
From the tips of my body where it does not belong it moves out,
From the tips of my fingers where it does not belong it moves out,
From the tips of my speech where it does not belong it moves out,
Every kind of evil sorcery,
   To a point above it has gone
   Opposite it has gone
   To a place inside it has gone
   It has become normal again.
   It has become normal again.
Just as you are the one who transforms evil by means of it,
   So may I transform evil because of it.
Just as you are the one who has become evil,
   So may I become evil with it.
Just as you are the one whom crowds of evils move away from,
   So may crowds of evil move away from me.
Just as you are the one dreaded by evil,
   So may I be dreaded by evil.

Just as you are the one who warns off evil by winking,
    So may I warn off evil.
Invisible to the weapon of evil sorcery may I go about.
Just as you are the one avoided by weakness,
    May weakness leave me on account of it.
Just as you are the one whom weakness merely grazes,
    May weakness merely graze me.
Just as you are the one who has become like evil,
    So may I become like evil.
Just as you are the one who stands (firm) because of it,
    So may I stand firm because of it.
Just as you are the one who gets well on account of it,
    So may I get well because of it.
Just as you are the one who gets well repeatedly by means of it,
    So may I get well repeatedly because of it.
Just as you are the one made holy by it,
    So may I be holy.
Surely this day every kind of evil, of evil sorcery which bothered me,
    May evil act as a substitute for me.
This day that which does not happen to you,
    This day do not let such things happen.
Surely this day the power of every kind of evil,
    To a point above has gone
    Opposite has gone
    To a place inside has gone
    It is normal again.
    It is normal again.
    Surely this day well may I go about,
Invisible to evil power of any kind may I go about,
    Restoration-to-youth According to beauty I have become, I say.
    Restoration-to-youth According to beauty,
    Natural Boy I have become again,
    These things I have become.
    These things I have become.
    It has become beautiful again.
    It has become beautiful again.

At Rumbling Mountain,
Holy Girl with the red-feathered arrow,
    This day I have become trustful
    This day I look to you.
Rise up to protect me,
Stand before me to protect me,
With your strong feet rise up to protect me,

With your sturdy legs rise up to protect me,
With your strong body rise up to protect me,
With your healthy mind rise up to protect me,
With your powerful sound rise up to protect me,
With your fine head rise up to protect me.
You are the one who carries the dark bow with the red-feathered arrow,
    These you will carry before me to protect me.
    By means of these you have kept harm away from me,
    Thus in their shelter evil will pass me by.
    Thus in their shelter evil has passed me by.
    Thus in their shelter it has passed by
    Thus in their shelter it has passed by.
    My mind being safe has been passed.
    My mind being safe has been passed.
Ghost power of every kind with which I may be bothered,
    Surely this day to a point at the tips of my toes where it does not
        belong will move out (in swelling fashion)
    From the tips of my body where it does not belong it moves out,
    From the tips of my fingers where it does not belong it moves out,
    From the tips of my speech where it does not belong it moves out,
Evil sorcery of every kind has gone away from me,
    To a point above it has gone
    Opposite it has gone
    To a place inside it has gone.
Surely this day surviving you stand protecting me,
Surely this day surviving you stand protecting me,
    May you return protecting me.
As you are the ones at the place where you tell me to be,
    May I be the one at the place where you tell me to be,
    May you be reciprocatingly dependable.
Surely this day invisible to the weapon of every kind of evil sorcery may
    I go about.
Surely this day you are the ones who put your feet down in it (cornmeal),
    So with it may I put my feet down.
Just as you are the ones who become evil,
    So may I become evil with it.
Just as you are the ones from whom evil is warned off with it,
    So may evil be warned away from me.
Just as evils swarm away from you because of it,
    So may evils swarm away from me.
The weapon of every kind of evil sorcery,
    From the tips of my toes where it does not belong may it move, I say.
    From the tips of my body where it does not belong may it move, I say.
    From the tips of my fingers where it does not belong may it move, I say.
    From the tips of my speech where it does not belong may it move, I say.

Surely this day I shall be well again.
Well I shall go about,
Good health may I be,
May my body be light,
May my body be cool,
May my feet be strong,
May my body be whole,
May my mind be clear,
May my sound power be strong,
May my hand be dependable,
May my gait be long,
Surely this day happily I get up.
The weapon of every kind of evil sorcery,
Away from me it has gone
To a point above it has gone
Opposite it has gone
To the inside it has gone.
Evil power which has been mentioned, evil intention which has been
mentioned,
All have returned to normal.
All have returned to normal.
Surely this day happily I go about, I say.
May it be beautiful before me,
May it be beautiful behind me,
May it be beautiful under me,
May it be beautiful above me,
May all be beautiful around me,
May my speech be controlled,
Restoration-to youth According-to-Beauty I have become, I say
May all these things be so.

Good having come to me from Rumbling Mountain may I go about.
Good having come to me from Rumbling Rock may I go about.
Good having come to me from Rumbling Cloud may I go about.
Good having come to me from Rumbling Water may I go about.
Good having come to me from Sun's House under the east may I go about.
From the Moon's house under the west it has become beautiful again for me.
From [the] home of Dark Wind, it has become beautiful again for me.
From the horizon, home of the Yellow Wind, it has become beautiful
again for me.
By my mother, Earth Woman from Earth Center, things have become
controlled for me, I say
Everything has become right for me from all around Where-they-
project-through.

From Mountain-fallen-away it has become beautiful for me again.

From Rock-projecting-through-the-sky it has become beautiful for me again.

From Black Mountain it has become beautiful for me again.

From the top of Mt. Taylor it has become beautiful for me again.

From the place called Water-vessel-hangs where the Fish people live it has become beautiful for me again

From Where-spruce-trees-lie it has become beautiful for me again.

From Where-snakes-are-strung-amongst it has become beautiful for me again.

From Red Mountain it has become beautiful for me again.

From Where snake lies around it has become beautiful for me again.

From Grinding-snake-place it has become beautiful for me again.

From all around Where-mountain-mahogany-rises-in-a-knoll it has become beautiful for me again.

From Alien-territory-where-groups-move it has become beautiful for me again.

From the Houses-of-the-zenith-people-within-which-dark-mists-move it has become beautiful for me again.

From Where-male-rain-falls it has become beautiful for me again.

From the Houses-of-the-zenith-people-within-which-dark-mists move it has become beautiful for me again.

From Where-female-rains-fall it has become beautiful for me again.

From Where-zigzag-lightnings-flash-out it has become beautiful for me again.

From Where-zigzag-lightnings-darts-out it has become beautiful for me again.

From Where-sunrays-flash it has become beautiful for me again.

From Where-rainbows-flash it has become beautiful for me again.

From everywhere it has become beautiful for me again.

From House-at-the-bottom-of-the-water it has become beautiful for me again.

From the home of the Water Monster People it has become beautiful for me again.

From the home of the Water Horse at the bottom of the water it has become beautiful for me again.

From the place called White-mountain-beyond-the-sky it has become beautiful for me again.

From the home of Dark Thunder, it has become beautiful for me again.

From White Mountain, the home of Blue Thunder, it has become beautiful for me again.

From White-mountain-beyond-the-sky, the home of Yellow Thunder, it has become beautiful for me again.

From White-mountain-beyond-the-sky, the home of Pink Thunder, it has become beautiful for me again.

From Taos, Monster Slayer has got things under control for me, I say.

From there it has become beautiful for me again.

From Taos, home of Child-of-the-water, it has become beautiful for me again.

From Taos, home of Changing Grandchild, it has become beautiful for me again.

From Taos, home of Reared-within-the-earth, it has become beautiful for me again.

From the center of the broad cornfield White Corn Boy has got things under control for me.

From the center ladder of the cornfield White Corn Girl has got things under control for me.

From the center of the broad cornfield Pollen Boy has got things under control for me.

From the center of the broad cornfield Cornbeetle has got things under control for me.

From the center of the broad cornfield Restoration-to-youth Boy has got things under control for me.

From the center ladder of the broad cornfield According-to-beauty Girl has got things under control for me.

With beauty before me may I go about.

With beauty behind me may I go about.

With beauty beneath me may I go about.

With beauty above me may I go about.

With beauty all around me may I go about.

With my speech under control may I go about.

Restoration-to-youth According-to-beauty I have become.

Restoration-to-youth According-to-beauty,

Perfection,

These I have become again.

These I have become again.

These I have become again.

These I have become again.

It has become beautiful again.

It has become beautiful again.

It has become beautiful again.

It has become beautiful again.

—20—

The Power of Positive Thinking

Craig R. Prentiss

No one can doubt the impact that *The Power of Positive Thinking* by Norman Vincent Peale (1898–1993) has had on American religious life. The book crested atop the best-seller list for more than two years, selling over two million copies in hardback and over seven million copies by the twentieth century's end. When scholars ranging from Will Herberg to Charles Glock to Sydney Ahlstrom attempted to document the evidence for what has been called a "revival" of religious life in America during the early to mid 1950s, Peale's name was always one of the first to come up. As an artifact in the history of American religious practice, *The Power of Positive Thinking* exemplifies a strand of religious thought with deep roots and which both admirers and critics alike have often labeled as quintessentially American: the belief that one's health, happiness, and prosperity are contingent on the attitude and will of the individual.

The Power of Positive Thinking is essentially a book of techniques. These techniques are applicable to nearly all of the troubles associated with life, as the chapter headings of the book attest. Whether one wondered "How to Break the Worry Habit," "How to Use Faith in Healing," "How to Get People to Like You," or "How to Create Your Own Happiness," Peale provided suggestions that included practical techniques such as mental imaging, repetition of biblical passages, and the cultivation of certain habits in conversation. Despite the claims of his critics to the contrary, Peale's theology of individualism and self-help was always tempered by his understanding that the power that was released through positive thinking was the power with which Jesus Christ had graced all of humankind. Peale's concept of divinity was of a profoundly immanent God, conceived as a source of energy who dwells in the mind and waits to be tapped. This immanent view was particularly ironic in light of Peale's career in the Reformed Church of America, a Calvinist community that had always stressed a transcendent God. Peale wrote in one of his earliest books, *The Art of Living*, that "essentially the function of the Church is that of the General Electric Company—to release power." The power of God existed for the service of "the individual and society." This divine power was

"inherent in the world and freely offered to those who want it and will take it."
The techniques elaborated on in *The Power of Positive Thinking,* Peale believed,
functioned precisely to release the power of God within us.

To make sense of the success and influence of Peale's work we must look at the
context for Peale's theology, as well as the atmosphere in which it was received.
Peale was the son of a Methodist minister and was himself ordained in the Methodist Church in 1922, while a seminary student at Boston University. After successful stints at two Methodist congregations, Peale agreed to take over as
minister of the Marble Collegiate Church in New York City in 1932, where he
remained throughout his career. His move to the Reformed Church came largely
because of the ministerial lifestyle the Marble Collegiate Church had offered him,
not because of a rejection of Methodist theology. This choice was indicative of the
lack of importance that Peale gave to denominational labels.

Although Peale was influenced by countless sources, two factors stood out as
paramount in his theological formation: psychotherapy and the New Thought
movement. During the 1920s and 1930s, Freudian theories of psychoanalysis
saturated American popular culture and remained influential for decades to
come. Peale was among those fascinated by the apparent power of the subconscious to influence human behavior and happiness. This fascination led to Peale's
partnership with Dr. Smiley Blanton, a Tennessee Methodist interested in Freud,
who had studied under the Viennese master himself in the late 1920s. Peale and
Blanton teamed up in 1937 to form a clinic connected to the Marble Collegiate
Church, where they would minister to the spiritual and psychological needs of
Peale's congregants. They were not the first to engage in the practice of coupling
religion and psychotherapy, but their program continued to expand well beyond
Peale's own congregation until it became reorganized in 1951 as the American
Foundation for Religion and Psychiatry, a nondenominational and nonsectarian
agency. By 1972, it had merged with the Academy of Religion and Mental Health
and was renamed the Institutes of Religion and Health.

Peale's own interest in psychoanalysis mirrored that of the larger culture.
E. Brooks Holifield has chronicled the rising import of psychology in changing the
shape of Christian ministry. Beginning especially in the years following World War I,
psychology became a permanent fixture on the popular culture scene. The mental
hygiene movement popularized the notion that virtually every individual and social
ill could be traced to psychological problems, and in turn, required only
psychological adjustment for its cure. After Freud's introduction to the American
audience in the years of the First World War, terms from the Freudian and neo-
Freudian vocabulary, such as id, oedipus complex, and collective unconscious soon
embedded themselves in the nation's vernacular and fed the rise of a host of often
pseudoscientific popular psychologists. World War II also fed the ascendancy of
psychology as the U. S. Army utilized the services of over 1,500 psychologists to
test soldiers, instruct leaders, and treat soldiers who had been traumatized in battle.
When the soldiers returned home, psychologists remained ever-present in the
burgeoning corporate environment. The American Psychological Association

reported in 1954 that nearly half of its nearly 14,000 members were employed as efficiency counselors, personnel managers, vocational advisers, pollsters, and advertising consultants. By the mid-twentieth century, Peale's fascination with psychology was the rule more than the exception.

Peale's understanding of psychology differed significantly from Dr. Blanton's. Where Blanton viewed the subconscious as a complex and sometimes troubling force that often played havoc with our minds, Peale's "unconscious mind" was a font of untapped powers and the key to success and well-being. This contrast was most evident in Peale and Blanton's 1940 collaborative work, *Faith is the Answer: A Pastor and a Psychiatrist Discuss Your Problems.* Peale wrote that it was the unconscious that makes for success, failure, misery, or happiness. Mental images in the unconscious could either defeat the individual or, if properly and wisely used, could endow men and women with great power. "Religion," Peale and Blanton wrote, "says that when these hidden energies are brought under the influence of Christ as Master of life, the most amazing results appear in people whose lives were hitherto commonplace or defeated."

In addition to the Freudians and neo-Freudians, Peale was also influenced by the work of the American psychologist and philosopher William James (1842–1910). James, one of the founders of a philosophy known as Pragmatism, was interested in the ability of the human will to overcome negative experiences, and he promoted the self-conscious cultivation of habits to promote healthy minds. Peale never tired of quoting James, to the point where his wife observed in later years that Peale was more likely to cite James than Jesus in his speeches and sermons.

The other major influence on Peale's theological formation was the New Thought movement. New Thought was a term given to an amorphous assembly of individuals and organizations bound by a common belief in a connection between the physical world and a supernatural realm, as well as a belief in our ability to harness supernatural energies for our benefit. The origins of New Thought are usually traced to the work of Phineas P. Quimby (1802–1866). Based on his experience with hypnotism, Quimby came to believe that by tapping into a divine energy that flowed through all living things, one could attain both physical and mental health. Illness resulted from our failure to be in touch with the Divine Mind, yet health and happiness could be restored through reestablishing a right relationship to God within us. Quimby's most famous disciple was Mary Baker Eddy (1821–1910), founder of Christian Science, though his influence extended to many others. Warren Felt Evans, an early promoter of the New Thought movement, who viewed Jesus as the prototypical mind healer, as well as Charles and Myrtle Fillmore, founders of the Unity School of Christianity, were among Quimby's intellectual heirs. Various attempts to create umbrella organizations for all New Thought adherents began at the advent of the twentieth century, beginning with the International Metaphysical League in 1915, which was followed by the International New Thought Alliance.

Another intellectual inspiration for the New Thought movement was the Transcendentalist Ralph Waldo Emerson (1803–1882). Steeped in the idealism of the

Romantic Age, Emerson taught in his 1838 address to Harvard Divinity School that "the world is not the product of manifold power, but of one will, of one mind; and that one mind is everywhere active, in each ray of the star, in each wavelet of the pool. . . . The perception of this law of laws awakens in the mind a sentiment which we call the religious sentiment, and which makes our highest happiness. . . . By it the universe is made safe and habitable." With such an outlook, Emerson's compatibility with the New Thought theme of the immanent Divine Mind made his writings ideal proof texts for the burgeoning movement. It was no coincidence, then, that Norman Vincent Peale, who came to admire Emerson while attending college at Ohio Wesleyan, cited Emerson almost as frequently as he did William James.

Perhaps his familiarity with Emerson and James planted the seeds that allowed Peale to be receptive to ideas of the New Thought movement, ideas to which he began to be exposed in the late 1920s. Although he never openly affiliated himself with New Thought, Peale shared the movement's confidence in the therapeutic use of mind power and the divine energy residing within each person waiting to be tapped. Peale, together with New Thought, Christian Science, and Swedenborgianism, may be examples of "Harmonial Religion," in which the mind can heal by tapping into divine energy.

The Power of Positive Thinking reflects the influences of both psychotherapy and New Thought. Like most of Peale's writings, it was built around inspirational stories taken from Peale's own experience. The characters in these stories were most often medical doctors (in keeping with the public's faith in science) or businessmen. I do mean *men,* since it was not until later, as Peale became more aware that his audience was largely made up of women, that women became more central to his narratives. Peale was particularly attracted to salesmen as the subjects of his stories; he believed them to personify the sort of optimism and perseverance that Peale preached was necessary for happiness.

Peale's business orientation was particularly apropos in the age of *The Organization Man* and *The Man in the Grey Flannel Suit.* Unprecedented economic growth in the 1950s ideally suited Peale's optimistic and self-reliant message. But more than this, cheaper automobile prices, coupled with road and highway construction, fueled suburbanization. This suburbanization had the effect of eroding previous long-standing communities, leaving individuals and families isolated from traditional sources of self-identity. The time was ripe for a do-it-yourself guide to happiness and spiritual fulfillment, and *The Power of Positive Thinking* did not disappoint those in search of such a guide.

The text was equally compatible with both a generic brand of Christianity and the mantra of success that went hand-in-hand with the rise of consumerism. After all, a generation raised in the Great Depression and thrown into World War II was coming of age. They were eager to take advantage of the promise of serenity and order that the suburban lifestyle advertised itself to be. Yet, as Peale was acutely aware, the comfort and tranquillity that the postwar middle class had hoped for was seemingly out of reach. Peale was confident that he had the antidote to suburban anxiety. Judging from the sales of *The*

Power of Positive Thinking, as well as the success of his magazine, *Guideposts,* published by his Foundation for Christian Living, many other people agreed with Peale's prescription for happiness and well-being. In simple terms, Peale was successful because his ideas succeeded in bringing happiness and peace to millions of frazzled homemakers, stressed salespeople, and anxiety-ridden executives.

Critics of Peale's work were never in short supply. Neo-orthodox theologian Reinhold Niebuhr called Peale's theology "easy religion," and the Methodist bishop G. Bromley Oxnam questioned whether Peale's work could fairly be called "Christianity" at all. At seminaries across the country, the expression "Paul is appealing, but Peale is appalling" became a catch phrase. The consensus among many theologians in the academy was that Peale's teachings failed to meet the intellectual standards necessary to be taken seriously, standards that these academics equated with a recognition of the reality of sin as well as a greater appreciation for the prophetic strands of the Christian tradition. Peale, on the other hand, understood his own theology to be consistent with the original message of the New Testament, though translated in a language for a modern audience.

Peale was correct in believing that his style would resonate with the public at large. Although accusations of intellectual shallowness or false consciousness seemed reasonable to a self-identified cultural elite, one need look no further than the simplest and most obvious answer to explain why Peale's work was eagerly consumed by so many.

While we cannot be certain how Peale's work was used by his readers, one would imagine that it was employed to inspire people to ask for better pay at work, overcome the anxiety associated with illness, turn around slumping sales, succeed in romantic life, achieve in school and job training, and even take home blue ribbons at the county fair. In short, as Peale taught, there was little that could not be impacted by a positive mental attitude. Peale's own stories (as you will read) were themselves collections of testimonials to the power of Peale's message, even if those stories were filtered through Peale's own narrative interests.

Peale's techniques succeeded in doing what Peale said they would do, at least for those readers who were inclined to accept his message. As a result, the theology and the methods that Peale elaborated on in *The Power of Positive Thinking,* as well as in countless other books, articles, and speeches, have become an important strand of religious practice in America and worldwide. Even today, a cursory browse through the Internet reveals that Peale's teachings remain popular at seminars, particularly those dealing with business success. Moreover, millions of individuals around the world carry pocket-sized booklets containing inspirational stories and phrases penned by Peale.

Further Reading

Carol V. R. George, *God's Salesman: Norman Vincent Peale and The Power of Positive Thinking* (New York: Oxford University Press, 1993); Martin E. Marty, *Modern American Religion, Under God, Indivisible, 1941–1960* (Chicago: University of Chicago Press, 1996); Donald Meyer, *The Positive Thinkers: A Study of the American Quest for Health, Wealth and Personal Power from Mary Baker Eddy to Norman Vincent Peale* (New York: Pantheon, 1965); Richard Weiss, *The Myth of American Success: From Horatio Alger to Norman Vincent Peale* (New York: Basic Books, 1969).

Try Prayer Power

In a business office high above the city streets two men were having a serious conversation. One, heavily troubled by a business and personal crisis, paced the floor restlessly, then sat dejectedly, head in hand, a picture of despair. He had come to the other for advice, since he was considered a man of great understanding. Together they had explored the problem from every angle but seemingly without result, which only served to deepen the troubled man's discouragement. "I guess no power on earth can save me," he sighed.

The other reflected for a moment, then spoke rather diffidently. "I wouldn't look at it that way. I believe you are wrong in saying there is no power that can save you. Personally, I have found that there is an answer to every problem. There is a power that can help you." Then slowly he asked, "Why not try prayer power?"

Somewhat surprised, the discouraged man said, "Of course I believe in prayer, but perhaps I do not know how to pray. You speak of it as something practical that fits a business problem. I never thought of it that way but I'm willing to try prayer if you will show me how."

He did apply practical prayer techniques and in due course got his answer. Matters ultimately turned out satisfactorily. That is not to say he did not have difficulties. In fact, he had rather a hard time of it but ultimately he worked out of this trouble. Now he believes in prayer power so enthusiastically that I recently heard him say, "Every problem can be solved and solved right if you pray."

Experts in physical health and well-being often utilize prayer in their therapy. Disability, tension, and kindred troubles may result from a lack of inner harmony. It is remarkable how prayer restores the harmonious functioning of body and soul. A friend of mine, a physiotherapist, told a nervous man to whom he was giving a massage, "God works through my fingers as I seek to relax your physical body, which is the temple of your soul. While I work on your outward being, I want you to pray for God's relaxation inwardly." It was a new idea to the patient, but he happened to be in a receptive mood and he tried passing some peace thoughts through his mind. He was amazed at the relaxing effect this had on him.

Jack Smith, operator of a health club, which is patronized by many outstanding people, believes in the therapy of prayer and uses it. He was at one time a prize fighter, then a truck driver, later a taxi driver, and finally opened his health club. He says that while he probes his patrons for physical flabbiness he also probes for spiritual flabbiness because, he declares, "You can't get a man physically healthy until you get him spiritually healthy."

One day Walter Huston, the actor, sat by Jack Smith's desk. He noted a big sign on the wall on which was penciled the following letters: A P R P B W P R A A. In surprise Huston asked, "What do those letters mean?"

Smith laughed and said, "They stand for 'Affirmative Prayers Release Powers By Which Positive Results Are Accomplished.'"

Huston's jaw dropped in astonishment. "Well, I never expected to hear anything like that in a health club."

"I use methods like that," said Smith, "to make people curious so they will ask what those letters mean. That gives me an opportunity to tell them that I believe affirmative prayers always get results."

Jack Smith, who helps men to keep physically fit, believes that prayer is as important, if not more important, than exercise, steam baths, and a rubdown. It is a vital part of the power-releasing process.

People are doing more praying today than formerly because they find that it adds to personal efficiency. Prayer helps them to tap forces and to utilize strength not otherwise available.

A famous psychologist says, "Prayer is the greatest power available to the individual in solving his personal problems. Its power astonishes me."

Prayer power is a manifestation of energy. Just as there exist scientific techniques for the release of atomic energy, so are there scientific procedures for the release of spiritual energy through the mechanism of prayer. Exciting demonstrations of this energizing force are evident.

Prayer power seems able even to normalize the aging process, obviating or limiting infirmity and deterioration. You need not lose your basic energy or vital power or become weak and listless merely as a result of accumulating years. It is not necessary to allow your spirit to sag or grow stale or dull. Prayer can freshen you up every evening and send you out renewed each morning. You can receive guidance in problems if prayer is allowed to permeate your subconscious, the seat of the forces which determines whether you take right or wrong actions. Prayer has the power to keep your reactions correct and sound. Prayer driven deeply into your subconscious can remake you. It releases and keeps power flowing freely.

If you have not experienced this power, perhaps you need to learn new techniques of prayer. It is well to study prayer from an efficiency point of view. Usually the emphasis is entirely religious though no cleavage exists between the two concepts. Scientific spiritual practice rules out stereotyped procedure even as it does in general science. If you have been praying in a certain manner, even if it has brought you blessings, which it doubtless has, perhaps you can pray even more profitably by varying the pattern and by experimenting with fresh prayer formulas. Get new insights; practice new skills to attain greatest results.

It is important to realize that you are dealing with the most tremendous power in the world when you pray. You would not use an old-fashioned kerosene lamp for illumination. You want the most up-to-date lighting devices. New and fresh spiritual techniques are being constantly discovered by men and women of spiritual genius. It is advisable to experiment with prayer power according to such methods as prove sound and effective. If this sounds new and strangely scientific, bear in mind that the secret of prayer is to find the process that will most effectively open your mind humbly to God. Any method through which you can stimulate the power of God to flow into your mind is legitimate and usable.

An illustration of a scientific use of prayer is the experience of two famous industrialists, whose names would be known to many readers were I permitted to mention them, who had a conference about a business and technical matter. One might think that these men would approach starch on a purely technical basis, and they did that and more; they also prayed about it. But they did not get a successful result. Therefore they called in a country preacher, an old friend of one of them, because, as they explained, the Bible prayer formula is, "Where two or three are gathered together in my name, there am I in the midst of them." (Matthew 18:20) They also pointed to a further formula, namely, "If two of you shall agree on earth as touching any thing that they shall ask, it shall be done for them of my Father which is in heaven." (Matthew 18:19)

Being schooled in scientific practice, they believe that in dealing with prayer as a phenomenon they should scrupulously follow the formulas outlined in the Bible which they described as the textbook of spiritual science. The proper method for employing a science is to use the accepted formulas outlined in the textbook of that science. They reasoned that if the Bible provides that two or three should be gathered together, perhaps the reason they were not succeeding was that they needed a third party.

Therefore the three men prayed, and to guard against error in the process they also brought to bear on the problem various other Biblical techniques such as those suggested in the statements: "According to your faith be it unto you." (Matthew 9:29) "What things soever ye desire, when ye pray, believe that ye receive them, and ye shall have them." (Mark 11:24)

After several thoroughgoing sessions of prayer the three men together affirmed that they had received the answer. The outcome was entirely satisfactory. Subsequent results indicated that Divine guidance was actually obtained.

These men are great enough scientists not to require precise explanation of the operation of these spiritual laws any more than in the case of naturalistic laws but are content with the fact that the law does operate when "proper" techniques are employed.

"While we cannot explain it," they said, "the fact remains that we were baffled by our problem and we tried prayer according to the formulas in the New Testament. That method worked and we got a beautiful result." They did add that it seemed to them that faith and harmony are important factors in the prayer process.

A man opened a small business in New York City a number of years ago, his first establishment being, as he characterized it, "a little hole in the wall." He had one employee. In a few years they moved into a larger room and then into extensive quarters. It became a very successful operation.

This man's method of business as he described it was "to fill the little hole in the wall with optimistic prayers and thoughts." He declared that hard work, positive thinking, fair dealing, right treatment of people, and the proper kind of praying always get results. This man, who has a creative and unique mind, worked out his own simple formula for solving his problems and overcoming his difficulties through prayer power. It is a curious formula but I have practiced it and personally know that it works. I have suggested it to many people who also found real value in its use. It is recommended to you.

The formula is (1) PRAYERIZE, (2) PICTURIZE, (3) ACTUALIZE.

By "prayerize" my friend meant a daily system of creative prayer. When a problem arose he talked it over with God very simply and directly in prayer. Moreover, he did not talk with God as to some vast and far-off shadowy being but conceived of God as being with him in his office, in his home, on the street, in his automobile, always nearby as a partner, as a close associate. He took seriously the Biblical injunction to "pray without ceasing." He interpreted it as meaning that he should go about every day discussing with God in a natural, normal manner the questions that had to be decided and dealt with. The Presence came finally to dominate his conscious and ultimately his unconscious thinking. He "prayerized" his daily life. He prayed as he walked or drove his car or performed other everyday activities. He filled his daily life full of prayer—that is, he lived by prayer. He did not often kneel to offer his prayers but would, for example, say to God as to a close associate, "What will I do about this, Lord?" or "Give me a fresh insight on this, Lord." He prayerized his mind and so prayerized his activities.

The second point in his formula of creative prayer is to "picturize." The basic factor in physics is force. The basic factor in psychology is the realizable wish. The man who assumes success tends already to have success. People who assume failure tend to have failure. When either failure or success is picturized it strongly tends to actualize in terms equivalent to the mental image pictured.

To assure something worth while happening, first pray about it and test it according to God's will; then print a picture of it on your mind as happening, holding the picture firmly in consciousness. Continue to surrender the picture to God's will—that is to say, put the matter in God's hands—and follow God's guidance. Work hard and intelligently, thus doing your part to achieve success in the matter. Practice believing and continue to hold the picturization finely in your thoughts. Do this and you will be astonished at the strange ways in which the picturization comes to pass. In this manner the picture "actualizes." That which you have "prayerized" and "picturized" "actualizes" according to the pattern of your basic realizable wish when conditioned by invoking God's power upon it, and if, moreover, you give fully of yourself to its realization.

I have personally practiced this three-point prayer method and find great power in it. It has been suggested to others who have likewise reported that it released creative power into their experience.

For example, a woman discovered that her husband was drifting from her. Theirs had been a happy marriage, but the wife had become preoccupied in social affairs and the husband had gotten busy in his work. Before they knew it, the close, old-time companionship was lost. One day she discovered his interest in another woman. She lost her head and became hysterical. She consulted her minister, who adroitly turned the conversation to herself. She admitted being a careless homemaker and that she had also become self-centered, sharp-tongued, and nagging.

She then confessed that she had never felt herself the equal of her husband. She had a profound sense of inferiority regarding him, feeling unable to maintain equality with him socially and intellectually. So she retreated into an antagonistic attitude that manifested itself in petulance and criticism.

The minister saw that the woman had more talent, ability, and charm than she was revealing. He suggested that she create an image or picture of herself as capable and attractive. He whimsically told her that "God runs a beauty parlor" and that faith techniques could put beauty on a person's face and charm and ease in her manner. He gave her instruction in how to pray and how spiritually to "picturize." He also advised her to hold a mental image of the restoration of the old-time companionship, to visualize the goodness in her husband, and to picture a restored harmony between the two of them. She was to hold this picture with faith. In this manner he prepared her for a most interesting personal victory.

About this time her husband informed her that he wanted a divorce. She had conquered herself to the extent of being able to receive this request with calmness. She simply replied that she was willing if he wanted it, but suggested a deferral of the decision for ninety days on the ground that divorce is so final. "If at the end of ninety days you still feel that you want a divorce, I will co-operate with you." She said this calmly. He gave her a quizzical look, for he had expected an outburst.

Night after night he went out, and night after night she sat at home, but she pictured him as seated in his old chair. He was not in the chair, but she painted an image of him there comfortably reading as in the old days. She visualized him puttering around the house, painting and fixing things as he had formerly done. She even pictured him drying the dishes as he did when they were first married. She visualized the two of them playing golf together and taking hikes as they once did.

She maintained this picture with steady faith, and one night there he actually sat in his old chair. She looked twice to be sure that it was the reality rather than the picturization, but perhaps a picturization is a reality, for at any rate the actual man was there. Occasionally he would be gone but more and more nights he sat in his chair. Then he began to read to her as in the old days. Then one sunny Saturday afternoon he asked, "What do you say to a game of golf?"

The days went by pleasantly until she realized that the ninetieth day had arrived, so that evening she said quietly, "Bill, this is the ninetieth day."

"What do you mean," he asked, puzzled, "the ninetieth day?"

"Why, don't you remember? We agreed to wait ninety days to settle that divorce matter and this is the day."

He looked at her for a moment, then hidden behind his paper turned a page, saying, "Don't be silly. I couldn't possibly get along without you. Where did you ever get the idea I was going to leave you?"

The formula proved a powerful mechanism. She prayerized, she picturized, and the sought-for result was actualized. Prayer power solved her problem and his as well.

I have known many people who have successfully applied this technique not only to personal affairs but to business matters as well. When sincerely and intelligently brought into situations, the results have been so excellent that this must be regarded as an extraordinarily efficient method of prayer. People who take this method seriously and actually use it get astonishing results.

At an industrial convention banquet I was seated at the speaker's table next to a man who, though a bit on the rough side, was very likable. He may have felt a bit cramped by his proximity to a preacher, which obviously wasn't his usual company. During the dinner he used a number of theological words, but they were not put together in a theological manner. After each outburst he apologized, but I advised him that I had heard all those words before.

He told me he had been a church attendant as a boy but "had gotten away from it." He gave me that old story which I have heard all my life and which even now people will get off as something entirely new, viz., "When I was a boy my father made me go to Sunday school and church and crammed religion down my throat. So when I got away from home I couldn't take it any more and have seldom been to church since."

This man then observed that "perhaps he should start going to church since he was getting old." I commented that he would be lucky to find a seat. This surprised him for he "did not think anybody went to church any more." I told him that more people attend church each week than frequent any other institution in the country. This rather bowled him over.

He was head of a medium-sized business and he fell to telling me how much money his firm took in last year. I told him I knew quite a few churches whose take exceeded that. This really hit him in the solar plexus, and I noted his respect for the church mounting by leaps and bounds. I told him about the thousands of religious books that are sold, more than any other type of book. "Maybe you fellows in the church are on the ball at that," he slangily remarked.

At this moment another man came up to our table and enthusiastically told me that "something wonderful" had happened to him. He said he had been very depressed, for things hadn't been going well with him. He decided to get away for a week or so and on this vacation read one of my books in which practical faith techniques are outlined. He said this brought him the first satisfaction and peace he had felt. It encouraged him as to his own possibilities. He began to believe that the answer to his trouble was practical religion.

"So," he said, "I began to practice the spiritual principles presented in your book. I began to believe and affirm that with God's help the objectives I was endeavoring to accomplish could be achieved. A feeling came over me that everything was going to be all right, and from then on nothing could upset me. I absolutely knew it was going to be O.K. So I began to sleep better and feel better. I felt as if I had taken a tonic. My new understanding and practice of spiritual techniques were the turning point."

When he left us, my table companion, who had listened in on this recital, said, "I never heard anything like that before. That fellow talks about religion as happy and workable. It was never presented to me that way. He also gives the impression that religion is almost a science, that you can use it to improve your health and do better in your job. I never thought of religion in that connection."

Then he added, "But do you know what struck me? It was the look on that guy's face."

Now the curious fact is that when my table companion made that statement a semblance of the same look was on his own face. For the first time he was getting the idea that religious faith is not something piously stuffy but is a scientific procedure for successful living. He was observing firsthand the practical working of prayer power in personal experience.

Personally, I believe that prayer is a sending out of vibrations from one person to another and to God. All of the universe is in vibration. There are vibrations in the molecules of a table. The air is filled with vibrations. The reaction between human beings is also in vibration. When you send out a prayer for another person, you employ the force inherent in a spiritual universe. You transport from yourself to the other person a sense of love, helpfulness, support—a sympathetic, powerful understanding—and in this process you awaken vibrations in the universe through which God brings to pass the good objectives prayed for. Experiment with this principle and you will know its amazing results.

For example, I have a habit, which I often use, of praying for people as I pass them. I remember being on a train traveling through West Virginia when I had a curious thought. I saw a man standing on a station platform, then the train moved on and he passed from sight. It occurred to me that I was seeing him for the first and last time. His life and mine touched lightly for just a fraction of an instant. He went his way and I went mine. I wondered how his life would turn out.

Then I prayed for that man, sending out an affirmative prayer that his life would be filled with blessings. Then I began praying for other people I saw as the train passed. I prayed for a man plowing in the field and asked the Lord to help him and give him a good crop. I saw a mother hanging up clothes, and that line of freshly washed garments told me she had a large family. A glimpse of her face and the way in which she handled the clothes of the children told me she was a happy woman. I prayed for her, that she would have a happy life, that her husband would always be true to her and that she would be true to him. I prayed that they might be a religious family and that the children would grow up strong, honorable young people.

In one station I saw a man leaning half asleep against a wall, and I prayed that he would wake up and get off relief and amount to something.

Then we stopped at a station, and there was a lovable little kid, one pants leg longer than the other, shirt open at the neck, wearing a too-big sweater, hair tousled, face dirty. He was sucking a lollipop and working hard on it. I prayed for him, and as the train started to move he looked up at me and gave me the most wonderful smile. I knew my prayer had caught him, and I waved to him, and he waved back at me. I shall never see that boy again in all likelihood, but our lives touched. It had been a cloudy day up to that point, but suddenly the sun came out and I think there was a light in the boy's heart, for it was revealed on his face. I know that my heart felt happy. I am sure it was because the power of God was moving in a circuit through me, to the boy and back to God; and we were all under the spell of prayer power.

One of the important functions of prayer is as a stimulus to creative ideas. Within the mind are all of the resources needed for successful living. Ideas are present in consciousness which, when released and given scope together with proper implementation, can lead to the successful operation of any project or undertaking. When the New Testament says, "The kingdom of God is within you," (Luke 17:21) it is informing us that God our Creator has laid up within our minds and personalities all the potential powers and ability we need for constructive living. It remains for us to tap and develop these powers.

For example, a man of my acquaintance is connected with a business where he is the chief of four executives. At regular intervals these men have what they call an "idea session," the purpose of which is to tap all the creative ideas lurking in the minds of any of the four. For this session they use a room without telephones, buzzers, or other usual office equipment. The double window is fully insulated so that street noises are for the most part eliminated.

Before starting the session the group spends ten minutes in silent prayer and meditation. They conceive of God as creatively working in their minds. Each in his own way silently prays, affirming that God is about to release from his mind the proper ideas needed in the business.

Following the quiet period all start talking, pouring out ideas that have come to their minds. Memos of the ideas are written upon cards and thrown on the table. No one is permitted to criticize any idea at this particular juncture for argument might stop the flow of creative thought. The cards are gathered up and each one is evaluated at a later session; but this is the idea-tapping session, stimulated by prayer power.

When this practice was inaugurated a high percentage of the ideas suggested proved to be without particular value, but as the sessions continued the percentage of good ideas increased. Now many of the best suggestions which have later demonstrated their practical value were evolved in the "idea session."

As one of the executives explained, "We have come up with insights that not only show on our balance sheet but we have also gained a new feeling of confidence. Moreover, there is a deeper feeling of fellowship among the four of us and this has spread to others in the organization."

Where is the old-fashioned businessman who says that religion is theoretical and has no place in business? Today any successful and competent businessman will employ the latest and best-tested methods in production, distribution, and administration, and many are discovering that one of the greatest of all efficiency methods is prayer power.

Alert people everywhere are finding that by trying prayer power they feel better, work better, do better, sleep better, are better.

My friend Grove Patterson, editor of the Toledo *Blade*, is a man of remarkable vigor. He says that his energy results, in part at least, from his methods of prayer. For example, he likes to fall asleep while praying, for he believes that his subconscious is most relaxed at that time. It is in the subconscious that our life is largely governed. If you drop a prayer into the subconscious at the moment of its greatest relaxation, the prayer has a powerful effect. Mr. Patterson chuckled as he said, "Once it worried me because I would fall asleep while praying. Now I actually try to have it so."

Many unique methods of prayer have come to my attention, but one of the most effective is that advocated by Frank Laubach in his excellent book, *Prayer, the Mightiest Power in the World*. I regard this as one of the most practical books on prayer, for it outlines fresh prayer techniques that work. Dr. Laubach believes that actual power is generated by prayer. One of his methods is to walk down the street and "shoot" prayers at people. He calls this type of praying, "flash prayers." He bombards passers-by with prayers, sending out thoughts of good will and love. He says that people passing him on the street as he "shoots" prayers at them often turn around and look at him and smile. They feel the emanation of a power like electrical energy.

In a bus he "shoots" prayers at his fellow passengers. Once he was standing behind a man who seemed to be very gloomy. He had noticed when he entered the bus that the man had a scowl on his face. He began to send out toward him prayers of good will and faith, conceiving of these prayers as surrounding him and driving into his mind. Suddenly the man began to stroke the back of his head, and when he left the bus the scowl was gone and a smile had replaced it. Dr. Laubach believes that he has often changed the entire atmosphere of a car or bus full of people by the process of "swishing love and prayers all around the place."

In a Pullman club car a half-intoxicated man was quite boorish and rude, talking in an overbearing manner and generally making himself obnoxious. I felt that everyone in the car took a dislike to him. Halfway down the car from him I determined to try Frank Laubach's method. So I started to pray for him, meanwhile visualizing his better self and sending out thoughts of good will toward him. Presently, for no seemingly apparent reason, the man turned in my direction, gave me a most disarming smile, and raised his hand in the gesture of salute. His attitude changed and he became quiet. I have every reason to believe that the prayer thoughts effectively reached out toward him.

It is my practice before making a speech to any audience to pray for the people present and to send out thoughts of love and good will toward them. Sometimes I select out of the audience one or two people who seem to be either depressed or even antagonistic and send my prayer thoughts and good-will attitude specifically toward them. Recently addressing a Chamber of Commerce annual dinner in a southwestern city, I noted a man in the audience who seemed to be scowling at me. It was altogether possible that his facial expression was not in any way related to me, but he seemed antagonistic. Before starting to speak I prayed for him and "shot" a series of prayers and good-will thoughts in his direction. As I spoke, I continued to do this.

When the meeting was over, while shaking hands with those around me, suddenly my hand was caught in a tremendous clasp and I was looking into the face of the man. He was smiling broadly. "Frankly I did not like you when I came to this meeting," he said. "I do not like preachers and saw no reason for having you, a minister, as speaker at our Chamber of Commerce dinner. I was hoping that your speech would not be successful. However, as you spoke something seemed to touch me. I feel like a new person. I had a strange sense of peace—and doggone it, I like you!"

It was not my speech that had this effect. It was the emanation of prayer power. In our brains we have about two billion little storage batteries. The human brain can send off power by thoughts and prayers. The human body's magnetic power has actually been tested. We have thousands of little sending stations, and when these are turned up by prayer it is possible for a tremendous power to flow through a person and to pass between human beings. We can send off power by prayer which acts as both a sending and receiving station.

There was a man, an alcoholic, with whom I had been working. He had been "dry" (as the Alcoholics Anonymous term it) for about six months. He was on a business trip, and one Tuesday afternoon about four-o'clock I had a strong impression that he was in trouble. This man dominated my thoughts. I felt something drawing me so I dropped everything and started praying for him. I prayed for about a half-hour, then the impression seemed to let up and I discontinued my prayers.

A few days later he telephoned me. "I have been in Boston all week," he said, "and I want you to know I'm still 'dry,' but early in the week I had a very hard time."

"Was it on Tuesday at four o'clock?" I asked.

Astonished, he replied, "Why, yes, how did you know? Who told you?"

"Nobody told me," I replied. "That is, no human told me." I described my feelings concerning him on Tuesday at four o'clock and told about praying for him for half an hour.

He was astounded, and explained, "I was at the hotel and stopped in front of the bar. I had a terrible struggle with myself. I thought of you, for I needed help badly right then, and I started to pray."

Those prayers starting out from him reached me and I began to pray for him. Both of us joining in prayer completed the circuit and reached God, and the man got his answer in the form of strength to meet the crisis. And what did he do?

He went to a drugstore, bought a box of candy, and ate all of it without stopping. That pulled him through, he declared—"prayer and candy."

A young married woman admitted she was filled with hates, jealousy, and resentment toward neighbors and friends. She was also very apprehensive, always worrying about her children, whether they would be sick or get into an accident or fail in school. Her life was a pathetic mixture of dissatisfaction, fear, hate, and unhappiness. I asked her if she ever prayed. She said, "Only when I get so up against it that I am just desperate; but I must admit that prayer doesn't mean anything to me, so I don't pray very often."

I suggested that the practice of real prayer could change her life and gave her some instructions in sending out love thoughts instead of hate thoughts and confidence thoughts instead of fear thoughts. I suggested that every day at the time for the children to come home from school she pray, and make her prayers an affirmation of God's protective goodness. Doubtful at first, she became one of the most enthusiastic advocates and practicers of prayer I have ever known. She avidly reads books and pamphlets and practices every effective prayer-power technique. This procedure revamped her life as is illustrated by the following letter which she wrote me recently:

"I feel that my husband and I have both made wonderful progress in the last few weeks. My greatest progress dates from the night you told me that 'every day is a good day if you pray.' I began to put into practice the idea of affirming that this would be a good day the minute I woke up in the morning, and I can positively say that I have not had a bad or upsetting day since that time. The amazing thing is that my days actually haven't been any smoother or any more free from petty annoyances than they ever were, but they just don't seem to have the power to upset me any more. Every night I begin my prayers by listing all the things for which I am grateful, little things that happened during the day which added to the happiness of my day. I know that this habit has geared my mind to pick out the nice things and forget the unpleasant ones. The fact that for six weeks I have not had a single bad day and have refused to get downhearted with anyone is really marvelous to me."

She discovered amazing power in trying prayer power.

You can do the same. Following are ten rules for getting effective results from prayer:

1. Set aside a few minutes every day. Do not say anything. Simply practice thinking about God. This will make your mind spiritually receptive.

2. Then pray orally, using simple, natural words. Tell God anything that is on your mind. Do not think you must use stereotyped pious phrases. Talk to God in your own language. He understands it.

3. Pray as you go about the business of the day, on the subway or bus or at your desk. Utilize minute prayers by closing your eyes to shut out the world and concentrating briefly on God's presence. The more you do this every day the nearer you will feel God's presence.

4. Do not always ask when you pray, but instead affirm that God's blessings are being given, and spend most of your prayers giving thanks.

5. Pray with the belief that sincere prayers can reach out and surround your loved ones with God's love and protection.

6. Never use a negative thought in prayer. Only positive thoughts get results.

7. Always express willingness to accept God's will. Ask for what you want, but be willing to take what God gives you. It may be better than what you ask for.

8. Practice the attitude of putting everything in God's hands. Ask for the ability to do your best and to leave the results confidently to God.

9. Pray for people you do not like or who have mistreated you. Resentment is blockade number one of spiritual power.

10. Make a list of people for whom to pray. The more you pray for other people, especially those not connected with you, the more prayer results will come back to you.

— 21 —

Shamanism in the New Age

Gary Laderman

The Way of the Shaman (1980) is, according to the publicity on the back cover, "the definitive handbook on practical shamanism—what it is, where it came from, how you can participate." The following excerpt from the book captures something of the allure, accessibility, and authority of this rendition of shamanism. The author, Michael Harner, is a trained anthropologist who has taught at such prestigious universities as the New School for Social Research in New York, University of California–Berkeley, Columbia, and Yale. Thousands of curious Americans have turned to these pages in search of spiritual transformation and the acquisition of sacred powers—enough for Harner to leave his academic post and devote himself full time to instructing these Americans, and others around the world, in the "Harner Method of Shamanic Counseling." Indeed, after its initial release, *The Way of the Shaman* quickly became a successful New Age handbook that introduced the wonders of shamanic practices to the American public. This anthropologist turned spiritual entrepreneur has discovered a "way" to open the doors of perception and to initiate students into the mysteries of ancient, though eternal and universal, truths about the cosmos and human consciousness.

Although many would argue that all shamanism is "practical," Harner wants to emphasize the pragmatic value of engaging in these prescribed shamanic rituals—follow his guidelines and your life will change. Today, many will testify about the effectiveness of the Harner Method, but the book's original authority hinges on the credibility of Harner's own "experiments" with shamanism. He identifies himself as a child of the Age of Science, as someone who prefers "to arrive first-hand, experimentally, at [his] own conclusions as to the nature and limits of reality" (xii). Ultimately, what validates these experiments is personal experience—one does not need to know why Harner's techniques work, only that they changed his life dramatically. Although personal experience is the best evidence for the truth of Harner's way, the book is loaded with references to shamanic experiments in cultures across time and space. The encyclopedic knowledge of shamanism throughout the text buttresses the central message: you, too, can become a shaman and change your life. This step-by-step guide to becoming a shaman is replete with exercises, activities, and suggestions that promise an existential transformation in consciousness.

Harner's shamanism is first and foremost a ritual strategy for breaking free of prosaic, everyday awareness and entering into an extraordinary, boundless state of consciousness that has real effects in everyday life. The detailed, easy-to-follow directions for discovering your guardian spirit, sucking intrusions out of patients, and dancing your power animal have led many, according to Harner, to tap into reservoirs of spiritual power that shamans have utilized for ages. The recognition that shamanic practices can be identified in countless human cultures attests to the truth of these powers and, for Harner, the unrestricted quality of relevant knowledge needed to access them.

As an anthropologist, Harner had years of access to shamanic cultures. In the late fifties and early sixties, he did field work in South America, living among the Jivaro and Conibo Indians and participating in a number of shamanic rituals. In fact, his own hallucinogenic experiences with shamans in the Ecuadorian Andes and the Peruvian Amazon, and ultimately his own initiation into the shamanic life by a Jivaro master, Akachu, transformed the anthropologist's life. From his first contact with hallucinogens in the jungles of South America, through his apprenticeship under Akachu, to his final day as an Anonshaman, Harner's training in the field and, equally important, his personal experiences beyond his field notes opened his eyes to a universal method for becoming a shaman.

One of the critical differences between the shamanism practiced in the field by Harner and the shamanism he promotes in the book relates to drug use. Although his own spiritual development rested on the ingestion of hallucinogenic plants, Harner's commercial method relies on other strategies for altering human consciousness, such as drumming and dancing. Again, the basis for his authority to teach others about drugless shamanism is a result of personal experiences, for he "studied briefly with shamans of a few western North American Indian groups. . . . From them I learned how shamanism could be practiced successfully without the use of the *ayahuasca* or other drugs of the Conibo and the Jivaro" (18–19). A spiritual primer that championed drug-free hallucinatory experiences to discover sacred powers could not have appeared at a more opportune moment. Americans in the 1960s and 1970s, who were disillusioned and downright angry with the confusing power of LSD, mushrooms, marijuana, and other substances, appreciated radical transformations of consciousness without mind-altering substances or the danger of arrest.

The book was first published in 1980, not long after the figure of the shaman became a fixture in American culture during the 1960s. Public interest in, and awareness of, the powers of the shaman was sparked by a combination of social trends and cultural shifts in the 1960s and 1970s. Carlos Castaneda's controversial tales of his drug experiences and apprenticeship with a Yaqui elder known as Don Juan shaped a generation's view about the potential links between spiritual growth, personal fulfillment, and altered states of consciousness. In addition, experimentation with drugs by cultural icons and young adults searching for genuine religious experiences and intimations of the sacred contributed to the growing spiritual turn in American religious culture. The popularity of depth psychology and the human potential movement also generated an image of shamans as exemplary technicians of psychic healing and transformation. Increasing attention to environmental issues and impending ecological disaster brought the shaman into sharp relief as a living embodiment of harmonious relations with the larger cosmos. Finally, an explosion of white appreciation and desire for Native American forms of religious life aroused a great deal of curiosity about the individual experiences of shamans, who are critical social figures in Native American communities.

Harner's writing is part of a larger popular spiritual movement in America many refer to as "neoshamanism" or "urban shamanism." In this movement, religious practices and bodies of knowledge typically associated with the traditional shaman in non-Western cultural settings are recast by Westerners to fit a modern, domesticated version of personal self-exploration and cosmic awakening available to anyone interested. In the words of anthropologist Jane Monnig Atkinson, "particularly appealing for its 'democratic' qualities that bypass institutionalized religious hierarchies, the new shamanism is compatible with contemporary emphases on self-help, self-actualization, and—not incidentally—rapid results" (322). In many ways, the success of neoshamanism has as much to do with market value as it does with democracy. Although shamanic truths are ultimately universal and personally available to all, neoshamans play the role of cultural brokers who can deliver the spiritual goods to inexperienced consumers.

Harner and other neoshamans extract a constellation of ideas and practices from a variety of cultural settings, historical circumstances, and individual encounters. They seek to produce seamless systems of shamanic practice available through texts, in workshops, or over the Web to eager novices looking for dramatic spiritual adventures and escape from the numbing routines and pains of daily life. One result of brokering the shamanic experience to a larger audience is the simultaneous distortion of local cultural histories and the invention of religious rituals that are customized for contemporary individuals living in the modern world. Harner draws on his own experiences and a wealth of cross-cultural knowledge to create his own version of shamanic ritual practice. As Harner himself notes, "The exercises presented in this book represent my own personal distillation and interpretation of some of the millenia-old shamanic methods that I have learned firsthand from South and North American Indians, supplemented by information from the ethnographic literature, including that from other continents" (xxi). It should also be noted that the methods Harner has developed are ideally suited for modern American life because they are safe ("classic drug-free method"), immediate ("classic shamanic methods work surprisingly quickly"), and convenient ("just as it was suited, for example, to the Eskimo [Inuit] people whose daily hours were filled with tasks of struggle for survival, but whose evenings could be used for shamanism") (xii).

Cultural variations and local integrity can be discounted in the face of what Harner contends is a primeval, universal religious force that transcends any particular shamanic expression. The sample exercise below illustrates the way in which Harner universalizes shamanism and assumes the authority to instruct others on how to follow the shamanic path. As a set of religious instructions, the method is a singular amalgamation of comparative knowledge about shamanism, simple instructions to ritually enter into the shamanic state, and the promise of spiritual fulfillment and psychic transformation as a practicing shaman. Its widespread appeal can be attributed to the successful way Harner integrates these three components, along with the crucial ingredient, personal experience, into a credible religious manual for the spiritual marketplace. Another reason for its success, of course, is that it works for many people.

The set of practices below, "Calling the Beasts," "The Starting Dance," and "Dancing Your Animal," are offered to the budding shaman as a means for contacting past and present guardian spirits. Like most of the text, the specific exercises are framed by a passage that anchors the reader in a dizzying array of brief cultural snapshots of shamanic practice. In this case, the sum of the snapshots add up to a safe, fast, convenient way to enter states of consciousness in which you can access your own personal power animals—guardian spirits that raise "one's physical energy . . . ability to resist contagious disease . . . [and] one's mental alertness and self-confidence" (69). At the very beginning of the book, Harner identifies a "Shamanic State of Consciousness" (SSC) that all shamans achieve; they are religious specialists par excellence, who can move between the "Ordinary State of Consciousness" (OSC) and a more expansive, powerful realm of cosmic reality. The comparative data Harner assembles in this particular section demonstrate how entering the SSC can reestablish a paradisal "animal-human unity" that has been lost in the OSC.

All of the data point to one unequivocal fact: shamans have a special relationship with animals. They can become an animal, talk with animals, and acquire a guardian animal spirit. Harner presents a litany of cultures that hold to these and other fundamental assumptions about the true nature of reality, including the Lakota Sioux, Osage, Pueblo Zuni, the Arunta in Australia, Lapps in Scandinavia, Indians in Mexico and Guatemala, and the Jivaro. In the Jivaro example, the last before turning to the first exercise, Harner returns to his days in the field, when a shaman actually "*saw* that I had a guardian spirit even though I myself was unaware of it" (65). Unfortunately, Harner did not know how to see at the time. The general structure of the book implies that the special knowledge contained therein—as "distilled" through Harner's education and experience—precedes practice. The vast range of cross-cultural evidence, coupled with the identification of a basic, universal message, establishes the requisite mind-set to acquire shamanic visions and powers.

As Harner promises, the exercises are surprisingly simple and can be executed with minimal preparation. Regardless of the complex systems of knowledge required of practitioners within each culture, Harner claims to have struck upon a nine-step, universal program to enter the SSC and "evoke or get in touch with [your] animal aspects" (65). All a modern shaman needs is an empty, darkened room, two rattles (or drums "for a more powerful transition into the SSC" [67]), and knowledge of the cardinal directions. By shaking the rattle or banging the drum at various speeds, moving the body in time and space, and mentally concentrating on the natural world, an individual can begin the process of breaking through to another reality. In this schema, by the eighth step the shaman will be embodying her or his power animal, though only for a short period of time (about ten seconds or so).

The spiritual rewards of "dancing your animal" are great, and Harner is clear about the payoff: self-empowerment. The price of obtaining the power of the guardian animal spirit is minimal, and definitely innocuous: the guardian spirit enters the body of the shaman to experience the "enjoyment of once again existing in material form" (68). This is not a form of spirit possession, according to Harner, for the shaman maintains control of her or his body while the spirit inhabits it. The exchange that takes place in this transaction has both material and spiritual consequences, and the enhancement of power for the practicing shaman has pragmatic value: the guardian animal spirits become allies who help the shaman direct sacred powers from a nonordinary reality into acts of healing in this one.

Although Harner briefly acknowledges a darker side of shamanic power, his method promises beneficial healing on personal, global, and cosmic scales: "The way I offer you is that of the healer, not of the sorcerer" (xxiv). The section reprinted here is only a preliminary step in learning how to enter into states of consciousness beyond normal, mundane awareness and to become a spiritual agent of positive change. The dances, visualizations, recitations, dream interpretations, healing practices, and other lessons outlined in the book do more than enhance individual health and well-being. According to Harner, these are sacred techniques that can help others and can ultimately restore the spiritual connections between humanity and "its relatives, the plants and animals of this good Earth" (139).

In *The Way of the Shaman,* Harner identifies a set of religious practices that simultaneously make sense and defy logic—a common characteristic of religious systems in general. On the one hand, like other religious manuals before it, the book contains the right mixture of sacred knowledge and ritual instruction. As the reader enters into the worldview established by the text (answering the question: what do shamans know about reality?), she or he can take action to "live" within it. Theory and practice are thus seamlessly interwoven in a unified metaphysical system. As many followers of the Harner Method eagerly attest, the method, once put into practice, makes a great deal of sense in their lives.

On the other hand, the shaman is in many ways a convenient fiction, a product of Western imaginations, and these practices are simply cultural flotsam crafted to appear coherent and systematic. As anthropologist Michael Taussig notes about shamanism's status as a conceptual category, it is "a made-up, modern, Western category, an artful reification of disparate practices, snatches of folklore and overarching folklorizations, residues of long-established myths intermingled with the politics of academic departments, curricula, conferences, journal juries and articles, [and] funding agencies." From the age of exploration on, European and American societies simultaneously destroyed native cultures around the world and remained fixated on the religious experiences of certain indigenous figures, variously labeled "witch doctor," "wizard," "soothsayer," "medicine man," "conjuror," "priest," and "shaman." Whether the goal has been to classify, analyze, convert, or emulate, the "shaman" has been an effective, and popular, category with which to think about fantastic human experiences—possession by animal spirits, travel to the land of the dead, miraculous powers of healing, and so forth.

Harner wants the reader to do more than think about shamanism as an all-purpose category that encompasses extraordinary human phenomena. Action is the key that unlocks the shamanic potential in readers who follow the practices described in the book or in workshops now available around the world. Experimental action is the only way scientifically to prove to yourself that the practices work, action taken in the privacy of your home, with others in drumming circles, or under more rigorous conditions in training workshops. Ritual action can be repeated by the shaman to enter states of consciousness that expand the frontiers of reality and bring practitioners into contact with other worlds of experience. The practices Harner outlines, what are identified as "core" shamanic techniques, promise to bring these worlds to life for anyone willing to follow the way.

The text below is from Michael Harner, *The Way of the Shaman* (San Francisco: Harper Collins, 1990), pp. 57–68. Copyright ©1980 by Michael Harner. Reprinted by permission of Harper Collins Publishers, Inc.

Further Readings

Catherine Albanese, "From New Thought to New Vision: The Shamanic Paradigm in Contemporary Spirituality," in *Communication and Change in American Religious History*, edited by Leonard I. Sweet (Grand Rapids, Mich.: William B. Eerdmans, 1993), pp. 335–54; Jane Monnig Atkinson, "Shamanisms Today," *Annual Review of Anthropology* 21 (1992): 307–30; Gary Doore, ed., *Shaman's Path: Healing, Personal Growth, and Empowerment* (Boston: Shambhala, 1988); Mircea Eliade, *Shamanism: Archaic Techniques of Ecstasy* (Princeton: Princeton University Press, 1964); Gloria Flaherty, *Shamanism and the Eighteenth Century* (Princeton: Princeton University Press, 1992); Paul K. Johnson, "Shamanism from Ecuador to Chicago: A Case Study in New Age Ritual Appropriation," *Religion* (1995): 162–75; Amanda Porterfield, "Shamanism: A Psychosocial Definition," *Journal of the American Academy of Religion* 55, no.4 (1987): 721–39; Wendy Rose, "The Great Pretenders: Further Reflections on White Shamanism," in *The State of Native America: Genocide, Colonization, and Resistance*, edited by M. Annette Jaimes (Boston: South End, 1992), pp. 403–22; Michael Taussig, "The Nervous System: Homesickness and Dada," *Stanford Humanities Review* 1, no. 1 (1989): 44–81.

The Way of the Shaman

POWER ANIMALS

Shamans have long believed their powers were the powers of the animals, of the plants, of the sun, of the basic energies of the universe. In the garden Earth they have drawn upon their assumed powers to help save other humans from illness and death, to provide strength in daily life, to commune with their fellow creatures, and to live a joyful existence in harmony with the totality of Nature.

Millennia before Charles Darwin, people in shamanic cultures were convinced that humans and animals were related. In their myths, for example, the animal characters were commonly portrayed as essentially human in physical form but individually distinguished by the particular personality characteristics possessed by the various types of animals as they exist in the wild today. Thus Coyote is distinguished in the stories by his mischievous behavior, and Raven often by his unseemly dependence on others to kill game for him. Then, according to various creation myths, the animals became physically differentiated into the forms in which they are found today. Accordingly, the myths explain, it is no longer possible for humans and animals to converse together, or for animals to have human form.

While the mythical paradise of animal-human unity is lost in ordinary reality, it still remains accessible in nonordinary reality to the shaman and vision-seeker. The Australian aborigines' concept of "The Dream Time" embodies this awareness, for it refers to a mythological past that still exists parallel in time to present-day ordinary reality, and which is penetrated in dreams and visions. The shaman, alone of the humans, is regularly able to effect the animal human unity by entering the SSC. For the shaman in the altered state of consciousness, the mythical past is immediately accessible.

North and South American Indian mythology is pervaded with animal characters in tales that tell not of the adventures of a coyote, a raven, or a bear, but of the adventures of Coyote, Raven, and Bear. In other words, the individual characters represent entire species or larger classes of animals. This is analogous to the unity of one's individual guardian animal spirit with the entire genus or species to which it belongs. This unity means that a person usually possesses not just the power of a bear, or of an eagle, but the power of Bear or of Eagle. The possessor of a guardian animal normally draws upon the spiritual power of its entire genus or species, although he is indeed connected into that power by an individualized manifestation of it.

The connectedness between humans and the animal world is very basic in shamanism, with the shaman utilizing his knowledge and methods to participate in the power of that world. Through his guardian spirit or power animal, the shaman connects with the power of the animal world, the mammals, birds, fish, and other beings. The shaman has to have a particular guardian in order to do his work, and his guardian helps him in certain special ways.

The guardian spirit is sometimes referred to by native North Americans as the power animal, as among the Coast Salish and the Okanagon of Washington. This is a particularly apt term, for it emphasizes the power-giving aspect of the guardian spirit as well as the frequency with which it is perceived as an animal. But the Coast Salish also sometimes refer to the guardian spirit as the Indian, for it can appear to them in human form as well. Such an animal-human duality of the guardian spirit is a common feature of North and South American Indian cosmology as well as elsewhere in the primitive world. Thus, among the Cocopa of the Colorado River valley, animals appear in dreams as human beings. Among the Jivaro, a guardian spirit usually first appears in a vision as an animal, and then in a dream as a human.

The ability of animals to appear as humans is not surprising, given the widespread belief that humans and animals are biologically related (are "relations") and in ancient times were able to converse together. In nonordinary reality, the animals continue to be able to manifest themselves in human forms to humans who have entered the SSC. It is only the shaman, or the person with shamanistic tendencies, who is able to resume the lost ability to communicate with the (other) animals. Thus, when a man becomes a shaman among the tribes of the western desert of South Australia, he acquires the power to speak to birds and other animals. When Castaneda engages in conversation with a coyote, he is making progress toward becoming a shaman. Among the Jivaro, in fact, if an animal speaks to you, it is considered evidence that the animal is your guardian spirit.

Among the Lakota Sioux, the guardian animal spirits often speak when they appear to the vision-seeker. As Lame Deer recounts, "All of a sudden I heard a big bird crying, and then quickly he hit me on the back, touched me with his spread wings. I heard the cry of an eagle, loud above the voices of many other birds. It seemed to say, 'We have been waiting for you. We knew you would come. Now you are here. Your trail leads from here . . . you will have a ghost with you always—another self.'"

The capability of the guardian animal spirits to speak to a human or to manifest themselves sometimes in human forms is taken as an indication of their power. Another indication of their power is when they make themselves visible navigating in an element that is not their "ordinary" environment. Common examples are a land mammal or serpent flying through the air, with or without the benefit of wings. All these capabilities show that the animal is indeed nonordinary, a bearer of power, able to transcend the nature of an ordinary animal and its ordinary existence. When its transformation into human form occurs, it is a magical act of power. When possessed by a shaman, the power animal acts as an alter ego, imparting to the shaman the power of transformation, and especially the power of transformation from human to the power animal, as well as back again.

The belief by shamans that they can metamorphose into the form of their guardian animal spirit or power animal is widespread and obviously ancient.

Among the Arunta of Australia they often took on the form of eagle-hawks. In the course of the initiation of a shaman of the Wiradjeri tribe in Australia, he had the nonordinary experience that feathers emerged from his arms and grew into wings. Then he was taught to fly. Subsequently he "sang off his wings," and returning to ordinary reality, walked back into camp and discussed his experience.

In northernmost Scandinavia, Lapp shamans changed into wolves, bears, reindeer, and fish; and Siberian and Eskimo shamans frequently transformed themselves into wolves. Similarly, among the Yuki Indians of California, shamans who were believed to have the power to transform themselves into bears were called "bear doctors." The bear doctor of the Yuki "was really a shaman who had the bear as a guardian spirit." An incipient bear shaman "associated with actual bears, and ate their food, and at times lived with them," sometimes for an entire summer.

The ancient shamanic belief in the ability to transform oneself into an animal survived in Western Europe until the Renaissance. The Christian Church, of course, considered persons engaged in animal metamorphosis to be wizards, witches, and sorcerers, and persecuted them through the Inquisition. Yet a colleague of Galileo, the alchemist and scientist Giovanni Battista Porta, in 1562 still possessed the ancient knowledge of how to experience such a metamorphosis and published the information in his famous book, *Natural Magick*. Thus he explains how, using a hallucinogenic potion, a man would "believe he was changed into a Bird or Beast." Porta observed, "the man would seem sometimes to be changed into a fish; and flinging out his arms, would swim on the Ground: sometimes he would seem to skip up, and then to dive down again. Another would believe himself turned into a Goose, and would eat Grass, and beat the Ground with his Teeth, like a Goose: now and then sing, and endeavor to clap his Wings." Similarly, Castaneda, with the aid of a hallucinogenic mixture, reports he had the experience of becoming a crow, and that don Genaro observed that shamans can become eagles and owls.

The use of a hallucinogenic drug, however, is by no means necessary for a person to experience the metamorphosis into a bird or other animal. Dancing, accompanied by drumming, is the far more common method employed by shamans throughout much of the primitive world to achieve a shamanic state of consciousness sufficient to having the experience. The initiation of shamans among the Carib Indians of northern South America, for example, involves nighttime dancing during which the neophytes move in imitation of animals. This is part of a process of learning how to turn into animals.

But it is not just shamans and shamanic initiates who utilize dancing to metamorphose into animal forms. In many primitive cultures, anyone with a guardian spirit may use dancing as a means of evoking his alter ego. Among the Coast Salish Indians of the Northwest Coast, the winter dance season provides an opportunity for an individual to consciously become one with his power animal. "The dancer's spirit finds its dramatized expression in dance steps, tempo, movements, miens and gestures: in the sneaking pace, then flying leaps of the ferociously yelling 'warrior,' or in the swaying trot of the plump, sadly weeping 'bear mother'; in the rubber-like reptilian writhing of the 'double headed serpent' in the 'lizard' who sheds tears over his devoured offspring or in the mighty 'whale' who grabs smaller fish." Often Northwest Coast shamans doing such dancing wore special masks and accoutrements to add to the unification with their power animals. Among the Tsimshian, for example, a shaman might dance not only wearing the mask of an eagle, but also claws of copper. The desire for unity with animals of power is well illustrated by this version by Cloutier of a grizzly bear song from the Tlingit tribe of the Northwest Coast:

> Whu! Bear!
> Whu
> Whu
>
> So you say
> Whu Whu Whu!
> You come
> You're a fine young man
> You Grizzly Bear
> You crawl out of your fur
>
> You come
> I say Whu Whu Whu!
> I throw grease in the fire
> For you
> Grizzly Bear
> We're one!

Much animal-like dancing in the primitive world has as its objective the unification of power animals with the dancers, whether or not the rituals are purely shamanic in other respects. Thus the dance of the Beast Gods by the shamanistic medicine societies at Zuni Pueblo in the American Southwest bears "a strong resemblance to seances among other peoples in which the shaman is inspired, in that the Beast Gods are summoned by dancing, rattling, and drumming, and the dancers work themselves into a frenzied condition in which they imitate the actions and cries of animals." Those dancers assuming the personality of the bear may even wear actual bear paws over their hands. But this dance of the Beast Gods is more than simple imitation, since the Zuni dancer, like a North American Plains Indian doing an Eagle or Buffalo Dance, is striving to go beyond imitation to become one with the animal. Thus, the Osage Indian song series, "The Rising of the Buffalo Bull Men," emphasizes the creation of a personal consciousness of unity with the animal:

> I rise, I rise,
> I, whose tread makes the earth to rumble.
>
> I rise, I rise,
> I, in whose thighs there is strength.

I rise, I rise,
I, who whips his back with his tail when in rage.

I rise, I rise,
I, in whose humped shoulder there is power.

I rise, I rise,
I, who shakes his mane when angered.

I rise, I rise,
I, whose horns are sharp and curved.

Likewise, a Zuni dancer wearing the mask of one of the kachina gods is doing more than impersonating the kachina. Transported into an altered state of consciousness by the dancing, drumming, rattling, and whirr of bull roarers, he "becomes for the time being the actual embodiment of the spirit which is believed to reside in the mask." As one Coast Salish said, "When I dance I don't act, just follow your power, just follow the way of your power." Shamans, in dancing their guardian animal spirits, commonly not only make the movements of the power animals but also the sounds. In Siberia, native North and South America, and elsewhere, shamans make bird calls and the cries, growls, and other sounds of their animal powers when experiencing their transformations. As Lame Deer says of bear power, "We make bear sounds . . . 'Harrnh' . . ." Similarly, Castaneda growls and makes a gesture of claws in response to don Juan's advice that showing his claws is "good practice."

What Lame Deer is speaking of is not the uncontrollable possession of the Carribean Vodun cults, but rather a reaffirmation by the shaman of his oneness with his animal companion. As Eliade notes, this is "less a possession than a magical transformation of the shaman into that animal."

Among the Indians of Mexico and Guatemala, the guardian spirit is commonly known by the term, "nagual," derived from the Aztec nahualli. "Nagual" refers to both a guardian animal spirit and to the shaman who changes into that power animal (compound words derived from nahualli have the meaning of being "disguised, masked"). "Nagual" is also commonly applied in Mexico to a shaman who is capable of making such a transformation, whether he is doing it at the time or not. Thus Castaneda refers to don Juan as a nagual, in addition to speaking of the broader ramifications of the concept.

Incidentally, Castaneda contrasts the nagual with the "tonal" in a lengthy, if somewhat confusing discussion. The confusion can be somewhat dissipated if one understands that "tonal" derives from the Nahuatl or Aztec term, tonalli. This word referred especially to one's vital soul, and the sign of one's day of birth, which was frequently an animal. The tonalli was part of an elaborate calendrical system with implications of predestination, somewhat analogous to one's sign in Western astrology. Thus the tonal concept carries the implications of fate, predestination, and the destiny of one's life from birth to death. Castaneda's discussion is generally consistent with this understanding. Thus one's life experiences in ordinary reality may be believed to be determined by the tonal animal; but this animal is not the same as the nagual of the shaman, which like guardian animal spirits elsewhere is connected with the SSC and, as Castaneda implies, lies beyond ordinary reality.

A confusion between a tonal animal and the nagual animal sometimes occurs in the anthropological literature on Mexico and Guatemala. This may be due both to faulty scholarship and to the merging of the two animals in their cosmologies by some native Mexican and Guatemalan groups in colonial times.

While for some tribes it is reported that virtually every adult had a guardian spirit, as among the Nitlakapamuk Indians of British Columbia or the Twana of western Washington, the more usual situation was that not all adults possessed guardian spirits. Thus, among the North American Plains Indians, individuals frequently failed to obtain them, and as a result were usually considered to be doomed to lack power and success in life. Among the Jivaro, most adult males believed themselves to possess them, having the certain knowledge that they had succeeded in the vision quest at the sacred waterfall. It was not so essential for women to obtain them formally, because the intra-tribal feuds, the most common cause of violent death, were primarily directed at adult males rather than at women and children.

The most famous method of acquiring a guardian spirit is the vision quest or vigil conducted in a solitary wilderness location, as among the Plains tribes of North America. The Jivaro pilgrimage to a sacred waterfall is a South American example of such a vision quest. Even among the Avaro, however, the beneficial power of a guardian spirit could be acquired without going on a vision quest. Parents of a newly born infant, in fact, typically gave it a mild hallucinogen so that it could "see" and hopefully thus acquire an arutam wakani or guardian spirit. The parents, of course, wanted the baby to have as much protection as possible in order to survive into adult life. There was also a somewhat stronger hallucinogen, uchich maikua, or "children's datura," that was administered for the same purpose when the child was somewhat older, but not yet ready to undertake the vision quest at the sacred waterfall.

The Jivaro assumed that a child would probably not even reach the age of six, seven, or eight without some protection from a guardian spirit. The parents, however, could never be sure that an infant or very small child had really obtained a vision and power, so it was considered essential for a boy eventually to go on the formal vision quest to be absolutely sure he had the protection of a guardian spirit. Life was perceived as not as dangerous for females as for males in that feud-ridden society, but girls did have a smaller version of the vision quest in the forest near the house.

In North America, the Southern Okanagon of the State of Washington held a view similar to that of the Jivaro. Among the Okanagon, guardian spirits commonly were acquired involuntarily by very young children without going on a vision quest. Small children's visions were usually similar to those seen on the formal vision quest by youths and young adults. "The spirit first appeared as human, but as it departed the child saw what kind of animal it was. It might come without any forethought on the part of child or parent, and at any time of day or night." Walter Cline reports:

> Only a very precocious child would know about his guardian spirit at the age of four or five. . . . Unless he were "very smart" [even a youth or young adult] immediately forgot the vision and what the spirit had said to him, and, in most cases, had no intercourse with the spirit for a number of years. . . . In the event of serious emergency during this time, however, it was ready to help him.

In other words, it is possible for a person to have, or to have had, the past protection and power of a guardian spirit without being conscious of it. Thus, in 1957, a Jivaro shaman saw that I had a guardian spirit even though I myself was unaware of it.

To a shaman it is readily apparent that many Westerners have guardian spirits, as evidenced by their energy, good health, and other outward manifestations of their power. It is tragic, from the point of view of such a shaman, that even these power-full people are nonetheless ignorant of the source of their power and thus do not know how to utilize it fully. A related tragedy, from the same point of view, is that lethargic, ill, and dispirited Western adults have obviously lost the guardian spirits that protected them through their childhood. Worse, they do not even know that there is a method to regain them.

Calling the Beasts

Now try an exercise in which you will have a chance to get in touch with one or more of your unknown past or present guardian spirits. You probably had at least one in the past, or otherwise you would not have survived childhood's hazards and illnesses. Even if it has long since left you, the exercise should awaken your hidden memories of it. This exercise is a simple, ancient shamanic technique. One name for it is "Calling the Beasts." There are different names for it in different cultures. It is a way whereby the people of the community, through dance, evoke or get in touch with their animal aspects.

Keep in mind that a single guardian spirit can appear either in animal or human form, although most likely you will see or feel the animal aspect of your guardian spirit.

Undertake this exercise in a quiet, half-darkened room free of any furniture that might interfere with your movements. It will help if you have two good rattles (see Appendix A on drums and rattles). Do not hesitate, however, to try this exercise without waiting to acquire rattles. There are two phases in the exercise: (1) the starting dance, and (2) dancing your animal. In both dances you steadily and loudly shake a rattle in each hand, and your dancing is in time with the rattles. In all the dancing you keep your eyes half-closed. This allows you to cut down on light, and at the same time enables you to know where you are in the room.

The Starting Dance

1. Standing still and erect, face east and shake one rattle very rapidly and strongly four times. This is the signal that you are starting, ending, or making an important transition in serious shamanic work. Think of the rising sun, that ultimately brings power to all living things. (A total time of about 20 seconds.)

2. Still facing east, start shaking one rattle at a steady rate of about 150 times per minute, standing in place. Do this about half a minute to each of the cardinal directions (rotating either clockwise or counterclockwise, depending on what seems better for you). Meanwhile, think of your plant and animal relatives in all the four directions who are ready to help you. Now face east again and shake the rattle above your head at the same rate for half a minute. Think of the sun, moon, stars, and the entire universe above. Next shake the rattle toward the ground in the same way. Think of the Earth, our home. (A total time of about 3 minutes.)

3. Still facing east, take both rattles in your hands and start shaking them at the same rate as in Step 2, simultaneously dancing as if you were jogging in place to the tempo of the rattles. In this starting dance, you are giving proof of your own sincerity to the power animals, wherever they may be, by making a self-sacrifice of your own energy to them in the form of dance. This dancing is a way of praying, and of evoking the sympathy of the guardian animal spirits. In shamanism it can truly be said that you dance to raise your spirits. (A total time of about 5 minutes.)

4. Stop dancing, and repeat Step 1. This signals you are about to make a significant transition to dancing your animal.

Dancing Your Animal

5. Start shaking your rattles loudly and slowly about 60 times per minute, moving your feet in the same tempo. Move slowly and in a free form around the room, trying to pick up the feeling of having some kind of mammal, bird, fish, reptile, or combination of these. Once you pick up the sense of some such animal, concentrate on it, and slowly move your body in accordance with being that animal. You are now touching the SSC. Be open to experiencing the emotions of that animal, and don't hesitate to make cries or noises of it, if you experience the desire. By keeping your eyes half-closed you may also see the nonordinary environment in which the animal is moving, and perhaps even

see the animal as well. Being and seeing the animal commonly happen simultaneously in the SSC. (The time for this tends to average about 5 minutes.)

6. Without pausing, shift into a faster rate of rattle-shaking and movement, about 100 shakes per minute. Continue everything else as in Step 5. (The time for this tends to average about 4 minutes.)

7. Without stopping, increase your rattle-shaking to approximately 180 times per minute, continuing your dancing as before, but at a still faster rate. (The time for this usually is about 4 minutes.)

8. Stop dancing, and mentally welcome the animal to stay in your body. As you do this, shake the rattles rapidly four times, drawing them toward your chest. (Time about 10 seconds.)

9. Repeat Step 1. This is the signal that the work is ended.

For a more powerful transition into the SSC when doing the above exercise, I recommend that a drum be used in addition to the rattles. For this, you will need someone to act as your assistant to beat the drum exactly in tempo with your shaking of the rattles (for information on drums, see Appendix A). Your assistant should stand at the side of the room and not attempt to participate in any of the movements while drumming. When the drummer becomes experienced with the steps of the exercise, you may find it possible to do the animal dancing without the rattles, thereby freeing your consciousness more from ordinary reality.

Typically, Westerners "dancing their animals" discover themselves to be such creatures as Crane, Tiger, Fox, Eagle, Bear, Deer, Porpoise, and even Dragon (for there are no "mythical" animals in the SSC; Dragon is as real as the others). One thing that usually becomes clear to the dancers is that underneath our ordinary human cultural consciousness is a near-universal emotional connection with wild animal alter egos.

Keep in mind that no matter how successful you were in dancing your animal, that in itself is not proof that you still have its power. You may only be dancing a memory. A successful experience does suggest, however, that you may have at least had such a guardian spirit in the past, if not now. The dancing itself, however, is no proof in itself, one way or another.

Incidentally, no matter how fierce a guardian animal spirit may seem, its possessor is in no danger because the power animal is absolutely harmless. It is only a source of power; it has no aggressive intentions. It only comes to you because you need help.

If one wishes to maintain shamanic practice, one has to change into one's animal regularly to keep the animal contented enough to stay. This involves exercising the animal through dance, singing songs of the animal, and recognizing "big" dreams as messages from the guardian, the power animal. Dancing your animal is an important method for keeping it content and thus making it reluctant to leave you. The guardian animal spirit resident in the mind-body of a person wants to have the enjoyment of once again existing in material form. It is a trade-off, for the person gets the power of the whole genus or species of animals represented by that guardian spirit. Just as a human may want to experience nonordinary reality by becoming a shaman, so too a guardian spirit may wish to experience ordinary reality by entering the body of a living human.

Even with the best of care, as I learned from the Jivaro years ago, guardian spirits usually stay with you only a few years and then depart. So, in the course of a long, powerful life, you will have a number of them one after another, whether you know it or not.

Dancing is not the only way you can physically exercise your power animal and keep it willing to stay with you. Another way is to exercise it in wilderness areas or, lacking that, remote areas of public parks. I remember one young Westerner trained in shamanism who worked weekdays in a bookstore and on Sundays went to a regional park where he took his Cougar for lopes over the hills. No one ever stopped him, and he found it more satisfying than going to church.

Of course, there is an obvious potential problem when you transform yourself into your animal in a public place: people are not likely to understand, at least in this culture. But then, as Castaneda once told me, don Juan had a somewhat similar problem even with his Mexican Indian public. He said don Juan explained that one of the reasons he had given up using the hallucinogenic datura ointment was that Indians had taken to shooting at him when he was jumping over trees. A shaman's lot is not always a happy one.

Remember, guardian spirits are always beneficial. They never harm their possessors. And you possess the guardian spirit; it never possesses you. In other words, the power animal is a purely beneficial spirit, no matter how fierce it may appear. It is a spirit to be exercised, not exorcized.

— 22 —

Jewish Mourning Practices

Vanessa L. Ochs

When it comes to death, most American Jews, whether they are generally observant or not, gravitate toward the traditional Jewish practices for funerals, burials, and mourning. This is neither surprising nor hypocritical; death leaves many feeling "scriptless," not knowing what to do, what to say, or even what to feel. Traditional Jewish practices provide an instant and wise roadmap, giving mourners a path that leads from grief and meaninglessness toward comfort and healing.

At the moment of death, some mourners may tear their clothing (*kriyah*) as a sign of their intense grief (though some do this only at the funeral and do so in a symbolic way, with the rabbi snipping a black ribbon that has been pinned to their lapel). The mourner and anyone who learns of the death say the words *barukh dayan emet* (blessed is the true and righteous judge), meaning that God is responsible for both life and death and, though God's intentions cannot be fathomed, there is no choice but to acknowledge God's will. In some observant communities, people will follow the practice of refraining from speaking words of comfort to the mourners until the funeral has taken place. Until that time, the mourners in their most intense grief are considered inconsolable as well as thoroughly absorbed in tending to the dead and making arrangements for the funeral. In many instances, this practice is not observed, and the mourners begin to receive words and gestures of consolation immediately. David Kraemer, author of *The Meanings of Death in Rabbinic Tradition,* suggests this "flagrant disregard of Talmudic . . . prescriptions" reflects a contemporary belief that the needs of the dead are best attended to by funeral professionals; the community can take care of the emotional needs of the living.

At the occurrence of a death, a Jewish family typically notifies their rabbi (if they belong to a synagogue) and "makes arrangements"; that is, they engage the services of a funeral parlor. Funeral plans begin immediately, since burial must take place as soon as possible, preferably the next day, unless it is a Sabbath or holiday.

Attending the body immediately after death until the burial are the *shomrim* (guardians), who take shifts staying with the body and reciting psalms. Never leaving the body is a sign of respect and a reflection of older fears that the soul of the dead person is vulnerable to evil forces. In observant communities, there is a specially trained group called the *chevra kadisha,* the sacred society that performs the ritual of *tahara,* purifying the body through a set of ablutions. For the sake of modesty, a men's group cares for men who have died and a woman's group cares for women. They wash the body, gently pouring bucketsful of water over it, and they dress the body in a plain white shroud. Traditionally, a man is wrapped in his prayer shawl (*tallit*), and the ritual fringes on the *tallit* are cut. All the tasks of the *chevra kadisha* are referred to as *chesed shel emet,* acts of ultimate loving-kindness that can never be repaid. These people are respected for the sacred work they do. In communities that have no *chevra kadisha,* the work of guarding, bathing, and dressing the body is performed by the staff of the funeral parlor.

Death means a sudden burst of prescribed activity not just for the mourning family but for their Jewish community as well. Among Jews, if you are at all acquainted with the deceased or the family, it is not only appropriate for you to make some response, it is obligatory. You do not wait to be invited, and you do not justify shying away by saying, "Given that we're not that close, I didn't feel it was appropriate for me. . . ." At the very least, you will acknowledge the death by a small donation to charity in the person's memory.

Many synagogues have a Caring Committee (*gemilut hassadim*), whose role it is to notify community members of the death and to announce when and where the funeral will be held (this is sometimes done through a phone chain or automated announcement). They will specify the place where *shiva,* the days of mourning, will take place, and will let people know when it will be helpful to have people join the mourners for morning and evening prayers. As mourners are not supposed to prepare foods for themselves, volunteers are asked to prepare foods for them and deliver it to their homes. They may be asked to do errands for the family, such as taking care of children or picking up out-of-town mourners at the airport.

Typically, the family's rabbi, or the rabbi assigned by the funeral parlor, meets with the mourners (that is, the immediate family of the deceased: the father, mother, wife, husband, sister, brother, son, or daughter) in order to learn more details about the deceased, so that a proper eulogy can be delivered at the funeral. Traditionally, Jews are supposed to bury their dead in a plain pine box, a sign of humility and a confirmation of the belief that, although the soul may ascend to heaven, the physical body returns to dust. Some families, however, find the cratelike box too stark and choose to honor their dead with one of the costly, lined wooden boxes the funeral director recommends as being more "dignified." Jews are not supposed to embalm their dead or hold a viewing. Both practices are considered disrespectful to the dead person, who would be displayed without his or her awareness. Nonetheless, some Jews still choose to hold a viewing for the sake of the finality it can bring to the immediate family. And if the body is to be transported to Israel for burial there, embalming becomes necessary.

The funeral service, usually held in the chapel of a funeral parlor, is simple and stark. There are supposed to be no flowers and no music to distract from the harshness of death. Although some will still send flowers to the funeral parlor, American Jews have long been urged by their rabbis to replace this gesture with a charitable donation in memory of the deceased. Sometimes the family will receive visitors in a room just prior to the service, and although the Jewish tradition is not to console mourners before the funeral, gentle expressions of consolation are frequently shared.

At the service, there is a reading of a few psalms and prayers, quite a contrast to the Sabbath or holiday Jewish services people are familiar with that last three or more hours. The rabbi will offer a eulogy and sometimes members of the immediate family will choose to speak, a practice that is becoming more common. The coffin, which had been in front of the funeral chapel, is then placed in a hearse by pallbearers, and the mourners and those who have come to the funeral form a caravan of cars behind the hearse, as they proceed to the Jewish cemetery.

At the gravesite, which has already been prepared, there are brief prayers. Then the kaddish prayer is recited by the mourners. The kaddish makes no mention of death or of the one who has died; it is a collection of extravagant praises for God that in ancient times was recited when the Torah had been studied. Nonetheless, for many, it is the sound of this prayer, in one's own throat or one's ears, that awakens one to the finality of death. At this point, it is customary for the mourners to each take hold of a shovel and place dirt on top of the coffin after it has been lowered into the ground. The sound of dirt and rocks falling on the wooden coffin is stark and poignant, bringing home the reality of the death. In some families, the mourners will fill the grave themselves; in others, the shovelsful of dirt are symbolic. Some mourners will choose not to perform this ritual at all, as it makes death more absolutely real than they can bear. If there are tombstones for other members of the family at the cemetery, stones will be placed on them as a sign of respect and memory. When the mourners depart from the gravesite, those who have accompanied them stand in two lines, creating a path for the mourners to pass through, and the words "May God comfort you among the mourners of Zion and Jerusalem" are spoken.

When the mourners return home, they wash their hands outside their door as a gesture of purification. This is, quite literally, a threshold ritual that marks the end of one state of being and the beginning of another. Some experience the washing as making a distinction between the cemetery and death and the home and life. The mourners are served a meal called se'udat havra'ah, a meal of comfort. Eggs are always served, symbolizing the cyclical nature of life.

In this way the *shiva* period begins seven days of intense mourning. The number of days may be shorter if the funeral falls during a holiday, and fewer still if the family elects to mourn for only three days or only one. The mourners observing shiva sit on low chairs, wear no shoes, do not go to work, prepare no food for themselves, and study no Torah. Shunning vanity, men are not supposed to shave and women are not supposed to wear makeup. Mirrors in the house have been covered. Mourners are visited by those who come to sit with them, to speak about the memory of the deceased, and to pray the daily services with them, so the mourners can recite the kaddish prayer with a quorum of ten people (in liberal Jewish traditions) or ten men (in Orthodoxy). Paying a call on mourners sitting shiva is not limited to those who are very close or know the family well—anyone who knows the family at all is encouraged to stop by, as a sign of caring, respect, and concern.

At the end of the shiva period, mourners perform a ritual of going outside and walking around their house or around their block, symbolizing a gradual but inevitable return to everyday reality. Afterwards, some will observe an additional, less restrictive mourning period of thirty days (*shloshim*). Others will continue to observe eleven months of mourning practice, which may include refraining from going to plays, concerts, parties, or celebrations. Many Jews will say the kaddish prayer for eleven months either on the Sabbath or, in observant families, by going to the synagogue twice a day. From then on, *kaddish* will be recited on the anniversary of the person's death (*yahrzeit*) and at memorial services (*yizkor*) held in synagogue on certain holidays.

At the end of the mourning period (and sometimes as early as six months after the funeral) the mourners return to the cemetery for an unveiling ceremony in which a tombstone is set at the gravesite, the kaddish is recited, and once again a consolation meal is served at home. The erected stone is supposed to be modest, but a visit to American Jewish cemeteries will reveal that some families do in fact, build more extravagant tombstones to express the importance of the deceased or the prominence of the family.

Mourning American Jews consistently say that Jewish practices of mourning, however strictly or loosely they choose to follow them, are psychologically brilliant and deeply healing. I believe this accounts for the many who observe Jewish mourning practices, even when they observe no other Jewish practices. They will typically point to the wisdom of having been surrounded by a caring community of relatives and friends at a time when they might have instinctively preferred to be alone. As the term "consolation" suggests, although the mourners may feel existentially alone, they are, in fact, still members of a living community. This community shares their pain and believes that, even in the face of grief, life can go on and that the memory of the deceased will be a blessed memory.

Two of the mourning practices included here are intended for mourners and those who have come to comfort them; one concerns the way in which those who come to make a shiva call should comport themselves; the other concerns the ritual walk taken by mourners at the end of the shiva period. These rituals have been prepared by CLAL—the National Jewish Center for Learning and Leadership—an interdenominational Jewish organization that makes sacred Jewish practices available to the Jewish community, especially when those practices may be insufficiently familiar or not readily accessible.

A third mourning practice is the ritual of *taharah*, the ritual purification of the dead. Recently younger Jews have decided to take on this most noble of *mitzvot* (commandments), by becoming members of their community's volunteer burial society. This act of extreme lovingkindness, which involves bathing the body in a ritual manner and dressing it, is all the more moving and emotionally taxing when performed for someone who is known. This account by Debbie Friedman, "Bubby's Last Gift" describes a granddaughter who performed her grandmother's *tahara*.

The translation of the kaddish prayer comes from *On the Doorposts of Your House,* edited by Chaim Stern (New York: Central Conference of American Rabbis Press, 1994). The rituals for consoling mourners and for ending shiva were taken from publications of CLAL (the National Jewish Center for Learning and Leadership): *Renew the Old, Sanctify the New* (New York: CLAL, 1998)(© 1998 CLAL) and *Shehecheyanu: Reaching Each Moment* (New York: CLAL, 1999) (© 1999 CLAL). The Blessing is adapted from Rabbi Jules Harlow, ed., *A Rabbi's Manual* (n.p.: Rabbinical Assembly, 1965). The third reading comes from Debbie Friedman, "Bubby's Last Gift," in *Wrestling with the Angel: Jewish Insights on Death and Mourning,* edited by Jack Riemer (New York: Schocken, 1995).

Further Reading

Ann Brener, *Mourning and Mitzvah* (Woodstock, Vt.: Jewish Lights Publishing, 1993); Hayim Halevey Donin, *To Be a Jew: A Guide to Jewish Observance in Contemporary Life* (New York: Basic Books, 1991); Jules Harlow, *The Bond of Life: A Book for Mourners* (New York: Rabbinical Assembly, 1983); Maurice Lamm, *The Jewish Way in Death and Mourning* (New York: Jonathan David Publishers, 1969); Jack Riemer, ed., *Jewish Insights on Death and Mourning* (New York: Schocken, 1995); David Kraemer, *The Meaning of Death in Rabbinic Judaism* (New York: Routledge, 2000).

Mourner's Kaddish

Let the glory of God be extolled, let God's great name be hallowed in the world whose creation God willed. May God rule in our own day, in our own lives, and in the life of all Israel, and let us say: Amen.

Let God's great name be praised for ever and ever.

Beyond all the praises, songs and adorations that we can utter is the Holy One, the Blessed One, whom yet we glorify, honor and exalt. And let us say: Amen.

For us and for all Israel, may the blessing of peace and the promise of life come true, and let us say: Amen.

May the One who causes peace to reign in high heavens, cause peace to descend on us, on all Israel, and all the world, and let us say: Amen.

May the Source of Peace send peace to all who mourn, and comfort to all who are bereaved. Amen.

Making a Shiva Call

When we make a *shiva* call, we sometimes worry: "But what shall I say?" We remind ourselves: "Trust and be patient. The right words—which may be no words at all, just a rich holding silence—will come from the heart.

MEDITATION

Dear God, help me to ease the pain of those who mourn by letting them know that my heart is breaking along with theirs. May my presence lessen their loneliness and bring comfort.

RITUAL

(When you make a *shiva* call)
Let the mourners initiate the conversation. Let them choose what you will talk about or let them choose silence. You may want to ask to hear stories about the person who has died or you can tell a story that would honor him or her. You are not expected to stay too long. Often, a brief visit is fine. As you leave, you may wish to speak the ancient wise words, "May God comfort you among the mourners of Israel and Zion," or more simply, "May you be comforted."

BLESSING

Hamakom y'nachem etkhem b'tokh sh'ar avelei tzion v'yerushalayim.
May God comfort you among the mourners of Israel and Zion.
Tinachamu min hashamayim.
May your comfort come from Heaven.

TEACHING

Moses said to the Lord: "Please, O Lord, I have never been a man of words. . ."
and the Lord said. . . "Who gives speech?. . . . Is it not I?. . . . Now go, and I
will be with you as you speak." (Exodus 4:10–12)

A man dies in the neighborhood of Rabbi Judah. Since the family had no
friends close by, the Rabbi went to them for seven days with ten of his students
and friends. In doing this, he comforted the mourners (Babylonian Talmud:
Shabbat 152).

Ending Shiva

MOVING OUT OF MOURNING AND BACK INTO LIFE

It is a custom that when *shiva* (the period of mourning) ends, the mourners
leave their house and walk around the block. The first step out the door is
surely symbolic of the return to the larger world outside of hearth and home
which, for a week, was a holding place for very wounded hearts. In their
home, the mourners were not permitted to greet or be greeted by their visitors,
a harsh rule, cutting through the pleasantries and to the bone of things. A living room without greetings makes the abruptness of human presence and
absence visceral. Now, stepping outside their home for the first time in a week,
the mourners may greet and be greeted by others they meet along the way. Terribly jarring at first, in the fullness of time, being woven back into a less heavy
world will become second nature.

MEDITATION

May it be your will that I slowly accept your comfort into my heart, O Lord.
Help me to return to your broken world by greeting all whom I meet with
"Shalom" (wholeness and peace) and wishing them "Shalom" as we depart.
Eternal one whose name is peace, grant my heart healing and shalom.

May the one who grants peace and wholeness above grant peace and wholeness upon us and upon all Israel, and let us say: Amen.

RITUAL

At the conclusion of *shiva*, the mourners leave their house and walk around
the block. Returning back home does not mean that mourning and being
comforted are over, but it does signify that the time has come to restore
connections to a living world and to begin to seek healing of one's broken
heart.

BLESSING

(As you end *shiva* and leave your home)
Almighty God, master of Mercy, healer of the brokenhearted, let neither death nor sorrow have dominion over us. Grant us comfort, strength, and consolation to those who mourn. May we always cherish what is imperishable in _____'s life. Bless this family with love and peace, that we may serve You with all our hearts. May_____'s memory inspire us to deeds of loving kindness. And let us say, Amen.

(As you return to your home)
Blessed is the one who comforts me, deepens my memory of my loved one and who helps me return to life.

TEACHING

Your loving kindness sustains the living. . .(*Amidah*)

> Your sun will not go down again
> Your moon will not depart;
> For the Eternal One will be your light forever,
> And your days of mourning ended.
> (Isaiah 60:20)

Saying hello and goodbye are so often covers for the many things that we would prefer not to say or don't feel safe saying. In the *shiva* house, we learn to be silent or to say what we mean.

> *Shalom aleikhem*

May you know wholeness and peace.

Bubby's Last Gift

She was so rigid. It was unlike her. There was a time when she was free and easy and open. When I touched her, she didn't respond to me at all. Her smile was gone, her touch was cold. She would not look at me. And no matter how loudly I called to her, she would not answer me.

It was hard to be angry with her. After all, this was all beyond her control. She would have been different if she could have been. I know that.

Once she was five feet two. She was only about four feet eight now. She was ninety-two. Soon she would be ninety-three.

She had put on some weight since she had stopped walking. She had forgotten her routine. Her body had more wrinkles than years. One knew by looking that this was a body that had endured years of challenge and hard times. One could see that perseverance and determination kept her alive. It filtered down to all of us as well.

Though our wrinkles were not yet showing, we were who we were because of her.

She was so cold. I guess they kept her in the refrigerator. It was hard to imagine that she didn't need a blanket or a sweater or something to keep her warm. I wondered if she was even there. I think that she had finally left to go be with all of the family and friends who she so loyally and routinely blessed in Gan Eden every Shabbat as she blessed the candles.

I have often stood at the kitchen sink preparing dinner. I have scrubbed the vegetables clean to make certain there was no mud and have attempted to use a special solution from the health-food store that would neutralize and ingest any toxic chemicals present.

I have stood at the sink night after night in preparation for bed. First I flossed, then I put toothpaste on my toothbrush, and soap on my hands and face, and washed myself so that I would be fresh for bed.

I have often snuggled with my dog and found a flea or two, and in a frantic neurotic moment, I have run her into the shower with me and covered her with herbal antiflea shampoo to suffocate the fleas and attempt to make the eggs very unhappy.

It was December 1992. It was not time for bed, there were no insecticides present, there were no fleas. Bubby had died.

I had called the mortuary to make arrangements for Bubby's Funeral. I explained that she was yo go back to Utica, New York, that she was not to travel on Shabbat, and that she was to have *taharah*. They charged $175 for the *taharah,* but I did not care about the money. There was nothing too good for my Bubby. I knew that this was a mitzvah and that it was appropriate to charge for such a service.

I found out also that the Palm Springs "*Taharah* Queen" did the *taharah* herself and when she finished, she called the undertakers to help her with the body. This was not acceptable to me. Bubby was going to have a kosher *taharah* even if I had to do it myself.

I called my friend Devorah Jacobson, who was a rabbi. She had been part of a Hevra Kadisha in St. Louis. I asked her if she would help me. She said, "It would be an honor."

"Devorah," I said, Would it be okay if my mom and I helped you?" She told me that it would be fine. Mom said she would do it and arrived at the funeral home the next morning to help. Two other close friends joined us. We would need at least four people to do this.

When I was little, I walked upstairs every morning to help Bubby get dressed. She wore a bra that had about a hundred fifty hooks and eyes. For her it was an arthritic nightmare, but I helped her fasten her bra every morning. It was a big job, but I always got my reward. I got to stay upstairs and have oatmeal with Bubby and Zadie every morning. I can only imagine how she managed all those years that we were separated.

The *taharah* was to begin. "Put on rubber gloves," they said. I didn't want to do it. There was nothing of which I was afraid. My Bubby was not diseased, she was dead. I put the gloves on at their insistence. They said that you never know what you might pick up in a hospital.

"Bubby," I said, If I do anything to humiliate you or cause you embarrassment during your *taharah,* I ask your forgiveness in advance. I ask that you know that I would never do anything to cause you shame or humiliation or enbarrassment."

Bubby said nothing to any of us. We all knew that she understood that we were there to help make her passage one of gentleness and comfort.

We had three very large pails filled with water. We read psalms, we read *Eishet Chayil* ("A Woman of Valor"), and poured the water from the head down to the feet as we held her and whispered, "*Taharah* he," "She is pure." We did it again and again. I took off the rubber gloves, figuring that throughout the course of history they did not have such gloves. I wanted to touch her, and I knew that God would not only understand but would keep me from contracting any disease.

As the water washed down her body, it splashed on our aprons and clothes and the floor. I flashed on what it was that I was washing away. I continued to recite, "*Taharah* he." I knew full well that the need for purification had nothing to do with the way Bubby lived or behaved. I winced as we took the third bucket of water. It was getting close to being finished and I did not want it to be over. I did not want her to go away. I continued to recite, "*Taharah* he."

She bathed me when I was little. She dried me and put the towel over my head and rubbed my head and chanted, "Where did Debbie go?" And I said, "There she is!" I was struck by the awareness of what was to come. I would never find her again from beneath a towel, or putting on a bra, or making my oatmeal. I would never watch her meditate or stretch or walk in her Nikes. I would nver hear her say to me, "Honey, I don't ever want to be a burden to you," or, "The old gray mare, she ain't what she used to be," or, "I'm having a hankering for something sweet," or, "Honey, when it comes my time to go, God will take me." Where did Bubby go? There she is. . . .

There she is. We took the towels and dried her. I wanted to put some powder and hand cream on her, but she did not need it where she was going.

Every part of her was dried now. We opened the package wrapped in cellophane. Out came three pieces: a shirt, and pants with "feeselach," little feet, attached. They were made of linen. They resembled Dr. Denton's pajamas. They were simple and not something that one would find at their local Bloomie's or Nordstrom's. They had a character all their own. The third piece was a bonnet to cover her head.

One arm at a time, one leg at a time. I thought: These were the arms that once cradled me, that kept me safe when I was terrified. These were the legs that walked with me and taught me to keep moving and trying even when it hurts. These were the legs that said, "You must always go forward." These were the little hands that always reached back to me when I reached to them— the same hands that "packed" my tushy when I stuck a napkin in the Shabbat candles and started a little fire in the house one Friday night.

Where did Bubby go?

I wanted to keep her false teeth. I loved them. I used to love them in my bathroom at night when she stayed with me. She told me that when she wanted to diet, she took them out so she wouldn't eat. Unfortunately, the Hala- kah said that they had to be with her. I could not keep them. Eating with Bubby was like being in the percussion section of the symphony orchestra. Those teeth, though functional, were very noisy. For every bite she took, we could get up and dance the samba.

It was time. We were almost finished dressing her.

In 1978, the man she married after Zadie's death had died. A week later, I received a phone call from a woman. Out of the blue, she told me that she was the granddaughter of a friend of Bubby's and that the two grandmothers were to arrive in Houston that evening. I though that it was a joke, but it wasn't. That evening, I picked her up at the airport.

I had a one-bedroom apartment. She slept with me in a queensize bed. The first day she was there, I was awakened suddenly by a set of seventy-eight-year-old gums sunk into my biceps. "Are you awake?" she said. I said, "Bubby, what are you doing?" She said, "I used to bite you all the time when you were a little girl."

I said, "Bubby, what time is it?" She answered, "Four-thirty. I have to medi- tate. Meditate with me. All you have to do is say, 'One, one, one.' Your sister Barbara taught me how to do it. Come on, it's good for you."

My sister had taught her "omm." Bubby did her own variations on a theme. Her arrival at my home reestablished our relationship as it had been when she and Zadie lived upstairs on Baker Avenue.

In 1980 she had a heart attack. We sent her to Pritkin. She walked three miles every day. She did her stretching and her volunteer work. She went three days a week and on Shabbat to the Home for the Aged, where most of the resi- dents were her age or older.

I would ask her to come visit me and her response was always, "Honey, if I am not at the home, the volunteers don't give the people the right Pokeno cards and the people are all confused. The volunteers don't help the residents with the Kiddush wine and cake. If they are not helped, they spill all over. They count on me. I'll come see you soon, but better you should come here."

When we were together, we walked every day. I ran from her and then back to her. And so continued our exercise routine. One day I lost her in the park. I told her where to turn around so that she could meet me, but she kept going.

Every jogger in Balboa Park had his eyes out for her. My hubby, the Queen of Balboa Park.

We sent my aunt out to look for her. Given that they were from the same gene pool, it came as no surprise to any of us: my aunt got lost as well. Both were well exercised.

On our walks together we would talk about ideas and feelings. I said, "Bubby, you and I need to talk about what you want when you die. You have to tell me so that I make certain that you have exactly what you want."

"I want it kosher," she said."

"You want *taharah*?"

"Yes."

"Does it bother you to talk about it?"

"Honey, when it comes my time to go, it's my time to go. God will take me when He's ready."

We put her into the coffin. I kissed her forehead just as she had done to me all of my life. I did not want her to go. I was flooded with memories but I would not cry. She did not like it when I cried. I was intent upon honoring her ways. These were, after all, her last moments.

When I turned to walk out of the room, I turned back one more time to see her. I talked to her under my breath and said, "I stayed as long as I could, Bubby. I was with you until the last possible moment. You will be with me forever, in every song and every thought and every act of loving kindness that I may muster up in my life. You taught me what I know about love. It felt funny to do *taharah* on you, Bubby, you were so pure. I'll miss you."

The undertaker waited for us to leave the room. In his funereal voice he asked, "How will you be paying for this?" Jokingly, I said, "Do you take Visa? I would love to get the mileage." He said yes. I could hear Bubby laughing at my having gotten mileage for her funeral arrangements. She loved a bargain. She loved life.

Some think that dead bodies are frightening. Some people flinch at the thought of touching or being in the presence of a dead body. I believe that the fear arises from the confrontation with our own mortality. There are those who have the same response to live bodies. The thought of closeness, the thought of touching or being touched either physically or emotionally by another human being is frightening. This fear may be connected to the idea of loss. The fear of death and the fear of life may be one and the same: that a being suddenly disappears from the realm of our physical existence may be more than we care to struggle with. This idea of potential loss may rule our lives and even keep us at a distance from the relationships we want most in our lives.

There was a great comfort in knowing that for the first time in my life I could do something for someone who could not say, "Thank you." For me, this was a special gift. My life has not been the same since then. I am aware of the fact that caring for the dead is the highest mitzvah that one may perform, but it seems that another lesson has to do with the notion of *kal v'chomer* (how much the more so!) If one is capable of giving to one who is dead, how much more so to those still in life. This insight was Bubby's gift to me.

— 23 —

The Latter-day Saint Word of Wisdom

Jana Kathryn Riess

Among the general American population, the Church of Jesus Christ of Latter-day Saints is probably better known for its dietary restrictions than for its distinctive beliefs. Mormons abstain from alcohol, tobacco, nonprescription drugs, and hot caffeinated drinks, such as coffee and tea. Mormons call their health code the "Word of Wisdom."

Joseph Smith received the Word of Wisdom as a divine revelation in 1833, when the Mormons were living in Kirtland, Ohio. Mormon legend states that Joseph's wife, Emma Hale Smith, detested the brethren's habit of chewing (and spitting) tobacco during church meetings. She approached Joseph and complained; he in turn inquired of God whether tobacco was appropriate for the Saints. The revelation he received addresses not only the use of tobacco but other health issues as well, such as wine, hard liquor, beer, meat eating, and herbal remedies.

Although the revelation occurred in 1833 and was duly recorded, Mormons of the nineteenth century did not abide by its precepts as strictly as Mormons do today. In fact, its recommendations were largely ignored. Coffee, tea, and tobacco were among the Mormons' few indulgences when they embarked on their perilous trek westward in 1847; indeed, each pioneer family was advised to bring along for the journey a pound of coffee, a pound of tea, and a gallon of alcohol. Brigham Young, who succeeded Joseph Smith as prophet and president of the church, periodically attempted to curb intemperate habits among the Mormons but conceded that alcohol was sometimes necessary for medicinal purposes. Young also chewed tobacco until 1860. Even after he had abandoned tobacco himself, he made allowances for moderate use by others, encouraging Mormon men to use small portions and chew in private. On one occasion, he requested that tobacco chewers wait until leaving the Tabernacle before opening their stash. After the meeting, Young said, they could chew a double portion.

Young and other leaders preached moderation but rarely demanded total abstinence. Many church leaders partook of wine, for example, but they rejected drunkenness, disfellowshiping or even excommunicating those who abused alcohol. Moderate enjoyment was accepted. Pointing to the revelation's phrase "not by commandment or constraint," they maintained that individual Mormons needed to abide by their own consciences about such matters. This attitude began to change around the turn of the century. A few church leaders then asserted that members needed to abstain entirely from liquor, tobacco, coffee, and tea. Others, such as Lorenzo Snow (president of the Quorum of the Twelve Apostles), added that the Word of Wisdom required restrictions on meat eating (see verses 12–15).

The Mormon discussion about the revelation's provisions mirrored a temperance debate that became increasingly important to other Americans in the first two decades of this century. As Prohibition gathered momentum in Washington, Mormons in Utah began to emphasize total abstinence from alcohol as a core tenet of the Word of Wisdom. In 1906, church leaders began to use water instead of wine for the sacrament, a practice that continues in Mormon wards to the present day (despite the revelation's specific recommendation that the sacrament drink should be "pure wine of the vine, of your own make"). In 1908, the president of the Church publicly endorsed Prohibition. In 1921, the Church instituted a requirement that all temple-going Mormons keep the Word of Wisdom. By this time, the restrictions on meat eating had dropped out of the health code, which now eschewed alcohol (including both beer and wine), tobacco, tea, coffee, and other drugs. Today, many Mormons do not imbibe caffeine, though this is still a matter of individual conscience, as is the consumption of herbal tea.

Historian Jan Shipps has proposed that the Word of Wisdom took on greater significance in the twentieth century as the Mormon understanding of the Kingdom of God palpably shifted. Early Saints, Shipps explains, resided in sacred time and sacred space; their identity as "God's peculiar people" was corporately defined. They had little need of external behavioral codes, since they "lived so clearly in the kingdom." As once-fundamental elements of Mormonism, such as the practice of polygamy or the commitment to a Mormon theocracy, had to be abandoned at the close of the nineteenth century, Mormon leaders began to emphasize obedience to laws of tithing, temple attendance, and of course dietary choices. "God's peculiar people" could remain chosen, special, set apart, through living the Word of Wisdom. Today, adherence to the Word of Wisdom is one of the most significant commitments Mormons make. It broadcasts their religious identity to others, reminds them of beliefs held, and connects them to the increasingly global Mormon community.

In addition to its spiritual and sociological implications, contemporary Mormons stand to reap considerable health benefits for abiding by the Word of Wisdom. Numerous studies have demonstrated that orthodox Mormons can expect a life span which is, on average, approximately a full decade longer than that of other Americans. In 1997, a UCLA study claimed that the Mormon death rate from cancer and cardiovascular disease was half the national average. Mormons see this longevity as a fulfillment of the revelation's promise: "And all saints who remember to keep and do these sayings . . . shall receive health in their navel and marrow to their bones" (v. 18).

The passages printed here are from the Revelation given through Joseph Smith at Kirtland, Ohio, February 27, 1833, in *The Doctrine and Covenants* (Salt Lake City: Church of Jesus Christ of Latter-day Saints, 1981); and Shirley R. Warren, "I Tried to Quite Dozens of Times," *Ensign* (March 1996), p. 65.

Further Reading

Thomas Alexander, "The Word of Wisdom: From Principle to Requirement," *Dialogue: A Journal of Mormon Thought* 14, no. 3 (Autumn 1981): 78–88; Lester Bush, *Health and Medicine among the Latter-Day Saints* (New York: Crossroad, 1993); Clyde Ford, "The Origin of the Word of Wisdom," *Journal of Mormon History* 24, no. 2 (Fall 1998): 129–54; Robert J. McCue, "Did the Word of Wisdom Become a Commandment in 1851?" *Dialogue: A Journal of Mormon Thought* 14, no. 3 (Autumn 1981): 66–77.

Doctrine and Covenants, Section 89

1. A word of wisdom, for the benefit of the council of high priests, assembled in Kirtland, and the church, and also the saints in Zion—
2. To be sent greeting; not by commandment or constraint, but by revelation and the word of wisdom, showing forth the order and will of God in the temporal salvation of all saints in the last days—
3. Given for a principle with promise, adapted to the capacity of the weak and the weakest of all saints, who are or can be called saints.
4. Behold, verily, thus saith the Lord unto you: In consequence of evils and designs which do and will exist in the hearts of conspiring men in the last days, I have warned you, and forewarn you, by giving unto you this word of wisdom by revelation—
5. That inasmuch as any man drinketh wine or strong drink among you, behold it is not good, neither meet in the sight of your Father, only in assembling yourselves together to offer up your sacraments before him.
6. And behold, this should be wine, yea, pure wine of the grape of the vine, of your own make.
7. And again, strong drinks are not for the belly, but for the washing of your bodies.
8. And again, tobacco is not for the body, neither for the belly, and is not good for man, but is an herb for bruises and all sick cattle, to be used with judgment and skill.
9. And again, hot drinks are not for the body or belly.
10. And again, verily I say unto you, all wholesome herbs God hath ordained for the constitution, nature, and use of man—

11. Every herb in the season thereof, and every fruit in the season thereof; all these to be used with prudence and thanksgiving.

12. Yea, flesh also of beasts and of the fowls of the air, I, the Lord, have ordained for the use of man with thanksgiving; nevertheless they are to be used sparingly;

13. And it is pleasing unto me that they should not be used, only in times of winter, or of cold, or famine.

14. All grain is ordained for the use of man and of beasts, to be the staff of life, not only for man but for the beasts of the field, and the fowls of heaven, and all wild animals that run or creep on the earth;

15. And these hath God made for the use of man only in times of famine and excess of hunger.

16. All grain is good for the food of man; as also the fruit of the vine; that which yieldeth fruit, whether in the ground or above the ground—

17. Nevertheless, wheat for man, and corn for the ox, and oats for the horse, and rye for the fowls and for swine, and for all beasts of the field, and barley for all useful animals, and for mild drinks, as also other grain.

18. And all saints who remember to keep and do these sayings, walking in obedience to the commandments, shall receive health in their navel and marrow to their bones;

19. And shall find wisdom and great treasures of knowledge, even hidden treasures;

20. And shall run and not be weary, and shall walk and not faint.

21. And I, the Lord, give unto them a promise, that the destroying angel shall pass by them, as the children of Israel, and not slay them. Amen.

I Tried to Quit Dozens of Times

As a young woman, I stopped going to church and later acquired a smoking habit that took control of my life. The years passed, and I married and was blessed with eight children. Seeing their need for the gospel, I sent each of them to Primary and Sunday School as they became old enough to go on their own. As they grew older, however, they began noticing that I stayed home while other parents attended church with their children. Soon it became clear to me that to keep them going to church, I had to go with them.

Because I'd been taught the Word of Wisdom as a young girl but did not abide by it, it was uncomfortable for me to go to church. The Church meetings I began to attend enkindled a desire in me to be a clean and active participant. I wanted to quit smoking. My non-member husband had quit smoking twice, once for a year and then for good. I had tried to quit dozens of times, but the cravings of my tobacco-conditioned body created an obstacle seemingly larger than any mountain I had ever climbed.

One day when my older children were at school and the little ones were sleeping, I knelt at the foot of my bed to ask the Lord's help in overcoming the habit that held me prisoner. As I prayed, a man's name came into my mind. Brother Fred Lisonbee had come to our home once as a stake missionary, but there was no reason I could think of that his name should mean anything to me. Yet his name refused to leave my mind. I decided that perhaps there was a reason for his name persisting in my mind. I got up and called him.

Dr. Lisonbee was a busy chiropractor; I realized that just as he answered the telephone. I suddenly felt foolish. He said he remembered me and asked what he could do for me.

"Brother Lisonbee, I am trying very hard to quit smoking, but I just can't do it. I was hoping you might have a suggestion."

Without hesitation, he said, "Why don't you ask the Lord to take away the desire to smoke?"

I was stunned. Unable to think of a reply, I thanked him and returned to my bedroom and thought about what he had said.

Finally I knelt again and prayed for my desire to smoke to be taken away. During my prayer, I felt as if someone were pouring a big pitcher of warm water over my head, the water rushing down, over, and through me. As the pitcher emptied, I was filled. Weeping, I got up from my knees and knew that somehow I was different; something wonderful had happened.

My desire to smoke and the seemingly unyielding addiction to tobacco were washed away as if I had never smoked. From that time on I attended church with my children. Now they attend church with their children. I am eternally grateful to a Heavenly Father who helps us as we strive to repent and keep his commandments.

Imagining: The Unseen World

24

Early Christian Radio and Religious Nostalgia

Philip Goff

A visit to the famed corner of Hollywood and Vine in Los Angeles today will demonstrate that the golden age of radio has not only passed, it has been entombed. Huge theaters that once held audiences enthralled as radio stars stood before them and beamed dramas, comedies, and musicals out to millions of listeners now stand as empty testaments to a bygone era. Nowhere in that neighborhood do the ghosts speak as loudly as at 1750 Argyle Street, one block northeast of the famous intersection. There sits what initially appears to be an abandoned Hollywood set on two acres, including a small rural-looking church, complete with a steeple and green shutters, hidden among a confused, overgrown garden of palms, banana trees, huge balls of pampas grass, and trailing roses—all set on a tiny hill across the street from the Capitol Records building, which was created to resemble a stack of LPs, itself an obsolete survival of an earlier period in entertainment. But this is no movie set. It is what remains of the once-vibrant radio phenomenon called the Little Country Church of Hollywood.

Not surprisingly, the Little Country Church's origins are in the country. Its founder, William B. Hogg, was a rural Southern minister whose provincialism was challenged by spending a year in France as a chaplain during the First World War. Wounded, he landed in the hospital with homesick and often dying American soldiers. To entertain them, he made the sound of hoof beats with his hollow hands and spun down-home tales that comforted the young men far from home. He discovered that these positive stories could boost their morale and strengthen their spirits, as well as enable him to speak directly to the inner needs of the wounded.

Hogg returned with a greater vision of Christian ministry. By the mid 1920s, he had joined Paul Rader at the Chicago Gospel Tabernacle, which was the center of a storm of evangelistic activities in the Windy City. Rader was among the first to take advantage of radio as a medium to proselytize listeners; he developed a daily four-hour program of religious music—jazzed up to attract members of the flapper age, of course—as well as preaching and prayer on Chicago's most powerful stations. In fact, Rader and his Tabernacle musicians put together the largest selection of Christian radio in the nation long before the advent of today's religious-owned stations. In this setting, Hogg developed the radio character of a simple, rural preacher interested in commonsensical religious values. Drawing on his experience in wartime France, he captured radio audiences with his moral stories of the simple ways of country folk.

When Hogg moved to Los Angeles in 1931 to direct Rader's new Gospel Tabernacle there, he found himself in a city filling up with rural folk seeking work and already full of broadcasting opportunities. Los Angeles was in the midst of a population boom that had started at the turn of the century with the arrival of railroads, increased during the "Roaring 'Twenties'" with Hollywood's emergence, and that now found fulfillment in the "California dreams" of many Midwestern and Southern farmers who fell prey to drought and the Great Depression. Not surprisingly, Hogg used the growing medium of radio to his advantage. "He was a master at telling stories," remembered one associate, "but it was not just the stories he told—it was the way he told them." Employing both humor and pathos, as well as a love for the Bible, "His manner caught on like wildfire in the Southland, and people in the Christian world began to love him like everyone loved Will Rogers in those days."

But Hogg did not rely merely on his own abilities. He wisely employed several talented musicians who, over time, became one of the top two quartets in a city built on entertainment. With Rudy Atwood at piano and a quartet consisting of Thurl Ravenscroft (later the voice of Tony the Tiger and the Jolly Green Giant), Al Harlan, Bill Days, and William McDougall, Hogg led a half-hour daily broadcast full of uplifting music and short messages. Pianist Atwood later recalled, "Because of his rising popularity and his generosity in sharing the limelight, he was as much responsible as anyone for bringing the musical part of evangelicalism . . . to the attention of the public."

After two years together, Hogg informed his costars that he intended to create a new type of program outside the aegis of the Los Angeles Tabernacle. It was a risky move. There were very few successful religious broadcasts in those days, and this one would be like no other. He planned to recreate a country community in rural Tennessee through music and a skit that played out the lives of villagers. Local station managers were unimpressed. Given the hard times, they believed, listeners wanted positive programming filled with dance music to lift aching spirits. Finally Hogg convinced the management at KFAC that his would, indeed, be an entertaining and uplifting program. It would evoke happy memories, feelings of bygone days for those who now struggled to fit into urban Los Angeles. The music would be soothing and optimistic, not dull and dreary-sounding "church music." Likewise, the skits would be humorous as well as moralistic.

The problems before Hogg were the same ones faced by other conservative Protestants hoping to use the radio waves to spread the gospel. As a response to the myriad of religious stations that applied for licenses in the early, heady days of radio, the Department of Commerce in 1927 attempted to place restrictions on programs that could too easily slip from public service to money-making ventures. Soon a federal commission was created to oversee radio, including religious broadcasting. Working with the Federal Council of Churches in New York, the commission created a required "sustaining time" for each station and network, which gave free radio time to mainline Protestants, Catholics, and Jews. Those who were too conservative for mainline denominations, therefore, were cut out of the free access to airtime on the major stations and networks throughout the country. Instead, conservatives had to buy time as they could afford and as they were allowed by local stations. By the early 1930s, however, even this practice had come under fire by the Federal Council of Churches, and the two major networks, NBC and CBS, began to consider whether they would continue to accept any paid for religious programming. If Hogg's program was to survive in this continually restrictive medium, he would have to find a way to please both his conservative listeners and his moderate and liberal broadcasters.

And so, in January 1933, Hogg and his quartet began broadcasting their daily program set in an imaginary rural town where neighbors knew one another, cared for one another, and helped each other through crises. Posing as Parson Josiah Hopkins—the character he had developed in Chicago radio—Hogg used his wife to play Sarah Hopkins, his two daughters to play instruments, and Atwood and the quartet to sing, play the parts of townfolk, and create sound effects of horses, buggies, and various farm animals. The cast arrived each morning at 7:30 A.M. to practice their songs and the skit before going on live radio at 8:00. The program was such a huge success throughout the city that the program went national on the Columbia Broadcasting System in April 1934. At the height of the Depression, it drew audiences who heard in its songs and conversations a bygone era when times were better. Children, who enjoyed morning programming before school, listened as they ate breakfast, urged by their parents to take to heart the lessons of the show. With such an enviable schedule, the national listenership—although impossible to quantify today— doubtless was extremely high. Religion now sat comfortably next to children's shows, baseball, and soap operas at the dawning of radio's golden age.

Each program ran according to a set script. The quartet sang the first verse of "Come to the Church in the Wildwood," a favorite among displaced conservative Protestants who pined for the old days:

> How sweet on a clear, Sabbath morning,
> To list' to the clear ringing bell;
> Its tones so sweetly calling,
> Oh, come to the church on the hill.

Then, Strollin' Tom—played by Thurl Ravenscroft, blessed with the most reso- nant bass voice in Hollywood—welcomed listeners by describing the rural town and the church's central position. He then directed the audience to listen in on the conversation of Josiah and Sarah Hopkins in their buggy, pulled by Dan the horse, as the couple talked about recent problems in the village en route to church. Along the way, they might stop to talk with others—all setting up the theme for the Parson's message to come. They usually arrived at church just in time to hear the first quartet number; then Parson Hopkins would request another song or two, telling a short anecdote—usually a moving one—about why that song is meaningful to him. Finally, the minister would give a five-minute message that drove home a nonsectarian religious truth most audiences would readily agree with: that helping others is really good for your own state of mind; that it is best to "throw away the scraps of life and let the chickens have them" rather than obsess on bad things; that your environment is not everything, rather what lies deep in your heart is what matters most; that some things cannot be learned from a book but are known only by intuition. All of this in only fifteen minutes each morning.

Given the times, it is miraculous that Hogg could get his program on the national CBS network and keep it there until his death three years later. After all, CBS was the very first network to ban sectarian and paid-for religious programming. Alert to the Federal Council of Churches' warnings against programming that was anything but mainline Protestantism, CBS agreed to keep sectarian Protestant shows away from the free time allotted each week for religious broadcasting, as well as to proscribe religious groups from buying time—in a sense, from being their own sponsor. But Hogg, a fundamentalist, had ingeniously toned down his message to a "feel good" show that struck the distant chords of memory for rural believers feeling the pain of dislocation during the Depression. Many of the songs used were revivalist standards, but only the first verse was sung, thus avoiding theological controversy with mainline churches. Humming replaced the remaining two or three verses in each song—thereby giving those sectarian believers "in the know" the opportunity to sing along, all the while explicitly following CBS's strict policy.

It worked. In fact, the show worked so well that many local listeners in Los Angeles began to clamor for a real "Little Country Church" to attend—one that replicated the rural oasis to which they escaped each morning with Josiah and Sarah Hopkins, and villagers Lige Guyton, Abe Snodgrass, Lem Gupton, and Jerry Potlucks—all members of the Goose Creek Quartet. Soon enough, they procured the property on Argyle Street and created the Little Country Church of Hollywood, complete with meandering sidewalks and climbing rose vines and a full-service radio studio inside the building. Now, not only could listeners enjoy hearing their rural friends each morning, they could join them on Sunday mornings for service. What had been merely a broadcast appealing to distant memories became, in fact, a church congregation seeking to recreate the past.

Umberto Eco referred to this phenomenon as "hyperreality," that is, part of the American imagination that seeks the real but to attain it must fabricate the fake— witness wax museums of the Last Supper, complete with hymns in the background. Yet the reproduction is experienced as if it were real, resulting in dedication to it as the ideal. In this sense, then, the Little Country Church of Hollywood helped to sustain the romantic revivalist tradition that characterized evangelicalism during this period. As Eric Hobsbawm points out, such created traditions hold "a set of practices, normally governed by overtly or tacitly accepted rules of a ritual or symbolic nature, which seek to inculcate certain values and norms of behavior by repetition, which automatically implies continuity with the past." Such traditions of imagination were especially meaningful at the height of the Depression.

How did Hogg accomplish all this in such difficult times? First, the times themselves were conducive for the program. With truckloads of "Dust Bowl" migrants arriving in California daily—one of the largest in-nation migrations of the twentieth century—there existed a built-in audience for such a program. Hogg could readily employ the rural vernacular, given his own Southern background. One popular topic for discussion was food, which tied these migrants to their region as much as any folkway could. Whether it was fried chicken, or boiled greens, or biscuits and gravy, the residents of Goose Creek could invariably make listeners' mouths water and connect with their ways. So, too, Hogg entered their shared memories through language. Utilizing contractions, subject-verb disagreement, and colloquial phrases, the Parson could communicate directly to thousands of listeners immediately. But Hogg was not above poking fun at the rural ignorance of larger political issues by introducing national affairs into the village's small world. Of course, the characters usually misunderstood what was under discussion. Such scripts appealed to both urbanites, who took pleasure in the stereotype, as well as those just off the farm, for they enjoyed laughing at themselves as they sought to understand and cope with their new lives.

Second, he purposefully hewed a middle path that appealed to both displaced conservative Protestants and less sectarian listeners. The hymns are a perfect example. As each show opened with the same song, those conservatives familiar with all four verses sang along and were transported back to their roots.

> There's a church in the valley by the wildwood,
> No lovelier spot in the dale;
> No place is so dear to my childhood,
> As the little brown church in the vale . . .
> From the church in the valley by the wildwood,
> When day fades away into night,
> I would fain from this spot of my childhood
> Wing my way to the mansions of light.

Those unfamiliar with the song, who simply liked the characters, enjoyed the "morality tale" involved in each story. Never was the message heavy-handed. Yet, those inside the movement could easily pick up on the "insider's language" that defined fundamentalism during this period. By avoiding doctrinal debates and instead emphasizing positive principles with which virtually all Protestants, Catholics, and Jews would concur, Hogg took his show to the pinnacle of success on a national network.

But it was Hogg's use of nostalgia that most obviously confronted the listener. The show literally dripped with it. And whether one were at home in the city or new to it, enough of the romantic tradition of "down home," "heartland," and "simple times" remained to draw thousands of daily listeners. To the modern ear, these might sound like clichés. Constant references to rose gardens, grandma's jelly, and patriotism strike a cynical post-Watergate crowd as syrupy-sweet and belying what was truly going on. But one must listen with the ear of a mid-1930s audience, who felt their world was turning upside-down, who were anywhere from a few days to a generation removed from rural life, and who questioned whether all the "progress" made so far in the twentieth century was really progress at all. By tapping into nostalgia, sentiments that ran both deep and wide among listeners, Josiah Hogg's program rocketed to national attention.

Religious nostalgia did not die with the Little Country Church of Hollywood. Although the building on Argyle Street long outlived its religious usefulness, the emotions it drew from listeners lives on in various forms of religious entertain-ment. When Paul Crouch, president and host of the international Trinity Broad-casting Network, stands before his weekly audiences—estimated at fifty million people—via satellite, dressed in his country-western clothes, and shouts, "Tonight we're gonna have CHURCH!"—the spirit of Josiah Hogg is not far away. Before long, discussion on the program has covered biscuits, dogs, old-time revival, and the merits of country life—all set in Southern California.

This episode of the "Little Country Church of Hollywood" exists, like many of those early religious programs, only on a reel-to-reel recording, without the script or cues the actors used to create it. Given the players in this episode, it likely dates to 1934 or 1935.

Further Reading

Ben Armstrong, *The Electric Church* (Nashville, Tenn.: Thomas Nelson, 1979); Hal Erickson, *Religious Radio and Television in the U.S., 1921–1991: The Programs and Personalities* (Jefferson, N.C.: McFarland and Company, Publishers, 1992); James Gregory, *American Exodus: The Dust Bowl Migration and Okie Culture in California* (New York: Oxford University Press, 1989); George H. Hill, *Airwaves to the Soul: The Influence and Growth of Christian Broadcasting* (Saratoga, Calif.: R & E Publishers, 1983); Michele Hilmes, *Radio Voices: American Broadcasting, 1922–1956* (Minneapolis: University of Minnesota, 1997); Eric Hobsbawm and Terence Ranger, eds., *The Invention of Tradition* (Cambridge and New York: Cambridge University Press, 1983); J. Fred MacDonald, *Don't Touch That Dial: Radio Programming in American Life, 1920–1960* (Chicago: Nelson Hall, 1979); J. Gordon Melton, Philip Charles Lucas, and Jon R. Stone, *Prime-Time Religion: An Encyclopedia* (Phoenix, Ariz.: Oryx Press, 1997); Mark Ward, *Air of Salvation: The Story of Christian Broadcasting* (Grand Rapids, Mich.: Baker Books, 1994).

A Hint to Better Things

> *Quartet:* [Singing opening chorus of "The Church in the Wildwood"]
>
> How sweet on a dear Sabbath morning
> To list' to the clear, ringing bell
> In sounds so sweetly calling
> Oh, come to the church on the hill.
> [Hum through next three verses]

Strolin' Tom. Howdy folks, howdy! Hmmm, strangers around these parts? Yes, this is the Little Country Church of Hollywood all right. Come right in, and welcome. The quartet and Brother Rudy's come in, and I'm Brother Strolin' Tom, so if the Parson and his good wife Sarah don't get here pretty soon, we—heh!—we might heist off and start the meetin' most anytime.

Parson and Sister Hopkins went by to howdy with Aunt Lu Salter. Aunt Lu prides herself on her preserves. So, I guess they enjoyed biscuits and preserves this morning along with a dish of fried chicken and the trimmin's. Heh! Heh! Ah, the best way to find out about it is to listen to Brother and Sister Hopkins and their old buggy horse Dan as they trot along to meetin'. Can you all hear 'em? Yeh, they're coming in on the Possum Trot Road from Aunt Lu Salter's.

[Sound of horse trot made by banging two coconut halves together]

Sarah: Oh, I intended to ask Aunt Lu for her recipe for putting up [unintelligible]

Josiah: Yes, they sure was powerful too.

Sarah: Josiah, what is your favorite preserve?

Josiah: Mine?

Sarah: Um-hum.

Josiah: Oh, well, blackberry jam is mighty good.

Sarah: Heh-heh!

Josiah: And you know plums ain't bad.

Sarah: No—

Josiah: Watermelon rind, too, that's another one of my favorites.

Sarah: Yes, that's good.

Josiah: But honey, you know the gov'nment is getting out a new kind?

Sarah: The government?!

Josiah: Yes sir! I reckon they give 'em away sorta like they do garden feed.

Sarah: Well, what kind of preserves is the government givin' away? I hadn't heard about 'em.

Josiah: Forest Preserves!

Sarah: Oh! Ha ha ha! Where did you get that idea, Josiah?

Josiah: Well, when we was all talkin' about it there in Lige Guyton's shoe shop.

Sarah: They was?

Josiah: Yes, they was! And I see they put up a thing over there at the post office, some sort of a showin' about the gov'ment furnishing forest preserves . . .

Sarah: Hmm-hmm?

Josiah: Yeh, and Bill Evans says that he thinks that the forest preserves is a mixture of all the sorts of wild berries that grow in the woods.

Sarah: You know it might be that!

Josiah: Yeah, it might. But [unintelligible], he thinks that—akerns [acorns]! You know, oak tree akerns? Put up some sort of way. But, law me, I says, you never could make no preserves that suit my tastes out of akerns.

Sarah: Nah . . .

Josiah: [To Dan the horse:] Git up there!

Sarah: Has [unintelligible] gone back to the city yet?

Josiah: Let's sit over here, honey. This here's a good quiet place right here to rest awhile and let Dan check his gut. [To Dan the horse] Whoaa! [Pulls horse off side of the road] Pretty place here under the tree, it'n it?

Sarah: Yes, it is. [unintelligible] was asking me about Brother Methuselah's uncle.

Josiah: Oh yeah. Luke said he was gonna take the hike into the center next Tuesday. That's what he said.

Sarah: Hmmm.

Josiah: You know his uncle sure is bald-headed, ain't he?

Sarah: Ha ha! I reckon he is.

Josiah: I reckon he is baldheaded.

Sarah: He hasn't got a hair, t'all, has he?

Josiah: No, he ain't. No, his head's as slick as a peeled onion! Ha, ha, ha!

[Bells ringing in background]

Sarah: What's you laughin' at?

Josiah: Ah, something Luke Mathuselah told me 'bout his uncle. Ha, ha, ha!

Sarah: Yeah? What was that?

Josiah: Yeah, you see Luke's uncle's an old bachelor.

Sarah: Yes, I know that.

Josiah: And he's powerful interested in the singin' school the [unintelligible] holdin' in the Red Onion School House everynight.

Sarah: He is?

Josiah: Yes. Well, he waxes his moustache and rubs off his shoes ev'rynight and goes to the singin'. Heh, heh, heh!

Sarah: So what are ya' laughin' at?

Josiah: Ah me. Git up there, Dan! Oh, it's the way he's a sparkin' Aunt Lu Salter. Git up Dan! What Luke said about bald-headed men in general . . .

Sarah: Luke Tate?

Josiah: Yeh. Luke said that all the bald-headed men had to do to get ready for the singin' was to straighten out his necktie.

Both: Ha, ha, ha!

Sarah: So what'ya gonna talk on today, Josiah?

Josiah: You know, I thought I'd talk on rememberin'. Git up there!

Sarah: Rememberin'. Well, where's that verse?

Josiah: Yeh, that verse is there, in Matthew, its 26th chapter and 75th verse where it speaks about, ah, Simon Peter rememberin' the words of the Lord. That's what it is.

Sarah: You better watch that bump now!

Josiah: [To Dan the horse] You slow down there. [To Sarah] I'm slowin' down right now honey.

[The couple arrives at the church, the quartet already singing.]

Quartet: [Singing]

> Upon a wide and stormy sea,
> Thou'rt sailing to eternity,
> And the great Admiral orders thee:
> "Sail on! Sail on! Sail on!"
> [Refrain] Sail on! Sail on!
> The storms will soon be past,
> The darkness will not always last;
> Sail on! Sail on!
> God lives and He commands:
> "Sail on! Sail on!"

Josiah: [Walking into church late] Well, howdy neighbors!

Crowd: Howdy! Hello! Howdy!

Josiah: Oh, we sure had a great time over at Aunt Lu's. Oh, she's got these preserves, and more preserves! Heh, heh!

[Crowd laughs]

Josiah: Yeh, you know I was tellin' her today that I was goin' to ask y'all to sing a few dedicated to her, . . . 'cause, . . . so in return for that big dessert eatin' we had. Heh, heh, heh! She likes that piece there . . . it's something about the hand that was wounded. Y'all got that'n?

Quartet: Oh yeah! Yes! Yes!

Josiah: Well, I wish y'all would sing that. It's "The Hand that was Wounded for Me." That's it! That's it!

Quartet: [Singing]

> The hand that was nailed to the cross of woe,
> In love reaches out to the world below;
> 'Tis beckoning now to the souls that roam,
> And pointing the way to the heav'nly home.
> [Refrain] The hand of my Savior I see,
> The hand that was wounded for me;
> 'Twill lead me in love to the mansions above,
> The hand that was wounded for me!

Josiah: Well, y'all done right well on that. That's a good feelin'. You know, if you just turn over there, I think it's about four pages further over there in that red book, there's a piece there that just makes my heart so tender [voice begins to tremble] ev'rytime I sing it. It gets me so homesick [voice breaking]. I'm a comin' home! Rudy, you know that, don't you? [Organ music starts] Go ahead and high step that. "I'm a Comin' Home!"

Quartet: [Singing]

> Jesus, I am coming home today
> For I have found a joy in thee alone.
> From the path of sin I turn away
> Now I am coming home.
>
> [Refrain] Jesus, I am coming home today,
> Never, never more from thee to stray.
> Lord, I now accept thy precious [unintelligible]
> I am coming home!

Josiah: Oh, what a lovely song. And there's a peace just comes floatin' over my mind like the perfume out of a rose garden when they sing that song. You remember there, when that Simon Peter feller, he . . . he sorta slid back and said things he ought not said and done things that he oughta not a done? Just about the time that he tore off and done something like that, it says there in Matthew 26:75, it says, "Then Simon Peter remembered the words of the Lord." I tell ya, folks, memories is put mighty deep in the human heart. And just as sure as you are born to die, they're deeper there than you think they're.

Now you take then during the war. Of course, I was sort of a [unintelligible] such as there was. I didn't know much but I done the best I could with what little I had. The thing that touched me was, them ol' boys would lay around there in those barrack places—that what they called the places where they stayed at, was the barracks. They'd find a little picture of an old gate, a picture of an old grapevine swing, and might nigh ev'rybody had a picture of a sweetest face old ladies. All off protectin' em, you see. [voice breaking] Memories of home. I don't care how bare them walls was, fellas would find some place to stick up a little memory of home.

But I think you'll understand about the tenderness in my own heart, and the most touchin', was the night that my orderly got killed. It was terribly difficult for me and I got up there and he didn't know nothin'. But you know them mem'ries had stuck in his heart? And when I come in, you see, he didn't know who I was. Who do you reckon he thought I was? Thought I was his mother. I just sort of put my hand on his forehead, you see, like that. And he said, "Mother, keep your hand there." Well, see it just got me so— I was scared. Well, I just hated to take my hand off. And then, when I did, he said, "Will you rock me, Mother? I'm so sleepy. Rock me to sleep." See he had got hit in the neck. Well, they had an old chair there. It didn't have no rockers on it, and so I just took him up in my arms. One of the boys said, "I'd go on and humor him. He don't know no better." So just reached down and took him, and put his head on my shoulder and I rocked backwards and forwards. And you know, he smiled. I was so glad I could do that.

And that's the fella, you know, I was a tellin' you all about. He sorta come to his self just before he went away, and kinda opened his eyes, and he see'd me. And he kinda hiked his hand up and waved it, and said, "Well, I'll be seein' ya tomorrow." That is the feller. I told you all about that feller.

Yes [organ music begins in background], this rememberin' is awful kind of bidness and it's mighty deep in the human heart.

Quartet: [Singing]

> [unintelligible] before the shadows lengthen,
> Across the [unintelligible] landscapes of our lives,
> We worship Jesus—[humming rest of verse and chorus, then next verse and chorus]

Josiah: [Quartet humming in background] Well neighbors, we was talkin' about memories. You know what I sort of think about them? That memories is put in the human heart sorta like the needle in a compass—to point to better things. Goodbye folks.

Sarah: Goodbye, ev'rybody.

Quartet: [Singing, fading to humming] We worship Jesus . . .

— 25 —

Martin Luther King, Jr., and the Making
of an American Myth

Craig R. Prentiss

On August 28, 1963, over one-quarter of a million people gathered on the Mall in Washington, D.C., between the Capitol Building and the Lincoln Memorial. At the end of a long day of speeches and songs, with the crowd tired, restless, and eager to return home, Martin Luther King, Jr., approached the podium to give the last speech. Literally in the shadow of the "Great Emancipator," King delivered a speech that is recognized by many as the apex of twentieth-century American rhetoric. The significance of King's "I Have a Dream" speech does not rest in his masterful delivery alone. King's words have woven their way into the fabric of American mythic discourse. As the words of the Hebrew prophets were invoked to call judgment on the nation, today the poetic images of King's "Dream" are also used to depict an imagined community of racial and ethnic harmony similar to the "beloved community" of which King often spoke. Two categories, civil religion and myth, will help explain the significance of King's "I Have a Dream" speech to religious practice in the United States.

In a 1967 article in *Daedalus*, sociologist Robert Bellah reintroduced the term "civil religion" centuries after its initial use by Rousseau in *The Social Contract*. Bellah employed the term to describe a tradition that "exists alongside of and rather clearly differentiated from the churches." He was pointing to "a collection of beliefs, symbols, and rituals with respect to sacred things and institutionalized in a collectivity," which had been evident since the founding of the United States. From the ritualized evocations of God in political discourse, to the early republican artwork depicting George Washington's apotheosis, to the millennialist impulses behind the ideology of an American manifest destiny, Judeo-Christian imagery has continually been brought to the service of American nationalism.

Although Bellah's category of civil religion has become standard among scholars, the concept is not without its critics. At the root of the problem lies the difficulty inherent in categorizing human activity as "religious." Though most do not question the characterization of beliefs or activities directly related to churches, temples, or mosques as being religious, the fact that beliefs and activities outside of these settings are sometimes indistinguishable for the purposes of description has led to interesting and fruitful debates about methods of analysis among scholars. Still, for our purposes, civil religion is a category that can help illuminate the significance of King's speech.

The second category that will enhance our understanding of the role the speech has played in American religious practice is myth. Like the category of civil religion, the term "myth" has also been the focus of much debate among religious studies scholars. Having long ago dispensed with the popular association of myth with falsehood, scholars have come to identify certain types of human discourse as taking on the status of myth. They recognize how vital this type of discourse has been in the formation of social order as well as the development of individual worldviews. A recent essay by Russell McCutcheon describes mythic discourse in a way that is particularly useful for our purposes. McCutcheon describes myth as "a technique or strategy . . . of social argumentation found in all human cultures." Unlike previous identifications of myths as things-in-themselves, referred to by nouns, McCutcheon suggests that myths should be thought of as "active processes akin to verbs." With these assumptions, he proposes three distinguishing characteristics of myth: "(1) that myths are not special (or 'sacred') but ordinary human means of fashioning and authorizing their lived-in and believed-in 'worlds,' (2) that myth, as ordinary rhetorical device in social construction and maintenance, makes *this* rather than *that* social identity possible in the first place, and (3) that a people's use of the label *myth* reflects, expresses, explores, and legitimizes their own self-image." In describing myth in this manner, McCutcheon recognizes that a myth is not a static reality located in a distant and archaic past. Instead, myth is myth precisely because it is used to shape current reality, in the same manner that ancient and long forgotten myths once shaped realities in the past.

With McCutcheon's definition in mind, we can see that King's "I Have A Dream" speech has taken on the status of myth in American culture, and in doing so it serves as another example of civil religion in the United States. We will look at the context in which the speech was made, the speech itself, and the way the speech has been appropriated in the United States today.

The speech was delivered only months after a particularly ugly confrontation in Birmingham, Alabama, between black civil rights protesters and white police officers. In the spring of 1963, millions of Americans across the country were exposed to newspaper photographs and television news reports chronicling the Birmingham Police Commissioner Eugene "Bull" Connor directing his officers to use angry dogs, clubs, and fire hoses on peaceful black demonstrators. The nationwide outrage that the brutality sparked has often been seen as a key moment in turning the tide of white opinion in favor of the black civil rights cause. The images of police brutality lingered in the memories of Americans as they witnessed the March on Washington in the following August.

Understanding the context for King's speech is vital for making sense of its impact. In 1963, the United States was at the height of Cold War tension with the Soviet Union. For both sides, the importance of scoring points through propaganda was vital. Therefore, the grim reality of both legal segregation in the South and white racism towards African-Americans in all parts of the country provided Soviet Communists ample fodder for their anti-American, anti-capitalist ideology. In this context, the civil rights movement was viewed simultaneously by many white Americans as evidence that American ideals ultimately promote freedom while at the same time as a potential powder keg through which revolutionary ideas (potentially Communist ideas) and even violence might be ignited.

It should be remembered that not all African-Americans were receptive to the message of King's speech. The nonviolent, direct-action tactics promoted by King and his Southern Christian Leadership Conference, with its emphasis on interracial harmony, were met with cynicism on the part of some African-Americans. Notably, the Nation of Islam and their most public spokesperson, Malcolm X, remained critical of King's message and his tactics. Interracial harmony was a utopian fantasy, they believed, and failed to take into account the entrenchment of white racism and white power. From the Nation of Islam's perspective, only fear of potentially violent retribution would inspire whites to grant blacks their civil rights and allow them to live in peace, separately, free from white oppression.

Each of these contextual items affected the way that King's "I Have a Dream" speech was received. The idea for the "March on Washington for Jobs and Freedom," at which King delivered his famous speech, was initiated by union activist A. Philip Randolph. The initial focus of the march was to draw the attention of Congress to the need for jobs. With the public relations success of the Birmingham campaign in the Spring, however, the focus shifted toward an emphasis on freedom and interracial unity. Furthermore, it was hoped that a demonstration would put pressure on Congress to pass important civil rights legislation. Eventually this envisioned legislation evolved into the 1964 Civil Rights Act.

The rally of over 250,000 participants, nearly one-third of whom were white, was remarkably smooth in terms of logistics. Though many white Washingtonians feared that violence was inevitable—an assumption rooted in racism—the march was peaceful. CBS carried the event nearly in its entirety, and ABC and NBC interrupted regular programming to present King's speech live. When King stepped to the podium, he began to read from a prepared speech that had been delivered to the press in advance. As he was finishing, King diverged from his original remarks and began to improvise. The improvisation was built around the refrain: "I have a dream." It was not the first time King had employed this refrain. In fact, for those who accompanied King to his many speeches and sermons across the country, most of his words were quite familiar. But to the many millions who watched from their television sets, King's words were fresh, inspired, and exciting.

Although he is known primarily as a political figure, King considered himself, before all other things, a Baptist preacher. His speech at the March on Washington was not simply a speech; it was a sermon. It was composed with the poetic symmetry and delivered with the sermonic cadence that were firmly rooted in the tradition of the African-American church. This preaching tradition was character ized not by the traditional three-point style of argument but instead by a pattern designed to lift an audience gradually to a crescendo of enthusiasm. King was a master of this style, and his delivery had as much to do with the impact of the speech as did the words themselves.

In choosing to describe the role of the "I Have a Dream" speech as myth, we could also recognize it as a myth made from myths: the myth of America's role in doing God's will on earth and the Judeo-Christian myth. The first myth is central to the American civil religion described earlier. King began his speech with an allusion to one of America's sacred texts, The Gettysburg Address, and its author, the martyr par excellence for the cause of national unity, Abraham Lincoln. Standing before his monument, which King called a "hallowed spot," his speech created a continuity between the civil rights struggle of the mid twentieth century and the process that Lincoln had begun with the Emancipation Proclamation. Yet, since the origins of the movement toward justice were more than a century old, King could invoke the two most sacred texts in American civil religion, the Declaration of Independence and the Constitution. He could argue that a prom- ise had been made from the nation's founding that "all men, yes, black men as well as white men, would be guaranteed the inalienable rights of life, liberty and the pursuit of happiness." What made these rights inalienable, of course, was their endowment by the Creator. Though the promise enshrined in these texts had not been kept, it was the task of all within range of King's voice to make that promise become a reality.

These sacred texts were at the heart of another element in the mythology of the nation's civil religion, the "American dream." King understood his own "dream" to be an amplification of a dream that resided at the core of American self-identity. It is worth noting that the value of referring to "*the* American dream" in discourse comes precisely from the ambiguous nature of the term itself. Americans have always imprinted their own values onto the mythic template of this dream, color- ing it with diverse and often contradictory characteristics ranging from material wealth, to egalitarianism, to religious freedom. In keeping with McCutcheon's description of myth, the American dream is presented, by King and so many oth- ers, as if there is agreement as to what it means. It is through his assertion that equal rights and racial harmony are central to the American dream that King sought to make it *the* dream. In this way, the speech itself helped to shape reality.

In addition to the myth of the American dream, King also tapped the Judeo- Christian myth in his speech. These references came naturally to a preacher, though he was acutely aware that having been raised in the Judeo-Christian tradition was a commonality for most blacks and whites at midcentury. It was in these terms that King felt most comfortable citing common ground. God, as revealed to them in the Bible, served as the ultimate authorizing agent. It was no coincidence, then, that King's speech refers to "God's children" three times, an image which emphasizes both God's power and the need for a childlike humble servitude.

Scripture was also brought to the service of authorizing King's call for equality. "We will not be satisfied," King said, quoting Amos 5:24, "until justice rolls down like waters and righteousness like a mighty stream." His "dream" included a vision from Isaiah 40:4–5, "that one day every valley shall be exalted, and every hill and mountain shall be made low, the rough places will be made plain and the crooked places will be made straight and the glory of the Lord shall be revealed and all flesh shall see it together." This imagery not only called attention to future judgment but paralleled the very social reordering that King was calling for in American society. Racial distinctions were imagined to be erased by the hand of God.

The appropriation of the Hebrew prophets for the cause of contemporary justice had a long history in African American Christianity. Since slavery, African-Americans identified with the suffering and oppression of the ancient Israelites and read the Hebrew story into their own travails in the United States. King's use of these prophets remained in line with countless black preachers who came before him.

With the intricate blending of mythology familiar to nearly all Americans culled from the civil religious and Judeo-Christian traditions, King created a text that went on to reach its own status as myth and helped to place the issue of interracial unity squarely within the grand narrative of America's history and future. Yet, not everyone recognized the potential impact of the speech. The *Washington Post* did not even mention it the following day, choosing instead to highlight the speech given by A. Philip Randolph. *U.S. News and World Report*, which had taken an editorial position consistently hostile to the civil rights struggle, focused only on King's use of the phrase "a marvelous new militancy which has engulfed the Negro community" as a means of portraying the marchers as troublemakers. Their coverage ignored the fact that this phrase was buried between a reaffirmation of the principle of nonviolence and a recognition of a common destiny for blacks and whites (both ideas put forth in direct response to critics from groups such as the Nation of Islam). Still, the *New York Times* ran a headline the following day that read, "I Have a Dream . . . ," and soon the various media outlets helped solidify King's speech as the defining moment of the March on Washington.

The varied initial media coverage is instructive insofar as it reminds us that words are never self-evidently authoritative; they are made authoritative by people in specific contexts for specific reasons. Three primary events helped to promote King's "I Have a Dream" speech to the status of myth. First, just over two weeks after the speech, white supremacists exploded dynamite in the Birmingham, Alabama, Sixteenth Street Baptist Church. The blast resulted in the deaths of four young black girls attending Sunday school. In addition to this tragedy, which sparked a national outrage, the juxtaposition of the carnage and devastation in Birmingham to the peace and idealism of the March on Washington and King's "dream" did not go unnoticed. The need to make the dream a reality intensified. Second, by the mid 1960s, frustration with slow progress toward true equality led to a more aggressive and sometimes violent strand of civil rights activism. The 1965 race riots in Watts, as well as in other cities in the months and years that followed, crushed much of the optimism felt in August 1963. The rise of the Black Power movement coincided with a loss of faith in the techniques of nonviolence to achieve true justice. These developments frightened many whites as well as moderate and conservative blacks, and King's dream was again employed as a model for what *ought* to be, as opposed to what was. Finally, the April 1968 assassination of King in Memphis, Tennessee, turned the words of "I Have a Dream" into the sacred phrases of an American martyr.

As happens with any death, King's murder left his legacy to be decided by others. Like the Hebrew prophets who King himself had quoted to call the justice of God's reign into being, the now dead leader, who had been likened to Moses for his people, was cast in the role of an American prophet. And like Isaiah, Jeremiah, and so many others, King's memory was molded to fit the needs of those who followed him. Some white Americans, content with Jim Crow and systematic segregation, continued to view King as a subversive agitator who threatened a divinely ordained social order. For most, however, King remained fixed as the great peacemaker of the Summer of 1963, who sacrificed his life for the dream that people would someday "be judged not by the color of their skin but by the content of their character."

Some are quick to point out that by trapping the memory of King in 1963, we lose sight of the man he became in the last years of his life. In the three years leading up to his death, King became an outspoken critic of the Vietnam War and what he viewed as American imperialism abroad. His focus turned to poverty, regardless of race, and he railed against the excesses of American capitalism. In short, the Martin Luther King, Jr., who was killed in Memphis was a more radical man than the man who told us of his dream in 1963. Some contend that preserving him in memory as the dreamer of lofty dreams was a convenient means of sidestepping the other challenges that he posed to the nation.

Martin Luther King, Jr., the mythic figure, and "I Have a Dream," the mythic speech, continue to be used for present-day purposes—all the more so since 1986, when the United States began observing the Martin Luther King, Jr., national holiday on the third Monday of every January. The institutionalization of King's memory has provided a platform on which individuals may annually assess not only the impact of King himself but, perhaps more importantly, the status of what has simply come to be known as "the dream." When King originally delivered the speech, it was in part the product of his own response to the community which surrounded him. Many accounts maintain that King's improvisational insertion of the "I Have a Dream" refrain was his reaction to a cry from the gospel singer Mahalia Jackson, who urged him to tell the people of his dream. It is fitting then that King's speech is today brought to life again in the retelling and rehearing of King's words in communities across the country, particularly on King's holiday. With each retelling, the words from the past speak to the present and are colored by a multitude of contexts that King himself may not have been able to imagine.

King's dream has been the subject of countless sermons in recent decades. Like a scriptural passage, the speech itself acts as a proof text for clergy in the same manner a passage from a Pauline epistle might be used. A sermon delivered in 1992 at the Chapel of Princeton Theological Seminary by E. K. Bailey, senior pastor of the Concord Missionary Baptist Church in Dallas, used King's speech to give insight into Joshua 1:1–9. The burden that Joshua faced in leading the Hebrew people after Moses had died was similar to the situation faced by those who sought justice when King, whom Bailey called both "the Dreamer" and "a modern-day Moses," was killed. The bulk of the sermon was an assessment of the state of "the dream" and a call to carry the torch as Joshua had done. A Martin Luther King Day sermon from 1994 at the Wilshire Christian Church in Los Angeles, California, by Joseph R. Jeter, Jr., compared Joseph's dreams in Matthew 2:13–23 to King's dream. Like Joseph, "Dr. King had a dream and then he woke up and did something about it. He walked, he preached, he went to jail, he wrote, he sought to build the beloved community." Jeter called upon his congregation to make King's dream come true. These two sermons are examples of the innumerable sermons that have been preached in American churches, synagogues, and mosques in recent years that utilized King's speech in much the same way as scripture is utilized. In doing so, speakers succeed in clothing the speech itself with a power and authority that almost transcends its earthly origins in the same way that scripture, to the faithful, transcends the earthly origins of those who wrote it.

A quick scan of Martin Luther King Day celebrations across the country in 1999 will further illustrate ways the speech is used in American religious practice. In Los Angeles, amid several commemorations taking place at senior citizens centers, community centers, and churches, hundreds attended celebrations paying tribute to King. The celebrations included gospel singing, testimonials, speeches, and sermons. In what the Los Angeles Times described as a "riveting sermon," Pastor Tony Simon of the Community Temple Baptist Church in Santa Ana reminded his listeners that "we can't have the dream if we don't know about the dream. . . . Where there is unity, there is power." The San Fernando Valley Interfaith Council sponsored their eleventh annual event entitled "Living the Dream." Further north, the San Francisco Chronicle noted that rain did not keep thousands from participating in a city march dedicated to King's memory, many with rain-drenched signs with the words "Living the Dream" painted on them. In St. Louis, Missouri, there were over ten official Martin Luther King day events, including poetry readings, skating parties, interfaith religious services, plays, and lectures focused on human rights. Florrisant, Missouri, a suburb of St. Louis, held its annual city- and countrywide commemoration entitled "Martin Had His Dream, What's Yours?" featuring politicians, ministers, and gospel choirs. The four hundred who gathered at St. Charles Borromeo Church outside of St. Louis listened to the St. Alphonsus "Rock" Catholic Church choir and a speaker who implored the crowd to work to fulfill King's dream. The headline on page one of the New Orleans Times Picayune read, "King's Dream Eludes Us Still, N[ew] O[rleans] Pastors Say." The article went on to describe two weeks of celebrations honoring King, including a parade and a march sponsored by the Knights and Ladies of St. Peter Claver Council and Court 267. In Atlanta, Georgia, at the Ebenezer Baptist Church, where King's own father had been a minister, South African Archbishop Desmond Tutu proclaimed that "God has a dream like Martin Luther King, Jr.," and went on to quote the final refrain of King's speech, "Free at last, thank God almighty we're free at last."

The importance of the Martin Luther King, Jr., holiday seems to be growing with every year, and the sacred text from which celebrants most often quote is the "I Have a Dream" speech. The mythical status of King's words, as they were spoken in 1963, was not self-evident. It is through communal recitation over time that his words have been used to authorize a vision of what the American social order should be. The speech has become embedded in the civil religion of the nation and is quoted freely by priests, rabbis, and other clerics as easily and as naturally as it is quoted by politicians. As with all myths, the content of King's dream is still contested. Lawsuits have been filed to prevent opponents of affirmative action from quoting King's speech in advertisements. In a trend that resembles the common complaint that American culture has taken the "Christ" out of Christmas, ritualistic articles are written each January bemoaning perceived improper uses of "the dream" that are said to debase it. As this essay is being written, the estate of Martin Luther King, Jr., is appealing a U.S. District Court decision that the "I Have a Dream" speech is public property and not the property of King's family. Whatever the eventual decision, there can be no doubt that, like all myths, people will continue to make the words their own to authorize their own dreams.

The following copy of King's 1963 "Address at March on Washington for Jobs and Freedom" is on file at the Martin Luther King, Jr., Papers Project at Stanford University and was transcribed from the audio recording at Martin Luther King, Jr., Library and Archive, Martin Luther King, Jr., Center for Nonviolent Social Change, Inc., Atlanta, Georgia. Reprinted by arrangement with The Heirs to the Estate of Martin Luther King Jr., c/o Writers House as agent for the proprietor. Copyright 1963 Martin Luther King, Jr., renewed 1991 by Loretta Scott King.

Further Reading

Russell T. McCutcheon, "Myth," in *Guide to the Study of Religion*, edited by Willi Braun and Russell T. McCutcheon (London: Cassell Academic, 1999); Taylor Branch, *Parting the Waters: America in the King Years, 1954–1963* (New York: Simon and Schuster, 1988); Richard Lentz, *Symbols, The News Magazines, and Martin Luther King* (Baton Rouge: Louisiana State University Press, 1990); David J. Garrow, *Bearing the Cross: Martin Luther King, Jr. and the Southern Christian Leadership Conference* (New York: William Morrow, 1986); *Martin Luther King, Jr., and* the Sermonic Power of Public Discourse, edited by Carolyn Calloway-Thomas and John Louis Lucaites (Tuscaloosa: University of Alabama Press, 1993); James H. Cone, Martin and Malcolm and America: A Dream or a Nightmare (Maryknoll, N.Y.: Orbis Books, 1991); E. K. Bailey, "The Anatomy of a Dream," Princeton Seminary Bulletin 13 (1992): 311–19; Joseph R. Jeter, Jr., "Waking Up from a Dream: Martin Luther King, Jr., Celebration: A Sermon, Matthew 2:13–23," Impact 32 (1994) 39–45.

Address at March on Washington for Jobs and Freedom
August 28, 1963, Washington, D.C.

I am happy to join with you today in what will go down in history as the greatest demonstration for freedom in the history of our nation.

Five score years ago, a great American, in whose symbolic shadow we stand today, signed the Emancipation Proclamation. This momentous decree came as a great beacon light of hope to millions of Negro slaves, who had been seared in the flames of withering injustice. It came as a joyous daybreak to end the long night of their captivity. But one hundred years later, the Negro still is not free. One hundred years later, the life of the Negro is still sadly crippled by the manacle of segregation and the chains of discrimination.

One hundred years later, the Negro lives on a lonely island of poverty in the midst of a vast ocean of material prosperity. One hundred years later, the Negro is still languished in the corners of American society and finds himself an exile in his own land. So we've come here today to dramatize a shameful condition.

In a sense we have come to our nation's capital to cash a check. When the architects of our republic wrote the magnificent words of the Constitution and the Declaration of Independence, they were signing a promissory note to which every American was to fall heir.

This note was a promise that all men, yes, black men as well as white men, would be guaranteed the inalienable rights of life, liberty and the pursuit of happiness.

It is obvious today that America has defaulted on this promissory note insofar as her citizens of color are concerned. Instead of honoring this sacred obligation, America has given the Negro people a bad check, a check which has come back marked "insufficient funds."

But we refuse to believe that the bank of justice is bankrupt. We refuse to believe that there are insufficient funds in the great vaults of opportunity of this nation. So we have come to cash this check, a check that will give us upon demand the riches of freedom and the security of justice.

We have also come to this hallowed spot to remind America of the fierce urgency of Now. This is no time to engage in the luxury of cooling off or to take the tranquilizing drug of gradualism. Now is the time to make real the promises of democracy. Now is the time to rise from the dark and desolate valley of segregation to the sunlit path of racial justice. Now is the time to lift our nation from the quicksands of racial injustice to the solid rock of brotherhood. Now is the time to make justice a reality for all of God's children.

It would be fatal for the nation to overlook the urgency of the moment. This sweltering summer of the Negro's legitimate discontent will not pass until there is an invigorating autumn of freedom and equality. Nineteen sixty-three is not an end but a beginning. Those who hope that the Negro needed to blow off steam and will now be content will have a rude awakening if the nation returns to business as usual.

There will be neither rest nor tranquility in America until the Negro is granted his citizenship rights. The whirlwinds of revolt will continue to shake the foundations of our nation until the bright day of justice emerges.

But there is something that I must say to my people who stand on the warm threshold which leads into the palace of justice. In the process of gaining our rightful place we must not be guilty of wrongful deeds.

Let us not seek to satisfy our thirst for freedom by drinking from the cup of bitterness and hatred. We must ever conduct our struggle on the high plane of dignity and discipline. We must not allow our creative protest to degenerate into physical violence. Again and again we must rise to the majestic heights of meeting physical force with soul force.

The marvelous new militancy which has engulfed the Negro community must not lead us to a distrust of all white people. For many of our white brothers, as evidenced by their presence here today, have come to realize that their destiny is tied up with our destiny. They have come to realize that their freedom is inextricably bound to our freedom. We cannot walk alone.

And as we walk, we must make the pledge that we shall always march ahead. We cannot turn back. There are those who are asking the devotees of civil rights, "When will you be satisfied?" We can never be satisfied as long as the Negro is the victim of the unspeakable horrors of police brutality.

We can never be satisfied as long as our bodies, heavy with the fatigue of travel, cannot gain lodging in the motels of the highways and the hotels of the cities. We cannot be satisfied as long as a Negro in Mississippi cannot vote and a Negro in New York believes he has nothing for which to vote.

No, no, we are not satisfied and we will not be satisfied until justice rolls down like waters and righteousness like a mighty stream.

I am not unmindful that some of you have come here out of great trials and tribulations. Some of you have come fresh from narrow jail cells. Some of you have come from areas where your quest for freedom left you battered by the storms of persecutions and staggered by the winds of police brutality. You have been the veterans of creative suffering. Continue to work with the faith that unearned suffering is redemptive.

Go back to Mississippi, go back to Alabama, go back to South Carolina, go back to Georgia, go back to Louisiana, go back to the slums and ghettos of our northern cities, knowing that somehow this situation can and will be changed.

Let us not wallow in the valley of despair. I say to you today, my friends, that even though we face the difficulties of today and tomorrow. I still have a dream.

It is a dream deeply rooted in the American dream.

I have a dream that one day this nation will rise up and live out the true meaning of its creed—we hold these truths to be self-evident that all men are created equal.

I have a dream that one day on the red hills of Georgia the sons of former slaves and the sons of former slave owners will be able to sit down together at the table of brotherhood.

I have a dream that one day even the state of Mississippi, a state sweltering with the heat of injustice, sweltering with the heat of oppression, will be transformed into an oasis of freedom and justice.

I have a dream that my four little children will one day live in a nation where they will not be judged by the color of their skin but by the content of their character.

I have a dream today!

I have a dream that one day, down in Alabama, with its vicious racists, with its governor having his lips dripping with the words of interposition and nullification; one day right down in Alabama little black boys and black girls will be able to join hands with little white boys and white girls as sisters and brothers.

I have a dream today!

I have a dream that one day every valley shall be exalted, and every hill and mountain shall be made low, the rough places will be made plain and the crooked places will be made straight and the glory of the Lord shall be revealed and all flesh shall see it together.

This is our hope. This is the faith that I will go back to the South with. With this faith we will be able to hew out of the mountain of despair a stone of hope. With this faith we will be able to transform the jangling discords of our nation into a beautiful symphony of brotherhood. With this faith we will be able to work together, to pray together, to struggle together, to go to jail together, to stand up for freedom together, knowing that we will be free one day. This will be the day, this will be the day when all of God's children will be able to sing with new meaning "My country 'tis of thee, sweet land of liberty, of thee I sing. Land where my fathers died, land of the Pilgrim's pride, from every mountainside, let freedom ring!" And if America is to be a great nation, this must become true.

And so let freedom ring from the prodigious hilltops of New Hampshire.

Let freedom ring from the mighty mountains of New York.

Let freedom ring from the heightening Alleghenies of Pennsylvania.

Let freedom ring from the snow-capped Rockies of Colorado.

Let freedom ring from the curvaceous slopes of California.

But not only that.

Let freedom ring from Stone Mountain of Georgia.

Let freedom ring from Lookout Mountain of Tennessee.

Let freedom ring from every hill and molehill of Mississippi, from every mountainside, let freedom ring!

And when this happens, when we allow freedom to ring, when we let it ring from every tenement and every hamlet, from every state and every city, we will be able to speed up that day when all of God's children, black men and white men, Jews and Gentiles, Protestants and Catholics, will be able to join hands and sing in the words of the old Negro spiritual, "Free at last, free at last. Thank God Almighty, we are free at last."

—26—

Spiritual Warfare in the Fiction of Frank Peretti

Peter Gardella

In a New York neighborhood where "things were tailored for the elite and discerning," limousines carried "VIPs from many different nations and races" to a meeting of the Universal Consciousness Society; "and within and on top [of the limousines] were demons, large, black, warty, and fierce, their yellow eyes darting warily in every direction." Two angels in disguise observed the movement. "Babylon the Great," said one to the other. "The Great Harlot arising at last." And the second angel replied, "Yes, Universal Consciousness. The world religion, the doctrine of demons spreading among all the nations" (Peretti, 174). Before Frank Peretti's novel *This Present Darkness* (1986) was finished, these angels would be locked in combat with a demon prince who had inhabited Babylon since ancient times. They would fight in a small town in the western United States, with the help of rural people, and their struggle would identify the values of that town with the cause of God and Christ. Even as the angelic victory meant defeat for many modern trends, it affirmed the nuclear family and a vision of rural, or at least suburban, simplicity.

Fiction can connect daily life with cosmic themes. For evangelical Christians of the 1990s, Frank Peretti offered a worldview complete with perspectives on history, geography, and politics. He created a world that set the prayers, family lives, and spiritual struggles of contemporary Christians at the center of the universe. Peretti continued the tradition of Charles Sheldon, whose *In His Steps* (1897) arose from battles over temperance and urban politics and still inspires Christians to ask, "What would Jesus do?" Peretti also continued an older tradition of believers, including C. S. Lewis, John Bunyan, and John Milton (and before them, medieval and ancient apocalyptic writers), who depicted angels and humans at war. Though Peretti's angels may seem cartoonish and his characters wooden, his imagination gave models to millions of Christians for practicing faith with regard to the issues and hostilities of their time.

Estimates of sales range as high as eight million copies for Peretti's six novels, with 2.8 million attributed to *This Present Darkness* alone; but his influence and his significance go beyond his own books. Theologians accuse each other of borrowing their worldviews from Peretti, while pastors and missionaries describe incidents from their own lives as episodes from a Frank Peretti novel. The Peretti phenomenon began when Christian pop singer Amy Grant plugged Peretti's book at concerts during her 1987 tour. Then, *This Present Darkness* almost single-handedly expanded the field of Christian fiction beyond the romance novels of the 1970s. Evangelicals began to write and read so many novels of spiritual warfare that separate sections of Christian bookstores and Barnes and Noble outlets were devoted to them, contributing to an explosion of evangelical culture that entailed a great deal of retailing. Riding a wave of apocalyptic fear around the year 2000, Tim La Haye's series of *Left Behind* novels became even more popular than Peretti's.

Both Amy Grant's CDs and Frank Peretti's novels thrived within the world of Christian bookstores, adding another dimension to religious life in the last third of the twentieth century. Like the Christian posters, T-shirts, bumper stickers, and jewelry sold in those stores, Christian fiction and music mutually reinforced a sense of separation and superiority, while connecting Christians with current events. When *This Present Darkness* turned New Age educational techniques and international organizations into tools of Satan, it provided entertainment while reinforcing faith and preparing readers to fight for Christian causes in politics and culture. At the bookstore, those interested in Christian fiction, music, videos, cards, and gifts could meet each other, exchange news about their families and communities, and possibly form opinions about social issues, with ramifications that extended from local school board elections to the votes of Congress.

Peretti represented a new readiness to accept concepts of angelic intervention and supernatural power, occurring both within and outside evangelical circles, which would have seemed bizarre in previous generations. In the 1950s and 1960s, intellectuals took it for granted that people believed less and less in angels, devils, and supernatural interventions in life. This process was widely known as secularization, and many assumed it would go on forever. Then the 1970s brought *Star Wars* and "the Force." By the late nineties, *Touched by an Angel*, *Sabrina the Teenage Witch*, *Charmed*, and *Buffy the Vampire Slayer* led the ratings races on television, while covens of witches danced at every full moon across the nation. A series of novels about the training of a young witch named Harry Potter dominated children's literature. Measured by the amount of consumer spending, Halloween had become the second leading holiday in American life. Although Peretti and his readers rejected video arcades and role-playing games featuring wizards and spells, such as *Magic: the Gathering* or *Dungeons and Dragons*, novels of spiritual warfare gave evangelicals a way to enjoy special powers while remaining within the Christian tradition.

Many of the readers of Peretti's novels consider themselves as "Third Wave" Christians. They see a Third Wave of religious enthusiasm after the Pentecostal revivals of the early twentieth century (which created the Assemblies of God and other Pentecostal denominations) and the charismatic movements that surged through non-Pentecostal denominations in the 1970s. Although they seek power from God in prayer, Third Wave believers do not emphasize the gift of speaking in tongues. Instead, they concentrate on the power of the Holy Spirit to work miracles that promote the growth of missions and the church. *This Present Darkness* has been called the "Bible of the Third Wave."

Some critics have seen the prominence of supernatural power in Peretti's work as a shortcoming. As Gary Corwin, an associate editor of *Evangelical Missions Quarterly,* recalled, "In a world that seemed to be heading down all sorts of bizarre paths of occult involvement," *This Present Darkness* "made sense of it all" and gave believers new "motivation for prevailing prayer" (148). But then Corwin complained that Peretti implied too magical a view of prayer. "Is God in control, or are we?" he asked (149). If the novel led people to forget that "the essence of prayer is communion with God for his sake alone," Corwin feared that "the demons will already have won a major battle." In a long and systematic article, Robert Guelich, a professor of New Testament at the same Fuller Theological Seminary that nurtured the Third Wave, found no biblical basis for the ways that humans empower angels with their prayers in Peretti's novels and particularly rejected the concept that people provide "prayer cover" for angelic warfare (56, 60). The concept of prayer cover, which means that the prayers of humans provide covering fire for good angels in their battles with demons, does seem to begin with Peretti, although many have found it congenial. Besides prayer cover, Guelich concluded, Peretti's books contain "numerous distortions about the person and work of Christ, the believers' role . . . , Satan and his hosts, and the nature of evil" (63). According to Irving Hexham, a professor at the University of Calgary and self-described evangelical Anglican, the laudable "emphasis on prayer and spirituality" in *This Present Darkness* caused people to overlook the new social boundaries that the novel erected between Christians and feminism, secular higher education, and meditation (288, 156).

As these critics claim, Peretti does advocate employing prayer to prevail against demons and does enclose evangelicals within boundaries, from which he shows them launching their prayers as weapons. Near the climax of *This Present Darkness,* a college classroom becomes the scene of an exorcism in which the prayers of Christians outside give an angel wielding a sword power to slash the demonic chains that bind a young woman so that they "burst outward and away from her, writhing like severed snakes" (365). The student then comes out of a trance induced by her professor, who had herself been possessed by the demon of Babylon.

The supernatural geopolitics implied in the novel—not only in Peretti's frequent references to Babylon but also in the roles of New York and the United Nations, and in the attempt of the demons to take possession of American towns and colleges—show the influence of a concept of "spiritual mapping" popular among Third Wave Christians. With spiritual mapping, believers see the world as a battleground in which Christian and demonic forces hold particular cities and territories. San Francisco may be held by a spirit of perversion, for example, while in San Jose, missionary actions are disrupted by a spirit of greed. In all mapping systems, Babylon has particular importance as the center of the "10/40 window," a vast rectangle defined on its short sides by the tenth and fortieth degrees of latitude above the equator and extending lengthwise from West Africa through Egypt and the Middle East to India, China, and Japan. Within this 10/40 window, according to many writers on missions, live 90 percent of those who have not had the gospel preached to them; from that region come leaders such as Saddam Hussein and Ayatollah Khomeini, who are literally possessed by the fallen angels who rule their lands. The new worldview provided a post–Cold War version of Hal Lindsey's *Late Great Planet Earth* (1970).

Although spiritual mapping and supernatural geopolitics may be considered exotic, sensational, and unbiblical by some critics, most of the doctrines and recommendations implied in *This Present Darkness* express nothing more than an ideal of rural peace that seems to reflect the story of Frank Peretti's life. Born in Lethbridge (a city in the Rocky Mountain region of Alberta Canada), Peretti married in 1972 at twenty-one years of age. After studying English and film at UCLA from 1976 until 1978, he left college without a degree. He then worked with his father Gene for six years as associate pastor in an Assembly of God church on Vashon Island in Washington. Leaving the ministry in 1984, Peretti worked making skis in a factory and lived with his wife in a trailer near Seattle. Presumably he wrote after the workday, because *This Present Darkness* was published in 1986, and by 1988 its success enabled the author to quit the ski factory.

Simplicity and privacy appear prominently among the values Peretti affirmed in published interviews. In 1992 he told Bob and Gretchen Passantino that Christians should "live a quiet life, mind our own business, work with our own hands, and walk properly toward those outside." When Gustav Niebuhr of the *New York Times* sought the author in 1995, he found him in "a large, rustically elegant log house deep in the woods of northern Idaho." On book jackets and publishers' information forms, Peretti lists hobbies such as carpentry, sculpturing, bicycling, hiking, music, aviation—all potentially solitary pursuits. According to Barbara Peretti, her husband often felt "left out, awkward, not in control of the situation" as a child, perhaps because he was a pastor's son. Working as a youth leader in church camp, Peretti says that he began to tell stories rather than trying to give "one inspiring, emotional message a day." He found that the continuing installments gave him more control, because "the kids couldn't wait to hear what happened next," and that a storyteller had more freedom than a preacher "to express the total lifechanging power of the Bible." Fiction gave Peretti an alternative form of preaching that allowed a committed, but shy, Christian to connect with others.

Just how the Bible changes life for the characters in Peretti's books has not seemed obvious to everyone. Reviewer Gene Doty wrote that nothing in *This Present Darkness* suggests "why one would be a Christian, except to escape the demons' assaults" (94). The sort of transformation that Peretti seeks may elude scholars, however, because it is so simple. A suggestion of his ideal of life appears in *This Present Darkness* when the hero reporter and his female sidekick approach the "quaint and unpretentious ten-acre farm" that the former dean of Whitmore College, driven from office by demon-possessed New Agers, has chosen for his retirement. As they drive up the "long gravel driveway" to the white house, they see a lawn "small and manicured, the fruit trees pruned and bearing, the flower beds soft with freshly turned and weeded soil" (154). As if to emphasize that this ideal is more rural than suburban, Peretti notes that "chickens meandered about, pecking and scratching," and that a collie ran out to bark at the approaching strangers. "Wow, a normal human being to interview for once," says the hero, who has clearly had enough of professors who teach meditation. A simple, rural, peaceful life—much like Peretti's own life in the woods of the Northwest—is the true Christian goal.

In times of war, the appeal of peace becomes compelling. Peretti's tales of spiritual warfare over rural values took hold in an era—the last three decades of the twentieth century—that witnessed more violence and more wars inspired by religion than any period since that of the Reformers and Puritans. Religious wars included the Protestant-Catholic "troubles" in Ireland; the Yom Kippur War of 1973; the Iranian Revolution; revolutions of the mujahedeen and Taliban against Soviet and secular rulers in Afghanistan; civil war between Buddhists and Hindus in Sri Lanka; clashes of Catholic and Orthodox Christians with each other and with Muslims in the Balkans; and Hindus fighting Muslims in India against the background of tension between India and Pakistan. Within the United States, terror at the World Trade Center, Waco, and Oklahoma City strongly implicated religion. Even the Gulf War of 1991, though it was fought over secular aims like land and oil, featured monumental portraits of Saddam Hussein next to Nebuchadnezzar, the king of ancient Babylon who destroyed Solomon's Temple. It was almost prophetic that, writing in *This Present Darkness* five years before the Gulf War, Peretti introduced his readers to a fallen angel named "Rafar, the Prince of Babylon." This "Baal-prince from ancient times" and "would-be pagan god" would lead the demonic invasion of a small town named Ashton in the American heartland.

For believers, demonic threats appeared not only in the violence and war reported in the media but also in moral and spiritual transformations that affected everyday life. Evangelical Christians of the late twentieth century lived through a revolution that swept away many values and laws derived from the Bible. During the 1960s and 1970s, premarital sex, cohabitation, and abortion moved from the realm of the hidden and illegal to that of acceptable status in law and public discourse. At the same time, Eastern religions, yoga, and other forms of meditation became commonplace. The 1980s and 1990s saw witchcraft and voodoo, which had been synonymous with superstition or insanity, gain respectability. By the 1990s, open homosexuals were appearing on network television, being elected to Congress, and seeking recognition of their partnerships as marriages under the law.

When Peretti published *This Present Darkness* in 1986, two years after he left the ministry, the cause of Christian faith in the world must have looked much as it did to John Bunyan when he published *The Pilgrim's Progress* in 1678, eighteen years after the restoration of English monarchy ended the Puritan Revolution. Bunyan and Peretti both represent a once dominant, Christian point of view driven toward the margins of their cultures in an age of religious warfare. Both used vivid images of devils to conjure up spiritual victories for their sides. In combat with Bunyan's hero, the demon Apollyon appears with "wings like a dragon, feet like a bear, and out of his belly came fire and smoke" (Bunyan, 57); just before the defeat of Peretti's Rafar, prince of Babylon, his "nostrils spewed deep red clouds" and his "words gargled through the tar and the froth" (Peretti, 372).

Yet a profound difference remains between Bunyan and Peretti. When the victory over Apollyon is won, Bunyan's Christian continues a solitary flight from the world to the Celestial City. He had already left his wife and children behind in the City of Destruction when he fled, with his fingers in his ears so that he would not hear them as he ran, crying out for "life, life, eternal life" (Bunyan, 19). When Peretti's heroes defeat their demons, they gather in their families and their churches; husbands reconcile with wives, parents with children, church members with pastors. These are very small families and small churches in a small town, but they are also real communities, and they remain in contact with the rest of the world. Everyone stays in Ashton, the little town that once stood on the front lines of a spiritual war. Presumably, they will live as Peretti recommends in various interviews and speeches. Although Christians "can't save the environment, feed all the poor, or stop all abortions," they will set an example. "Recycle your kitchen trash," Peretti prescribes. "Volunteer your family for one Saturday helping at a local soup kitchen. Show your children love for all life, born and unborn, by loving them unconditionally." For entertainment, these victorious Christians will no doubt "turn off the tube and read to their kids and talk things over" (Hile, 179). Such images of Christian life show that Peretti's vision owes less to the "Moral Majority" Christian politics of the 1980s than to the "Jesus people" of the 1960s and 1970s, who promoted a drug-free Christian lifestyle while affirming the romanticism of the counterculture.

Meanwhile, above and below the peaceful town of Ashton stand rank upon rank of angels and demons. In the following selection from *This Present Darkness,* the main human characters of the novel appear in conjunction with their spiritual allies and enemies. An evil spirit pursues Marshall Hogan, the hero of the novel, who has come to Ashton because he was neglecting his family as a newspaper reporter in New York. Without Hogan's knowledge, God has called him to help rescue the town in response to the prayers of a local minister, Hank Busche. Peretti allows us to overhear Hogan's argument with his daughter Sandy, a college student, and to watch Busche pray as he mows the grass. Soon, all of these people, and more, will be brought together in a spiritual war alongside twenty-four angels, whom we also see assembling, passing through walls to enter Busche's church. These are not the loving guardian angels of Victorian sentimentality or the chubby cupids of Baroque art. They are warriors, giant men with beards dressed in tan military fatigues. On their waists are golden belts and strapped along their legs are copper scabbards holding swords with gashed and discolored blades. Their wings burn like lightning, and their names ring with foreign power—Krioni, Triskal, Guilo, Armoth. Tal, the captain of the host, has often stood "near the throne room of Heaven itself, in conference with none other than Michael" (44). In the exaggerated masculinity of these angels, the traditional gender roles of Ashton stand confirmed and protected.

The demons that these angels fight, like the spirit of complacency and despair who fastens to Marshall Hogan in this excerpt, usually have no names. At the head of the demons, however, stands Rafar of Babylon; Rafar in turn serves the Strongman, "one of the few majesties intimate with Lucifer" (132). Rafar and the Strongman control Professor Langstrat, a svelte psychologist who teaches Sandy "The Psychology of Self" at Whitmore College. Langstrat's interactions with Hogan and his daughter quickly demonstrate her intellectual arrogance, humanistic self-preoccupation, and controlling nature. A powerful woman, the lover and corrupter of Ashton's male chief of police, Professor Langstrat becomes one of only two people Peretti depicts as knowing collaborators with Satan's angels.

This Present Darkness presents a world filled with angels, demons, and exotic humans, in which true Christians, true Americans, and true women and men must arm themselves with spiritual power to survive. Because supernatural and alien human powers fight over Ashton, it becomes more than an American backwater town adrift in world culture. Because the prayers of Ashton prevail, the cosmos centers on Christian families nestled in small-town America.

The selection below is from Frank E. Peretti, *This Present Darkness* (Wheaton, Ill.: Crossway Books, 1986), pp. 36–48. Copyright © 1986. Used by permission of Crossway Books, a division of Good News Publishers, Wheaton, Ill. 60187.

Further Reading

A brief introduction to spiritual warfare appears in Damian Thompson, *The End of Time: Faith and Fear in the Shadow of the Millennium* (Hanover, N.H.: University Press of New England, 1996), pp. 139–166. Sources used in this introduction include John Bunyan, *The Pilgrim's Progress* (Orig. 1678; New York: New American Library, 1964); Gary Corwin, "This Present Nervousness," in *Evangelical Missions Quarterly* 31 (April 1995): 148–49; Sara Diamond, *Not by Politics Alone: The Enduring Influence of the Christian Right* (New York: Guilford, 1998); Gene W. Doty, "Blasphemy and the Recovery of the Sacred," in *Violence, Utopia, and the Kingdom of God,* edited by Tina Pippin and George Aichele (London: Routledge, 1998); Robert A. Guelich, "Spiritual Warfare: Jesus, Paul and Peretti," *Pneuma* 13 (Spring 1991): 33–64; Irving Hexham, "The Evangelical Response to the New Age," in *Perspectives on the New Age,* edited by James R. Lewis and J. Gordon Melton (Albany: State University of New York Press, 1992); Kevin S. Hile, ed., *Something about the Author* 80 (Detroit: Gale Research, 1995); Colleen McDannell, *Material Christianity: Religion and Popular Culture in America* (New Haven: Yale University Press, 1995); Gustav Niebuhr, "The Newest Christian Fiction Injects a Thrill into Theology," *New York Times,* October 30, 1995, p. A1; Bob and Gretchen Passantino, "Battling for the Minds and Hearts of Our Children: A Discussion with Frank and Barbara Peretti," http://answers.org/Issues/peretti.html Nov. 15, 2000.

This Present Darkness

Could anyone have seen him, the initial impression would not have been so much his reptilian, warted appearance as the way his figure seemed to absorb light and not return it, as if he were more a shadow than an object, a strange, animated hole in space. But this little spirit was invisible to the eyes of men, unseen and immaterial, drifting over the town, banking one way and then the other, guided by will and not wind, his swirling wings quivering in a greyish blur as they propelled him. He was like a high-strung little gargoyle, his hide a slimy, bottomless black, his body thin and spiderlike; half humanoid, half animal, totally demon. Two huge yellow cat-eyes bulged out of his face, darting to and fro, peering, searching. His breath came in short, sulfurous gasps, visible as glowing yellow vapor.

He was carefully watching and following his charge, the driver of a brown Buick moving through the streets of Ashton far below.

Marshall got out of the Clarion office just a little early that day. After all the morning's confusion it was a surprise to find Tuesday's Clarion already off to the printer and the staff gearing up for Friday. A small-town paper was just about the right pace . . . perhaps he *could* get to know his daughter again.

Sandy. Yes sir, a beautiful redhead, their only child. She had nothing but potential, but had spent most of her childhood with an overtime mother and a hardly-there father. Marshall was successful in New York, all right, at just about everything except being the kind of father Sandy needed. She had always let him know about it, too, but as Kate said, the two of them were too much alike; her cries for love and attention always came out like stabs, and Marshall gave her attention all right, like dogs give to cats.

No more fights, he kept telling himself, no more picking and scratching and hurting. Let her talk, let her spill how she feels, and don't be harsh with her. Love her for who she is, let her be herself, don't try to corral her.

It was crazy how his love for her kept coming out like spite, with anger and cutting words. He knew he was only reaching for her, trying to bring her back. It just never worked. Ah well, Hogan, try, try again, and don't blow it this time.

He made a left turn and could see the college ahead. The Whitmore College campus looked like most American campuses—beautiful, with stately old buildings that made you feel learned just to look at them, wide, neatly-lawned plazas with walkways in carefully laid patterns of brick and stone, landscaping with rocks, greenery, statuary. It was everything a good college should be, right down to the fifteen-minute parking spaces. Marshall parked the Buick and set out in search of Stewart Hall, home of the Psychology Department and Sandy's last class for the day.

Whitmore was a privately-endowed college, founded by some landholder as a memorial to himself back in the early twenties. From old photos of the place one could discover that some of the red-brick and white-pillared lecture halls were as old as the college itself: monuments of the past and supposedly guardians of the future. The summertime campus was relatively quiet.

Marshall got directions from a frisbee-throwing sophomore and turned left down an elm-lined street. At the end of the street he found Stewart Hall, an imposing structure patterned after some European cathedral with towers and archways. He pulled open one of the big double doors and found himself in a spacious, echoing hallway. The close of the big door made such a reverberating thunder off the vaulted ceiling and smooth walls that Marshall thought he had disturbed every class on the floor.

But now he was lost. This place had three floors and some thirty classrooms, and he had no idea which one was Sandy's. He started walking down the hall, trying to keep his heels from tapping too loudly. You couldn't even get away with a burp in this place. Sandy was a freshman this year. Their move to Ashton had been just a little late, so she was enrolled in summer classes to catch up, but all in all it had been the right point of transition for her. She was an undeclared major for now, feeling her way and taking prerequisites. Where a class in "Psychology of Self" fit into all that Marshall couldn't guess, but he and Kate weren't out to rush her.

From somewhere down the cavernous hall echoed the indistinguishable but well-ordered words of a lecture in progress, a woman's voice. He decided to check it out. He moved past several classroom doors, their little black numbers steadily decreasing, then a drinking fountain, the restrooms, and a ponderously ascending stone and iron staircase. Finally he began to make out the words of the lecture as he drew near Room 101.

". . . so if we settle for a simple ontological formula, 'I think, therefore I am,' that should be the end of the question. But *being* does not presuppose meaning . . ."

Yeah, here was more of that college stuff, that funny conglomeration of sixty-four-dollar words which impress people with your academic prowess but can't get you a paying job. Marshall smirked to himself a little bit. Psychology. If all those shrinks could just agree for a change, it would help. First Sandy blamed her snotty attitude on a violent birth experience, and then what was it? Poor potty training? Her new thing was self-knowledge, self-esteem, identity; she already knew how to be hung up on herself—now they were teaching it to her in college.

He peeked in the door and saw a theater arrangement, with rows of seats built in steadily rising levels toward the back of the room, and the small platform in front with the professor lecturing against a massive blackboard backdrop.

". . . and meaning doesn't necessarily come from thinking, for some have said that the Self is not the Mind at all, and that the Mind actually denies the Self and inhibits Self-Knowledge . . ."

Whoosh! For some reason Marshall had expected an older woman, skinny, her hair in a bun, wearing horn-rimmed glasses with a little beady chain looped around her neck. But this one was a startling surprise, something right out of a lipstick or fashion commercial: long blonde hair, trim figure, deep, dark eyes that twitched a bit but certainly needed no glasses, horn-rimmed or otherwise.

Then Marshall caught the glint of deep red hair, and he saw Sandy sitting toward the front of the hall, listening intently and feverishly scrawling notes. Bingo! That was easy. He decided to slip in quietly and listen to the tail end of the lecture. It might give him some idea of what Sandy was learning and then they'd have something to talk about. He stepped silently through the door, and took one of the empty seats in the back.

Then it happened. Some kind of radar in the professor's head must have clicked on. She homed in on Marshall sitting there and simply would not look away from him. He had no desire to draw any attention to himself— he was rapidly getting too much of that anyway, from the class—so he said nothing. But the professor seemed to examine him, searching his face as if it were familiar to her, as if she were trying to remember someone she had known before. The look that suddenly crossed her face gave Marshall a chill: she gave him a knifelike gaze, like the eyes of a treed cougar. He began to feel a corresponding defense instinct twisting a knot in his stomach.

"Is there something you want?" the professor demanded, and all Marshall could see were her two piercing eyes.

"I'm just waiting for my daughter," he answered and his tone was courteous.

"Would you like to wait outside?" she said, and it wasn't a question.

And he was out in the hall. He leaned against the wall, staring at the linoleum, his mind spinning, his senses scrambled, his heart pounding. He had no understanding of why he was there, but he was out in the hall. Just like that. How? What happened? Come on, Hogan, stop shaking and *think!*

He tried to replay it in his mind, but it came back slowly, stubbornly, like recalling a bad dream. That woman's eyes! The way they looked told him she somehow knew who he was, even though they had never met—and he had never seen or felt such hate. But it wasn't just the eyes; it was also the fear; the steadily rising, face-draining, heart-pounding fear that had crept into him for no reason, with no visible cause. He had been scared half to death . . . by nothing! It made no sense at all. He had never run or backed down from anything in his life. But now, for the first time in his life . . .

For the first time? The image of Alf Brummel's gazing gray eyes flashed across his mind, and the weakness returned. He blinked the image away and took a deep breath. Where was the old Hogan gut strength? Had he left it back in Brummel's office?

But he had no conclusions, no theories, no explanations, only derision for himself. He muttered, "So I gave in again, like a rotted tree," and like a rotted tree he leaned against the wall and waited.

In a few minutes the door to the lecture hall burst open and students began to fan outward like bees from a hive. They ignored him so thoroughly that Marshall felt invisible, but that was fine with him for now.

Then came Sandy. He straightened up, walked toward her, started to say hello . . . and she walked right by! She didn't pause, smile, return his greeting, anything! He stood there dumbly for a moment, watching her walk down the hall toward the exit.

Then he followed. He wasn't limping, but for some reason he felt like he was. He wasn't really dragging his feet, but they felt like lead weights. He saw his daughter go out the door without looking back. The clunk of the big door's closing echoed through the huge hall with a ponderous, condemning finality, like the crash of a huge gate dividing him forever from the one he loved. He stopped there in the broad hall, numb, helpless, even tottering a little, his big frame looking very small.

Unseen by Marshall, small wisps of sulfurous breath crept along the floor like slow water, along with an unheard scraping and scratching over the tiles.

Like a slimy black leech, the little demon clung to him, its taloned fingers entwining Marshall's legs like parasitic tendrils, holding him back, poisoning his spirit. The yellow eyes bulged out of the gnarled face, watching him, boring into him.

Marshall was feeling a deep and growing pain, and the little spirit knew it. This man was getting hard to hold down. As Marshall stood there in the big empty hall, the hurt, the love, the desperation began to build inside him; he could feel the tiniest remaining ember of *fight* still burning. He started for the door.

Move, Hogan, *move!* That's your daughter!

With each determined step, the demon was dragged along the floor behind him, its hands still clinging to him, a deeper rage and fury rising in its eyes and the sulfurous vapors chugging out of its nostrils. The wings spread in search of an anchor, any way to hold Marshall back, but they found none.

Sandy, Marshall thought, give your old man a break.

By the time he reached the end of the hall he was nearly into a run. His big hands hit the crash bar on the door and the door flung open, slamming into the doorstop on the outside steps. He ran down the stairs and out onto the pedestrian walkway shaded by the elms. He looked up the street, across the lawn in front of Stewart Hall, down the other way, but she was gone.

The demon gripped him tighter and began to climb and slither upward. Marshall felt the first pangs of despair as he stood there alone.

"I'm over here, Daddy."

Immediately the demon lost its grip and fell free, snorting with indignation. Marshall spun around and saw Sandy, standing just beside the door he had just burst through, apparently trying to hide from her classmates among the camellia bushes and looking very much like she was about to take him to task. Well, anything was better than losing her, Marshall thought.

"Well," he said before he considered, "pardon me, but I get the distinct impression you disowned me in there."

Sandy tried to stand straight, to face him in her hurt and anger, but she still could not look him squarely in the eye.

"It was—it was just too painful."

"What was?"

"You know . . . that whole thing in there."

"Well, I like coming on with a real splash, you know. Something people will remember . . . ."

"Daddy!"

"So who stole all the 'No Parents Allowed' signs? How was I to know she didn't want me in there? And just what's so all-fired precious and secret that she doesn't want any outsiders to hear it?"

Now Sandy's anger rose above her hurt, and she could look at him squarely. "Nothing! Nothing at all. It was just a lecture."

"So just what is her problem?"

Sandy groped for an explanation. "I don't know. I guess she must know who you are."

"No way. I've never even seen her before." And then a question automatically popped into Marshall's mind, "What do you mean, she must know who I am?"

Sandy looked cornered. "I mean . . . oh, c'mon. Maybe she knows you're the editor of the paper. Maybe she doesn't want reporters snooping around."

"Well, I hope I can tell you I wasn't snooping. I was just looking for you."

Sandy wanted to end the discussion. "All right, Daddy, all right. She just read you wrong, okay? I don't know what her problem was. She has the right to choose her audience, I suppose."

"And I don't have the right to know what my daughter is learning?"

Sandy stopped a word halfway up her throat and inferred a few things first. "You *were* snooping!"

Even as it happened, Marshall knew good and well that they were at it again, the old cats-and-dogs, fighting roosters routine. It was crazy. Part of him didn't want it to happen, but the rest of him was too frustrated and angry to stop.

As for the demon, it only cowered nearby, shying from Marshall as if he were red hot. The demon watched, waited, fretted.

"In a pig's eye I was snooping!" Marshall roared. "I'm here because I'm your loving father and I wanted to pick you up after classes. Stewart Hall, that's all I knew. I just happened to find you, and . . . ." He tried to brake himself. He deflated a little, covered his eyes with his hand, and sighed.

"And you thought you'd keep an eye on me!" Sandy suggested spitefully.

"Got some law against that?"

"Okay, I'll lay it all out for you. I'm a human being, Daddy, and every human entity—I don't care who he or she is—is ultimately subject to a universal scheme and not to the will of any specific individual. As for Professor Langstrat, if she doesn't want you present at her lecture, it's her prerogative to demand that you leave!"

"And just who's paying her salary, anyway?"

She ignored the question. "And as for me, and what I am learning, and what I am becoming, and where I am going, and what I wish, I say you have no right to infringe on my universe unless I personally grant you that right!"

Marshall's eyesight was getting blurred by visions of Sandy turned over his knee. Enraged, he had to lash out at somebody, but now he was trying to steer his attacks away from Sandy. He pointed back toward Stewart Hall and demanded, "Did—did she teach you that?"

"You don't need to know."

"I have a right to know!"

"You waived that right, Daddy, years ago."

That punch sent him into the ropes, and he couldn't fully recover before she took off down the street, escaping him, escaping their miserable, bullish battle. He hollered after her, some stupid-sounding question about how she'd get home, but she didn't even slow down.

The demon grabbed its chance *and* Marshall, and he felt his anger and self-righteousness give way to sinking despair. He'd blown it. The very thing he never wanted to do again, he did. Why in the world was he wired up this way? Why couldn't he just reach her, love her, win her back? She was disappearing from sight even now, becoming smaller and smaller as she hurried across the campus, and she seemed so very far away, farther than any loving arm could ever reach. He had always tried to be strong, to stand tough through life and through struggles, but right now the hurt was so bad he couldn't keep that strength from crumbling away from him in pitiful pieces. As he watched, Sandy disappeared around a distant corner without looking back, and something broke inside him. His soul felt like it would melt, and at this moment there was no person on the face of the earth he hated more than himself.

The strength of his legs seemed to surrender under the load of his sorrow, and he sank to the steps in front of the old building, despondent.

The demon's talons surrounded his heart and he muttered in a quivering voice, "What's the use?"

"YAHAAAAA!" came a thundering cry from the nearby shrubs. A bluish-white light glimmered. The demon released its grip on Marshall and bolted like a terrified fly, landing some distance away in a trembling, defensive stance, its huge yellow eyes nearly popping out of its head and a soot-black, barbed scimitar ready in its quivering hand. But then there came an unexplainable commotion behind those same bushes, some kind of struggle, and the source of the light disappeared around the corner of Stewart Hall.

The demon did not stir, but waited, listened, watched. No sound could be heard except the light breeze. The demon stalked ever so cautiously back to where Marshall still sat, went past him, and peered through the shrubbery and around the corner of the building.

Nothing.

As if held for this entire time, a long, slow breath of yellow vapor curled in lacy wisps from the demon's nostrils. Yes, it knew what it had seen; there was no mistaking it. But why had they fled?

A short distance across the campus, but enough distance to be safe, two giant men descended to earth like glimmering, bluish-white comets, held aloft by rushing wings that swirled in a blur and burned like lightning. One of them, a huge, burly, black-bearded bull of a man, was quite angry and indignant, bellowing and making fierce gestures with a long, gleaming sword. The other was a little smaller and kept looking about with great caution, trying to get his associate to calm down.

In a graceful, fiery spiral they drifted down behind one of the college dormitories and came to rest in the cover of some overhanging willows. The moment their feet touched down, the light from their clothes and bodies began to fade and the shimmering wings gently subsided. Save for their towering stature they appeared as two ordinary men, one trim and blond, the other built like a tank, both dressed in what looked like matching tan fatigues. Golden belts had become like dark leather, their scabbards were dull copper, and the glowing, bronze bindings on their feet had become simple leather sandals. The big fellow was ready for a discussion.

"Triskal!" he growled, but at his friend's desperate gestures he spoke just a little softer. "What are you doing here?"

Triskal kept his hands up to keep his friend quiet.

"Shh, Guilo! The Spirit brought me here, the same as you. I arrived yesterday."

"You know what that was? A demon of complacency and despair if ever I saw one! If your arm hadn't held me I could have struck him, and only once!"

"Oh, yes, Guilo, only once," his friend agreed, "but it's a good thing I saw you and stopped you in time. You've just arrived and you don't understand—"

"What don't I understand?"

Triskal tried to say it in a convincing manner. "We . . . must not fight, Guilo. Not yet. We must not resist."

Guilo was sure his friend was mistaken. He took firm hold of Triskal's shoulder and looked him right in the eye.

"Why should I go anywhere but to fight?" he stated. "Here I was called. Here I will fight."

"Yes," said Triskal, nodding furiously. "Just not yet, that's all."

"Then you must have orders! You *do* have orders?"

Triskal paused for effect, then said, "*Tal's* orders."

Guilo's angry expression at once melted into a mixture of shock and perplexity.

Dusk was settling over Ashton, and the little white church on Morgan Hill was washed with the warm, rusty glow of the evening sun. Outside in the small churchyard, the church's young pastor hurriedly mowed the lawn, hoping to be finished before mealtime. Dogs were barking in the neighborhood, people were arriving back home from work, kids were being called in for supper.

Unseen by these mortals, Guilo and Triskal came hurriedly up the hill on foot, secretive and unglorified but moving like the wind nevertheless. As they arrived in front of the church, Hank Busche came around the corner behind the roaring lawn mower, and Guilo had to pause to look him over.

"Is he the one?" he asked Triskal. "Did the call begin with him?"

"Yes," Triskal answered, "months ago. He's praying even now, and often walks the streets of Ashton interceding for it."

"But . . . this place is so small. Why was I called? No, no, why was *Tal* called?"

Triskal only pulled at his arm. "Hurry inside."

They passed quickly through the walls of the church and into the humble little sanctuary. Inside they found a contingent of warriors already gathered, some sitting in the pews, others standing around the platform, still others acting as sentries, looking cautiously out the stained glass windows. They were all dressed much as Triskal and Guilo, in the same tan tunics and breeches, but Guilo was immediately impressed by the imposing stature of them all; these were the mighty warriors, the powerful warriors, and more than he had ever seen gathered in one place.

He was also struck by the mood of the gathering. This moment could have been a joyful reunion of old friends except that everyone was strangely somber. As he looked around the room he recognized many whom he had fought alongside in times far past:

Nathan, the towering Arabian who fought fiercely and spoke little. It was he who had taken demons by their ankles and used them as warclubs against their fellows.

Armoth, the big African whose war cry and fierce countenance had often been enough to send the enemy fleeing before he even assailed them. Guilo and Armoth had once battled the demon lords of villages in Brazil and personally guarded a family of missionaries on their many long treks through the jungles.

Chimon, the meek European with the golden hair, who bore on his forearms the marks of a fading demon's last blows before Chimon banished him forever into the abyss. Guilo had never met this one, but had heard of his exploits and his ability to take blows simply as a shield for others and then to rally himself to defeat untold numbers alone.

Then came the greeting of the oldest and most cherished friend. "Welcome, Guilo, the Strength of Many!"

Yes, it was indeed Tal, the Captain of the Host. It was so strange to see this mighty warrior standing in this humble little place. Guilo had seen him near the throne room of Heaven itself, in conference with none other than Michael. But here stood the same impressive figure with golden hair and ruddy complexion, intense golden eyes like fire and an unchallengeable air of authority.

Guilo approached his captain and the two of them clasped hands.

"And we are together again," said Guilo as a thousand memories flooded his mind. No warrior Guilo had ever seen could fight as Tal could; no demon could outmaneuver or outspeed him, no sword could parry a blow from the sword of Tal. Side by side, Guilo and his captain had vanquished demonic powers for as long as those rebels had existed, and had been companions in the Lord's service before there had been any rebellion at all. "Greetings, my dear captain!"

Tal said by way of explanation, "It's a serious business that brings us together again."

Guilo searched Tal's face. Yes, there was plenty of confidence there, and no timidity. But there was definitely a strange grimness in the eyes and mouth, and Guilo looked around the room once again. Now he could feel it, that typically silent and ominous prelude to the breaking of grim news. Yes, they all knew something he didn't but were waiting for the appointed person, most likely Tal, to speak it.

Guilo couldn't stand the silence, much less the suspense. "Twenty-three," he counted, "of the very best, the most gallant, the most undefeatable . . . gathered now as though under siege, cowering in a flimsy fortress from a dreaded enemy?" With a dramatic flair, he drew his huge sword and cradled the blade in his free hand. "Captain Tal, who is this enemy?"

Tal answered slowly and clearly, "Rafar, the Prince of Babylon."

All eyes were now on Guilo's face, and his reaction was much like that of every other warrior upon hearing the news: shock, disbelief, an awkward pause to see if anyone would laugh and verify that it was only a mistake. There was no such reprieve from the truth. Everyone in the room continued to look at Guilo with the same deadly serious expression, driving the gravity of the situation home mercilessly.

Guilo looked down at his sword. Was it now shaking in his hands? He made a point of holding it still, but he couldn't help staring for a moment at the blade, still gashed and discolored from the last time Guilo and Tal had confronted this Baal-prince from the ancient times. Guilo and Tal had struggled against him twenty-three days before finally defeating him on the eve of Babylon's fall. Guilo could still remember the darkness, the shrieking and horror, the fierce, terrible grappling while pain seared every inch of his being. The evil of this would-be pagan god seemed to envelop him and everything around him like thick smoke, and half the time the two warriors had to maneuver and strike blindly, each one not even knowing if the other was still in the fight. To this day neither of them even knew which one finally delivered the blow that sent Rafar plummeting into the abyss. All they remembered was his heaven-shaking scream as he fell through a jagged rift in space, and then seeing each other again when the great darkness that surrounded them cleared like a melting fog.

"I know you speak the truth," Guilo said at last, "but . . . would such as Rafar come to this place? He is a prince of nations, not mere hamlets. What *is* this place? What interest could he possibly have in it?"

Tal only shook his head. "We don't know. But it is Rafar, there's no question, and the stirrings in the enemy's realm indicate something is in the making. The Spirit wants us here. We must confront whatever it is."

"And we are not to fight, we are not to resist!" Guilo exclaimed. "I will be most fascinated to hear your next order, Tal. We cannot fight?"

"Not yet. We're too few, and there's very little prayer cover. There are to be no skirmishes, no confrontations. We're not to show ourselves in any way as aggressors. As long as we stay out of their way, keep close to this place, and pose no threat to them, our presence here will seem like normal watchcare over a few, struggling saints." Then he added with a very direct tone, "And it will be best if it not be spread that I am here."

Guilo now felt a little out of place still holding his sword, and sheathed it with an air of disgust.

"And," he prodded, "you do have a plan? We were not called here to watch the town fall?"

The lawn mower roared by the windows, and Tal guided their attention to its operator.

"It was Chimon's task to bring him here," he said, "to blind the eyes of his enemies and slip him through ahead of the adversary's choice for the pastor of this flock. Chimon succeeded, Hank was voted in, to the surprise of many, and now he's here in Ashton, praying every hour of every day. We were called here for his sake, for the saints of God and for the Lamb."

"For the saints of God and for the Lamb!" they all echoed.

Tal looked at a tall, dark-haired warrior, the one who had taken him through the town the night of the Festival, and smiled. "And you had him win by just one vote?"

The warrior shrugged. "The Lord wanted him here. Chimon and I had to make sure he won, and not the other man who has no fear of God."

Tal introduced Guilo to this warrior. "Guilo, this is Krioni, watchcarer of our prayer warrior here and of the town of Ashton. Our call began with Hank, but Hank's presence here began with Krioni."

Guilo and Krioni nodded silent greeting to each other.

Tal watched Hank finishing up the lawn and praying out loud at the same time. "So now, as his enemies in the congregation regroup and try to find another way to oust him, he continues to pray for Ashton. He's one of the last."

"If not *the* last!" lamented Krioni.

"No," cautioned Tal, "he's not alone. There's still a Remnant of saints somewhere in this town. There is always a Remnant."

"There is always a Remnant," they all echoed.

"Our conflict begins in this place. We'll make this our location for now, hedge it in and work from here." He spoke to a tall Oriental in the back of the room. "Signa, take as your charge this building, and choose two now to stand with you. This is our rest point. Make it secure. No demon is to approach it."

Signa immediately found two volunteers to work with him. They vanished to their posts.

"Now, Triskal, I'll hear news of Marshall Hogan."

"I followed him up to my encounter with Guilo. Though Krioni has reported a rather eventless situation up to the time of the Festival, ever since then Hogan has been hounded by a demon of complacency and despair."

Tal received that news with great interest. "Hm. Could be he's beginning to stir. They're covering him, trying to hold him in check."

Krioni added, "I never thought I'd see it happen. The Lord wanted him in charge of the *Clarion*, and we took care of that too, but I've never seen a more tired individual."

"Tired, yes, but that will only make him more usable in the Lord's hands. And I perceive that he is indeed waking up, just as the Lord foreknew."

"Though he could awaken only to be destroyed," said Triskal. "They must be watching him. They fear what he could do in his influential position."

"True," replied Tal. "So while they bait our bear, we must be sure they stir him up and no more than that. It's going to be a very critical business."

Now Tal was ready to move. He addressed the whole group. "I expect Rafar to take power here by nightfall; no doubt we'll all feel it when he does. Be sure of this: he will immediately search out the greatest threat to him and try to remove it."

"Ah, Henry Busche," said Guilo.

"Krioni and Triskal, you can be sure that a troop of some kind will be sent to test Hank's spirit. Select for yourselves four warriors and watch over him." Tal touched Krioni's shoulder and added, "Krioni, up until now you've done very well in protecting Hank from any direct onslaughts. I commend you."

"Thank you, captain."

"I ask you now to do a difficult thing. Tonight you must stand by and keep watch. Do not let Hank's life be touched, but aside from that prevent nothing. It will be a test he must undergo."

There was a slight moment of surprise and wonderment, but each warrior was ready to trust Tal's judgment.

Tal continued, "As for Marshall Hogan . . . he's the only one I'm not sure about yet. Rafar will give his lackeys incredible license with him, and he could either collapse and retreat, or—as we all hope—rouse himself and fight back. He'll be of special interest to Rafar—and to me—tonight. Guilo, select two warriors for yourself and two for me. We'll watchcare over Marshall tonight and see how he responds. The rest of you will search out the Remnant."

Tal drew his sword and held it high. The others did the same and a forest of shining blades appeared, held aloft in strong arms.

"Rafar," Tal said in a low, musing voice, "we meet again." Then, in the voice of a Captain of the Host: "For the saints of God and for the Lamb!"

"For the saints of God and for the Lamb!" they echoed.

— 27 —

Charismatic Renewal among Latino Catholics

Manuel A. Vásquez

The Catholic Charismatic Renewal Movement emerged in the late 1960s, inspired by wide-ranging changes in the Catholic Church following the Second Vatican Council (1962–1965). Vatican II, as the council came to be known, inaugurated a period of *aggiornamento* (updating), opening the Church to the modern, secular world it had consistently condemned. As part of this climate of openness and change, the Church recognized the laity's centrality in theological, liturgical, and pastoral matters. In particular, Vatican II documents emphasized the need to nurture lived Catholicism, that is, Catholicism as experienced in everyday life by the laity, as a way to revitalize and reform institutional structures. The Church's recognition of the importance of the faith-life link among the laity thus created a favorable climate for the emergence of relatively autonomous lay pastoral initiatives such as the base Christian communities in Latin America and the Catholic Charismatic Renewal in the United States.

Although Latinos have had a significant place in the United States since the end of the Mexican-American War (1848), changes in immigration laws in 1965 facilitated the rapid growth of immigration from Latin America. Thus whereas in the 1920s, 87 percent of foreign-born Americans came from Europe and only 4 percent from Latin America, today 50 percent come from Latin America and only 17 percent from Europe. The large and rapid influx of Latino immigrants is having a powerful effect on the Catholic Church, since about 75 percent of the estimated thirty-two million U.S. Latinos are Catholics. It is not surprising that Latino Catholics are now the largest Catholic group in places such as Los Angeles, Houston, and Miami. Latino Catholics, however, have also become numerically dominant in places such as New York City, long a stronghold of Irish American and Italian American Catholicism. To minister to this growing Latino population, when only 4 percent of priests are Latino, the Catholic Church has come to rely heavily on post–Vatican II movements, among which the Catholic Charismatic Renewal has been one of the most successful.

Scholars point to a gathering of faculty and students at Duquesne University in Pennsylvania in February 1967 as the starting point for charismatic renewal among Catholics. News of the Holy Spirit's work at the "Duquesne Weekend," as this event became known, spread quickly to other campuses, including Notre Dame and Michigan State University. The Duquesne Weekend included intense prayer and small-group reflection on the biblical book of the Acts of the Apostles, a seminal text for the charismatic movement. According to one participant, as the gathering proceeded, many began to receive the Holy Spirit. They praised God in new languages, wept, and sang. From late at night until early the next morning, they prayed and each person there felt that God was dealing with him or her in a new, special way.

Nationally, the movement caught fire, moving rapidly from its initial base among the white, educated middle class, to other groups such as Latinos. Mexican-Americans, Puerto Ricans, and Dominicans have been particularly receptive to the Catholic Charismatic Renewal, becoming leaders of various charismatic circles and assemblies. It may be the case that Puerto Ricans and Dominicans are drawn to charismatic renewal because it reflects the more festive and emotive cultures of the Caribbean. It also may be that the movement itself has a longer history in Puerto Rico than in other countries in South America, thus facilitating the creation of Puerto Rican leaders.

After its beginnings in the early seventies in the United States, the Catholic Charismatic Renewal also gained popularity in Latin America. The movement has achieved considerable visibility and draws its supporters from diverse racial and class backgrounds. This expansion has been facilitated by the crisis of liberation theology and base Christian communities. Liberation theology and base communities sought to link faith and transformative action against persistent social injustices in the region. During the 1960s and 1970s, liberation theology and base communities played a key role in opposing repressive military dictatorships in many countries in the Americas. Nevertheless, with the disorderly transitions to democracy and the economic crises of the eighties and nineties, many people have been forced to retreat from political activism and to focus instead on personal and family survival. In this context, the Charismatic Renewal, with its strong stress on individual regeneration and on sustaining communities of feeling, has proven very attractive. This emphasis also appeals to U.S. Latinos. On the one hand, the Charismatic Renewal offers Latinos strong, intimate, and expressive communities in the face of what they see as an impersonal and consumerist society. On the other hand, the movement reaffirms the individual, with all his or her rights and duties, in a way that dovetails with mainstream culture in the United States.

The rapid growth of evangelical Protestantism—both North and South American—in the late 1980s has facilitated the growth of charismatic Latino Catholicism. Although the Duquesne Weekend marks the birth of the charismatic movement for Catholics, the foundational source of the movement can be traced back to the Pentecostal revival in 1906 at the Apostolic Faith Mission on now-famous Azusa Street in Los Angeles. Indeed, although there are significant differences, charismatic Catholicism shares several key theological and liturgical features with Protestant Pentecostalism. These similarities have led some scholars to refer to the Charismatic Renewal as "Catholic Pentecostalism" or to locate both it and Protestant Pentecostalism within the overarching umbrella terms "charismatic Christianity" or "neo-Pentecostalism." Consequently, factors both within and without Catholicism have encouraged the development of charismatic expression in parishes throughout the Spanish-speaking world.

The Catholic Charismatic Renewal functions simultaneously at both the local (parish) level and in global settings, through its national and international gatherings. As a result of this multiplicity and dispersion, charismatic Catholicism is increasingly becoming an ecclesial and worship style rather than a highly structured and centralized movement. Boundaries between charismatics and conventional Catholics can be very ambiguous. Sometimes those who no longer attend regular charismatic prayer meetings will remain active in their parishes. Others, who have no charismatic involvement in their parishes, become attracted to large public healing services conducted by charismatics. Latinos in the United States and Latin America move easily between charismatic expressions of their faith and "normal" Catholicism.

The hymns reprinted here are taken from a book of songs and hymns published by the parish of Our Lady of El Carmen in San Salvador, El Salvador. The songs are a part of a Christian global culture articulated through a dense and rich tapestry of activities and strategies. This global culture connects charismatics living in the United States and in Latin America. Songs such as these are not relegated to the parish that produces them because, due to modern modes of communications, they may be distributed at retreats, brought to international conferences, reprinted in grassroots publications, and sung at missionary crusades. By using high-tech media, communities of charismatics are linked across national and regional borders. Not only do the songs move throughout the Latino charismatic communities, so do the people. There is a constant back-and-forth movement between congregations in the United States and their sending countries. Transnational migration of the faithful makes it possible for charismatic Latinos to form a territorially borderless community of faith and practice across the Americas. Salvadoran immigrants living in Washington, D.C., Los Angeles, and Long Island who express their religious commitments in charismatic communities would be familiar with these songs. At the same time, the songs are well known among other Latinos, who have no connection with El Salvador.

The unseen world that the songs describe centers on the believer's experience of Christ. Like Pentecostalism, the Catholic charismatic expression is Christocentric, placing the experience of personal salvation through Jesus' passion and resurrection at the heart of all activities. Catholic Charismatic Renewal's Christology stresses two complementary aspects of Jesus Christ's nature. On the one hand, songs such as "There Is a Celebration [*Fiesta*]" and "Even Though in This Life" portray Jesus as an omnipotent Redeemer who "heals the sick, expels the demons, and calms the seas and the storms." He is capable of overturning the status quo of poverty and corruption and of building "a home, a beautiful home, far beyond the sun." On the other hand, charismatics see Christ as a companion, walking beside the sinner, consoling him or her at every tribulation and protecting him or her against temptations. In other words, Christ is both all-powerful and radically embodied; he can transform one's life completely through an ongoing I-Thou encounter in prayer, meditation, chanting, and in charismas (divine gifts) expressed in the redeemed sinner's body and in the body of the Church. The Christ of charismatics is not the abstract Christ of high theology but a familiar Christ, who fulfills his salvific telos or goal through tangible actions such as healing and casting out demons. The song "Fire, Fire" is unequivocal about Christ's presence: "someone is here and I know it is Christ, someone is here and I know it is the Lord."

The effectiveness of Christ's works stems from his multiple charismas, which are anchored and made manifest in the activities of the Holy Spirit. Like Protestant Pentecostals, charismatics see themselves as contemporaneous with the primitive Christian community. As described in Acts, the originative moment for this community is Pentecost, when the beleaguered apostles received the Holy Spirit in the form of tongues of fire that empowered them to speak in different languages (Acts 2:1–4). Armed with the power of the Holy Spirit, the apostles began to announce the gospel and perform miracle cures and exorcisms. These are the same wondrous acts taking place in small Charismatic Renewal circles today, when many among the faithful speak in tongues (glossolalia). The continuity between the earlier Christian community and the Charismatic Renewal explains not only the emphasis on the Holy Spirit but also the imagery of justification as a baptism of fire. As "Holy Spirit Come Here" makes clear, divine fire has a powerful cleansing effect, erasing a past of sin and confusion and producing a new state of joy and ecstasy. This state is not just expressed in songs ("I will praise him with all my heart, I will praise him saying: Glory to God!") but also in the festive worship style that characterizes charismatic assemblies, with plenty of clapping, dancing, and embracing. It is also part of a lived faith: "Now that I know what real life is, I can laugh, I can sing. Now I know I can love with your power inside of me."

In the face of criticism from traditional Catholics, who tend to emphasize the more formal and penitential dimensions of the faith, charismatics find in the work of the Holy Spirit every reason to celebrate. In this regard, charismatics also share with Pentecostals a belief in Jesus' imminent Second Coming. Fulfilling all promises, Jesus' return is close at hand, and charismas—glossolalia (speaking in an unknown language), miracle healings, and the power to exorcise and to prophesize—are signs and instruments of the *eschaton,* the end of times. The eschatology involved here is paradoxical; the reign of God is both seen and unseen. Christ is coming to create a new Jerusalem, a city of God that will put the corrupt and contingent city of man to shame. Those saved will "walk the streets of gold with Jesus," leaving behind once and for all the life of poverty, temptation, and tribulation. This new Jerusalem is an altogether different place than any we know, a realm "beyond the sun." However, although divine geography seems here to supercede human space, the simple allusion to Jerusalem, a human-made city, demonstrates that charismatic eschatology is bound up with human history. Heaven is "beyond the sun"; nevertheless, its essence is represented through earthly attributes, through objects such as gold, which stand for human power. In a way, Heaven does not erase human power but, to the contrary, it maximizes such power. By being in Heaven, the sinner leaves behind his life of lack and enters one of abundance in the company of God. Here we encounter the second dimension of charismatic eschatology. The reign of God is also this-worldly; it is immanent, already here but not fully realized. The works of the Holy Spirit are an anticipation of things to come. Just as Jesus' miraculous works pointed to the formation of a new community constituted not by outward rules and rituals but by laws inscribed in the heart, so today's charismas in the Church give a foretaste of complete salvation.

This is where charismatics begin to depart from Pentecostalism. Works are essential, making believers coparticipants in the salvific project. And "works" here refers to the activity of the Holy Spirit through the Church as the only legitimate holder of tradition. This tradition was built on the principle of apostolic succession and on the exemplary lives of saints. Whereas Catholic charismatics diminish the role of saints (and to some extent that of Mary, although she remains the intercessor par excellence), there is an unambiguous recognition of the clerical authority and the centrality of the sacraments. The Catholic Charismatic Renewal has "domesticated" some of the most powerful and potentially destabilizing elements of Pentecostalism. Indeed, the combination of respect for hierarchy (continuity) and relative lay autonomy, expressed in the intense and transformative personal relationship with Jesus (rupture), has been extremely appealing to Pope John Paul II as he has sought to carry out a "new evangelization."

The pope, however, has recently tempered his endorsement of the Catholic Charismatic Renewal as the movement begins to show some limitations and contradictions. One of the most common complaints among Latin American and Latino pastoral agents is that charismatics forsake the social aspects of the faith, concentrating mostly on prayer and celebration. This is not entirely true, for charismatics place a great emphasis on charity toward the poor. Nonetheless, unlike Christian base communities and liberation theology, which saw the transformation of structural injustices as a key component in building God's reign, Catholic charismatics concentrate more on individual and spiritual renewal, hoping that aggregate personal change will eventually translate into more just societies. Within this framework, good works for the poor tend to take a strongly paternalistic tenor.

Some critics also see the danger of the Catholic Charismatic Renewal movement becoming an end in itself, setting itself against the parish structure (which charismatics see as lacking the power of the Holy Spirit). This critique has renewed attempts to integrate the movement into the life of the Church as a whole, as yet another reform initiative. But as the songs below indicate, there might be something irreducibly antistructural in the exuberant and polymorphous manifestations of the Holy Spirit.

The songs printed here, translated by Manuel A. Vásquez, are from *Amémonos de Corazón* ["Let Us Love Each Other with Our Hearts"] (San Salvador, El Salvador: The Parish of Our Lady of El Carmen, 1995).

Further Reading

The research of Thomas Csordas has been of particular importance in this area. See his "Catholic Pentecostalism: A New Word in the New World," in *Perspectives on Pentecostalism: Case Studies From the Caribbean and Latin America*, edited by S. D. Glazier (Washington, D.C.: University Press of America, 1980), pp.143–175; "Religion and the World System: The Pentecostal Ethic and the Spirit of Monopoly Capitalism," *Dialectical Anthropology* 17 (1992): 3–24; *The Sacred Self: A Cultural Phenomenology of Charismatic Healing* (Berkeley and Los Angeles: University of California Press, 1994); and *Language, Charisma, and Creativity: The Ritual Life of a Religious Movement* (Berkeley and Los Angeles: University of California Press, 1997). See also Marjo De Theije, "CEBs and Catholic Charismatics in Brazil," in *Latin American Religion in Motion*, edited by Christian Smith and Joshua Prokopy (New York: Routledge, 1999); Manuel A. Vásquez, *The Brazilian Popular Church and the Crisis of Modernity* (Cambridge: Cambridge University Press, 1998); Anna Peterson, Manual A. Vásquez, and Philip Williams, eds., *Christianity, Social Change and Globalization in the Americas* (New Brunswick, N.J.: Rutgers University Press, 2001); Pierre Hegy, "Images of God and Man in a Catholic Charismatic Renewal Community," *Social Compass* 25 (1978): 7–21; Danielle Hervieu-Leger, "'What Scripture Tells Me': Spontaneity and Regulation within the Catholic Charismatic Renewal," in *Lived Religion in America: Toward a History of Practice*, edited by David Hall (Princeton: Princeton University Press, 1997); Mary Jo Nietz, *Charisma and Community: A Study of Religion in American Culture* (New Brunswick, N.J.: Transaction, 1987); Harvey Cox, *Fire from Heaven: The Rise of Pentecostal Spirituality and the Reshaping of Religion in the Twenty-First Century* (Reading, Mass.: Addison-Wesley, 1995); Edward O'Connor, ed., *Perspectives on Charismatic Renewal* (South Bend, Ind.: University of Notre Dame Press, 1975); Karla Poewe, *Charismatic Christianity as Global Culture* (Columbia: University of South Carolina Press, 1994); Richard Quebedeaux, *The New Charismatics: The Origins, Development, and Significance of Neo-Pentecostalism* (New York: Doubleday, 1976); Meredith B. McGuire, *Pentecostal Catholics: Power, Charisma, and Order in a Religious Movement* (Philadelphia: Temple University Press, 1982).

I Want to Walk the Streets of Gold

In the new Jerusalem, "the street of the city was pure gold, transparent as glass"
(Rev. 21:21)

I want to walk
The streets of gold with Jesus. [*repeat*]
I want to walk the streets of gold,
Want to walk the streets of gold
Want to walk the streets of gold with Jesus.
And to walk the streets of gold with Jesus,
One has to live under the shelter (*amparo*) of his light,
Obey his word, have his spirit,
To walk the streets of gold with Jesus.

Even Though in This Life

Even though in this life
I have no riches,
I know that there, in the glory,
As a soul lost
Amid my poverty,

Jesus has compassion for me
Far beyond the sun [*repeat*]
I have a home,
A home, beautiful home,
Far beyond the sun [*repeat*]

Thus through the world
I keep walking
Surrounded by tests and temptation.
But at my side,
Consoling me
Is my blessed Christ
In my tribulation

To all the peoples
Of the human race,
Christ wants to give
Complete salvation,
Also a house
For each brother
He went to prepare
In Holy Zion.

Fire, Fire

Someone is here and I know it is Christ
Someone is here and I know it is the Lord.
He can baptize and I know it is Christ,
He can baptize and I know it is the Lord.

Fire, fire, fire is what I want
Give it, give it, give it to me Lord.
All the faithful promises I anticipate
That you give me the Fire of the consoler.

I want to feel Christ's power;
I want to feel the Holy Spirit,
I want to feel heaven's angels
Camping by my side and help me triumph.

There Is a Celebration (*Fiesta*)

There is a feast, feast, feast,
Continuously in me [*repeat*]
There is a feast, feast, feast,
Since I met Christ.

This is the Christ that I preach
And never tire of preaching.
He heals the sick,
Expels the demons,
Calms the seas and the storms.

I will praise him [*three times*]
With all my heart
I will praise him [*three times*]
Saying: Glory to God!

Holy Spirit Come Here!

Holy Spirit come here;
Holy Spirit come to me;
I want to live, to be happy
With your power inside of me.

Now that I know what real life is
I can laugh, I can sing,

Now I know that I can love
With your power inside of me.

Brother, do you want to live in
God's glory? Then accept this blessing
Which will be your salvation.

Raise your arms,
Now close your eyes,
Rejoice brother,
Filled with joy.

28

Visualizing Chenrezi in American Tibetan Buddhism

Richard Hughes Seager

Traditional Tibetan Buddhist practices have come to play an increasingly important role in American Buddhism since the 1970s, when a substantial number of lamas, or teachers, began to arrive in America in the wake of the Chinese invasion of their homeland. These traditions have a highly distinctive character for a variety of reasons. They originated centuries ago, when the Buddhism of ancient India took root in central Asia, where it fused with regional shamanic traditions. As a result of Tibet's isolation during the heyday of European colonialism, these traditions remained largely untouched by a range of powerful modernization movements that transformed much of Buddhist Asia. In response to the Chinese policy of destroying Tibetan religion, moreover, pioneering lamas arrived in a state of crisis, which led many of them to place emphasis on the preservation of tradition. To accomplish this, they, along with their American students, soon engaged in the translation and publication of texts, many of which were once considered secret teachings. They also began to create places where Tibetans and Americans could study and practice these texts together.

To an important but limited degree, Tibetan Buddhism in America is modeled on the institutional structure of Tibet, where four schools or orders—the Sakya, Gelugpa, Kagyu, and Nyingma—predominate. Within these four, there are numerous teaching and practice lineages, each with traditions that include founders, philosophies and practices, wrathful protectors, and guardian spirits. Within this framework of school and lineage, lamas teach in accord with the tradition of their own teachers and, in doing so, perpetuate lines of transmission thought to have their origins in ancient founders of Tibetan Buddhism and, beyond that, in the teachings of the historical Buddha. With a few notable exceptions, there has been little effort to recreate in the United States the kind of large monastic compound that figured predominantly in the history of Tibetan Buddhism. But in the last thirty years, the Tibetan practice community has burgeoned, as groups that once met in rented rooms have purchased and refurbished houses, apartment buildings, and schools and have built new structures to create an extensive network of shrine rooms, practice halls, and dharma centers. Religious practices once performed in remote Himalayan regions are now routinely practiced on farms in Vermont, in hunting camps in Colorado, at conference centers in Atlanta, and at numerous other locations.

In some respects, Tibetan Buddhist meditative practices resemble those in other traditions. For instance, Dzogchen, a Nyingma practice, is considered akin to Zen meditation, a Japanese technique that is highly influential in the United States. Tibetan Buddhists also practice *vipassana,* the major form of meditation in South Asia, which in this country has inspired the highly popular Insight Meditation movement. All of these share an emphasis on watching the activity of the mind during seated meditation. Many Americans, however, now practice them to reduce stress, achieve peace of mind, build character, or deepen personal relations, a reorientation of value that some applaud and others decry but is often seen as typically American.

Other Tibetan practices, however, are resistant to this kind of reorientation of value, due to their highly specific and fundamentally traditional character; a case in point is the Chenrezi sadhana under consideration here. *Sadhana* is literally translated as "means of accomplishment" but more colloquially as "visualization." Visualization techniques are not unknown in other forms of Buddhism, but in Tibet they were raised to a religious performance artform in a uniquely rich practice tradition called Vajrayana. *Vajra* means "diamond" or "adamantine" and *yana* "vehicle," the two words together conveying both the idea of clarity and immutability in the experience of total liberation and the means to attain it. In the philosophical language of many Buddhist traditions, this experience is characterized as one of emptiness, a state of nonduality beyond all possible human conceptions. To achieve this state, a visualization is used to harness the body, speech, and mind of a practitioner with the body, speech, and mind of a buddha or bodhisattva—fully realized beings often referred to in translation as "deities." Visualization techniques include the use of mudras (ritual gestures) and mantras (syllables or phrases thought to express in sound the essential qualities of a particular buddha or bodhisattva). Mandalas, symbolic representations of the personified forces of the universe, are also used as aids to visualization. Those who practice Vajrayana understand it to be the most complete form of the teachings of the Buddha, one that leads to liberation in a single lifetime if practiced assiduously.

Many different visualization practices have been transmitted from teacher to students within Tibetan schools and lineages. In the United States, however, this transmission process has been opened up to a large degree, at least in some reaches of the Buddhist community. In traditional Tibet, many texts and oral teachings were closely guarded by teachers and transmitted to students only when they had been ritually empowered to practice them. As a result of efforts to translate and publish texts that might otherwise have been lost, teachings that once may have been kept secret can now be purchased in book stores and found posted on the Internet. In the often free-form atmosphere of American Buddhism, there is also a tendency for some seekers to frequent different centers and receive empowerments from a number of lamas, without ever taking up practice. This "collection" of empowerments is viewed critically by some lamas and serious students but tolerated by others. Whatever else this may be, it is a not wholly surprising aspect of the Americanization process, given that many spiritually restless Americans have developed a romantic fascination for all things Tibetan.

Despite these developments, the basic process of transmitting and practicing a visualization remains largely unchanged among lamas and highly committed students. First, a mutual relationship must be established in which a lama assumes spiritual responsibility to teach and the student to learn diligently. This relationship is informed by a strong tradition in Tibetan Buddhism of unapologetic, devotional regard for lamas, many of whom are considered reincarnations of highly realized beings. A student is also expected to undertake a series of preliminary practices to clear away negativity and accumulate merit in preparation for performing a visualization. Each practice must be done one hundred thousand times (the number varies from lineage to lineage), so the preliminary stage itself can take several years. A teacher will then empower the students to practice, choose for them a deity for their visualization practice, and instruct them in the appropriate mantra, mudra, mandala, and written and oral teachings.

Most visualizations follow a fairly standard form, although some are brief and simple, others lengthy and highly elaborate. A typical one opens with a prayer of taking refuge in the Buddha, his teaching or dharma, and the community or sangha. This is followed by an expression of intent to become fully realized and by a dedication of the merit gained from performing the visualization to all sentient beings. The core of the practice is performed in several stages. The first is a step-by-step process of building up a mental image of the buddha or bodhisattva to be visualized—its characteristic gestures, clothing and ornaments, colors, the place in which it resides, and so on. Once the image is established, a second stage is entered in which the practitioner becomes fully identified with it. When masterfully accomplished, this stage is marked by the seamless union of practitioner and deity, complete in every detail. The intent is for a practitioner to experience being the deity with an immediacy more concrete than a vivid, colorful, and sound-filled dream, more real than everyday life, a state that may last for hours or, according to Tibetan lore, even days. Finally, the practitioner dissolves the image entirely. This stage is extremely important insofar as it underscores the fact that the ultimate goal of the practice is not to visualize a deity per se, but to experience within oneself the clear and immutable emptiness a deity represents as a fully realized being. To conclude the practice, one again dedicates the merit accrued from performing it to all living beings.

This schematic description only does partial justice to the complex metaphysics and philosophy a serious practitioner encounters in the practice of visualization. It takes a great deal of concentration to perform one with mastery and, once this is achieved, a student will then move on to another that marks a further stage on the path. Many Americans, perhaps several thousand, have pursued this kind of meditation in the course of rigorous three-year retreats that are considered an essential step in becoming a teacher oneself. Practice centers consisting of a number of one-room cabins secluded on mountainsides or in valleys have been built expressly for these retreats, recreating in America the isolated huts and caves traditionally favored by many practitioners in Tibet. But visualizations are also practiced by others at home, in a shrine room, or dharma center, and the practice of visualizations can be undertaken virtually any place and under many circumstances. One can practice visualizing a deity while eating, during sleep, and even within dreams.

The text below includes key sections of a relatively simple visualization, but it is one devoted to the bodhisattva of compassion, who is among the most important figures in the Buddhist pantheon of Central and East Asia. In Tibet, he is known by the name of Chenrezi and is an immensely popular figure. The text is taken from a sadhana distributed by a Kagyu temple in New York state under the direction of Lama Norlha Rinpoche. It was printed on a series of unbound, narrow, rectangular pages to roughly replicate the form of palm-leaf manuscript pages of ancient Buddhist Asia. The text in the original runs in three parallel lines: one in Tibetan characters, a second in phonemes to enable practitioners to chant it readily, and a third in English.

The visualization opens with a lengthy litany (not reproduced here), which in an understated way illustrates the epic quality of the transmission of the teachings of Tibet to the United States. It consists of over forty names of key teachers in the Kagyu lineage from King Tilopa, a tenth-century founder of the lineage, down through the sixteenth Gyalwa Karmapa, an important pioneering teacher in the West during the 1970s and head of the Kagyu school until his death in 1981 in a Chicago suburb. The first part of the text reproduced below is a characteristically Tibetan formula for taking refuge, which makes an appeal to a wide range of personified forces (*yidams, dakas, dakinis, dharmapalas,* and the like) familiar in Tibet as well as to the Buddha, dharma, and sangha. The second part includes a more conventional formula for taking of refuge, an expression of intent to become fully realized, and a dedication of merit.

In section three, the creation of the image of Chenrezi is undertaken. Note in the text that he emerges from the syllable HRIH, his mantra or sound vibration. This conveys the idea that the spiritual qualities he represents are inherent in the fabric of the universe. Note also that he wears as an ornament the buddha Amitabha, whose name signifies the clear, radiant light of emptiness. This section is followed by a fourth that consists of a brief prayer to Chenrezi. There are two lengthy prayers, in roughly equal parts praise, expression of intent, and supplication, which have been omitted.

The fifth section marks the union of the practitioner and Chenrezi, a state of light and purified awareness in which the self, world, and Chenrezi are one in emptiness. The Realm of Dewachen to which the text refers is an abode of the buddhas, a "pure land" that is a spatial symbol of liberation. *Om Mani Peme Hung* is a variant rendering of the greatest of all mantras, the use of which is ubiquitous in both spontaneous prayer and ritual formulas in Tibet. *Om* represents the totality of sound and the inexpressible vastness of the universe. *Mani* means "jewel" and *peme* "lotus," two traditional symbols of liberation. The mantra is later referred to in the text as the "Six Syllables." Note the instruction to recite it "as much as you can," which may be ten, one thousand, ten thousand, or more repetitions. During this time, the union of deity and practitioner is complete and the practitioner engages in a range of visualizations focused on selected aspects of Chenrezi, all of which have specific transcendental meanings.

When this stage is completed, the image is dissolved, gradually if time permits and quickly if not, a process that is not explicitly indicated in the text. But the practitioner has already been instructed to melt Chenrezi's image back into the HRIH syllable from which it was originally generated, underscoring that he emerged from and reverts back into a sound vibration. The sixth section marks the critical transition in which the practitioner attempts to continue to dwell in emptiness, even though the image of the deity has dissipated. This is explicit in the direction to maintain one's mind in equanimity, free from all conceptualizations. The cultivation of emptiness within oneself and its embodiment in everyday life is the ultimate point—what is to be accomplished—in practicing the visualization. The text concludes with a number of dedications of merit, one of which is reproduced in section seven. Here the practitioner expresses an aspiration to be reborn in the highest realm of the Buddha's pure land, where the benefits from his or her ongoing practices can emanate through the universe.

Vajrayana practices, such as this Chenrezi sadhana, form the spiritual core of the traditional Tibetan Buddhist visualization practice in the United States. But more innovative kinds of visualizations have been recently developed by lamas in an effort to provide a path more in tune with the style and ethos of mainstream America. Tarthang Tulku has recast elements of the Tibetan tradition, including its visualization techniques, in the volumes of his "Time, Space, Knowledge" series. Chogyam Trungpa's "Shambhala training" is also a path for the practice for contemplative living. The details of the visualizations used in it are closely held by the community, but basic elements of its philosophy are outlined in Trungpa's *Shambhala: The Sacred Path of the Warrior*.

This reading is published in "A Chenrezi Sadhana: Benefit for Beings Pervading Space, the Visualization and Recitation of the Great Compassionate One" (Wappinger Falls, N.Y.: Kagyu Thubten Choling Monastery, 1985).

Further Reading

John Blofield, *The Tantric Mysticism of Tibet: A Practical Guide to the Theory, Purpose, and Techniques of Tantric Meditation* (New York: Penguin Books, 1970); Rinpoche Bokar, *Chenrezig, Lord of Love: Principles and Methods of Deity Meditation*, edited by Dan Jorgensen (San Francisco: Clearpoint, 1991); Jane Gyatso, "An Avalokitesvara Sadhan" in *Religions of Tibet in Practice,* edited by Donald S. Lopez (Princeton: Princeton University Press,

1997), pp. 266–270; Richard Hughes Seager, "The Tibetan Milieu," in *Buddhism in America* (New York: Columbia University Press, 1999), pp.113–35

A Chenrezi Sadhana

1. I and all sentient beings as limitless as the sky,
   from this moment until the heart of enlightenment is reached,
Go for refuge to the glorious and holy Lamas,
Go for refuge to the Yidams, all the deities of the Mandala,
Go for refuge to all the Buddhas, the Bhagavans,
Go for refuge to all the holy Dharma,
Go for refuge to the Noble Sangha,
Go for refuge to the Dakas, Dakinis, Dharmapalas and Guardians,
   the assembly of those who possess the eye of wisdom.

Repeat the refuge prayer three times

2. In Buddha, Dharma, and the Supreme Assembly,
I take refuge until enlightenment.
By the merit of practicing generosity and the other perfections,
May I achieve Buddhahood for the benefit of beings.

Repeat three times

3. On the crown of the heads of me and all sentient beings vast as space,
And on a white lotus and moon is a HRIH,
Which becomes the Noble Supreme Chenrezi.
He is luminously white, and radiates light of five colors;
Beautifully smiling, he gazes with compassionate eyes.
He has four hands; the first pair with palms joined,
And the lower two hold a crystal rosary (right) and a white lotus (left).
Silks and precious jewels adorn him;
A deerskin covers his upper body.
Amitabha is his crest adornment.
His two legs are in the Vajra posture.
A stainless moon is his backrest.
He is the essence that embodies all the sources of refuge.

4. *While saying the following prayer, think that all sentient beings are saying it with you, with one voice.*
Lord not veiled by any fault,
Your body white in color,
your head adorned with a perfect Buddha,
your compassionate eyes see all beings—
To you, Chenrezi, I bow down. . . .

Repeat three times

5. In this manner after I have prayed one-pointedly,
The body of the Noble One radiates light.
This purifies the deluded mind and impure karmic appearances.
The outer environment becomes the Realm of Dewachen;
The inner essence, the body, speech and mind of beings,
Becomes the body, speech, and mind of Chenrezi;
Appearance, sound, and awareness become inseparable from Emptiness.

Meditate in accordance with this meaning

Om Mani Peme Hung

Recite as much as you can

6. *Afterwards, place the mind in equanimity, in its very nature free from the conceptualization of the Three Wheels, subject, object, and action.*

The body of myself and others and all appearances are the Noble One's body,
All sound is the melody of the Six Syllables,
All mental events are the vastness of great Wisdom.
By means of this virtue,
Having quickly achieved the state of powerful Chenrezi,
May I establish all beings without exception on that level.

7. By the merit of having recited and meditated in this way,
May I and all the beings connected with me
As soon as we leave this impure body
Be born miraculously in Dewachen.
As soon as we are born there,
having progressed to the exalted Tenth Ground,
May we perform the benefit of others by our emanations through the ten directions!

29

The Rite of Baptism in Haitian Vodou

Elizabeth McAlister

On a Saturday night in March in the year 2000, the members of an Afro-Haitian *sosyete* (society, congregation) in New York City gathered to celebrate an important religious holiday. They recited prayers, sang, and offered food at the feast days of two important deities: Danbala, the ancient and venerable serpent, and Loko, patron of the priesthood. The service was also the occasion for a rite of passage; the smallest member of the sosyete, a one-year-old baby, was baptized and put under the protection of God, the angels, and the spirits of Afro-Creole traditional religion.

It was a small gathering of perhaps twenty-five people, most of whom were extended family. "Papa Emmanuel," the godfather, was an *oungan* (priest) initiated into the mysteries of the tradition. He, in turn, had initiated most of his family, and they gathered often to pray. Although most of the family had been born in Haiti, they had lived in the United States for many years, and Emmanuel's sosyete was probably the oldest Vodou congregation in the United States. They were multigenerational, spoke both English and Haitian Creole at home, and worked at a variety of occupations, including teaching, social work, and the performing arts. In the sosyete were several non-Haitian members who had married Haitians or were initiated by Papa Emmanuel in New York.

The prayer service was held in March on the Saturday night closest to Saint Patrick's Day, because the Vodou deity Danbala has been associated with the Catholic Saint Patrick ever since the colonial period in Haiti. To understand Afro-Haitian religion, it is important to remember the conditions under which it was formed. Its history goes back to the terrible time of slavery, when French Catholic slaveholders bought and forced African peoples of different backgrounds into plantation work. These Africans came from diverse cultures, including the Fon of Dahomey, the Yoruba, and the Kongo. Finding themselves thrown together under the brutal regime of the French, they developed common ways to practice their religions. They forged a worldview that encompassed cosmology, philosophy, belief, ritual, medicine, and concepts about justice and aesthetics. Some parts of this worldview we can trace to its Dahomean roots, others to the Kongo. There is also a great deal of Catholic influence in the religion, and this is clear, when Haitians who are initiated in Vodou also practice Catholicism, perform the sacraments, and maintain special devotions to the saints.

Afro-Haitian religion was unknown to most Americans before the 1970s—or it was only known through the incorrect and demonized images of "Voodoo" seen in Hollywood movies. The reality of Haitian Vodou is becoming better known now that hundreds of thousands of Haitians have immigrated to the United States since the 1970s. There are large Haitian communities in Miami, New York, Boston, Chicago, and Montreal. Most Haitians in the United States are Catholic, and some of them are also sèvitè (servants), who serve the spirits of Vodou.

The religious world of Vodou is populated by numerous unseen forces who originate in various African and European societies. The most important force is undisputedly God the Creator, who is called by his French name, Bondieu (the Good Lord) or by his name in Haitian Creole, Gran Mèt (literally, the Great Master). Because Gran Mèt seldom reveals himself to humans, they rely on a series of other spiritual beings. Haitians pray to Jesus Christ, the Blessed Virgin Mary, and all of the Catholic saints. In addition to these Christian entities, there are many lwa (spirits, angels), who communicate with sèvitè through divination, dreams, and possession. These lwa have names such as Legba, Marasa, Loko, Danbala, Ezili, Kouzen Azaka, Ogou, Jean Petwo, Bawon Samdi, and many others.

The unseen world of the spirits is conceived as an elaborate universe that mirrors our world. The dead and the spirits are separated from the living by an invisible body of water, a vast sea that recalls the Atlantic Ocean that the African ancestors had to cross during the slave trade. The spirits and the dead live in the land an ba dlo (under the sea), a land called Ginen (mythical Africa). In a ceremony that must be done at least one year and a day after a sèvitè dies, priests or priestesses call the recently dead back from under the waters, and send them on to God. Ancestors who were particularly important, powerful, or memorable may cycle back again as spirits, to help in healing, guidance, and protection, to make life more bearable for the people still alive on this earth.

Afro-Haitian religion can be understood as an ongoing set of relationships and conversations between humans and the world of their ancestors, the Afro-Creole spirits, and the Catholic saints. The living are connected to one another through family and social networks and can become "brothers and sisters" who are initiated by the same godmother or godfather. The living also remain connected to those who have recently died. Prayers are regularly offered to les morts [the dead], who are believed to be making their way on a spiritual journey to God. People perform complicated rituals for family members who have died recently, in order to help them on this journey. But it is the lwa [spirits] who guide people through the unseen world into life and through unto death, and it is the lwa who accompany the dead back to God.

Vodou and Catholicism are similar in that they both look to God as creator, judge, and ultimate animator of the life of the world. But the spiritual worlds of the two traditions are different. Vodou sees the universe as two mirrored worlds separated by an ocean, whereas the Christian cosmology consists of the earthly, the heavenly, and the infernal realms. Vodou offers the lwa and the recently dead as spiritual guides, whereas Catholicism features the Trinity, the Blessed Virgin Mary, and the saints.

How, then, do people in Haiti manage to live in the worlds of Catholicism and Vodou at the same time? It is a complex question that scholars and theologians have tried to answer, with much disagreement in the process. Haitian people do manage to practice both Catholicism and Vodou, sometimes separately and sometimes together. To see just how, we have to look at the way that people live their religious lives, how people pray, and how they mark important rites of passage such as birth and death. We must try to understand which spiritual entities people "work" with, and how. One way to do this is to look to see which world people are engaging with when they perform religious ritual.

The unseen worlds of Vodou and Catholicism do overlap in fundamental ways; spiritual beings are appointed by God to reveal truths, to protect people, to help people make moral choices, and to guide them in living and dying. The saints and the spirits, as well as the ancestors, are all forces it is possible to petition through prayer and through spiritual "works." The religious work of Vodou sometimes calls for Catholic rituals to be performed. Besides holding novenas, baptism is probably the most common ritual. Not only can people be baptized, but most ritual objects in Vodou are also baptized in order to be prepared for contact with the spirits. The process of baptism does several things; it singles out a person or a thing to be consecrated, it introduces the person or thing to the spirits and angels, and it gives the person or thing a new name that the spirits and angels can recognize. In this way, the person becomes a new member of the unseen worlds of both Catholicism and Vodou. The person is now a child of God in a renewed way, ready to continue on the spiritual journey toward God.

There is a proverb in Haiti that says "*Pitit se richès*" (Children are wealth). It is very important that a baby's life begin properly and that its relationship to God, the angels, and the spirits be clear and direct. The baptism of a baby in the Afro-Haitian religious world accomplishes several things. Though they hold baptisms in houses or Vodou temples, sèvitè believe baptism to be exactly the same as the Catholic ritual. As a Roman Catholic sacrament, baptism removes original sin from the baby and makes of the baby a new person who, through the grace conferred by baptism, enters into the Christian community. The ritual of baptism recalls the New Testament story of John's baptism of Jesus at the Jordan River, told in Matthew 3:13. By following Jesus' example, Christians believe they can join Jesus to become a child of God, and be saved after death.

Through the rite of baptism, sèvitè see themselves as belonging to the world of Catholicism, and generally perform all the other Catholic sacraments as well. Ironically, sometimes parents who have already baptized their baby in a Vodou house, will also baptize in a Catholic church, because in Haiti it is only there that they can obtain the important baptismal certificate needed to enter school or get a passport. In this way, the world of Catholicism overlaps with the official world of government bureaucracy. This is not the case with Vodou, which, because it is the religion of the poor majority, has been devalued and unrecognized by most governments in Haitian history.

Besides engaging with the unseen world of Catholicism, removing original sin from the baby, and joining the baby to the Christ, baptism in a Vodou house formally introduces the baby to the world of Vodou. After receiving the sacrament of baptism, the baby is presented to the spirits and angels. This introduction is appropriate because it is thought that babies can actually see the spirits. A baby is considered to be pure innocence, incapable of intending harm. In this state of innocence, babies are thought to be able to communicate directly with the spirits. Consequently, it is important that they be baptized and placed under divine protection.

Baptism rituals can be stand-alone ceremonies participated in by family members who bring their baby to a priest or priestess of Vodou. Baptism can also be done in the middle of other rituals, as is the case with the rite reprinted here. Catholic rites performed within Vodou rituals use the formality of European ceremony to signal moments of importance, and also to remember that to live in a Creole community means one must be able to move constantly between two cultural worlds.

In the ritual performed in New York, the ceremony had arrived at the point where the congregation was invoking the powerful spirit called Papa Ogou. Papa Ogou is the patron of metalworking, especially of iron, but his command extends to all matters of war and soldiering, discipline, and technology. Papa Ogou is one of the most important lwa in this house in New York, and at this point, Papa Ogou had emerged from an ba dlo to possess Papa Emmanuel. Possession by the spirits, although it sounds foreign and scary to anybody not familiar with it, is a very common ritual behavior in many of the world's religions. The spirit is believed to come from the unseen world and materialize in the present world, to inhabit briefly the body of the worshiper. A similar principle is at work in the Pentecostal and Holiness worlds, where the Holy Spirit "comes down" and physically touches believers in Christ, who "speak in tongues" in a special spiritual language.

In Vodou, spirit possession is one of the most important goals of many rituals, because the spirits not only arrive in our world from the other side of the waters but also often arrive with a kind of human consciousness; they can talk, sing, and communicate with people. The members of a Vodou society will typically salute the spirit with special ritual movements, and then they will wait to see whether that spirit has a special message for them. The spirit may stop and talk, bring advice, a healing touch or even an admonition to people within the group. All in all, the arrival of the spirit is an important moment and gives sèvitè something they cannot necessarily find in Catholicism: direct, face-to-face contact with the divine. In Vodou, the unseen world of the spirits often, and regularly does, break through into the material world.

Let us return to the baby and his baptism. The small New York apartment of the oungan has been tidied and the furniture has been pushed back against the walls to make room for prayer. Against one wall a table makes up a large altar. A statue of Saint Patrick is at the center, and a large vase of flowers sits before it. On either side of the statue are dishes of diverse foods, two cakes, candles, and bottles of liqueurs, rums, and gin. Lit candles illuminate a crucifix, a gourd strung with beads (called an *ason*), a small bottle of holy water, and a simple white enamel cup of water.

Papa Ogou has arrived to possess the priest Emmanuel during the celebration ceremony for Papa Danbala and Papa Loko. Papa Ogou/Emmanuel is busy giving advice to the family members, who have gathered around to talk with him. He looks over and catches sight of one his goddaughters with her baby, sitting at the edge of the room. He beckons for them to make their way over to him, and within seconds Papa Ogou has called the congregation together to baptize the baby. It is a spontaneous ritual but virtually the same as if it had been planned in advance.

The mother explained that she was pleased that Papa Ogou decided to conduct the ritual himself. The new mother had been planning to come to Papa Emmanuel especially for baptism. When she was pregnant, he had called on God and the spirits for special blessings for the health of the unborn child. He had also given her a spiritual "work" to perform for Saint Claire, together with a series of prayers, so that the birthing would not hold complications. As it turned out, the baby came quickly and easily.

The baptism began with standard Catholic prayers: the recitation of the Lord's prayer and three Hail Marys, all in the formal French of the Haitian Catholic world. After that, the congregation sang a French canticle special to baptism. Its last line, "Accept my promise, Lord Jesus," represents the baby, who is promising himself to Jesus. Because the baby was too young to speak, the congregation spoke for him. A second song reiterated the same theme, and then it was time to baptize the child.

Papa Ogou/Papa Emmanuel turned to the baby's godmother (whom he had himself appointed from among the women in the family). "What will you name this child?" he asked. At this, the godmother gave the child a *non pwen* (literally, point name), also called a *non vanyan* (honor name). This special name is particular to Vodou and is usually a cryptic phrase with many meanings, depending on the context. These special names in Vodou are not gendered, and they can be given to both boys and girls. This is the name that the person will use when communing with the spiritual world. If the child grows up to become initiated, he or she will likely be given a different non vanyan, and this newer name will reflect the developed, adult self. One's name, like one's personality, moral life, and circumstances, then, can change over time in the world of Vodou.

Holding her baby, the mother, who was initiated years earlier, sucked in her breath and waited to hear the name of her child. Her own name, *La Paroisse* (the parish [bell]), referred to the parish church bells that announced the mass. The name indicated that she was mandated to be vocal, to bring people together in the religious world, and to work in the community. She wondered what name her child would be given. In an instant, the godmother spoke. "*Sa'w wè-a, se sa*" [What you see is what it is], she pronounced. Heads nodded in agreement. This polyvalent name expressed that the child has no secrets but is as he appears. It could also indicate that the child would be received just as he presents himself. This would be an admonition that the child must have good manners and present himself properly to the world.

Papa Ogou/Papa Emmanuel dipped a sprig of leaves into his bottle of holy water, and shook some droplets of water onto the baby. As he did this, he recited a prayer, which began with his own name in Vodou, Big Rock: "Big Rock, who has achieved the rank of priest, who holds the ason, and who understand the mysteries of Africa." After identifying himself, he baptized the baby "in the name of the Father, the Son, and the Holy Spirit."

Immediately the congregation recited the next prayer, which is a basic prayer in Vodou that mirrors the form and the function of the Nicene Creed. In this prayer, the sèvitè acknowledges the primary sovereignty of God, and next, of the saints, the spirits, and the angels in the unseen world, as well as all that exists in this world. The prayer goes on to state that God has created two roads for each person: a road close to God and a road far away from God. Everyone has free will to choose which path he or she will take. This statement explicates the morality within Vodou and the idea that God has offered people the free choice to live a moral life or an immoral one. It is clear that within the world there are moral choices, both seen and unseen, that can be productive or destructive.

The prayer finishes "by the power of the great judge who rules the heavens, the earth, the great judge of Ginen." The close of this prayer refers to the judgment that people will be subject to at the crossroads, that is, at the moment they move from the living world to the world of the dead. This concept of judgment after death is akin to the Judgment Day of scripture, yet the reference to Africa moves the judgment to the other world below the waters, the world of Afro-Creole spirits. Interestingly, the end of the prayer moves from French to the Creole language, signaling again the move from the Roman Catholic world into that of Vodou.

After this prayer, the priest typically launches a very long prayer that invokes the lwa, each in turn, in a particular ritual order. The invocation, all in Creole, begins with Legba, the deity who stands at the crossroads, at gates, and in doorways, and who is the unseen usher who controls movements of spirit and people from one world to the next. Legba is creolized, or "syncretized," with Saint Anthony of Padua, and so Saint Anthony is invoked at the same time. After Legba, the other spirits that the particular congregation worships are called one by one by the priest, many of them together with their Catholic counterparts. This is an Afro-Creole ritual that is added onto the Roman Catholic baptism. It is done here because in time each person in Vodou will begin a relationship with their mèt tèt (literally, the master of the head), a kind of "guardian angel" specially protecting and governing that person. Since a small baby does not yet have a guardian angel, the priest invokes all of them, so that each spirit is invited to guide and protect the baby.

It is likely that somebody will be possessed by one of the lwa at this point during the general celebration. In this baptism, Papa Ogou had already come to "dance" in the head of the priest himself. It may have been a sign that Papa Ogou wished to claim the child as his mèt tèt. Generally, however, the mèt tèt is not revealed until the person is much older.

At the end of all the prayers, the atmosphere of the baptism becomes light and celebratory. The final song is a happy one the congregation sings as they parade the baby around the room with his new godparents. In New York, Papa Ogou/Papa Emmanuel handed the baby's mother a bottle of champagne from the altar, a form of congratulations for introducing her baby to the grace and protection of the unseen world.

The ritual reproduced here was recorded by the author in March 2000 in New York City. I would like to express my deep thanks to Papa Emmanuel and his Société La Fleur d'Or for their permission and assistance with this essay. Much of the interpretation of the ritual presented here is from interviews with Papa Emmanuel and with his son, "Après Dieu." This essay is dedicated to the sweet little boy "Sa'w wè-a, se sa."

Further Reading

Karen McCarthy Brown, *Mama Lola: A Vodou Priestess in Brooklyn* (Berkeley and Los Angeles: University of California Press, 2001); Donald J. Cosentino, ed., *Sacred Arts of Haitian Vodou* (Los Angeles: UCLA Fowler Museum of Cultural History, 1995); Maya Deren, *Divine Horsemen: The Living Gods of Haiti* (New York: Chelsea House, 1953); Elizabeth McAlister, "Vodou and Catholicism in the Age of Transnationalism: The Madonna of 115th Street Revisited," in *Gatherings in Diaspora: Religious Communities and the New Immigration,* edited by R. Stephen Warner (Philadelphia: Temple University Press, 1998, pp. 123–60).

The Ritual of Baptism

The priest asks the mother to bring the baby forward and asks the godfather and godmother to join them. He presents the godfather with a candle, which he is to hold throughout the ceremony.

Oungan (in French): In the name of the Father, the Son, and the Holy Spirit
Society in chorus (in French):

> Our Father, who art in heaven
> Hallowed be thy name
> Thy kingdom come, thy will be done
> On earth as it is in heaven
> Give us this day our daily bread
> And forgive us our trespasses
> As we forgive those who trespass against us
> And lead us not into temptation

But deliver us from evil
Amen

Hail Mary, full of Grace
The Lord is with you
Blessed art thou among women
And Blessed is the fruit of thy womb, Jesus
Holy Mother of God, Have mercy on us sinners,
Now and at the hour of our death
Amen
[Three times]

Society sings this hymn together:

Before all I take this oath, on my honor
And I give glory to my God
I want to love you without end
More and more
Accept my promise, Lord Jesus

And then this hymn:

I pledge my promise in this baptism
On my behalf others have sworn
On this day I speak for myself
I pledge myself today freely
I pledge myself, I pledge myself, I pledge myself today freely
I pledge myself today freely

Oungan (in Haitian Creole): What name do you choose for this child?
Godmother: I call him "What you see is what it is."

The oungan asks for a small bottle of holy water (collected on a visit to a Catholic Church). With a small sprig of leaves he shakes several droplets of water onto the baby.

Oungan (in Haitian Creole):

By the power of the great oungan "Big Rock"
Oungan of Africa
Oungan of the highest rank
Oungan who holds the sacred rattle
Ki gweto Ki Gwewun Bogidi [*ritual language; untranslatable*]
I baptize you in the name of the Father, the Son, and the Holy Spirit

Society together chants this prayer in French:

Yes God, Yes God
I believe that you are in your place
I believe that the mysteries (spirits; angels) are in place
I believe that all is in its place
Oh God, hear my words and grant my prayers

Lord, you have created two roads
Everyone has the right to take the road he pleases
Without interfering in the choices of others
By the power of God

Prayer continues, switching to Haitian Creole:

By the power of the great judge in heaven
By the power of the great judge on earth
The great judge of African Guinea

By the power of Saint Antoine de Padua Legba Atibon
Ago Agosi Agola
[*Then the other lwa are invoked; here is a partial listing:*]

Marasa
Loko
Aiyzan
Danbala
Sobo
Bade
Silibo
Agasou
Bosou
Belekou
Agwe
Mètres Ezili Frèda
Dereal
Papa Pierre
Jean Dantò
Manbo Ezili Dantò
Adjedje
Agawou
Kouzen Azaka Mede
Ossagne
Ogou
Bawon
Grann Brijit
Gede
Petwo

At the end of the long invocation, the congregation breaks into celebration, and people take the elbows of the godfather, godmother, and the mother holding the baby and parade in a circle. The drummers present play a simple beat while the congregation parades and sings, in Haitian Creole.

Oliban's baptism was good, Yes God!

Oliban's baptism was good
I'm carrying the *koyo* [homebody] in a rocking chair.

After a short break while people admire the baby and drink a bit of water, the congregation returns to finish the original ritual, the celebration of the spirits Danbala and Loko.

Persuading: Witnessing, Controversies, and Polemics

—30—

Millions Now Living Will Never Die

Iain S. Maclean

Through the zealous door-to-door promotion of their message of this present world's imminent end, the Jehovah's Witnesses have become perhaps the most well-known North American new religious movement. Their leader, Joseph Rutherford, adopted the name from Isaiah 43:10, and the term "Jehovah's Witnesses" was formally accepted at a conference in Ohio in 1931. The name reflects the belief that members represent the end-time "faithful remnant," who alone keep the name and laws of Jehovah. The founder of the movement, Charles Taze Russell (1852–1916), was initially a follower of a group called the Second Adventists, who believed in an imminent second return to earth of the Messiah. These Adventists were part of a much wider Adventist movement that emerged out of the teaching of the Baptist layman William Miller, who preached that Jesus Christ would return to earth in 1844 and rescue his people from a collapsing social order.

Adventist belief in the imminent coming of Christ indicated a shift from the postmillennial beliefs of many nineteenth-century Protestant denominations. Postmillennial Protestants argued that progressive social advance, accompanied by a general optimism for the future, would culminate in the return of Jesus Christ after a one-thousand-year "millennial" period. Adventists rejected this hopeful belief in human betterment and replaced it with a more pessimistic belief about the possibility of social and political improvement. This shift in expectations also reflected a change from a postmillennial to a premillennial interpretation of Scripture. Premillennialists preached that Jesus Christ was now expected to return before the millennial rule of the Messiah was established. This shift in eschatology—the doctrine of last things—assumed a darker view of human progress and of the immediate future. Such preaching resonated with contemporary political populism that emerged as a protest against the perceived corruption of government and its consequences for the poor. The eschatological and millennial teachings of the Jehovah's Witnesses served to critique all existing ecclesiastical, political, and social orders as well as to distinguish them from all other religious groups.

Charles Taze Russell broke with the Adventists in 1879 and founded the Zion's Watchtower Tract Society, which became in 1896 the Watchtower Bible and Tract Society. He published the magazines *Zion's Watch Tower* and *Heralds of Christ's Presence,* the precursors to the *Watchtower* magazine. Russell's movement continued the Adventist emphasis on the imminent return of Jesus Christ, followed by the establishment of a literal millennium, or one-thousand-year rule of Jesus Christ on a restored earth. Although Russell's Adventist and millennial beliefs were not original, his eschatological claims were. Other new religious movements eventually gave up insisting on specific dates for the Second Coming, but Russell continued to predict the imminent end of the world. Much Jehovah's Witness literature used in door-to-door proselytizing, such as the *Watchtower, Announcing Jehovah's Kingdom,* and the booklet *The Truth That Leads to Eternal Life,* emphasized eschatological or "end time" teachings through the emphatic setting of dates.

Although he agreed with most Adventist eschatology, Russell held that the Adventists were mistaken in setting the date of Christ's return in 1844. He preferred the date 1874 and later changed this to the year 1914. When the Second Advent failed to occur in 1914, Russell argued that the final end was to occur within the lifetime of those alive in 1914. Along with later Jehovah's Witnesses, Russell believed that only 144,000 faithful witnesses would have "the heavenly hope" actually to rule with Jesus in heaven. He based his idea on a specific exegesis of the Book of Revelation 7:4 and 14:1 and the notion of a chosen or the "faithful and discrete slave" from Matthew 24:45–47. Jehovah's Witnesses believe that all those who are to rule in heaven had already been chosen by 1935, only a remnant of whom still remain on earth. The remaining Jehovah's Witnesses will continue to live on an earthly paradise during the millenium. After the defeat of Satan, Jesus Christ will return in judgment and deliver a perfected earth to God. Those who survive the judgment will live with God in this paradise for "the ages to come."

Although Russell's and later Jehovah's Witnesses' teaching emerged from a Christian matrix, as a theological system it denied almost all major tenets of Christianity, such as the doctrines of the Trinity, the deity of Christ, his bodily resurrection and physical return, and the existence of hell. In addition, Russell taught that no earthly institution was redeemable since all were controlled by the devil. Consequently, he drew a sharp, dualistic distinction between his adherents and all others. In addition to condemning all political and business institutions, he advocated a virulent anticlericalism and denunciation of established Christianity. As the American religious historian Sydney Ahlstrom has noted, the movement's beginnings were marked not only by apocalyptic speculation but also by opposition to Satan's three great allies: the false teachings in the Christian Churches, the tyrannies of human governments, and the oppression of business.

The most well-known end-time prophecies were those made by Russell and his successor, Judge J. F. Rutherford. Russell had claimed that the year 1914 (and then later 1918) was to be the year of the return of Jesus Christ and the end of the present world. These dates were calculated through a convoluted exegesis of the phrase "seven times" used in the book of Daniel. Russell, clearly influenced by the Adventist

N. H. Barbour, claimed, after the failure of his 1914 prediction, that Christ had in fact come invisibly. Russell concluded that Christ was not bodily resurrected but re-created as a spiritual being. He argued that this return was unseen to human eyes and that Christ was invisibly installed and enthroned as the messianic king in 1914. These invisible events he stated, marked the beginning of the end that would culminate in the Battle of Armageddon with the complete overthrow of earth's present rulers and the establishment of God's earthly millennial reign.

Russell's views of this future earthly millennium had been set out early in his career, as early as 1886, when he wrote *The Plan of the Ages* (later reprinted as *The Divine Plan of the Ages*). The book's most striking feature is its frontispiece, a fold-out "Chart of the Ages," which presents the book's teaching in dispensational form (see Figure 30.1). The eschatology of Russell and later Jehovah's Witnesses' (though they often deny any connection with "Russellism" or Adventism) was deeply influenced by the nineteenth-century tradition of charts based on the dividing of sacred and ecclesiastical history into specific time periods or dispensations. In addition to distributing pamphlets and magazines, Jehovah's Witnesses used charts to illustrate their understanding about the march of human history toward destruction. Such an approach naturally encouraged the calculating and setting of dates for the end of time. *The Divine Plan of the Ages* was the first published in the Millennial Dawn or "Studies In the Scriptures" series of books. In this work Russell clearly set out the Jehovah's Witness understanding of history and salvation. The chart placed in the front of the book is similar to those popularized by the Adventists (Millerites, later called the Seventh-Day Adventists) and reflects dispensationalist theology.

Dispensationalism is a form of biblical interpretation developed by J. N. Darby, a founder in the 1840s of the separatist English Plymouth Brethren. Taking the words of 2 Timothy 2:15 ("rightly dividing the Word of truth") as a programmatic ideal, this method of interpretation began by distinguishing ages, time periods, or "dispensations" in Scripture. Each age, or dispensation, is clearly defined historically by a change in God's method of dealing with humanity. Every historical period ends in human failure and God's judgment, which in this chart are marked as "harvests." Such a division of God's actions into distinct time periods results in extremely literal interpretation of Scripture. Thus the insistence on the literal fulfillment of all prophecy leads to the argument that Old Testament prophecy referring to Israel is to be fulfilled literally in a future kingdom and not figuratively in the church, as most traditional Christian exegesis had maintained.

Dispensational ideas are clearly illustrated in the "Chart of the Ages." A basic timeline is divided by numerous arcs, lines, and pyramids into three major dispensations. The First Dispensation runs from Adam's creation to Noah and the Flood. The Second Dispensation runs from the Patriarchal Age through the "present evil world" (Gal.1:4; 2 Pet. 3:7) to the second harvest. The Second Dispensation is further divided into three ages: the Patriarchal Age, the Jewish Age, and the Gospel Age. The second two dispensations ends with a harvest that illustrate the results of the age. The Jewish Age ended with the harvest period of

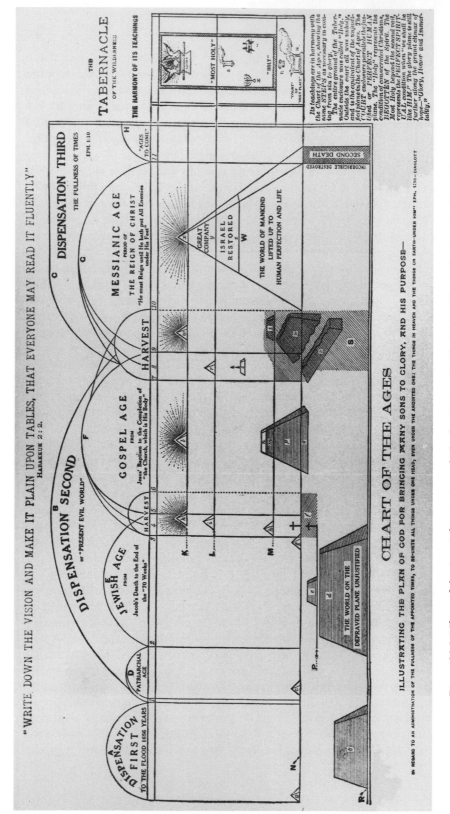

Figure 30.1 "Chart of the Ages," frontispiece of Charles T. Russell's *The Divine Plan of the Ages, Studies in Scriptures.*

Jesus' ministry, whereas the Gospel Age ends in a harvest period overlapping with the millennium. This age, our own "present evil age," is characterized by the rule of Satan. Here is the rationale for Jehovah's Witness claims that they should have as little to do with the social, political, and ecclesiastical orders of this age as possible. The Third Dispensation, the "dispensation of the fullness of times" (2 Pet. 3:13) or the establishment of Christ's kingdom, extends from Christ's advent through the millennium and beyond. Thus Russell held that it was a great error to identify the Church Age with the Kingdom of Christ, for the Church Age was one under the rule of Satan, "the present prince of this world." A further complication is provided by the intersecting arcs that divide each "harvest period, connected by vertical lines running down to parallel planes all connected at the right of the chart to a diagram of the Jewish Tabernacle. The Tabernacle of the Wilderness is understood here as a type, illustrating the same stages more graphically illustrated in the larger chart from the world of sin to the glory of the kingdom age.

Throughout the chart, Russell has placed a series of capital letters that represent different planes of human existence. The "N" located in the First Dispensation represents human nature as expressed by Adam as well as the state of all justified individuals. Below it the "R" represents the sinful plane of Adam's posterity. The "P" represents justification by sacrifices under the law. Alongside the "P" are levels of human perfection; the letter "M" is spiritual initiation, the "L" is the plane of perfect spiritual being, and the "K" stands for "the glory that shall follow," or everlasting life. Lower-case letters are also used to illustrate the importance of world history. Within the Gospel Age is a type of pyramid that represents four distinct classes within the nominal Church. The s and t represent two classes of followers, namely, the one (s) that is justified and sanctified, the other (t) that is only justified. In the Jewish Age, the letter e represents the "fleshly Israel" that will be restored during the millennial age.

Russell's successor, Judge Joseph Rutherford, largely followed Russell's eschatological teachings. He did modify them somewhat by downplaying the 1874 "Coming" and by reinterpreting 1914 (rather than 1874) as the beginning of the end of "the time of the Gentiles" and as the start of Christ's active ruling and judgment through the Watchtower organization. He argued rather for a date in 1925 for the end of the world, when all would be devastated, except for the 144,000 chosen who would go to heaven, while the rest of redeemed humanity lived on in an earthly paradise. As this was to occur in 1925, then certainly many of those alive in 1918 would witness the fulfillment of these events. Thus, Rutherford coined the slogan "millions now living will never die" to emphasize the importance of the year 1925.

This slogan became the core of an active preaching and propaganda campaign by Rutherford during the 1918–1922 period and became the title for the booklet that outlined these latest Jehovah's Witness end-time claims. The booklet *Millions Now Living Will Never Die* was first published in 1920 during his campaign, the centerpiece of which was a lecture with the same title. The pamphlet contained the major idea of the Jehovah's Witnesses: the world was mired in wars, famine, and disasters that would eventually lead to the establishment of a Messianic kingdom. The pamphlet's slogan, "millions now living will never die," and date of 1925 were spread by door-to-door canvassing and through Jehovah's Witness periodicals, such as the *Watch Tower* and *Herald of Christ's Presence*. The date 1925, for instance, was printed on the first page of its September 1, 1922, edition.

Rutherford's claim that 1925 was the year that the millennial kingdom would begin was based on the following argument in *Millions Now Living Will Never Die*. First, Scripture, he argued, predicted seventy jubilees (each being a period of fifty years) before the end of time. Second, the period involved was calculated as beginning with the entry of Israel into Canaan in 1575 B.C. and lasting for 3500 years (the sum of the jubilee years), thus ending in 1925. Further evidence that this date was certain was found in the increasingly chaotic political and social conditions of the period, conditions supposedly identical to the "signs of the times" described by Jesus in his apocalyptic discourses. The end, when it came, would replace the present world order. Rutherford predicted that "the new order is coming in, and that 1925 shall mark the resurrection of the faithful worthies of old and the beginning of reconstruction, it is reasonable to conclude that millions of people on the earth will still be on the earth in 1925. Then, based upon the promises set forth in the divine Word, we must reach the positive and indisputable conclusion that millions now living will never die." This would mark the actual inauguration of the kingdom secretly begun in 1914. In addition, 1925 would witness the resurrection of the "faithful worthies of old." This was understood as a physical resurrection to life on earth of Abraham, Isaac, Jacob, and all those not included in the 144,000, who alone would live in heaven.

Witness teachings concerning the return of Jesus Christ in 1914 and the imminent end of the world were promulgated through street preaching, and later by door-to-door canvassing and the distribution of literature. *Millions Now Living Will Never Die* was distributed by Witnesses as both a testimony to their own faith and as a warning to those living in the world. During the 1920s, members even used portable phonographs to spread their message. Such canvassing for proselytes was and is still regarded as a sacred duty and an essential means of salvation. Jehovah's Witnesses understand that separation of the saved from the damned is an activity that prepares people for the end of the world. Thus almost every Jehovah's Witness is involved in one of four categories of missionary activity: as special pioneers, pioneers, auxiliary pioneers, or as publishers. Special pioneers volunteer for 150 hours per month of door-to-door canvassing, and pioneers and auxiliary pioneers volunteer for sixty and thirty hours per month. Members work in pairs, modeling their approach on Jesus' commission to the Seventy in Luke 10:1.

Such activity was required in large part precisely by the Jehovah's Witnesses' critique of the present world order, contrasting it with another, better world and, no doubt, by the leader's emphasis on setting rather specific dates for the end and subsequent transformation. Despite the failure of such endings to materialize, specific times (such as 1979, 1981, and 1991) continue to be set, and the basic pattern of Russell's and Rutherford's millennial interpretations continue to be taught. This focus on another place—indeed, an alternative society—serves not only to critique present American society but also to inculcate a sharp separationist ethos among adherents. The more sharply this distinction is maintained, the more clearly it is claimed that the rest of society, if not apostate, is at least disobeying the laws of Jehovah, and, as a "faithless generation," thus serves as a sign of the imminent end so devoutly awaited.

Figure 30.1, "Chart of the Ages" is the frontispiece of Charles T. Russell, *The Divine Plan of the Ages, Studies in the Scriptures,* vol. 1, (1886; reprint, Brooklyn, N.Y.: International Bible Students Association, 1923). The text below includes selections from pp. 87–97 of J. F. Rutherford, *Millions Now Living Will Never Die* (Brooklyn, N.Y.: International Bible Students Association, 1920).

Further Reading

James A. Beckford, *The Trumpet of Prophecy: A Sociological Study of Jehovah's Witnesses* (Oxford: Basil Blackwell, 1975); Paul Boyer, *When Time Shall Be No More: Prophecy Belief in Modern American Culture* (Cambridge: Harvard University Press, 1992); Gruss Edmond, *Jehovah's Witnesses and Prophetic Speculation* (Nutley, N.J.: Presbyterian & Reformed Publishing Co., 1975); David Morgan, *Visual Piety: A History and Theory of Popular Religious Images* (Berkeley and Los Angeles: University of California Press, 1998); M. James Penton, *Apocalypse Delayed: The Story of the Jehovah's Witnesses* (Toronto: University of Toronto Press, 1985).

Millions Now Living Will Never Die

KINGDOM COMING IN

The wars, famine, pestilence, distress of nations, etc., upon the earth are but the forerunners of the establishment of the Messianic kingdom. The Lord through his prophet said: "I will shake all nations, and the desire of all nations shall come." (Haggai 2:7) And while this great shaking is in progress and monarchs are losing their crowns, aristocratic and autocratic thrones are tumbling to the earth, the words of the prophet ring out clearly in the ears of the followers of Jesus: "And in the days of these kings shall the God of heaven set up a kingdom, which shall never be destroyed: and the kingdom shall not be left to other people, but it shall break in pieces and consume all these kingdoms, and it shall stand forever." (Daniel 2:44)

Elijah was a type of the followers of Christ Jesus; and the Lord used him to picture the events transpiring in the end of the world, as we have heretofore mentioned. . . . In fulfillment of the anti-type, the Elijah class knew that the war was coming and one of them, the Lord's faithful servant, pastor Russell, for forty years pointed out from the prophecies that it would come in 1914. The Lord is not in the war, meaning that the Lord's kingdom is not yet in full sway. Then follows the earthquake, symbolic of revolution, which has already swept some of the countries. Then shall follow the anarchy—destructive troubles. Anarchy means a disregard of all law, certain classes assuming to exercise power and authority where it is not granted, causing indescribable suffering and sorrow. In this the Lord is not, but it is another means of clearing away the ground preparatory to establishing the kingdom. Then Elijah heard the still small voice. This still small voice is a message from the Lord. The voice is used to symbolize a message or messenger. The Lord has long ago put the message in his Word the Bible for the benefit of those who should live in this hour of stress. The multitudes of earth are clamoring everywhere. They are confused; they are distressed. They are in sorrow, in tears of bitterness. They are almost at their wits' end. But if they could be heard to express their hearts' sincere desire now, without a doubt there would come up from every quarter of the earth this request: Give us a government of righteousness with a wise ruler who will administer the laws in behalf of all; give us peace and not war; give us plenty and not profiteers; give us liberty and not license; give us life and not suffering and death. Back from the past comes the sweet small voice of the Lord saying that this request shall be fulfilled: "For unto us a child is born, unto us a son is given: and the government shall be upon his shoulder: and his name shall be called Wonderful, Counselor, The mighty God, The everlasting Father, The Prince of Peace. Of the increase of his government and peace there shall be no end, upon the throne of David, and upon his kingdom, to order it, and to establish it with judgment and with justice from henceforth even forever. The zeal of the Lord of hosts will perform this." (Isaiah 9:6, 7)

THE JUBILEE

An understanding of the jubilee system which Jehovah inaugurated with Israel throws a great light upon the immediate future events. The Scriptures clearly show that Israel, while God dealt with them for more than eighteen centuries, was a typical people. Their law was typical, foreshadowing greater and better things to come. The Lord commanded Moses to institute the Sabbath system the year that Israel entered the land of Canaan, which was 1575 years before A.D. 1 (Leviticus 25:1–12), and that every fiftieth year should be unto them a year of jubilee. This was done on the tenth day of the seventh month, the day of atonement. "And ye shall hallow the fiftieth year and proclaim freedom throughout the land unto all the inhabitants thereof; it shall be a jubilee unto you and ye shall return every man unto his possessions and ye shall return every man unto his family." Other Scriptures show that there were to be seventy jubilees kept. (Jeremiah 25:11; 2 Chronicles 36:17–21) A simple calculation of these jubilees brings us to this important fact: Seventy jubilees of fifty years each would be a total of 3500 years. That period of time beginning 1575 before A.D. 1 of necessity would end in the fall of the year 1925, at which time the type ends and the great anti-type must begin. What, then, should we expect to take place? In the type there must be a full restoration; therefore the great anti-type must mark the beginning of restoration of all things. The chief thing to be restored is the human race to life; and since other Scriptures definitely fix the fact that there will be a resurrection of Abraham, Isaac, Jacob and other faithful ones of old, and that these will have the first favor, we may expect 1925 to witness the return of these faithful men of Israel from the condition of death, being resurrected and fully restored to perfect humanity and made the visible, legal representatives of the new order of things on earth.

Messiah's kingdom once established, Jesus and his glorified church constituting the great Messiah, shall minister the blessings to the people they have so long desired and hoped for and prayed might come. And when that time comes, there will be peace and not war, as the prophet beautifully states: "In the last days it shall come to pass, that the mountain of the house of the Lord shall be established in the top of the mountains, and it shall be exalted above the hills; and people shall flow unto it. And many nations shall come, and say, Come, and let us go up to the mountain of the Lord, and to the house of the God of Jacob; and he will teach us of his ways, and we will walk in his paths: for the law shall go forth of Zion, and the word of the Lord from Jerusalem. And he shall judge among many people, and rebuke strong nations afar off; and they shall beat their swords into plowshares, and their spears into pruning hooks; nation shall not lift up a sword against nation, neither shall they learn war any more. But they shall sit every man under his vine and under his fig tree; and none shall make them afraid; for the mouth of the Lord of hosts hath spoken it."(Micah 4:1–4)

EARTHLY RULERS

As we have heretofore stated, the great jubilee cycle is due to begin in 1925. At that time the earthly phase of the kingdom shall be recognized. The Apostle Paul in the eleventh chapter of Hebrews names a long list of faithful men who died before the crucifixion of the Lord and before the beginning of the selection of the church. These can never be a part of the heavenly class; they had no heavenly hopes; but God has in store something good for them. They are to be resurrected as perfect men and constitute the princes or rulers in the earth, according to his promise. (Psalm 45:16; Isaiah 32:1; Matt. 8:11) Therefore we may confidently expect that 1925 will mark the return of Abraham, Isaac, Jacob and the faithful prophets of old, particularly those named by the apostle in Hebrews chapter eleven, to the condition of human perfection.

RECONSTRUCTION

All the statements of the world, all the political economists, all the thoughtful men and women, recognize the fact that the conditions existing prior to the war have passed away and that a new order of things must be put in vogue. All such recognize that this is a period now marking the beginning of reconstruction. The great difficulty is that these men are only exercising human wisdom and have ignored the divine arrangement. We are indeed at the time of reconstruction, the reconstruction not only of a few things but of all things. The reconstruction will not consist of patching up old and broken down systems and forms and arrangements, but the establishment of a new and righteous one under the great ruler Christ Jesus, the Prince of Peace. The Apostle Peter at Pentecost, speaking under divine inspiration and referring to that time, said: "Times of refreshing shall come the presence of the Lord; and he shall send Jesus Christ, which before was preached unto you: whom the heaven must receive [retain] until the times of restitution of all things, which God hath spoken by the mouth of all his holy prophets since the world began." (Acts 3:19–21)

Examination of the prophecies from Moses to John discloses the fact that every one of the prophets foretold the time coming for restitution blessings. Reconstruction and restitution mean the same thing, i.e., the restoration of mankind to the things which were lost. The reward of the church in heaven is not that which man originally had; but is given as a great reward for faithfulness to the Lord under trying conditions and circumstances. Restitution means the blessings that will be given to mankind in general through the divine arrangement and therefore restoring him to life, liberty and happiness on the earth, once enjoyed by the perfect man Adam and which was included in the promise made to Abraham. This blessing comes to the world through the seed, the exalted, elect class, the Messiah, the Christ.

The Scriptures clearly show that this great time of blessing is immediately preceded by a great time of trouble. This trouble is now on the world. The word Michael used in the following text means "who as God," or representing God-Christ Jesus the great captain of our salvation. His second coming and the establishment of his kingdom has been the hope and desire of Christians for centuries past. In referring to this time, then, the prophet Daniel under inspiration wrote "And at that time shall Michael stand up, the great prince which standeth for the children of thy people: and there shall be a time of trouble such as never was since there was a nation even to that same time: and at that time thy people shall be delivered, every one that shall be found written in the book. And many of them that sleep in the dust of the earth shall awake, some to everlasting life, and some to shame and everlasting contempt." (Daniel 12:1, 2)

MILLIONS WILL NEVER DIE

Every part of the divine arrangement must be fulfilled; not one jot or tittle shall pass away unfulfilled. Every portion of the divine promise, therefore, is important. Answering the question as to the conditions prevailing at the end of the world, Jesus quoted the above prophetic statement from the Book of Daniel, or used words similar saying: "Then shall be great tribulation, such as was not since the beginning of the world to this time, no, nor ever shall be; And except those days should be shortened, there should no flesh be saved: but for the elect's sake those days shall be shortened." (Matthew 24:21, 22) Thus he shows that the distress upon the earth will end with a time of tribulation such as the world has never known and that this will be the last. There will never be another. Then he adds that for the sake of the elect those days shall be shortened; and much flesh shall be saved.

We ask, Why would the Lord carry through this time of trouble a large number of people, sparing them from death in the time of trouble, unless he intended to minister unto them some particular blessing? And since God has promised a blessing of restitution to that which Adam lost, and since these promises point to a beginning of fulfillment immediately following this trouble, and since the promise clearly is that the elect, constituting the seed of Abraham, according to the promise, shall be the instruments through which the blessings shall flow, then this statement of Jesus clearly and conclusively proves that many peoples living on earth at the end of the trouble will be the first ones to be offered the blessings of restoration, which blessings will be offered through the elect, the Messiah. It follows as a matter of course that those accepting the offer as made and rendering themselves in obedience to it shall be restored to that happiness which was lost in Adam, viz., life, liberty and happiness.

The prophet of God offers other testimony in corroboration of this: "And it shall come to pass, that in all the land, saith the Lord, two parts therein shall be cut off and die; but the third shall be left therein. And I will bring the third part through the fire, and will refine them as silver is refined, and will try them as gold is tried: they shall call on my name, and I will hear them: I will say, It is my people: and they shall say, The Lord is my God." (Zechariah 13:8, 9) Here, then, is a clear statement to the effect that one part God will spare in this time of trouble and that these shall ultimately be his people and he will be their God.

Having in mind that it was an earthly home, human life and attendant blessings, that Adam lost, and that these are the blessings God promises shall be restored to man, we can understand the words of the prophet David when he wrote: "Blessed is he that considereth the poor: the Lord will deliver him in time of trouble. The Lord will preserve him, and keep him alive; and he shall be blessed upon the earth; and thou wilt not deliver him unto the will of his enemies." (Psalm 41:1, 2) Here he plainly states that those who deal righteously in this time of trouble shall be blessed upon the earth.

HOW TO LIVE FOREVER

The church systems would have the people believe that only those who become church members can be saved. The Bible never taught any such doctrine. The Lord never organized the nominal systems and the true church is but a little flock, who shall inherit the kingdom of heaven, and the others of the world do not inherit it. To the church Jesus said: "Fear not, little flock; for it is your Father's good pleasure to give you the kingdom." (Luke 12:32) Jesus died not only for those who will constitute the members of the church, but for all. St. John plainly stated: "He is the propitiation [satisfaction] for our sins: and not for ours only, but also for the sins of the whole world." (John 2:2)

The Apostle Paul, discussing the great Redeemer and his office, said: "We see Jesus, who was made a little lower than the angels for the suffering of death, crowned with glory and honor; that he by the grace of God should taste death for every man. For it became him, for whom are all things, and by whom are all things, in bringing many sons unto glory, to make the captain of their salvation perfect through sufferings." (Hebrews 2:9, 10) Thus we see that Jesus died for every man, not only for a few. Again says the Apostle: "There is one God, and one mediator between God and men, the man Christ Jesus; who gave himself a ransom for all, to be testified in due time." (1 Timothy 2:5, 6) By this Scripture it is clearly seen that in God's due time every creature must hear the testimony as to what Jesus has done for him and know of the plan of salvation. Again says the Apostle Paul: "The gift of God is eternal life through Jesus Christ our Lord." (Romans 6:23) There can be no gift without both a giver and a receiver, and this could not operate without knowledge on the part of both. In other words, the giver must intelligently offer the gift to another, and the other must intelligently know of this fact before he can receive it. It would be impossible for the human race, therefore, to accept the gift of life everlasting before it is offered. It will be offered only in God's due time and the divine plan shows that his due time is after the seed of promise is developed, after the kingdom is set up; and then each one in his order will be brought to a knowledge of the fact that a plan of redemption exists and that the way is open for him to accept the terms of it and live. Knowledge being essential, it precedes the reception of blessings from the Lord; and knowing this fact, it is easy to be seen why the adversary, the devil, and his agencies so diligently strive to prevent the people from knowing the truth. But when Messiah's kingdom is established we are definitely informed (Revelation 20:1–4) that Satan will be restrained of his power that he might deceive the nations no more; and then the people shall know the truth and nothing shall hinder them from knowing it.

POSITIVE PROMISE

The words of Jesus must be given full force and effect because he spake as never man spake. His speech was with absolute authority. And in God's due time his words must have a fulfillment, and they cannot have a fulfillment until that due time. Jesus plainly said: "Verily, verily, I say unto you, If a man keep my saying, he shall never see death." (John 8:51) As above stated, no one could keep the saying of Jesus until he hears it, until he has a knowledge of God's arrangement. Throughout the Gospel age none but Christians have had this knowledge and all who have kept this saying and keep it faithfully until the end will receive life everlasting on the divine plane. (Revelation 2:10) The remainder of mankind have not heard it: therefore could not keep it. They will hear however, in due time after the establishment of the kingdom. Then it shall come to pass that every one who will keep the saying of the Lord shall never see death. This promise would not have been made by Jesus if he did not intend to carry it into full force and effect in due time.

Again he said "Whosoever liveth and believeth in me shall never die." (John 11:26) Do we believe the Master's statement? If so, when the time comes for the world to know, then they who believe and, of course, render themselves in obedience to the terms have the absoute and positive statement of Jesus that they shall never die.

Based upon the argument heretofore set forth, then that the old order of things, the old world is ending and is therefore passing away, and that the new order is coming in, and that 1925 shall mark the resurrection of the faithful worthies of old and the beginning of reconstruction, it is reasonable to conclude that millions of people now on the earth will be still on the earth in 1925. Then, based upon the promises set forth in the divine Word, we must reach the positive and indisputable conclusion that millions now living will never die.

Of course it does not mean that every one will live; for some will refuse to obey the divine law; but those who have been evil and turn again to righteousness and obey righteousness shall live and not die. Of this we have the positive statement of the Lord's prophet, as follows: "When the wicked man turneth away from his wickedness that he hath committed, and doeth that which is lawful and right, he shall save his soul alive. Because he considereth, and turneth away from all his transgressions that he hath committed, he shall surely live, he shall not die." (Ezekiel 18:27, 28)

RETURNING YOUTH

The Lord, in the exercise of his loving-kindness toward man, has graciously given many illustrations and pictures of the outworkings of his great plan. In the book of Job he gives us a picture of the perfection of man, of his fall, of the redemption by the great Ransomer, and then the subsequent restoration. When the times of restoration begin there will doubtless be many men on the earth who will be very old and almost ready for the tomb. But those who learn of the great ransom-sacrifice and who accept the Ransomer shall return to the days of their youth; they shall be restored to perfection of body and mind and live on the earth forever. We note the words of the prophet:

"He [Jehovah] keepeth back his [man's] soul from the pit, and his life from perishing by the sword. He [man] is chastened also with pain upon his bed, and the multitude of his bones with strong pain: so that his life abhorreth bread, and his soul dainty meat. His flesh is consumed away, that it cannot be seen; and his bones that were not seen stick out. Yea, his soul draweth near unto the grave, and his life to the destroyers."

Thus is given a vivid description of the dying human race, individually and collectively. Then the prophet shows how the message of truth will be brought to him and he will learn of the great ransom-sacrifice. Continuing, he says: there be a messenger [one who brings a message of glad tidings] with him [man], an interpreter [one who expounds and makes it clear], one among a thousand [the Lord will provide here and there teachers for the benefit of others], to show unto man his [the Lord's] uprightness: then he [the Lord] is gracious unto him (man), and saith, Deliver him from going down to the pit [grave; and the man joyfully says:] I have found a ransom. His flesh shall be fresher than a child's: he shall return to the days of his youth." (Job 33:18-25)

When God expelled Adam from Eden he said: "And now, lest he [Adam] put forth his hand, and take also of the tree of life, and eat, and live for ever: therefore the Lord God sent him forth from the garden of Eden, . . . and he placed at the east of the garden of Eden cherubims, and a flaming sword which turned every way, to keep the way of the tree of life."(Genesis 3:22–24) Thus the Word shows that had Adam remained in Eden, feeding upon the perfect food it afforded, he would have continued to live. The judgment was executed against him by causing him to feed upon imperfect food.

— 31 —

Ordaining Women Rabbis

Pamela S. Nadell

For two millennia, rabbis, the religious leaders and teachers of the Jewish people, were always, without question, male. A rabbi, literally "my master," was a scholar certified to rule on matters of Jewish law, to teach its sacred texts and preach their lessons, and to lead his community. But late-nineteenth-century American Jews began questioning men's exclusive hold on the rabbinate. As they watched women becoming the first female doctors, lawyers, and ministers, they asked "Could not our women become rabbis?" Nevertheless, it took nearly a century of debate and argument before the first women entered this ancient profession.

Debate and argument are time-honored traditions in Judaism. Since antiquity sages have wrangled and reasoned, staked out their positions and backed them with proof texts from the sacred literature, in order to persuade their fellow Jews to accept their interpretations of Jewish law. For example, during the rebellion that gave rise to the holiday of Chanukah, some pious Jews, refusing to profane the Sabbath by taking up arms when attacked, were slaughtered. Subsequently, the leaders of the rebellion, the Maccabees, reasoned that they would fight any enemy who attacked on the Sabbath in order to live (1 Macc. 2:29–41). Later, rabbis engaged in a very different debate about Chanukah. Should Jews light eight candles on the first night and then take one away each successive night, or should they start out with a single candle (plus the candle that lights all the others) and count up to eight?

Eventually, nearly every aspect of individual and collective life sparked rabbinic debate. Ancient rabbis disagreed over whether a man who prayed out loud but failed to hear his own words had fulfilled his religious obligation. Medieval rabbis argued over how to respond to Jews who had, when faced with the sword, bowed to Christianity and Islam. And modern rabbis struggled over whether those starving in concentration camps during the Holocaust had to fast on the Day of Atonement. As long as those engaged in these debates followed time-honored rules of analysis and interpretation, grounding their arguments in the historic Jewish experience and the authority of Jewish law, such debates were deemed a positive good, essential to enabling Jews and Judaism to change to meet the times. The debate about ordaining women rabbis thus becomes a prism through which to view this historic Jewish practice of religious debate.

It also shows how the subjects of these debates so often came from the challenges Jews faced by living as Jews in a wider world. The particular question of ordaining women emerged out of Judaism's encounter with modernity. Scrutinizing virtually every aspect of historic religious practice and law, modernizing Jews sometimes adjusted and at other times abandoned laws and customs that historically had set the patterns of Jewish life from birth to death and all that lay in between. Although the men who became the first Reform rabbis hoped all Jews would welcome their revision of Judaism, crafted to allow Jews to remain Jews and to participate fully in the wider society, other Jews and their rabbis constructed different responses to these challenges. Their interpretations of the proper balance between the Judaism of the past and the changes they believed it permitted launched the other modern Jewish religious denominations, Conservative Judaism and Orthodox Judaism.

Not surprisingly, this encounter with modernity that reshaped Jewish life also revolutionized the rabbinate. Traditionally, Jews appointed rabbis as spiritual heads of their communities. They needed these men to interpret and to apply Jewish law and to judge, tasks mandatory to the proper functioning of Jewish society. Barricaded behind piles of sacred Hebrew tomes, rabbis searched in the traditions of the past to judge the affairs of their day.

In the modern era rabbis lost most of these powers. Jews no longer turned to rabbis to ask if a chicken was kosher or to settle a business dispute. Jews now required rabbis less for their ability to interpret Jewish law than to stand as exemplars of Judaism, men with a broad experience of Jewish life and culture and the ability to convey that to their congregants and their Christian neighbors. Nineteenth- and twentieth-century Jews came to expect that their rabbis would lead them in their synagogues and temples and preach at every service. They asked them to solemnize their weddings and to speak words of comfort at their funerals. They wanted men capable of inspiring their children and of discussing great Jewish books with the women of the sisterhood. They required rabbis to counsel the sick, the dying, the divorcing, and the disenchanted. In short, they expected their rabbis to minister, much like parsons, preachers, and pastors.

Just as examining Judaism in light of modern sensibilities had reshaped the rabbinate, so too it compelled a rethinking of the status and religious responsibilities traditionally assigned to Jewish women. And that reappraisal led eventually to the question: could not our women become rabbis?

This question was of particular interest to Reform Jews, for Reform Judaism had already paved the way for the expansion of Jewish women's religious roles. Reform Judaism evolved in Germany at the turn of the nineteenth century. There Jews, influenced by the scientific rationalism of their day, first tested Jewish laws and customs against their newfound sensibility that religious faith is largely moral. Subsequently, they revised those practices which seemed to conflict with this stance. They abandoned ancient Jewish laws regulating diet and dress as not in keeping with the spirit of the age, and they came to pray and to preach in the language of the land, abandoning the Hebrew that so few any longer understood. Not surprisingly, they often found in the churches of their neighbors models for change. Thus, Reform Jews replaced bar mitzvah, the ceremony marking the religious maturity of a thirteen-year-old boy, with confirmation for boys *and* for girls. They prepared their children for these confirmations in Sunday schools. In America, Reform Jews broke with the custom of separating men and women in the synagogue, and allowed husbands and wives to sit together when they prayed. Accordingly, as Christians ordained the first women ministers (a term nineteenth-century Jews also applied to their own rabbis), Reform Jews too came to debate whether or not Jewish women could, in fact, be ordained.

The ordination of women ministers—the first was Antoinette Brown Blackwell in 1853—belongs to the history of the nineteenth-century woman's rights movement. Launched in 1848 at the Seneca Falls Convention in New York, the woman's rights movement is best known for demanding woman suffrage, a battle its leaders waged for three-quarters of a century. Yet its founding text, the Declaration of Sentiments and Resolutions, envisioned far broader reforms. Specifically, it railed against men for excluding women from the professions—from law, medicine, and the ministry. In fact, some came to deem women's advancement in the professions even more significant than their winning the right to vote.

Late-nineteenth- and early-twentieth-century Americans anticipated, often with great excitement, that soon women would take on new roles in American society. Especially after 1920, when the battle for woman suffrage reached its long-awaited conclusion with the ratification of the Nineteenth Amendment guaranteeing that the right to vote could not be denied "on account of sex," some Americans began testing the promises of expanded roles for American women. By 1930, the number of women attending college had mushroomed to 481,000 from 85,000 in 1900. The vast majority of the female college graduates of the 1920s anticipated either taking a job after graduation or continuing to study for a profession. In fact, the 1920s saw the number of women employed in the professions rise by 50 percent, although the vast majority remained in the highly feminized fields of teaching, librarianship, social work, and nursing. Nevertheless, some found new places as journalists, editors, professors, civil servants, and in business; or as doctors, lawyers, and ministers. Stories of their success were frequently featured in a press eager to broadcast the news that women's status in American society was indeed changing.

American Jews came to wonder whether expanding women's roles meant they should now become rabbis. In the 1920s and 1930s, a handful of women who wanted to be rabbis spent enough time in seminaries to compel their faculties, alumni, and American Jews more broadly to take up the issue. Yet none of these women succeeded in winning seminary ordination. Consequently, the debate dragged on. It closed finally for Reform Jews in June 1972, when Sally Priesand was ordained a rabbi. Thirteen years later, in 1985, Amy Eilberg became the first female Conservative rabbi. And soon thereafter, Orthodox Jews began asking if there would be Orthodox women rabbis.

What follows is but one chapter in this century-long controversy over women's ordination: Reform Judaism's engagement with Martha Neumark's petition to become a rabbi. The debate over Neumark reveals not only how Jews negotiate the process of change but also illuminates the complexities of modern Judaism, how and why so many different interpretations of the same historic tradition emerged. For example, those debating women rabbis—or, in fact, any other change from the past—had to decide what was more important: the weight of Jewish tradition or the need to adapt Judaism to modernity. Seeking guidance in the great body of Jewish literature, the rabbis failed to find a single statement specifically prohibiting women rabbis. Did that mean that women could be rabbis? Or was the fact that Jewish women had never been rabbis and Judaism's preference for assigning woman her particular sphere decisive? At the same time, the men also looked around. Must Judaism change to accommodate women's new status in American society? Or had it already made sufficient accommodations by allowing women to take on the new role of religious educator? Thus, debating the woman rabbi shows modern Jewish men and women negotiating and, indeed, reaching very different conclusions about what Judaism permits and prohibits.

Martha Neumark (1904–1981, Martha Neumark Montor) claimed her place in the history of ordaining women rabbis when, in 1921, she stood at the center of a two-year long debate at Cincinnati's Hebrew Union College (HUC), Reform Judaism's rabbinical seminary, over whether its leaders would break with tradition and permit women to become rabbis. Born in 1904, the second of the three children of David and Dora Turnheim Neumark, Martha Neumark had come to America in 1907 with her family, a trip made so that David Neumark could become a philosophy professor at HUC. His young daughter Martha was a prize-winning pupil at Sunday school. As a teen at her confirmation, she read from the Torah and was so deeply moved that she began to think about becoming a rabbi.

In 1918, fourteen-year-old Martha Neumark entered HUC's Preparatory Division, following in the footsteps of the other girls who had taken this precollegiate course since the founding of the college in 1875. So Neumark, who had already set her sights on becoming a rabbi, began studying Bible, Hebrew, Aramaic, rabbinics, liturgy, and Jewish history.

Apparently, not until 1921 did the prospect of ordaining her actually come up. That spring Martha Neumark asked the college to assign her a high holiday pulpit for the following fall. In October her classmates would begin practical rabbinical training, and she wanted to join them; Jews, living in small communities without full-time rabbis, hired student rabbis to lead them in prayer and preach on the holiest days of the Jewish calendar—the New Year (Rosh Hashanah) and Day of Atonement (Yom Kippur). HUC president Kaufman Kohler well understood the implications of honoring Neumark's petition for a high holiday placement. He reported to his Board of Governors: logic dictates that if she is sent out to preach and then completes the required course of study, she should be ordained.

For the next two years the men of the college struggled with the question. It swirled beyond college faculty, alumni, and lay leaders to their wives and daughters, and even to leading American Jewish figures not then confronted with challengers to the male rabbinate in their seminaries. What followed was the first, but by no means the last, intricate dance by American Jews around the question of women's ordination in which faculty met, rabbis debated, scholars searched the tradition, and the women who wanted to become rabbis opened up to the press. Asserting conflicting claims upon the Jewish past, just as modernizing rabbis reinterpreted traditional texts to validate their reforms, the adversaries in the debate on women's ordination squared off. In the end, after faculty and rabbis, seminary leaders and laity had fixed their positions behind closed doors, out of sight of the women whose lives their decisions would affect, Neumark was not ordained.

From the beginning, as HUC faculty debated the prospect of a woman rabbi, the men kept dividing the question along the lines of Reform Judaism vs. Jewish tradition. Some asserted that since Reform Judaism's adaptation to modernity included proclaiming the equality of women with men in the synagogue, they could find no logical reason to bar women from becoming rabbis. But others, notably HUC Professor Jacob Lauterbach, objected vehemently, arguing against women's ordination as utterly contrary to Jewish tradition.

Another member of the faculty, Professor David Neumark, disagreed. His reading of the sacred texts of the past led him to assert that nowhere in the entire corpus of Jewish legal literature had the sages ever raised the topic of ordaining women rabbis. What was not discussed, concluded the father of the daughter who would be a pioneer, was not prohibited. Having heard from the faculty, the HUC Board of Governors decided to canvass their alumni, the men who had become rabbis; but they would not meet until the summer of 1922. Meanwhile, no women students at the college could plan to officiate on the high holidays.

Since 1889, Reform rabbis had met annually as the Central Conference of American Rabbis (CCAR). For five days every summer, the men, often with their wives and families, gathered in comfortable vacation settings such as the beach resort of Cape May, New Jersey, where they convened in 1922. Here those who had been classmates and those who over the years had become firm friends saw one another again. They worshiped, and then, while their wives walked on the beach, the men studied and heard committee reports, debated responsa (Jewish legal opinions), and weighed the questions they believed were challenging all Jews. They paused to memorialize colleagues who had died the year before and argued, sometimes heatedly, over resolutions on the timely issues of their day. They knew a professional stenographer would record their remarks and preserve them for posterity in the annual yearbooks of the Central Conference of American Rabbis.

Over the years the discussions of the CCAR set directions for Reform Judaism. For example, the year after its founding, the men had a protracted debate over which prayer book revision their synagogues should adopt. Sometimes rabbinic responsa (singular, responsum) dictated the parameters of their debates. Just as rabbis of old had written opinions on the questions of their day, so too modern

American rabbis wrote responsa about the questions of their moment in time. Responsa (in Hebrew, literally questions and answers) are much like legal briefs, texts in which rabbis stake out a position on a question and craft an argument based on the great corpus of Jewish literature, historic Jewish custom, and often contemporary realities. At the CCAR conventions the rabbis would respond to a responsum sent out in advance, argue its strengths and weaknesses, and then decide whether they and the Reform Jews whom they guided would accept or reject its conclusions.

By 1922, the men of the CCAR had already grappled with a variety of difficult legal issues. The rabbis had argued over whether a man converting to Judaism had to be circumcised and whether the historical Sabbath observed on Saturday could be moved to Sunday to accommodate American realities. They had tussled with the thorny problem of mixed marriage, and ruled then, in 1909, that it was contrary to Judaism. These questions raised, the responsa written, and the debates they provoked reveal modern Judaism negotiating change, sometimes abandoning old customs, and creating new traditions. Thus, in 1922, the rabbis followed a time-honored pattern when they gathered to discuss the topic of a new day, the "Responsum on Question, 'Shall Women be Ordained Rabbis?'"

In the months preceding the CCAR convention, HUC Professor Jacob Lauterbach had written a full-length rabbinical opinion on women rabbis and sent it in advance to the men, many of whom had been his students. Here Lauterbach began by arguing that women's admission to other customarily male professions drove the question, but he held that Judaism, unlike law or medicine, demands its official representatives to be male. And he found his proof in the key passages of Jewish law that excluded women from representing the congregation.

Lauterbach also went beyond classical Jewish sources to consider sociological realities. Women could not possibly enter the rabbinate as they did any other profession, for it was unique in its arduous demands. No woman could marry and raise a family and give the rabbinate the whole-hearted devotion it required. On the contrary, a successful rabbi required a helpmate for a wife, one to make his home a model for the entire congregation. Excluding women from the rabbinate, Lauterbach continued, in no way deprecated them. It merely affirmed Judaism's wisdom in assigning men and women their respective spheres. A woman's sphere remained the home where she reigned as wife and mother, but he conceded that the modern world offered women new avenues for religious and educational work in Sunday schools and in women's organizations. Thus, he saw no injustice done to women in upholding the rabbinate as a male preserve.

When the CCAR met to consider Lauterbach's responsum, most of the fifteen rabbis on the record revealed that their professor's arguments had not persuaded them. They decried his traditionalism as not in keeping with the revolution in women's status of their day. They criticized his legal argument, for he had not found a single statement in all of Jewish tradition that prohibited ordaining women. Although some worried about the "practicability" of women's ordination—whether this step would precipitate a decisive break between Reform Jews and all other

Jews—the rabbis, in the end, proved to be progressive men. They expected woman's social and economic emancipation to follow quickly in the wake of her new right to vote, and they wanted to extend that to the profession of rabbi. These men understood that the woman rabbi would enter a transformed, modern rabbinate, preaching and teaching, appealing to the young and the old in the congregation, and presenting Judaism to a wider world. Surely, so they argued, women with the requisite academic training could take on these functions.

Professor David Neumark joined the men who had been his students that summer. He came to refute Lauterbach's interpretation of the sources that excluded women from the rabbinate. Where Lauterbach argued that women were prohibited from leading congregations, Neumark countered that rabbis traditionally did not represent their congregations. Where Lauterbach quoted Talmud to prove that women had never historically studied in the academies where students trained to become rabbis, Neumark retorted that women were not *often* found in those settings. Where Lauterbach saw tradition denying women the privilege of reading Torah before the congregation, Neumark observed that Reform Jews had parted with this.

In the end, after taking the unusual step of hearing from some of the women present during the debate, the liberal spirit prevailed, and the rabbis voted 56 to 11 to declare that "woman cannot justly be denied ordination." When Martha Neumark advanced to HUC's Collegiate Department in the fall of 1922, she had every reason to expect that soon she would become the first woman rabbi in the history of Judaism.

The ultimate responsibility for college policy, however, rested neither with the faculty nor their former students, but rather with the Board of Governors. In February 1923 its members voted, so Martha Neumark recalled, six laymen to two rabbis that "no change should be made in the present practice of limiting to males the right to matriculate for the purpose of entering the rabbinate." Although the board held a full discussion of the topic, its minutes recorded only the decision and not the debate. Although the faculty and the rabbis favored women's ordination, the Board of Governors set policy. The board's decision reveals once again the complexities of how modern Judaism develops as different authorities, clergy and lay, in diverse settings, inside seminary board rooms and at beach resorts, exercise religious power and make decisions in the modern world.

The decision surely disappointed Martha Neumark. In fact, she continued to study, earning for her seven-and-a-half years in rabbinical school a certificate qualifying her to become a religious school principal. Now she too finally recorded her views. Although, in 1922, she had traveled to Cape May with her father, she apparently did not speak when the other women present voiced their opinions. Only now did she speak for the record. Yet, since she was neither a member of the college faculty, nor an ordained rabbi, nor on the Board of Governors, she had to seek out a space in which to voice her opinion. She turned, as had so many other women trying to crash the barriers to the male-dominated professions, to the one space open to her—the press.

In 1925, Martha Neumark published a two-part autobiographical essay in the national Jewish weekly, *The Jewish Tribune and Hebrew Standard*. She described how she came to set her sights on becoming a rabbi, her studies at the college, her personal theology, and why she saw ordaining women as but another aspect of the historic woman's question. There the matter rested for half a century. Many decades later, in 1964, just as Sally Priesand was making her way into rabbinical school, Martha Neumark Montor once again tried to persuade her alma mater to ordain women rabbis. Finally, in 1972, against the backdrop of the second wave of American feminism, the young Sally Priesand, following in Martha Neumark's footsteps, succeeded in becoming the first woman rabbi in the history of American Judaism.

The selections here are Jacob Z. Lauterbach, "Responsum on Question, 'Shall Women Be Ordained Rabbis?'," *Central Conference of American Rabbis Yearbook* 1922, pp. 156–77; Martha Neumark, "The Woman Rabbi: An Autobiographical Sketch of the First Woman Rabbinical Candidate," *The Jewish Tribune and Hebrew Standard*, 10 April 1925; pp. 1ff; and Neumark, "The Woman Rabbi: Difficulties That Beset Path of First Woman Rabbi Outlined in Brief Autobiographical Sketch," *The Jewish Tribune and Hebrew Standard*, 17 April 1925, p. 5.

Parenthetical citations appear in the original text and refer to different works of rabbinic literature. Bracketed items contain translations of quotations from rabbinic literature, which Lauterbach included in their original language, or transliterations where his English sentence conveys the meaning of the original.

Further Reading

Simon Greenberg, ed., *The Ordination of Women as Rabbis: Studies and Responsa* (New York: Jewish Theological Seminary of America, 1988); Pamela S. Nadell, *Women Who Would Be Rabbis: A History of Women's Ordination, 1889–1985* (Boston: Beacon Press, 1998); Haviva Ner-David, *Life on the Fringes: A Feminist Journey towards Traditional Rabbinic Ordination* (Needham, Mass.: JFL Books, 2000); Ellen M. Umansky and Dianne Ashton, eds., *Four Centuries of Jewish Women's Spirituality: A Sourcebook* (Boston: Beacon Press, 1992).

Responsum on Question, 'Shall Women Be Ordained Rabbis?'

The very raising of this question is due, no doubt, to the great changes in the general position of women, brought about during the last half century or so. Women have been admitted to other professions, formerly practiced by men only, and have proven themselves successful both as regards personal achievement as well as in raising the standards or furthering the interests of the professions. Hence the question suggested itself why not admit women also to the rabbinical profession?

The question resolves itself into the following two parts: first what is the attitude of traditional Judaism on this point, and second, whether Reform Judaism should follow tradition in this regard. At the outset it should be stated that from the point of view of traditional Judaism there is the following important distinction to be made between the rabbinate and the other professions in regard to the admission of women. In the case of the other professions there is nothing inherent in their teachings or principles which might limit their practice to men exclusively. In the case of the rabbinate on the other hand, there are, as will soon be shown, definite teachings and principles in traditional Judaism, of which the rabbinate is the exponent, which demand that its official representatives and functionaries be men only. To admit women to the rabbinate is, therefore, not merely a question of liberalism, it would be acting contrary to the very spirit of traditional Judaism which the rabbinate seeks to uphold and preserve.

It should be stated further, that these traditional principles debarring women from the rabbinate were not formulated in an illiberal spirit by the rabbis of old out of a lack of appreciation of women's talents and endowments. Indeed the rabbis of old entertained a high opinion of womanhood and frequently expressed their admiration for woman's ability and appreciated her great usefulness in religious work. Thus, e.g., they say: "God has endowed woman with a finer appreciation and a better understanding than man." (Niddah 45b). "Sarah was superior to Abraham in prophecy" (Tanhuma Exodus beginning) "It was due to the pious women of that generation that the Israelites were redeemed from Egypt" (Sotah 11b) and "The women were the first ones to receive and accept the Torah" (Tanhuma Buber, Mezora 18, p. 27a); and "They refused to participate in the making of the golden calf." These and many other sayings could be cited from rabbinic literature in praise of women, her equality to man and in some respects, superiority to him. So that we may safely conclude that their excluding of women from the rabbinate does not at all imply deprecation on their part of woman's worth.

But with all their appreciation of woman's fine talents and noble qualities, the rabbis of old have also recognized that man and woman have each been assigned by the Torah certain spheres of activity, involving special duties. The main sphere of woman's activity and her duties centered in the home. Since she has her own duties to perform and since especially in her position as wife and mother she would often be prevented from carrying on many of the regular activities imposed upon man, the Law frees her from many religious obligations incumbent upon man, and especially exempts her from such positive duties the performance of which must take place at certain fixed times, like reciting the Shma, or at prescribed seasons, like Succah. (M.Kiddushin I, 7). [All positive commandments which are time-bound: men are obligated and women are exempt.]

This fact, that she was exempt from certain obligations and religious duties, necessarily excluded her from the privilege of acting as the religious leader or representative of the congregation [sheliah tzibbur]. She could not represent the congregation in the performing of certain religious functions, since, according to the rabbinic principle, one who is not personally obliged to perform a certain duty, cannot perform that duty on behalf of others and certainly cannot represent the congregation in the performance of such duties. [This is the general rule: any on whom an obligation is not incumbent cannot fulfill that obligation on behalf of the many.] (R. H. III, 8, Berokot 20b).

On the same principle she was expressly disqualified from writing Torah scrolls. Since she could not perform for the congregation the duty of reading from the Torah, the text prepared by her was also not qualified for use in connection with the performance of that duty (Gittin 45b Mas. Soferim I, 14). Women were also considered exempt from the obligation to study the Torah (Erubin 27a; Kiddushin 29b–30a). Some rabbis even went so far as to object to women studying the Torah (M. Sotah III, 4). This opinion, of course, did not prevail. Women were taught the Bible and given a religious education and there were some women learned in the law even in talmudic times. But to use the phrase of the Talmud (M. K. 18a) [ishah bi midrashah lo shekiha] women were not to be found in the [bet midrash] academies and colleges where the rabbis assembled and where the students prepared themselves to be rabbis. Evidently, for the reason that they could not aspire to be rabbis, the law excluding them from this religious office.

This law that women cannot be rabbis was always taken for granted in the Talmud. It was considered to be so generally known and unanimously agreed upon that it was not even deemed necessary to make it a special subject of discussion. The very idea of a woman becoming a rabbi never even entered the mind of the rabbis of old. It is for this reason that we find only few direct and definite statements to the effect that women cannot be rabbis. Only occasionally when the discussion of other questions involved the mentioning of it, reference, direct or indirect, is made to the established law that women cannot act as judges or be rabbis. Thus in a Baraita (Pal. Talm. Shebuot. IV, i 35b and Sanhedrin IV, 10 21c) it is stated [Harei lamadnu shehaishah ainah dinah] "We have learned that a woman cannot act as judge, i.e., cannot render decisions of law." The same principle is also indirectly expressed in the Mishnah (comp. Niddah VI, 4 and Shebuot IV, i). In the Talmud (Gittin 5b) it is also indirectly stated that a woman cannot be a member of a Beth Din, i.e., a rabbi, or judge. For there it is taken for granted that she could not be one of three who form a tribunal or [bet din] to pass upon the correctness of a bill of divorce or of any other document. (See Rashi ad. loc.)

In the Midrash. Num. R. X, 5, it is also quoted as a well known and established principle that women may not have the authority to render decisions in religious or ritual matters, [that women are not qualified to render decisions].

These talmudic principles have been accepted by all medieval Jewish authorities. Maimonides, Yad, Sanhedrin II, 7, declares that the members of every tribunal or [bet din] in Israel, which means every rabbi, Dayyan [judge] or More Horaah [teacher of religious subjects or rabbi] in Israel, must possess the same qualities which characterized the men whom Moses selected to be his associates, and whom he appointed judges and leaders in Israel. These qualities, Maimonides continues, are expressly stated in the Torah, as it is said: "Get you from each one of your tribes *men*, wise and understanding and full of knowledge, and I will make them heads over you" (Deut. I, 13). Maimonides here has in mind the idea, entertained by the rabbis of all generations, that the rabbis of each generation continue the activity and are the recipients of the spirit of those first religious leaders of the Jewish people. For as is well known, Moshe Rabenu [Moses] and the seventy elders who formed his council were considered the prototypes and the models of the rabbis of all subsequent generations (comp. Mishnah R. H. II, 9). Likewise, R. Aaron Halevi of Barzelona (about 1300 C. E.) in his Sefer Ha Hinuk (Nos. 74, 75, 77, 79, 81, 83) as well as Jacob Asheri in Tur Hoshen Mishpat VII and Joseph Karo in Shulhan Aruk, Hoshen Mishpat VII, 3, all expressly state the principle that a woman cannot officiate as judge or rabbi. It hardly need be stated that when some of the sources use in this connection the term judge [*dayyan*] they, of course, mean rabbi for which Dayyan is but another name. In rabbinic terminology the functions of a rabbi are spoken of as being to judge [*ladin ulehorot*] and decide religious and ritual questions. And even in our modern rabbinical diploma we use the formula [*yoreh yoreh yadin yadin*] giving the candidate whom we ordain the authority to judge and decide religious questions, and to give authoritative rulings in all religious matters.

To be sure, the rabbis do permit the women to be religious teachers, such as Miriam, who, according to the rabbis, taught the women while Moses and Aaron taught the men (Sifre Zutta quoted in Yalkut, Shimeoni Behaaloteka 74i end) and Deborah, whom the rabbis believed to have been merely teaching the law (Seder Elijahu R. IX–X Friedmann, p. 50, compare also Tossafot B. K. 15a s.v. [*asher tasim*] and parallels). Some authorities would put certain restrictions upon women even in regard to her position as teacher (see Kiddushin 82a and Maimonides, Jad. Talmud Torah II, 4) but in general the opinion of the rabbis was that women may be teachers of religion (see Hinuk 152 and comp. Azulai in Birke Joseph to Hoshen Mishpat VII, 12); and as a matter of fact, there have always been learned women in Israel. These women-scholars were respected for their learning in the same manner as learned men were respected (See Sefer Hasidim, 978 and comp. also Sde Hemed I, letter Kaf No. 99), and some of these women scholars would occasionally even give lectures in rabbinics, but they have never been admitted to the rabbinate since all the rabbinic authorities agree, at least implicitly, that women cannot hold the office of a rabbi or of a [*sheliah tzibbur*, representative of the congregation] and cannot perform any of the official functions requiring the authority of a rabbi.

This is the attitude of traditional Judaism towards the question of women rabbis, a view strictly adhered to by all Jewry all over the world throughout all generations even unto this day.

Now we come to the second part of our question, that is, shall we adhere to this tradition or shall we separate ourselves from Catholic [worldwide] Israel and introduce a radical innovation which would necessarily create a distinction between the title rabbi, as held by a reform-rabbi and the title rabbi in general. I believe that hitherto no distinction could rightly be drawn between the ordination of our modern rabbis and the ordination of all the rabbis of preceding generations. We are still carrying on the activity of the rabbis of old who traced their authority through a chain of tradition to Moses and the elders associated with him, even though in many points we interpret our Judaism in a manner quite different from theirs. We are justified in considering ourselves the latest link in that long chain of authoritative teachers who carried on their activity of teaching, preserving and developing Judaism, and for our time we have the same standing as they had (Comp. R. H. 25a). The ordination which we give to our disciples carries with it, for our time and generation, the same authority which marked the ordination given by Judah Hannasi to Abba Areka or the ordination given by any teacher in Israel to his disciples throughout all the history of Judaism.

We should, therefore, not jeopardize the hitherto indisputable authoritative character of our ordination. We should not make our ordination entirely different in character from the traditional ordination, and thereby give the larger group of Jewry, following traditional Judaism, good reason to question our authority and to doubt whether we are rabbis in the sense in which this honored title was always understood.

Nor is there, to my mind, any actual need for making such a radical departure from this established Jewish law and time honored practice. The supposed lack of a sufficient number of rabbis will not be made up by this radical innovation. There are other and better means of meeting this emergency and that is, by the rabbis following the advice of the Men of the Great Synagog, to raise many disciples and thus encourage more men to enter the ministry. And the standard of the rabbinate in America, while no doubt it could be improved in many directions, is certainly not so low as to need a new and refining influence such as women presumably would bring to any profession they enter. Neither could women, with all due respect to their talents and abilities, raise the standard of the rabbinate. Nay, all things being equal, women could not even rise to the high standard reached by men in this particular calling. If there is any calling which requires a whole-hearted devotion to the exclusion of all other things and the determination to make it one's whole life work, it is the rabbinate. It is not to be considered merely as a profession by which one earns a livelihood. Nor is it to be entered upon as a temporary occupation. One must choose it for his lifework and be prepared to give to it all his energies and to devote to it all the years of his life, constantly learning and improving and thus growing in it. It has been rightly said that the woman who enters a profession, must make her choice between following her chosen profession or the calling of mother and home-maker. She cannot do both well at the same time. This certainly would hold true in the case of the rabbinical profession. The woman who naturally and rightly looks forward to the opportunity of meeting the right kind of man, of marrying him and of having children and a home of her own, cannot give to the rabbinate that wholehearted devotion which comes from the determination to make it one's lifework. For in all likelihood she could not continue it as a married woman. For, one holding the rabbinical office must teach by precept and example, and must give an example of Jewish family and home life where all the traditional Jewish virtues are cultivated. The rabbi can do so all the better when he is married and has a home and a family of his own. The wife whom God has made as a helpmate to him can be, and in most cases is, of great assistance to him in making his home a Jewish home, a model for the congregation to follow.

In this important activity of the rabbi, exercising a wholesome influence upon the congregation, the woman rabbi would be deficient. The woman in the rabbinical office could not expect the man to whom she be married to be merely a helpmate to her, assisting her in her rabbinical activities. And even if she could find such a man, willing to take a subordinate position in the family, the influence upon the families in the congregation of such an arrangement in the home and in the family life of the rabbi would not be very wholesome. Not to mention the fact that if she is to be a mother she could not go on with her regular activities in the congregation.

And there is, to my mind, no injustice done to woman by excluding her from this office. There are many avenues open to her if she choose to do religious or educational work. I can see no reason why we should make this radical departure from traditional practice except the specious argument that we are modern men and, as such, we recognize the full equality of women to men, hence we should be thoroughly consistent. But I would not class the rabbis with those people whose main characteristic is consistency.

DISCUSSION

Rabbi Levinger: I feel very strongly on this question. When we look at the various denominations in this country who are opposed to ordaining women as ministers we find that they are those who like the Episcopalians and Catholics look upon their ministers as priests. To us the Rabbi is merely a teacher and preacher. The question is not whether there are a great many women who want to become rabbis. Perhaps there are none at all. But we are called upon to act on a matter of principle and if in the next thirty or forty years we produce but one Anna Howard Shaw, we want her in the rabbinate.

Rabbi Witt: I was present at the meeting of the Board of Governors when the matter came up, and it was decided to refer it to the Conference. After reading the responsa that was prepared by Rabbi Lauterbach I feared that there would be much opposition. I trust that our action in this matter will be unanimous. It is not a matter of tradition at all. I must confess I was not in the least interested in Rabbi Lauterbach's presentation. It seemed reactionary to me. I did not feel that it was the proper presentation of the subject.

I need not say that I honor Dr. Lauterbach for the learning contained therein but the point he presents is not the point at issue. We have witnessed the revolution in the status of woman. Five years ago I had to argue in favor of women's rights when that question came up in the Arkansas legislature, but I did not feel that there would be need to argue that way in a liberal body of men like this.

There is a principle involved, and I hope that the stand we take will be one in line with all the progressive tendencies of our day: That we will have the vision to see what is before us and from the standpoint of to-day shall we say to women that they shall not have the right to function as we are functioning?

The question is, Have they the qualifications to function as spiritual leaders? What does it require to be a spiritual guide? It requires a great spirit and the quality of leadership. Some women have it and some women have not. Some men have it and some men have not. If we had a great leadership we would not have the questions which were so ably presented yesterday among the practical questions of the ministry. The one thing that was stressed was that if we had devoted leaders who could inspire following all the problems would vanish.

I believe that this body of men should do nothing that would stand in the way of any forward movement in behalf of the womanhood of America. I cannot believe that a religion that is so splendidly spiritual and forward-looking as our religion will stand in the way of such a movement. I feel that this Conference can only act in one way, and that is to fall in line with what is the destiny of the women of the future.

Rabbi Weiss: In a large measure I agree with the previous speakers. I agree with all that has been said in favor of ordaining women as rabbis. I believe I am second to none in the rabbinate in the matter of idealism. But a vast measure of compromise must enter into all situations of life. I do not believe that we can have life exactly as we would like to have it. There is a vast debt due to cold, austere justice, but there are fourteen million Jews in the world and they must be considered. In the City of New York alone there are a million and a half who look upon you with a degree of respect but who have their own mode of procedure and who would look upon any radical action on your part as a line of cleavage in the House of Israel. I merely mean that we should proceed slowly. I believe that some compromise can be effected such as allowing women to be teachers or superintendents, but I believe that it were unwise at the present time to have them ordained as rabbis. Let me give one concrete illustration. Suppose one were to sign a marriage document. To many in New York today such a ceremony would hardly be recognized as binding.

Rabbi Brickner: There is much merit in what Dr. Lauterbach has said. He has not stressed the question of opinion, but the question of practicability. Modern psychologists agree that women do not differ from men so much in intellect. In fact experiments prove that women are the peers of most men. There are women occupying positions in modern industry in which she could not be equaled by many men. It is not a question of equality. All that Dr. Lauterbach has said, has already been said against women entering other professions. The question with us is one of practicability. The tendency in modern Judaism is to conserve Jewish values. We wish to be in touch with the masses of Jewish people. When I came away from Toronto the other day I clipped from the newspaper the vote of the Methodist Church in Canada. It represents the liberal traditions in Canada. And yet it voted by a small majority against permitting women into the ministry. It is not a question of principle or equality—on that we are all agreed. It is purely a question of practicability.

Rabbi Charles S. Levi: The matter before you is not a matter of the hour, but a matter of all times. It is a matter that touches upon the acknowledged leadership of our people, and reaches the lives of uncounted thousands of our American co-religionists. We are the links in the chain of time. We are the spokesmen who give expression to the great truths which bind the past to the future, and it is for us to keep alive the chain of tradition.

Rabbi Rauch: I listened with great interest to Dr. Lauterbach's presentation and was at first inclined to agree with him but as he proceeded it struck me that there was a great omission. He gave a fine presentation of the traditional point of view and even hinted at certain modern needs, but I regret to say that he failed to touch on what reform Judaism has to say on the subject. And yet our whole interpretation of religious life is supposedly based on the principles of reform Judaism. Now what has the philosophy of reform Judaism to say in regard to woman? I know from experience because I was born in an orthodox environment. There was a very clear line of distinction between the boy and girl, and the education given to the boy and girl. The boy had to learn Scriptures while the girl was not expected to learn them. Many duties were imposed upon the boy, few upon the girl. This went on for centuries. What happened when reform came in? One by one the barriers separating the boy from the girl educationally began to be broken down. We admitted the girls into the same schools, and we tried to teach them the same things. Even in the important ceremony of barmitzva we brushed aside the traditional point of view and we said that the girl should be educated and confirmed the same as the boy. And in our congregations, which is the practical side of our religious life, we have given to women exactly the same status as the men. In my own congregation women conduct the summer services and they conduct them just as well if not better than they used to be when we got some one temporarily for the summer. In every line of endeavor in our temples we have proceeded on the theory that woman is the equal of man. What do they ask us to do? They want us to make it possible for women to work along the same lines as we men are working. We do not ask privileges for them. Let there be the same demands, the same rigorous training and let the congregation decide whether the woman is doing the work well or not. I do not think that our cause will be hurt by a liberal attitude.

Rabbi Englander: Personally I was surprised to learn that the Board of Governors submitted this question to the Conference. I thought that after the faculty, a body composed of the teachers, had taken action that would be sufficient guidance for action on the part of the Board of Governors. However, I wish to touch on one argument which has been raised to the effect that if we admit women as rabbis we would tend to create a schism in Israel. During all the conferences in recent years there are many actions that we would not have taken had we feared this. We would not have set ourselves on record against Zionism. Had fear been taken into consideration we would not have taken a stand on many subjects. Twenty years ago this Conference put itself on record favoring absolute religious equality of women with men. Are we going back on our own action? In spite of all the arguments advanced by Dr. Lauterbach, the faculty set itself on record as favoring the ordination of women although it stated that at the present time it believed it was impractical for women to enter the rabbinate. But I do not believe that the question of practicability is for us to decide. The only question before us is, shall we in the light of reform Judaism put ourselves on record in favor of admitting women to the rabbinate.

A motion is made that further discussion be discontinued.

Rabbi Morgenstern: I do not care to express any opinion upon this subject, because you can readily understand, inasmuch as this question has been submitted by the college authorities to the Conference to get an expression of opinion, I am here rather to listen than to offer any opinion I myself may have. I realize that the time of the Conference is very precious and that you cannot afford to give more time than is necessary to the discussion of this question, but I believe that the question is of such importance that it ought to justify the expenditure of as much time as may be necessary for a thorough discussion of the question. Several of the men lay emphasis upon the significance of the principle of not breaking with Catholic [worldwide] Israel. We have heard the arguments but there are several valuable thoughts which have not yet been presented. And there is one phase of the question which has not been adequately discussed. We can all accept the opinion of Dr. Lauterbach as authoritative, namely, from the point of view of traditional Judaism the ordination of women would not be permitted. We need not discuss that. But the practical aspect of the question has not been discussed. Namely, is it expedient, and is it worth while?

Rabbi Abrams: I cannot feel but in thorough sympathy and agreement with Rabbi Lauterbach. We are paying too much attention to what is being done by other denominations. It is the spirit and practice of Israel that should guide us. It would be a mistake to break with the traditions of the past.

Rabbi Raisin: It seems to me that the question resolves itself into three parts. First, what is the principle? Second, is it consistent? Third, is it practical?

As a matter of principle women ought to be ordained as we now recognize that they are entitled to the same privileges and rights as men. Our ancestors never asked, is it practical? They asked, is it the will of God? And thus they settled the question for themselves. But we must ask the question, is it in keeping with the tradition of the past? In the whole paper of Rabbi Lauterbach we do not find the statement that women could not be ordained as rabbis. Indirectly we inferred that she may not be ordained because we do not find any women who were ordained. At the most sentiment was against it, but sentiment was against women going into many of the professions even to-day. But that does not mean that they should not be ordained or could not be according to traditional laws.

What is our ordination to-day? In spite of our claim that we are the descendants of the ancient rabbis, we must admit that the function of the modern rabbi is entirely different from the function of the rabbi of old. In olden times, he was the judge. That was his chief function. Preaching and teaching were secondary. If we were to lay claim to be lineal descendants of the ancient teachers we must go to the prophets of the Bible. We are the followers of the prophets more than of the rabbis. And if we would follow the example of the women of the Bible, we would find that many women served as prophets and that during Talmudic times many of them taught. So we are not inconsistent with the past, if we put ourselves on record as favoring the ordination of women.

Rabbi Joseph L. Baron: I enjoyed thoroughly the scholarly paper of my teacher on the negative view of the question, and I shall not deny that the admission of women into the rabbinate will, like any innovation, shock some people and call forth opposition and ridicule. But I wish to point out several flaws in the negative argument. Professor Lauterbach intimates that the matter has hitherto never arisen as a practical issue because it has been taken for granted that a woman cannot, in the capacity of rabbi, carry out, or represent the people in, a function in which she is not personally obliged to participate. How, then, can we infer from this that with the full entry of woman in all the religious functions of home and synagog, she must still be denied the privilege of ordination? We broke with tradition long ago when we granted women an equal standing with men in all our religious functions.

I disagree entirely with the remark that by taking the proposed step, we shall create a schism. The Russian Jews, to whom reference has been made, do recognize and follow women leaders, as in the radical factions. And if women are not recognized as leaders in the orthodox synagog, let us not forget that neither are we recognized as such. There is a distinct difference made, even in the Yiddish terminology between a *Rav* and a *Rabbi*. Again, we broke with tradition long ago when we declared that a rabbi need not be an authority on questions of *Kashruth* [dietary laws]; and I need not mention which, from the point of view of orthodoxy, is the greater offense.

When I received the responsum of Dr. Lauterbach a week or two ago, I inquired as to the attitude of the members of a Unitarian Church in Moline, where a woman has been officiating for about half a year, and the reply was very favorable. That minister is not falling behind her male predecessors in her zeal and ability in handling all the problems of the church. So, as to the practicality of the matter, I believe that should be left entirely with the individual congregation.

Rabbi James G. Heller: I do not believe that the Conference has the right to appeal to its duty to "Catholic Israel" in order to settle this question. In the past many decisions have been taken which evidenced no regard for mere keeping of the peace. The one question at issue, the one question that should be discussed by this Conference, is whether in principle the admission of women into the rabbinate is desirable, and whether it is in accordance with the historic teachings of reform Judaism. The entire content of Dr. Lauterbach's responsum can, to my mind, be summed up in that very logical inconsistency to which he refers toward the end of his paper in so laudatory a manner. He must complete the syllogism contained in his remarks. Since traditional Judaism, Orthodoxy, did not require women to perform certain duties or functions, did not permit them to share in certain duties or functions, did not permit them to share in certain religious acts, it could not allow them to become teachers of these same duties. And, per contra, since reform Judaism requires and asks of women the performance of every religious duty in the catalog, it cannot deny them the right to become teachers and preachers.

Rabbi Samuel S. Cohon: I wish to call your attention to the fact that in other professions there is a great deal of prejudice against women even where they administer with considerable success. You would imagine that women would welcome the services of women physicians. But in actual practice it is stated that women are more bitterly opposed to female practitioners than are men.

In the legal profession we also know that in many instances women are debarred from practice. But I believe that many of us who realize how much our wives have helped us, how they have co-operated with us, how they have borne many of the responsibilities also realize that they should be given the opportunity to assume this work on their own accord if they so desire. Of course there will be prejudice against women in the rabbinate but if one congregation is found that will welcome a woman the opportunity should be granted.

Rabbi Frisch: We have made greater departures from tradition in reform Judaism than the one which is before us so we can afford to dismiss this question without further discussion. But I regard the ordination of women as the last step in the removal of restrictions in the Jewish faith. She is fitted by temperament and by all of her qualifications to the position of teacher and she has been granted the right to participate in all our congregational activities as the equal of man. Civilization has had cause to regret every restriction which it has placed in the way of those who wanted to be free.

I have been wondering whether we are not denying ourselves a new source of strength, a new source of inspiration by our reluctance in admitting women to the rabbinate. I recognize the handicaps, but I believe that the women who surmount the obstacles will be greater spirits than the men who are in the rabbinate today. Will it be any greater reproach for a woman to give up the ministry for the sake of maternity than it is for a man to give it up to seek a livelihood in other work? I think it will be for a nobler reason. If we get women into our midst as rabbis I believe that we will be enjoying some of the inspiration and strength which we feel we need. So I plead that we place ourselves on record as in full sympathy with a further emancipation of women by their ordination as rabbis in Israel.

Rabbi Stern: Emotionally I am conservative and I do not like to break with the past, but I cannot agree with Rabbi Lauterbach in this instance. Is it not essential for us first to decide what is the principle? I believe the practical will take care of itself. It is very interesting to note that in the city of New York a professor in the Seminary, the rabbi of an orthodox congregation had a Bar Mitzva of girls. This is very interesting and shows that the other wing of Judaism is also making progress.

A motion that the opinions of members which have been sent in should be read was introduced. The motion was lost.

Rabbi Morgenstern: I think there is one possible source of information that we have not heard from and whose opinion would be very helpful to us. I mean the wives of the rabbis present. It would help us to get an expression of opinion from the women, if some of the wives would be willing to give us their ideas based on many years of experience in this work. I would ask that opportunity be given to the ladies to express their opinion.

It was moved that the courtesy of the floor be extended to any of the ladies present who cared to take part in the discussion.

Mrs. Frisch: When I entered the hall this morning, I was opposed to the ordination of women as rabbis. I am now in favor of it. I have been much impressed with what I have heard.

The reason I was opposed to the ordination of women was what you would call the practical reason. I now feel that whatever practical reasons I may have had cannot be compared in value with the matter of principle which has been mentioned here this morning.

The practical reason that I had in mind was that I as a wife and mother did not understand how a woman could attend to the duties which devolve upon a rabbi and at the same time be a true home-maker. Candidly, I do not see at this moment how it can be accomplished. I cannot solve this question, but there may be some women who would prefer a life of celibacy in order to minister to a congregation.

Personally I am selfish enough not to be willing to give up the happiness of wifehood and motherhood for this privilege, great though it be. But I love the work of the rabbinate so much that could I have prevailed upon myself to forget the joys that come with wife-making I should have become a rabbi. And I do not believe that privilege should be denied women and it behooves us to go on record as being in favor of this movement.

Miss Baron: I am connected with Jewish work in New York City and I know that since the Jewish woman has entered the work it has intensified the value of Jewish education; and I believe that should the Jewish woman enter the rabbinate she will be able to intensify the religious feeling of our people.

Mrs. Berkowitz: I am more than satisfied to be the silent member of our partnership, but I believe it is the function of women to give spiritual value to the world and especially the Jewish woman imbued with the Jewish spirit will naturally bring a certain quality to the ministry which some of our men lack. I think that might be enlarged and strengthened and therefore I should like to see our women become rabbis if they wish to do so.

A motion that action on this resolution be postponed until next year was lost.

A motion that a referendum vote of the members of the Conference be taken was lost.

A motion that this resolution be referred to the Committee on Resolutions was lost.

Rabbi Joseph Leiser: The objections of Professor Lauterbach concerning the admission of Jewish women to the rabbinate are inadequate. His thesis, that the rabbinical profession is a career and involves the totality of life to the preclusion of even the function and offices of motherhood, is not valid and is no more applicable to the Jewish woman as rabbi than it is to the Jewish woman as lawyer, doctor, dentist, newspaper writer, musician, business woman or teacher. In all these trades and professions, Jewish women are actively engaged beyond the consideration or limitations of sex, and independent of previous sex-taboos. As a profession, the rabbinate ought to be open to women on a parity with that of man, providing women receive a degree for academic training carried on according to approved standards.

But my objection to the position maintained by Prof. Lauterbach rests on more fundamental contentions than of sex discrimination in the rabbinate. The Professor fails to analyze the rabbinate in the light of its function and activity in the world to-day. He carries over into America, a modern America, the methodology and outlook of an orthodox rabbi whose function is that of a lawyer, one who renders decisions in an ecclesiastical court from codes drawn up by established standards of behavior. Orthodox Judaism rests upon laws of conformity. One discharges his duties. One learns them and fulfills them, whereas reform Judaism releases the individual to enable him to realize his own nature and therefore allows him to contribute whatever there is implanted within his soul and mind to humanity.

This difference in motivation is translated to the profession of the rabbi, as it is interpreted in reform Judaism.

The mere repudiation of the authority of the Talmud and Schulhan Aruk is not sufficient to constitute one a reform rabbi nor does the accepting of it make one an orthodox rabbi. To be sure, the orthodox rabbi is learned in the law, since the very nature and constitution of his profession require it. But the reform rabbi is not primarily a legal expert. The modern rabbinate has become an institution, just as the synagog has developed other functions than those pertaining to worship and the discharging of ceremonial observances. In these days it serves more than one purpose and therefore requires more than one type of professional labor.

The variety of activities that are now released in the ordinary synagog calls for a number of workers all of whom must be filled with the knowledge of God. The new work recently developed in the synagog appeals particularly to the woman who by nature and training is singularly fitted to undertake it.

It will be said in rebuttal that, while the need and utility of these modern activities within the synagog may require the professional assistance of woman these functions do not require the training and professional equipment of a rabbi.

This is a mistake. Mere inclination provides access to those qualities of emotionalism and undisciplined enthusiasm which endanger the assistance of a woman. Professional training is required for the expert in the religious institution of the synagog. In the department of education as our synagogs are elaborating them a Jewish woman is particularly well qualified, providing her training in rabbinics is grounded in a thorough knowledge of the literature.

A Jewish woman is the logical adjunct to young people's societies and organizations, and no synagog is complete without these new features.

The social activities of a congregation are dependent on the social instincts of a woman. Her rabbinical training enables her to link up these activities with tradition and provides the background of Jewish consciousness to this work.

The pulpit and whatever pertains to it is, and remains, a plane wherein man is by nature and temperament best qualified, although not exclusively so. Nor is woman by reason of self limitations, disqualified. Viewing the rabbi in the light of a prophet and the man of vision, he more than woman responds to this unusual endowment. Men are prone to be idealists. They are quick to see visions. They are the dreamers. To men is given the gift of prophecy but not exclusively, as the careers of Hulda and Deborah testify. Men are called upon by God to be pathfinders, liberators, protagonists of right, brandishing the shining sword of justice before the hosts of evil-doers. In the defense of right, men will face the outrages of the world alone.

On the other hand, women are conservative, and seldom are impelled to stand forth and proclaim these eternal convictions. They are pacifists, importunists, moderators, trimming their sails to whatever winds blow on the seven seas of thought. Remember, that while it was due to the merit of women that the children of Israel were redeemed from Egypt, it was only merit not the fierce rebellion of a Moses, saying, "Let my people go free!" that wrought the miracle.

Were the woman as rabbi merely confined to pulpit discourses and the formal aspects of ceremonials, her admission to the profession would be inept and otiose. The synagog, however, has enlarged its tent cords of service. It is an institution of which the pulpit is part, not the totality. Being only a feature of the institutional labor, there are spheres of activity in the synagog that can not only be filled by woman, but are primarily her province.

Rabbi Neumark: I. "This fact that she was exempt from certain obligations . . . she could not . . . represent the congregation in the performance of such duties (R. H. III, 8; Berakot 20b)." Against this argument is to be said:

First: The traditional functions of the rabbi have nothing to do with representation of the congregation in the performance of certain religious duties from which women are freed. There are certain categories of men, such as are deformed and afflicted with certain bodily defects, who could not act as reader, but could be rabbis for decisions in ritual matters and questions of law. The same holds true of people with a "foreign accent" in Hebrew.

Second: Women are not free from the duties of *Prayer, Grace after meal* and *Kiddush*, and they can read for others.—cf. Mishnah and Bab. Gemara Berakoth 20a, b. Thus even in our modern conception of the function of the rabbi which includes reading, woman can act as representative according to traditional law. (Of course, "Tephillah" here is used in its technical meaning—"Eighteen-Prayers"—, while the Prayer in its general meaning of Divine Service had the Sh'ma in its center from the obligatory reading of which woman was free. But no orthodox Jew ever waited with the obligatory reading of the Sh'ma for the public service; it has, at least in post-talmudic times, always been done right in the morning privately.

Third: The practice within reform Judaism has decided in favor of admitting women as readers of the Divine Service. And since we are interested in the traditional law on the subject only in order to take from it a clue for reform practice, this argument would be of no consequence even if it were valid as it is not: If woman is to be debarred from the rabbinate in orthodox Judaism because she cannot serve as a reader, then the only logical consequence would be that reform Judaism which has decided in favor of the woman reader, should disregard the orthodox attitude, and admit woman to the rabbinate.

II. The reason why a Torah Scroll written by a woman was considered unfit, is not, as Dr. Lauterbach claims, because she could not be reader of the Torah, but quite a formal one: Whosoever has not the obligation of binding (T'phillim [phylacteries]), has not the fitness of writing (a Torah-Scroll—Gittin 45b; Men. 42b). The above reason is given in Sopherim I, 13, but there, woman is not debarred from writing a Torah-Scroll (I have before me ed. Berdyshew 5657—one-volume Talmud and 12 vol. Talm. ed. Wien, Anton Schmidt, 1832).

III. In Babli Moed Katan, 18a, it is not said that "women were not to be found in the academies and college where the rabbis assembled and where the students prepared themselves to be rabbis." It is only said: [*ishah bi midrashah lo shekiha*] "a woman is not *often* to be found in the Beth-ha-Midrash." The academies and colleges of those days were not institutions for training of rabbis, but institutions of learning, most of whose students were pursuing other vocations. A woman in those days was supposed to keep away from all public places, such as courts, and the like, and even, as much as possible, from the streets: [The king's daughter is all glorious within; Ps. 45:14].

IV. As to the direct question of the legal situation, I have discussed that matter in the opinion which I have submitted to the faculty of the Hebrew Union College. I want to add the following remarks: I. The statement of Jerush. Synh. 21c and Sheb. 35b, that woman cannot serve (occasionally) as judge, is not from a Baraitha, as Dr. Lauterbach claims; but occurs in a discussion between two Amoraim. 2. [*Lamadnu*] does not mean "we have learned," but is a technical term for an inference on the virtue of an hermeneutical rule; in this case a [*gezerah shavah;* inference]. 3. Nowhere in talmudic but always by [*tanya*] literature is a Baraitha introduced by [*lamadnu tani*] and the like. 4. The emphasis on "men" in the quotation from Maimuni is *not* justified.

V. As to the practical question of the advisability to ordain women at the Hebrew Union College, I do not believe that the orthodox will have any additional reason to object. They themselves employ women in their schools as teachers and readers, and more than this our woman rabbi will not do. In fact the entire question reduces itself to this: Women are already doing most of the work that the ordained woman rabbi is expected to do. But they do it without preparation and without authority. I consider it rather a duty of the authorities to put an end to the prevailing anarchy by giving women a chance to acquire adequate education and an authoritative standing in all branches of religious work. The practical difficulties cannot be denied. But they will work out the same way as in other professions, especially in the teaching profession, from the kindergarten to post-graduate schools. Lydia Rabbinowitz raised a family of three children and kept up a full measure of family life while being a professor of bacteriology. The woman rabbi who will remain single will not be more, in fact less, of a problem than the bachelor rabbi. If she marries and chooses to remain a rabbi, and God blesses her, she will retire for a few months and provide a substitute, as rabbis generally do when they are sick or meet with an automobile accident. When she comes back, she will be a better rabbi for the experience. The rabbinate may help the women, and the woman rabbi may help the rabbinate. You cannot treat the reform rabbinate from the orthodox point of view. Orthodoxy is orthodoxy, and reform is reform. Our good relations with our orthodox brethren may still be improved upon by a clear and decided stand on this question. They want us either to be reform or to return to the fold of real genuine orthodox Judaism whence we came.

The Woman Rabbi: An Autobiographical Sketch

Reputable psychologists tell us that the children have no religious sense properly speaking. Thus, though I might have said: as a child I was deeply and sincerely religious, I mean only that I held tenaciously to religious decorousness. Religion and everything over which religion haloed its glamour appeared particularly sacrosanct to me. This was evident in my attitude toward the Sunday School. I remember how, in the early days, I was shocked at the misbehavior of the other children in the Sunday School. They were so quiet in the day school, and on Sunday they were young devils. I myself was quite a behavior problem in the public school (how often my poor father had to come and rescue me from the principal's office). But such conduct seemed the height of impropriety in the Sunday School.

I have always wondered why I was imbued with the idea of becoming a rabbi. The first distinct recollection I have of a definite feeling toward communal work is connected with my confirmation service. I was one of those who read from the *Torah* in Hebrew, and the recitation of those ancient words crystallized a vague restlessness of mine into a desire to serve my people. The easiest way to enter that field was to enter the Hebrew Union College and become a rabbi! My youthful impetuosity was not concerned with the difficulties of such an undertaking. The doubt never entered my mind as to whether I, a girl, would be ordained. I wanted to serve Judaism and Jews. What other requisite was necessary for admission to the rabbinate? Surely, ancient precedent justified me.

WAS LAUGHED AT

At first everyone laughed at me (indeed, perhaps, they have never stopped), but as time went on, and I remained steadfast in my purpose, my parents, at least began to consider the matter more seriously. They never were wholly in favour of the idea, and especially not of *my* entering the struggle for admission to the ministry, but they never deterred me, and even encouraged me.

I was fourteen when I entered the Hebrew Union College. During the preceding summer I had taken some lessons in Hebrew Grammar from my dear friend, Dr. Englander, but even with that I was hardly as well prepared for the work as the most *goyish* [Gentile] of the boys. Something occurred during that first year which strengthened my purpose. A senior student at the college, reputed to be the best student of that period, had succumbed to the influenza epidemic. It was the first time that anyone with whom I was intimately associated had died. I was deeply impressed. I vowed to myself, in youthful ardor, that I would try to take his place in the world of Jewish scholarship; I would carry on the work which had been torn from his hands. Whenever my zeal flagged, because of the persistent discouragement and laughter, I needed only the thought of him to buoy me up.

My years at College have been rich with contacts, both cultural and social. What religious joy I experienced in beholding and listening to the deceased Dr. Gotthard Deutsch. What a majestic figure! That long, snow-white beard, with deep reflective eyes. His most typical movement was playing with his beard, stroking it, combing it, curling it. All that I remember of my first examination with him is his beard. His intimate friends called Dr. Deutsch "a walking encyclopedia", but his knowledge was only of minor significance for me. It was the way in which he presented his material. A phrase here and there, a sentence, and one obtained a splendid panorama of Jewish history.

Beards savor of the patriarch; they lend a nimbus of sacredness and authority. In my early days at the College, most of the professors were bearded, and they gave the College walls a certain touch of the old *Yeshivoth* [Academies]. It was only the modernity of the surroundings which kept one from believing that one was in ancient Sura or Pumbeditha.

Dr. Kaufman Kohler was not "the Nestor of American Judaism" to me, but a kindly, deeply-religious, tolerant teacher. Occasionally, the boys had little differences with him, on religious points, and although he was firm in presenting his point of view, he never insisted that his ideas be accepted. It was his sermons that always gave me the greatest intellectual pleasure. Militant in his Judaism, yet peaceful and just, he was defiant of sham, and a sworn enemy of hypocrisy. I always used to marvel at the beauty which this scholar was able to superimpose upon the power of his sermons.

INFLUX OF LOVE NOTES

Four years ago, for some unaccountable reason, the newspapers began featuring me, so to speak. My picture was printed in almost every sheet, together with the subtitle that I was studying at the College, and was destined to be the only and first woman in the rabbinate. Then a queer, but I suppose to be expected, result ensued. I was flooded with love-letters and proposals from everywhere and everybody. Even a Filipino medical student from far-away Manila made a shy bid for my hand. Thus at a time when I was preparing to provide for my own subsistence, some one was offering to provide it for me. Interesting paradox! Gruff, uncouth, illiterate, boring letters were intermingled with the suave, the courteous, the refined.

Although the teachings of the Hebrew Union College, as far as the College can be said to require a certain definite affirmation, were in keeping with my secular education; though they in no way conflicted with the changing points of view I acquired at the University, I was yet disappointed with one phase of modern Judaism. Reform Judaism is for the rational; those who desire to harmonize their past and their present, their heart and their mind. But in some ways it impresses me as too academic. My first years at the College, spent in the midst of adolescence, were robbed of that emotional development which was my due. With Santayana, I hold that religion can be made into beauty, and that true religion always is. The ritual and ceremony were what I missed. The mystic, Oriental atmosphere, necessary for the encouragement of any aesthetic soul was lacking. It was only in my later years at College, in the classes of Dr. Henry Slonimsky, that my mystic nature was given its proper cultivation.

To be a pupil to one whom one has always called "daddy"! In a way it was interesting and amusing, but it was always quite difficult for me to adjust myself. When I first entered my father's class room I felt somewhat estranged. That man with the magnetic soul and the philosophic mien, sitting on the rostrum, seemed someone else than the wonderful father I knew at home. In time I became adjusted to the idea, and relished the impersonal, and yet vitally engrossing manner, in which Professor David Neumark described abstruse philosophic principles. Socrates, Plato, Aristotle, and the Arabic peripatetics, Maimonides, Bachya, and Jehuda Halevi assumed meaning for the problems of present-day Judaism. What a trenchant, incisive way he had of attacking the fallacies of others. With what naive simplicity he acknowledged his own great philosophic stature.

At home, my father became my tutor. For examinations and recitations, we would always prepare together. How rigorous he was; how insistent upon the mastery of every detail. Questions that no other professor would have dreamed of asking, my father coached me in thoroughly. But we were also spiritual companions. Often, we would spend the evenings discussing a religious problem. Sometimes, I might break in with the remark that Stirner had said so and so, and my father would smilingly rejoin: I read him when I was eight years old, and even then I realized his stupidity. I remember when I took a course in aesthetics, how my father used to ridicule the professor's view of art. Harmony, color, line, rhythm, representation, how asinine he declared the professor's definitions.

From my father I obtained my God-concept. It was he who converted me from a belief in God as a being, anthropomorphic or attributeless, into a belief in God as a process. God is a thinking process. Every individual is born with a minimum consciousness, or soul, if you will. The growth of the individual increases that consciousness. The same holds true with the world as a whole. Thus, he would end up: God is the thought of the individual and the world. This almost sounds Roycian, by my father's explanation too involved for record here, would have convinced anyone to the contrary. My father's most characteristic resume of the problem was this: If you believe in anything else than that God is a process, that is, if you think of Him in any sort of material way, then you might as well conceive of Him as a piece of cotton or a piece of cheese. Almost facetious, but it is his theory in a sentence.

My work at the Hebrew Union College, my gradually enlarging acquaintance with Jewish lore, philosophy and history has made more firm my conviction that in no manner are women incapable of entering the ministry, either by reason of tradition, or because of their inherent incapacity. Women would add new blood to the ranks of the ministry, a thing much needed at present. In another article I shall describe what particular benefits they could render.

The Woman Rabbi: Difficulties

Because of the publicity that had been showered upon me, other women began to think of entering the Hebrew Union College, with a view toward the rabbinate. Their application blanks received the identical replies: they might enter the College, and take all the work, but under no conditions would they he granted the regular scholarships nor the privilege of being ordained. The faculty had no choice in the matter—under the present regime, scholarships and ordination were available only to *male* students, who had signified their desire of entering the ministry.

The problem had reached its highest stage. What was to be done with these women applicants; was I to be regarded as a "regular student", with the prospect of being ordained? The faculty decided to take official action with the result that it declared itself in favor of ordination for any woman rabbinical candidate who had undergone training under the same rules as those of the men students. I was particularly grateful for this decision, because a short time previous I had applied to the faculty for a fall "holiday position", which request had been refused. (Even though my position had been assigned me, it is highly problematical whether any congregation would have accepted a woman—and so young—to officiate at the high holiday services.)

The question was finally referred to the Board of Governors, which has the final authority in such matters. The Board declared that it was a problem too weighty to be decided arbitrarily, and transferred the decision to the Central Conference of American Rabbis, despite the fact that the Faculty of the College, a representative body of the foremost Reform Jewish scholars had decided in favor of ordination.

RITUAL INVALUABLE

Two summers before this time I had read services at a certain summer resort, while my father preached the sermon. I shall never forget the occasion. The curious, yet sympathetic, interest of the congregation (the women relished the idea more than the men did), the unique quality of the event, the generous approval of my father inspired me to persist in my intention of becoming America's first woman rabbi. It was as I incanted the Hebrew that the witchery and charm of the service surged through me. I began to feel the value of ritual in a religious service. The formal and academic nature of the Reform service became emphasized. Since then I have come to the belief that ritual and ceremony are invaluable adjuncts to a religious communion. The next summer (1921) I read services in conjunction with one of my college class-mates, which experience, more than the one with my father, gave rise to an idea which I shall broach later.

In the summer of 1922, the Central Conference, at Cape May, debated the question of women in the rabbinate. Dr. Jacob Lauterbach, Professor of Talmud at the College, read the first paper, contending that it would be in violation of tradition and prejudicial to the best interests of modern, Reform Judaism to have women admitted to the rabbinate. But in what a kindly, tolerant vein he spoke. He is the soul of gentleness and generousness; and I believe it was more because he thought he owed a duty to Judaism than that he himself opposed it that he was openly against the admission of women into the rabbinate.

But Dr. Lauterbach met with very little approval. As a body the Conference was overwhelmingly in favor of the ordination of women as Rabbis. It was interesting to observe some of the rabbis, dignified impressive men, who regarded the whole affair with an amused smile. These were the true scholars of the assembly. They scorned this petty concern with a matter that should have been settled long ago. Women or men in the rabbinate—their scope was to broaden and advance the culture of Judaism. It was mostly the younger rabbis who joined in the combat with zest.

The liberals among them conceived this to be an excellent point of vantage from which they could demolish some of the hoary, encrusted Jewish traditions. To have women admitted as rabbis would give them an excellent wedge with which to pry further into the crumbling dogmas of a moribund Judaism. But, probably to the regret of these latter, there was no struggle involved. Almost unanimously the Conference was in favor.

ATTITUDE TOWARDS WOMEN RABBIS

The Board of Governors, however, decided otherwise. At the meeting where this decision was arrived at, there were two rabbis present and six laymen, who voted unanimously and respectively Aye and Naye. This illustrates, in general, the attitude of rabbis and laymen toward the admission of women to the rabbinate. The rabbis, who know the duties, functions, and handicaps of their profession assert that women can enter the ministry; whereas layman, for the most part unacquainted with the ministerial technique, aver that the duties of the office are too burdensome on a woman. The irony of fate! My father, who from the beginning had advised me against my purpose, was primarily interested in the principles of the question, and tradition's attitude toward it. I repeat verbatim his reply to the assertions of some of the opposition:

". . . If woman is to be debarred from the rabbinate in orthodox Judaism because she cannot serve as reader, then the only logical consequence would be that Reform Judaism, which has decided in favor of the woman reader, should disregard the orthodox attitude, and admit women to the rabbinate. . . . The entire question reduces itself, to this: women are already doing most of the work that the ordained woman rabbi is expected to do. But they do it without preparation and without authority. I consider it a duty of the authorities to put an end to the prevailing anarchy by giving women a chance to acquire adequate education and an authoritative standing in all branches of religious work. The practical difficulties cannot be denied. But they will work out the same as in other professions. . . . Lydie Rabbinowitz raised a family of three children while being a professor of bacteriology. The woman rabbi who will remain single will not be more, in fact, less of a problem than the bachelor rabbi. If she marries and chooses to remain a rabbi, and God blesses her, she will retire for a few months and provide a substitute, as rabbis generally do when they are sick, or when they have met with an accident. When she comes back, she will be a better rabbi for the experience. The rabbinate may help the woman, and the woman rabbi may help the rabbinate."

The discussion [about] the admission of women as rabbis is merely another phase of the woman question. Despite the fact that so many women have achieved eminence in their chosen fields, a struggle ensues each time that a woman threatens to break up man's monopoly upon any industrial, political, or social province. The usual feminist recapitulation of the achievements of women from Sappho down to George Sand and George Eliot has become too threadbare for use. We need but look at the noteworthy contributions which our own American Jewesses have made to their people and to the country. Henrietta Szold stands out as the most zealous worker in the cause of the restoration of the Jewish homeland. Indefatigable, ceaselessly energetic she sacrifices herself and her interests for her people. Mrs. Rebekah Kohut has distinguished herself as a communal worker. Edna Ferber has, acknowledgedly, enriched American Literature.

WOMEN BETTER FITTED

Surely, a woman rabbi is more adapted to the needs of the Reform synagogue as it exists at present than is a man. Our services have become haunts mostly for women, and no one can doubt that the spiritual struggles which a woman has had will be more vitally interesting to these women parishioners than those of the man. At least, their paths of spiritual storm will coincide more.

But why be restricted to the question: Should a man or a woman be the rabbi? Those who phrase the problem thus, misunderstand or misstate it. Many congregations have two rabbis. In fact, this practice is becoming more general all the time, due to the fact that one man is fitted for a certain type of work, the next for another. One is adapted to pastoral work; one is brilliantly gifted as an orator. One is interested in social service; the other has powers as a religious teacher. Why could there not be a division of labor between the man and woman rabbi? The division of their work would be entirely dependent upon their capacities; the same standards would hold as in the division of labor when there are two men rabbis. There are many, very many problems which members of the community, men and women, have, with which they feel they cannot go to the man rabbi, because of the delicacy of the matter, or their sensitiveness. Men and women compose the congregation; a man and a woman should serve this congregation's needs.

The present attitude of some of the laity is to be regretted, in view of the fact that women rabbis will benefit them incalculably. Women can aid in the solution of the problem by devoting themselves to Jewish study, by fitting themselves for ordination. The general community can help by showing a willingness to accept women as their spiritual leaders.

—— 32 ——

Mother India's Scandalous Swamis

Stephen Prothero

Americans encountered Hinduism in the late eighteenth century, when sea captains from ports such as Salem, Massachusetts, first sailed into Indian waters. But immigration from India to the United States did not begin in earnest until over two hundred years later, in the first decade of the twentieth century. What Americans learned of Hinduism in the interim they typically got from books, notably missionary accounts, travelogues, and translations of Hindu scriptures. In those books, Americans learned both to love and to hate Hinduism. Christian missionaries, at least until the late nineteenth century, typically denounced living Hindus as heathens. But some intellectuals, from the Sanskrit scholars of the eighteenth century to the Transcendentalists and Theosophists of the nineteenth, praised ancient Hindu scriptures for their lofty literature and sublime spiritual ideals.

Still, the dominant tone was condemnation. In *Following the Equator,* a travelogue published in 1897, Mark Twain lent the critics an able pen, popularizing a host of negative stereotypes about India and Hinduism. Both Hinduism and its homeland, Twain wrote, were ancient yet childish. The country was unspeakably dirty and its people oversexed. The Hindu religion, moreover, amounted to idol worship, and Hindu yogis were more intent on making money than seeking spiritual liberation. Of the images of the Hindu gods in the Indian city of Banares ("Idolville," he called it), Twain wrote, "And what a swarm of them there is! The town is a vast museum of idols—and all of them crude, misshapen, and ugly. They flock through one's dreams at night, a wild mob of nightmares."

As long as Asian Indians remained in their homeland, such "nightmares" were visited only on tourists and missionaries, who, under the aegis of the American Board of Commissioners for Foreign Missions first went to India in 1812. But when Hindus began arriving in the United States, Hinduism became a domestic matter. Asian Indians came to the United States long after the Chinese and Japanese immigration waves, and they disembarked in far fewer numbers. Although there are records of an Asian Indian visiting Massachusetts as early as the 1790s, Indian immigrants did not arrive in significant numbers until the first decade of the twentieth century, and even then the figures were modest. By 1920 only about sixty-four hundred had come. Although Asian Indian immigrants were all called "Hindoos," most were actually Sikhs, practitioners of a religious tradition that originated in the Punjab region of north India in the sixteenth century. Roughly one-third were Muslims, and only a small portion practiced what we now refer to as Hinduism.

Like the Chinese and Japanese who preceded them, Asian Indians were met with hostility. This hostility led to violence in September 1907 in Bellingham, Washington, where a riot spearheaded by hundreds of white workers caused seven hundred Indian laborers to flee across the border into Canada. Soon the Asiatic Exclusion League which in the past had fulminated against the "yellow peril" from China and Japan, was denouncing Indian immigrants.

Rather than rebuking this nativism, the government codified it. In 1917, Congress severely restricted Asian Indian immigration by placing India in a "barred zone" of Asian countries. In 1923, in *U.S. v. Bhagat Singh Thind,* the Supreme Court ruled that Asian Indians, while admittedly Caucasian, were not "white persons" in the popular sense of that term and, therefore, were not eligible for naturalization. One year later, Congress passed a law cutting off immigration for people not eligible for naturalization, effectively terminating Asian Indian immigration.

Ethnic animus toward Indian immigrants veered into religious bigotry early in the twentieth century. In 1893, Swami Vivekananda became the first Hindu missionary to the United States when he accepted an invitation to represent the Hindu tradition at the World's Parliament of Religions held in Chicago in conjunction with the World's Columbian Exposition. A follower of the Indian teacher Ramakrishna, Vivekananda practiced both *bhakti yoga* (Hindu devotionalism) and *Advaita Vedanta,* a form of Hinduism that affirms the essential equivalence of God (Brahman) and the human soul (Atman). In Chicago and in subsequent lectures in cities across the United States, Vivekananda spoke against Christian missions in India and for religious tolerance. For the most part, he received a respectful hearing as an intelligent spokesman for an ancient faith and an able leader of his Vedanta Society (established 1894), the largest Hindu organization in the United States through the first quarter of the twentieth century.

As the Vedanta Society gathered strength, however, American Christians began to denounce both the organization and its swamis, drawing on stereotypes that went back to Twain and the missionary critics of the nineteenth century. In "The Heathen Invasion," published in *Hampton-Columbian Magazine* in 1911, Mabel Potter Daggett lashed out at Hinduism for luring unsuspecting American women into the "worship of men." "Women who were formerly Baptists and Presbyterians, Methodists, Episcopalians, Catholics, and daughters of Abraham," wrote Daggett, were being seduced into embracing Hinduism by dark-skinned yogis, who were far more interested in their followers' money and affections than in their souls. This view—that American Hinduism amounted to worship of swarthy Indian men by eccentric American women—also figured in a high-profile lawsuit in Boston in 1911. At issue was the will and mental competence of Sara Bull, a high-society woman whose Cambridge salon had attracted authors such as Julia

Ward Howe, Irving Babbitt, and Gertrude Stein and intellectuals such as psychologist William James and social reformer Thomas Wentworth Higginson. After hearing Swami Vivekananda speak in the late 1890s, Bull had embraced Hinduism. On her death in 1911, it was discovered that she had left a large sum of money to the Vedantists. Her daughter challenged the will on the grounds that swamis had duped her gullible mother. That argument carried the day and the bequest was nullified.

This theme of Hindu swamis as seducers of naive women was repeated in Mrs. Gross Alexander's *Methodist Quarterly Review* article, "American Women Going after Heathen Gods" (1912), and in books such as *Hinduism in Europe and America* by Elizabeth A. Reed (1914) and *The Indian Menace* (1929) by Mersene Elon Sloan. It reached a mass audience in Katherine Mayo's *Mother India* (1927), which denounced India and Hinduism as filthy in both senses of the term. According to *Mother India,* which was a top-ten bestseller in 1927 and 1928, virtually all of India's social and religious problems could be traced back to one source: Hinduism's obsession with sex. And thanks to immigrant swamis, that obsession was crossing the oceans to the United States—the "largest and richest hunting ground" for that "sex-hungry" faith.

Mayo's blockbuster was widely denounced by Indians, who resented the author's insistence that their homeland was unfit for home rule. Mohandas Gandhi, who led the nonviolent fight against British colonization, dismissed the book as a "Drain Inspector's Report" intent not on fostering women's rights but on shooting down India's bid for independence. The book was also criticized by liberal American missionaries, who in the spirit of E. Stanley Jones's conciliatory *The Christ of the Indian Road* (1925), blasted the book for its ethnocentrism. One of the cleverest retorts appeared in Dhan Gopal Mukerji's *A Son of Mother India Answers*, published in New York in 1928. Mukerji, after denouncing Mayo as a tourist suffering from "racial myopia," suggested that she write an equally biased account of social conditions in the United States. Such a book, he said, would include chapters on "The Only Land Where Lynchings Occur," "The Land of Marital Scandal—One Divorce to Every Seven Marriages," "The Land of Industrial Strife—Incessant Strikes and Lockouts," and "Child Laborers—A Million and a Half No Older Than Thirteen— in the Richest Land in the World."

In the wake of the immigration restrictions of 1917 and 1924, the Asian Indian population in the United States declined, and controversies about a Hindu invasion of the United States subsided. With the opening of immigration from Asia in 1965 and the arrival of a new generation of Indian gurus, however, controversy resurfaced. Now groups such as the International Society for Krishna Consciousness (ISKCON) were denounced as dangerous "cults," and again the criticism took a sexual turn. Whereas some Hindu-based groups were denounced for practicing celibacy, others were condemned for sexual licentiousness. Hinduism, meanwhile, continued to be denounced as sexist. In *Gyn/Ecology* (1978), the feminist theologian Mary Daly took a page out of *Mother India* when she reduced Indian culture in all its complexities to the outlawed practice of suttee.

The following selections come from the Hindu controversies of the teens and twenties rather than the eighties and nineties, and all address four interrelated questions: Should Asian Indians be allowed to come to the United States and become citizens? Are Hindu swamis taking advantage of their female followers? Is Hinduism antiwoman? Is India fit for independence?

Indian immigrants did not write many responses to these questions, in part because they did not have the means to be published in widely read magazines and newspapers. In 1908, however, the *Overland Monthly* of San Francisco invited Girindra Mukerji, an Indian immigrant studying at the University of California, to respond to the anti-Indian climate, more specifically to the Bellingham riot of the previous year. In "The Hindu in America," Mukerji presents a measured appeal for religious and racial toleration ("from the oldest civilization to the newest") and urges Americans to permit young people such as himself to continue to come to the United States to study. He reminds his readers that Hindu swamis are not trying to make American converts and that Indians are, like most Americans, Caucasians. Although Mukerji does not identify himself religiously in the article, it is fair to assume from the contents of the piece and from his name that he was a Hindu from Bengal, a province in northern India.

In *Hinduism in Europe and America* (1914), Elizabeth Armstrong Reed makes the alarmist case against Hindu swamis. The bitter fruit of their "hypnotic influence," argues Reed, is nothing less than "abject slavery" and insanity. Although this book represents a fairly standard critique in this genre, it is noteworthy because Reed was widely known before 1914 as a disinterested scholar of Hinduism and Buddhism. Before she wrote *Hinduism in Europe and America,* Reed produced scholarly books on ancient Hinduism and early Buddhism. In the process, she earned the praise of respected Orientalists such as F. Max Müller and election into the Royal Asiatic Society. A devout Christian, Reed was married to Hiram V. Reed, a preacher in the Campbellite tradition, an outgrowth of frontier Presbyterianism which sought to revive Christianity by reshaping it along the lines of the primitive church.

A short selection from Katherine Mayo's *Mother India* (1927) comes next. In this excerpt, taken from a chapter called "Slave Mentality," Mayo lays down her main argument: that India is a dying nation whose weakness can be traced to one cause, namely, a national obsession with sex. Here Mayo clearly betrays a promise, made at the beginning of *Mother India,* to confine her analysis to secular matters such as public health and to "[leave] untouched the [realm] of religion."

Two replies to *Mother India* follow. First is a book review published in 1928 in the *Atlantic Monthly.* Written by an American missionary, this review shows that not all Christian missionaries in India embraced Mayo with open arms. The second selection attends to Mayo obliquely rather than directly. It is written by Laura Glenn who, like Sara Bull, was a prominent American convert to the Vedanta Society. Like Bull, Glenn came to Hinduism after listening to Swami Vivekananda lecture. But Glenn eventually took Swami Paramananda, the founder of Vedanta outposts in both Boston and Los Angeles, as her guru. On her conversion to

Hinduism, Glenn took the name Sister Devamata ("Divine Mother"). A prolific writer and editor, she edited *The Message of the East,* a Boston-based Vedantist journal, and lectured widely on Hinduism both in the United States and in India. She was also Swami Paramananda's most valued assistant. In this selection, from *Days in an Indian Monastery* (1927), a memoir of her years spent in India, Sister Devamata presents a picture of women in Hinduism very different from Mayo's representation. Although Devamata's claims will no doubt sound old-fashioned to contemporary feminists, they represented a significant departure from conventional wisdom at the time she first wrote them down.

The selections are from: Girindra Mukerji, "The Hindu in America," *Overland Monthly* 51, no. 4 (April 1908): 303–08; Elizabeth A. Reed, *Hinduism in Europe and America* (New York: G. P. Putnam's Sons, 1914); Katherine Mayo, *Mother India* (New York: Harcourt, Brace, 1927)(© 1927 by Harcourt, Inc. renewed 1954 by M. Moyca Newell, reprinted by permission of the publisher); Alden H. Clark, "Is India Dying? A Reply to 'Mother India'," *Atlantic Monthly* 139, no. 2 (February 1927): 271–79; Sister Devamata, *Days in an Indian Monastery,* 3rd ed. (La Crescenta, Calif.: Ananda Ashrama, 1927) (by permission of Vedanta Centre Publishers, Cohasset, Mass.).

Further Reading

Thomas A. Tweed and Stephen Prothero, *Asian Religions in America: A Documentary History* (New York: Oxford University Press, 1999); Robert S. Ellwood, *Alternative Altars: Unconventional and Eastern Spirituality in America* (Chicago: University of Chicago Press, 1979); Carl T. Jackson, *The Oriental Religions and American Thought: Nineteenth-Century Explorations* (Westport, Conn.: Greenwood Press, 1981); Sydney Ahlstrom, *The American Protestant Encounter with World Religions* (Beloit, Wis.: Beloit College, 1962); Harold R. Isaacs, *Scratches on Our Minds: American Views of China and India* (Armonk, N.Y.: M. E. Sharpe, 1980); Spencer Lavan, *Unitarians and India: A Study in Encounter and Response* (Boston: Beacon, 1977).

The Hindu in America

Five centuries ago Columbus started out for India; the nuggets of India had been the great attraction of the ambitious merchants, mariners and monarchs of Europe. The wealth of India has been the theme of the poets—Milton, in his famous epic, "Paradise Lost," talks of "the wealth of Ormuz and Ind." After years of adventures, Columbus struck on land which, though not India, more than satisfied the cravings for gold. Columbus, mistaking this land as the long searched for India, named the aborigines Indians. Thus, America, from the day of her discovery, becomes associated with India.

The people of India, on the other hand, never knew how they were discovered in some other land, how they had been classed with the aborigines of some other race quite distinct from their own. They did not know how they were made known to European people as dressed up in blankets, feathers and tattooed all over the body.

But real India was not forgotten. The great navigators sailed their vessels round the farthest end of Africa. The route retains the name of "Good Hope." In spite of the perilous voyage and the tropical heat which they had to encounter, the hope of reaching India meant so much to them that they named the point in South Africa the Cape of Good Hope. At last, the Europeans reached India. The East India Company was organized. The exploitation of India began with all the energy of the hardy Briton. With the years, America grew as a civilized country, and finally became an independent State, and during this period, India fell completely a victim to English dominance. India continued to exist only to be exploited and all but destroyed. America became one of the great nations of the earth. The varied destinies of these two nations went on with time, until today each represents the opposite pole of advancement. The people of India come from the same race as the Europeans who have transformed the vast waste territory of America into the most interesting place on the earth. India, linked politically for 150 years with England, with her grand history and her centuries of civilization, is an object of pity and compassion all over the world. . . .

Hopefully, India looks to this great country of the United States. . . . The year 1901–1902 brought the first pioneer Hindu students to the schools of the Pacific Coast. . . . The State of California had no Hindu student till the year 1904. With the advent of some energetic and public spirited young men, the University of California became the headquarters of the largest number of Indian students in the whole union. . . . These young men are highly patriotic, and they have easily adapted themselves to the American environments. The American or casual observer would hardly notice any semblance or vestige of the caste system in their lives; here are the students of the highest caste, as well as from the lowest, living in amity. The unity of thought and purpose has harmonized their mode of living and association has smoothed away the mystical myths of centuries. No family or social distinction amongst themselves or any restriction as to food stuffs which might have been considered most objectionable in India, does stand in their way of fitting themselves, in American homes, as representatives of a new race in India. . . .

Official statistics show conclusively that the emigration of the Hindus . . . is invariably limited to the Sikhs and the Pathans, formerly in the English army. These Sikhs and Pathans are the inhabitants of the Punjab—the most fertile part of all India. The Punjab watered by five rivers was once the granary of this northern country, and is now quite unable to provide a living for a most abstemious and easily contented people. Of late, the emigration has been reaching such an alarming point that great consternation has been felt by the British, and in the United States threatens to bring on another racial and international complication. The laboring class sees the great danger of low wages as a result of competition with Asiatic labor, and the probability is not remote that the Indian will be ousted from the means of earning a livelihood in factories and on the railroads. The American, especially the inhabitant of this Western coast, sees the spectre of another "yellow peril," and one prominent newspaper declared the Hindus "outlaws" in this country. The public mind seemed to be in such a disordered state that the better class of the Hindus here blushed for shame for their fellow man. The law courts declared the Hindus as "undesirable," not fit to become citizens of the State. The riot in Bellingham was the culminating point of the Hindus' distress. . . .

The Hindus, driven from pillar to post, at present, are mostly working on railroads, in factories and few are peddling in the streets of San Francisco and Oakland. About one to two thousand is estimated as their total number in the whole union. Many are employed in the silver mines, Nevada. When the writer was associated with an official enquiry by the United States Government it was found that the Hindus are the most peaceable of all the laboring element and their neighbors unanimously declared that "we are never bothered by the loss of our chickens or other property through them." These men are born agriculturalists. Much can be done in inducing them to cultivate lands and thereby they may prove themselves valuable assets to the state. . . .

There is yet another class of Indians in the United States. Their coming dates from the year 1893, with the opening of the congress of religion at Chicago. India had, in her representative, her only pride and glory—in Philosophy—in Vedantism. Swami Vivekananda, whose name has become almost a household word in this country, was the delegate from India. With the exposition of the Vedantic Philosophy as the most rational of all intellectual conceptions of life and death, Swami Vivekananda, duly realizing the situations created by the enthusiasm evoked in the International Congress of Philosophy and Religion, established centers of the Vedanta Society in different States. The most prominent achievement was made by the patience and energy of Swami Abhedananda, in New York. He has been in this country ten years, and has published many books on Hindu Philosophy. For the first time in America, a systematic attempt at an intellectual appreciation of India began with this movement. "Vedanta," the monthly organ of this society, is now making headway in many homes. A permanent home has been established by the erection of a building in the city of New York. This activity, though similar to the missionary activities of the Occident in the Orient, has kept as its distinctive trait the Indian method. The chief difference is that it is non-proselyting. It aims to disseminate the Indian thought to a broad and intellectual people. It does not profess to have any creed or religious belief to be enforced on those who study, and who are sympathetic intellectually. On the Pacific Coast, the society established its branch in San Francisco, now popularly known as the Hindu Temple. The works are being carried on by two Swamis of the Vedantists. . . .

It will easily be seen that the [commercial] relations with the United States, via the Pacific, are as yet nominal, but there is the prophecy of an immense inter-communication, a great future exchange of commodity and thought, to be found in the development along American lines of the minds of the youth in your colleges. Who shall say, if we give it in exchange, that a leaven of Hindu philosophy would not improve the humanity and even the business instinct of the strenuous American. India looks to America for a certain kind of help—and it will not be denied. It is an appeal from the oldest civilization to the newest.

Hinduism in Europe and America

Modern Hindu Gurus. The guru is a modern money-making invention who is not mentioned in the earlier literature of India. The word originally meant a teacher of the Vedas, and as such it conveyed the idea of respectability, but the Vedic mantras are too voluminous, and prosaic, to attract many pupils, and women are not allowed to study them at all, neither are the lower castes, hence pupils in these classes were so few in number that the income from them was exceedingly small.

The Tantriks, however, were equal to the emergency of furnishing profitable employment for any Brahman who could read, in this way: They gave the name of mantra to some mystic and meaningless syllables, which might be given to the pupil, and taught at a single setting. The lowest castes, and even women, were made eligible to these classes, and almost any Brahman was enabled to collect around him an army of *chellas* who were bound by their vows to worship him as their god, and to pay a yearly tax to him and his descendants from generation to generation. In this vow the victim swears that: "My soul, mind and body, are irrevocably sold to my guru," whose name is given and then the ownership of his victim becomes absolute. When the sons of a deceased guru make a division of his property, the *chellas* are counted as so many slaves, and are distributed among the heirs in the same way as other properties belonging to the estate. . . .

The gurus are mostly of two classes, the Tantrik and the Vaishnava. The Tantriks inculcate and enforce the homage to the wives of Shiva, and the worship of courtesans. They also claim that while meeting together for the practice of the Bacchanalian rites, all the members of their orgies have a higher position than that of the most exalted Brahmans.

The Vaishnavas enforce the equally degrading worship of either Krishna, or some other incarnation of Vishnu. . . . Both sects agree that the gurus are a necessity, and that they must be well paid by those who have sold themselves, "body, soul, and mind," into this abject slavery. . . .

European and American Fanatics. One would hardly expect to find this confessedly corrupt cult flourishing in the United States, but a book recently written by a Krishna priest and published on American soil is dedicated: "To my Guru, to whom my Soul, Mind, and Body are irrevocably sold, in payment of the grace of this illumination which lighted my path to the Lotus feet of Krishna, my Beloved."

Hence we can easily see the character of the vows which must finally be taken by this man's devotees, and cease to wonder that so many of them find at last a refuge—not in Krishna, but in the asylums.

And yet, knowing these things, the Swamis are constantly advocating Krishnaism on both European and American soil. They know their own official works are the exponents of the character of the boy thief, the dishonorable warrior, the licentious lover, and all of the unspeakable obscenity connected even with his public worship, in places where they dare go through with the whole ceremony, and they know that this idolatry is utterly degrading to all who are tainted therewith, and yet they are persisting teaching it. . . .

Family ties are not allowed to intervene in any way between the Swamis and their devotees, for the official statement is:

> It knows no barrier! We know thee, O Krishna or thy representatives, as one greater and nearer to us than our husbands, brothers, and fathers; and even at the risk of their displeasure to us, we come to lay at thy feet our poor offerings and our hearts.

It was in harmony with this creed that the wife of a prominent educator abandoned her family with the announcement: "My husband and children are no more to me than others who are equally deserving of my regard. My religion teaches me that they have no claim on me!" . . .

A well-known New England woman, having fallen under the hypnotic sway of a Swami, made over her entire fortune at his dictation. After the papers were safely made out, the "further mysteries" were revealed to her. Can we wonder that she then went hopelessly insane and was for years in the asylum?

The Gurus do not, as yet, bring their most hideous idols with them—only some little image before which to say one's prayers "so as to aid in concentration." But far worse than idolatry before images is the man-worship which they inculcate and enforce—the slavish devotion to the priests.

One well-known Swami was in the habit of receiving the adoration of his followers, when he came out of his "daily meditation." Then these American women were ready to caress his robe, and kiss his sandaled feet. . . .

Let the white women beware of the hypnotic influence of the East—let her remember that when her Guru, or god-man, has once whispered his mystic syllables into her ear and she has sworn allegiance to him, she is forever helpless in his hands. . . .

Certain it is, that if our clean-hearted American women were acquainted with the true character of the cult, they would flee its contaminating influence. But "the further mysteries" are not revealed until the victim is beyond the reach of any returning mental health, and the descent to heathenism has been so gradual, and the way has been painted in such alluring colors, that she has been unconscious of her destination until it was too late.

Let our people read the standard Hindu works on this subject—let them look into the pages of the Vishnu-purana, which may be found in English translation in our large libraries, let them study the Bhagavata-purana; they are both devoted to the glorification of Krishna, and they both show him to be the worst type of a shameless sensualist, faithless lover, and undutiful son. Lacking these, let them read the works of English scholars like Sir Monier Monier-Williams or Prof. F. Max Müller. If they will only investigate the matter in any sane and scholarly way, all illusions on the subject will quickly vanish, and the priests of Hinduism will no longer be able to "creep into houses and lead captive silly women."

Mother India

The whole pyramid of the Indian's woes, material and spiritual—poverty, sickness, ignorance, political minority, melancholy, ineffectiveness, not forgetting that subconscious conviction of inferiority which he forever bares and advertises by his gnawing and imaginative alertness for social affronts—rests upon a rock-bottom physical base. This base is, simply, his manner of getting into the world and his sex-life thenceforward.

The Indian girl, in common practice, looks for motherhood nine months after reaching puberty—or anywhere between the ages of fourteen and eight. The latter age is extreme, although in some sections not exceptional; the former is well above the average. Because of her years and upbringing and because countless generations behind her have been bred even as she, she is frail of body. She is also completely unlettered, her stock of knowledge comprising only the ritual of worship of the house of idols, the rites of placation of the wrath of deities and evil spirits, and the detailed ceremony of the service of her husband, who is ritualistically her personal god.

As to the husband, he may be a child scarcely older than herself or he may be a widower of fifty, when he first requires of her his conjugal rights. In any case, whether from immaturity or from exhaustion, he has small vitality to transmit.

The little mother goes through a destructive pregnancy, ending in a confinement whose peculiar tortures will not be imagined unless in detail explained.

The infant that survives the birth-strain—a feeble creature at best, bankrupt in bone-stuff and vitality, often venereally poisoned, always predisposed to any malady that may be afloat—must look to his child-mother for care. Ignorant of the laws of hygiene, guided only by the most primitive superstitions, she has no helpers in her task other than the older women of the household, whose knowledge, despite their years, is little greater than hers. Because of her place in the social system, child-bearing and matters of procreation are the woman's one interest in life, her one subject of conversation, be her caste high or low. Therefore, the child growing up in the home learns, from earliest grasp of word and act, to dwell upon sex relations.

Siva, one of the greatest of the Hindu deities, is represented, on highroad shrines, in the temples, on the little altar of the home, or in personal amulets, by the image of the male generative organ, in which shape he receives the daily sacrifices of the devout. The followers of Vishnu, multitudinous in the south, from their childhood wear painted upon their foreheads the sign of the function of generation. And although it is accepted that the ancient inventors of these and kindred emblems intended them as aids to the climbing of spiritual heights, practice and extremely detailed narratives of the intimacies of the gods, preserved in the hymns of the fireside, give them literal meaning and suggestive power, as well as religious sanction in the common mind. . . .

And, even though the sex-symbols themselves were not present, there are the sculptures and paintings on temple walls and temple chariots, on palace doors and street-wall frescoes, realistically demonstrating every conceivable aspect and humor of sex contact; there are the eternal songs on the lips of the women of the household; there is, in brief, the occupation and preoccupation of the whole human world within the child's vision. . . .

Once more, then, one is driven to the original conclusion: Given men who enter the world physical bankrupts out of bankrupt stock, rear them through childhood in influences and practices that devour their vitality; launch them at the dawn of maturity on an unrestrained outpouring of their whole provision of creative energy in one single direction; find them, at the age when the Anglo-Saxon is just coming into full glory of manhood, broken-nerved, low-spirited, petulant ancients; and need you, while this remains unchanged, seek for other reasons why they are poor and sick and dying and why their hands are too weak, too fluttering, to seize or to hold the reins of Government?

A Reply to *Mother India*

In *Mother India*, a book which has received remarkable attention both in England and in America, Miss Katherine Mayo presents India as "a sick man growing daily weaker, dying body and brain, of a disease that only himself can cure." What this disease is she states in the following way: "The whole pyramid of India's woe, material and spiritual . . . rests on a rock-bottom physical base. The base is simply this, his manner of getting into the world and his sex life thenceforward." To support this contention Miss Mayo marshals a mass of quotations, tells vividly of her own investigations during some months of feverish activity in India, and makes some startling general assertions, which, if true, would go far to establish her claim.

A perplexed Western public is naturally asking, "Are Miss Mayo's charges true?" I shall attempt in this article to prove, beyond any reasonable doubt, that her basic assertions are not true, that she has leaped with magnificent agility from one-sided and limited evidence to her general conclusions, and that India remains the same land of mingled sorrow and hope, darkness and vision, weakness and strength, that she was before Miss Mayo made her very American, whirlwind tour. Above all I hope to show that India is on the upward road, with her face toward the morning.

Miss Mayo's chief sin against India was her almost complete blindness to every evidence of health and progress and her morbid overemphasis on every evidence of sickness and decay. The pity is that she has gathered material which, used discriminatingly, might have stung India to the speeding up of reform. It seems to me that she had a fresh and very powerful message on the baleful effects of sex exaggeration and on other prominent abuses, if only she had been able to present it in a balanced and friendly way. If she had pictured the encouraging aspect of things with the same emotional effect which was given to the evils that still exist, we, who have been working for decades for India's physical and social progress, would have welcomed the book as an ally. As it is, *Mother India* has struck a blow both against truth and against interracial understanding and good will. . . . The influence of this book is, indeed, calculated to lower the tone of civilization by stimulating people in both East and West to interpret each other by whatever is indecent and beastly. . . .

Should I now add to my argument the weight of the most reliable opinion? Miss Mayo has guarded herself against any effect of expert opinion in India by disposing summarily of us all. We missionaries are looking to our support at home and to the effects of our statements upon Indians, and so cannot tell the truth. The position of the official imposes "the policy of the gentle word." Indians see the problem only partially. India is a dying man with "no one, anywhere, enough his friend to hold the mirror up and show him plainly what is killing him." Miss Mayo regards herself as the only one left to do this, and so, single-handed, she shouldered the task. Yet let me venture to call attention to what a few, who know their India well, think of her effort. Mrs. Cousins, who is neither a government servant nor connected with official or missionary circles, and who for twelve years has lived in intimate friendship with the women of India, says, in an article in the October *Young Men of India:*

> While my experience corroborated a large number of her facts and illustrations regarding sex, health, untouchability, and the treatment of animals, I aver that the total impression she conveys to any reader, either inside or outside India, is cruelly and wickedly untrue. Unless read in conjunction with supplementary books on other aspects of India's life and culture . . . it will create nothing but race-resentment. . . . All the sins of India which Miss Mayo marshals with such weight of depression are balanced by her own sins of omission.

Next turn to one of the ablest of India's missionaries, Miss M. M. Underhill. In the *International Review of Missions* for October, 1927, she says:

> The book shows throughout a lack of any background knowledge of India; and, what is more serious, it shows a lack of appreciation—one might almost say of power to appreciate—in face of a civilization foreign to

previous experience. For example, Miss Mayo quotes freely from Mahatma Gandhi, but has completely failed to understand either the man or what he stands for in India. One cannot help asking, "Does Miss Mayo know even now much more of India than she did before going?" We doubt it.

. . . I will cite only one more opinion. It is that of the acknowledged leader of the Social Reform Movement in India, Mr. K. Natarajan, editor of the *Indian Social Reformer.* . . . This man, whose great life purpose Miss Mayo professes the desire to serve, is stirred by the book to such feeling as I have never known him to show before. In his eyes Miss Mayo reveals "mortal aversion to things Indian." . . . Her statement about the rearing of children in intensive vicious practices he denies with impressive vehemence. He says, "Not only has Miss Katherine Mayo grossly exaggerated the extent and nature of actual evils, but she has, as we shall show, freely indulged in half-truths and untruths without any attempt to verify them."

I cannot see how, if the testimony even of this brief paper is read with any open mind, it is possible to resist the conclusion that Mr. Natarajan and the other friends of Indian progress who have resented Miss Mayo's attack are substantially right. Her assertions about the average age of motherhood are proved to be inaccurate both by census figures of marriage and by carefully gathered medical data. Her statement about the absence of sport from child life is only a glaring instance of what pervades the book. India is not a human beast dying of her indulgences and her corruptions; she is a great people whose remarkable vitality has carried her through many evil customs and mistaken ideals to a new day of hope and renewed vigor of life in which she is beginning to purify herself for her great part in future world service.

Interracial understanding is of all things to be cultivated at this juncture of Indian progress. Those of us who know India can give assurance that her response to open-mindedness and good faith is as immediate, as warm and whole-hearted, as her present bitterness is deep.

Days in an Indian Monastery

Indo-Aryan tradition gives great freedom to women. The *Purdah* system has no place in it. That sprang up in India as a reflex of Mohammedan domination, which preceded British rule. The Mohammedan did not understand feminine liberty and wherever he prevailed it became necessary to veil the women and withdraw them from public gaze. In Bengal, where Mohammedan influence was strong, even today ladies do not go into the street except in palanquin or carriage. In Madras, where the Mohammedan influence has always been negligible, ladies go about freely, even at nightfall, sometimes followed by a servant, more often alone and with face and head covered. . . .

The mother is the ruling spirit of the house. She holds the key to the strong box and dispenses the money and family treasure. She directs the course of life of the various members of the household and she has sometimes twenty-five or thirty to look after. She regards it as her special privilege to serve them all before she thinks of herself. By choice she sees that every one is fed before she will eat. . . .

Unselfishness is a living, ever-present quality in the Indian woman's heart, a natural, spontaneous attribute of her character. She does not come last because she is put last, but because she covets the place. Many of the usages that are misunderstood by the Occidental world are based on a desire to honor, protect or cherish woman—not to subordinate or dishonor her. Take the custom of the wife walking behind the husband: it arose in the days when to go abroad meant facing many dangers and the first place was a place of peril, the second was a place of protection. With that idea behind it, it has come down the ages.

When a custom is imbedded in the Indo-Aryan social structure, it is extremely difficult to uproot it, for the Indo-Aryans are tenacious of tradition. I do not discuss the problem of the widow, as her position is in a state of transition; old conditions are breaking down and I feel confident that a new order will be established for her in the social readjustment now in progress. She will become, I believe, the teacher and helper and reformer of modern Indian society.

Indian women possess unusual executive abilities. Indo-Aryan annals contain the record of able rulers and administrators among them. One salient instance is known to me. It is that of Rani Rashmani, who lived in the last century and built the Temple on the Ganges where Sri Ramakrishna spent the larger part of his life. She sprang from a humble station and had little schooling, but she managed a large property with great efficiency and even had the courage to oppose the Government in a controversy over some land. She not only defended her rights with fearless determination, but she carried the dispute to the Court, pleaded her own case and won it.

There have been notable spiritual teachers also among the women of India. They are declared to be the authors even of some of the Vedic Scriptures. Sri Ramakrishna's first teacher after his initiation was a woman. I was told by one who was very close to him that she remained with him for eleven years, then went away one day suddenly. She could recite by heart in Sanskrit one hundred thousand lines of Aryan Sacred Writings and was possessed of astounding scriptural learning. She seemed to have acquaintance with all the religious literature of the Aryans and could tell just where even unfamiliar injunctions were to be found. . . .

There have been various gifted poets among the women of modern India, but the Indian woman is primarily a mother and guardian of the sanctity of the home. The home in India is sacred and inviolable. . . . Although house-keeping is simpler in India, the Indian housewife has not fewer duties. She takes many upon herself out of devotion and a feeling of consecration. In homes where there are ample resources and servants the mother still prepares the daily meals by preference. She realizes the physical and spiritual value of food cooked with love and a sense of sanctity and does not wish to deprive her family of this advantage. Indian women have a remarkable gift for cooking and cooking is for them almost a religion. As the food prepared is nearly always offered in the Shrine before it is eaten, its preparation becomes an actual part of the daily worship. In homes where a cook is employed, the ladies of the house frequently keep as their task the paring and cutting of the vegetables for the curry.

The care of the household Sanctuary also is claimed as the mother's privilege. She cleans it, polishes the vessels used in the worship and often conducts the Service. Sometimes the younger members of the family help her. The order of the day in a Madras home is this. Every one is up by six or before. While the women are busy with their house or with the children, the gentlemen see clients, transact business, visit the sick or teach the little ones. Next comes the bath, which is taken by rubbing the body first with soap or a cleansing earth, then pouring water over head and body until earth or soap is rinsed off. The Indian says if you get into a tub of water dirty, the water is no longer clean; how can you get clean by washing in it?

After the bath comes meditation or worship or a pilgrimage to the Temple. Then follows the main meal of the day and when this is over the men of the family go to their office or business. Government offices open at eleven. At one or two o'clock many take *Tiffin,* a light luncheon usually brought from the home by servants. The restaurant habit is alien to Indian traditions of purity and cleanliness. When the office closes at five, the men on their way home go to a *Math* or a holy man for an hour of spiritual refreshment and ladies go to the Temple. Evening worship and a late meal close the routine of the day.

—— 33 ——

The Wit and Wisdom of *The Door*

Michael McClymond

Religion is among the most serious of human preoccupations, dealing with issues of life and death, good and evil, salvation and damnation, God and the devil. So a connection between religion and humor may not be immediately apparent. If the business of humorists is to be funny, is it not the business of religionists to be as serious as possible? Certainly there have been religious movements in American history, especially those of a more zealous or puritanical character, that have regarded almost any form of humor or wit touching on sacred matters as irreverent or even blasphemous. The great colonial theologian Jonathan Edwards made a resolution as a young man never to utter anything "sportive, or matter of laughter, on a Lord's day," and, outside of some rare moments of satire or sarcasm, his voluminous writings contain almost nothing of a humorous nature. Harvey Cox, in his work *The Feast of Fools* (1969), attributes the demise of humor and satire within Western religion to the impact of the Protestant Reformation, pointing out that humor and satire were integral parts of medieval Catholicism. Laughter was allowed in the Catholic cathedral but not in the Protestant meetinghouse. Although Cox has a point regarding the moral earnestness and sobriety of the earlier Protestants, his thesis is one-sided. Martin Luther's writings are rich in humor. Moreover, Doug Adams's *Humor in the American Pulpit* (1975) shows that many of the leading Protestant preachers of the 1700s and 1800s—from George White-field to Lorenzo Dow, Timothy Dwight, Peter Cartwright, and Henry Ward Beecher—were witty fellows in the pulpit. They often used humor to puncture the pretensions of power, wealth, and intellect.

Humor is a term difficult to define, and one recent treatment of the topic described it simply as a type of stimulation that tends to elicit laughter. Just as a Geiger counter registers the presence of radioactivity, so laughter signals the arrival of the humorous. A motor reflex, such as the contraction of the pupil in dazzling light, serves the obvious function of protecting the sensitive tissues and functions of the eye. Yet the laughter reflex does not seem to have any necessary function in human life. On the other hand, humor may be more important for society than is commonly recognized, because humorlessness and cruelty seem to go hand in hand. Neither Stalin, nor Hitler, nor Pol Pot were known for having a sense of humor. Humor provides a release of tension, a form of social criticism, and a revelation of life's incongruities. Recent theories of humor emphasize the presence of incongruity, or incompatible frames of reference, as a key factor in the buildup and release of tension that occurs in the telling and hearing of a good joke. Humor, according to Arthur Koestler, compels the listener to perceive the situation in two self-consistent but incompatible frames of reference at the same time, to operate simultaneously on two different wavelengths.

Religion offers an especially rich field for the human mind to perceive incongruity and hence to discover humor. The argument for the humorlessness of religion can be stood on its head: if religion is among the most serious of human endeavors, then it is potentially among the most humorous, most comic, and most permeated with incongruity and laughter. Sometimes religious humor takes the form of ribald and scatological tales—the minister has eaten beans before the worship service and is passing gas as he preaches on "the sweet aroma of Christ," and his parishioners pretend not to notice. Sometimes it treads on sacred ground and there finds something ridiculous. Woody Allen offers the following dialogue between Abraham and Isaac after the patriarch is commanded to sacrifice his son: "And Isaac trembled and said, 'So what did you say? I mean when He brought this whole thing up?' 'What am I going to say?' Abraham said. 'I'm standing there at 2 A.M. in my underwear with the Creator of the Universe. Should I argue?' 'Well, did he say why he wants me sacrificed?' Isaac asked his father. But Abraham said, 'The faithful do not question. Now let's go because I have a heavy day tomorrow.'" Here one of the pivotal moments in Judaic history—an occasion on which the whole survival of the promised nation was at stake—becomes the butt of Allen's joke, and the story concludes with the observation that Abraham "proves that some men will follow any order . . . as long as it comes from a resonant, well-modulated voice." The humor arises from an incongruity between the sacred narrative and the comedian's embellishments.

Conrad Hyers identifies four different dimensions to religious humor—the iconoclastic, the confessional, the celebratory, and the paradoxical—and has tried to correlate each of these with the prevailing ethos of Protestantism, Roman Catholicism, Eastern Orthodoxy, and Judaism, respectively. The iconoclastic approach to humor calls into question all human claims to rightness and self-righteousness. It deflates pretensions and abases the proud. It unmasks the overt or subtle idolatries of wealth, power, privilege, and intellect. The philosophy and practice of humor in *The Door* (formerly *The Wittenburg Door*) falls mostly into this first category of the iconoclastic. The confessional strain of humor differs from the iconoclastic in that it not only protests against what it sees as pride and pretension but also confesses its own involvement in the universal human condition. It recognizes the murkiness and ambiguity that characterize the human condition. In Shakespearean comedy, even the most roguish characters are finally included rather than excluded from the final feast or plot resolution—Falstaff in

The Merry Wives of Windsor, Caliban in *The Tempest,* Angelo in *Measure for Measure.* This confessional sort of humor is tolerant, compassionate, and purgatorial, unlike satire and sarcasm, which create a chasm between those who are laughing and those who are being laughed at.

Confessional shades off into celebratory humor, which is magnanimous in spirit and involves an affirmation of life and laughter. Celebratory humor rests on the recognition that the human condition is not only to be confessed as sin or error but also embraced despite its faults and foibles. It is able to laugh at the very people and situations that otherwise dismay or annoy us. It fits in with the natural rhythms of life and dwells on the perennial themes of children, love, sex, marriage, work, food, drink, and sleep. In the early Greek Orthodox tradition, a custom developed of gathering together in the sanctuary on the day after Easter for the purpose of telling jokes and humorous anecdotes. This was conceived as a fitting way of following up Easter, when God pulled his biggest joke on the devil.

A fourth and final strand of religious humor is the paradoxical, which is especially characteristic of Jewish humor. Often the Bible itself exhibits a startling contrast between faith's aspirations and life's realities. The aged Sarah laughs when she is told that she will bear a son, and when the promised child is born, he is given the name Isaac, related to the Hebrew word for laughter. Throughout their history, the Jewish people have been keenly aware of the contrast between their scriptural designation as the "chosen" people and their political situation as unwanted outsiders among the nations. In the famous play "Fiddler on the Roof," the milkman Tevye finally puts the question directly to God: "Lord, couldn't you find *another* chosen people?" As a minority people, the Jews often told stories that emphasized role reversals, whereby the lowly Jew was able to outsmart even a Gentile ruler.

The Door, which bills itself as the world's only religious satire magazine, began publication in 1971 under the title *The Wittenburg Door,* named after the cathedral where Martin Luther affixed his "Ninety-Five Theses" and so commenced the Protestant Reformation. The title was in fact a misspelling, since the town in Germany is "Wittenberg," yet the founding editor, Mike Yaconelli, explains that the calligrapher spelled the word phonetically on the first issue of the magazine and they decided to leave it as it was. The periodical was born at the height of the Jesus Movement, and it soon became an underground favorite with youth ministers, seminary students, pastors, and a fair number of disenfranchised Christians, who all appreciated the magazine's wacky and irreverent tone. The articles took on the established church, denominations, Christian celebrities, and televangelists, and often exposed the quirkier side of American religion—as for instance in the regular column "Not So Good News," featuring recent events. *The Door* is still an underground publication in the sense that it runs no advertisements and does no marketing. The current circulation is around twelve thousand, and subscribers have typically learned about it by word of mouth.

Currently *The Door* is published by the Dallas-based Trinity Foundation, founded in 1973 by the activist Ole Anthony, now in his early sixties, who has a very eclectic background. Anthony did analysis of nuclear weapons systems in China and Russia for the Defense Intelligence Agency until the mid 1960s and then made and lost a fortune in the offshore drilling business. He was also involved in Republican politics and fund-raising. Anthony had never been devout, but that changed in 1972 when a public relations firm that he owned was hired to help launch a Christian television station in Dallas and he was deeply affected by one of the lecturers that he heard. Although he had (and still has) no formal theological training, Anthony pursued an independent study of the Bible, the Talmud, and other sacred texts. Soon he was hosting Christian radio and television programs, and today some affectionately refer to him as "Rabbi." Anthony believes that most of Christianity has lost touch with its Judaic roots, and the seventy-five people who live in the community connected with the Trinity Foundation celebrate Jewish as well as Christian holidays.

After being exposed to the world of Christian broadcasting, Anthony became disillusioned with what he regarded as the endemic greed and hypocrisy of many radio and television preachers. In 1982 he led a group of followers into a low-income neighborhood in East Dallas and began his ministry to the homeless. Among the men that showed up at the door of Trinity's homeless shelter was Harry Guetzlaff, who said that he lost his home, marriage, and video-production business by giving thousands of dollars away to Robert Tilton, a Dallas-based preacher. Tilton had urged his viewers to pledge money that they did not have and promised that God would return their gifts a hundredfold. Guetzlaff now manages the production of *The Door,* and he has also been among the most dedicated investigators seeking to uncover fraud on the part of televangelists and religious broadcasters.

The Trinity Foundation moved into investigative work as many television preachers became increasingly influential and money-driven during the 1980s and 1990s. One detective, after a midnight trash run to obtain financial information on a media evangelist, explained to *U.S. News and World Report* that "these preachers are turning people off God with their hypocrisy and greed" and "by exposing that, we can turn people toward the true faith." Trinity sleuths helped research a nationally broadcast "PrimeTime Live" television feature, which concluded that televangelist W. V. Grant's alleged ability to read minds owed a lot to interviews that Grant and his staff conducted with audience members before the services. The same television segment disclosed that Robert Tilton had received thousands of letters, some of them containing desperate appeals for prayer and spiritual support, and that Tilton had simply removed the donations from the envelopes and discarded the unanswered letters. (Tilton and his lawyers say that the letters were planted in the dumpster behind Tilton's bank.) Another target has been the televangelist and faith healer, Benny Hinn. According to a CNN report, based on a Trinity Foundation investigation, detectives found evidence that in 1996 Hinn spent $35,000 to fly on the Concorde to London with his bodyguards and then stayed with them in a $2200-per-night hotel suite. Such lavish spending clashes stands in stark contrast to the ethos of the Trinity Foundation, where twenty or so employees—including Ole Anthony—live on $80-per-week salaries and work with the homeless.

Anthony has described the Trinity Foundation as "a challenge to the vanity and hypocrisy of the religious world" and says that the purpose of *The Door* is "to make fun of anyone who takes himself seriously in the name of God." Regularly skewered in *The Door* are James Dobson of "Focus on the Family," politician and Christian broadcaster Pat Robertson, the Promise Keepers movement, Southern Baptists, religious merchandisers of all stripes, Christian rock stars, Christian weightlifters, and "I Love Jesus" bumperstickers. In recent years *The Door* proclaimed "Beavis and Butthead" (of MTV fame) as "theologians of the decade," featured a nude centerfold (viewed from a side angle) of televangelist W. V. Grant, and ran a cover photo of a gun held to the head of Billy Graham with the headline: "Buy This Magazine, Or Billy Gets It!" As a result of the "Beavis and Butthead" cover story, the magazine was banned from many Christian bookstores. The answering machine at *The Door* office frequently contains messages from offended Christians who attempt to "exorcize" the magazine's evil spirits by means of telephone. In retrospect, one of the more intriguing articles was done in 1988 on a then-obscure Texan group known as the Branch Davidians and their leader Vernon Howell (later known as David Koresh). At that time Howell was trying to forge a career as a rock guitarist and hoped to win a hearing for his music with Robert Darden, who not only was editor for *The Door* but also had a weekly column in *Billboard* magazine.

Although *The Door* is filled with articles and cartoons that make fun of various religious groups—from liberal Catholics to conservative Muslims—the texts reprinted here perhaps reflect what it does best; point out the silliness of modern society and poke fun at evangelical Protestant culture. In the first text, "The Ten Commandments Re-Written for Gen-Xers," the humorist Ed L. Weir uses the common convention of rewriting a classical text. In the next, the American fascination with new religions is derided. In the other two, writers invoke the sacred beliefs and righteous personalities of conservative Protestants and liberal Christians to laugh at both. Throughout the texts we see a clever sense of humor paired with irreverent insight into American religious and secular culture.

Part religious collective, part investigative unit, part satire squad, the Trinity Foundation may be unique in the annals of recent American religious history. Trinity's opponents, and especially the televangelists investigated and/or lampooned in *The Door*, have criticized the detective techniques used by the group and assert that the Trinity Foundation is simply seeking notoriety. Martin Marty, in a 1998 National Public Radio segment on Ole Anthony and Trinity, describes *The Door* as a magazine of religious humor that has a purpose that goes beyond humor. The satire seeks to effect social change. Whatever else one says about the Trinity Foundation, the people associated with it seem willing to poke fun at themselves. In 1997 the group staged a skit in which Ole Anthony received a mock Academy Award. "If we took ourselves too seriously," said the emcee Judy Buckner, "we couldn't make fun of anyone else."

The selections below are: Ed L. Weir, "The Ten Commandments Re-written for Gen-Xers," *The Door*, November/December 1999, p. 25; Randall F. West, "Mix and Match—Design Your Own Cult Kit," *The Door*, January/February 2000, pp. 30–31;

John Green, "Witness Wipes," *The Door,* November/December 1999, p. 31; and Scot Marvin and Doug Duncan, "The Conservative Christian Hierarchical Scale of Sin," *The Door,* July/August 1996, p. 36. Reprinted courtesy of *The Door Magazine.*

Further Reading

Doug Adams, *Humor in the American Pulpit: From George Whitfield through Henry Ward Beecher* (North Aurora, Ill.: Sharing, 1975); Conrad Heyers, "A Funny Faith," *Oneworld* 78 (July/August 1982): 10–11, and *The Comic Vision and the Christian Faith: A Celebration of Life and Laughter* (New York: Pilgrim Press, 1981); Theodor Reik, *Jewish Wit* (New York: Gamut, 1962); Cal Samra, *The Joyful Christ: The Healing Power of Humor* (San Francisco: Harper and Row, 1986); Joseph Telushkin, *Jewish Humor: What the Best Jewish Jokes Say about the Jews* (New York: William Morrow, 1992); William Willimon, ed., *William Willimon's Last Laugh* (Nashville, Tenn.: Abingdon, 1991); "About the Human. Christian Humor with Greg Hartman," http://christianhumor.about.com/comedy/christianhumor (April 6, 2001).

The Ten Commandments: Re-written for Gen-Xers

I. "I am the Lord your God, who brought you out of the land of inconvenience, out of the house of disco. Keep helping yourselves, and I will help you. Do your best unless you can't. Deal?"

II. "Don't try to imagine what I look like, and if you do, don't, under any circumstances try to realize it, sing or write about it, make a web-page, paint, or scan it. You are bound to get it wrong every time. It was cute at first. Now it just irks Me. I am NOT a slob like one of you."

III. "Learn a language. Use Hooked on Foniks. Eliminate verbal pauses. Don't punctuate your sentences with needless expletives and don't use My name for emphasis. It really irritates Me. Seriously."

IV. "Take Sunday off. Sleep late, talk sweet to your liberal girlfriend, drink herbal tea and read esoteric novels. Cook out. (No pork) Run scan disk. Notice My glory in nature, but not enough to really matter. Go mountain biking. Watch Sunday Morning. Cruise the mall. Change your wallpaper. Wash your car. But don't, and I repeat, don't do any work unless it's something you enjoy. Church attendance is optional."

V. "Honor your father and mother unless they have unmistakably inhibited your personal growth through ignorance and selfishness. In that case, just stay away, send cards when appropriate, be polite, and don't enable them. And don't you dare go having children either unless you want them to be politicians or blues musicians."

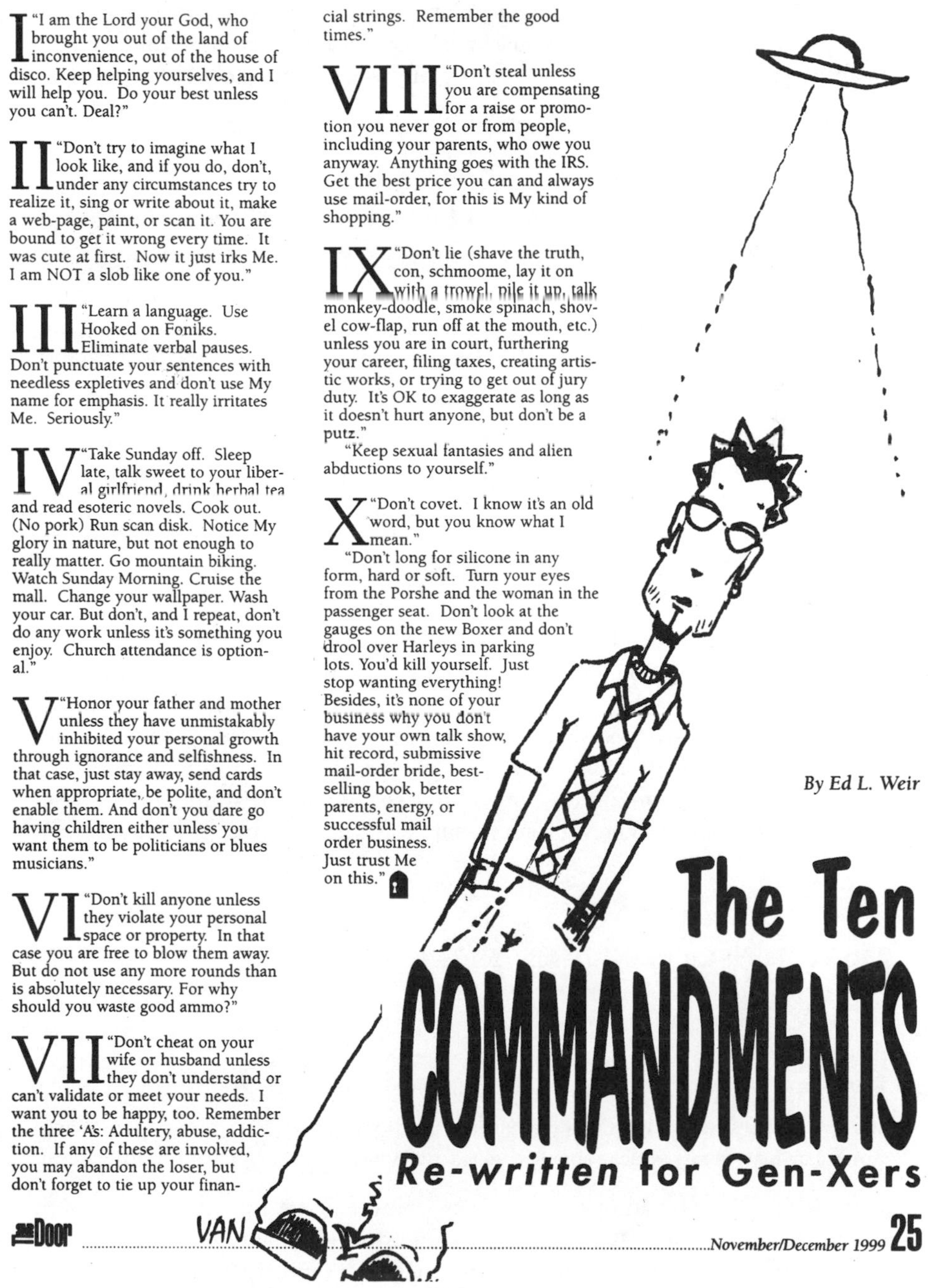

I "I am the Lord your God, who brought you out of the land of inconvenience, out of the house of disco. Keep helping yourselves, and I will help you. Do your best unless you can't. Deal?"

II "Don't try to imagine what I look like, and if you do, don't, under any circumstances try to realize it, sing or write about it, make a web-page, paint, or scan it. You are bound to get it wrong every time. It was cute at first. Now it just irks Me. I am NOT a slob like one of you."

III "Learn a language. Use Hooked on Foniks. Eliminate verbal pauses. Don't punctuate your sentences with needless expletives and don't use My name for emphasis. It really irritates Me. Seriously."

IV "Take Sunday off. Sleep late, talk sweet to your liberal girlfriend, drink herbal tea and read esoteric novels. Cook out. (No pork) Run scan disk. Notice My glory in nature, but not enough to really matter. Go mountain biking. Watch Sunday Morning. Cruise the mall. Change your wallpaper. Wash your car. But don't, and I repeat, don't do any work unless it's something you enjoy. Church attendance is optional."

V "Honor your father and mother unless they have unmistakably inhibited your personal growth through ignorance and selfishness. In that case, just stay away, send cards when appropriate, be polite, and don't enable them. And don't you dare go having children either unless you want them to be politicians or blues musicians."

VI "Don't kill anyone unless they violate your personal space or property. In that case you are free to blow them away. But do not use any more rounds than is absolutely necessary. For why should you waste good ammo?"

VII "Don't cheat on your wife or husband unless they don't understand or can't validate or meet your needs. I want you to be happy, too. Remember the three 'As: Adultery, abuse, addiction. If any of these are involved, you may abandon the loser, but don't forget to tie up your financial strings. Remember the good times."

VIII "Don't steal unless you are compensating for a raise or promotion you never got or from people, including your parents, who owe you anyway. Anything goes with the IRS. Get the best price you can and always use mail-order, for this is My kind of shopping."

IX "Don't lie (shave the truth, con, schmoome, lay it on with a trowel, pile it up, talk monkey-doodle, smoke spinach, shovel cow-flap, run off at the mouth, etc.) unless you are in court, furthering your career, filing taxes, creating artistic works, or trying to get out of jury duty. It's OK to exaggerate as long as it doesn't hurt anyone, but don't be a putz."
"Keep sexual fantasies and alien abductions to yourself."

X "Don't covet. I know it's an old word, but you know what I mean."
"Don't long for silicone in any form, hard or soft. Turn your eyes from the Porshe and the woman in the passenger seat. Don't look at the gauges on the new Boxer and don't drool over Harleys in parking lots. You'd kill yourself. Just stop wanting everything! Besides, it's none of your business why you don't have your own talk show, hit record, submissive mail-order bride, best-selling book, better parents, energy, or successful mail order business. Just trust Me on this."

By Ed L. Weir

The Ten COMMANDMENTS
Re-written for Gen-Xers

VAN

Figure 33.1. "The Ten Commandments Re-written for Gen-Exers," from *The Door*.

VI. "Don't kill anyone unless they violate your personal space or property. In that case you are free to blow them away. But do not use any more rounds than is absolutely necessary. For why should you waste good ammo?"

VII. "Don't cheat on your wife or husband unless they don't understand or can't validate or meet your needs. I want you to be happy, too. Remember the three 'A's: Adultery, abuse, addiction. If any of these are involved, you may abandon the loser, but don't forget to tie up your financial strings. Remember the good times."

VIII. "Don't steal unless you are compensating for a raise or promotion you never got or from people, including your parents, who owe you anyway. Anything goes with the IRS. Get the best price you can and always use mail-order, for this is My kind of shopping."

IX. "Don't lie (shave the truth, con, schmoome, lay it on with a trowel, pile it up, talk monkey-doodle, smoke spinach, shovel cow-flap, run off at the mouth, etc.) unless you are in court, furthering your career, filing taxes, creating artistic works, or trying to get out of jury duty. It's OK to exaggerate as long as it doesn't hurt anyone, but don't be a putz."
"Keep sexual fantasies and alien abductions to yourself."

X. "Don't covet. I know it's an old word, but you know what I mean."
"Don't long for silicone in any form, hard or soft. Turn your eyes from the Porsche and the woman in the passenger seat. Don't look at the gauges on the new Boxer and don't drool over Harleys in parking lots. You'd kill yourself. Just stop wanting everything! Besides, it's none of your business why you don't have your own talk show, hit record, submissive mail-order bride, best-selling book, better parents, energy, or successful mail order business. Just trust me on this."

Mix & Match Cult Kit—Design Your Own

AMAZE YOUR FRIENDS!
ASTONISH YOUR PASTOR!
IMPRESS YOUR FAMILY!

YOU, TOO, CAN BE A DIVINE MASTER JUST BY CREATING YOUR OWN BRAND NEW, WILD AND WACKY PERSONAL CULT.

Just pick any combination of items from columns one, two, three, and four. (Note: if you pick four items from the same row, you may be mistaken for a member of an established cult and spiritual kneecap-breaking [or lawsuits] may result. Also, some of the items you choose may be mutually exclusive, but that's ok, because it's your cult, and you can conflict if you want to. The real cults sure don't worry about it.)

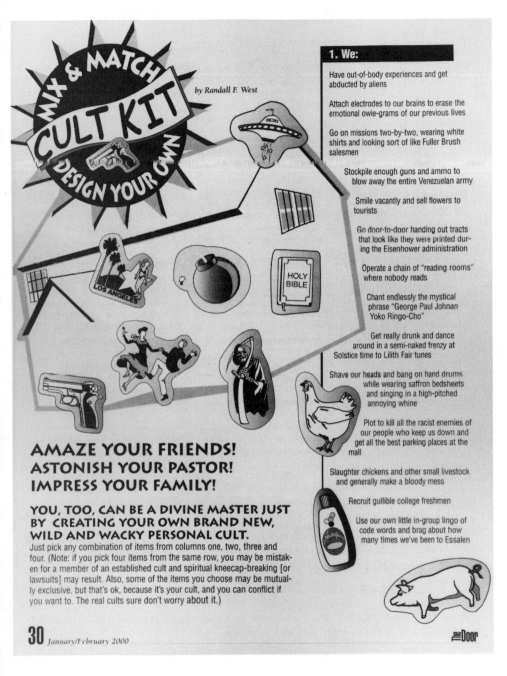

Figure 33.2. "Mix & Match Cult Kit" from *The Door*.

1. We:

Have out-of-body experiences and get abducted by aliens

Attach electrodes to our brains to erase the emotional owie-grams of our previous lives

Go on missions two-by-two, wearing white shirts and looking like Fuller Brush salesmen

Stockpile enough guns and ammo to blow away the entire Venezuelan army

Smile vacantly and sell flowers to tourists

Go door-to-door handing out tracts that look like they were printed during the Eisenhower administration

Operate a chain of "reading rooms" where nobody reads

Chant endlessly the mystical phrase "George Paul Johnan Yoko Ringo-Cho"

Get really drunk and dance around in a semi-naked frenzy at Solstice time to Lilith Fair tunes

Shave our heads and bang on hand drums while wearing saffron bedsheets and singing in a high-pitched annoying whine

Plot to kill all the racist enemies of our people who keep us down and get all the best parking places at the mall

Slaughter chickens and other small livestock and generally make a bloody mess

Recruit gullible college freshmen

Use our own little in-group lingo of code words and brag about how many times we've been to Essalen

2. And We Also:

Talk endlessly about the fact that we're all gods (well, we are, but what are you?)

Sue the pants off everyone who gets in our way

Go to business school

Read Revelation over and over, and over, and over, and over, and over. Then do it again. Repeat until nicely glazed

Give all our possessions to the Master and blow off parents, relatives, and friends

Teach that Jesus is our brother and we can get to heaven if we give out enough tracts and keep our noses clean

Publish a really thin international newspaper

Sit on meditation pillows until our rear ends begin to resemble the lower half of a pear

Write meandering screeds about the phallic imperialism of traditional patriarchal religion

Burn a lot of incense to sooty little green statues of Sumo wrestlers

Plot to kill any racist enemies of our people who are left after Step 1 while calculating the numerological value of the commas and semicolons in the Greater Detroit phone book and their important message for today

Dress up in scanty costumes of feathers and face paint and prance around to bongo music

Make them recruit other gullible freshmen

Talk endlessly about human potential while charging huge amounts of money for an endless series of seminars

3. And We Abstain from:

Rational thought

Obsequiousness to the IRS

Caffeinated beverages (tough luck, Starbucks!)

Any social interaction except gun shows

Sex (unless the Master's in the mood)

Reading any version of the Bible except the approved one prepared by our cousin Luke from Macon

Medical treatment, because the material world is an illusion and—hey, what are you doing with that knife? Get away! Hey, stop!

Meat (except Mickie D's cheeseburgers on two-for-one days because that's not really meat anyway)

Men

Shampoo

Violence

Good Taste

Any contact with Christians who weren't baptized by our special "Triple Dip Deluxe" method

Discounts

4. So that we can:

Evolve to a higher plane of Consciousness, or at least feel at home in L.A.

Get filthy rich (and maybe get our picture taken with Tom Cruise or John Travolta)

Achieve godhead, get our own planet, marry a nice girl or two from BYU and have a jazillion kids (not necessarily in that order)

Destroy the Minions of the Antichrist and the Evil Satan (or at least take as many of them with us as dare to attack our headquarters)

Improve the bottom line of the Master's international empire of spiritual investments dba The Divine Son, Ltd. (Patent Pending)

Finally quit having to go around door-to-door

Become gods, or at least get a piece of the celestial action

Get whatever we want: including good sex, a better job, a hot car, great sex, a bigger house, fantastic sex and, oh yeah, enlightenment

Live the reality of the Goddess, or at least shop like one

Become One with the Zero That is the Sum of All (and wipe away the memory that we could have bought Microsoft back in 1985 and retired to Bermuda by now)

Displace the evil oppressors and get all the Microsoft stock that is our right and heritage, then get on the Mother Ship

Protect ourselves from the Powers of Darkness to Which We Sacrifice and of Whom We Actually Become the Servants and Hey, How Did We Get in This Situation, Anyway?

Say, when the end is near, "we did it our way"

Achieve our fullest potential as human beings by maximizing our return on investment and self-actualizing our bank accounts with fees from dweebs and losers

Witness Wipes

Reverend Mike Purkey says: "Witness Wipes are the future of evangelism. The simple beauty of the plan lies in the fact that sooner or later, everyone has to go to the bathroom! Witness Wipes simply meet people at their point of need. They minister to the body and the soul."

WITNESS WIPES—EVANGELISM FOR THE NEW MILLENIUM

At the heart of this bold new plan is specially formulated rolls of two-ply bathroom tissue. Each tear-away sheet contains a salvation verse printed in non-

Witness Wipes

by John Green

Reverend Mike Purkey says: "Witness Wipes are the future of evangelism. The simple beauty of the plan lies in the fact that sooner or later, everyone has to go to the bathroom! Witness Wipes simply meet people at their point of need. They minister to the body and the soul."

WITNESS WIPES— EVANGELISM FOR THE NEW MILLENNIUM

At the heart of this bold new plan is specially formulated rolls of two-ply bathroom tissue. Each tear-away sheet contains a salvation verse printed in non-toxic, non-allergenic vegetable dye. Our toilet paper must meet the highest quality control standards, and samples are regularly tested at the paper mill.

Witness Wipes are sensitive to your aesthetic needs—you get to pick the color of both the paper and the printing from a wide selection of choices.

Our Vision:

All over America, Christians will begin capturing the bathrooms of their city for Jesus. In backpacks and purses, they will carry spare rolls of the Good News, switching out the plain paper rolls they encounter. Hurting people sitting on toilets all over the U.S. will find help and healing in a new sort of scroll. They will leap up in liberty, their faces flushed with new joy. What a glorious opportunity!

So now it's up to you. My friend, will you do your part and help wipe out the works of Satan? Will you be a part of this mighty movement? When the roll is called up yonder, will your name be one of those who brought many into the Kingdom? Are your bowels moved with compassion?

Call today for your free sample roll and a full-color brochure explaining more about this wonderful opportunity, and ask for our free "Toilet Training Kit." Call now.

1-888-Wit-Wipes

Door ....

Figure 33.3. "Witness Wipes" from *The Door.*

toxic, non-allergenic vegetable dye. Our toilet paper must meet the highest quality control standards and samples are regularly tested at the paper mill.

Witness Wipes are sensitive to your aesthetic needs—you get to pick the color of both the paper and the printing from a wide selection of choices.

Our Vision:

All over America, Christians will begin capturing the bathrooms of their city for Jesus. In backpacks and purses, they will carry spare rolls of the Good News, switching out the plain paper rolls they encounter. Hurting people sitting on toilets all over the U.S. will find help and healing in a new sort of scroll. They will leap up in liberty, their faces flushed with new joy. What a glorious opportunity!

So now it's up to you. My friend, will you do your part and help wipe out the works of Satan? Will you be a part of this mighty movement? When the roll is called up yonder, will your name be one of those who brought many into the Kingdom? Are your bowels moved with compassion?

Call today for your free sample roll and a full-color brochure explaining more about this wonderful opportunity, and ask for our free "Toilet Training Kit." Call now. 1-888-Wit-Wipes.

The Conservative Christian Hierarchical Scale of Sin

Engaging in homosexuality 100
Engaging in bestiality 99
Voting for a democrat 98
Skipping church on Sunday morning 97
Skipping church on Wednesday night 96
Adultery with member of the same sex 95
Adultery with an animal 94
Adultery with member of opposite sex 93
Ordaining a lesbian for ministry 92
Ordaining a heterosexual woman for ministry 91
Showing concern for the environment 90
Getting divorced 89
Masturbating while thinking about a member of the same sex 88
Masturbating while thinking about a member of the animal
     kingdom 87
Masturbating while thinking about a member of the opposite sex 86
Neglecting to read the Bible 85
Reading any translation other than the King James Version 84
Drinking any imported beer or wine 83
Drinking American beer or wine 82
Skipping over the Leviticus passages in your "Year With the Bible" 81

Reading a book passage about a homosexual act (Bible excluded) 80
Reading a book passage about an act of bestiality (Bible excluded) 79
Reading a book passage about a heterosexual act (Bible excluded) 78
Reading non-Christian based fiction 77
Reading non-Christian nursery rhymes 76
Murdering a heterosexual 75
Giving homeless people money without first winning them to the Lord . . 74
Dancing with a member of the same sex 73
Dancing with an animal 72
Watching secular television channels 71
Not tithing 70
Tithing only 1% of income 69
Tithing only 2% of income 68
Tithing only 3% of income 67
Tithing only 4% of income 66
Tithing only 5% of income 65
Tithing only 6% of income 64
Tithing only 7% of income 63
Tithing only 8% of income 62
Tithing only 9% of income 61
Tithing on monies from business transactions with people who
    might be homosexuals 60
Not spanking your child 59
Spanking an adult 58
Not attending at least one Promise Keepers event 57
Neglecting to watch each entire broadcast of *The 700 Club* 56
Reading *The Door* 55
Neglecting to write that letter to CBS asking for a Saturday morning
    "Power Team" cartoon 54
Not calling Sunday "the Sabbath" 53
Letting your wife do the family bills 52
Letting your wife work more than 10 hours per week outside
    the home 51
Forgetting to send in your pledge to help Benny Hinn go once
    more to "da Hoelee Land" 50
Missing more than one broadcast per week of Rush Limbaugh 49
Missing one broadcast per week of "Focus on the Family" 48
Missing one broadcast per week of "Insight for Living" 47
Not reading every book by James Dobson 46
Not reading every book by Chuck Swindoll 45
Not reading every book by Frank Perretti 44
No reading every book by Ron Blue 43
Stepping inside a Catholic church 42
Skipping over the Precious Moments collection in the family
    magazine 41

Not being able to defend capitalism using Biblical texts 40
Not buying the "Davy and Goliath" video series for your
    children 39
Attending any mainline denomination that does not have a strong
    conservative leadership 38
Not believing that America's Founding Fathers were all Christians . . . 37
Having coffee with a liberal 36
Not saluting the American Flag at least twice a day 35
Allowing children to watch those demonic Disney movies 34
Likewise I'm sure 33
Says who? 32
Says me 31
I'd like to see you try it 30
Oh yeah? 29
Yeah! 28

THE LIBERAL CHRISTIAN HIERARCHICAL SCALE OF SIN

Refusing to embrace every value system on the planet except
    conservatism 100
Failing to use gender neutral terms when referring to Deity 90
Opposing the ordination of women 80
Opposing the ordination of gays and lesbians 70
Lack of self-righteous zeal in condemning racism 60
Wearing fur 50
Not reading every book by Tony Campolo 40
Not reading everything by Mike Yaconelli 30
Not donating to public broadcasting 20
Opposing the Brady Bill 10
Driving a domestic gas-guzzler 5

34

Battling Spiritism and the Need
for Catholic Orthodoxy

Manuel A. Vásquez

Ever since its emergence in the mid nineteenth century, spiritism has posed a difficult challenge to Catholicism in the Americas. On the one hand, spiritism tapped into the Catholic notion that the supernatural-spiritual and natural-material worlds intersect. Like Catholicism, spiritism developed an elaborate cult of the dead. On the other hand, spiritism grew in response to the disenchantment of the world brought by Protestant missionaries working among the urban, educated elite in South and Central America. These Protestants questioned the everyday appearance of the supernatural and stressed reason and personal conscience. In the nineteenth-century Catholic mind, within a context of secularization and increasing religious pluralism in Latin America, spiritism came to be associated with a Masonic conspiracy against the papacy.

Spiritism's adaptability, the fact that it simultaneously borrows from and delegitimizes Catholicism, continues to be a concern for the Catholic church in the United States as it struggles to minister to a growing Latino population. Given the scarcity of Spanish-speaking priests and the superficial knowledge of Catholic doctrine among Latino laity in the United States, the danger of losing church members is very real. In the face of the radically pluralistic religious market place, some Catholic leaders feel that Latinos are particularly vulnerable to spiritism and other New Age religions, faith communities that claim to accept certain aspects of Catholicism while rejecting its official doctrine. The ambivalent relationship between spiritism and Catholicism, as well as the massive conversions to evangelical Protestantism among Latinos, has created a religious environment of mutual suspicion in the Americas. The two polemical pamphlets reprinted here are examples of the tense relationship that can exist between believers.

The roots of modern spiritism in Latin America can be traced to Hippolyte Léon Denizard Rivail (1804–1869), a Parisian educator and translator of scientific books, who took the name of Allan Kardec from two of his previous incarnations.

Kardec sought to establish a spiritist canon by borrowing and synthesizing varied elements from Christianity, Eastern religions, and parapsychology. From Christianity, Kardec took ethical values, particularly the emphasis on following the Golden Rule and practicing charity. He rejected doctrines such as the Trinity, the Divinity of Christ, and the existence of miracles, angels, demons, heaven, and hell as unenlightened. In this regard, Kardec was simply operating within the Kantian conception of religion—religion within the limits of reason alone—that dominated liberal theological circles at the time.

Kardec was also a creature of his time in his enthusiasm for Eastern religions, which had become the focus of European orientalists and philosophers such as Schopenhauer. Borrowing piecemeal from Hinduism and Buddhism, Kardec held the existence of disembodied spirits closely connected to the material world. Sensitive to the effects of good and bad actions (the karmic law), these spirits seek to purify themselves through various reincarnations. Along their evolutionary path, the spirits may communicate with us through mediums to guide us in our own spiritual development or request our help. Finally, under the influence of Auguste Comte's positivism, Kardec presented his beliefs as a philosophical system capable of scientific validation through (para)psychological experimentation. This allowed him to appeal to the growing urban and secular intelligentsia in Europe.

Kardec articulated his spiritist synthesis in a series of books, beginning with *The Book of the Spirits* (1855), based on mediumistic communications with evolved spirits. In this book, Kardec set the essential tenets of his philosophy, particularly the notion of linear spiritual progress through multiple reincarnations. *Book of the Spirits* was followed by several works, including the philosophical treatise *The Book of the Mediums* (1859) and *The Gospel According to Spiritism* (1864). In these works, Kardec took a more "evangelical" approach to religion, gathering maxims and aphorisms derived from Christianity.

In the United States, Kardecian spiritism found a place alongside (and sometimes in tension with) a vigorous strand of Swendenborgian spiritualism. Emanuel Swedenborg (1688–1772), a Swedish theologian and scientist, advocated a more mystical, intuitive approach to the spirit world, one that stressed the importance of dreams, vision, and trances. His spiritualism became very popular among the growing middle class in the urban Northeast and Midwest. The popularity of Swedenborgian spiritualism in the nineteenth century has been attributed to a crisis of republican values following the death of the nation's founding fathers and the rapid transition to modernity. Kardecian spiritists, however, do not see a connection between their teachings and those of Swedenborgians. Kardecian spiritists see their beliefs and practices as part of a secular philosophy and science, in contrast to spiritualism, which they argue is more of a religion of the supernatural.

Kardec's spiritism, then, did not arrive in the United States through the Victorian elites of the nineteenth century. It came with immigrants from Latin America in the twentieth century. Kardec's *Book of the Spirits* reached Brazil barely two years after its publication in France and rapidly gained popularity in Mexico, Puerto Rico, Cuba, and Venezuela. Like Santería and folk religions such as *curanderismo* (healing involving a combination of prayer, mediumship, and herbal medicine), Latin American spiritism entered the United States through the migratory circuits that have linked the Americas since the Mexican-American War.

While in Latin America, spiritism became entangled in the region's complex racial and class hierarchies. On the one hand, urban liberal elites appropriated a more scientific, rationalistic version of spiritism (*espiritismo de mesa blanca*, white table spiritism) in order to set themselves against the Catholic Church, which they saw as conservative, even obscurantist. The association of anticlericalism with spiritism explains in part the Catholic Church's strong and long-standing opposition to it. On the other hand, a more devotional, mystical spiritism evolved among the popular classes. This spiritualism combined with other local traditions, including Native American beliefs in the spirit world and in faith healing, African-based cosmologies built around the ancestor spirits, and the cult of the saints among traditional Catholics. In the eyes of white table spiritists, these popular versions of spiritism deal with lower, less-educated disincarnated spirits, such as those of slaves, indigenous people, prostitutes, and rogues—all inherently dangerous to the middle-class social order. In a certain sense, the two texts reproduced here illustrate the split between scientific and devotional spiritism. Although these two strands are always in tension, the line between the popular versions of spiritism and its more educated, "whitened" counterparts is often blurred. For example, Umbanda, a popular religion in Brazil, brings together varying combinations of European spiritism, Catholicism, and African-based religions. Umbanda is also practiced across class and racial lines.

What kind of Catholics would buy these pamphlets? Even though one of the texts has a *Nihil Obstat,* indicating that a church censor acknowledges that the document does not contain anything contrary to the faith, neither of them can be said to represent official Catholic teaching, particularly in the post–Vatican II ecumenical atmosphere. Although Catholic leaders assert the truth of their religion, they try to create and foster an environment of respect and understanding between faiths. Rather, the texts are an attempt to defend the faith at the popular, street-life level. Both texts can be purchased for a nickel apiece in many church stores in Spanish-speaking parishes. Although it is impossible to determine precisely which Latino communities circulate antispiritist texts, there is a tendency to see such literature more frequently among Latinos of Caribbean origin—Puerto Ricans, Dominicans, and Cubans. These immigrants would have had more contact with African-based religions, such as Santería, in their homelands and so would be familiar with some of spiritism's claims. On the other hand, Catholics from Brazil and Mexico would also be aware of spiritist criticisms of Catholicism. Consequently, such pamphlets move easily throughout urban centers in the United States, from Brooklyn neighborhoods to Miami suburbs to Los Angeles barrios.

Frequently, polemical pamphlets are produced by "committees" and have no individual author. The information presented is asserted as truth, not as carefully reasoned arguments that cite supporting evidence. Polemical pamphlets do not include bibliographies or footnotes. Consequently, it is difficult to ascertain where the author(s) found their information and thus to judge their conclusions. However, in the case of these pamphlets, a specific individual takes credit for writing the texts. At the end of both pamphlets is the sentence: "If you would like more copies, write or call Father Prudencio Sanchez, . . ." Attempts to contact Father Sanchez have been unsuccessful, and so the biography of the author remains as unknown as that for the anonymous pamphlets.

The pamphlet "Christian and Spiritist?" takes the "high road" in disputing spiritism by offering a point-by-point refutation of spiritism's doctrinal errors after a polite, if restrained, acknowledgement of Kardec's contributions. The pamphlet is careful to distinguish various versions of spiritism although still linking the latter to Vodou and Santería, through mentioning Haiti and Cuba. This clever rhetorical device allows the author to raise the specter of demonic possession, bloody sacrifices, and all other stereotypes of African-based religions without being overly polemical. Nevertheless, the real heart of the pamphlet is what the author sees as spiritism's stress on individual rational agency. By affirming that each spirit can of his or her free will enlighten him-or herself and attain happiness, spiritism denies the role of the Catholic Church as a collective body with a monopoly over legitimate religious goods (such as the sacraments). Moreover, spiritism's stress on reason eliminates faith and divine grace as key elements in attaining salvation. Here, however, the author must walk a fine line in order not to privilege faith and God's sovereignty, which are hallmarks of Protestantism. In fact, the importance of good works, which makes the human a coparticipant in the salvific project, shares more with spiritism's reading of karma than with Protestant dualism. As I shall argue later on, this Catholic response to spiritism should be seen against the larger backdrop of an increasing religious pluralism in Latin America and among Latinos in the United States that is dramatically illustrated by the rapid growth of evangelical Christianity.

In sharp contrast to "Christian and Spiritist?" the pamphlet "Worse than a Virus" by the same author strikes a highly polemical tone, connecting spiritism with primitive superstitions and practices such as cannibalism and human sacrifice, which are said to characterize humanity's darkest, less-evolved aspects. Gone are all distinctions between European spiritism and African-based mediumship religions. Arising from original sin, spiritism in all its forms stems alternatively from confusion or ignorance or from fear and dependence. Here the author partakes of the same critical attitude toward religious excesses that informed the works of Ludwig Feuerbach and Sigmund Freud: rather than issuing from a true religious impulse, spiritism is merely a projection of, and compensation for, our limitations. Sanchez's examples of "the woman with a depleted mind" and the "big but terrified man" evoke the Freudian images of "neurasthenic women" and the child paralyzed by fear of castration by an omnipotent father. Without specifically mentioning the negative position of psychoanalysis toward all religious experience, Sanchez resorts to pop psychology to connect the practice of spiritism with abnormal behavior.

Parallel to the clinical diagnosis of reasons behind the emergence and persistence of spiritism, the author offers an interesting reading of Christianity. In a turn of phrase reminiscent of Plato's famous allegory of the cave, the author affirms that Jesus Christ is the light that can help us leave the "the night, the spiritist cave" to be able to see Truth in the highest form. Consciously or not, in order to assert Christianity's superiority over spiritism, the author deploys a notion of spiritual progress. Sanchez uses the metaphors of light and darkness and of civilization and prehistory to set up a dualism that white table spiritists would find very familiar. Christianity, then, becomes the search for fixed, finished essences, obscuring the mystery and suprarational core behind notions such as the Trinity and Christ's incarnation and resurrection.

A final element in the author's refutation of spiritism is the accusation of fraud. Here Father Sanchez returns to nineteenth-century America and the mysterious activities of Catherine Fox (1841–1892) and Margaret Fox (1838–1893). The Fox sisters were real, historical figures who played a pioneering role in the development of spiritualism in the United States. Early on in their lives, there were reports of raps, knocks, and other noises in the various houses inhabited by the sisters in Hydesville and Rochester, New York. Although the fledgling spiritualist movement took these noises to be communications from the spirit world, many skeptics attributed them to the skillful flexing of the knee and toe joints. Historical records also confirm the author's assertions that the sisters declared spiritualism to be a fraud both to the press and at public gatherings. Margaret Fox, however, later retracted her confession, alleging that she was under great financial and emotional stress at the time. Sanchez, however, ignores this part of the history and evokes the sisters as evidence of the long history of spiritualist fraud.

The deeper question posed by these two texts is: Why spend so much time on a long-discredited religion, a "religion that should have disappeared 2000 years ago"? After all, while there are active spiritist circles and federations throughout the Americas, at least numerically, the religion is a fairly weak competitor with the Catholic Church, especially when compared to the growing evangelical Protestant population. It is true that the explosion of New Age religions, many of which began in the United States, have attracted the interest of an emerging managerial and technocratic class in Latin America. It is also true that among North American Latinos it is plausible that the rejection of Catholicism and adoption of spiritism can help ameliorate the impact of migration. Spiritualism, for instance, provides support networks and may speed up the process of Americanization through an emphasis on individualism and progress. Nevertheless, these arguments are limited. The managerial-technocratic class, while growing, still constitutes a very small sector of the Latin American population, with the vast majority being poor people who seem to opt for Pentecostalism in great numbers. Among both Latin Americans and Latinos living in the United States, one is more likely to encounter Catholics who dabble in spiritist practices—who might attend a séance or visit a *curandero* at times of crisis—than fully declared spiritists.

It is precisely the proximity and cross-fertilization of grassroots Catholicism and popular versions of spiritism that poses a thorny problem for the Church and demands such vigorous responses as those penned by Father Sanchez. The leaders and members of the Catholic Church are faced with vociferous criticisms by evangelical Protestants that Catholicism is not a true faith freely chosen by mature, committed believers. Evangelical critics insist Catholicism is a superstitious form of magic performed by priests to deceive the people. Consequently, the Church must defend the uniqueness of Catholic faith by asserting clear and authoritative boundaries against evangelicals and spiritualists. In other words, the overriding goal of pamphlets such as "Christian and Spiritist?" and "Worse than a Virus" is to demonstrate that, unlike spiritism, Catholicism is not about fear and superstition. Catholicism is true Christianity and thus it is impossible to be both Catholic and spiritist. This stress on orthodoxy vis-à-vis spiritism dovetails with what many scholars have called a "conservative restoration movement" within the universal Church. This movement seeks to rein in some of the secularizing dynamics unleashed by Vatican II through reaffirming orthodoxy and clerical authority. Controversial pamphlets such as these must be read in the light of global changes within Catholicism in response to increasing religious pluralism in the Americas.

The pamphlets reproduced below are Father Prudencio Sanchez, "Christian and Spiritist?" and "Worse than a Virus, Spiritism Alters the Mind and Damages Physical and Spiritual Health," translated by Manuel A. Vásquez (Waldolf, Md., n.p., n.d., [late twentieth century]).

Further Reading

Roger Bastide, *The African Religions of Brazil* (Baltimore: Johns Hopkins University Press, 1978); Bret Carroll, *Spiritualism in Antebellum America* (Bloomington: Indiana University Press, 1991); Diana Brown, *Umbanda: Religion and Politics in Urban Brazil* (Ann Arbor: University of Michigan Press, 1986); Robert Carpenter, "Esoteric Literature As a Microcosmic Mirror of Brazil's Religious Marketplace," in *Latin American Religion in Motion,* edited by Christian Smith and Joshua Prokopy (New York: Routledge, 1999), pp. 235–60; Ralph Della Cava, "Vatican Policy, 1978–1990: An Updated Overview," *Social Research* 59, no. 1 (1992): 171–99; Alan Harwood, *Rx: Spiritists As Needed: A Study of a Puerto Rican Community Mental Health Resource* (New York: John Wiley & Sons, 1977); David Hess, *Spiritists and Scientists: Ideology, Spiritism, and Culture in Brazil* (University Park: Pennsylvania State University Press,1991); June Macklin, "Folk Saints, Healers, and Spiritist Cults in Northern Mexico," *Revista Interamericana* 3 (1974): 351–76; Anna Peterson and Manuel A.Vásquez, "The New Evangelization in Latin American Perspective," *Cross Currents* 48, no. 3 (1998): 311–29.

Christian and Spiritist?
The Church Condemns Spiritism

The Catholic Church's rejection of spiritism does not mean that everything the latter teaches is bad or a lie. It is difficult to give a definition of Spiritism that covers all its forms. What we can say about spiritism in Haiti or in Cuba may not apply to Puerto Rican Spiritism and vice versa. And certainly, what in general is practiced in these three nations will not be recognized as spiritism in Anglo-Saxon countries. Thus, limiting ourselves to Allan Kardec's spiritism, as it is presented in *The Book of the Spirits, The Book of Mediums,* and *The Gospel According to Spiritism,* it is fair to say that there are truths contained therein, a fact that gives due credit to the author. For example, Kardec believes in the existence of one God, Creator of the universe. Kardec also praises the Decalogue; encourages love among all men, civilized or not; condemns abortion and the death penalty; admits in its own way, that there is life after death, where there will be rewards and punishments. Despite all this, the Catholic Church condemns spiritism. Why?

Because Kardec, who writes beautiful pages in his books, falls into many and grave errors. He also proposes ideas totally opposed to Catholic doctrine, and, at the same time, omits important things that a disciple of Christ cannot ignore. I will mention [these errors] below:

1. Not even by far does Kardec believe in the mystery of the Holy Trinity: One God and three persons—Father, Son, and the Holy Ghost. And this is the fundamental truth in Christianity.

2. In Kardec's doctrine there is no place for Christ, both God and true man, who, with his life, passion, death, and resurrection, reconciles God and man. According to Kardec, man reaches his perfection, his supreme joy, and becomes pure spirit through many reincarnations. This happens all by man's own efforts, since Kardec does not speak of God's grace and the channels by which we receive it: the sacraments.

This goes against Catholic doctrine, which teaches that salvation requires: a) to have true faith; b) to belong to the Church; c) to receive baptism and the other sacraments; and d) cooperate actively in salvific work. Total salvation will happen at the end of times, that is, in the Lord's day. Then, already reconciled with God through His Son's death and justified by [Christ's] blood, will we be saved by Him from wrath:

"Since, therefore, we are now justified by his blood, much more shall we be saved by him from the wrath of God. For if while we were enemies we were reconciled to God by the death of his Son, much more, now that we are reconciled, shall we be saved by his life" (Rom. 5:9–10).

3. Kardec attributes to spiritism the mission that the Catholic Church places on the Holy Spirit: to guide and help the Church to proclaim the mysteries revealed by Christ.

4. In *The Gospel According to Spiritism*, Kardec does not say anything about Christ's incarnation or about his virgin birth. Why? I suppose because he does not want to recognize Jesus Christ's divinity and the virginity of his mother, Mary.

5. The Church does not share with Spiritism the belief that souls reincarnate, which is its basic teaching. The Church does not believe in reincarnation for two reasons: because there is no proof of it and because the Bible offers strong arguments against it.

6. The Catholic Church condemns spiritism because it defies the biblical injunction against calling on the dead to learn, through their alleged revelations, hidden things that only God knows. The Church teaches that souls, with the exception of those temporarily detained in purgatory, are in their resting homes [*moradas*]. No human power can dislocate them from there without divine permission, a permission that mediums do not have because they disobey the Bible and call forth the dead.

7. The Church cannot agree with spiritism's notion that disembodied spirits fulfill one of the Church's functions: to interpret faithfully Jesus' message. *"He who hears you hears me, and he who rejects you rejects me, and he who rejects me rejects him who sent me"* (Luke 10:16).

8. The Church disapproves of spiritism because many take it as a religion, a religion without ritual [*culto*], ministeries, and sacraments.

9. The Church distances itself from spiritism because it confuses the resurrection of the dead with the reincarnation of the spirits, thus negating the only true resurrection. The Christian doctrine on resurrection is clear in the Bible:
   "But in fact Christ has been raised from the dead, the first fruits of those who have fallen asleep. For as by a man came death, by a man has come also the resurrection of the dead" (1 Cor. 15:20–21, see also 1 Thess. 4:14–17 and other texts).

10. The Church rejects spiritism because it confuses angels and demons with the disembodied spirits (of the dead).

11. The Church disapproves of spiritism because it gives a totally erroneous understanding of heaven, purgatory, and hell. According to Kardec, purgatory and hell are in this world. For Christianity, heaven is not a physical place but a state of the soul, which, being forever with the Lord, enjoys complete happiness.
   "And this is eternal life, that they know thee the only true God, and Jesus whom thou hast sent" (John 17:10).

12. The Church repudiates spiritism because it denies that all those condemned will be punished eternally. Spiritism affirms that all spirits or souls will attain supreme joy.

13. The Church condemns spiritism because it falsifies the nature of the human soul. The list can be extended, but what I have stated suffices to understand that Christianity and Spiritism are incompatible. This condemnation of spiritism is not new. Already in 1856, a few years after the birth of modern spiritism, the competent authorities in Rome asked the bishops throughout the world to oppose by all necessary means *the practice of calling forth spirits and other spiritist superstitions. This call had the goals of protecting the faithful against the enemy, safeguarding the well of faith [depósito de la fé], preserving Christians against moral corruption.*

Another Vatican decree, dated April 27, 1917, prohibited participation in all spiritist activities, including the mere passive attendance to séances.

A Christian who fails to see the incompatibility between his faith and spiritism is a badly educated [*mal formado*] Christian. She or he must educate her or himself, ask for help, attend formation courses for adults in the closest parish. Through these means she or he will be able to understand and live the new life that Christ gave us. It is a pity that, knowing something about Christianity, she or he lets her or himself be involved in the shadows of something that belongs to man's darkest past. This was a time when the human being, alienated from God, searched for the Creator guided by ignorance. This ignorance persists in today's spiritism.

The spiritist who believes that what he practices is somehow related to Christianity simply ignores what Christianity truly is. However, his [situation] can be remedied. Many of the first Christians were in the same situation: They were pagans but docile to the teachings of Paul and the other apostles, and they finally abandoned their former lives: *"Many also of those who were now believers, came confessing and divulging their practices. And a number of those who practiced magic arts brought their books together and burned them in the sight of all; and they counted the value of them and found it came to fifty thousand pieces of silver. So the word of the Lord grew and prevailed mightily"* (Acts 19:18–20).

Worse than a Virus, Spiritism Alters the Mind and Damages Physical and Spiritual Health

A woman with a depleted mind . . .

Although I knew something about spiritism through my studies, I did not come into contact with it until two years after my ordination as priest. In an asylum I met a woman, who in the afternoons, could not, even with her eyes closed, stop seeing shadows on the wall. "It is an agony [*martirio*]," she would say. For many years she had practiced spiritism. And while she didn't believe it anymore, her mind and imagination were degraded [*desgastadas*] and tired; they were out of control.

A big but terrified man [muerto de miedo] . . .

Some years later, a man measuring two meters in height entered my parish office. He was terrified. A witch doctor [*brujo*] had "found" a pouch filled with strange things in the man's backyard, just a few days after the death of his wife. The man and the witch doctor went one night to the cemetery, but someone threw stones at them from a nearby sugarcane stand just at the moment they were placing one hundred pesos on a tomb. Later, the witch doctor brought the man again to place eighty pesos more, because with the stoning "the work had not been done right. . . ." The man, however, didn't have any more money. . . .

Spiritism and paradise lost

Spiritism is as old as original sin. When man lost God, he was filled with confusion, ignorance, grief [*llanto*], and anxiety. Disoriented, man felt and was vulnerable to all his limitations: lack of affection, physical weakness, the travails of survival, and his impotence before death and the unknown. Love, money, health, luck, [and] future are the most common words used by those who traffic on tribulations of being human.

The exploiter's apparition

The "witch doctor" of every epoch (experts on necromancy, soothsayers, oracles, magicians, mediums, psychics, etc.) emerged as the administrator of all personal fears. His name varies across time, or takes different shades following the means available to manipulate those fears. The exploiter evolves with the times, but his condition of exploiter and terrorist [*aterrorizador*] remains the same.

The most ancient terrorism

Terrorism is usually associated with the violent ways (kidnappings, bombs, political assassinations) of our days. We think of terrorism as something modern, but nothing can be less true. Terrorism is as old as spiritism and all forms of superstition. For the time the witch doctor appears in its diverse forms, there has been a constant: the use of fear and ignorance to advance his personal goals and to *terrorize* his victims.

Cannibalism and human sacrifices

Spiritism and superstition have gone from terrorizing minds to terrorizing bodies, from eating up the brain [*comerse el coco*] to eating the body. From psychological terrorism, [spiritism] went to cannibalism and human sacrifices, so frequently present in human history.

Even though today cannibalistic terrorism is not common, there are many deaths in those environments of superstition. Even in the so-called civilized societies, there are today cases of people killed "because they have been possessed by the devil or by evil spirits." In June 1995 in the United States, some drivers saw in terror how a father cut the head of his fourteen-year-old son, "because he was possessed by an evil spirit." Another twelve-year-old son could escape.

Spiritism scientific?

With scientific progress in the last two centuries, spiritism wanted to modernize itself. It wanted to convince us of their lies through science. Especially in the middle of the last century, there was an attempt, magnified by the means of communication, to give modern spiritism a scientific and honorable character.

Repentant exploiters

But this was all in vain. Time and time again, spiritism was unmasked as a lie [patraña] and a fraud. The most famous case of repentant exploiters was that of the Fox sisters (Margaret and Catherine)—two North Americans who emitted strange sounds. These sounds were taken as conclusive proof of the possibility of communication with the spirits.

Supported by the popularity of these sounds, Allan Kardec (a famous spiritist) mounted a whole propaganda apparatus for spiritism. But spiritism, which pretended to be scientific, should be by now nothing more than a quaint item from the past [antiguallada del pasado]. In February 1851, after an examination of the Fox sisters, a commission of three doctors and some professors from the University of Buffalo, USA, came to the conclusion that the sounds came from the girls' knee joints and possibly from foot joints. The fraud-game lasted several more years, because the [propaganda] "managers" were reaping abundant profits.

Years later, the sister, now married, declared first to the New York Herald and then to a public gathering at the Musical Academy in New York (October 21, 1888), that the spiritism they created and propagated was a sheer farce. In the presence of her sister, Margaret said: "I am here tonight as one of the founders of spiritism to denounce it as an absolute fraud from beginning to end, as the most sickly of all superstitions and the most evil blasphemy that the world has known."

Empty shelves

Have you seen how pharmacy employees remove from the shelves a medicine that has been discovered to be poisoned? Have you seen supermarket workers throwing a contaminated product into the garbage? Spiritism should have been discarded two thousand years ago as a poisoned and contaminated product, a product dangerous to physical and mental health and to the pockets of those disingenuous enough to get close to spiritism in search for solutions to the problems.

Mental pollution

We know now that tobacco contaminates the lungs, that alcohol destroys the liver, and that nature can be poisoned and contaminated. In the same way, we need to be clear that spiritism has beliefs that rip apart [*descuartizan*] the human mind, that poison and sully it. Spiritism is mental pollution.

What a pity to see tormented people, tortured by superstitious and spiritist practices. To leave that situation is difficult; sickly fears paralyze. It is difficult but not impossible. Particularly pitiful are those spiritists who mix Christianity with their spiritist practices. Worse than not entering in the "temple," is going into it to debase [*profanarlo*] it. This is what spiritists do. Spiritism is contrary to the teachings of the Bible and the doctrine of the Church.

The effects of mental pollution

Spiritism produces a state of passivity damaging to intelligence and will. It erases or disintegrates personality. It causes hallucinations and all sorts of aberrations, especially in individuals predisposed to madness, and exposes those who are not to grave physical and mental disorders. It uses fraud to inquire about life beyond the grave. It cancels moral responsibility.

In sum, plainly stated, the beliefs and practices guided by healers [*curanderos*], spiritists, mediums, or psychics on TV is the best way to end up with a fried brain [*el "coco" aguachinado*] and as a psychiatrist's client. It is clear that those convinced that they were once cows will end up acting like cows, and those who believe they once were dogs will end up "barking." These people do not understand themselves or others.

Children and spiritism

The terrors that beset adult spiritists assume gigantic proportions for children who witness or hear about this pseudospiritual underworld. It is important that those superstitions apparently most harmless (horoscopes, beliefs in the evil eye, and other related silliness) not be transmitted to children. Children are very impressionable and will become easily influenced by stupidities, fears, and insecurities.

Christ? Yes—Spiritism? No

I said before that spiritism should have disappeared two thousand years ago. Why? Because [its existence] is due to man's distancing from God. [Because man] was diminished through the consequences of sin, he end up falling in aberrations and falsehoods. Spiritism has no reason to exist once God begins to illuminate man: "*Do not turn to mediums or wizards; do not seek them out, to be defiled by them. I am the Lord your God*" (Lev. 19:31).

Through revelation God extracted man from the dark night. When God reveals himself through his own son, Christ, there is no reason for walking blindly [*andar a tientas*]: "Jesus said to him: '*I am the way, and the truth, and the life*'" (John 14:6). And these other words remind us of the darkness in which spiritists act: *"I am the light of the world; he who follows me will not walk in darkness, but will have the light of life"* (John 8:12)

Exit prehistory

Christ responded to all of man's questions and anxieties. He quenched man's thirst for love, showing him a God that is love. [Christ] gave redemptive value to all our weaknesses and sicknesses, taking our nature. [Christ] filled us with richness by making us participants in Heaven's goods [*bienes del Cielo*]. He defeated our death through his death and introduced us to victory through his resurrection. This is true luck! Not the one which spiritism searches for in vain in the shadows of fraud! Get out of prehistory and the shadows; enter the light of the Church that Christ left us.

There are many things that man's limitations cannot overcome. [Nevertheless], Spiritism can be overcome. One can leave the night, the spiritist cave, and enter the spring that Christ inaugurated for us.

INDEX

This index contains select proper names, terms, and titles of books and other publications. The names of individual American Indian tribes may be found as subentries under the general heading "Native Americans."